Kemmy's Limerick Miscellany
New Anthology of Limerick Writing

Acknowledgments

Many people have contributed to the compilation of this Miscellany, and we wish to thank them, particularly the sponsors: The Heritage Council of Ireland, McManus Charitable Thrust, Limerick City Council, Limerick County Council, Paddy Hoare, Jan O'Sullivan and the Irish Labour History Society

Special thanks to Joe O'Donoghue whose generous contribution made the completion of this project possible.

Thanks also to Ken Bergin, librarian, and Jean Turner, assistant librarian, for access and copying of extracts from the Leonard Collection in the UL Special Library; Mike McGuire, assistant librarian Limerick City Library; Joe Kemmy, Tom Donovan, Denis Leonard of Limerick Civic Trust; Bríd Frawley, Larry Walsh, curator Jim Kemmy Museum; Margaret O'Donoghue, Patsy Harrold, Liam Irwin and also those associated with the Limerick Writers' Centre - Anne Marie O'Kelly, Clare Dollard, Marian Cody, Mark Lloyd, Mike Finn, Dermott Petty & Dominic Taylor.

Irish Labour History Society Museum and Archives

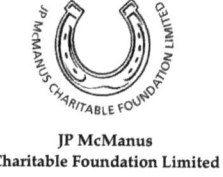
JP McManus
Charitable Foundation Limited

Limerick City Council

Kemmy's Limerick Miscellany
New Anthology of Limerick Writing

Edited by Denis O'Shaughnessy

Published by
The Limerick Writers' Centre

Limerick - Ireland

Published by
The Limerick Writers' Centre
12 Barrington Street
Limerick
Ireland

http://limerickwriterscentre.wordpress.com/

This selection © the Limerick Writers' Centre
Copyright in the stories and poems is that of the individual authors and publishers

All rights reserved

No part of this publication may be reproduced or transmitted in any form or by any means, electronic or mechanical without permission in writing from the publisher, except by a reviewer who may quote brief passages in a review
Sales enquiries:
E-mail: limerickwriterscentre@gmail.com
Web: www.kemmyslimerickmiscellany.com

Book design: Kelly Richards Printing
Cover design: Aisling Burke
Cover image: Michael Collins from his painting Jim 1999
Editor's Photograph: Deirdre Power
Photograph of Jim Kemmy courtesy of Michael Martin
Printed and bound by: ColourBooks Ltd. Dublin

ISBN 978 - 0 - 9562810 - 0 - 5

A CIP catalogue record for this book is available from The British Library

This publication has received support from the Heritage Council under the 2009 Publications Grant scheme

Dedication

Photo © Michael Martin

JIM KEMMY
1936 ~ 1997

Contents

Preface   xi
Introduction   xiii

One: People

Donogh, Hilda and Patrick Kavanagh, P.J. Browne   3
Women in Bloom, Christine Gonzalez   6
Death of Kate O'Brien, Limerick Socialist   9
Jim Kemmy, Mayor, Matthew Potter   10
Terry Wogan Growing Up, Terry Wogan   13
Fonsie and Benny, John Liddy   16
What the Buckley Saw, Limerick Socialist   16
Brendan Foley's Story, Alan English   18
The Tragedy of the Poet Ryan, Limerick Socialist   21
Defining a Limerickman, Michael Curtin   29
Eamon Casey: a Curate in Limerick, Joe Broderick   29
Two Limerick Historians, Jim Kemmy   31
Wit of the Famous Judge Adams, Denis O'Shaughnessy   34
Memoriam to Michael Hartnett, Dan McMahon   36
A Reporter in Court, Fergal Keane   38
The Last Hours of Sean Bourke, Gerry O'Hare   39
Stevie Insults Dev, Limerick Leader   41
My First Day in the Leader, Fergal Keane   43
Bridge over Ma Murphy, Seán Bourke   45
Richard Harris: his Early Days, Gus Smith   48

Two: Religion

The Confraternity, Brendan Behan   57
First Communion Dress, Mae Leonard   58
Distinguished St. Michael's Clergyman: Bishop T. E. O'Dwyer, Frank Prendergast   60
Proselytisers at Work, M. Ó Corbui   61
A Visit to St. Jude, Michael Quinlan   64
The Old Registers, Canon Brendan Connellan   65
The Decade of Moving Statues, Limerick Leader   66
Pork Butchers' Present, Sean Curtin   67
Confraternity Men to the Fight, Denis O'Shaughnessy   68
Troubled Times in St. Mary's, Canon Brendan Connellan   70
Student Pranks at Louvain, Rev. Jeremiah Newman   72
Covering the Visit of Pope John Paul, Fergal Keane   74
The Sign of the Cross, Annals of the Sisters of Mercy   76
To the Inhabitants of this City, Edward Alexander   77
Duties of a Confraternity Director, James A. Cleary   78

Three: Stage and Screen
The Bishop and the Cinema, Limerick Leader — 83
The Atheneum: A Civic Culture Centre, Frank Prendergast — 84
The Closed Lyric, Kevin O'Connor — 85
Catherine Hayes sings for the Queen, Basil Hayes — 86
Memoirs of a Savoy Pageboy, Joe Malone — 87
A Visit to The Pirates, Michael Quinlan — 91
When the Lyric rose up against 'Biddy,' Denis O'Shaughnessy — 93
'A Matter of Principle' Vincent Prendergast — 96
Dracula Rises Up, Michael Quinlan — 97
Pigtown, Mike Finn — 100
Liszt in Limerick, Richard Aherne — 102

Four: Fiction
The Eve of all Saints, Kate O'Brien — 107
The Soup Kitchen, J.M. O'Neill — 113
Some Critical Notes on Kate O'Brien, Paddy Lysaght — 118
Crossing the Line: The School Inspector, John McGahern — 119
After Father Cletus, Michael Curtin — 120
Angela in New York, Frank McCourt — 122
Death in Claughaun, Helena Close — 125
Happy Days in Laurel Hill, Lorna Reynolds — 131
The First Day, J. Carroll — 132
Daddy is Dying, Roisin Meaney — 137
One Funeral and a Weddin', Pat Shortt — 139
Broken Bread, Joan McDonnell — 141

Five: History
The Funerals, Des Fogerty — 149
Feeling hard done by, Michael McCarthy — 151
Limerick's Fighting Women in the Siege of 1690, Maurice Lenihan — 154
The Fighting Women of Limerick: fact or fiction? Kevin Hannan — 157
1916: A Stupendous Piece of Folly, Limerick Leader Editorial — 159
Queen Elizabeth I and Limerick, Matthew Potter — 160
Death in Mount St. Vincent — 163
The lighter side of Patrick Sarsfield, Paddy Lysaght — 164
It's a long way from the Markets Field, Tess Guerin-Letendre — 166
Bishop O'Dwyer and Maxwell, Anon. — 167
King William in Limerick, Henri and Barbara van der Zee — 169
Death in Brookeborough: Seán South's last hours, Kevin Haddick Flynn — 170
Death on the Irish Sea: The Tragedy of the Goulds, Michael J. McNamara — 173
Limerick in 1916, Mannix Joyce — 175
Letters of John FitzGibbon, Earl of Clare, 1798, D. Fleming/A.P.W. Malcomson — 178
The Orphans — 181
More wretched than any other town, Bob Ryan — 181

Some City and Liberty Place-names, Gearóid MacSpealáin, M.A. (F. G. Spencer)	183
Hell is an emigrant ship, Eitienne Ryan	184
MacAdam the Traitor, Maurice Lenihan	187

Six: The County

The Dog Hoaxes of West Limerick	191
A Glenstal Boyhood, Fitzwilliam Barrington	192
Angling in Castleconnell, Kevin Hannan	195
Pigkilling, Micheal Hartnett	197
Men of Annaholty: their measure taken, Denis O'Shaughnessy	198
Burning of Mansions and the Friendly Ghosts of Curragh Chase House, Joan Wynne Jones	199
Play, James Kennedy	202
Gold rush in Bulgaden	205
The Hiring Fair at Kilmallock, John Gallahue	206
Memories of Crecora, Canon Punch, P.P.	211
A Comic Look at Adare, Paddy Lysaght	212
Despair in West Limerick, Gerard Curtin	214
When the Limerick people came to Castleconnell, Joe Carroll	215
A distinguished Co. Limerickman, Liam Irwin	217
Growing up in Newcastle West, Lindie Naughton	218
The First Trans-Atlantic Flying-Boat Passenger Flight, Valerie Sweeney	221
Bruree in World War II, Mainchín Seoighe	223
Sad Day in the Manor, Ann Morrow	226

Seven: Songs and Poems

Thirty-two Bob! (anon)	231
Death of an Irishwoman, Michel Hartnett	232
Why? Rubbish, Paddy Lysaght	233
Portrait of an Old Woman, Frances Condell	233
A rural sing-song, Constantine Fitzgibbon	234
The Fág a Balla Hall (anon)	236
Johnny Come Lately, Jonath Dillon	237
Poem for a Local Historian, Keith Armstrong	237
Shanagolden, Sean McCarthy	239
Rumour Has It, Maureen Sparling	240
An Muince Dreoilíní, Micheal Hartnett/Micheál Ó hAirtnéide	240
Mission Week, Tim Cunningham	241
Abbey Fishermen Elegy, Arthur Lysaght	242
The Miser's Grave, Michael Hogan	243
McNamara's Band, Willie W. Gleeson	244
A Farewell to English, Michel Hartnett	246
To an Infant, Aubrey de Vere	247
On the One-day-dead Face of my Father, Richard Harris	248

Eight: Sport

Limerick My Lady! Tony Ward/John Scally	251
A journey to an All Ireland - by lorry! C. B. McKernan	254
The Munster Monster, Pat Shortt	255
My Beloved Bohemians, Sean J. Fielding/Aidan Corr	257
A Shattered Dream, Thomas Toomey	259
A reunion of the heart, John Scally	262
How Tom Clifford Became a Forward (and other sporting memories), Sean J. Fielding	265
Limerick v. Wexford, Con Houlihan	267
Be a Proud Shannon Man, Maureen Sparling	268
My Early Hurling Days, Séamus Ó Cinnéide	269
Munster and the All Blacks 1978, Moss Keane with Billy Keane	271
Limerick Boating Song	274
The Great John Burke, Ivan Morris	275
Crimson and Blue, Hugh Flannery	278
Limerick Rugby full of Heroes, Richard Harris	278
Munster v Biarritz 2006, Gerard Nix	281
It all goes back to Thurles: when Mick Mackey was still King, Raymond Smith	281
Don't Cry for me Garryowen, Tommy Creamer	284

Nine: The City

Memories of Limerick, Sean J. Fielding	289
A pint for the Stevedore: hard times in Limerick Docks, Pat Doran	290
O'Rahilly strongly opposes University	292
Limerick Bells, Finbarr Crowe	293
The Parish, Willie W. Gleeson	294
Franco says thanks	295
"My Dear Native Place" Michael O'Toole	297
I can remember, Mrs. Manning	300
The Local Defence Force, Séamus Ó Cinnéide	301
Recovery, John Liddy	302
The Magdalene Asylum, Kevin Hannan	305
Duffy's Circus Limerick, Desmond O'Grady	306
Memories of St. John's, Ciarán MacMathúna	307
Some Limerick Characters, Thomas Ryan	309
The Park, Dominic Taylor	312
Paradise Lost, Criostoir O'Flynn	313
Limerick Bands and the Parnellite Split, John McGrath	318
Origins of some Limerick City Street Names, Gerry Joyce	320
Limerick City, Desmond O'Grady	323
Remembering Professor King-Griffin, Eoin Devereux	325

Ten: Politics

The Poor Hoor Was Killed, P.J. Browne	329
The Night de Valera Came to Town, Mae Clancy-Leonard	330
Stevie Coughlan and the IRA, John Liddy	332

Carry-on at the 'Monument', David Lee	335
The O'Malley Dynasty, Dick Walsh	338
'The Liberator', Edward O'Dwyer	342
Dev's train journey to Limerick, Eamon de Valera	343
The Bishop and the Poor, Thomas J. Morrissey, SJ	344
The night Che Guevara came to Limerick, Martin Hannan	346

Eleven: Travellers

A peek at 1950's Limerick and its beautiful, chaste women, Constantine FitzGibbon	351
A very odd place, Charles Dickens	355
Visit of the Marquis of Lansdowne to his Limerick Estate, Liam Irwin	356
Charlotte Bronte's Kilkee Honeymoon, Thomas J. Byrne	357
Belgian Refugees in Limerick during the First World War, Tadhg Moloney	360
Stop-start journey to Limerick in an old car, John B. Keane	362
An unhappy experience in Cruise's Hotel, Liam Irwin	364
A Frenchman's Experiences on his Walk through Limerick, Chevalier de La Tocnaye	366
A Swede in Limerick, Mikael Fernström	371
I wish we were out of it, William Wordsworth	374
A Frenchman's view of the Clergy, Paschal Grousset	375

Twelve: Miscellany

The Hell that was Daingean, Sean Bourke	379
In praise of a reformatory	383
Skipping, Jim McInerney	384
Milford House – it owners and occupiers, Tony Browne	386
A bountiful salmon harvest, Pat Doran	388
Keeping the lid on things, Michael McCarthy	389
The Korean War, Michael Browner	392
Jane Austen's Limerick Romance, Harriet O'Carroll	395
The Brave Shannon Pilots	400
The Bonny Baby Competition, Fergal Keane	403
Does anyone give a Curse? Rev. Frank Moriarty, C.C.	404
Words spoken at the graveside of Jim Kemmy, Gearóid O Tuathaigh	407
Acknowledgments to Publishers	411

Preface

THE late, great, Jim Kemmy left many valuable legacies behind him, not least amongst them being his valuable treasure-throve of local history and literature, which we have inherited in the *Old Limerick Journal*, and his *Limerick Anthology* and *Compendium*, the latter pair now collectors' items.

It is exactly thirty years since Jim edited the first edition of the *Old Limerick Journal*, which we are happy to say, is still going strong, a remarkable tribute to a small group of history buffs and a prolongation which must be unique in this country. Jim would be pleased, I am sure, to know that interest in local history continues unabated, the spark of which he and other local enthusiasts helped to ignite so many years ago.

While an anthology is not all about local history, it is, as would be described in business terms, its anchor tenant. Anthology is derived from the Greek word for garland, or bouquet of flowers, a colourful derivation indeed, but editing one is no bed of roses. Why wasn't such a piece included? What was he thinking of by putting that in? As Michael Hartnett wrote, *the question of exclusion sometimes comes to be more worrying than that of inclusion: the luminary of today may be the footnote of tomorrow and vice versa.*

Yet, the beauty of a miscellany (an earlier description of anthology) such as this is that there are no hard and fast rules. Like a housewife baking a cake, you can throw in your own choice of this, and a bit of that, hoping the end product will prove tasteful. What Jim Kemmy did successfully, and hopefully I can repeat, is to reveal pages that have long remained dormant, and open windows with excerpts from books that not everyone has got around to perusing.

Down the years, many diverse writers, poets and historians, novelists and journalists, local and otherwise, have left impressions of Limerick and its people, its history and lore, culture and sport. This is the essence of this publication. Since Jim's premature death in 1997, many more compilations, good and bad, have been written of the city and county, and we include a selection of these. Wedded to the old, these hopefully, should prove an attractive miscellany, as the title of this new publication suggests, with something for everyone.

Limerick has often been described as the gateway to the west. Whether this was a factor or not in attracting diverse luminaries to its gates is not clear, but not many small cities can boast of having Dickens lecturing ('a very odd town'), Lizst playing, Thackery and Wordsworth ('I wish we were out of here') visiting. Che Guevara (tasting Guinness), Sasoon, Graves, Isherwood, were all here and have left their impressions (not all laudatory) as did Brendan Behan ('a city of piety and shiety'), Frank O'Connor, and Sean O'Faolain, who described the city as being feminine. While natives such as Richard Harris and Kate O'Brien ('my own dear native place') professed their love, Frank McCourt, with his miserable (but happily eventually highly successful) childhood, founded a world-wide industry of this genre.

In this collection I have dropped some chapters that were part of the *Limerick Anthology* and *Compendium*, but at the same time adding others, such as stories from the cinema, a medium that at one time played a huge part in the social lives of the city and county. The city, particularly, was a 'picture' mad town, and even as far back as the 1930's the eminent Lord Longford, on expressing disappointment at such small houses at his travelling plays, was told 'they were all at the pictures!' I have also given local poets a chance to display their wares, who knows, amongst them may be another Desmond O'Grady or Michael Hartnett.

Songs, too, are added, as a tribute to a once great convention, sadly waned. Frank O'Connor, when incarcerated in the Glass House in the Curragh, remarked that the Limerickmen there were the greatest harmonisers he had ever come across. Michael Curtin captures the essence of a former great tradition in this quote from his evocative *Defining a Limerickman*:

> He is not the man he was in many ways and none more so than in the statistic: he used to sing. He used to sing everywhere, that ubiquitous accomplishment explicable by the fact that Limerick is one half pub and the other half church. He has received the best compliment he could dream of - dubbed a great public house singer. Let the other guy have Carnegie Hall. Having put politics, sport and religion to bed a voice would call on him: Limerickman, give us an oul song. A bit of order. Limerickman is about to sing. And his audience could depend upon it being an oul song. Nobody could put the ngnaw into *Remembering You* like Limerickman. But he's not asked to sing anymore. Shhh is only heard now in the pub when the Young Turks can't hear the commentary on the seven days a week soccer matches.

As a former classmate of the late Jim, it is a privilege for me to be asked to edit *Kemmy's Limerick Miscellany*. Both of us, in a desperately deprived era of the early 1950's and the emigrant ship *lán go doras* (what's new!) had to leave Sexton Street CBS in the early days of our secondary education, to follow our fathers' trades: he as a stonemason, and I as printing compositor. Little did I think, so many years afterwards, that our footpaths would cross again when I was called to continue his compilation of writings and impressions of a place he loved so well.

We wish the Limerick Writers' Centre, recently formed, under whose aegis this book has been published, every success in its efforts to encourage and foster the works of local writers and to provide a forum for them, a laudatory and worthwhile venture.

Denis O'Shaughnessy
October, 2009

ONE
PEOPLE

Donogh and Hilda . . . and Patrick Kavanagh
P.J. Browne

'I saw the danger, yet I walked along the enchanted way,'
Patrick Kavanagh, 'On Raglan Road'

IN 1946, the same year as the death of Audrey Harris, Donogh O'Malley met Hilda Moriarty. Hilda was born in Dingle in 1922. She had aspirations to be a writer, but when she sixteen, her father, who was a doctor, brought her to Dublin and enrolled her in the medical school at UCD. One of the classmates at the time was Paddy Hillery.

According to his son Daragh, 'Donogh met Hilda for the first time at a rugby match in Tralee. He was playing with Shannon, and he spotted Hilda watching from the sidelines. When he got back to Limerick, he sat down and wrote her an eight-page letter in green Biro, and they later met in Dublin.'

Donogh and Hilda married in Adare in August 1947. They set up home at 29 Lanarone Avenue, Corbally, which was around the corner from the Mill Road and the house Donogh grew up in, Riverview.

'When Hilda came to college in Dublin (Con Houlihan reflecting) she was a very beautiful girl. She associated with another beautiful girl, Kathleen Ryan. When Hilda and Kathleen were seen together walking down Grafton Street, they were quite a sight. Your heart would jump up. Kathleen's brother John Ryan owned the Bailey and patronised the literary scene.

'Kathleen was a reluctant film star. She took part in one fairly good film, *Odd Man Out*, and one great film, *Esther Waters*, based on the book by George Moore, which was set in the English racing world of the late nineteenth century. Kathleen was brilliant in that.

'Hilda was a friend to the poor in Limerick. Ask the people down there. I know this to be true from my rugby friends around Young Munster and the Parish. In her own way she was a counterpart of her husband. Donogh's contribution was on a national scale, the whole country benefited. Hilda, in her own way, carried on locally what Donogh had started nationally.

'Their son Daragh O'Malley is a very fine person and a great actor. He's a friend of mine and was often here in the house. The O'Malley name in Limerick will forever be held in great esteem. It will be similarly revered in west Kerry.'

'More Prosaic Than Poetic'. Patrick Kavanagh wrote in the *Standard* of 28 March 1947: 'Romantic love is not quite the fortuitous happening it is made out to be. There is a considerable element of will about falling in love. There is more of a suicide than an accidental death about it.'

It's intriguing that an inconsequential friendship should continue to resonate so enduringly in the mythology of modern Irish poetry. Patrick Kavanagh and Hilda Moriarty were not lovers. Their friendship (such as it was) has been tailored and exaggerated to suit various points of view. The truth is more prosaic.

As Kavanagh indicated, love is an act of will. It is useless to seek perfection in someone else. To love someone is to see all the faults and love anyway. In the end, this is the way to accept oneself. Hilda Moriarty was not impressed by Kavanagh or his poetry. She would have known many a similar character around Dingle.

Kavanagh's persistence in befriending her and pursuing her is the stuff of popular legend. Though not malicious or hurtful to those involved the story enables us to perpetuate a myth we find comforting. Hilda was intelligent and blessed with the insouciant Kerry pragmatism. That she strung Kavanagh along until she found a better author is fiction.

She was fond of the poet, but no more than that. She never felt sorry for him and was disappointed that he was drifting along in life hoping for an opportunity that he felt was rightfully his; that's how life was lived in west Kerry, and Hilda's compassion was withdrawn when she saw through this.

Patrick Hillery, who preceded Donogh O'Malley as Minister for Education, knew Hilda when they were both at UCD:

'She was in the same class as me in medical school. She was a very beautiful looking girl, and before you ask, I was already seeing a girl at the time! Hilda was well got, one of the Moriartys from Dingle. They were a great family and her father was legendary in the way he looked after his patients.

'The association with Kavanagh has been well documented I'd say. But he wasn't Hilda's type at all. He was kind of slovenly and maybe that was the best he could do but Paddy Moriarty wouldn't have wanted his daughter hanging around with the likes of him. I used to see him around Dublin when I was a student, but I never had anything to do with him.

'The inspiration for 'On Raglan Road' was hardly romantic. She met the poet one evening in Dublin by accident, to learn that he was unemployed and on the touch. He had been having a difficulty writing, he added. She suggested that he write something more marketable and move away from the bogs and cattle and sheep of rural Monaghan. Write about people, she told him, something interesting. She continued to challenge him to do this and he finally relented and said he would write a poem about a woman. "Of course I can write a poem about a woman. In fact I'll write a poem about you, Hilda. I'll immortalise you in poetry." '

Kavanagh was as good as his word, but even he could not have predicted the enduring popularity of this song, especially in versions by Luke Kelly and Sinéad O'Connor.

Peter Kavanagh, a formidable if contentious intellect, was the defiant keeper of his brother's flame, accumulating an impressive body of source material that might otherwise have been lost. According to him: 'Patrick's association with Hilda came to nought, as might be expected . . . . Just the same, the romance could not be called a failure. He got several good poems out of the misery.'

Kavanagh got a lot more than that from the O'Malley's. Donogh was fond of him and gave him a few quid whenever they met. Hilda used to tell her husband: 'You must do something about Kavanagh. Tell Haughey to give him a few pounds.' John A. Costello was good to Kavanagh after humiliating him in the libel case in 1954. Kavanagh said he voted for him anyway; he said the same thing to Fianna Fail.

'It was probably a country thing with him,' says Daragh. 'Every so often Kavanagh would send a telegram to Sunville addressed to Dr Hilda O'Malley, the telegram usually had a tip for a horse in an upcoming big race.

'One time his tip hit the jackpot. This was in 1961 when he tipped Nicolaus Silver to win the Grand National. The horse, trained by Fred Rimell and ridden by Bobby Beasley, came in at 28/1 and I think my mother had three quid each way on him. With the winnings she bought a grand piano which was thereafter known as Kavanagh's Grand Piano. It was Kavanagh who got Hilda interested in the horses when they were friends in Dublin – Kavanagh was always doing doubles and trebles at the betting shop in Duke Street, next to the Bailey, and in later life, Hilda loved nothing more than placing a weekly bet in McWilliams's betting shop in Henry Street in Limerick.

'When Kavanagh died in 1967, both my parents were saddened. Hilda did say that Paddy never fully recovered from lung surgery. She sent a wreath to the funeral. I read somewhere that this gesture was a token of her undying love for him. That's absolute rubbish! It reminds me of one of Kavanagh's great lines – "Gods make their own importance." '

'Enduring Fidelity'. In her biography of Patrick Kavanagh, Antoinette Quinn writes of Donogh O'Malley: 'His courtship of Hilda was lavish and spectacular. He travelled from Limerick to take her for romantic dinners in Dublin and showered her with expensive gifts.' There is no basis for this observation; O'Malley was not particularly well-to-do at this point of his life. Handsome, yes, charismatic, yes, but not affluent enough for the kind of courtship alluded to.

Joe O'Toole had a sense of Hilda Moriarty being a quintessential west Kerry woman: matriarchal, pragmatic, not likely to defer to the likes of an O'Malley or any man. 'When I first came to Dublin,' said O'Toole, 'I found the women's liberation movement bewildering, to say the least. My formative years were spent in Dingle, a town where businesses were dominated by women. There was no doubt about who was in charge, and who made the important decisions. Hilda would have had those imposing traits as well.'

Father Tom Stack, himself the author of a book on Patrick Kavanagh (*No Earthly Estate: God and Patrick Kavanagh*, 2002) says that Donogh was not in the slightest bit threatened by Kavanagh. 'He was fond very fond of Kavanagh and would give him a few pounds every time they met. Kavangh was alert to these of course and would sometimes show up at a function when he knew Donogh might be there. Shortly after he was made Minster for Health, Donogh was the principal speaker at a medical conference in Dublin. It would have been well publicised and Kavanagh got wind of it so off he went. He was a bit worse the wear from the drink. As I remember it, the building was very warm, the heating was working too well.

'The combination of heat and drink was too much for Kavanagh and he fainted, or appeared to faint. There was a bit of a panic and the meeting was interrupted. Next thing I heard Donogh shouting: "Will someone effin' do something for Kavanagh." It was more comical than life-threatening and I think Kavanagh was able to get up and walk away, no doubt with a few quid in his pocket.'

Political journalist and author Bruce Arnold was also acquainted with Patrick

Kavanagh.: 'I knew him. We lived in Wilford Place and he used to frequent Baggot Street Bridge. He wasn't an easy man to know, but he was much more of a gentleman than people thought, and he was a lot more educated than he was given credit for.'

Bruce Arnold was never timid about voicing his convictions: 'He deserved the Nobel Prize for his poetry, but he blotted his copybook in other ways and didn't get it.'

From *Unfilled Promise: Memories of Donogh O'Malley*, Currach Press, 2008.

Women in Bloom
Christine Gonzalez

(Diary of a Limerick Merchant's Daughter, 1838-1840)

ELLEN O'Callaghan was 17 years old when she decided to start a diary, relating her debuts into Limerick society. After several years spent in the Presentation Convent in Cork, she was back at No. 9 George's Street, where her father, Patrick O'Callaghan, ran a grocery and spirits establishment. Ellen had a younger sister, Maryanne, while her elder sister Kate introduced her to a new life of frills, thrills, music and romance, which Ellen stepped into with enthusiasm. During the following year and half, she wrote every day in her large, 500-page leather-bound diary, describing her doings and her frame of mind with great precision. The following excerpt is the final chapter of the diary:

MATTERS OF THE HEART

Like any teenage girl, Ellen's thoughts revolved a great deal about romance, and her diary is rich in considerations on the matter. She was easily moved by sentimental novels; in August, 1838, she commented on one of her books '.... and it excited me almost to tears; death is described most beautifully and as to Love, genuine sincere love that has to suffer all blame, disgrace and trouble for the loved object! It is too exciting.'

Her own life, unfortunately, was less thrilling, as Ellen and Kate complained that 'every nice young man in Limerick had no money while all those who were rich or had the name of it were all ugly, ignorant and horrid.'

Two men, yet, attracted her favours: they were James Hogan and John Owens, who had a 'very ardent affection' for both sisters. It is difficult for the reader to assert with certainty the developments of this particular 'Victorian soap,' since Ellen related the events for an initiated few and avoided disclosing too many details in her diary, for fear it would fall into the wrong hands.

We can however assume that Ellen's elder sister Kate, who was married to John Sheehy, attorney on Thomas Street since 1835, had an 'affair' with James Hogan in the Autumn of 1838, while her husband was in Dublin to cure his lame leg. They simply went for walks, had private *tête-à-tête* and kept up a correspondence; but in early Victorian times, that was enough indeed to ruin a women's reputation. Kate had to suffer her husband's wrath when, in April 1839, 'some friend (sic - presumably 'fiend') in human shape informed [him] of every act of Kate and James last December, and this to a mind confined and petty as his operated so much that the beating of his spleen was quite intolerable to Kate who requested Mamma to arrange matters today.' A family council was held in relation to Kate's behaviour, and Ellen was shocked by the general uproar as, after all, Kate was still a young lady and did not mean any harm.

> [John Sheehy] seems to have it fixed on his mind that her conduct is very improper whatever her motives may be . . . It is a dreadful thing to downface and convict a person of evil when there is none meant and what ever levity or folly and indeed I am quite sure it does not exceed gaity that Kate indulged was made a mountain of and decided on a grievous offence against John.'

But Ellen did not harbour any particular affection for John Sheehy anyway, who had taken her dearest sister away from their family home, and who prevented Kate from going out as often as she fancied. John could also be quite harsh in his remarks, and strict in his notions of a wife's discipline. In February 1839 he 'went back to his matrimonial arrangement past intentions, present situation, expectations . . . and included Kate in a great deal of it not being very complimentary to say the least of it.' Ellen was shocked by his lack of respect for the rules of etiquette, when he childishly insisted that his wife should follow him whenever he wanted to leave. Ellen avoided their house in Thomas Street after a series of cutting remarks from John, and promised herself that she would never get married to such an obnoxious personage, even if that meant finishing her life in single blessings.

Ellen, for her part, spent two years hesitating between James Hogan and John Owens, who both wooed her discreetly. John was the brother of Mr. Henry Owens, a cabinet-maker on Cecil Street. He was serious, 'steady', and quite reserved, and shared with Ellen a taste for literature. He offered her many books, poems and music sheets, often annotated by his hand, which could be quite compromising for a respectable young lady. In November 1849, they were elaborating a stratagem to spend a full day together, but their plans were thwarted by James Hogan's sudden marriage proposition. Ellen had been seeing James since 1838, and was very fond of him, although he appeared more interested by her sister. He was a very humorous, lively person (the very opposite of his rival John Owens) and himself and Ellen often got engaged in endless conversations. James was also very playful: in June 1839, Ellen recorded a particularly turbulent visit:

[James Hogan called] and really this visit comprised more modes of amusement than any I ever knew before. First began dragging and tying chairs and tables to me then backgammon was proposed, hairdressing, boxing to such a degree that I was quite bothered the last amusement was a feat of strength required which we always rendered impracticable; after all this work we rested ourselves for a good while and that was the pleasantest part of the day. James in his fiddling and ragging displayed my incognito watch of course I did not appeared bothered.'

James Hogan was a perfect suitor, helping Ellen choosing ribbons for her bonnet, getting her books at the Institution . . . but he seemed unable to commit himself, always regaining his formal manners wherever things were getting a bit too serious. After two years of the erratic courtship, he suddenly asked Ellen's hand, to her greatest surprise; she had long resigned herself to be no more than a friend to him. But his request met with a stubborn refusal from Mr. O'Callaghan, whose illness had rendered him quite moody and unpredictable. Despite all her filial obedience, Ellen could not but resent her father's resolution, and confided in her diary: 'My father is a very odd man he is the cause of all my trouble he is so rude. God forgive me.' At the end of the diary in early June 1841, Ellen was still annoyed with her father, but did not think that his decision could be appealed. Nevertheless, the records in Limerick Archives and Ancestry Office show that Ellen O'Callaghan eventually got married with James Hogan at St. Munchin's Catholic Church on 15 November 1842, after four years of courtship and nearly two years of engagement.

In the early Victorian times, a girl was meant to be demure, affable and gentle, and to smile softly like a picture of the Madonna. However, it was not easy for Ellen to adhere to that ideal of sanctity when her heart was in turmoil and she suffered from excruciating boredom. In the summer of 1839, when she was left alone in Limerick, deprived of the company of her sister and her friends, she opened her heart in her diary: 'Indeed I am not all well in myself, besides being in great loneliness of heart, Mamma goes to Dublin on Wednesday and Kate this day week, and in fact everyone I care about [is] going out for an indefinite period. In the second half of her diary, she often complains about her *ennui*, her desperation of being alone, with no one to confide in. She did not even have the heart to play the piano, so she spent endless hours staring through the window, comparing the tediousness of her life to the excitement of the precedent season:

'I was just recalling in memory what a very gay pleasant Christmas we spent and now the three families who when assembled constituted all the gaity are laced in position very nearly approximating to miserable if not particularly unhappy, Death in one sickness and uncertainty of life in the other. For my part, I have lost all taste of what I then considered gaity and never expect to enjoy anything further in the way of pleasure for the future.' (*Ellen refers here to families who were gathered together for Christmas 1839, and who suffered greatly during the winter of 1839, when Mr. John Hogan's brother, Fr. Patrick Hogan, died of a short illness. Mrs. Hackett died, and Mr. O'Callaghan's state of health was a subject for deep concern*).

And indeed, Ellen's prospects did not look very bright: the few chances of entertainment that offered to her were obliterated by the temper of her father, who systematically refused her to participate in any social event. Even when she was invited for dinner in Kate's house, which was situated on Thomas Street, he would come and collect her at nine o'clock, to her great embarrassment. Visitors, daunted by Mr. O'Callaghan's moods, were getting less and less numerous, and no more parties were organised at the family home, at No. 9 George's Street.

Ellen admitted however that she ought to be satisfied with her fate, and she often apologised to God for being so sullen. In December 1840, as a last resort, she decided to join the teetotallers, hoping that it would bring her more luck. At least, she had not lost all of her idealist temper, even if she had undoubtedly matured over the two years spanned by her diary. She recognised herself having changed: 'This [diary] is a most contradictory piece of composition. I am so changed from what I fancied I should wish to occur and I feel almost ashamed when I alight on any passage of it.'

Later on she declared: 'there are some sentences rather inclined to the sentimental but now I do not think it is so ridiculous I will finish this book for Kate who likes it; but it will not surprise myself at all if some day in a penitential or rather cowardly mood I should sponge and wash a great deal of it out.'

And in fact, a change in Ellen's personality between June 1838 and January 1840 is uncontestable: when she started her diary, she was a fresh 17-year-old girl filled with energy and fascinated by the new world that opened to her. Throughout the months, she discovered the realities of a monotonous routine and the severity of her parents; she learnt that friendship was often superficial, and that health and wealth were not to be taken for granted. Even though she never formally stood against the values of her parents, she did not either adhere to them unconditionally. Although she was anchored in a rigid education, Ellen O'Callaghan drew the blueprint for the new type of women that was to emerge in the nineteenth century: pretty, but thoughtful, dignified but subject to passions.

From *Georgian Limerick*, 1714-1845, Vol II. A Limerick Civic Trust Publication.

Death of Kate O'Brien

ON August 13, Kate O'Brien, the finest writer produced by the Limerick middle classes, died in England at Canterbury Hospital. She had been in poor health for the last few years and when she died at the age of seventy-seven years she had few friends and little money. No serious effort was made by the local press to analyse Kate O'Brien's literary work in the articles written about her death. In a brief outline of her writings, Joseph H. O'Donnell, in a piece published by the *Limerick Leader* on August 17, accurately placed Kate O'Brien as a writer when he stated:

Kate O'Brien wrote with a deep understanding of the milieu of the prosperous middle class family. She wrote with affection of houses and families, the homes that had been built by years of successful trading by the merchants of provincial Ireland. She was and remained a middle class writer . . .

Kate O'Brien wrote with an intimate understanding of the people and houses of the Ennis Road and the Catholic convents of Laurel Hill and the Presentation. Despite the sympathetic manner in which she wrote about the prosperous middle class families and merchants and their successful business activities, these people and their political representatives treated Kate O'Brien with scant respect.

Over the past twenty years, Mrs. Mary Hanley, the most indefatigable champion of Kate O'Brien in Limerick unsuccessfully petitioned four merchant Mayors to grant the Freedom of Limerick to their 'own' writer. Ted Russell refused because Kate O'Brien's books were still banned and he feared the reaction from the Redemptorists. The mild Frank Glasgow also shied away from the idea because he claimed the decision would not be unanimous. Vincent Feeney was asked in May 1967 but he believed that the election was far too close for such a controversial matter. Jack Bourke made an effort to do something about the proposal but he, too, failed.

There is some irony in the fact that during Jack Danagher's year as Mayor, President Kenneth Kaunda of Zambia was given the Freedom, after some successful lobbying by the Jesuits. This ceremony took place a few hundred yards away from Brian Boru House, the Mulgrave Street home of Kate O'Brien. For all her sympathetic treatment of Limerick middle classes, the shabby treatment she received in return was more in character and much closer to reality than anything contained in Kate O'Brien's fiction.

From *Limerick Socialist*, September, 1975

Jim Kemmy, Mayor
Matthew Potter

JIM Kemmy was one of the leading figures in the political history of twentieth-century Limerick. He was born in the city on 14 September, 1936, the son and grandson of stonemasons and was educated at the CBS, Sexton Street and the Municipal Technical Institute, O'Connell Avenue. He left school at the age of fifteen and became an apprentice stonemason. In the same year his father had to cease working as he was suffering from tuberculosis and he died two years later.

Kemmy spent much of the 1950s completing his apprenticeship but was often unemployed and on one occasion was dismissed for seeking a pay increase. After being unemployed for six months, he emigrated to Britain in 1957 and lived there for three years, working on building sites. It was during this period that he first became interested in reading and greatly assisted by the paperback revolution, embarked on a lifelong pursuit of self-instruction that resulted in his becoming, in the words of Desmond O'Malley, a 'highly educated man.'

Kemmy returned to Limerick in 1960, and as a result of the economic boom of the Lemass era, was able to secure employment as a stonemason. Later he worked for Limerick Corporation in the same capacity. He was soon drawn into the trade union movement and became branch secretary of the Brick and Stonelayers Trade Union and secretary of the Limerick Buildings Trade Group. He also became a member of the Limerick Council of Trade Unions and eventually became President.

Jim Kemmy was a life long socialist, but throughout his career, his advanced views often left him at odds with many of his fellow Leftists. He joined the Labour Party in 1963 and in the 1969 general election was director of elections in the Limerick east constituency. However, he became disenchanted with Labour as a result of the controversies associated with Steve Coughlan during his 1969-70 mayoralty and what Kemmy regarded as the inadequate response of the party leadership to these events. In 1972 Kemmy and forty of his supporters resigned from the Labour Party and he remained an Independent until 1982 when he founded the Democratic Socialist Party.

Kemmy was elected to Limerick City Council in 1974 and having successfully contested three subsequent local elections, remained a member until his death in 1997. During the 1970's, he became one of the most controversial figures in the public life of Limerick City. In an era when religious practice was almost universal in Ireland, Kemmy was a non-believer and opposed the still powerful influence of the Catholic Church in Irish life. In 1975 he founded the Limerick Family Planning Clinic and in the process caused uproar at a time when artificial contraception was still banned in Ireland.

Kemmy was widely criticised by the Catholic clergy and by large sections of the general public while the women who attended the clinic were dubbed 'Kemmy's Femmies' by one irate parish priest. Kemmy was also a critic of what he believed to be old-fashioned nationalist and republican attitudes to the North of Ireland and was a fierce opponent of the Provisional IRA. Consequently, he was often accused by many of having too much sympathy for the position of the unionist community in Northern Ireland.

He also became a contentious figure in the city council. He was one of the first members of the council to refuse to wear the ceremonial red robe, saying that 'while some councillors act like clowns, there is no need to dress like them' and another occasion referring to some of his colleagues as being dressed like 'Father Christmas.' His contribution to council meetings were often critical of housing conditions, poverty, the provision of family planning and other social problems, and as a result became the focus of fierce arguments that sometimes resulted in proceedings breaking up in disarray. In some quarters, Kemmy became a sort of 'hate figure' and a focus for persistent and hostile criticism. However, he was a highly intelligent, burly and formidable man, and tackled his many opponents with vigour, wit and a wide command of the subject.

Inevitably, Kemmy entered the sphere of national politics and stood unsuccessfully for the Dáil in 1977. However, he was first returned in the general election of June 1981 and became a figure of national importance for the first time.

In February, 1982, he became the central player in the crisis that brought about the collapse of the Fine Gael-Labour Coalition administration, when he voted against the budget introduced by the then Minister for Finance, John Bruton, as it included a provision for VAT to be levied on children's shoes for the first time. In the ensuing general election, Kemmy retained his seat, and the leader of Fianna Fáil, Charles Haughey, who was attempting to put together a government, offered to support him for the position of Ceann Comhairle. Predictably, Kemmy declined. He lost his seat in the general election of November 1982, but regained it in 1987 and held it until his death, having been returned in the 1992 and 1997 general elections. In 1990, Kemmy and the Democratic Socialist Party merged with the Labour Party of which he became vice-chairman in 1991 and chairman in 1993. However, he was disappointed to receive no ministerial position in either the Fianna Fáil-Labour administration of 1992-94, or the Rainbow Coalition administration of 1994-97.

Kemmy was elected mayor of Limerick for the first time in June, 1991, the year of the Treaty 300 celebrations marking the anniversary of the Treaty of Limerick in 1691. It was a belated tribute to a man who had been a councillor for seventeen years and had been elected a TD on three occasions. By this time, Kemmy's views on family planning, the role of the Catholic Church in Ireland and the Northern troubles were becoming more mainstream and he was recognised as having been far in advance of his time on these and on many other issues. The hostility and criticism that he had endured in the 1970s and 1980s was now replaced by widespread respect and affection. He was mayor for a second term in 1995-1996 and on both occasions was lauded for the manner in which he filled the position, although he never wore the principal mayoral chain in public, preferring one of the smaller sheriff's chains instead. Kemmy was the last person to be simultaneously mayor of Limerick and a TD, a circumstance that it not likely to be repeated, due to the abolition of the dual mandate in 2003.

Despite a long and busy political career, Kemmy found time for a varied and stimulating intellectual life. His ruling passions were the history of the labour movement and the history of Limerick City. In the early 1970s he founded and edited a controversial magazine entitled the *Limerick Socialist*. In 1979, along with the veteran Limerick local historian Kevin Hannan, he founded the *Old Limerick Journal*, which is still flourishing at the time of writing and which has published numerous articles by various historians (including the present writer) on the history of Limerick city and its environs. In 1996, he edited the critically acclaimed and best selling *Limerick Anthology* and an equally successful companion volume, the *Limerick Compendium*, appeared shortly after his death.

At the height of his political career, Jim Kemmy died on 25 September 1997 and was buried in Mount St. Lawrence Cemetery. His close friend, the distinguished Limerick-born academic, Professor Gearóid O Tuathaigh of NUI Galway, delivered a very stirring oration at his graveside. In 2000, the Limerick City Museum was named the Jim Kemmy Municipal Museum and soon after the College of Business in the University of Limerick was named the Jim Kemmy Business School.

From *First Citizens of the Treaty City*, published in 2007 by Limerick City Council.

Terry Wogan Growing Up
Terry Wogan

SO, without knowing too much of the details, Michael Terence Wogan was born to Rose and Michael Wogan, in Mother Cleary's Nursing Home, Elm Park, Limerick, on the 3 August 1938. It was a dark and stormy night. Or maybe it was the morning? Or the middle of the day? I never asked.

My mother used to make great play of the thunder and lightning that lit up Limerick upon my birth, but if Apollo was trying to tell me something, it has never been made clear. Rose used to claim that on the first day she took her beloved first-born out in his pram, a great gust of wind tried to pull it from her grasp. Perhaps I should have been a weather forecaster. I wonder if the same thing happened to Michael Fish? He missed a Great Wind, too, remember?

Born in the town of Limerick, then, Ireland's third biggest town. Not a city. No cathedral, you see. But more churches than Nashville, Tennessee. But, unlike Nashville, Tennessee, all of the same denomination: Roman Catholic.

Limerick was more Roman Catholic than the Vatican. Not a lot of Christianity, if by that you mean love and tolerance of your fellow man, but plenty of religion. They had something called the 'Arch-Confraternity', a sort of Catholic Freemasonry, except that there was no secrecy. If you got into the Arch-Confraternity, you let the whole of Limerick know about it. You had arrived: a pillar of the Church, a pillar of the community, people bought you drinks, paid your fare on the bus. 'Ah, don't stir, Seán. I have it here.'

The Da never joined. Maybe he was never asked, but he wasn't exactly big on religion. Neither was my mother. I think she had too much of a sense of humour for it. Oh, they went to Mass, ate fish on Fridays, kept the Lenten Regulations, and made sure their two sons had a good Catholic education and kept the Faith, but I never felt, at least in retrospect, that their hearts and souls were entirely in it. Maybe I am trying to make my own agnosticism easier to understand.

In his great Pulitzer Prize-winning book, Frank McCourt makes Limerick childhood seem like growing up in the Black Hole of Calcutta, and in the poverty-stricken slums behind St John's Castle, with a ne'er-do-well for a father, it surely was. In the lower-middle-class environs of Elm Park, Ennis Road, it was okay. It was not the lap of luxury – we didn't have a car or a telephone. We did have a radio, though. Along with the books, it saved my life. No, it made my life.

There, in that provincial Irish town on the banks of the Shannon, many miles from London, and light years away from its culture and sophistication, I grew up in the BBC, with the Light Programme. It became my window on the world, my magic carpet to another place. It influenced my thoughts, my speech, my attitudes, my sense of humour. Everyone else of my contemporaries seemed to be listening to Irish Radio, but I struggled towards puberty with the help of Workers' Playtime, Mrs Dale's Diary, Dick Barton: Special Agent, Much Binding in the Marsh and then, Take it from Here, Educating Archie, The Goons and Hanncock's Half Hour. I was a right little West Brit…

They piled me off to school at five, about a mile down the Ennis Road, to Ferrybank, a preparatory school run by the Salesian nuns. It was just up the road from Barrington's Pier, where the sallies grew, and Cleeve's Toffee Factory, which filled the air with the very scent of heaven.

Mother took me there with my little schoolbag, and left me in the care of the kindly nuns. She had barely returned home, before there was a knock on the front door. There I was again. Fresh-faced and fine-featured, I declared myself home, and enquired civilly on the prospects of lunch. That'll be enough of school, I had felt, after about ten minutes, and had walked out of the front gates and home...

After four gentle dream-like years at preparatory school, the Salesian nuns showed me the door and the nightmare began. They sent me off to the big boys' school, Crescent College, Limerick. It was not really nightmarish, but the end of innocence. It could have been worse, much worse. It could have been boarding school. It could have been the Christian Brothers, men whose legendary cruelty and brutality could only be compared to a particularly bad-tempered Mongol horse.

The Jesuit fathers who took charge of me were no Mary Poppinses, but glimmerings of humanity occasionally broke through their ascetic severity. The Jesuits dressed in black and had wings – panels to their black coats, that flew back as they walked. Black angels. Frightening – at least for a nine-year-old.

Over the years of growing up, fear was replaced by a certain amount of respect, and even a grudging affection – not for those who doled out the corporal punishment, though. You got beaten for everything: bad homework, wrong homework, inattention, misbehaviour – anything. Not that you got punished on the spot. No, they wanted you to think about it, before you got the works.

Corporal punishment was the way forward in education in those days, even for the highly educated and civilized Jesuits. And they had a most peculiarly sadistic way of dealing it out. A grammatical mistake in homework, or a moment of foolishness in class, and the good father would write out a little chit from his docket-book. Depending on the seriousness of the error or transgression, that chit would be good for three or six heavy welts across the hands with a reinforced leather strap, administered by a cheery, burly priest named Father Bates.

Here was a man who took real pleasure in his work, obviously deriving considerable spiritual benefit from offering your suffering up to God. The sadistic bit was that this was no instant, spur-of-the-moment leathering. No, you had to wait until lunchtime, to join a queue of other unfortunates, and watch them get their hands knocked off, until it came to your turn.

With no feeling in my swollen hands, I would cycle off home for lunch, then back an hour later, into class again, and a couple of hours after that, find myself queuing up again for more gratuitous violence, before the kindly Jesuits let me out for the day.

And in case you think you are dealing with a junior combination of Jack the Ripper and Joey the Eejit here, let me tell you that this ongoing torture was the lot of all but the brightest and most dutiful... Extraordinary to think that men as sophisticated and supposedly intelligent as the Jesuits could use terror as their main tool in the education of young minds, even allowing for the fact that it was the norm in those days.

At Crescent, I played rugby from the time I was about ten, and tennis. Strangely enough, it was when playing tennis rather than rugby that I received my most serious injury: missing a forehand I knocked my own front tooth out. No great loss, although a more accurate shot would have knocked both of them out. Early pictures show a pair of front teeth more suited to a rabbit. These, combined with a pair or ears that would have given Mr Spock a run for his money, were the subject of many a cruel jibe from my peers, none of whom, incidentally, were oil paintings themselves.

The removal of one tooth pushed back the other one a bit, deflecting the slurs, and acting as a frightener for opposing prop-forward, when I took the false tooth out for rugby.

We didn't play football, a game for hooligans and the lower orders; and cricket and hockey regarded as Protestant activities. The Irish national games, Gaelic football and hurling, were for 'National' and Christian Brothers schools, that is non-fee-paying ones. Middle-class Irish schoolboys played middle-class British games. (There was no 'upper' class. If you were that high up the totem pole you went to a Catholic public school in England.) 'Garrison' games, they were called, by the true sons of the Gael: games played by the former army of occupation, the British soldiery.

Now that I think of it, given my maternal grandfather, I was entitled ... Golf, another game introduced by the British, got in under the wire somewhere and avoided stigma – perhaps because it was played by officers, and the Irish always had respect for anyone on a horse.

The prejudices and hatreds generated by religion in Ireland are well documented over hundreds of years, and all too familiar over the last three decades, but, in my formative years, and well into the 1960s, there was a fair amount of fear and loathing attached not just to where you prayed, but what you played. The Gaelic Athletic Association (GAA) bestrode the island like a colossus, forming the third point of the triumvirate that ruled: Church, State and GAA.

Restrain the urge to laugh – it was not funny. Well, it was not meant to be. The GAA rule was simple: play rugby or football, and you were forbidden the joys of Gaelic football and hurling – and vice versa. We all knew it was ridiculous then, but, in retrospect, it is almost impossible to believe. The rugby and football fields of Ireland were crawling with pseudonyms. Woe betide anybody who was found out! Expulsion and disgrace – and if the local priest could have excommunicated you from the Holy Roman Catholic Church, he would have, and laughed at your chances of salvation.

There were a lot of ways of putting your immortal soul in peril in the Ireland of my youth: the non-observation of Lenten Regulation; the eating of meat on Fridays; non-attendance at Sunday Mass; impure thoughts... The occasions of sin were all around us. Guilt – that's what kept you going. . . . .

From *Is It Me?* BBC Worldwide Limited, 2000.

PEOPLE

Fonsie and Beni
John Liddy

When Beniamino Gigli alighted from Limerick station
he met Fonsie Renihan outside The Railway Hotel.
"Welcome" he said, "you brought the house down
in Dublin last night and I was glad you met a friend
from long ago, Madam Sheridan - Maggie from Mayo."

Gigli, surprised to hear this news vendor's rapport
enquired if he were coming to the concert that evening.
"I would if I had a ticket", replied Fonsie, "everybody
wants to hear Caruso's successor" and with that
Gigli insisted he accept a complimentary.

The next morning he came for the papers and Fonsie
mentioned that his rendering of Ponchielli's La Gioconda
was superb and thanked him for the invitation. "No, no"
Gigli protested, "Thank you for allowing me to see."

Years later Fonsie talked about postcards from Beni.
But what did he mean by 'allowing him to see'?
I often asked and never got an answer. Perhaps it was
as Montaigne said: *because it was him; because it was me.*

From *Revival Poetry Journal* Issue 8 July 2008

What the Buckley saw

God bless the Squire and his relations,
To keep us in our proper stations

IT was most certainly the most exclusive piece of social journalism in the *Limerick Leader* since Seamus O Cinneide reported on the An Taisce bun-fight at Killaloe. The assignment was a challenging one for any young Limerick reporter: to confront and interview three blue-blooded members of the aristocracy at their ancient ancestral seat of power at Adare Manor.

The choice of reporter was an automatic one: Miss Helen Buckley, well versed in social airs and graces, rose to the occasion in impeccable style, her vignette of the nobility as parents even upstaged O Cinneide's salmon-sniffing act among the rather ratty professional members of An Taisce.

The low-keyed title, 'At Home with Elizabeth', had just the right, quiet, dignified air about it. The article itself was written in the very best of good taste and judgment, and exuded that essential reverence so necessary in serving our betters. Miss Buckley pulled out all the elegant stops and left no superlative unturned in matching her prose to the classical surroundings. Her story (June 10) set the scene in the very first instance:

'In a paradisiacal nursery suite overlooking the banks of the Maigue, Ana Elizabeth Wyndham Quin, daughter of the earl and countess of Dunraven, is in her twelfth week of life.

'The baby, whose weight has risen from its chartered birth size of seven and half pounds and already measures over twenty-one inches in length, is coolly stoical about having its hours of nullity interrupted for photographs and looks like a tiny but bemused anachronism in its long flowing gown.'

Here her narrative picks up pace as Miss Buckley moves on to describe the small oasis of bliss, where the baby had spent her first twelve weeks:

'The flat relegated to Ana on the ground floor of Adare Manor, which was for a time inhabited by a member of the estate staff, has been completely re-decorated to produce a wonderful of baby folklore. It consists of a living-room replete with yellow curtains fringed in white, lemon covered chair, turquoise line-tiles, lighter torquoise walls, blue chinz covered chairs, a picture, flowers in abundance, TV, rocking horse and one of the Countess's favourite inanimate 'furry animals.'

The main room leads onto a perfectly equipped kitchen, a bathroom, a bedroom and the nursery proper. The highlight of the small sleeping quarters is the crib used by Lady Dunraven and her sister, and now done up by her in the flimsy loveliness of tucks of broiderie anglaise, (bought in Cassidy's) over a basic material layer of lemon. Hanging over the cot's side is a minute pillow embroidered with images of the infant sphere which sent out tones of Brahms' Lullaby.'

Miss Buckley allowed herself to luxuriate in the neat little haven and her prose rises to lyrical heights giving the pen-picture of the riot of colour. But the well dressed and fashionable conscious reporter was relegated to the ha'penny place when she came up against the tiny infant, whose display of clothes was a complete one-baby fashion show. 'Ana's clothes, which her mother describes veritably as 'a marvellous trousseau,' came in every length and style and certainly size. A red Italian coat fringed in white lace, which Daddy invested in, will be kept cupboard bound for a while. So also one would imagine will the beige cat-suit with it pale turquoise sweater. Among the other occupants of the wardrobe are two very lovely full-length Victorian dresses bought by the Countess for their 'workmanship', and because she does not like 'short dresses on tiny people - they could get cold legs'

Presents which Ana Elizabeth received were laid out in pleasant profusion ranging from tiny silver and gold bracelets to large ones (Geraldine Dunraven: 'With some of the large ones I requested the permission of the god-parents not to wear them until she is older') from a miniature silver rosary beads in an equally silver sized silver case, to an entire set, composed of silver brush, silver photograph frame.

The baby was not, however, actually born with a silver spoon in her mouth, but she did manage the next best thing, by way of a mother of pearl teething ring with silver boot attached and a tiny silver comb.

But silver without gold was not quite enough, so 'even a gold nappie pin was included in the offerings. The presents were bought from Irish and British jewellers and some in Tiffany's in New York.'

But all this was just a little bit too much for even Miss Buckley but, like the servant tilting his cap at his master, she could not resist a slight tongue-in-cheek, but nicely balanced, in her concluding sentence; "So whatever the latent characteristics of the little girl, known to her parents among other things, as 'Charlie Bubbles', 'Ana B-a-n-a-n-a' and 'Buttons', few people feel any trepidation about her future security.'

As they say in proletarian Prospect, 'You can chalk it down, girl.'

From *Limerick Socialist*, July 1972

Brendan Foley's Story
Alan English

THE first years of my life were spent in another family's parlour on the Quarry Road in Limerick city. My family rented the room for four shillings a week. There was me, my brother Gerard and my father and mother, Anthony and Rosaleen Foley. In the autumn of 1952 we were given a two-bedroom house of our own in Ballynanty Beg, a new Corporation house that overlooked Thomond Park. I suppose it came not a day too soon. My mother was heavily pregnant with her third child.

She hung a new pair of curtains and pulled them across on the night she felt the baby coming. They preserved her dignity and helped to drown out the clatter of builders working late into the night. It was seven o'clock and dark outside. There were twelve days to Christmas Eve.

My father went to fetch the doctor, but he couldn't be found. He eventually turned up shortly after a local nurse had helped my mother give birth to another boy. Afterwards, everybody said he was hardly in the door when he was walking back out again. Half an hour later, at half past eight, my new brother was dead. Nobody ever found out what the cause was because at nine o'clock my mother was dead herself and they buried her without giving my father an explanation; buried her in a nun's habit alongside my dead baby brother, Michael. Nobody in Ballynanty asked questions, because who was going to give them answers. Some said it might have been because my mother had been so good to her own mother, taking care of her when she had suffered a stroke and gone childish, forever lifting her on to the toilet and back into her favourite armchair in the corner of her parlour on the Quarry Road. Maybe the strain had been too much, they said. But the next thing they knew, it wasn't really their business any more because once the funeral was over my father closed the front door behind him and he never came back.

After the burial in Mount St. Laurence he made his way through the Christmas shoppers in William Street hand in hand with Gerard and myself, and out to his sister's house in St Mary's Park. Madgie McNamara had agreed, at the funeral mass the night before, to take us in and raise us as her own. Hospitality was the only thing she could offer us. Her house had three bedrooms, including a box room. She had four children of her own and her husband, Fred, was out of work more often than he was in it. On occasion he helped clean the turbines out at Ardnacrusha power station and sometimes he made a few bob up at St Mary's church, mowing the grass and ringing the Angelus Bell when Willie Bartlett, the parish clerk, wasn't around. But mostly he didn't do much.

The night we arrived my father looked my uncle in the eye on the doorstep. 'Thanks, Freddie,' he said. 'Thanks very much.' Some nights my father cried and called us over to comfort him, and Uncle Fred would say, 'Look, Tony, enough's enough now.' But all this I didn't find out until later, much later. When it happened, I was two years old.

The McNamaras had once lived in Sheep Street, but the house collapsed one summer's evening after heavy rain and they were relocated to 59 St Munchin Street in the Island Field. There was a small vegetable garden at the back, and a spot where they kept a few chickens. My aunt was a great woman for baking apple tarts, rhubarb tarts, griddle cakes and soda bread. My father paid for our keep, bought our shoes and our schoolbooks, and told us that Madgie was our mother because our mammy was dead. He was a labourer for Molloy's, a famous building firm in Limerick. He was tall and thin, rakishly thin. He had gone bald early in life.

When I was still a young boy my father got married again and moved out of the McNamara's house. He would call to see us once or twice a week on his bicycle and take us for a spin, Gerard on the metal seat behind him, me on the timber square in front.

At the Christian Brothers school in Creagh Lane, it was quite rare to have a pair of football boots. The school had a big bundle of old-style boots and you went through them and found a pair. I was one of the first in my class to have my own. They were new but they were on sale in a second-hand shop for a pound. I looked at them for weeks, hoping nobody would buy them. Eventually my aunt took me in and we got them. I was ten.

Every day after school we played soccer on a small patch of grass opposite Eddie Price's house. Sometimes forty or fifty of us kicked a ball up and down the street, from boys of ten to men of sixty. We played hurling with broken sticks scavenged from the Gaelic Grounds and we skinned orchards.

One day, when I was fourteen, five or six of us went down to the Scouts Field where the St. Mary's rugby club trained. They were only too delighted to see us coming. Throughout their history the Saints had been thrown off every pitch they ever trained on. They would take a chance on a new field and somebody would come along. 'Out!' If they had nowhere to go they would run the Island Bank, often in the fading light, taking care not to hop off a passing horse. The only bath or shower they had was the Abbey River, or the contents of a zinc bucket.

They were formed in 1943 by a fella called Whacker Casey and their headquarters then was a broken-down house in Glueyard Lane owned by a character called Hadah Sweeney. Most nights he stumbled in drunk singing his song, 'Ireland Mother Ireland.' There were no chairs, just a couple of timber benches and a fireplace. He had no electric light, just a paraffin lamp, so they paid for it out of God knows what. Then they got him a bag of coal a week to keep the place warm.

By the time I joined, Saints had bought an old timber hut from Shannon airport and put it up directly in front of Hadah's house. This became the new clubhouse. They called it the Casbah. There was a potbelly stove inside, where Peter Hayes would boil oxtail soup. Between Hadah's and the Casbah was a piece of waste-ground about fifty feet long and twenty feet wide. That was another of our training grounds. It was such a cramped space that fellas had to throw lineout balls from inside Hadah's house.

Next to Glueyard Lane was Flag Lane, home to the famous Hayes family. The one who started me off in rugby was Mick Hayes. He was a labourer up at CIE, the railway station. The older men who played with him for Saints called him the Red Fella, said he was a fabulous player. He told us if we backed away from anything on the field, we were cowards, not fit for rugby. If you got on the wrong side of him, even once, that was it for life. At training, my attention would wander over to where Star Rovers were playing a soccer match. If they were a man short, I'd ask Mick if I could fall on. He didn't like that. He said I was always dragging myself together. He didn't mince his words.

'Brendan – you're lazy! You've always been lazy. The others are making a laugh out of you. There's a young kid there and he's up first. You're last. Every time there's a loose ruck, you're last. You're not putting it in, Brendan. You don't want to put it in. And if you don't want to put it in, Brendan, there's only one thing for it. Chuck it up.'

After training, myself and Mick and a handful of others would go walking, the length and breadth of Limerick, and I'd hear all the stories about Saints. Mick saw something in me, he thought. I had potential, I was long and lean. When I was seventeen we won the Junior Cup for the only time in the club's history. I joined Shannon then, the senior team in the parish. They had a few promising young players, including a fella with red hair who talked a lot. Gerry McLouglin was his name. By then I was working at the Good Shepherd Convent, driving a van. I've always loved open spaces and the open road.

After serving my time in the Shannon pack I was picked to play for Munster. I knew if I could play well in a big match, against one of the overseas teams, the Irish selectors might notice me. In 1976 the Australians came and we gave it a real go, should have beaten them. The following Sunday morning I heard my name being called out on the radio: picked for Ireland against France. Straight away my friend Thady Coughlan drove me into Shannon and we had a party in the clubhouse. My father was very proud, but he wasn't a drinking man so we had to make up for him. I was the first Shannon man capped in ten years and only the second ever. For people like Mick Hayes, and the lads I'd grown up with in the Island Field, it meant the world. My friend John Ryan said: 'To think that one of us could be picked for Ireland, after comin' from our stable.'

The following year I lifted the Munster Senior Cup at Thomond Park, one of the best moments of my life. Three of us were picked for Munster against the All Blacks. For the other two lads, Locky and Colm Tucker, it was their chance to show the Irish selectors they were good enough. Maybe having three Shannon fellas in the Irish team was too good to be true, but we thought we were good enough. Not many teams got the better of the Shannon pack.

From *Stand Up and Fight*, Yellow Jersey Press, 2005.

The Tragedy of The Poet Ryan

LIMERICK is famous for its 'characters.' They can be found in every level. From people like 'Dunnick' O'Malley of conventional Corbally to 'Gurky' McMahon of swampy St Mary's Park. Generally, they are by nature non-conformist and this gives them their curiosity value.

That popularity is usually determined by their ability to act the part of 'a gas man' and so amuse the attentive audience, many of whom appear to have a secret longing to be a 'character' and to receive even this fleeting acclamation to compensate for some inner insecurity.

One of Limerick best known 'characters' died over a year ago. He had been a familiar sight on the city's streets. Deep lines on his face, white unruly hair, an aloof bearing, and a general aura of public disorder.

Gerard Ryan lived out an existence dictated by the fact that he was a poet. In ill health, he had no constant job. He was careless about his finished poems, and left no manuscripts. Over the years, in many moves from one shabby room to another, his papers and poems had perished. Landladies had burned and dumped his life's literary work when the room had remained unpaid. In fact, during his life, he never had a book of poems published. That had to wait until he was dead a year.

However, during his life, he was a character in 'literary' Limerick. The Poet Ryan they called him. He was an old man, and usually hung out in the 'White House' bar; that is when he was not suffering from cold and hunger in his run-down room or coughing his guts up in the City Home. However, between bouts of his pain and suffering he was a character. He provided talk and laughter for the price of a few pints. The 'artistic' circle could, at least, give him that much.

After his death, it was decided that he should be remembered. Last May, 'An April Morning Walk', Poems by Gerard Ryan, was launched at a press conference in O'Malley's Roundhouse in High Street. Drink and talk flowed fast. People who had little connection with the unhappy life and times of the Poet Gerard Ryan were present and recalled suitable anecdotes to prove what a fine man Ger had been.

It was a sad and strange event. As one 'outside' observer remarked, 'If all those had given Ger five bob a week it would have kept him in comfort.' So it would. But then 'characters' are taken for granted and in the end very few visited the Poet Ryan in the City Home.

One was Desmond O'Grady, who one Christmas in an outburst of seasonal excess, ran wildly through the wards of incurables telling them to cheer up, as they had everything to live for . . . O'Grady, however, with Peter Donnelly and a few of the more sensitive people who tried to help The Poet, showed a genuine if far off appreciation of Ryan's poetry. The only note of realism was introduced when a review of the book appeared in the Limerick Weekly Echo. Written by Frank Hamilton, it said:

Gerard Ryan lived and died in a small provincial place. I remember him. Sitting alone. At an Art Exhibition. While the trendy young things talked the clichéd jargon of the spiritually faded.

He wrote nature poems. He was close to the earth. Yet for me one of the most memorable is simple, stark, terrifying, called 'Unit Six, St. Camillus.'

> On the window sill
> Beside my bed
> In St Camillus
> A bowl of dying flowers . . .

Other images come like:

> The nurse leads off
> With a trolley of clean clothes
> Slowly they move
> To the long ward of incurables . . .

It is all there. In the end. And as Gerard Ryan would say: 'Let me tell you something for nothing . . . that is what life is all about . . .'

Desmond O'Grady, writing an introduction to the book, took a more familiar line. He wrote: 'Devoted to the art of good conversation, story telling and high song he spoke only of people and poetry, the human affair and those mad enough to try to record it through art.'

It is indeed a sad commentary that Gerard Ryan had to suffer pain, poverty and hunger enduring the 'human affair' while people in his pub audiences could return to their safe and secure jobs and homes. But, like the fate of 'Gurky' McMahon and many more, that's the way it happened ... the silent tragedy of a Limerick 'character.'

From *Limerick Socialist*, July, 1974.

A reply

THE article in our last edition on the Poet Ryan and the recent publication of some of his poems provoked some local comment. One reader and friend of the dead poet wrote to this paper and gave some more details of the poet and his friends:

'I have just finished reading your scathing remarks about Ger Ryan's superficial friends and I am blushing to think that I may have been one of them. To tell the truth, there were times when he nearly bored me out of my mind with his blather. I must confess, however, that I enjoyed his funeral. I would like one exactly the same for myself. It's seldom I envy anybody anything but I envied him the dozen red roses placed on his coffin by the Poetry Circle, the organ music played by Kevin Imbush, Stephen O'Shea's rendering of Handel's 'Largo' and 'A' raibh tú ag a' gCarraig', the interment in the little hillside cemetery under a dripping sky.

'One thing: I could do without being left there whilst the mourners wended their way homewards not missing a pub until they reached the White House in the late evening, there to do final homage to his picture before which had been placed a large lighting candle draped in black.

'But I must tell you that Ger had more friends than you knew of. Frank McNamara, a cousin of the Poet's, made him a decent weekly allowance and went to see him every Tuesday. It was in the home of Darina and Claude Byrne that Ger spent his last Christmas, as he had done on many a previous Christmas. The late Dr. McPolin and Dermot O'Donovan were, I believe, also good to him in their time.

'Your article on Ger and your reference to other 'characters' together with one Matt Talbot put me in mind of another character named Father 'Fitz'. About thirty years ago this 'silenced' priest in a dirty black suit, the lapels covered in snuff and porter stains, was a familiar sight in the area around William Street and Gerald Griffin Street. He lived for a period in some doss-house in Mungret Street and later lived with the Noonan brothers at Geraldine Villas, Garryowen. Fr. 'Fitz' frequented pubs in the Market-place district and was decently treated by the workers who drank in these bars. I was told by my grandmother that though he was silenced, I must still greet him with 'God bless you Father' when he passed. 'As a child I often wondered about what heinous crime he was guilty of that he should be so cast out by Mother Church. How much more New Testament figure he was than Matt Talbot.

'Another well-known character at that time was 'Jimmy the Lady'. He was a vivid figure leaning over his half-door in Corry Lane, a bag tied around his waist for an apron. A big, soft man with a prickly beard and more than his share of female chromosomes, he supported two orphaned nieces by taking in laundry.'

The 'Limerick Socialist' is glad to add the names mentioned in this letter to the list of people who helped the Poet Ryan during his lifetime. The main points made in last month's article however were that poetry is not considered a financially productive trade in capitalist society, and that many of the so-called friends of the poet, who extravagantly proclaimed their regard for him after his death, showed only a shallow concern for his well-being during his life. This criticism could also be extended to editors and owners of local newspapers who could not be considered over-generous in their payments (if at all) to Ger Ryan for the publication of his poems in their papers.

From *Limerick Socialist*, August, 1974.

Defining a Limerickman
Michael Curtin

THERE is no more a monolithic Limerickman than there is a Dubliner who hasn't read *Ulysses*, yet who is supposed to be more Joycean than Joyce himself. But imagine that such a superman of the Shannon once existed and became victim of a Big Bang and is now diffused throughout the city, his gemlike qualities coated in strata of ordinariness.

Consider the boiling pot from which he came: Viking, Dane, Norman, English, Dutch, German, Scottish; the milieu in which the brew was stirred: imperialist and republican godparents; and the assorted ingredients that were added: the pictures, the music hall, the light opera, sport, faith.

How can he be put together again?

Employ the indefatigable exertions of Frankenstein - *Igor more steam* - and the indiscrimination of *The Three Stooges* to throw everyone who is not nailed down into the pot.

The trawl for components is most likely to be rewarded among those in their sixties who still manifest the traditions that shaped them though the inheritance is odds on to have been somewhat stultified by television's global village. Unlike all the king's horses and all the king's men, having succeeded in putting Limerickman together again, here he is - though he is not the man he was.

Wherever there are two or three gathered together in anybody's name he will grab the first chance he gets to tell them how he once danced with Movita while she still wore one of the black eyes that Jack Doyle gave her backstage in the Savoy. He's told the story so often he believes it himself. And, this whopper of a kite still in the air, he follows on as the three-thousandth claimant to have broken the nose of Richard Harris on the rugby pitch.

He has free travel now and deservedly so because in the bad old days when times were tougher for some than others, his wife would nudge him on the bus when the conductor approached: Don't let Mrs O'Brien pay - she has a houseful. Like his wife he is indoctrinated with a slew of Limerickisms the provenance of which is rooted in the garrison city influence. Such as: when his blood pressure rises and he momentarily forgets that he was young once himself he roars at larky children: go on, hop it or I'll give you a fong up the hole. From the thong on the soldier's boot that the Cockneys couldn't pronounce when they were stationed here. Sassoon and Graves served in the old Strand Barracks. There is nothing of the Brits Out mentality infecting Limerickman.

He is not the man he was in many ways and none more so than in the statistic: he used to sing. He used to sing everywhere, that ubiquitous accomplishment explicable by the fact that Limerick is one half pub and the other half church. He has received the best compliment he could dream of - dubbed a great public house singer. Let the other guy have Carnegie Hall. Having put politics, sport and religion to bed a voice would call on him: *Limerickman*, give us an oul song. And by way of seconding the motion the publican would come in: Quiet please. A bit of order. *Limerickman* is about to sing. And his audience could depend upon it being an *oul* song.

Nobody could put the ngnaw into *Remembering You* like Limerickman. And for an encore dip into *The Old Refrain* or *Oft in the Stilly Night* or whatever you fancy from *Maritina, The Bohemian Girl, The Lily of Killarney*. His wife invariably obliged with *I Dreamt I Dwelt in Marble Halls*.

He is very close to his wife now. Since his bypass he has rediscovered the childhood sweetheart whom he had begun to take for granted as someone handy to have around the house to cook and answer the rosary. Now she is again his indispensable companion - along with the stick and the dog to accompany the walking regime imposed by his doctor.

But they're not asked to sing anymore. Shhh is only heard now in the pub when the Young Turks can't hear the commentary on the seven days a week soccer matches. He may not be the man he was in the singing stakes but there is the odd sighting. When there is an electricity supply board industrial dispute or a night of the big wind and the candles flicker strategically in the Stygian pub and the customers fidget and scratch their heads trying to remember how they lived before they were brainwashed, an atavistic longing is given expression again: Limerickman give us an oul song.

Though he is an authority on rugby - as is his wife and dog - he will die happy in the knowledge that he has left his children a love of hurling. Where the greatest game in the world is concerned he is riddled with inferiority. He passes on what has been handed down to him: *You have to be twice as good as Cork to beat them*. But when he talks about rugby he allows his megalomania out for a walk. *Any fifteen Limerick players would beat that Irish team*. Not quite a delusion of grandeur on his part because as his wife and dog will corroborate: it's true.

He is a much travelled man who has been to Cardiff Arms Park, Murrayfield, Twickenham, Lansdowne Road, and recently Santa Monica where his youngest son, the software engineer, has been headhunted. Limerickman sits silent upon a deckchair in California staring at the Pacific with a wild surmise unlike that of Stout Cortez: what in the name of God am I doing here. His wife and family knocked all his objections to the visit with the sworn promise that civilization had reached the Coast at last in the shape of draught Guinness on tap. He could no longer hold out.

So he sits crucified with hospitality as only the open handed Americans can inflict it: sunshine, cold cans, hot dogs, barbecued steak while he licks his lips homesick for the Limerick rain, a warm pint of Guinness, fish and chips and his own bed. He came back from his honeymoon in Salthill, Galway, to the rented room where the two eldest were born, qualifying for a council house when three more came into the world. He put in extra hours at night as a telephonist so that he could at last buy his own home, an abode he kept in better nick than an Englishman would his car on a Sunday morning. It took a lot of time, a lot of rearing and a lot of hard work. Yet along comes this shakings of the bag of a youngest son, hardly with a foot outside the graduating gate of Limerick University and he's living it up in a mansion in the sun like a film star.

He thought he'd see one but they're all dead, those he might have recognised. *Boys' Town*, there was a picture. They don't make them like that anymore. He shook hands with a film-star once, Rock Hudson, outside St. Joseph's church, when Rock was here to make Captain Lightfoot. Also in Limerick he shook hands with three presidents of the United States and one Pope. Yet even though he has shaken hands with the Pope he no longer thinks of himself as the paterfamilias in the religious stakes where this youngest hot shot son is concerned. Or any other stakes if he is to be honest. It started early enough with this young fellow when he was fourteen and the wife asked did you get mass and he answered I was at half seven in the Fathers. His wife pointed out that there was no mass at half seven at the Fathers only devotions. Well, the young fellow insisted - and it checked out he was telling the truth - the priest was there in all his gear, it seemed like mass to me. But then the boy had shown earlier signs of a liberal education when he had no school on the eighth of December which fell on a Tuesday that year and in answer to his fathers probe: what feast day is it, answered with an educated guess : Pancake Night.

How did it happen overnight? Where is it all gone? *Gear*? Alb, cope, chasuble, surplice, biretta, he'd been taught all that in Senior Infants. Forty years a member of the Arch-confraternity of the Holy Family in the Redemptorist church, he could still sing for you now: *Faith of our Fathers, Through Jesus' Heart All Burning With Fervent Love Towards Men, Soul of my Saviour, Tantum Ergo, Confraternity Men to the Fight, Sweet Heart of Jesus, Hail Queen of Heaven, O Mother I Could Weep For Mirth*: this last maybe appropriate when he accepts that there isn't a hymn among all the young men today.

Boys' Town. The know-alls used to point out that it was a true story, that there was a real Father Flanagan. All he knew was there was a *real* Spencer Tracy and that the boys of *Boys' Town* were as real as the boys from Limerick when Limerickman was a boy and that they stayed out of trouble with the help of authority in the form of parent, teacher, priest and Hollywood. He asked his son - the oldest, not the youngest: what's the name of Hopalong Cassidy's horse and he had a supplementary clue at the ready (you'll be a topper if you get it) but the boy answered: who's Hopalong Cassidy?

Youngest son was born standing on Limerickman's shoulders and his inheritance was a state of the art university, a state of the art rejuvenated city through which a mighty river flows that is in the process of being reclaimed for swimmers once again. Assuming youngest son will wake up and tear himself away from the Pacific to come home and dive into the Shannon. He will, he will. Limerickman clings to that. Of course he will. Although the night they had the farewell party for Limerickman in Santa Monica, with all the American pals in, and they demanded:

Limerickman's youngest son, get out the guitar. And he could sing, why wouldn't he coming from a singing family. But *Born in the USA*? Even if he did do a damn fine job of it. They can't help it, Limerickman told himself as the night grew older and the guitar was passed around, they don't know any better. Until the youngest son showed that he was a damn fine boy as well as a damn fine singer: Mam, what about *Marble Halls*? Limerickman only listened to herself until he was sure he'd grabbed them and then he set about clearing the throat of his soul. He was ready when the youngest son a little shamefacedly half-asked: what was the one you used to sing Dad? *Used*. By God did he give it to them. Closed his eyes and imagined himself back home where the humblest messenger boy who'd duck into the concert hall and hang by the ankles from the rafters would have a better ear than the cognoscenti of London, Paris, Milan. *Remembering You* of course. He knocked them out. The youngest son who had reddened in anticipation of sophisticated thumbs down from his American pals blinked a tear back and swallowed with pride. Limerickman, to show he wasn't all fogey, and to shake them out of his spell, chose the bouncy encore *I've Got a Luvelly Bunch of Coconuts* and then tried to shrug off the California seal of approval: hey, your dad can sure whack it.

No religion, no old songs, doesn't know the name of one cowboy's horse from another no more than the older brothers, is this youngest son his pride or his despair? Then again didn't Father Spencer Tracy himself say that there was no such thing as a bad boy. And now that he thinks of it when he compares youngest son with anyone else but himself, isn't the boy a topper just like Hopalong's horse. It's just all this change that confuses Limerickman. He can't help missing the old slums, the old lanes, the old heavy hand of authority that gave a certainty to his life in his obedience, the old frugality, the old rotten teeth and consumption and emigration and joblessness even though he knows its madness to be nostalgic simply because the old package was wrapped up in the old songs.

Look on the bright side: youngest son will come home. He will flash the same open orthodontic smile that he brought with him from Limerick to California and he will stand a little beefier from the celebrated American excess in the cuisine department and look authority straight in the eye with his own authoritative in-built hypocrisy detector and he will have no chip on his shoulder other than the positive awareness: that Limerick has its own Silicone Valley. He will stand tall as befits one born on Limerickman's shoulders and he will grow to become Limerickman himself. And some day when he has it all he will notice something is missing as will Everyman experience the niggling lack of proper fulfilment. Limerickman nurtures the dream that the catalyst might appear in the form of a late night showing of *Somebody Up There Likes Me*. Youngest son would cop on: they don't make them like that anymore. It might give him a taste. What with all those late night movies not to mention the video shops: he might yet learn the names of all the cowboys' horses. He might begin to think that there was something in what Limerickman used to say after all. Maybe even in that old religion. Come Back Shane and all the homesteaders going to church. Maybe even in the old songs.

Meanwhile, as youngest son shapes up to become the new superman of the Shannon, present incumbent Limerickman marks time. You'd have to kneel on his chest and pull it out of him with a forceps that he shook hands with John F. Kennedy, Richard Nixon, Bill Clinton and Pope John Paul the Second. Let the other fifty thousand have that celebrity. Let Rick and Ilsa have Paris.

He'll always have Movita.

From *Limerick: Images of a Changed City*, Limerick Chamber of Commerce, 2000.

A curate in Limerick: Eamonn Casey
Joe Broderick

IN the Autumn of 1951 Eamonn Casey was appointed curate to the parish of St Patrick's in Limerick. He already knew something of the city. He had done his secondary schooling at St Munchin's seminary which was housed in a mid-eighteenth century mansion backing on to the River Shannon. As a boy he had often attended Mass with his father at the Jesuit church in Limerick before going up to Dublin to pay a visit to his mother in hospital.

The city he had known in those days was a place of handsome brass-plated doors with peacock-tail fanlights, smart English sedans driving along clean streets and a faint tang of the sea wafting from the estuary. He would have seen street urchins and 'tinker' women begging beside the railways station; they might have seemed picturesque. He would certainly not have imagined, behind the city's genteel façade, how many Limerick people lived in dire poverty. Casey had never seen poverty. In his boyhood, he says, it 'was equally there ... but I didn't know it.' Now he went out to meet it. And to combat it.

From the outset he was an assiduous visitor to his parishioners. He marched along with his jaunty stride, knocking on every door and introducing himself. Behind those doors he discovered the hardships of working class Limerick: abandoned wives and unmarried women alone with a crowd of hungry and ragged children; lonely old people unable to warm themselves against the approaching winter; families whose breadwinner had taken the emigrant boat to England but had not been able to return or even earn enough to take their wives and children with them.

Young people were leaving in droves to search elsewhere for employment. 'I was visiting houses,' he says, 'and suddenly Jimmy was gone, Mary was gone, Joe was gone. I asked what happened to them. Did they get a job? Did they get digs? Were they practising their religion? I got their addresses and wrote to them ... at Christmas and on St. Patrick's Day.'

'I am by nature a compassionate man,' Casey had said. He certainly showed compassion to his parishioners during those distressing days in Limerick. Eamonn Casey did not restrict his ministry to dispensing sacraments and religious counsels; of course he did perform the liturgies and bring Holy Communion to the sick, and he visited those who needed him time and again, far beyond the call of duty. But, as well as spiritual comfort, he looked for solutions to their material problems.

'I remember one morning visiting a woman of twenty-eight. She was expecting her eighth child. My god, she looked like death. I couldn't just give that woman a blessing and leave. I sat down and had to talk with her about things that, as a priest, I should not have had to. It was embarrassing for me, and it was more embarrassing for her.

'That day, my bishop happened to be visiting us. I asked to see him in my room after lunch and told him what had happened to me that morning. I said to him that there should be some place to which I could send that woman where she could meet another woman who would talk to her with understanding and sympathy. Casey proposed an advice centre with pre-marriage counselling, but the bishop's first reaction was to ask: if our parents got along without marriage counsellors, why do couples need it now?

Dr. Patrick O'Neill was considered a holy bishop, but he was not readily approachable. Even the official Church obituary, on his death in 1958, described him as 'locked within himself, aloof and detached,' a man who 'hid a golden heart under a strange exterior.' In time Casey manoeuvred his way beyond the strange exterior. With help from some fellow priests and the mediation of a senior curate who carried a lot of weight with the bishop, Casey finally got permission to set up the Catholic Marriage Advisory Council in 1955.

By that time Casey was curate in St. John's, an inner-city parish where many lived in dilapidated and overcrowded tenements. Some of these were Georgian buildings, reduced to decaying skeletons of their former glory. Late one Friday night Casey was called out by neighbours to stop a man from beating his wife. When the priest appeared, the drunken husband slunk off into to a corner. But a week or two later neighbours urgently phoned up Casey again; the brutal scene was being repeated. The curate hurried around to break it up and restore some kind of order. He called back on the Saturday morning to make sure the man was behaving himself. Casey found him unashamed and defiant.

'What are you going to do about it, Father,' he asked insolently.

Casey, much to his own surprise, as the husband's, picked up a rickety chair, held it aloft for a split second and brought it down across the man's back. The chair shattered into pieces. It was the last time Fr Casey was called to make the peace in that house.

Some problems required drastic remedies; others seemed to have none. Nothing could be done to arrest chronic unemployment in what had once been a prosperous harbour town. The exodus of young people had reached alarming proportions. In October 1955 the diocesan magazine carried an editorial on the plight of the emigrants. 'Our worry is about their souls,' it read. Casey worried rather about their well-being; many of them were lads and lasses from his parish who were now battling to survive in London, Manchester and Birmingham.

He took his holidays and went to look for them, to see how they were making out, to bring messages from their worried parents in Limerick. He recalls those first visits to the daunting metropolis: 'I'd get lost in London and the Irish conductors would put me from one bus to the other, the real *sagart* (county priest) with the hat on me, and the smell of the bog off me.'

He soon got to like the excitement of London, enjoyed the company of the young emigrants, and they were glad to see this cheerful priest 'coming across the sea, not to upbraid them, not to look for money, but simply to bring them news from home.' Casey understood the importance for Irish workers of having something lined up when they arrived: employment, if possible; if not, at least a bed in a hostel. He realised that the first days in a strange and hostile land were critical. Without assistance, many young men and women became what Casey called 'social casualties'; the Catholic Church and the established Irish community lost track of them, and some, in their loneliness, took to drink, drifting from one badly paid job to another and finishing up in the gutter. Casey's first attempt at a remedy for this was to establish the Emigrants' Advisory Office in Limerick. Its task was to prepare the way for those obliged to emigrate.

During the fifties, about 40,000 men and women left the country every year, mostly from the west of Ireland. In 1957 the emigrants numbered 58,000, the highest figure this century. Farm jobs had become scarce in Ireland, and industry almost non-existent. Post-war Irish found work on building sites, in electricity plants and factories, and on road gangs constructing the M1 and other giant motorways. They lived in the camps.

Archbishop McQuaid of Dublin engaged the Columbian Fathers to make a survey of the conditions of these Irish emigrants. Fr. Aeden McGrath was chosen for the mission in England because of his 'extraordinary knowledge of the communist technique' which would enable him to 'counter the activities of left-wing groups, such as the Connolly Clubs, who were having some success in recruiting Irish emigrants.' As a result of reports from Fr. McGrath and other Columbian missionaries, the Irish hierarchy established a permanent chaplaincy for emigrants. When priest volunteers were called for, Eamonn Casey was amongst the first to offer his services.

There is no evidence that he showed an anti-communist bias. Both at home in Limerick and later in England, his chief concern was to find practical remedies for the causes of human misery. He did not stop at individual cures; he tried to create institutions with their own dynamic, capable of solving problems that were common to many.

The institutions he helped to create were not particularly original: emigrants' advice bureaux and marriage guidance centres already existed in Dublin before he set them up in Limerick. Nonetheless, in the context of Limerick at that time, they were revolutionary. Up to this the clergy's main concern had been purely religious and moralistic. The Redemptorist Fathers with their Confraternity of militant extremists had been strong in the city for decades; and they were still rampant. One of Casey's contemporaries described them with 'sashes and medals gleaming, marching Orange Order-style to church behind brass bands and banners. In those days the Confraternity members gave the straight-hand facist salute to their spiritual director.' Early in the century they had whipped up a campaign against the Jewish community in Limerick; now they hunted out and chastised couples embracing in the back seats of the cinema.

Limerick in the fifties was a depressing place: a mixture of religious fanaticism and physical drabness. Brendan Behan summed it up rather crudely as 'a city of piety and shiety.'

Eamonn Casey's bouncy enthusiasm would have distinguished him anywhere; in these circumstances his energy made him quite remarkable. In his speedy little Volkswagen he darted around Limerick, raising dust and getting things done. He organized a crowd of youngsters to collect waste paper for pulp but then the paper company moved out of town and the lads were left without their jobs. So Casey started up his own paper mill, kept the boys employed and ran the business at a profit. He used the money to fund a new school.

A fellow priest who worked with Casey in those early years of his ministry defined him as a 'man who refused to stay in the middle of the crowd . . . the average curate comes out of Maynooth and goes into the old structures, and he looks down the years and sees himself as a PP by the time he reaches sixty. And so he starts carving out a niche for himself. So you get fellows of thirty years of age with almost nothing to do. They wouldn't even be asked to build a henhouse for themselves! As an old priest said to me: 'Keep your mouth shut, keep your ears and eyes open, you'll get the respect of your people, and you'll make your money!'

Safe middle-of-the-road priests were inclined to mistrust Casey; he was too pushy for their liking. He, in turn, felt hampered by their provincial mediocrity. When he volunteered for the overseas chaplaincy, he was probably keen to get away from this stifling atmosphere. In October 1960 he left Limerick for wider horizons. He was assigned to the parish of Slough in Buckinghamshire, west of London . . . . .

From *Fall from Grace*, Brandon Book Publishers Ltd., 1992.

Two Limerick historians
Jim Kemmy

JOHN Ferrar, the first major historian of Limerick, was born in 1743. His father was a bookseller and bookbinder in the city from 1729 to 1754. His grandfather, Captain William Ferrar, served with the Williamite Army in Ireland and married Marie Lloyd of Drumsallagh, Co. Limerick. The Ferrars came from Huntington, England, where the family was engaged in the bookbinding trade. In addition to being a bookseller and bookbinder in the city from 1729 to 1754, John Ferrar edited the *Limerick Chronicle*, which he also printed, from 1768 to 1781, when the paper was taken over by Andrew Watson. Ferrar's History of Limerick appeared in two editions, the first in 1767 and the second in a much enlarged volume in 1787. In his *Recollections*, John O'Keefe, the actor and dramatist, gives the following description of the historian:

"His little shop was at the corner of Quay Lane. Ferrar was very deaf, yet had a cheerful and animated countenance: thin and middle size."

Ferrar was a political and religious ecumenist long before his time. In the preface to his history, completed on Christmas Day, 1786, he wrote:

"Controversy in religious matters is of all others the most unyielding, most unentertaining if not handled with charity and politeness. The heaps of books on this subject on the continent in the last century which contributed to deluge several parts of Europe with blood, were a disgrace to humanity. What! Shall we quarrel with an honest man because he differs from us in his manner of worshipping the Supreme Being? . . . The author, therefore, in writing the following pages, was extremely anxious to unite his fellow citizens, and, as far as lay in his power, to lessen the little jealousies which have divided men living in the same land under the same roof . . . . Toleration is the basis of all public peace."

A. J. O'Halloran, in his book, *The Glamour of Limerick*, re-creates an attractive image of the historian at work:

"You can picture him in his house in Sir Harry's Mall pouring over dusty tomes by candle-light, rejoicing when he discovered some new fact redounding to Limerick's credit; or in fancy you may see him, horn-rimmed spectacles on nose, peering into some dusty corner of St. Mary's Cathedral in the hope of alighting on some ancient inscription that might help him in his labours; or you can think of him clad in his suit of sober brown, white stockings, buckled shoes and cocked hat, trotting nimbly off to invite Doctor O'Halloran's aid in elucidating some knotty point."

A year after his work was published he was made a Freeman of his native city on September 2, 1768. When he began his undertaking, Ferrar admits that "he was then little acquainted what a respectable figure this city makes in the history of Ireland." Written "amidst the avocations of a laborious employment and the duties of a citizen," the book has won for Ferrar a permanent place in the memory of his fellow-citizens. Perhaps some enterprising publisher would consider republishing this history , written by a man who simply describes himself on the title-page of his book as J. Ferrar, Citizen of Limerick."

Maurice Lenihan was born in Waterford in 1811, sixteen years before Rev. P. Fitzgerald and John James McGregor published their two volume *History of Limerick*, and twenty-six years before *A History and Topography of Limerick City and County*, part of a *Topographical Dictionary of Ireland* by Samuel Lewis, appeared. After a long lifetime's work as a journalist and editor, Lenihan died in poverty in Limerick in 1895. His major work of 'no inconsiderable toil' *Limerick: Its History and Antiquities*, was published in 1866 but it was not until after his death that the book began to attract attention. For many readers, one of the attractive features of the work is to be found in the search for an item and the excitement of finding some other unexpected gem. A careful reading of the book will reveal many little known aspects of the history of Limerick, often hidden away in all-embracing footnotes.

The Jesuit historian, Francis Finegan, in his 1946-48 Studies articles, has made the most comprehensive study of Maurice Lenihan's life, including his services as a Town Councillor and Mayor of Limerick in 1884. Though he is generous in his praise of Lenihan and his work, he is not uncritical.

"It would be rash to deny that Lenihan's History of Limerick, taken as a whole, is free from error. Indeed, the wonder is that Lenihan did not fall into more errors than he actually did . . . occasionally, in his presentation of some historical episode, Lenihan wanders off to import some reminiscences of his own to the reader. Yet, perhaps, this very discursiveness is just one of the qualities that gives this book its endearing charm. The outstanding fault of the History consists in its attempt to crowd so much matter into so small a space – though the book, strictly speaking, cannot be called a small book."

Maurice Lenihan's book is not enhanced by his ungracious and sometimes inaccurate carping at John Ferrar. Historical studies in Limerick owe much to the ecumenical Ferrar and his pioneering work. Though Lenihan states in his preface: "the reader will find in the Index the fullest references to almost anything in the book besides what is contained in the table of contents," this claim is not always accurate. Many readers will have their own stories to relate about their explorations of the book, On one occasion, when researching the building of New Town Pery, I spent days searching through footnotes of the book only to find the information I impatiently sought in the body of the book. But the search was not in vain and the author's personal recollections of his 1851 meeting with Captain Creagh vividly links the old and the new cities and fixes the scene indelibly in the mind.

"The New Town, now the finest portion of the city, and the great centre of trade, was not built for seventy years afterwards (1760). Meadows and corcasses then occupied the grounds down to the water's edge. Captain Creagh, an old and highly respectable gentleman, who died some years ago in Cashel, informed me in 1851 that he remembered shooting snipe in Parick Street . . . a marsh which the tide covered . . . "

With his failing eyesight, Lenihan fell on hard times in the last years of his life. He moved his newspaper to smaller premises in Catherine Street and he was forced to sell his books and manuscripts in order to survive. The sale of the Arthur manuscript to the British Museum was an incalculable loss to Limerick historical studies. The story is told that he could not afford a pair of shoes to go to Mass on Sundays. To add to his grief, five of his children predeceased him. He died on Christmas Day, 1895, and is buried in Mount St. Laurence Cemetery. Despite its flaws and shortcomings, the book is by any standard, a monumental work and will continue to be read and quoted while the river Shannon flows through the author's adopted city.

With the passage of time, Ferrar's and Lenihan's works have become the two best-known Limerick histories. But there has long been a need for a comprehensive study from where Lenihan left off in 1866, though it should be acknowledged that a number of historians, notably Francis Finnegan, Robert Wyse Jackson, Mark Tierney, Mainchin Seoighe, Patrick O'Connor and Kevin Hannan, have written widely and well about different aspects of the period.

From *Limerick – Historical Reflections*, Oireacht Publications, 1966.

Wit of the famous Judge Adams
Denis O'Shaughnessy

RICHARD Adams was County Judge in Limerick from 1884 to 1908 and was universally noted for his wit. His fame crossed the Channel and according to Bart Kennedy, a well known English writer, 'his fame had penetrated the heart of dull London.'

Bart came over specially to hear the judge in action and wasn't disappointed. He spent the day in court in Limerick and this was his verdict: 'A wit and philosopher who dealt in genial wisdom of comedy,' the writer said, and waxed lyrical on how the judge, by his wisdom, kindness and wit, dealt with the cases that came before him in Limerick that day.

Con Cregan, long time editor of the *Limerick Leader*, as a young reporter attended court when the judge was in action, and has recorded some hilarious incidents about him:

The judge was strolling towards the railway station one day following a sitting in Rathkeale. With him was Fr. Jerry Murphy, then a local C.C. Passing the church tower the judge looked at the time and remarked that he should hurry as he would be late for his train.

'Ah,' said Fr. Murphy, 'you're in plenty of time, that old clock is wrong.'

The judge, in mock indignation, replied: 'I'm amazed at you Fr. Murphy. Do you mean to tell me that the Church can err?'

According to Con Cregan, Judge Adams was at his best when local 'characters' were in court. On one occasion a man was sued for the balance of his daughter's fortune. The defendant, in the course of his evidence, said he didn't like the match at all and had advised his daughter against the marriage.

'What advice did you give her?' asked the Judge.

'I wouldn't like to tell you what I said,' replied the witness.

'Oh, but you must,' said His Honour with a twinkle in his eye. 'This is a court of Law and we must hear everything.'

'Well,' said the witness, 'I told her that if she burned a certain part of her anatomy (in fact he used a plainer description than that) she should lie on her blisters.'

The Judge almost exploded with laugher at this piece of evidence.

A case that provided the judge with a perfect platform to show off his wit took place in Newcastle West in 1904 when a farm labourer cum fiddler named Daly sued a farmer named Mullins for breaking the fiddle over his head.

Judge Adams presided and was in his element, even if all the laughs were provided against the poor plaintiff, who obviously wasn't the brightest.

Plaintiff accounted how he, playing the fiddle, and another young lad playing the tambourine, were passing the defendant's house when he defendant rushed out, grabbed the fiddle and broke it over his (plaintiff's) head.

Mr. Kelly, for the defendant: Is this broken fiddle a Stradivarius (laughter). The plaintiff looked blankly at him.

Judge Adams: You are slightly going astray, Mr. Kelly. It should be Antonio

Stradvario of Cremont (laughter). To witness: You claim to be a musician. If this fiddle was made by Stradvario it is worth £500. What do you say to that?

Witness said he did not know (laughter).

Mr. Kelly, who was vying with His Worship for the laughs, said, 'this fiddle is not a dangerous instrument to strike a man with; it was deadly only when the plaintiff played it' (laughter).

His Honour, now having a field day, added that the defendant played the fiddle on plaintiff's head and though intended to be musical, it was a most discordant blow, every string being out of tune (great laughter).

At this stage the court was convulsed with the defendant giving evidence that his cows were upset by the music. When queried as to the tune being played, the boy on the tambourine said he was playing the 'Wearing of the Green', but the defendant said it was 'God Save Ireland.'

His Honour: According to this ye were playing two different tunes, no wonder the cows hissed at such a performance. Either that or they were Northern, Orange cows, rising in revolt at the rendering of 'Wearing of the Green' (laughter).

Mr. Liston, for the plaintiff, asked the defendant: 'If the King's Army Band were playing passing your door would you demand they cease playing?'

Witness said he would make the fiddles stop.

Mr. Liston: Oh, it was the fiddles the cows objected to and not the class of music? (laughter).

Judge Adams, summing up, said they had the organ grinder in London but those objecting did not go out and smash it. The fiddle was not by Stradvarius, or it would have cost the defendant £500 to replace it, but fortunately it was purchased from Mr. Patrick O'Shaughnessy, of Newcastle West, 'a personal friend of mine and an eminent musician, for 27s. 6d.'

'It was absurd to say that these poor innocent cows in their native Munster would object to this music (laughter). He believed defendant was angry at the musical promenade, came out, and did strike plaintiff, breaking the fiddle. He would give a decree for £1.10s. and 7s. 6d. costs.'

Described in another article as a 'fellow of infinite jest,' the Judge used to come up against a very rural policemen whose style of giving evidence was so diffuse and unconnected as to irritate his honour on every occasion it was inflicted on him. One day the policeman, described as not being a very brilliant specimen, gave evidence in a case in which a horse, usually quiet, saw a red petticoat fluttering on a line and not knowing what it was, bolted.

Judge Adams interjected: 'Res ignota pro magnifico.'

'Begorra yer Honour,' retorted the policeman, 'you took the words right out of my mouth,' The judge collapsed.

From *Limerick: One Hundred Stories of the Century*, 2000.

PEOPLE

Memoriam to Michael Hartnett
Dan McMahon, Dublin Memorial, 1999

IF you can picture this scene. It is 1985 in John B's in Listowel, a few friends are sitting at a table with Michael and John B. "Look at him" John B. says pointing at Michael "he is like an exotic bird." And exotic is how I found him when we first met in 1969. We were both night telephonists in Exchequer St Telephone exchange.

It's worth recounting that when he first met the Knight of Glin, the good Knight introduced himself "Desmond Fitzgerald Knight of Glin" and Michael replied "Michael Hartnett Night Telephonist." He was the first poet I knew and he shattered some preconceived notions. I thought all poets were layabouts who just thought themselves more sensitive than the rest of us. But I found that Michael was more sensitive, in fact, although it may sound like a cliche, he was a tortured soul.

He was fostered out to his grandmother, Bridget Halpin, as a child and he never recovered from it. "I was abandoned to (their) tragedies" he says "minor but unhealing". He knows the child in the Dal Riada poem "Craving an Absent Breast". If it's true what Kavanagh said that God enters through a wound, God would have no difficulty in entering the soul of Michael Hartnett. He believed he had magical powers, indeed that all poets had magical powers. Part of that magic was that if he stated something to be true, it would come true, even if this was impossible. It was exasperating.

Still, I knew he had some magical powers. Going to the west some 10 years ago, he managed to change his suit in the rear seat of a tiny car: He just bobbed up and down and there he was in a different suit. A feat worthy of Houdini. And then there was the tiny armchair. It had been made for my son Aziz when he just 2 years old and although physically impossible, Michael often slept soundly in it. He could be a marvellous companion and he loved people, he spoke to everybody and he even suffered fools gladly. He needed a drink to kick-start his amazingly gregarious nature and although alcohol makes most people dull, coarse and ugly, Michael became a kind of dancing dervish full of talk, stories and song.

He could sing from all the famous operas, not just the well- known arias and his party piece was the duet from Bizet's "The Pearl Fishers". He sang both Zurga's and Nadir's parts. Duirt Liam O Muirithe mar gheall air "Ba Tuisce leis dan na saol agus do bhi an cheart aige ". Agus uireannta ba tuisce leis deoch na saol.

And he was a good cook. I can still picture him cooking with the glass of wine in one hand and cigarette in the other, and magically producing wonderful food. He cooked often but most notably a sumptuous feast for my wife's 40th birthday, it was his way of repaying the odd borrowed fiver. As well as poet, balladeer, singer and raconteur. He taught me about St John of the Cross, Gerard Manley Hopkins, John Donne, O Bruadair and O Rathaille. He was always broke but he was stylish. He hired a chauffer driven Austin Princess for Lara and Niall's christening in the priory in Tallaght. And on the day he left the Telephone exchange he bought 100 pints for his colleagues in O'Neill's in Suffolk St.

He would like to have been compared to Andreas McCraith the Limerick rake poet, but he was much too frail for that role. If he had 5 pints do bhi a dhotain aige, beioir tareis sos no codhladh tiocfaidh se har nais. But mostly his capacity was small, although he won't mind if there is myth about his drinking. It was only later when he took the shorts that the terrible damage was done. And if his spoken word relied too much on hubris, there was no doubting its written counterpart: the adjective that cropped up most at the Newcastle West funeral was "authentic". And I think that when his work is reassessed the Inchicore Haiku will have a special place. It is flawless. The steady 17 syllables never waver, never appear forced and Hartnett is always at eye level with the Inchicore people. Haiku No. 13 goes:

"In the Richmond House
A good priest pressed in my hand
glad absolution"

This was Fr. Tom Stack who celebrated the Mass today. Michael would be pleased also that the Seannos singer who sang during the offertory, Eamonn O Donnacadh, is from Bluebell here in Inchicore. And also that his goddaughter Bonnie Alexandra Hickey (BAH), to whom the last poem of "Poems to Younger Women" is dedicated, is here this evening. I think it's no exaggeration to say that Michael was a big influence in my life. I last saw him a month ago and I noticed that the no admission sign which he often generated was gone and we had arranged to meet at his friend Christine Dwyer Hickey's New Year's Eve party. Instead I am trying to think of an epitaph. I think that Dean Swift's epitaph would have suited Michael:

He is gone
"where savage indignation can no longer lacerate his heart.
Go traveller and imitate if you can"

Also very apt would be the lines Seamus Heaney wrote a few days ago. It's a translation of Taigh O Huiginn, writing 400 years ago about his brother. He substitutes Michael's name for O'Huiginn:

"O hAairtneide is dead.
Poetry is daunted.
A stave of the barrel is smashed
And the wall of learning broken"

But perhaps just as apt would be one of his own Haikus, the last of the 87:

"My dead father shouts
From his eternal labour
"These are your, people!"

Michael, "Ar Dhes De go raibh do anam uasal."

A Reporter in Court
Fergal Keane

COVERING the courts was different. Real life was on display here, not mentioned by any blathering politician. To someone who had spent his secondary school years in middle-class Ireland – as Louis MacNeice wrote: '. . . banned forever from the candles of the Irish poor' – the experience was shocking, an intensive immersion in the social collapse of large swaths of one Irish city.

The defendants were almost exclusively drawn from the city's council estates. Their crimes ranged from theft of a church poor box to hideous gang rape. They were whey-faced and thin, coughing from cigarettes; they smirked at the police and waved to friends, shuffling into court and into the maw of a criminal justice system which processed them as indifferently as it had processed their fathers and uncles and cousins.

They were destined for jail, followed by unemployment and jail again. The system regarded these young men with contempt and they returned the compliment. Everybody in the little courtroom understood that there wasn't going to be any attempt at rehabilitation: the judges, lawyers, the defendants most of all. It wasn't going to happen. The criminal poor were written off as irredeemable, a nuisance and occasional source of horror but never enough of a critical mass to disturb the dreary calm of the Republic. The system was designed to keep criminals out of circulation, not transform them into useful citizens.

So they travelled across the city to the Victorian misery of Limerick jail, or up to one of the state reformatories to be brutalised until their sentence was done and they were thrown back into the world from which they'd come. They came from estates like Southill and St Mary's Park and Ballynanty, grey estates and ugly, like Finglas, where I'd spent my early childhood. You knew as you sat there, hunched under the pink-faced little judge, crammed in beside the solicitors, that you would very rarely, if ever, hear a defendant give an address from one of the wealthier areas of the city.

Meanwhile anybody who suggested that the city's crime problem might be getting a little out of control was roundly condemned. It was in Limerick that I first heard that favourite phrase of the politicians: 'You're after blowing that out of proportion.' A journalist who hears that should realise he is onto something good. The reckoning in Limerick would come long after I left the city.

In my time in Limerick a gun-related crime was a rarity. But by the early part of the new century shootings were no longer unusual. Twenty years after I left Limerick the city exploded in gang warfare. Rival families murdered each other and anybody unlucky enough to stand in their way. The social problems that created the crime had been centuries in the making: tenements had existed in all the Irish cities since the collapse of agriculture during the Famine; successive British and Irish governments had made either half-hearted efforts or no effort at all in dealing with the problem. Those who didn't get out to England or America scrabbled for jobs in factories. When the factories closed they joined the people who had never had jobs and became our long-term unemployed.

They were given dole money and offered places on training schemes that trained them for non-existent jobs. The worst cases washed up at the offices of the St. Vincent de Paul in search of charity. In Ireland's cities nobody ever entertained any serious thought that this order might change, or that there might spring from these desolate estates a violent breed of criminal whose activities would give Limerick the reputation as the home of the country's most violent armed gangs.

I was appalled by the idea that the poor would fester away for ever on their estates. But along with the rest of the city's comfortable classes I never really believed they could pose a major threat to anybody but themselves. The arrival of drugs on Ireland's big council estates changed the equation. Heroin began flooding into Ireland in the 1980's. With drugs came the opportunity to make big money. The guns came in and local Al Capones emerged. Suddenly the politicians began talking about a breakdown of the social order. By that they meant their order – the order that had existed since the foundation of the state, a country where the poor were encouraged to be happy with their lot and offer up any suffering for the repose of the Holy Souls.

Words like alienation and social justice sprang into the vernacular. The poor had arrived. They could hardly walk out their front doors without finding an earnest young person with a clipboard anxious to canvas their views, or go to the shops without stumbling into a journalist eager to expose the wretchedness of their lives. Those early years on the crime-beat taught me an important lesson, one I would carry with me to the most conflict-ridden regions of the earth; the poor and downtrodden will stay poor and downtrodden; they will always be unseen, people who are talked about rather than talked to, until they do something terrible. Then we pay attention.

From *All of These People: A Memoir*, HarperCollins 2005.

The Last Hours of Sean Bourke
Gerry O'Hare

LAST Tuesday was a normal day for Sean Bourke, the man who sprang Russian agent, George Blake, from an English jail. He awoke in his mobile home, parked discreetly off the main crossroads that lead into the little seaside town of Kilkee, Co. Clare.

He rummaged around and made breakfast. Glanced at the unfinished manuscript of his new book and decided to leave it alone for another day.

A quiet stroll into the town for the morning paper, a few hellos to the locals and a stroll to the seaside shelter where he was often to be seen sitting typing away at his battered typewriter. Today he just gazed out at the Atlantic rollers, possibly pondering on the cruel quirks of life that has seen him become an international figure, a guest of the Russians, living in comparative luxury, much sought after by feature writers of the world's press. And now . . .

Now he was practically penniless and with few prospects, except for his new book, of ever being a part of the jet set again.

Despite his obvious sadness and apparent loneliness, he decided to perform his daily ritual. An eight mile walk to Kilrush and back. Sixteen miles that he walked in all weathers, ending in one of the local bars, usually the Marine, where he drank and drank.

Nobody paid much attention to him as he set out past the crossroads and onwards to Kilrush, walking stick in hand and a hatful of memories.

About five o'clock he was seen approaching the crossroads on the return journey. Larry Collins, who lives at the crossroads, takes up the story. 'I heard a shout and looked around. A few people were standing over Sean, who had collapsed. Two local doctors were called to give him aid and we carried him into the house.

'The ambulance arrived with a nurse and for ninety minutes we fought to save him, but he died without ever opening his eyes or saying a word.'

Next day in Kilkee several of the locals stood around genuinely saddened by Sean's death. 'He was the perfect gentleman,' said local restaurateur Manuel di Lucia. 'He never bothered a soul, and was totally inoffensive. I would chat with him for hours over a drink and I doubt if I ever heard him say a harsh word about anybody. There was no doubt that he was bitter but he kept it to himself.'

Town Clerk Timmy McInerney said that Sean was adamant, up to his death, that he was the man responsible for springing Blake. 'He was working on this new book which I believe may have been a follow-up to his first book,' Timmy said. 'I understand that from talking to him it was going to be quite controversial.'

Sean's last manuscript is now believed to be in the hands of friends. Nobody is quite sure. But one thing is for sure, the quiet spoken Limerickman who mixed with the KGB, writers, poets, smugglers and barmen has written his last chapter.

'He died the way I believed he would have wished,' said Larry Collins. 'Out in the fresh air, on the road with the smell of a good brandy on his breath.'

. . . .

Sean Bourke, the Limerickman who made world headlines after he had master-minded the escape from Wormwood Scrubs prison of Soviet spy George Blake in 1966, died unexpectedly in Kilkee, Co. Clare, yesterday evening. He was 47 years of age.

Bourke had spent more than a year in Kilkee re-writing the manuscript of a book which was based on the psychological approach of prisoners to long-term sentences. Although he had a drink problem, Bourke seemed to have overcome it. He was a member of a well-known old Limerick family. His father was a British ex-serviceman but at the age of 13 the young Bourke was given a sentence in Daingean for a petty offence. This seemed to have embittered him and later he wrote at length on the subject. He went to England and worked in the building trade but many times clashed with the authority.

It was the sending of a bomb through the post to a policeman that he was sentenced to seven years in Wormwood Scrubs. He served only four years because of good behaviour. During that time he became friendly with Blake and after he was released he engineered Blake's escape. He then went to Moscow where he was the guest of the KGB and lived there for about 18 months.

In October, 1968, he arrived back at Shannon Airport and later the British Government succeeded in obtaining an extradition order in the District Court in Dublin on a charge of aiding Blake to escape.

Bourke successfully contested this and returned to Limerick where he continued his writing. He received close on £40,000 for the film rights of his book about how he helped Blake to escape.

Burke lived for a number of years in a converted grain store in Limerick. One of his proudest possessions was a certificate from the Revenue Commissioners which proclaimed him an artist exempt from income tax from his earnings.

While in prison in England he was allowed to study for part of the London University Bachelor of Arts course in English Literature.

Just over a year ago he said that he was feeling the psychological pressure of being cut off from Britain. He then decided that he would hand himself over to the British authorities in the hope that he would get off with a short sentence. Later, he changed his mind and went to live in Kilkee.

From *Irish Times*, 27-1-1982.

Stevie insults Dev

OF all the local politicians mentioned in local newspaper files down the years, Stevie Coughlan stands out as the most outspoken and controversial. From his early days as a local councillor, agitation was his middle name. One of the first major controversies in which he was involved in came in February 13, 1952, when the *Leader*, in large headlines, proclaimed, 'City Council Repudiates Mayor's Letter to Sunday Newspapers.'

Stevie was Mayor at the time, and in his anxiety to land his pet project, the establishment of a chocolate crumb factory for the city, he wrote a letter to the Sunday newspapers making disparaging references to an Taoiseach, Mr. de Valera.

In a very conservative era, the letter caused a sensation and at the following Monday night's City Council meeting, 'the public gallery was crowded to capacity, but hundreds more were unable to gain admittance,' said the *Leader* report.

Fianna Fail members of the Council were incensed.

'If you were behind the Iron Curtain you would tremble in your skin before you would dare address the head of the Government as you have,' thundered Cllr. Dan Bourke, Fianna Fail TD and former Mayor himself.

Stevie, well able to defend himself, retorted: 'Are you comparing this country to the Iron Curtain? Thank god we have our freedom here.'

The debate got highly personal when Ald. Burke accused the Mayor thus: 'We have watched you pitifully since you scraped into the Corporation. You were elected under very shady circumstances.'

Stevie: 'You are making a most serious charge.'

Ald. Bourke was the Mayor's chief protagonist, defending the honour of his beloved 'Chief' at all costs, even going so far as quoting the Provincial of the Holy Ghost Fathers as describing Mr. de Valera 'as eminently suitable for the high office of Taoiseach.'

Cllr. Kevin Bradshaw took up the cudgel on behalf of his Party, outlining what the Chief had done for the country, especially keeping us out of the War. Pointing his finger at the Mayor, he added, 'You took no hand, act or part in any of the Emergency services.'

Stevie: 'I was lucky not to be inside de Valera's glasshouse in the Curragh. You yourself tried to join Clann an Poblachta and paid 30 shillings to the party funds.' He accused another Fianna Fail man, Cllr. Gerry 'Paver' Dillon of being a former Blue Shirt.

The debates raged hot and heavy with all the councillors, no matter what their affiliations, condemning the letter, and some calling for the Mayor's resignation. 'As far as I know, Mr. de Valera never used an offensive word, even to an opponent,' said Cllr. Pa O'Connell, and Cllr. Finnan threatened: 'There was only one apology the people will take from you and that is your chain. Councillor Coughlan, ex-mayor of Limerick, that's what I call you.'

One of the senior councillors, P J Donnellan said: 'You may have been over enthusiastic in trying to do your best for Limerick but I and all my associates condemn you.'

Ald. G E Russell was one of the few sympathetic voices and while admitting that the letter was not above criticism, he made an appeal for the motion censuring the Mayor to be withdrawn. 'Of any of the mayors I have served under, Mr. Coughlan has done more than any to bring about more employment and bring a little happiness into the lives of the poorer people.'

The Mayor, defending his action, said it had been said that in insulting Mr de Valera he had committed an unpardonable sin, but he (Mayor) said when he saw the way he had been treated and kicked about, in his fight for the factory, and the unemployed, he decided to fight or die.

'I do not regret that letter,' he added. 'I fired that shot and have another up the breach if necessary. I owe no apology to anybody for trying to create employment in Limerick.'

When a proposition was made that the Mayor should resign, the law agent intervened and said it was out of order. The meeting eventually decided unanimously to repudiate the letter.

During the course of the meeting, the Mayor had requested the Town Clerk (Mr. McHugh) to hand out samples of the famous chocolate crumb to the councillors, some of whom refused, with a just a few sampling it.

Alas, this was the nearest anyone every got to partake in Stevie's dream of a chocolate crumb factory: his valiant efforts, which afterwards were to make regular headlines in the *Leader* pronouncing false dawns, came to naught in the end.

From *Special Millennium Feature*, Limerick Leader, January 1, 2000.

My first day in the *Leader*
Fergal Keane

MY heart pounded as I climbed the stairs. The girls at reception had told me to go on up. I was expected, she said. The editorial room was the first door on the right, halfway up the stairs. I could hear typewriters clattering furiously and smell of cigar smoke. I knocked on the door. There was no answer. I knocked again. Still no reply. Shaking with nerves, I opened the door and walked in.

The room was crowded with middle-aged men. They were either typing or talking on the phone. At the end of the room there was an elderly, dignified looking figure who sat behind a larger desk, sucking extravagantly on a sweet and making notes in a large diary. On the walls there were black and white photographs of older reporters, men who wore old-fashioned suits and, I presumed, were long deceased. Also on the walls, the effects of cigar smoke could be seen in a vague brown shading that covered the original paint.

I had only ever seen one other newsroom, the vast and bristling acre across which Dustin Hoffman and Robert Redford strode in *All The President's Men*. By contrast, this little room looked like the back room of a bookie's office. One of the typists paused from his work and looked up at me. He was balding, portly, wore thick glasses and was smoking a cigar. He took the cigar out of his mouth in order to address me. 'Yes? What do you want? he barked.

I stepped backwards. 'I'm here to see the editor. My name is Fergal Keane. I'm the new reporter.'

'Keane?'

The cigar smoker smiled. Then he addressed his companions: 'Well, lads, he's here! The junior. At last we get to see the cut of him.'

The others raised their heads to take me in.

The cigar man stood up and came forward to shake my hand. 'The name is Cormac Liddy,' he said. 'Mr. Liddy to you.'

One or two of the others snickered, as he said this.

'What are you laughing at, Phelan, you fucking ape?' he shouted.

A fair-headed youth sitting near the door burst out laughing.

'Mister my arse,' said Phelan in reply, leaning back with his hands behind his head.

Liddy turned to me smiling: 'You needn't take any lessons in manners from that customer.'

Liddy knocked on the editor's door and then ushered me in ahead of him. Sitting behind the desk was a silver-haired, pipe-smoking man who was busy laying out the front page of that day's paper. 'That's Mr. Halligan. He's the editor.'

Liddy then slipped discretely out of the room, trailing a cloud of cigar smoke. Halligan stood up and shook my hand. 'Good to have you with us. I'm sure Cormac and the rest of them will make you welcome.'

Halligan was a brilliant newspaperman. He was also, I would soon find out, the toughest of editors. Halligan had been born of Irish parents and brought up in the north of England. He had worked on local papers in England before becoming the *Daily Mail* correspondent in Dublin. Halligan was passionate about Ireland. It is often said that the children of Irish parents growing up in England tend to view Ireland in one of two ways: they either want to shed their parents' identity and be British or, feeling like exiles in the country of their birth, they embrace them and cross over the water. Halligan was definitely in the latter category. He quit the *Mail* to edit a newly established local paper in Ireland, and then moved to the job in Limerick.

Brendan Halligan liked me, which was just as well for I would've hated to have him as an enemy. Sharp, rigorous, a man of emphatic views, when Halligan turned his questioning eye on you, you prayed to heaven you'd got the facts. I came to fear his red pen slicing through copy, pointing out errors of grammar and spelling or demanding that I check the accuracy of some point of fact. He once threatened to throw me out of his office window when I mis-attributed a quote. To this day I cannot be sure if he was joking.

After a few words of welcome Brendan Halligan introduced me to the newsroom. My daily boss would be the elderly man in the corner, nicknamed 'Chum.' He was the news editor. When the atmosphere in the newsroom became especially raucous – a not infrequent occurrence – Chum would gently rap on his table and call out: 'Settle, lads, settle for the love of God.' This would be followed by a long muttering. It never had a great effect. Chum was a gentleman journalist, a man from a different age when lunches were long and deadlines more elastic. He enjoyed regular refreshment and we would set our watches by his morning visits to the pub behind the building. When he returned he would interrogate each of us on the progress of whatever story we were working on.

The great terror of the junior reporter was the Chum 'special.' This usually arose after a call from a source who would have overhead a rumour in a pub. On the basis of that the junior would be expected to produce a front page lead. Too often the trail proved false. I was once sent off in search of a secret NATO radar station in County Limerick on the basis of a rumour picked up in the pub. Ireland was not a member of NATO. To erect a secret radar station under the noses of the preternaturally suspicious county Limerick peasantry would have required stealth well beyond the combined abilities of the CIA, M16 or anybody else. I was laughed out of every shop, pub and house I visited. By the time I returned Chum had forgotten he'd even sent me on the story.

He was a kind-hearted man though. On my first day in the *Leader* Chum sent me to the annual general meeting of the Limerick Harbour Commissioners, knowing that, as a junior reporter with no money, I would appreciate the free lunch. I was to shadow one of the other reporters – a long-haired, bearded denims-wearing character called Billy Kelly. Billy had made a name for himself with a series exposing police brutality in the city, and also penned a weekly satirical column. He was a tough reporter and quickly became my hero.

The Harbour Commissioners' meeting was stupefyingly dull. But its aftermath was a delight. A local councillor got to his feet, and simpering in our direction, asked the 'gentlemen of the press join us for lunch in Hanratty's Hotel.' I followed Kelly and we were soon joined by the cigar-smoking Liddy. Having been assured by Kelly that it was permissible, I ordered a pint of stout. A waiter and menu arrived.

'I'll have Duck á l'Orange,' I said.

'You will in your arse have duck. You'll have steak,' interjected Liddy. 'On your wages you'll never pay for steak yourself.'

Like so many of my countrymen, Liddy put great faith in the power of steak, it was food for the 'quality.' Steak suggested abundance and prestige. So I ordered the fillet steak.

Walking back to the office I offered the opinion that journalism was a grand job. Liddy and Kelly simply nodded, too stuffed to disagree. To a young man earning around £40 a week after tax, such receptions were a godsend. As the months wore on I was regularly glutted with the good meat of Limerick's hotels.

From *All of These People*: A Memoir, HarperCollins 2005.

Bridge over Ma Murphy
Seán Bourke

LIMERICK was always a dump, but now it was dirtier and more dismal than ever. I walked up William Street and went into the red-brick public lavatory in the middle of the road. The doors were hanging off the cubicles, and the plumbing was out of action, but people went on using them and they were piled high with excrement. I went to the urinal. The same glass-fronted panel that was there when I was going to school was still fixed at eye level. In it, printed in an immaculate copperplate, there was a prayer to God beseeching Him to protect the beholder from all temptation.

Years before, some anonymous ecclesiastic in an inspired moment had hit on the idea that man's immortal soul was in greatest danger when he held his penis in his hand. At the top of the panel, pointed in large letters, were the words: *Not for ourselves but for your country*. The panel and the neatly printed prayer seemed incongruous in the surrounding squalor. I found this difference of approach between the Irish lavatory authorities and the English rather interesting. The Irish exhorted you to avoid sin, whilst the English assumed that you had already sinned and gave you the address of the place where you could get treatment. Both tried to make you feel guilty for having a piss. Outside the lavatory I was accosted by one of the gypsies who always hung around there. He wanted the price of a pint . . .

I walked up Mulgrave Street and approached the Munster Fair Tavern, one of the few pubs in Ireland which does not sell Guinness, it sells Murphy's instead. Outside, I met Ger Carey, a man I had gone to school with.

'Hello Seán,' he said. 'Your mother told me you were coming home today. God, 'tis a long time since I saw you now. It must be fifteen years.'

'Is it is as long as that, Ger?' I said.

'Indeed it is. Sure you left Limerick when you were only seventeen. I wasn't long after you myself. And since then we were never home on holiday at the same time, sure.'

'When are you going back?' I asked.

''I'm off on Wednesday,' he said.

'Will you come in for a pint, Ger?'

'Indeed I will.' Then, lowering his voice confidentially: 'Can you lend me a pound before we go in and I'll send it to you when I go back.'

'I will, Ger.' I gave him a pound and we went into the pub.

'Well, good luck,' he said, raising his pint of stout.

'Good luck Ger.'

We drank.

I wanted to know if my neighbours in Limerick knew I had been to jail. Ger, I felt sure, could tell me. I was wondering how to bring up the subject when he himself gave me the opening.

'So you're not working,' he went on. 'Well now, I thought you'd be on the stage or in the films by this time.'

'Why is that, Ger?'

'Didn't I read about you having a romance with some actress in London when the two of ye were in the one play? You were playing the part of a doctor, the paper said. 'Twas on the front page, sure.'

That incident had been a misunderstanding in the drama group at Wormwood Scrubs. There had been a photograph on the front page right enough, with a caption that said 'proposed in jail.' It had all been very embarrassing.

'And do the English daily papers get sold in Ireland these days?' I asked.

'They do indeed. They've been sold there this many a year sure.'

'So you all know where I was when that incident occurred, then?'

Ger hesitated, a little embarrassed. 'Well,' he said, looking into his pint, 'I heard you got into a little trouble all right. But sure that could happen to anyone.'

We started to talk about our schooldays. Despite his absence, Ger knew everyone in our district who had been born, got married, or died in the past fifteen years. The *Limerick Leader*, I thought, must be sold in Birmingham.

'Old Ma Murphy is dead too, the Lord have mercy on her soul,' he said presently.

'Who's Old Ma Murphy?'

'Don't you remember?' Ger was surprised.

'She's the old woman with the shawl,' he said, 'who used to come in the road with a donkey and cart selling milk at a penny a quart an' we going to school. Don't you remember her Seán?'

'Oh, of course,' I said. 'Isn't that the woman who was passing underneath when a gang of us were up on the railway bridge that day?'

'That's her,' said Ger, draining his second pint. 'And didn't my brother Fonsy destroy the poor woman.'

I ordered another couple of pints. 'Destroy' was putting it very politely, but then Ger had never been one for vulgarity or bad language. He was a better Christian than any of the rest of us in the gang could ever hope to be. I remembered the incident as if had happened only yesterday. The gang of us had been up on the railway bridge just beyond Bengal Terrace, where the countryside abruptly begins. Old Ma Murphy was coming in from the country where she had a cottage and half an acre near Ballyneety village. She was sitting up on the little cart next to the tank of sour milk and the jaded donkey was pulling her towards the town at the rate of about two miles an hour.

We all saw her coming. There was a hurried conference, as there usually is when there are a few very young boys on a bridge and a likely target comes into view. But we had no missiles handy. Stones were out of the question and there was no water near by. 'I have it!' said Fonsy, Ger's brother. 'I have it!' he dropped his trousers, placed one foot on either side of the wide gap in the boards and squatted down. His rectum was poised with precision over the centre of the opening. 'Give me the signal Seán,' he said, looking up at me with a grin. 'And you better allow me a few yards because 'tis a high bridge.'

I took up a strategic position and raised my hand in the manner of a battery commander, like I had seen it in the films. Ma Murphy came closer, her eyes fixed permanently about half-way along the donkey's burdened back, completely oblivious to the impending danger. The rest of the boys were all down on their hands and knees peering through other gaps in the boards. She was under the bridge. A couple of yards to go. 'Now!' I said, dropping my hand suddenly. The first one tapered like a bomb, landed dead centre between the donkey's ears, exploding on impact to splash all over the animal's neck. Ma Murphy stared disbelievingly for a moment at the brown mess. She was sixty years of age and had never before seen shit falling from the sky. Hail, rain and snow, yes, but shit, never.

She looked up, her eyes and her mouth wide open in an expression of shocked incredibility. But the second one was already on its way. It might have missed her, if it weren't for the donkey. Even that docile creature was so taken aback it stopped dead in its tracks. And by now Ma Murphy was staring straight up at Foncy's bare arse. She saw it coming but couldn't believe it. She just stared at it, mesmerized. Then it landed, right on her forehead, and splashed smoothly all over her face.

'Jesus, Mary and Joseph,' she screamed. 'I'm destroyed! Holy Mother of God, what's happening at all!' A dozen pairs of eyes, like cats in the night, were staring down at her through the gaps in the boards and Fonsy's arse was still poised there menacingly. 'Ye dirty blaggards!' she screamed. 'Ye dirty blaggards! May God forgive ye!' And her face was brown all over.'

'My God, Ger', I said, 'that was along time ago. We were only ten or eleven then, weren't we?'

'That's all sure.'

From *The Springing of George Blake,* Cassell & Company Ltd., 1970.

PEOPLE

Richard Harris: his Early Days
By Gus Smith

WHILE Crescent College turned out students who would become lawyers, doctors and bankers, it also put much emphasis on sport and over the years a number of its former pupils played rugby for Ireland. The Jesuits maintained a tight discipline and students who caused trouble or neglected their homework were punished. The punishments, which were carried out by the College Prefect of Studies, ranged from two slaps, or biffs as they were called, on the hand, to six slaps, depending on the gravity of the offence. The prefect used a leather strap and this became a dark symbol in itself. Boys came to fear the strap, but young Dickie Harris shrugged it off as something to be endured like a hard rugby tackle on the field.

The Harris family was close-knit and resided in a large house known in the area as *Overdale*. It was full of vitality and its doors were always open to the children's pals. For young Dickie it was a particularly happy and vigorous childhood. His father's flour mill provided the money to ensure that the family lived a life of quality. Young Harris was born into a conservative, class-conscious Limerick where the madcap antics of wealthy young men were accepted with stoic understanding by the barmen and hotel porters of the city.

It was a city, small and compact, that was emerging from the deprivation of a world war, with attitudes firmly rooted in faith and morals. Any display of new thinking or challenge to the established order was frowned upon. Harris and his youthful pals were the first generation to break away from the values inculcated down the decades. They represented a more open and liberal approach, a foretaste of the new generation whose confidence and social standing were dictated by family tradition.

He was a young rebel, always the centre of fun and mischief, admired by youth, regarded with some intolerance by an older generation. 'Dickie's incorrigible' was a phrase often used about him, but he ignored public opinion. In the streets he was conspicuous by his flaming red hair, gangling figure, and loud, musical voice. He could be quick and devastating with his tongue. Pretty girls – and Limerick had more than its share – tagged along after him and sometimes joined in his mischief-making and pranks, though it was generally accepted that he preferred at that time the company of boys of his own age.

Cinema-going was a popular pastime in the city and as long as he can remember Dickie Harris loved movies. They fired his lively imagination, fed his fantasies, and created for him new heroes. He was able to run off the names of screen cowboys and gangsters with admirable speed. 'One of my most abiding memories of Dickie,' recalls a schoolboy friend, 'was of seeing him falling down the wide staircase in the Savoy Cinema as he imitated the contortions of the cowboy star he had just seen in the cinema. He was very good at that. We used to be entertained by his rather robust gymnastics and he liked to show off.'

It was ironical, therefore, though no great surprise to some of his pals, that he was banned at different times from all the city's cinemas. 'I often went to the cinema and stayed there all day,' he recalls. 'I would go in for the matinee, stay for the middle show and evening performance. I used to do that when I had nothing else to do, especially in the summertime when I was on holidays. Later on when I started drinking I would go into the cinema drunk and I would stand up, sometimes on my seat, and start to say the lines with the actors.'

'There is a famous story about the time I got drunk and went into the Lyric Cinema where Marlon Brando was playing in *Julius Caesar*. When I got there I proceeded to repeat the immortal lines, "Friends, Romans, Countrymen, lend me your ears." Then I went on, "I have not come to praise Caesar but to bury him," which immediately made the audience laugh. Well, a Garda squad car pulled up outside and I was taken away for causing a disturbance.'

It was not long before he was recognized by cinema doormen and stopped. But life continued to be fun. His first love was a girl called Grace Lloyd, but he was to say sadly, 'We grew up together but she had no love for me. Grace was always the 'humdinger' in my life, the girl I cared most about.'

He was not unaware of the fact that he was growing up in a fairly privileged family, whose lifestyle contrasted with the poverty and poor housing conditions not a mile away from his home. The Harrises were among the lucky families at that time, for they were never short of food at *Overdale*. They kept a nanny, a servant and a gardener, and there seemed to be plenty of money for the good things of life. Gradually however, the flour-milling business began to decline, which meant that one or two of the house staff had to be let go.

'When this happened I realized change was coming,' he recalls, 'and the full realization struck me when my mother began to do the washing.' It was an exaggeration, however, to claim that the family fell, as Harris occasionally says today, on 'poor times'. It never came to that.

He admits he did a lot of foolish things as a youth, yet he invariably takes intense pleasure in recalling those childhood days in Limerick. 'I remember going to Cruise's Hotel every Saturday night at nine o'clock to wash dishes. My payment was free entry to the dance, and that was the highlight of the week, my big night out.

'Between dances, rugby and music I was kept going twenty-four hours a day. Myself and my pals, Gerry Murphy and Paddy Lloyd, would go out together. When one of us was inside then he would go to the fire escape and duck the other two in. This worked at the Savoy, Lyric and the Carlton, but it was difficult at the City Theatre and the Grand Central.'

In Kilkee, the popular County Clare seaside resort more than sixty miles from Limerick, he became known as the 'lively lad'. In summer half the population of Limerick repaired there for holidays. It became known colloquially as Limerick Summer. Harris's red hair and long, lean body could be easily picked out on the expansive beach, or when he played volley ball against the whitewashed wall at the sea front.

In the local Arcadia Cinema he was among the Limerick lads who shouted remarks at the screen and each other, or chanted along with the ads. The cinema bill changed nightly. Occasionally Harris's voice could be heard above the din and the usher would shout, 'Silence!' Sometimes the audience chorused along with a popular ad of the time to the tune of Danny Kaye's 'Wonderful Wonderful Copenhagen':

> *Wonderful wonderful golden*
> *Amber...*
> *A beautiful flavoured tea*
> *When you drink a cup*
> *It will cheer you up*
> *Wonderful golden*
> *Aaaammmbbberrr.*

When he left Crescent College his father suggested that he go into the flour-milling business. 'There was not much else I could do,' says Dickie. He became popular with the customers as he sold flour over the counter and in a jokey voice would count out aloud their exact change. The old ladies enjoyed his easy manner and sense of humour. As flour millers they had big barns and lofts and sometimes the wiry young Harris spent his time frightening the mice away from the flour.

His ambition to be an international rugby player was still a top priority with him. He had wanted to play for Young Munster but his father persuaded him to join the famed Garryowen club, and in 1952 he won a Munster Senior Cup medal with Garryowen. Good rugby judges considered he had a promising career provided he concentrated on the game. However, he still found time to play pranks. Once his father insisted that he attend a special tennis tournament being held at the local county tennis club where the Harris family were founder members. It was reckoned an important competition. The West of Ireland Championships always attracted a big entry of talented players.

On arrival at the club with his pal young Harris's attention was instantly drawn to the giant winner's cup surrounded by plaques, medals and trophies placed on a table near the gents' toilet. He also realized that a fellow could easily open a small window at the rear of the toilet and remove the cup.

'So without further thought, I quietly entered the toilet,' he recalls, 'went to the window, opened it, leaned out and removed the cup. I then placed it in the boot of a car and waited to see what would happen. It took a little while for anyone to notice but eventually there was consternation and havoc when word got out that the cup had gone missing.'

The finger of suspicion almost immediately was pointed in his direction. As he says today, 'It was generally believed that Harris was responsible for nicking the cup but nobody dared challenge me on it and when I left the grounds afterwards there were no questions asked.'

The newspapers published the story. Harris hid the cup in an unused corner of his home and thought no more about it, although he had intended returning the cup in a few days. The next morning when he arrived home he was confronted by his father.

'Jesus, Mary and Joseph, Dickie, get that cup out of this house.' He ordered his son. Ruffled, Dickie tried to explain away the prank but his father would not hear of it, repeating instead the words, 'Get the cup out of here.'

He went to Cruise's Hotel where his brother-in-law Jack Donnelly was the general manager, and quietly went to the ladies' toilets, the cup under his arm, and locked himself into one of the cubicles. He placed the cup on top of the toilet seat, then unlocked the door and hurried through a corridor to the rear of the hotel, where he hopped over a wall. He then went into a public phone and rang the Garda station and told them where the cup could be found. Within minutes a Garda squad car arrived outside the hotel and four officers ran inside and, in a few moments, emerged with the cup.

Later, the cup was presented to the tennis tournament winner by politician Donogh O'Malley and when he heard who was suspected of taking it in the first place, commented 'I wouldn't put it past the blackguard.'

In 1952, just when it appeared that his rugby career was taking off with Garryowen, Harris was stricken with tuberculosis but his mother would not allow him to be sent to a sanatorium; instead she decided to nurse him at home in *Overdale*. At the time in Ireland the disease was rampant and there was a certain stigma attached to anyone going to a 'San'. It took young Harris weeks, perhaps months, to accept that he would be confined to the house. For a restive and athletic young man it was sheer agony.

During the long, tedious days and nights he began to read and think a lot. Gradually he came to terms with himself and at the same time discovered who his real friends were.

'At first people came to see me every day, then after a while they got bored with me just lying there so they left me alone and I continued to develop my imagination; light bulbs, doorknobs, pillows became animated objects and I began playing scenes with them as if they were real people. I also read a lot – letters of Van Gogh in particular, and they turned me on to a kind of self-search that has never stopped.'

In the room, as he lay propped up in bed, he recited lines from plays aloud, especially Shakespeare and soon he was able to close the book and recite whole passages. He imagined himself on the stage playing Hamlet or Romeo and the thought made him want to get better quickly. 'I want to be an actor,' he told himself as the sunshine lit up the room. 'But how am I going to go about it?'

When he was finally told he was clear of TB, he announced his decision to become an actor to the whole Harris household. He also convinced others that he was deadly serious. One day in O'Connell Street he met a former school friend, Tom Stack, who was then studying to be a priest. They talked about little else except acting.

'I remember Dickie had a copy of John Steinbeck's *East of Eden* under his arm and this was a revelation to me because I remembered that at school he showed little interest in literature. When he told me what he was reading I was fascinated and knew he wanted to be an actor. I could see, despite his illness, that he had lost none of his humour and zest for living.'

Although Harris had seen McMaster and MacLiammoir and Siobhan McKenna when they visited Limerick, he claimed it wasn't their influence that made him become an actor. His motivation came from his reading. He conceded however that he learned a lot about acting from professional touring companies. 'I remember the Lord Longford Group came to Limerick with their production of Pirandello's *Henry IV* and I was staggered by the play. I swore that one day I would play the lead.'

He began to take an interest in local amateur drama companies like the College Players. As his interest grew, he thought of going to live in Dublin and applying to the Abbey Theatre for work but he dismissed the thought from his mind: he knew nobody in the theatre there and doubted that he would get a job. His mind was made up for him when the Anew McMaster company visited Limerick. 'If you want to be an actor, my boy, you must go to London,' McMaster advised him.

Around 1954, a combined university drama group arrived at Kilkee to present plays. Harris got friendly with them and agreed to cook their meals in the big house overlooking the sea called Hector's Castle. At night he helped backstage with props and scenery. It was the first time he had worked with a drama group and he enjoyed the experience enormously.

On summer nights the hotels held sing-alongs and the entertainment proved very popular with visitors. Everyone was expected to do their party piece. One Sunday evening in the Victoria Hotel, a very popular venue, Harris was drinking with his Limerick friends and listening to a singer belting out a big ballad to piano accompaniment when a voice was heard exclaim, 'Give us Brando, Dickie.'

When the singing stopped, the request was repeated. Everyone knew it was Harris's favourite party piece and they never tired of asking for it. It was a lengthy sequence from the movie *On The Waterfront*, featuring Marlon Brando. Harris stepped forward and took the centre of the floor. Silence fell in the large room.

Using an American accent, and in a hushed voice he began to 'take off' Brando convincingly. 'There was a touch of the method-acting school about his performance,' recalls Tom Stack. 'His gestures, whispered words like "I coulda been somebody, instead of a bum..." caught the flavour of the movie to perfection. The audience was captivated.'

To Stack at that time, Harris was a great extrovert and possessed both personality and presence. They talked together again about the vocation of acting and he felt that Harris was then more determined than ever to pursue his chosen career. 'It was eating him up and I could see he would never be satisfied until he was an actor.'

It was clear too, that Limerick was becoming too small for him. He was misunderstood by many of its citizens who confused his Bohemian ways with lack of purpose and talent. Once when the veteran editor of the *Limerick Leader*, Con Cregan, met him on the stairs of the building, he nodded his head and told a member of staff, 'I met that eccentric young Harris on the stairs just now. Whatever is to become of him?'

Joe Mulqueen, the stocky middle-aged chief reporter drew on his pipe and replied, 'They say he wants to act.'

Cregan shook his head, and said, 'My God, that young man has been play-acting all his life. And he's such a sturdy fellow, you know. Couldn't he do something useful with himself?'

Harris knew he had to get out of a city that thought more of shopkeepers than of actors. For an aspiring actor, there were few opportunities to learn techniques of the art of acting. When he told his father he was leaving the mill job, he wished him well but he was not surprised by his son's decision.

Harris was able to look back on a happy time in Limerick. As he says, 'I had a great childhood, and I don't regret a single day of it. Limerick was good to me. Sure I had troubled and happy times but all in all, I love the place.'

'Dickie was as wild as he was painted,' mused Limerick show-business columnist Earl Connolly. 'But it was only mischief and a bit of devilment; I don't remember him ever being vicious or nasty. I knew he wanted to go on the stage but I wasn't sure about the extent of his talent and had no idea how far he would go.'

Michael English, whose mother had a deep interest in theatre, knew of Harris's ambition to be an actor. They were friends and Harris confided in him his hopes for the future. 'My mother once made Dickie and myself go on stage with Anew McMaster when he visited Limerick with his company. He was proud of that. Dickie knew what he wanted.'

One of Harris's best pals at that time was the aspiring poet Desmond O'Grady who remembers Limerick as 'caste-divided city of Catholics and Protestants, urbanites and suburbanites, Laurel Hill and Presentation girls, Jesuit and Christian Brother boys. The rugby, rowing and church clubs were equally divided.'

To O'Grady, the arts were very local and low key but there was himself seriously writing poems and Dickie Harris dedicated to becoming an actor. They both had their personal epiphanies; through his lonely reading Harris discovered plays and books and O'Grady discovered poetry.

'During this hiatus of adolescence,' recalled O'Grady, 'Harris realized the radiance of Marlon Brando and the modern New York School of method acting. I discovered James Joyce and the modern movement in literature. Our painter friend Jack Donovan discovered Cézanne and modern painting. We three became fast friends.'

They met frequently in the Savoy tea-rooms to talk endlessly about the arts and their own particular ambitions. Because they had little money they were grateful to the 'innocent waitress' who grew to like their presence there and kept their teapot refilled with hot water. Sometimes they even imagined they were in some famous café in London or Paris, aspiring artists discussing their future work.

At other times, they went along to the Carlton Cinema to see the early Brando films and any forbidden Continental movies. They dressed in 'arty clothes', with young Harris prominent in his newly fashionable duffle coat and O'Grady looking like James Joyce in his clerical black coat and sweater. The painter Donovan wore crumpled country clothes and a battered tweed hat.

Being different from most others of their age in Limerick, they were labelled 'eccentrics'. O'Grady had made up his mind to try his luck in Paris, Harris talked about art schools in London. And Jack Donovan was content to go on painting wherever he could. With a poet's imagination, Desmond O'Grady was particularly anxious to leave the narrow confines of a city which he described as 'the last bollard on the dark edge of Europe, and O'Connell Street seemed a Desolation Row for anybody with a curious imagination'. Young Dickie Harris did not see Limerick in such black shades, nor did he wish to. Perhaps it was because of his abiding love for rugby football and his favourite teams, Garryowen and Young Munster.

His previous confinement through illness had had the effect of tending to make Harris more introspective on occasions, though it was never for long. Soon the old impetuosity would surface as well as his unquenchable humour and penchant for clowning. But if some Limerick people believed that there was little more to him than a mere prankster, they were wrong. He was ambitious, determined, and had a specific goal. Yet certain facets of life puzzled him. He sometimes wondered, for instance, what mark he had made on his parents; he was closer to his mother than his father.

'There were six boys and two girls in the family,' he likes to recall, 'and I was lost in the middle of this Harris brigade. I was the non-commissioned officer in the middle! I can't remember the parental stroke, the touch from mother or affection from father, that sense of being singled out, so I had an identity crisis when the tuberculosis eased off. I was free to become something, but what?

'I chose acting partly because I knew I'd have to create an identity for them to recognize I wasn't just child number five. I wanted them to realize who I am, for my mother and father to say. "Hey, we've got a friend called Richard Harris in the family. That's him there on the stage."'

He has always spoken of Limerick with passion and a tinge of sadness. His memories are vivid and mostly happy. He once recalled his earliest memory:

'My brother Noel was just born and one day I was pushing him in the pram. My mother and the maid were behind us and we were walking down Post Office Lane and the maid said, "Richard, whatever you do, do not take your hands off the pram." Then, for some reason, I looked into the pram and saw Noel and asked my mother would I ever be that young again? She leaned over to me and said, "No, Richard, you won't."'

Harris had always been able to tell a joke against himself. Once, he recalled, 'I remember well an American journalist who went to Limerick some time ago to do a story on me. She knocked at the school door and asked to speak to the Head. When he came down she asked did Dickie Harris go to school here? and explained that she was doing an article for an American magazine. He said, "I'd prefer you did not mention him in relation to this school."'

If the Jesuits at Crescent College failed to make an abiding impression on Harris, at least he carried away with him a love of rugby football and the meaning of friendship, for over the years he has retained an interest in rugby and kept friendly with former classmates. Now, in 1955, at the age of twenty-four, he was preparing to start a new career in London.

Being an extrovert the city would scarcely overwhelm him. Some people in Limerick heaved a sigh of relief when the news broke that he was leaving; others continued to retell funny stories about his zany escapades, and a few wondered if he would ever make it as an actor.

Dickie Harris was determined to prove everyone wrong.

From *Richard Harris: Actor by Accident*, Robert Hale Ltd., 1990.

TWO
RELIGION

Brendan Behan and the Confraternity
1960

THINGS, of course, die hard in people's memories, and betrayal looms very large in the history of England's government of Ireland. The city of Limerick is north of Kerry on the Shannon and was subjected to a long siege during the Williamite wars. In the end, although the citizens stood their hardships very bravely – I think because they had to – a treaty was concluded between the two sides; but the ink was hardly dry on the paper before every article of the treaty was broken by the English authorities and most onerous Penal Laws enforced against Catholics all over Ireland.

Maybe it's that race-memory of that broken treaty that had Limerick such a fervently Catholic city, for, apart, from its ham, it is main claim to fame is that it has a huge Catholic Confraternity which is said to comprise over ninety per cent of the city's population. The Confraternity, besides being very large, is also very enthusiastic, and they hold a mission every Lent, at which, for a week, a priest comes and preaches them about their sins, and they have prayers and Benediction every night lasting for hours, but ending before closing time. On the final Sunday, they go to Mass and Holy Communion in the morning, and in the evening there is a final service at which the congregation renew their baptismal vows. So every man gets a candle and takes it with him to the church and, at the appropriate time, the priest tells them to light their candles. It's a marvellous sight – and I say it quite genuinely and sincerely – to see thousands of candles all lighting up the cathedral. Anyhow, they hold up their candles and the priest calls upon them to renounce the devil and all his works and pomps and they all say, 'We do.'

'Louder,' says the priest, 'louder and scare away the devil and all his works and pomps.'

As one man they shouted, 'We do.'

'Louder still,' said the priest, 'let him hear you in hell or wherever he is. Do you renounce the devil with all his works and pomps?'

'We do,' shouted the congregation, and one very enthusiastic member roared: 'We do, we do, the dirty bastard.'

There was one famous member of the Limerickmen's Confraternty known as the Daddy Crowe who accompanied the group on a pilgrimage to Rome. They were well received in audience by the Pope, and at the end of the audience each member went up to the throne, took the Pope's hand and kissed his ring. But the Daddy Crowe didn't merely kiss his ring – he took him by the hand, shook it heartily and said: 'Jaysus, Holy Father, there's not a man in Limerick that wouldn't go to hell for you.'

Taking a girl out in Limerick as you might guess, has its difficulties. 'O Limerick girls are beautiful as everybody knows,' as the song has it, but they're also very careful about keeping their legs shut, if not their mouths. A boy who takes a girl out in Limerick gives her tea, brings her to a picture or a dance, treats her to drink or something at the dance, and some supper afterwards. Then he asks can he bring her home. He takes her to the gate of her house, puts his arm round her and she says breathlessly: 'Good night now it's nearly twelve o'clock Jasus I'll be kilt thanks for everything,' and she's gone.

And sure, there's no harm in it at all. Down on the Limerick-Cork border, there was a sturdy farmer of about forty years of age who, suddenly to his parish priest's dismay, upped and married a Protestant lady from the Palatinate in the county. However, the priest was agreeably surprised when, after three months of marriage, the wife came along to him and asked for instruction in the Faith. In due course, she was received into the Church and the couple lived happily together until her death about seven or eight years later. After a couple of years of widowhood, the farmer, to the priest's horror, married another Protestant lady, but again the priest was overjoyed when she, in turn, came long after a few months of marriage and was received into the Church.

She too died about ten years later and the farmer again was left alone in the world. After a year, he entered the bonds of wedlock again and for the third time to a Protestant lady. The parish priest made no fuss about the matter this time seeing that the two previous wives had ended up in no time as good-loving devout Catholics. The third wife, however, showed no hurry in going down to the parish priest and, by the end of the year, he began to get worried. Up he goes to the farm and sees the farmer.'

'What's the meaning of this,' John? says the parish priest, 'your wife hasn't come near me since you were married. It's a shame for you, John, and you after giving such good example for the whole county by converting your previous wives. What on earth is the matter at all?'

John, who was by this time well past sixty, sat there dejectedly in the chair looking at the parish priest.

'Ah! Father,' says he sadly, 'sure the oul' convertor isn't what it was.'

From *The Grand Tour of Limerick*, compiled by Cornelius Kelly. Cailleach Books, 2004. (Adapted from *Brendan's Behan's Island*)

First Communion Dress
Mae Clancy-Leonard

MY mother looked up from the letter, her face a picture of excitement – "your dress is coming from The States. You'll be gorgeous. Nobody in the whole of Ireland will have a dress like it."

You could say one thing for sure about my mother. She believed in miracles. How a be-freckled, gap-toothed creature like me could be elevated to 'gorgeous' was nothing short of one. But she was away in a hack – "I'll get Mrs. Tierney to curl your hair with rags and I'll get the nuns at the Good Shepherd Convent to make you a Limerick Lace veil . . ."

Her excitement was infectious. I wanted to rush out and tell everyone. "No, No," Mam cautioned, "nobody must know. You've got to keep this a secret and we'll stun them on your First Communion Day."

But that size of secret weighed far too heavy for a seven-year-old to carry around all by herself. Soon the entire class was in on it. Naturally, they were all green with envy. The next day someone brought in photograph of their American cousin in a frothy, flounced Communion Dress. Yes. Yes. I believed that anybody could be gorgeous in such a creation.

Sr. Bonaventure was finding it more and more difficult to curb our idle chatter. Religious Instruction was taking a back seat.

"If ye don't behave yerselves, I'll get Canon Lee to cancel the First Communion altogether. Now, how would ye like that?"

We applied ourselves more diligently to our Catechism then.

We knew the Ten Commandments backwards and we struggled through the Seven Deadly Sins. Sins in such high flown language that we couldn't understand a word. Asking meaning of avarice, adultery or lust was met with a dismissive -

"Learn it, ye're not supposed to understand it."

Two weeks before the big day Mam wore a worried frown. There was no sign of my dress. She pestered the postman and bombarded the GPO. She sent Dad up to the Harbour Office to find out if there were any boats due in from America. Granny began a Novena to St. Anthony or it might have been St. Jude. But, if all fruit failed she had a few bob saved in the cracked black teapot with the blue flowers. Granny's prayers worked. The postman whistled a fanfare as he handed over the many-stamped package. He was invited into the kitchen for the unwrapping. String zinged and brown paper crackled as it was removed and carefully saved. Then when the cover was lifted there was that distinctive American smell wafting the air. Mam eased out the glorious white dress.

My lips formed an awed "O..o..h." as the sun dazzled on its blue whiteness. I had never seen anything so exquisite. I reached out to touch it.

"Don't," my Mam howled, "your hands are dirty."

At this stage the postman beat a hasty retreat. He closed the front door on an agonising scream.

My hair stood on end - "wh..a..t's wrong mam?"

"Oh God! The sleeves, look at the sleeves."

"I can't see anything wrong with them Ma."

"Are you blind or something? See, they're short."

"So?"

"Canon Lee won't let you into the church with short sleeves."

I went numb. Neighbours were consulted and olagóned with my Mum.

They all agreed that short sleeves would not be tolerated in church and any attempted alteration would destroy the style of my dress.

There was nothing for it but to count the money from the black teapot and go shopping.

My First Communion dress was a lank, crepe-de-chine, long sleeves thing that I hated. The Limerick Lace veil was so different from all the others. I hated that too.

Then there were the photographs. We went down to Athlunkard Boat Club for the scenic background. It took half the day to take them because we had to have two sets. One lot in my long-sleeved dress and the other in my beautiful dress to satisfy the American cousin who sent it. By the time the film ran out I was cross-eyed with vexation.

I was so pleased when it rained and we all went home to our tea.

From *My Home Is There*, Isle Publications, 1996.

St. Michael's Clergyman: Bishop T. E. O'Dwyer, D.D.
Frank Prendergast, MA

UNDOUBTEDLY the most widely renowned member of the parish clergy was Bishop Thomas Edmund O'Dwyer, D.D. By any standards he was a colossus in the Irish Hierarchy of his day. He was of the same Tipperary stock as Seatrún Céitinn (1570-1649) another distinguished scholar in the Irish church of the 16th and 17th Centuries and author of "Foras Feasa ar Eirinn", an encyclopaedia of Irish History and heritage.

Even as a student of St. Michael's CBS in Sexton Street, Dr. O'Dywer displayed the intellectual prowess that marked his whole life. In Maynooth, he was a member of a brilliant class that included five future bishops and the noted Irish scholar and author from County Cork, an Canónach Peadar Ó Laoire. As a young curate at St. Michael's he was asked to preach the month's mind sermon for Bishop George Butler who had died on the 3rd February, 1886. His eloquence undoubtedly influenced his fellow priests greatly, as they selected him on the 3rd of March to succeed Dr. Butler. The delight of the people was shown by a parade of all the city's bands and blazing tar barrels that evening. His consecration the following June marked the beginning of one of the most notable and controversial bishoprics of the 19th or any other century in Ireland.

Having campaigned for Isaac Butt, M.P., the founder of the Irish Home Rule Party and a freeman of Limerick whose father was a native of Adare, he nonetheless opposed the Hierarchy and John Dillon, of the Irish Parliamentary party on the question of the Land Campaign. In matters of education he was widely regarded by the British Government and cited in editorials of the London Times.

His bishopric was marked by controversy: he was denounced publicly by Limerick politicians for his stances on various public issues of the day, Mayor John Daly and half of the newly elected Corporation walked out of a ceremony in St. John's Cathedral, following what they claimed was the insulting behaviour of the Bishop towards the mayor. He had a huge influence on the everyday life of his flock intervening for example in the bitter strike of the Limerick Pork Butchers' Society in 1891.

As a curate in the parish he was responsible for the establishment of St. Michael's

Temperance Society and the purchase and conversion of the former Munster and Leinster Bank premises in Sarsfield Street into the Catholic Literary Institute. Canon Sheehan of Doneraile, the author of "My New Curate" and other literary giants, was a guest speaker there and stayed with his cousins in William Street during his visits to Limerick.

He bought the former residence of Lord Limerick in Henry Street and had it adapted as a Diocesan seminary for the students who up to then had been training for the priesthood under the Jesuits at Mungret College. Hs decision to build St Joseph's Church so near the Jesuit Sacred Heart church at the Crescent did nothing apparently to enhance his status in the latter community.

He was also responsible for founding the Artisans' Dwelling Company to build houses for the ordinary worker; some of their homes can still be seen in Mary Street.

However, he will best be remembered in history here, for his stinging rebuke and chastisement of the Commanding Officer of the British Army, General Sir John Maxwell, on the 17th May, 1916, who had asked him to punish two of his priests, Father Hayes and Fr Wall, for their sympathy with the Republican movement. He was the toast of Nationalism in Ireland and especially in Limerick where he was conferred with the freedom of the city. His speech on that occasion is a model of its kind and worthy of study by every student of Limerick's history. But he was not finished yet; he vindicated in a pamphlet, the orthodox views of Cardinal Newman against the modernists of his day. The Pope, Pius IX, was so pleased with its sentiments that he addressed an autographed letter to Dr O'Dwyer congratulating him on "vindicating the memory of a most good and wise man." He died on August 19th, 1917, and in Archeadcon Begley's words, "he passed away in a blaze of glory, his acts and achievements having been far beyond the expectations of the multitude."

From *St. Michaels Parish, Limerick - Its Life and Times.*

Proselytisers at work
M O Corrbui

Oh! weep those days, the penal days,
When Ireland hopelessly complained;
Oh! weep those days, the penal days,
When Godless persecution reigned.

THE ruthless oppression of which Davis thus wrote was initiated and pursued with the sole intention of destroying the Catholic faith of the Irish people and rendering them poor and ignorant – mere hewers of wood and drawers of water for their Protestant overlords.

In the field of education Penal Laws excluded Catholics from the university and forbade them to act as guardians or tutors, keep a school, or send their children to be educated abroad.

With that magnanimity so typical of them, however, the English offered alternative sources of learning, and so came into being the Eramus Smith Schools, Charter Schools, and other educational establishments. But whatever the title by which these buildings were known, the policy of the founders was always the same: to further the cause of proselytism and Anglicisation. Henry VIII, of inglorious memory, was the first to order these schools to be set up, but little progress was made during his lifetime or for long afterwards.

In 1726, however, a Charter School was founded at Newcastle West, and in 1733 Primate Boulter set about increasing their number in order, as he said, 'to rescue the souls of thousands of poor children from the dangers of Popish superstition and idolatry, and their bodies from the miseries of idleness and beggary.'

In cases where the Catholic parents were in dire poverty, as many of them no doubt were, it was proposed to take children between the ages of six and ten, to feed, clothe and educate them, and train them suitably for the humble positions they would fill in life. Laudable objectives indeed, but as the Protestant historian Lecky records: 'The indispensable condition was that the children should be educated as Protestant; the alternative offered by law to the Catholics was that of absolute and compulsory ignorance.'

Hunger in the home caused some Catholics to allow their children into the Charter Schools, with the unspoken provision that as soon as times improved they would withdraw them again. But after a while the proselytisers saw through this ruse and a law was passed to ensure that once children were placed in a school they could not be taken out again and the parents had no longer any rights over them. The same law empowered the authorities to place in a Charter School any child between the ages of five and twelve found begging.

The schools were known as 'Charity Schools' and, because the children were dressed in blue, as 'Blue Schools.' Besides Newcastle West, such schools were started in Kilfinane, Kilmallock, Shannongrove and Limerick city. At Shannongrove, formerly Cill na Siurach, the local landlord, Mr. Bury, was in charge of a school for twenty boys and twenty girls. Sometimes the boys worked for Mr. Bury and twopence per day was paid for their services. This income helped to keep the schools going for some time.

When the supply of children began to fall off, 'nursery' schools for infants were started to act as 'feeders.' The ruins of the nursery school at Shannongrove (known locally as the 'babby' school) are still to be seen, but the Blue School which stood at Shannongrove has been completely demolished. Visitors to Ringmoylan cannot but have noticed the circular ruin overlooking the quay, but may not be aware that this was formerly a windmill from which came the wheaten flour for the Blue School.

In spite of the stated intention to 'feed, clothe, educate and train' the children, the schools were very badly run, and none of these objectives being realised or even actively pursued. Following investigation in 1788, it was reported that Shannongrove was 'a well built house, properly adapted for a schoolhouse. In it were 91 children. They were not kept properly clean and had not been washed or combed on the day of the visit. Many had skin diseases. Six had died in the last quarter of 1787, nine since, and fourteen were ill.'

The same investigation – conducted by an English protestant named Howard and covering other schools besides that of Shannongrove – found that although money had been poured into the project by the government and by wealthy English and Irish Protestants to see the Catholic religion and the Irish language wiped out, the children were not being educated at all. They were 'worked like slaves in the fields for the profit of their masters for eight hours at a time.' Children of eight, ten and twelve years were unable to read or spell. They were 'sickly, naked and half-starved; whole schools were suffering from itch or other maladies due to dirt, cold or insufficient food.

The rooms, the bed-covering, the scanty clothes of the children were alive with impurity, and the sad expressions on their countenances showed but too plainly how effectually they had been severed from all who cared for them, and, in many cases, how near was the last sad deliverance that awaited them.

When the Charity Schools began to fail, Shannongrove became completely a 'nursery' school and infants were regularly transferred from it to other schools in the country. This procedure was naturally opposed by the parents, who saw in it a further attempt to destroy their own influence, and efforts were made to rescue the children being transferred.

We find recorded, for instance, that in 1776 one George Downes, yeoman, of Pallaskenry, and Mary Moore, spinster, of the same place, were before Limerick Court charged with rescuing Timothy Moore and Sarah Vanston from William Dollard when he was taking them from Shanagolden to Dunkerrin in Offaly. Transfers were even made between Dublin and Cork, many children dying on the 170 mile journey in open carts.

The opposition to transfers caused the plan to be abandoned, as was eventually the whole system of Charity School proselytising. 'But,' to quote another Protestant writer, 'the fixed determination of the Government, in the interests of religious proselytism, was felt by the Catholics much more keenly than any measures against their faith which have obtained a far higher place in Irish history.'

From *Catholic Life*, Summer, 1959.

A visit to St. Jude
Michael Quinlan

O'CONNELL Street is always busy; I wonder where all those people go and where they are coming from? Every time I've been down here with mama it's always the same, busy till six o'clock then they all tear away home.

I will cross over here at William Street to Todd's Corner. Mama says it's the safest place to cross O'Connell Street during the day against all the traffic. And here on

Todd's side I have always wanted to see the inside of the Augustinian church just up the road a bit. That's where St. Jude is Mama said, and like Mama I own him as my favourite saint. St. Jude, the patron saint of lost causes and hopeless cases, the workingman's friend.

Mam never had the time to bring me in to see him, now I'll go in and have a word to him myself. Gees I must have passed the church already. God I am an eejit, but it's in the middle of all those shops and it's easy to miss with all the gawking I'm doing in the windows. As Mam often said, keep your bloody eyes open and watch where you're going, and don't be an eejit all your life. All right then, back to see St . Jude.

I know for sure that St. Jude is a dead saint, so I don't expect to see him walking around like I saw St. Francis. Inside here it's all white, everything is white even the pillars and arches. There are lots of windows along the walls with coloured glass in them, and low down too, not like other churches where they are so high up. And here he is himself, the altar of St Jude, and a little marble fence where I can kneel down and say a prayer to him.

There's his statue on the left hand side, he's dressed in a dark brown robe with jet black hair, and he's looking straight at me. Yes he knows I'm here all right, so I'd better ask him to tell Dad not to drink any more so we can be happy at home. And also take away Mam's asthma. Amen.

Because it's killing her slowly you know, she says. I think he heard me that time. But I'll say it all again just to make sure. And Holy St. Jude, I see people have been throwing money in there to you, but I'm sorry I haven't any to put in just now. Anyway the floor is covered with pennies and sixpences, so I suppose you have enough coins to cover your wages today. If you happen to see my dog Teddy up there in heaven, tell him I miss him. Amen, again. Thank you Holy St. Jude, I will visit again as soon as I can.

Well, this must be the brightest church in Limerick and I love those big lone windows with the coloured glass in them. But I need to be going soon. I was not bothered to be telling St. Jude I was mooching, none of his business anyway. That sin is a matter for Jesus.

From *Mickey Slabdabber*, 2005.

The Old Registers
Canon Brendan Connellan

BAPTISMAL and Marriage Registers of St. Mary's, Limerick, began in 1745, not the oldest in the country, but certainly the oldest in Munster. There was a time when previous to this, because of the Penal Days, it was forbidden to record theses events for Catholics. But with the appointment of Dr. John Creagh (controversial)* in 1745, and with the help of the scribe and historian Fr. James White who was curate in the

Abbey area, these records were undertaken with meticulous care and copperplate hand-writing, in very small hand and all in Latin, but perfectly legible today, with just two lines recording each sacrament, just giving date of Baptism (not birth), parents' names, sponsors' names, and the priest who administered the Sacrament. Baptisms took place very soon after birth, because of the high rate of infant mortality, sometimes on the same day of birth, but seldom more than a day or two afterwards. The infant was brought to the Church by the Godmother, who looked after all the arrangements for the mother.

In the records there are many historical anecdotes noted that are of special interest: the name of the priests of the parish are written at the top of each page, beginning with Dr. Creagh as Parish Priest of the Cathedral, and St. Mary's Church and Dean of the Diocese. At this time, the Cathedral had passed out of Catholic hands, but this was obviously stating a claim to the Cathedral. Fr. Michael McMahon was Parish Priest of St. Nicholas, and Fr. James White, Curate of the Abbey of St. Francis near the walls of Limerick.

The details of Dr. John Creagh's final acceptance by the people and the Bishop is described on 22nd May 1747 (Fr. White had been acting as P.P. since Dr. Creagh's original appointment in 1745, which was questioned by Bishop Lacy and the parishioners).

Fr. McMahon's death (P.P. of St. Nicholas) is recorded on 21st August, 1750, and how the following day, Bishop Lacy appointed Fr. James White to his position as curate of St. Mary's. Dr. Creagh announced this the following Sunday at the Masses. Obviously little time was lost in making appointments of Curates. Fr. James White notes that on 15th July, 1746, he buried a Don Joseph de Urculli Callabriensis from Bilbao (Spain) after giving him the Last Rites of the Church the day before. That year a Baptismal Certificate was issued to Pat O'Halloran of Madrid, and another to a Stephen White going to Spanish Indies.

In September, 1752, there is a reference to the change of the calendar year from the Julian to the Gregorian system, when in Ireland and England, 12 days had to be dropped, so that the 1st Sept. that year became 13th September. There is an insertion in Latin stating briefly that "because of the change from the old to the new way of counting, in the following month, 12 days were dropped." The change was nearly 200 years behind the times, because following the direction of Pope Gregory XIII in 1582, the rest of the Continent of Europe dropped 10 days, but England would not accept this at the time because of the Reformation in England, having fallen out with Rome.

Baptisms and marriages of some notable people are recorded in these Registers: Gerald Griffin (parents, Patrick Griffin and Ellen Geary), later to become poet and novelist and Christian Brother, with Quay Lane School named after him. Bryan, son of Michael Ryan and Catherine Merriman, a grandson of the Brian Merriman, author of 'Cuirt on Mhean Oiche.'; marriage of the famous East Clare "Biddy Early" on July 27th 1869 – Bridget Connors and Thomas Meaney; witnesses were Cornelius McNamara and Suzanne McNamara; ceremony performed by Fr. Richard Scott, P.P. It appears that Thomas Meaney only lived six months and it is rumoured that she married six times, as her husbands had the habit of dying after a short time!

RELIGION

*Dr. Philip Creagh, Dean and Parish Priest of St. Mary's, was appointed Co-adjudicator Bishop of Waterford in 1745. He asked Bishop Lacey for a letter of recommendation for his younger brother, Dr. John Creagh, who had just completed a brilliant course of studies in Rome. The Bishop gave him an excellent reference, thinking that he might be appointed as lecturer in some Continental College. But Philip sent it on to the Pope with a strong recommendation that he be appointed in his place, as P.P. of St. Mary's and dean of the Diocese.

He arrived two years late in 1747, and in the meantime, Fr. James White, C.C. of the Abbey area acted as P.P and started recording the baptisms and marriages in the parish from 1745, which have survived to the present day. This Fr. White was a historian and a scribe. Dr. Creagh succeeded in amalgamating the Abbey (then under St. John's Parish) and St. Nicholas Parish with St. Mary's. Dr. Creagh proved to be an outstanding choice and it was he who got the old church built in 1749. He remained on as P.P. for 45 years until he died in 1790; this must be a record for a tenure of pastoral office.

Fr. John Creagh set about building a new church, which would have to be sited outside the walls in the county of Limerick and he was granted in 1748 a site by John Ingram who lived in the present Town House. The site was that of a failed brewery where Ingram had been brewing Scotch whiskey, but it appears that the Irish preferred their own brew. Copy of title still in town-house.

By 1749 the church was opened, and it was very much appreciated at the time that many contributions were received from the Protestant trading population. We must remember that nearly all the hard work was done by the Catholic poverty stricken people, so their masters probably wanted to keep them on hands. It turned out to be the biggest post-penal church in Munster and lasted for 200 years, in spite of the fact that it was regularly flooded by high tides, when the congregation had to stand up in the seats during Mass.

Light on the Past: Story of St. Mary's Parish, Limerick, 2001.

The decade of the Moving Statues

THE mid-eighties saw the start of the moving statues syndrome. In August, 1985, reports came in from Mountcollins that a statue of the Blessed Virgin had been seen to move. In the following months there were reports of the same phenomenon coming from Cahermoyle and Manister.

Many people from the county and Clare travelled to Limerick to view the statue at Garryowen, near the Markets Field, following reports that some people had seen blood coming from one of the hands of Our Lady. The Rosary was recited several times each night as hundreds converged on the shrine.

In the county, Foynes was one of the top attractions when it was reported that Our Lady had been observed moving. Cratloe was also proving a huge draw with crowds visiting the shrine there and reports of people having seen movement. Cahermoyle and Manister, two of the first to report the phenomenon, drew constant crowds of believers, and the curious.

The Prior of the Dominicans in Limerick, Very Rev. Killian Dwyer, said that the attitude of the Church to the phenomenon of moving statues bordered on the 'sceptical.' 'These alleged happenings had a tendency in provoking numberless counterfeit imitations. As soon as one incident is purported, another is recorded elsewhere, triggering off a reaction that tends to escalate to the confusion of ordinary people,' he said.

Fr. Matt O'Shea of the Oblate Monastery at Cahermoyle said he 'was impressed by the extreme reverence and goodness of people praying there.'

A *Leader* Editorial said the alleged sightings 'tended to trivialise religion in the media and amongst the community and have yet to be supported by established fact. The case has yet to be tried let alone proved.'

A Blackpool man, John D. Vose, however, was a believer and claimed in Kilfinane church he saw the Statue of Our Lady change into the agonised face of Christ. He also claimed that children in the village 'saw a vision in the sky, with several different colours,' and got their mother's permission to talk to them. 'I believe in it implicitly.' He said he would be publishing a book, 'The Statues That Moved a Nation,' in the near future.

From *Limerick Leader Special Millennum Feature,* January 1, 1000.

Pork Butchers' Present
Sean Curtin

ON Wednesday, December 8, 1954, the closing day of the historic Marian Year, the Limerick Pork Butchers Society presented the Bishop of Limerick, Most Rev. Dr. P. O'Neill, with a cheque for £1,000. The money was part of the fund for the renovation of Our Lady's Shrine Altar at St. John's Cathedral. The Amalgamated Limerick Pork Butchers Society, since its foundation, has shown a deep-rooted love for the Mother of God, the *Limerick Leader* wrote shortly after.

"For the past 64 years," the paper said, "the Limerick Pork Butchers Society has looked upon the feast of the Assumption each year as one of their most important days. It has, during all that time, observed Our Lady's Day on August 15th as a holiday and when it fell on a week day it was observed at their own expense," the report concluded.

The presentation of the cheque was made by Mr. John Bennis and by Mr. George Judge, chairman and secretary of the Pork Butchers Society.

The story began for the Pork Butchers in 1891 when the then Bishop of Limerick, Dr. Edward Thomas O'Dwyer intervened in seven week strike in the four Limerick meat factories, Dennys, O'Mara's, Matterson's and Shaws. He presided at a public meeting where he discussed settlement proposals with the butchers who were by this stage at the end of their tether.

Sitting astride a horse in Mulgrave Street, he took a head count, those for, on one side, those against, on the other.

As a result of the settlement the society decided that in future August 15th – the Feast of the Assumption – would be a holiday taken at the men's own expense. They maintained this custom right up to the end.

Dr. O'Dwyer, for his efforts in settling the strike, was elected honorary president of the Amalgamated Limerick Pork Butchers Society which we are told, was formed during the even week long strike. Every succeeding Bishop of Limerick also held that honour.

From *The Marian Year Golden Jubilee* book, 2004.

Confraternity men to the Fight
Denis O'Shaughnessy

Hymns by him singers, *Raise up your banners on high*.
2,000 men up for Jesus and His Holy Mother.
Throats throttled wide to let Him know we were His.
Outpourings of exultation, exaltation, adoration and adulation.

No gentle folk songs here. Triumphalism rules OK.
Raise the roof on the high notes of *Sweet Heart of Jesus*:
Oh touch our hearts, so cold and so ungrateful.
Satan reaching for his ear muffs.

Coalman Paddy Hickey in our section, *Star of the Sea*,
Harmonising *Tantum Ergo* in Latin that was Greek to us.
Heil the visiting preacher with stiff armed facist salutes.
Warming us up with a joke before he threw the book at us.
Ha, Ha, Ha, we laughed to make him feel at home,
Even though we had heard the joke twenty times:
'At the blessing of religious objects at the Mission, the preacher
said hold up your cross, and a man at the back held up his wife.'
Then he left us have it with fire and brimstone.

Strengthen our Faith Redeemer, guard us when danger is nigh.
A candlelit renouncement of the devil and all his works and pomps.
Shouts of condemnation to stave off temptation.
We do! Louder. We dooo! Louder still: WE DOOOO!
Do ye renounce Communism? We do! Louder: WE DOOOO!
Let them hear it in the Kremlin. We DOOOOOOOOOH!

One set of Reds warning the other that they were being watched.
Confraternity Vigilantes patrolling cinemas
To break up couples snogging in the back seat.
Girls safe on Retreat Week from members who were tackin'.
No dark corners, occasions of sin,
No close dancing, groping, passionate kissing, impure thoughts.
Out! Out! Out! Hell's fires only a breath away.

The Retreat:
Dawn chorus of studs on hob-nail boots
Striking sparks on frosty pavements.
Retreat how are you. It was a full frontal attack
On Beelzebub and his cohorts.
Marching from damnation to salvation.
Members knocking up one another
And waking the whole house in the process for 6 a.m. Mass
So that factory workers could be at work on time.
Office and shop workers up too, though they hadn't to be at work till nine.
Some went walking after breakfast,
Others got a spot of salmon fishing in Corbally.
For most, it was back to bed after their gu-gu and toast.
With their frozen extremities shoving into wives' deliciously warm bodies.
Aaaaah! Take away your cold hands.
Any chance of a bit of how's your father?
Harder to get up the second time than the first.
Those who didn't get back to sleep often nodded off at work.
Happy we who thus united, join in cheerful melody.
Dozing off at saintly priests' sermons
On holiness at Devotions that night.
Head drooping onto chest, dawn start taking its toll.
Waking up with a start from a next door neighbour's nudge.
Or when a preacher loudly reaches his climax.
No nodding off at the sermons on death.
Riveted, ye know not the day nor the hour.
We must hasten to conquer the world,
With the Sign of the Lamb who bleeds.
Prefect calling to houses looking for non-retreating members.
Could warrant a visit from the preachers too
If the member was neglecting his religious duties.
Directors adored. Roads named after them.
Purposely moved on when at the height of popularity
For fear of cult status.
A social night out, meet the lads, hear the latest sca.
Munster and Garryowen supporters having a cut at one another.
Snooker in the Mechanics,' St. Michael's, Burton's, Todsie's

Or the cheapest, Polo Ryan's, afterwards.
A few pints with cronies, or a walk around Parteen for the Pioneers.

Fear of damnation kept us on the straight and narrow.
But keys could be left untouched in doors overnight.
Girls on their own walking safely home from the Stella or the George.
Disputes settled with fisticuffs:
Come outside the door, somebody hold my coat.
Only stabbing victims were pigs in Mattersons.

Unwanted pregnancies rare, not for wives in many marriages though.
Were we better off? For and against.
Doesn't matter now.
The past is a foreign country.
What we were, we were.
Oh that we could wed the best of then and now
The hymn anthem could be:
Oh Mother I could weep for mirth,
Joy fills my heart so fast,
My soul today is heaven on earth.
Oh could the transport last.

From *How's Your Father, Stories of Limerick*, 2002.

Troubled Times in St. Mary's Parish
Canon Brendan Connellan

THE early 1770's were troubled times in St. Mary's parish especially with regard to the appointment of priests. It will come as a great surprise to residents in the Abbey, and those whose ancestors came from there, to learn, that the Abbey was part of St. John's parish where the Canons Regular of St. Augustine were the parish priests. The Franciscan Abbey was outside the walls of the old city and was thus located in Co. Limerick; it was not until the coming of Dr. John Creagh as the new Parish Priest of St. Mary's in 1745, that he eventually succeeded in joining up St. Nicholas parish and the Abbey area under St. Mary's, and special arrangements were agreed with Fr. James White (Abbey) and Fr. Michael McMahon (St. Nicholas) about their respective duties and financial provisions, under the direction of Dr. Robert Lacy, Bishop of Limerick (1738-1759).

During the episcopacy of the previous Bishop, Dr. Cornelius O'Keeffe (1720-1737) there were serious problems with regard to the priests of St. Mary's. He was from the Cork diocese and had been lecturing in Nantes (France) when appointed to Limerick. His first task was to stop young men being ordained as priests who had not done any course of studies (common in Penal Days) and to get those who had been ordained to go back to some college to study theology.

Disputes in St. Mary's parish were serious. Fr. William Ryan, PP, who came in 1704, was in poor health, and gave the running of the parish about 1730 to Fr. Richard Hennessy, also from the Cork Diocese. He offended some of the people with his strong advice, and had to retire in 1725, on the orders of the Bishop, who could not withstand the violence of the people. He was succeeded by Fr. Tim Sheehan who withdrew in 1727. He was succeeded by a great favourite with the whole parish, Fr. Matt Geeran (Guerin).

But now Fr. Hennessy returned in 1728 supported by a papal letter, to the disgust of the parishioners. It was finally agreed in 1730 that Fr. Geeran would be curate but no peace ensued as two parishioners brought a very serious charge to the Bishop against Fr. Geeran, who fled the city, but the Bishop of Killaloe prevailed on him to return where he caused grave scandal by bringing a court case against the two parishioners before the Protestant Bishop. The two parishioners' case was before the Catholic bishop and the two cases went on for a long time, causing serious scandal. Eventually Bishop O'Keeffe suspended Fr. Geeran and deprived him of the curacy of St. Mary's.

During the episcopacy of Dr. Cornelius O'Keeffe (1720-1737), he went to visit the Irish College in Paris to found a Clerical Students' fund for the education of future priests for Cork and Limerick Dioceses. The money, it seems, came from the O'Keeffe family inheritance (Glenville, Co. Cork) and three students from that family and its connections were to benefit. This Burse caused a serious controversy during the time of the next Bishop, Dr. Robert Lucy, as to whether these students were for Cork or Limerick Dioceses. It was finally settled by a Tribunal in Paris deciding in favour of the Bishop of Limerick.

Bishop O'Keeffe had another dispute on his hands when the Augustinians wanted to set up a church in the city. The Dominicans and Franciscans already had foundations in the city and objected to others coming in, where there would not be sufficient numbers of people to support all these priests. The Bishop refused them permission, but the Augustinians appealed to the Archbishop of Cashel, then to the Primate of Armagh, then to the Nuncio in England, and finally to Rome. They were granted permission to set up a temporary church.

Bishop O'Keeffe died in May 1737 and Dr Robert Lucy was appointed the following year. He had been Superior of the Irish College in Bordeaux (France); soon after he ordained Fr. James White in St. Mary's, who had finished his studies in Salamanca (Spain), and appointed him to the Abbey area.

When Dean Hennessy died in 1736, Dr. Pierce Creagh was appointed new P.P. and Dean. He had been one year in St. Michael's after coming back from his studies in Rome. Then, in 1745, he was appointed Co-adjutor Bishop of Waterford. He had a brother Dr. John Creagh, just finished his Doctorate in Rome, and the older brother got a glowing reference from Bishop Lacy for John Creagh, expecting him to get a professorship in one of the Irish Colleges.

But it was used to get him appointed to succeed his brother in St. Mary's as P.P. and Dean of the Diocese. The Bishop and priests objected, and would not allow him to take over the Parish. Fr. James White stood in, as Administrator until Rome confirmed Dr. John Creagh in his position in 1747.

He then began to build the 'old' church which opened in 1749. Up to then, the two parishes, St. Mary's and St. Munchin's, used a 'Mass House' on the other side of the Shannon, near where the present St. Munchin's Church now stands. He continued the good work begun by Fr. White in keeping records of Baptisms and Marriages from 1745. He had to get the help of an Augustinian, Fr. Tom Walsh, after Fr. White's death in 1767. He remained P.P. until his death in 1790 – 45 years in office.

From *St. Mary's Parish Bulletins*, May 5/12, 2002.

Student Pranks at Louvain
Rev. Jeremiah Newman

STUDENT life in the Catholic University of Louvain has many and interesting aspects. This is only to be expected in a large university of very nearly twelve thousand members. Study of course is the main feature of any university and in particular this famous centre of scholarship. But there is a lighter side to student life everywhere and in this respect Louvain yields place to none.

There is great rivalry between the Flemish students and the French speaking Walloons and the tricks they play on one another are a constant topic. There are times, however, when the factions combine, usually to play a well-organised prank. Such was the case a couple of years ago when a stunt was pulled off which must rank high in the history of student jokes.

There is a convent in Louvain, in a suburb called Heverle, to the nuns of which the students owed a debt. It all began during the war when a priest arrived from Brussels to give a retreat to the two thousand strong girl population of the convent's large yet very select school. He was met at the station by two students dressed as Gestapo men, who detained him and relieved him of his soutane. A student then presented himself at the convent dressed as the priest and managed to get away with one address to the retreatants. When the prank was discovered the reverend mother felt it her duty to complain the tricksters who duly found themselves in trouble with the authorities.

But students' memories are long lived and they awaited their chance to pay back their debt to the good reverend mother. The chance came when a student arrived at Louvain who was the living image of the young King Baudhouin. And so the plot was hatched. After much planning the convent was rung up one morning and it was announced that the King would shortly pay it a visit as part of an unofficial tour of educational establishments in company with some friends of his own age. In point of fact, he would be coming in half an hour. We can imagine the feverish haste of the nuns to get ready for this signal honour which was about to be conferred on them.

At exactly the time appointed he arrived. A guard of honour (composed of students who had done their military service and possessed uniforms) clicked their heels and stood rigidly to attention. A first car carrying 'Detectives' drew in. Then another with a number of 'Counts' and 'Barons.' The 'Kings' ' – a magnificent 1951 black Buick – loaned for the occasion by a Government Minister's student son. Lastly a car-load of 'Pressmen' and photographers, who made very sure to bring away a record of the proceedings.

Everything was inspected in order, including the serried ranks of the convent school pupils. It was at this point that disaster almost overtook the venture. One of the girls thought she noticed a really striking resemblance between one of the 'courtiers' and a student from her native town. Her whispered comments brought suspicion to the mind of the chaplain who hurried away to make frantic investigations by telephone. Sensing danger, the visitors insisted they really had to depart and withdrew quietly, still with the greatest dignity.

The photographers had been busy in the meantime and the following week saw an issue of the student's newspaper giving full details of the 'royal' visit. It showed the reverend mother receiving the party on their arrival, conducting them around the convent, the grounds, etc. An open letter contained six points which it was suggested she would observe in case of future royal visits to her school. That champagne should be provided in large quantities was among them. The students had indeed got their own back.

Among the larger scale of hoaxes was that concerning one of the better-known Belgian dailies. As far as the eye could judge this was an ordinary morning newspaper. Printed exactly the same as that which it purported to be, one could never guess until beginning to read it that it was a student imitation. But on perusing it one's eyes were truly opened. The first page contained a large photo of 'the rector of the university conferring honorary degrees on two famous scholars.' Closer attention showed that the two recipients were really waiters in student cafes, whose photos had been welded with that of the rector to give the impression that they were indeed receiving degrees. The news columns were intensely interesting, as might well be expected, while the death notices and advertisements sections were screams.

On a rag day about four years ago a regiment of troops from Brussels had to be drafted into 'retake' the town from the students. From that day the students didn't like the police and every rag day now is a minor crisis. I well remember passing through the barrack square on the evening of one of these and seeing the garrison prepared for attack with mounted horses. Yes, on a rag day the students can take over, though their pranks are by no means confined to it.

There are professors who object strongly and surely not without reason, when toy bombs are exploded under their rostrums during lectures. There are clerics who feel aggrieved when a rag day procession features a 'friar' who pours water indiscriminately on the onlookers from a jeep carrying a large barrel marked 'beer' and there are very many who see little fun in being manhandled by 'Congo Negroes' who parade the streets on rag day in war paint.

But students will always be students and there is never malice in their fun and their tricks. Louvain indeed, like any another university, would be very much the poorer without these. The professors close their eyes to much that they could see; sometimes in fact one finds among them a collaborator. And so the student pranks go on, the lighter side of Louvain University life.

Catholic Life, April, 1954.

Covering the visit of Pope John Paul
Fergal Keane

POPE John Paul's visit gave us our first taste of international celebrity. It was also a landmark in the history of the modern Irish state. For those who imagined that the changes of the sixties and seventies had laid the foundations of a modern secular republic the public response to John Paul was a surprise. From the moment *Il Papa* arrived at Dublin airport on 29 September 1979 the country erupted in an ecstasy of faith. Not since Kennedy came nearly twenty years before had we been so flattered. Twenty thousand people turned out at Dublin airport to greet him while television carried live coverage of every holy minute. More than a million people – one third of the population – attended the first papal mass in Dublin's Phoenix Park, the same place were my grandparents had witnessed the Eucharistic Congress in 1932.

The Pope travelled to Drogheda and publicly appealed to the IRA to end its violence. On bended knees he beseeched the gunmen: '. . . to all of you who are listening, I say: do not believe in violence, do not support violence. It is not the Christian way.' But the papal appeal had the same effect as the denunciations of an earlier generation of religious appellants during the War of Independence – that is to say it didn't make a blind bit of difference. A few days later the IRA gave their answer by killing a Protestant father of three. That atrocity seemed to pass us all by in the excitement of the moment.

By the time the Pope reached Limerick the city was vibrating with anticipation. Yet to me the mood was not triumphalist. The atmosphere resembled a giant picnic rather than an assertion of Church power. People thronged to the Limerick racecourse to hear the Pontiff speak but I remember above all the brightness and good humour of the crowd.

On the day of the Limerick appearance I got up at around three in the morning to find Mrs C already in the kitchen making sandwiches. I showed her my laminated press pass which she touched gently as if it were some sort of precious relic.

People were on the move across the city. More than a quarter of a million flooded into the racecourse. The majority spent the night camped out to get the best view of the Pope. They sang hymns and said prayers. The *Limerick Leader* would later report that 300 children had been separated from and then re-united with their parents. For the first time I watched the international media in action. There were brash, loud people from the Associated Press; they looked rough, tough, travelled, everything I wanted to be. I felt like a hick with my brown three-piece suit and notebook. Then my determination to do the best job I could took over. The *Limerick Leader* had despatched its entire editorial staff to cover the visit and was producing a special commemorative edition.

Our opposition, a much smaller paper called the *Limerick Echo*, had gone to great lengths to produce exclusives, one of its reporters even promising a priest that she would join the Legion of Mary if he would give an exclusive account of his own meeting with the Pope. (I would later marry this pious journalist.). My own part in the *Leader's* grand operation was relatively small. I'd only been in the job a couple of weeks and Halligan was still taking my measure. The cigar-smoking Liddy was despatched to Rome to travel on the papal plane back to Ireland. His account of the journey caused some mirth in the editorial room:

> Never in all these years have a found a story so hard to write as I try to describe my feelings of intense joy that I had been privileged to meet this saintly man, or perhaps more appropriately this saint of a man. It has taken me nineteen attempts to write these few paragraphs.

Nobody doubted Liddy's genuine joy and emotion. But various other disrespectful suggestions were offered as to why Liddy, a talented writer, took so long to compose his epic.

The Pope came to earth in a helicopter, the first of those machines I had ever seen. My memory is of a white-clad figure emerging surrounded by priests, beyond them a cordon of Irish police, and then a vast, unending crowd which erupted into sustained cheering. All around me people were weeping. Until I began research for this chapter I had no memory of what the Pope actually said. After everything that had happened in the previous few days, not least the passionate appeal to the IRA in Drogheda, the media were in thrall to this most charismatic of men. When he met the press after Drogheda the assembled journalists burst into a spontaneous rendition of 'For He's a Jolly good Fellow'. Swept away by the excitement we missed the real import of his words in Limerick and the marker he was laying down for the future direction of the Catholic church.

In Limerick John Paul II revealed his conservative self. It was the voice that had rung out from pulpits of Ireland for decades, but diverted by the magic of his evident kindness, we barely heard his message to the Irish faithful. The Pope used Limerick to denounce the evils of abortion, contraception, divorce and working motherhood. 'Ireland must choose,' he declared. Whoever advised him was well out of touch with the changing social mores of the Republic.

But in the enthusiasm of the moment nobody in the press thought of shouting: 'Hold on a minute! It's not that simple here any more.' It would have been the equivalent of farting loudly in Mass. For the forces of revanchism in Ireland the papal speech in Limerick acted as a rallying cry. In the wake of the visit the Catholic right set out to change the Constitution so that it would include a ban on abortion, above and beyond the existing strict legal ban on termination.

It led to the bitterest public debate in the history of the modern state. Nobody took up arms but the (ultimately successful) attempt to have a Pro-Life amendment inserted into the constitution set liberal and conservative Ireland at each other's throats in the early 1980's and prepared the ground for future divisive struggles over contraception and divorce.

From *All of These People, A Memoir.* HarperCollins 2005.

The Sign of the Cross

THE Scripture Lessons – a Protestant Version – though supplied gratis were not obliged to be read, while the Class Books contained interesting solid information – with the great fault that nothing whatsoever in them bordered on Catholicity in Ireland. Still there was little interference and our children were not prohibited from making the Sign of the Cross and reciting silent prayer each time the clock struck, though the Board – by no means – liked such a manifestation of the Old Faith was quite evident when witnessed by them.

Inspectors' visits were made as a matter of right at least three times a year for the examination of the children, while as many more incidental calls as could be conveniently given, were strongly inculcated in the printed form, regulating the duties of that office. Notice of the intended visit was never sent at this period – on the contrary, it seemed their object to come at all times unexpectedly: that practice even had been turned to profit, as it showed great necessity for vigilance and unceasing preparation of all through the classes. It was not until a few years later on that the Board began to make formal objections to every external practice of Religion during Secular Instructions, and to have a sharp look out for Catechisms left carelessly about the rooms, etc. except at the hour marked on the Time Table for their use (1839).

For some years the National Board had been making rules from time to time which tended to restrict any religious practices during school hours. As long as possible we continued 'never minding them' when we could until at last they became so peremptory with all Convent Schools about having children making the Sign of the Cross at the striking of the clock at each hour that we should either discontinue it or cease our connection with them altogether, but that the girls might not know the cause or that the nuns had to yield, the striking weight was taken off the clock. This idea is said to have come from Archbishop Murray to get his nuns out of the difficulty in Dublin. The children resumed the Sign of the Cross in schools at the striking of the clock in 1894. (1876)

From the *Annals, Sisters of Mercy,* Limerick.

In 1831, Edward Alexander, a native of the city, felt obliged to have the following printed in large sized posters and posted up throughout the city, which was accordingly done:

To the Inhabitants of this City:

'I AM very much grieved, day after day, in beholding the sins which abound among us. It is sin which causes the Divine displeasure to fall upon us, whenever it does; and why should we run the hazard of exciting it against us, merely to gratify our sensual passions and appetites.

'This, therefore, is to exhort and beseech you, my dear fellow-citizens, both collectively and individually, to cease from sin and iniquity, lest the just judgments of a long-offended and long-suffering God fall with weight upon our heads. Is He not able to crush us in a moment, and shall we not fear and dread to continue sinning against, and offending Him day and night?

'Oh! I call upon you to remember how it is recorded, that His judgements fell with dreadful weight upon those cities and kingdoms, the inhabitants whereof lived in sin, and in forgetfulness of their God! Remember Sodom and Gomorrah – Jerusalem – Babylon! – how they were overthrown and destroyed under heaven, together with their inhabitants, because of their sins!

'Do not imagine that because Lord's judgements have never fallen on us, in the way of public calamity, that it will continue to be the case. Oh no! It is because he is a long-suffering and merciful God that they have not hitherto fallen upon us; but assuredly, if we continue in the same course of sin and iniquity, we cannot reasonably expect to escape his righteous judgments; and, perhaps, when it may be too late, we shall have to call upon Him for that mercy, which, though repeatedly offered to us, we have hitherto neglected and disregarded.

'Oh! May we never forget the memorable expressions of our blessed and holy Redeemer, in the days of His personal appearance amongst men, 'If ye die in your sins, whither I go ye cannot come.

'I remain your friend,

'EDWARD ALEXANDER,

'Limerick, 6th month, 1831.'

From *A Memoir of Edward Alexander*, Charles Gilpin, London, 1849.

Duties of a Confraternity Director
James A. Cleary, C.SS.R.

THE functions of the Director of a confraternity are in the highest degree important.

RELIGION

He is its heart and soul. A good Director implies a successful confraternity, and *vice versa*. The most excellent of confraternities, if entrusted to an inferior Director, begins to halt, to languish, and to die; time alone is necessary to compass its destruction. On the other hand a capable man, working on right lines, will build up, from the most uncompromising materials, a magnificent fabric, that will shelter and save innumerable souls which would otherwise be shipwrecked amidst the tempests of the world. Every priest of experience can recall to his memory examples of confraternities which after years of prosperity, fell to pieces in the hands of men who were unwilling or unable to direct them, and which were revived and restored to their former glory when they were once more entrusted to capable and willing men. It is no exaggeration to state that the most flourishing of confraternities might be brought to ruin by an incompetent Director, within a period of four or five years.

Now, it is not every man, even though pious and virtuous, who will succeed as the Director of a confraternity. A man may be pious, yet lacking in zeal; or zealous, yet wanting in tact; or tactful, yet without order or method. The interest in the work, or, as I might call it, this love for the confraternity, must spring from a zeal for the salvation of souls, which recognises in the confraternity a powerful means to attain this end; and it should result in a zeal of another and more definite character, namely, zeal for the good of the confraternity. Interest in the confraternity must be brought in to action by zeal and industry in working at the practical details that must be carried out in order to ensure success. Love that does not result in action for the well being of the object loved is mere barren and fruitless sentiment. But interest, as well as zeal may be, to a great extent, frustrated, when they are found in a character which is devoid of the spirit of discipline.

Human nature is weak and stands in need of supervision. Nor must the supervision exercised by the Director be a mere general survey; it must descend to the most minute particulars and the most trivial details. During the meetings he must see that every man is in his right place, and wearing his medal; at the monthly Communions he must see that benches are reserved for the sections, and occupied by members only. He must observe carefully the attendance and conduct of the members; but, above all, he should watch over the prefects of sections.

In order that the prefects may discharge their office well, it is absolutely necessary, that, from time to time, they give an account of their stewardship to the Director. This interview with the individual prefects does a marvellous amount of good. Besides applying a remedy to present evils, it keep the prefects alert and attentive to their duties; for whenever they become careless they know that they have to face an interview with the Director, which will put them to shame.

The report should be made in private, none being present save the Director and the prefect, and, if need be, the sub-prefect of the section. When the appointed hour has come, he will go through the names of the members on the section-book, glancing at the attention of each, and will ask such questions as seem needful. He has here an excellent means of testing the efficiency of a prefect; for a good prefect will be able to at once to give a satisfactory account of his members, where as a careless prefect will know little or nothing about them; or if he is cunning, will give accounts or reasons which are the product of his own imagination.

The Director, when he comes to the name of member who seems negligent, will ask: "Why is so-and-so not attending?" "Could he attend better?" "Indeed, he could, your Reverence," may be the answer. "Did you visit and warn him?" "I did, several times." Then the Director will fill in the man's name with a small printed *warning* which he will ask the prefect to deliver to the man in question. The Director then comes to the name of a still more careless member, who has received a warning before, with little or no result. For this member he fills in a printed *summons*, requesting him to visit the Director as soon as possible. He gives this to the prefect to be delivered as before.

At the same time he notes it down in his own "Report Book". This is a book in which the sections are arranged alphabetically. When a member receives a summons his name is written down under the name of his section, with the letter "S." to denote "Summons" immediately after the name. If the member *answers* the summons, and gives an explanation of his conduct the letter "A." is marked after his name in the "Report Book"; if however, his explanation be unsatisfactory, the letter "U." is placed after his name. Thus, the Director has always at hand the past confraternity history of his careless members. And now let us return to the examination of the section.

The Director comes to a third name. "Why is so-and-so not attending?" "He is drinking, your Reverence, send him summons, and make him take the pledge." This suggestion is adopted; or the Director takes a private note of the man's name, and calls to see him personally later on. Thus all the names are gone through, and various remedies are applied in the different cases. A friendly visit to a careless member is in general the best remedy of all; it is amazing what influence an Irish priest can exercise in this manner.

The Director should always appear to the men as acting on his own initiative, and not on the suggestion of any layman. Even when he thinks it necessary to take action from information given by laymen, or on the lines suggested by them, he should carefully conceal the source or motives of his conduct. Irishmen, as a rule, will bear almost anything from a priest when it is done honestly for their spiritual good; but there is nothing they detest more than unauthorized lay interference, they will either become rebellious or, at least, grow resentful and bitter. If the Director listens to some persons and acts on their suggestions against others, or takes part with some against others, he will soon stir up strife and dissension where formerly peace prevailed. He may receive and ask advice and information; he should be always ready to listen to suggestions; but he, and he alone, must be the Director. He must originate all action in the confraternity; he alone must admit new members, he alone must appoint or dismiss officials. In proportion as he proves himself unbiased in his motives, just in his conduct, and zealous for his work, he will win the love, trust, and gratitude of all the members.

From *Confraternity Work*, Browne and Nolan, 1932.

THREE
STAGE AND SCREEN

The Bishop and the Cinema

Most Rev. Dr. Hallinan,
Bishop of Limerick,
The Palace, Corbally, Limerick,
18th March, 1918.

DEAR Sir – Glancing quite recently through the columns of your journal quite recently my eye fell on an advertisement of a performance in a place of amusement, the location and proprietor of which are unknown to me. From the nature of the advertisement I take it to be a picture show house.

In that advertisement the Episcopal Consecration of the Most Rev. Dr. Hallinan is wedged in, in large characters, between two sensational titles of pictures. Whoever the author of this programme may be, nothing in worse taste could possibly be conceived. My first impulse on reading it was one of burning indignation. I asked myself was the spirit that animated him, a desire to insult me, or was it the spirit of avarice that used my Episcopal consecration, in which all the Catholics of the city took an interest, for the purpose of drawing the multitudes to witness the representation of it, and thus gathering in the coppers of the curious and thoughtless.

On reflection, I rejected the first hypothesis – there remains the second. Now, sir, if these were questions only of my personality, I would take no notice of it, nor would I ask you for space to insert this letter. There is something of more importance involved. There is the question of the moral and religious well-being of those committed to my spiritual care. The consecration of a Bishop is one of the most solemn and sublime of the religious functions of the Catholic Church. I need not dwell on what certain sensational title of films symbolises. Anything better calculated to lower the religious and moral tone of the spectators of this entertainment than this combination of piety, with profanity, of sublimity with vulgarity, it is hard to imagine.

And this is the kind of pabulum with which the minds of the rising generation of Irish boys and girls are being daily fed in these institutions called picture palaces. They are a fitting complement to the tons of filthy literature that are being daily imported from across the Irish sea, and if allowed to go unchecked, will gradually pave the way for the establishment in our midst of the leper hospitals for the treatment of the horribly revolting and highly infectious disease begotten of the immorality of the British soldier and of those who come in contact with them.

And these shows are injurious not only to the moral tone of those who frequent them; they also sap the national spirit of the country. For in their advertisements and performances there is a cunningly devised blend, not only of piety and profanity, but also of nationalism and Anglicisation. The very titles that one sees on the public advertising boards suggests this. You will see in large type some noble episode of Irish history calculated to stir up the spirit of a patriotic Irishman and side by side with that, something suggestive, even in word, of what is low, vulgar and degrading.

I take this opportunity of raising my voice in protest against the abuses connected with these establishments. Would it be too much to ask the proprietors of such houses in town to close them down during the remainder of the holy penitential season of Lent? They should never have opened them at this season. Whether they close them or not, I would wish that the managers of the schools in the city visit their respective schools these days, and warn the children against patronising them, and I request the clergy all, both secular and regular, to use all their opportunities in the pulpit and confession, to explain to the people the dangers connected with them.

DENIS HALLINAN, Bishop of Limerick.

From *Limerick Leader*, March 21, 1918.

The Athenaeum: a Civic Culture Centre
Frank Prendergast MA

THE Commissioners' writ ran effectively for almost to a hundred years when their powers had been transferred back to the reformed Municipal Corporation in 1853. For twenty years prior to that date Newtown Pery had its own headquarters or Town Hall in the Athenaeum building in Upper Cecil Street. This was to the front of the old Athenaeum Hall – later the Royal Cinema (now closed). This fine building has retained its historic role as a main office of the Limerick City Vocational Education Committee since 1930.

Two memorable events in particular which took place in the Athenaeum will be of interest to a Limerick audience. The first was the performance there on the 29th April 1857 of Catherine Hayes in Handel's Messiah. A native of St. Michael's parish, where she was born at No. 4 Patrick Street in 1825, she was then one of the world's leading Prima Donnas, having sung at a Royal Command performance for Queen Victoria and at Operatic/Concert Halls throughout Europe, America and Australia. Her performance at Limerick was a tour de force and got great applause.

The second item of interest in relation to the Athenaeum was a lecture on Irish Music given by a Dr. O'Connor of a Sunday evening c. 1870 during which he reminded his audience that the Irish words of what is one of the most beautiful melodies in Ireland or indeed anywhere else in the world "An Cúilfhionn" – were written by a County Limerick priest. He was Fr. Ailbe Hanley, a native of Knockainey, who was ordained by Archbishop James Butler at the cathedral in Thurles on 26th July, 1752. He retired on pension in 1801 as PP of Ballybricken and died 5 years later. He is buried in Knockainey's Protestant Churchyard where a headstone to his memory was erected by Rev. John Dwyer in 1814. A noted athlete, he is described in his obituary as having the gift of versification and as being the author of "Cúilfhionn". He was regarded as being the best of the Irish poets of his time. How the words of such an impressively beautiful love song came to be written by a priest I do no know but the girl of the poem is reputed traditionally to have been a native of Lough-Gur/Fedamore area.

Irish of course was the predominant language in the County Limerick of his day. The 1851 census – almost 50 years after his death – showed returns of 77,982 native Irish speakers in the County and 42,004 in the City. My mother's grandfather

William Murphy, an activist in the early Gaelic League in the city, was an Irish speaker from the Irishtown, the district where the last native Irish was spoken in the city.

From *St. Michael's Parish, Limerick - Its Life and Times.*

The Closed Lyric
Kevin O'Connor

The poster claps
'A thousand items of cash-and-carry
Watches, clocks, jewellery and clothes
At the cheapest prices you can afford'
To carry away . . .

To tinsel time. For time was tinselled here
To dancing moths in a slanted beam
Swooning above the wrinkled screen
Of prairies, canyons and brooklyn sets
Bowery boys and old costelloed gets
Bore you down into your seat
A bucket well of velvet deep,
The poster flaps . . .

The clapered past. When light was here
Covered you safe in the lurking dark
Safe from outside world, stark
Laureld hardy and mickey mouse
Sight and sound and senses trounced
Life was here . . .

In time-gone time. Now a curled-end poster cries
The flop of Superman's last glide
Founders the columns of Graeco Art
And peels the shabby stucco part
Surrender the city . . .

To those who pass. But soft, imagine
A moonbeam faintly flickers still
There on the wall above the hill
Hear the husky Doris, syrabic
Cooing away within the Lyric.

STAGE AND SCREEN

Catherine Hayes sings for the Queen
Basil Hayes

NEXT came a formal request and invitation from Buckingham Palace to selected members of the Royal Italian Opera and Her Majesty's Theatre to perform at a state concert for Queen Victoria and her guests on 2 June at Buckingham Palace.

Over 570 guests were invited to the concert. In addition to the Queen and Prince Albert attendees included the Duchess of Kent, the Duke and Duchesses of Cambridge and various other members of the royal family, visiting Royalty from Germany and the Netherlands, and members of the aristocracy and clergy.

The singers from the two Italian opera companies included: Giulia Grisis, Marietta Alboni and Catherine Hayes, Mario, Italo Gardoni, Filippo Coletti and Luigi Labache. Michael Costa the conductor was the accompanist.

The first part of the concert started with the beautiful quartet 'Mi manca la voce' from Rossini's *Mosè in Egitto*, with its opening harp accompaniment and soprano vocal line. Catherine, Alboni, Mario and Gardoni were the performers. Catherine's first solo came a short while later when she sang an aria completely unknown today called 'Oh vane pompe' from *La marescialla d'Ancre*, a tragic opera by the composer Nini which was first performed in Padua in 1839. This is an aria she later sang at several concerts; obviously she felt it suited her voice. This was well received. During the second half of the concert Catherine, Luigi Lablache and Italo Gardoni performed a trio from Mozart's Il Flauto Magico (The Magic Flute), sung in Italian and called 'Dunque il mio ben.' Since Lablache was Queen Victoria's singing teacher, presumably he had some say in the pieces like the Mozart trio. It was not something that Catherine would normally have sung.

There were various encores given by the performers during the concert. For her encore, Catherine chose to sing 'Kathleen Mavourneen,' which she had not sung since her early days in Dublin. It is interesting that she decided this was the appropriate moment to sing the Irish song once again. Could it have been her sense of humour, or perhaps the desire to make a point about her nationality, that made her select this song for the Queen of England and 500 royal guests at Buckingham palace? Perhaps it was her mother (who would not have been present) who suggested it as a possibility, should she be asked for an encore. She must have brought the music with her so that Michael Costa could accompany her, therefore it is reasonable to assume it was not an impulsive decision. In any event, it was probably the only time during the nineteenth century that anyone ever sang an Irish song in Buckingham Palace for Queen Victoria!

Whoever or whatever prompted the idea, it pleased the audience. Following the concert Queen Victoria made a note in her diary as follows: 'The concert was a very good one but hardly as much as the last ; Grisi's voice has sadly gone off. Alboni sang beautifully and Miss Hayes very nicely & with much feeling, & a good method. Mario was in excellent voice.'

Quite some time later, when Catherine spoke about this concert during an interview in Dublin, she mentioned that: 'The Queen entered into conversation with her, complimenting her on that the Queen was pleased to term her 'deserved success' and Prince Albert and the Duke of Cambridge both paid her flattering attention.'

Catherine's prominence on the London musical scene prompted one of the leading management agents and music publishers, Cramer & Beale of 201 Regent Street, to sign a contract with her. Shortly after the Buckingham Palace concert, Cramer & Beale published the sheet music of 'Kathleen Mavourneen' with a picture of Catherine and a headline that said 'Kathleen Mavourneen, Ballad sung by Miss Catherine Hayes at Her Majesty's Concerts, Buckingham Palace.'

From *Catherine Hayes,* Irish Academic Press, 2000.

Memoirs of a Savoy Pageboy
Joe Malone

IN my messenger boy days we were paid five bob a week. You spent your half-day cutting your boss's lawn. The payment for that job was a couple of apples, usually bad, or a cut of bread and jam. But I could never keep my eyes off the big fat maid who was kind of slow on top and who could blame her after 16 years in the Good Shepherd Convent, mis-named because most of the girls came out of there fat, foolish and ill-prepared for outside the walls. If you didn't do the work to your boss's satisfaction your job might be gone next day. The Protestant employers were far more decent that their counterparts, with a few exceptions.

Once we tried to organise a messenger boys' union, but we were threatened by the shopkeepers and jobs were scarce. They put the fear of God into us. So our attempts at forming a union died a sudden death. Some of the kids started work at 6 am and after a long round on foot, starting from Catherine Street and finishing at Barrington's Pier, the young boys and girls had to walk back home, their hands blue with the cold. At home they ate a few cuts of brown bread and then went to school.

After a few months as a messenger boy there was a job going at the Savoy Cinema for a page boy, or 'buttons.' My father was active in the trade union movement in the city and pulled a few strings with a man who later became a senator and vice-president of the union. I was very keen on this job. After the bike job it was full of colour, and I liked the idea of the uniform, pillbox hat, white gloves and black patent shoes. Most important of all to my impressionable mind was the status. It meant the respect of your fellow messenger boys. Strutting through the city, going to the bank, the newspaper and other offices, I felt like a real glasscock and was as proud as Punch when I heard an old woman say one day as I passed by, 'isn't he the real Ally Daly?' I really had notions about myself in those days. God help me.

The first picture I saw there was 'The Keys of the Kingdom' with Gregory Peck. The cinema was owned by the Ellimans and the company was known as Irish Cinemas Limited and also included the Savoys in Dublin and Cork and the Theatre Royal. The Ellimans were a very theatre-minded family and took a personal

STAGE AND SCREEN

interest in the Savoy. They sold on to Odeon Theatres, an English company owned by Joseph Rank, who had a large interest in British film-making and produced many second-rate pictures. The British industry was then in its infancy. With a few exceptions, picture-making in England was not in a healthy state. Richard Attenborough gave an accurate account of British film-making when he said it was all money and little talent. In the late forties, it cost one million pounds to make Hamlet, which was a financial disaster. With Lawrence Olivier and Janet Leigh playing leading parts, it was wasted. The film was shown to empty cinemas all over Britain and America. Limerick had it for nine days. One evening I counted 11 people in the cinema, with nearly 1500 seats.

Then came cinema variety and celebrity concerts with leading singers from Sadliers Well, Covent Garden and other opera houses. I often though to myself that they came to Ireland for the good food, steaks, mutton, beef, and were flabbergasted at the sight of a butcher stall. England still had rationing. The artistes weren't paid much money but they enjoyed the Limerick audiences. Once I remember they gave a concert at the Limerick prison where the audience was entertained by Owen Brannigan, Gwen Catley, James Johnston, and Victoria Sladen. We had concerts every Friday night with Stanley Bowyer at the famous Compton organ.

At that time the bishop would not allow Sunday pictures. After a long struggle by a lone councillor, long since dead, the argument was won and we got pictures on Sundays.

Most of the artistes for the Sunday night concerts were local ones, such as Michael McNamara, James Penny, who could sing a C sharp, which he did in the Rossini Stabet Mater. Josephine Scanlon, Hilda Roche, Michael McCann, Delia Murphy and Elsie Moloney, were among the others who took part. Music, and especially opera, has a very long tradition in Limerick going back to the old Theatre Royal. The Bowyer-Westwood, Carl Rosa, D'Oyly Carte, Elster-Grime, the Clonmel-born singer Frank Land and of course our own Joseph O'Mara and his company were the leading lights.

The cine-variety came in 1947/48. The first performance I can remember was by Frank O'Donovan, later to become Batty in the Riordans. Frank also wrote a few songs, including 'Sitting on the Bridge Below the Town.' Limerick people were ardent cinema goers. Among the Savoy's regular patrons were Donogh O'Malley and his wife Hilda and that great playboy Richard Harris. We spent a lot of our time trying to keep him quiet. There was also Paddy Clancy, who is now a successful fishmonger at Ellen Street corner and fruit vendor on market days. Maybe he should have become an actor. He is certainly a talented mimic.

When cine-variety came, it brought artists from all over the world. Europe was still in a shambles after the war. Theatres, cinemas were blown to smithereens. The musicians, singers, dancers, acrobats had limited outlets so neutral Ireland was the ideal place. Russian dancers, Hungarian acrobats, singers from Poland came with many more. We in Ireland were starved for good entertainment. The artistes needed an audience and some good food. After a few weeks of variety which was not a financial success, someone got a brainwave. Eddie Byrne was doing a programme in Dublin called Double or Nothing, with full houses most nights of the week, so Limerick had a go. That was the beginning of a very colourful career for Eamonn Andrews, who was the right man for the job. He had all the qualities, charm, unaffected manner of a man who liked people. He used to do a live programme on radio every Monday for the Imco cleaning concern called 'Spotless and Stainless' and be back in Limerick on the same afternoon – if he didn't crash into a pub or Garda Barracks which he once did.

I was asked to do the show, looking at it every day and night, I had a fair idea about the routine. Just as I was about to go on stage, he arrived with bits of straw hanging from his hair. He looked more like a cattle dealer than quiz master. Being a champion amateur boxer made him a great favourite with Limerick people, there being a strong tradition of boxing in the city. The Savoy was well known for its staging of boxing tournaments, including Ireland v. England, Ireland v. Belgium, and Ireland v Wales. Many of the tournaments were brought to Limerick by Jim Casey, the man who became Mayor after the two Mayors, Clancy and O'Callaghan, were murdered. Another active man in the promotion of sport in the city was Dermot O'Donovan. St. Bridget's and St. Francis were the two leading clubs at the time.

The Savoy was a focal point for all these activities. It was a meeting place, especially the snack-bar, and its famous dish of tripe and mash was great for soaking up the porter. Boggy men, horsey men, bookies and retired jockeys were among the regulars. Some of them retired quite young for reasons best known themselves. 'Thumbs Up' was the most notorious of the lot of them. He was a retired jockey, about four foot six in height, and wore a large peak cap, jodhpurs and a faded Crombie overcoat, a regalia which, like himself, had seen better days. He made a slight mistake at Longchamp and the French Racing board gave him his marching papers. He finished his days giving tips to some district justices, one of whom he pushed at Listowel Races. The same Justice had to bail him out that evening. 'Thumbs Up' was a funny little man, whose wife was a large country woman. They would have a few jars together during the day, and at night they would part company. He would then go to a vault in a graveyard three miles outside the city.

The other two characters well known to the snack bar and indeed the Savoy stage, were the Poet Ryan and Major Roche-Kelly, who lived as a recluse in Cappanty More at the foot of the Clare Hills. He was an ex-British army man who was badly shell-shocked and had little to say for himself. When Ger Ryan was feeling poorly, as he would say himself, he would take part in the quiz and easily win the jackpot. He would then adjourn to the Bedford Hotel and the next day the Major would repeat the Poet's performance. That went on for weeks. The two familiar drooped figures would cross from the Savoy smiling like two children who just got money from their favourite aunt. They were crossing the street at their usual slow pace when a big motor car came down the street, jammed on the brakes and wound down the window. The woman driver left a roar out of her like a bull. 'Do you think you own the road?' The Poet frowned, dropped his thick eyebrows, and said in a sharp biting tone: 'Madam, I wonder who owns the car?'

Alas. Their good time was coming to an end. Andrews twigged the caper. He walked into the snack bar and sat between the Poet and the Major, who were plotting their next move. He called three glasses of sherry and said, 'Gentlemen, I think we'll call it a truce.' The Poet, with his usual charm, lifted his glass and smiled.

A frequent visitor to the snack bar was a tall man dressed in a white trench coat, a soft hat, a piercing look and one eye that always seemed to be closed. He spoke

STAGE AND SCREEN

out through the side of his mouth. I knew he was an IRA man. After he had come in a few times, my curiosity got the better of me and I asked Rose, the waitress, who he was. She smiled and said, 'I thought you knew him.' 'No,' I said. 'That's the famous Eric 'Lanty' Hannigan, Lanty was the officer who trained Brendan Behan and Cathal Goulding in explosives in the Dublin Mountains for the IRA bombing campaign in England.'

Another visitor was a detective named Kenny who seemed to very interested in Lanty's movements. Kenny, I was to discover later, had shot a Republican up the country somewhere and was posted to Limerick. For his own safety, he used a carry a gun. The day Lovely Cottage won the Grand National, he came in fluthered drunk and waving his gun. I managed to get the gun from him, wrapped it in his overcoat, pushed him into the cloakroom, locked the door and left him to sleep it off. It was about that time some of the bookies left Limerick in a hurry. Some wag wrote on one bookies window above his name, 'Also Ran.'

The most colourful pair to appear on the stage in my time were Jack Doyle, all six feet three inches of him, with a red rose in his button hole, and Movita, with a head of massive black hair, dark beautiful eyebrows and brown eyes. She just about reached his shoulder, as they both sang their favourite song, 'South of the Border.' Movita sang 'The Kerry Dances.' She didn't have a very big voice but she sang in a charming manner.

I met jack in 1970 in a pub in London called The Hoop. He was pretending to tear up £5. I was reading the Irish Press when he left a roar at me. 'Paddy, come and join us,' which I did. We had a sing-song and when I told him that I brought his bags from the Limerick Railway station he paused for a few minutes and shouted to the barmaid, 'Two large Jamesons.' The two girls behind the counter who were from Thomondgate were getting a great kick out of our antics. We sang for hours until Jack got a phone call; he was due to sing at an Irish night in Camden Town.

My memories of the Savoy days would not be complete without a mention of Jimmy O'Dea, Maureen Potter and that fine baritone Denis Cox. O'Dea was always a favourite with Limerick audiences, especially if you could hear the sly jokes which was a very effective trick to get the first six rows laughing and then he had the whole house in the palm of his hands. Winston Churchill was one of the statesmen he used to send-up, but, looking back, Napoleon was his man. He would take his stance, drop one eye, and stare at the audience with magnetism. The while audience would go up in an uproar.

One Sunday night O'Dea and Cox were coming through the back stalls door. I was instructed not to leave anyone into the cinema. I put my hand across the door and said, 'Sorry gentlemen, you can't go through, there's a show on.' O'Dea looked at Cox, the two of them looked at me (we were all about the some height). O'Dea said in a caustic voice, 'out of my way young man, or I'll put you down the street talking to yourself.' With that he gave my pill-box hat a thump knocking it down over my ears, stormed down the middle and left me to the height I grew. Denis and Jimmy later measured me with a tape borrowed from the magician Albert le Bas. My lack of inches was always a joke between them.

Then came the opening of Feile Luimni by Sean T. O'Kelly. I was appointed to act as a page boy to the President. After weeks of drill in William Street Garda station under Sergeant Morgan, and after perfecting the Presidential salute, we were all set for the big night. Out of a big black motor car hopped this jovial little man, beside him a fine big stately woman. After the salute, we went into the cinema. I walked too far ahead of the President and found myself beside Ban Ui Cheallaigh. I got a tap on the head from his aide to allow O'Kelly to walk beside his wife.

The next day I was in Luke Larkin's bookie office studying the form, which was illegal because I was under age, but knowing Luke so well he turned a blind eye. While looking over the *Cork Examiner*, I heard her saying to a fellow punter, 'isn't the President looking like a little dote?' The caption read: 'President and wife open Feile Lumni.' I looked again. Sure enough there I was with my pill-box hat perched on the side of my head right beside his wife and Sean T. behind my back.

The most colourful manager in my time was 'Uncle' Cliff Marsden who first came to Limerick to cover a story for Fox Movie News about two German fliers. He came back to Limerick about 1948. When he died in 1953 he got a military funeral, much to the surprise of many of his friends who did not take him too seriously. But many a head shook when they found out he was one of Michael Collins agents, though he was English.

George Brent, who was in Limerick buying horses at the same time, was also a dispatch rider with Collins. I saw Marsden and Brent having a great chat; no doubt it was about the old days. Father Flanagan of Boys' Town was at the Savoy but he didn't live up to his reputation. He was a bitter man and he certainly didn't have the angelic smile of Spencer Tracey when he berated Mickey Rooney for his childish prank in the film about the priest's work.

From *Old Limerick Journal*, December, 1979.

A visit to The Pirates
Michael Quinlan

THE year 1935 in Limerick ushered in a few changes in that city's long history. For example, it was the year the City council became a management corporation, getting rid of the last semblance of the British system of local government. It was also to mark the first and last term of office of a Quinlan as Mayor of the city. From 1197 to 1933, the Quinlan mayor was a long time coming, but although we lost one Quinlan in 1935, we gained another, because that was the year I was born. Oh no, Limerick wouldn't be getting rid of the Quinlan's that easy.

1935 was also the year when the Savoy cinema first opened, the finest picture theatre ever seen in the city. Strangely enough, the first film to be screened here was *Brewster's Millions*, a movie of many incarnations that was first made under Cecil B. De Mille in 1914, the opening year of Britain's dreadful Great War. In 1921 when England was desperate to find a settlement to the 'Irish question', and planning to send the Black and Tans across the water to terrorise the people into submission, a remake appeared, still black and white and silent, starring the famous Roscoe 'Fatty' Arbuckle . . . .

STAGE AND SCREEN

British films were very successful in Limerick cinemas right up to the time I left the city in 1953. I must admit that they were my favourites as well, rather than the Hollywood alternatives. I was always fascinated too to read the certificates on the screen just before the movie started. Such as the intriguing 'Passed for distribution in the United Kingdom and the Irish Free State, and approved by the British Board of Film Censors' which seemed to imply an unrepublican collusion between someone high up in Dublin and the British government. And as it happened even the first live theatre show I ever saw was an English play, *The Pirates of Penzance* at the Limerick Playhouse.

One day out of the blue mama told me that the *Pirates* she had mentioned long before were back in town, and we would be off to see this live show at last on Sunday evening. Mama said *Pirates* was set in Cornwall, and was written by the famous Gilbert and Sullivan.

All very fine, but I had no idea where Cornwall was and as for Gilbert and Sullivan only some vague recollections of reading a piece about them in Dad's Pears Encyclopaedia, during one of the my furtive raids on his private library in the loft. But even that it was mostly the name Sullivan that had attracted my attention, just because I had a friend at school with the same moniker. As for opera, comic or otherwise, I possessed no idea of what it really was until that night. Mama added only that I would be delighted with it, and that it was as different as chalk is to cheese. As I could fancy a good piece of cheese for munching on but not at all on chalk, that was not necessarily encouraging.

Of course it would all be a new experience, for although I thought I knew every cinema in town from the Thomond to the Tivoli – flea houses both – and all the other assortment in between, I had no idea even where the Playhouse was. All I knew about it was that Grandad Tom Casey in his younger days had been part of the cast of a play there called the Colleen Bawn (The White Lady), as in fact was Patrick O'Connell, later to be mayor in 1947. Apparently Tom Casey and Patrick O'Connell were cast members in many Playhouse shows in earlier days, although Grandad Casey would have been much older than Mr. O'Connell at the time.

It was just after my Confirmation, and some of the money I had collected from that lucrative event was now to be used up for this entertaining purpose. As we strolled down Perry Street that evening our first call was to the little kiosk near Hayes' garage, where the customary bag of movie sweets was purchased along with the ten woodbines for mama. Then down Glentworth Street across O'Connell to Lower Glentworth, and now I was beginning to wonder if Mama was lost, because I had never seen a theatre of any sort down this way in my ramblings. But halfway along we turned into an alley called Theatre Lane, and sure enough there was a big wooden gate down there with the sign Limerick Playhouse.

Painted on the front were two strange facemasks, one happy, the other sad. That means drama and comedy, said Mama. The outer gate was open inwards, and buzzing crowd of people were milling around in the yard waiting for the theatre door to open. A young fellow came up to us, and gave Mama a big grin like the happy mask and a program headed *the Gilbert and Sullivan Theatre Group Presents* . . . then the door opened wide and we all trooped in, the young fellow from the yard having already raced into his second happy role of taking the money as we entered. This was a very small theatre, but it was cosy too. Lights were on, but not as brightly as in the Lyric, although the place did possess a beautiful red curtain just like the one at the Savoy.

There was stirring music also, pouring out of an overdressed group of people ensconced just below the stage, my first encounter with a theatre orchestra. Not a full orchestra of course; some had violins and others clarinets, and one man was surrounded by an intriguing variety of drums. Oh, and there was a passionate fellow conducting.

I was very surprised that I knew the tune they were playing. It was one we had sung sometimes at school, although vexingly I could not recall the name. Others later in the show were familiar in the same way. Suddenly the regular music fell away and a magnificent drum roll resounded. The lights dimmed, and the curtain opened to reveal a brightly lit stage of colourful live figures, with a back drop of cliffs and sea and a sailing ship nearby. But instead of talking to each other the characters were singing. Shades of the musical chemist, what could this be?

I just sat there transfixed, fascinated by the idea. Mama was right again; this was certainly different and better than the pictures. Soon Mama could not believe her ears either, for she heard me singing along with the actors. So she kept nudging me to shut up and be quiet. I was so excited that I knew many of the songs, or others with the same tunes, making the show a real treat for me.

Unlike the cinema, there was an intermission half way though, and we all ambled out into the yard, people standing around in little groups, chatting, smoking and laughing. Even the musicians were over in a corner there, all smoking like demons and animated amongst themselves. The second half of the show as just as exciting, with sword fights and more lively singing in between.

To top it off, the ending was another surprise to me. All the actors, even the ones that were supposed to be dead, came out to bow to us, and we all clapped and cheered wildly. In fact we clapped every time the curtain opened and closed, all the way through the show. Whatever the origins of the play this was grand Limerick entertainment.

Only the week before, Mama and I had been to the Coliseum in O'Connell Street, to see a double feature of Charlie Chaplin and the Keystone Kops. My first silent movies, which I found fantastic. But the *Pirates* show featured real live people. I felt the Frederick character to be the best actor that night, probably because he was the youngest and looked terrific in the part. Indeed afterwards I most fervently fancied myself in the role; likely it would never happen but there was no harm in dreaming.

From *Mickey Slabdabber*, 2005.

When the Lyric rose up against 'Biddy'
Denis O'Shaughnessy

BACK in December 5, 1927, an English touring company called the Union Jack

STAGE AND SCREEN

Photo Players came to the Lyric Theatre in Glentworth Street for a week's run with a play called 'Biddy.' Described as an 'Irish Stew', the play was written by an Englishman, Laurence Cowen, and the group looked forward to an enjoyable stay with good houses.

Little did they know what lay in store for them as the *Leader* report unfolded the story:

First indications of trouble ahead started on the opening night, December 5, when a group of young men picketed the play, distributing leaflets quoting adverse criticism from some Derry newspapers.

Rumours swept the city that on the second night there would be more vehement protests and crowds gathered outside the theatre to witness the fun.

But it was all happening inside and as the play progressed the cast were subjected to a continuous verbal fusillade consisting of booing and hissing. 'Leave Limerick immediately.' 'Pack up', and 'Go back to Houndsditch' were some of the cat-calls the actors had to endure. The play was stopped several times with the stage manager appealing to the audience to give the actors a chance. 'This is an all-Irish cast, with just one exception,' he stated.

One of the actors, named Charles Keogh, later came on and appealed for order stating that he was as good an Irishman as anyone in the audience. 'So was Judas an Apostle,' a member of the audience shouted back. 'Beat it as quickly as you can. This show must be closed down, you're only a renegade.'

Keogh had enough and moving closer to the footlights, invited anyone who would care to come up and he would show them whether he was a renegade or not. His invitation was not accepted. At this stage people in the pit took up the refrain of the hymn 'Faith of our Fathers' while Keogh, obviously demented at this point, just jibed at them from the wings. Tension was now so high that the Guards present were put on full alert and the Inspector sent for reinforcements.

Most outspoken of what was described as 'the vigilants' was Mr. Denis O'Dwyer, reported to be of the Harbour Commissioners, who addressed the crowd from the stalls: 'the piece that night was worse than immoral; it was an insult to the Catholic faith and the Catholic clergy. He would appeal to all those people who took exception to the piece to follow him and leave the building,' which was greeted by cheers and several left but some stayed on to make sure no attempt was made to go on with the play.

At this stage a member of the orchestra, who speaking in broken English, said he was glad he was not an Irishman. 'You are a disgrace to the world,' he added, which elicited cries from the audience: 'to go back to Germany or the Shannon Scheme.'

It was all too much for a female member of the orchestra, who frightened at the attitude towards her, swooned and the other members immediately disappeared from view with her limp form and did not return.

The end was drawing near and the last sally was made by a woman who was understood to be connected with the management of the theatre. She took up a position in the balcony and, addressing the twenty or so young men left in the theatre, said with a marked English accent that it was enough to make her tired. 'They (meaning the management) had tried to do good for the people of Limerick and that was the thanks they got.' She was interrupted at this stage by a man, who said they would not allow shows of that kind. 'I will show you some of your dirty, immoral Limerick some day.' she concluded in a high-pitched excitable voice, but her promise was only greeted with taunts, a young man nearby telling her to take them back to England with her.

At this stage the crowd on the street outside had grown to huge dimensions, a state of congestion existing from Tait's Clock to the door of the 'gods' and from the clock tower to the junction of Glentworth Street and Catherine Street, on the other side (good humoured).

Inside, the last verbal fusillade had been fired and the house was empty within the subsequent few minutes, and the surging throng outside was informed by Mr. O'Dwyer, who had been in consultation with the management, that 'Biddy' was finished and Limerick would know her no more, a statement that evoked a loud outburst of cheers.

So, what should have been a week's performance ended after two nights. The play moved on the Gaiety theatre in Dublin, and before its performance the author, Mr. Owen, remarked on the scenes in Limerick, saying 'it was the argument of the shillelagh; it was the method employed by the primitive man,' adding for good measure, that 'it was the procedure known as hanging a man first and then trying him.'

He was taken to task in the columns of the *Leader* by Mr. O'Dwyer, the leader of the 'Vigilants', with an address at North Strand, Limerick. 'Our protest was made in a most dignified and orderly manner. A strong feeling of resentment was produced in the great majority of those who witnessed the production that it culminated in compelling the cessation of the performance on the Tuesday night, when the most objectionable part was reached. It is significant to note that this part was deleted from the edition of the play as produced at the Gaiety Theatre.'

According to the *Leader* reporter, the most objectionable part of the play, and when the main trouble started, was a scene where 'the priest, who spoke the English of an uneducated person, was about to get 'the whole hierarchy of Ireland' a marriage dispensation for the 'squire' provided the latter paid for it by giving a piece of ground.'

The sequel to the scenes in the Lyric came a year later when in the London King's Bench Division the Union Jack Photo Plays Ltd. sued the leasees of the Lyric, Messrs. G. Lawrence and S. H. Parsons, for damages, claiming that as a sequel to the scenes which followed the production of the play 'Biddy, there was a breach of contract on the part of the Lyric management inasmuch as the play was discontinued after the first night. The defendants denied there was any breach of contract, as the then manager of 'Biddy', withdrew the production of his own free will. A number of Limerick people were subpoenaed to give evidence.

The judge held that after the second night's disturbance plaintiffs and defendants mutually agreed to rescind the contract (for a week's production) as they realised it was hopeless to go on with the play. Consequently he dismissed the claim, with costs. In the claim against the Gaiety Theatre, for £300 for alleged breach of contract in connection with the same play, judgment was given in plaintiffs' favour as the judge held that there was no legal excuse for breaking the contract in that case.

So ended the extraordinary story of 'Biddy's' aborted visit to the Lyric with a judgemental *Leader* reporter summing up: 'that the people of Limerick were not disposed to digest plays with Irish settings which have their birth in the brain of an outsider who was unacquainted with the native mentality as demonstrated in a most unequivocal manner in the Lyric Theatre last night.'

From *Limerick: 100 Stories of the Century,* (2000)

'A Matter of Principle'
Vincent Prendergast

IN his first year as Superior, things could hardly have gone better for Br. Murray. The Plain Chant Festival, the Intermediate and Leaving Certificate results, successes at the Thomond Feis, had all brought much prestige to the C.B.S. True, the Harty Cup had failed to arrive at Sexton Street for yet another year, but that aside, there were many other sporting achievements to compensate. And rounding out his first year then, the magnificent success of *The Gondoliers*. But there was one note of discord, the most painful I would suggest of his term of office. It was the unnecessary matter of a 'principal', that quite rapidly hardened into a near disastrous matter of 'principle.'

For the operas the rule was – the boys chosen to play the principal roles would perform in the evenings, while their understudies would perform in the matinees. That had been the clear, unequivocal understanding from the very beginning. For the role of the Duke of Plaza-Toro in The Gondoliers, Michael Power was the obvious choice of both Lionel Cranfield and Br. Murray. Another boy, Conleth Beare, was chosen as his understudy. Conleth was a relatively new boy in the school. His father, a Bank Manager, had been transferred to Limerick some time earlier. Mr. Beare was a generous benefactor to the school, for which Br. Murray was anxious to show his appreciation. Conleth was a brilliant student, but in truth, in his appreciation of Gilbert and Sullivan, not to mention the vital role of the "Duke of Plaza Toro", he was woefully out of his depth. He was certainly no match for Michael Power, but then what boy in the school was? If wiser counsel had prevailed Conleth Bere would never have been chosen in the first place.

On the Thursday evening, Michael Power, who had been outstanding throughout the week, was made up and costumed well in advance of curtain-up, and as was his custom, was pacing to and fro in the wings. Suddenly he was approached by Br. Murray and told to get changed, that Conleth Beare was going on as "The Duke." Michael did as he was told. When Jim Scallan arrived at the theatre and learned of the change, he was furious, and challenged Br. Murray at once. There was an almighty war of words but Br. Murray held firm. Conleth Beare was going on and that was that. Here was the perfect example of Br. Murray at his most obstinate, giving way to no man, but sadly, breaking one of his own golden rules to suit himself. On the Friday evening Michael Power went on as normal.

For the last performance of the week, the Saturday evening, the house was as always packed to capacity, and included dignitaries from all walks of life. Conleth Beare's parents were also in the audience and for reasons already mentioned, Br.

Murray felt they were entitled to see their boy in the principal role. It was his way of thanking them for their generosity. Word of this startling decision spread quickly through the theatre, the boys, the Brothers and back-stage staff. All were appalled. The earlier Thursday evening episode had been bad enough, but to take Michael out now on this final performance, having been excellent all week, amounted to treachery, but nobody dared question Br. Murray. Jim Scallan, who half suspected something like this might arise, arrived earlier than usual at the theatre and sure enough heard the "news." Up on stage he met Br. Murray and asked "who is playing the 'Duke' tonight?" "Conleth Beare" was the reply, Jim had already made up his mind up, "If he is," he said, "you can conduct the opera yourself." There was an icy silence.

Now both these very strong-willed men knew each other well – they had taught side by side in the same classroom for many years, and it was clearly the irresistible force versus the immovable object. But Br. Murray's first duty was to the school, the opera and the waiting audience. "Very well Mr. Scanlon," he said (he never got Jim Scallan's name right in all their years together) "You can have your way tonight, but let me assure you you will never put me in this position again."

Nor did he. Michel Power played the "Duke of Plaza-Torro" that memorable evening with his customary brilliance, unaware of the courageous stand that Jim Scallan had made on his behalf, and Jim Scallan conducted the orchestra . . . for the very last time. It was a sad and quite unnecessary end to what had been a formidable partnership.

From *A Set of Curious Chances – A Decade of Opera at Limerick C.B.S. 1939-1949* (1998)

Dracula rises up
Michael Quinlan

THE one and only time Dad ever took me the pictures I was about twelve, and the cinema was in Cecil Street, a theatre called the *Athenaeum*. This was for a musical called *Easter Parade*, the very first colour movie I ever saw. Mama told me Dad had been given free tickets because he was doing some work for the owners.

I was to see many free movies in that cinema years later, when I too worked for the new owner, Mrs Collins, and the cinema's name had changed to the *Royal*. Denny, the doorman, became a very good friend of mine, so much so that any time he saw me in the queue he would beckon me to come in ahead of everyone else, and never allowed me to pay for a ticket. Naturally I liked Denny. I never paid to see a movie at the *Royal* once, thanks to Denny, and no doubt to Mrs Collins, who I had gathered had instructed him to do so. I was later as an awkward teenager in two minds over my good fortune; the shy young man in me feeling so embarrassed at this favouritism that sometimes I would even consider going to the *Royal*. Other times I would try to hide in the queue so I could finally buy a ticket, but even the girl in the box office knew me well and wouldn't accept my money.

STAGE AND SCREEN

As a child, money for the movies was certainly a problem of the opposite order. By far the easiest cinema in Limerick to sneak into without paying was the Lyric, at the corner of Glentworth Street and Baker Place, which most people called Pery Square. (This may have been because the real Pery Square near the Library didn't look like a square at all).

Most cinemas in Limerick unfortunately lacked side doors like those of the *Lyric* near its front stalls. The front stalls were the cheapest, because the screen was practically in your face. It was not easy to keep looking up all the time without getting a crick in you neck; I always had a headache when I came out and my eyes hurt too.

The *Carlton* and the *Central* were just like the *Lyric* in having front stalls that were very uncomfortable, and the screens too high up. The *Savoy*, by contrast, the biggest and best cinema in the city, owned a screen set thoughtfully well back from the front seats. The *Savoy* stage was low as well, also you could see the whole film without having to move your head from side to side like some Wimbledon tennis fanatic. But then the *Savoy* didn't have serials like the Lyric did every Saturday matinee, and that was something that couldn't be missed either, money or no bloody money. So the *Lyric* was a place we couldn't help sneaking into in peril of our mortal souls.

Sometimes I had two glorious pennies to my name but no more, just half the price to get in. Then I would promise McGurk or Ger Downey twelve guilty sweets if he would open the door inside the first chance he ran into. While the boys who were rich with the entrance money queued up in a proper and decent manner, I skipped across the street to Enright's little kiosk and splurged all of my two pence to buy twenty-four wanton wrapped toffees.

I never had to lurk too long before the side door of the Lyric would develop an unauthorised angle, and I would scamper, swallowed up by the immediate pitch darkness between the stalls and the high front of the stage. It was always like a secret passage, and there were always two or three more sneaking in behind me before the door clicked discreetly shut again.

Periodically the usher would come down the aisle and shine his flashlight on the illegal portal to make sure it was still closed. He must be deaf not to have heard that click, I think, but then again maybe he really is. Cinema ushers in Limerick were said to own eyes in the back of their heads though, but they still couldn't catch us. Still, I knew it would be too hard to do this at the Savoy. Although there was a similar door near the stalls there, there was too much space between the stage and the front seats to creep in observed, and no secret dark way there to cover you either. I always felt bad in my conscience about having to sneak into the Lyric, but not to the point of denying the urge.

The Lyric's serials were a crock of course, sometimes literally so. There might be a hero tumbling off a cliff into a pit of crocodiles, and just as the croc yawns wide open to devour the bold fellow as he drops the fillum cuts off suddenly, to our moans and yelps of disappointment. You are cordially invited to return same time same place next week, to find out whether or not the strapping hero really did achieve his comeuppance by being satisfactorily eaten up.

All week you look forward to the feast, only to find out that the vexatious fellow manages to grab a tree branch on the way down, and the hungry croc misses out on his dinner altogether. But not to worry, before that session ends the hero is in another impossible jam, for example tied to the railway lines and a train rushing towards him at breakneck speed. Then cut again, you have to come back next week once more, most annoying for the urchins like me who were never in the least sure of the money for legitimate access. So the remote moguls of Hollywood made the sinning for boys in illegal entrances almost compulsory.

The classy and serial-free Savoy, I recall, had the best ads however. For example, the shoemaker's advertisements, where Rip Van Winkle was seated under a tree in a field, and a very serious adult voice informed you that:

> *Rip Van Winkle fell asleep, it was a longish snooze,*
> *His clothes indeed were sadly worn, but not his rebuilt shoes.*

Next, a big orange-coloured seashell appeared on the screen, and as it opened up there was a jar of Brylcream inside, like a funny-shaped pearl in an oversize oyster. The voiceover sang:

> *Brylcream, a little dab will do ya,*
> *Brylcream, you look so debonair,*
> *Brylcream, the girls will pursue ya,*
> *Simply dab a little in your hair.*

Seats in the middle of the cinema were a fearsome shilling and six pence, and only if Uncle John took me to the pictures did I ever get to plonk my bum on one of those. The balcony upstairs was out of the question, though. Everybody called the balcony the Gods, and it was only the rich people who could ever think of going up there. A huge two shillings and sixpence they cost. I brooded on this, and thought I would love to go up there some day and see the view that the high and mighty had. Meantime I asked Mama, were the people with the most money up higher to be near God? Jaysus, she replied, you do ask the most awkward questions sometimes.

Of all my movie experiences in Limerick the treat to the Savoy was undoubtedly the best. When the main lights were on before the picture you could gaze around and see the whole place rigged out like some fantastic castle. There were mediaeval windows with coloured lights in them and lines of wall with traditional turrets surrounding your view. The seats were grand too, lined with soft red velvet, and the carpets were a fancy red plush pile. Instead of cheap plywood around the front of the stage like the other theatres there were authentic wooden railings with a polished top on them, shaped like the great stone balustrades on Sarsfield Bridge.

Lean your head back on the seat and stare up at the ceiling, it looks like the open sky itself. Anyone would think you were inside a giant bubble, the immense curve of the roof cascading down inside the castellated walls like east and west horizons. Within the walls a hidden glow resembles the setting sun reflected on billowing clouds, while tiny lights scattered across the ceiling seem to be the very stars twinkling above. It was worth a visit just for the heavenly vistas.

But that wasn't the only attraction at the Savoy. The first time I was there I gasped in amazement, and for once it was Mama who was doing the snickering. For a great Compton organ rose up out of the floor like magic, revealing to my disbelieving eyes no one less than Norman Metcalf, vampire of the lanes. Dressed in his long black, funeral tail coat and immaculate shiny hair, he was not just sitting there at the organ but perched like Dracula triumphant, with outstretched claws raised up in front of him the spotlight surrounding him like an unhallowed moonbeam.

Not content to appear out of nowhere in such a supernatural fashion, he starts to play that instrument and all the theatre shakes. The sound bursts out so loud at first, like a thunderclap from hell, then softens to an eerie whisper. Now it swells again to a frightening pitch like a giant drowning wave, overwhelming you without hope of rescue. When the music reaches a huge crescendo he pounds out one last shattering chord, and stops all at once. The silence is spectacular. Then the noise of clapping hands is deafening, everyone is clapping, even me, applauding the triumph of Nos Fearatu.

All at once the magic organ starts to sink back into the floor again, but I could never see any sign of a hole there afterwards. Gees I wondered how that was done, but the moonbeam spotlight disappeared too quickly to figure it out, or maybe dimmed to conceal something unholy. But I marvelled; no other cinema in Limerick offered up any experience as wonderful as that one.

Mama always tried to make sure that we went to a cowboy picture in preference to any other kind, for she loved the singing cowboys like Gene Autry and Roy Rogers, and was crazy about how the bad guys never started shooting till the singing stopped. Maybe they were enjoying the melodies too, and didn't want to interrupt the proceedings with dead bodies until the music was fully sung out.

Sometimes we went to see a Sherlock Holmes picture, and I liked them better. Dracula was good too and we sometimes chanced the silent movies at the old Coliseum. The problem there was that the picture would keep breaking down part way through. So the whole audience would stamp the floor with their feet until it came back on again. That was great fun. It was freezing cold in there, and stomping the floor warmed us all up till the picture resumed. Then you forgot about the cold because the fillums were all so funny and we couldn't stop with the laugher.

My imagination there ran wild. I always believed I knew exactly what Charlie Chaplin was saying, and the Keystone Cops too. Although there wasn't any sound, bar the piano, I could hear every crash and whistle, and the train roaring down the track towards the girl tied to the line. Then her frantic screams, Help! Help! for pity's sake! Fortunately for her the pity usually responded, generally in the shape of a handsome young man keen to oblige a young lady in dire need.

From *Mickey Slabdabber*, 2005.

Pigtown
Mike Finn

Tommy: 'Long White Lob. Tamworth. Gloucester Old Spot. Cumberland. Belted

Kentucky. Saddleback. Old Ulster. Lincolnshire Curlycoat. The pig - now there's one beautiful animal. Stout, proud, cheerful, loyal. Wallowing in the succulent pleasures of his callipygian rotundity! The man that isn't moved to poetry by the sight of a plump pig's arse isn't a real man! Lazy? Never! Dirty? Hardly! Misunderstood? Definitely! Dog me arse! Man's best friend is the pig! I should know. I've killed thousands of 'em. In a century and a half, fifty million porkers have met their end in this town. Pigtown. Light o' heaven to their souls. Tommy Clohessy from Squeezegut Lane - Clocks for short - Pork Butcher. Up every mornin' at five o'clock. Five rashers, five sausages, half a black puddin' and I'm off! Ten paces and I'm on Athlunkard St.

'In every house a pig buyer, in every yard some swine. Pig Street. I loves the smell of pig swill in the mornin'! The pig is the saviour of the workin' man. Buy em' small. Feed em' shite. Sell em' big. Extra cash when it's most wantin'. A pig is for Christmas, not just for life. He's the gentleman that'll pay the rent. With me clogs on me feet an' me knives under me oxter. I'm skipping up the streets and lanes of this town. Up past Dick Devane's and the Cathedral, past the Custom House and under Cannock's Clock. It's a minute slow - again. George's street before me - misty, silent and empty. My town. Pigtown.

'The pork butchers are the back bone of this town and don't you forget it! Not just this town. Oh no. Moscow, St. Petersburg, Kiev. I'm not coddin' ya. When the Tsar wanted to teach the Russians how to save their bacon, who did he call? The Pigtown pork butchers, that's who. Every mornin' we march, like extras from a Lowery painting, toward the stone and tile palaces. Shaw's, O'Mara's, Denny's, Matterson's. Shrines to the Limerick rasher.

'And the sound. Oh, that sound - Madame Butterfly me bollix! The squeal of a pig as he slides along the bar towards his destiny is like the Hallelujah Chorus! Then, bam! *(He slams a cleaver onto the table.)* One blow to the back of the neck and the pig begins his journey to Sausageville. The pungent aroma of the singeing room and the bristles fall like leaves off a sycamore. Then off with the head, slice the carcass and out with the entrails. Blood flows rich and red, down the chute and into the veins of Pigtown. The pig is the most generous animal on God's earth. Ham and bacon. Rashers and sausages. Skirts, kidneys, liver, eyebones, backbones, pig's heads, pig's toes, lard. Bladders for footballs. Bristles for brushes and shit for roses. Nothin' wasted but the squeal. A fair lad too. A classless beast.

'The crowned heads of Europe line their regal bellies with Limerick bacon and ham while the courtin' couples of Pigtown dream their dreams over pig's toes from Tracey's wrapped in last week's Chronicle. Limerick Bacon, famous from Quebec to Queensland and the pork butcher was king. Like every king, my subjects come in all shapes and sizes.'

....

Elsa Reininger. 'When she asked me I gev my address as Schottengasse No 2, Vienna, Austria. There is no longer such a place. Oh, there is a Vienna. There is an Austria. I haf lived there. But Schottengasse No.2? No! Still, Schottengasse No. 2 sounds better than Volfe Tone St. Especially ven you are coming to a hotel in O'Connell St. Volfe Tone St. Volf Tonestrasse! Doesn't make it any better. It is now my address, but is not my home. Hmm. Vot is my home? I signed the register - Elsa Reininger. But vot does dat mean? Not a lot. Elsa Reininger of Neulistritz. In Bohemia. In the Hapsburg empire. Dat is, ven der vas an Hapsburg empire. The map changes like a table being set und set again for tea. But alvays, alvays at the centre, like a beautiful iced cake,

'Vienna! Wien! Oh! Vot a place! Vot a time ve had! The music, the valtzing, the dinners, the gowns. Mine husband, Berish, vorked in the bank. Ve knew everybody und everybody knew us. Ve had house. Ve had car. Ve had maids. *(She laughs.)* Me! Little Elsa Reininger, mit maids! Och! I vos like a princess! *(Pause.)* Und then, the change. Vot is hard to explain is how slowly it vos at first. Almost as if it vos not happening at all. So slowly. It grows cold. Like someone, somewhere has left a vindow open. So slowly. Oh, there is still valtzing. But why no longer do I get an invitation? So slowly. I am at home for tea and cakes, like alvays, but one day, no one calls. So slowly.

'Then, they cross the street from me und sit away from me on the tram. Soon, the tram is not for me. So slowly. One day, a boy vit armband spits at me in the street. He looked just like my son. I am not angry vit this boy. He is vearing a swastika. Vot else vould he do? But, beside him is Anja Meuller. To me she vould call each Tuesday at eleven for tea und little cakes. She loved those little cakes. *(Pause)* I cried vhen the spit hit my face. Not because he spat. But because she did not say stop. Then, they vould do no business vit mine husband. Then they beat him. Then they burned our house.

'Schottengasse No 2. And so, here ve are come. Mit nothing. Limerick. A town full of pork. So different. Here, sex is verboden. It might lead to valtzing! So much I do not understand. Ve came here because mine daughter lives in Volfe Tone St. Did you know, there used to be two synagogues there? Used to be. Nobody said stop. De vorld is not a bad place. But, there is a time to say nothing. Und there is a time ven nothing is not enough. My curse is to have lived in a time vit too much nothing. *(She gestures with the gun to the crucifix behind her.)* I did not do dis to your Jesus! *(With great pride.)* Elsa Reininger killed nobody. *(Pause)* Until tonight.

Liszt in Limerick
Richard Aherne

FRANZ Liszt was the most popular pianist of his day. He had everything in his favour – good looks, magnetism, power, a masterly technique, and an unprecedented rich sound. Born on October 22, 1811, in Raiding, Hungary, he was an accomplished pianist at the age of seven, composing at eight, making concert appearances at nine and studying in Vienna at ten. In 1827, at the age of 16, after the death of his father, he made Paris his headquarters.

In January, 1842, Liszt and his troupe played in Limerick, driving by stage coach from Dublin through the early hours of the morning. At 6 am they were disturbed by a dreadful commotion – they had run over a pig being brought to market. Over an hour later, after a journey of 20 hours, they stopped at the Royal Mail Hotel Cruises. Monsieur Liszt went directly to Major Vokes' residence in the fashionable Pery Square, while his associates went straight to bed in the hotel.

Advertisements for their 'Two Grand Concerts' appeared in the local papers. These were to take place at 1 pm that day (Saturday the 9th) and at 8 pm and on Monday 11 January, in Anthony Swinburn's Rooms in Brunswick (Sarsfield) Street. Tickets for the occasion were 5 shillings (25p) each and could be obtained from Corbett and Sons' Music Warehouse in Patrick Street.

Having had no more than 4 hours sleep, they were up at mid-day and on their way to Swinburn's. They arrived fifteen minutes late, and sweeping past the proprietor, made their way into 'a poor dirty place . . . where they were about 100 people present. They were uncommonly lively for the Morning Concert and gave everything applause. Unfortunately, Joey Richardson was not well – out in the cold all night. He played very queer and threw his flute down and nearly broke it after missing a passage in 'Rosseau's Dream' . . . Liszt was encored once.

That afternoon they took a walk along George (O'Connell) Street and decided it was 'a nice street, like the back-bone of a fish, one long street.' They returned to their hotel to eat and Liszt went back to Major Vokes – 'a grand man' – to play whist and games, etc.

It was their intention to attend to their religious duties the next morning but they were late in rising. Two local men, Messrs. Corbett and Rodgers, visited Liszt and spent most the day with him 'smoking and dining.' At the invitation of Bishop Knox, he gave a recital in the drawing-room of the then Bishop's Palace (now the headquarters of Bord na gCon) at 104 Henry Street.

Their big concert was scheduled for the next evening, Monday the 11th. A few hours prior to it, Parry and Miss Bassano went shopping and he bought 'a pair of Limerick Gloves, which are so small they go into a nutshell.' Mrs. Rodgers brought them to see the Grand (Pery) Square then being laid out.

At 8 pm Swinburn Rooms were visited by 200 of the elite of Limerick and Clare . . . a full and fashionable audience. Liszt's first piece, the 'Hexameron' was most exquisite and masterly.' The audience was 'at one moment astonished by the rapid brilliancy of his passages, and at another were spellbound by the sweet and delicate softness of his touch. He also performed 'Galop Cromaatique'. Such was 'the impress of his execution', combined no doubt with 'fevered gestures, and hair flying in all directions' that 'some thought the instrument would fall to pieces in his hands – it was a marvellous piano to stand up to it.'

And if that was not enough, 'the audience was kept in roars of laughter by John Parry's inimitable amusing compositions . . . during the interval they were very much pleased with Joe Richardson's beautiful variations on the flute, and Miss Bassano and Miss Steele sang several well-known duets.'

Their performance finished at 11pm and returning to their respective abodes, they packed their belongings and 'had a capital supper'. In the very early hours of Tuesday morning, with their adrenalin still flowing, they set out from a foggy Limerick to return the 94 Irish miles to Dublin.

Some years later, in February, 1852, Miss Bassano again appeared in Limerick in the Theatre royal and her visit, eleven years earlier, was alluded to as follows: 'Miss Bassano is not unknown to Limerick audiences for she appeared here some years go when Liszt was astonishing the public with his extraordinary pianoforte playing.'

Back in the Rotunda in Dublin, they prepared for yet another concert. On this occasion, the remarkable Catherine Hayes (referred to later as the Pearl of la Scala and the Irish Nightingale) performed. She was then only 15 years of age and was introduced to Liszt at this time.

A number of misconceptions, surrounding Liszt's stay here, have crept into reminiscences of the event. It was erroneously reported that he gave his performances in the Theatre Royal, Henry Street, but he, in fact, did so in Swinburn's Hotel. Tradition has it that he performed his Hungarian Rhapsody No. 2 for the first time in public, in Limerick. This is highly unlikely as there is no evidence anywhere to offer support and Parry's Diaries, so detailed in all aspects, would surely have recorded this.

It was also thought that Catherine Hayes sang at one of his concerts in Limerick but this is inaccurate as it was in Dublin that she performed, a few days later. She did perform in Limerick some weeks later, on 5 and 6 February.

By then Liszt was already back in England and was on his way to Halifax where they proceeded 'to the Oddfellows Hall . . . the last concert on this awfully long tour.' Awfully long it may have been, but the accounts of their episodes are rich and picturesque. Through their concerts, they experienced the various characteristics of the Irish, English and Scottish gatherings.

Many of Liszt's Hungarian Rhapsodies came following his tour. He continued to captivate and his life was constantly being discussed. More scandal followed when his pupil, the rich Olga (the Cossack Countess) tried to shoot him and then herself. Everything about him was of interest to a gossip-hungry world. Even his hands received special attention – plaster casts were made of them and his pupils wrote prose-poems about them.

Throughout his life, he was always talking about joining the church; that was part of his romantic posture and it was mostly talk. Even when he did join, late in life, he had the best of both worlds, and probably never took his religion very seriously, but only made a great a show of doing so. He took four minor church orders in 1865, wore a cassock, and was addressed as the Abbé Lizst.

In the course of his career, he insulted nobles and even kings, when the manners were rude while he was playing. He was Liszt , the only one of his kind, and royalty had to bow to his will. He continued up to the last year of his life. The old Liszt idly sketched music that hinted at a world still unknown. He did this merely to amuse himself, not caring if it was ever played.

And so, the man who made his own rules, the exceptional figure who had his own cake, and ate it too, the Grand Old Man of Music Franz Liszt, died on 31 July, 1886.

From *The Old Limerick Journal* Winter Edition, 1992.

FOUR
FICTION

The Eve of All Saints
Kate O'Brien

SUNDAY afternoon devotions began at half-past four in the Jesuit Church in Mellick, and on this Sunday, which combined the last of the month of the Rosary with the Vigil of All Saints, they were long and ceremonious.

As Agnes entered the dark porch of the church she could hear the high voice of a young priest giving out from the pulpit the First Glorious Mystery of the Rosary. "Our Father Which Art in heaven, Hallowed be The Name, Thy Kingdom come, They Will be done on earth as it is in Heaven – " and sweeping in passionate depth and incoherency against him, the great voice of the congregation in response. "Give us this day our daily bread."

"Hail Mary, Mother of God –" the massed voice of the people as wordless and passionate, like the voice of the sea.

Agnes slipped into the shadowy end of a long bench. When, as a child of eight, she had first heard this tremendous-sounding form of prayer she had burst into sobbing for which she could offer no explanation to her exasperated mother. Was she frightened? Was she sick? Was there a pin sticking into her? No. Would she like to go home? Oh no! Teresa, unwilling to slap her before the Tabernacle, had looked a great many slaps, and then rejoined her calm contralto to the prayer-thunder which was crushing her little daughter's heart.

Agnes was reminded of that now, and smiled as she settled in her place. Nearer the communion rails, in the more chic benches of the centre aisle, she recognised the bonnets and back views of certain aunts and cousins, and was thankful that she was well placed for the strategy of avoiding them at the conclusion of Benediction. Normally she would not have minded a cousinly word with some of them, or even a lift home in one of their carriages, but it would be embarrassing to have to explain that one tarried this evening to go to Confession. Respectable young ladies did not ring the emergency Confession bell; to have to do so proclaimed either religious morbidity or, god forbid, a state of sin. And though it was often done on the quiet by ladies, young or old, as unimpeachable as Caesar's wife – still it was done on the quiet.

"Second Glorious Mystery - the Ascension of Our Lord Into Heaven. Our Father Which art in Heaven –" Agnes, who wished to be at the slow and difficult business of examining her conscience, held her breath nevertheless to await the startling rush of the antistrophe – "Give us this day –" that it might lift, as it could hardly fail to, her flattened, springless heart to God. But having felt the prayer-surge of the congregation catch her, she pulled back, jibbing, as always, against the easy way. She had not come here to gush at God, having so long dodged Him. She had come to examine her sin and purpose amendment.

How long since she had last confessed?

Vincent and Marie-Rose – she winced at the immediacy with which they plunged into her affair – had last left Roseholm on August 7th – she remembered Vincent saying at breakfast: "Saturday, no luck at all", and that she had made the flurries of their afternoon departure an excuse to herself for avoiding her weekly confession.

However, still refusing to think of the thing that was hurting her, and therefore, as she had insisted to herself, still innocent of sin, she made her usual confession on the following Saturday, the 14th, but had, to her own alarm, been unable to go to Communion all the same for the Feast of the Assumption.

August 14th, But that was ten weeks ago. And since then, quite apart from the central trouble, oh, how over all that time, was she to recall and marshal her million sins against God, her neighbour and herself?

Against God – she must accuse herself, though she supposed no theologian would be dogmatic here, of which seemed to her the offence of lip-service, the cautious adherence to routine. She had said her usual prayers and attended Sunday Mass, had paused in her household affairs to say the Angelus when its bell came over the river to her. In such submission to her training she did not find herself all guilty, for she knew that if she could only bring herself to face these prayers with vigour, they would help her – and she hoped from day to day for that. But she also knew that human respect and a deeper kind of cowardice were elements of her conventional devotions. Against God, then, there were ten weeks of hypocritical tepidity.

Against her neighour. Much pride and detachment always. A critical rather than a sympathetic front to the world. Some gestures of impatience, which she had tried to remember, against her kindly old father. No words, but many inexcusably impatient thoughts against her brother Reggie, and from those thoughts the occasional withholding of impulses of kindliness, half out of shyness, but half out of contempt. Against her mother – oh, a million small sins of omission, moods of despair and weariness, slackness in prayer for her, slackness in hope. Against Doctor Curran – she smiled. In spite of his rage of this morning, she could not find much guilt in herself against him. She had not flirted, and she had quite honestly come to like and trust him. That he loved her was no surprise, but secretly, rather distressingly, a comfort. And in that, no doubt, she must admit unscrupulousness that she should take comfort in receiving that for which she could offer no adequate return. And in accusing herself she had to smile again for thinking how well met they two would have been as man and wife. Ah well! Where was she in this long examination? Against Vincent? She took a long breath, then bent her head still deeper into her covering hands. She listened awhile to the torrential rise and fall of prayer about her – ". . . Blessed is the fruit of thy womb, Jesus . . . Holy Mary, Mother of God . . ." Vincent. No sin against him. Oh, God, there is no sin. Love happens – out of the simple fact that one's eyes can see, that's all – and in itself it is pure, it has no evil in it. Sins ring it round at once – ah, yes, because we are so weak and sensual that we cannot love and let be. But against the thing we love, how can we sin, however we offend against the world that parts us from it?

Passionately, as if afraid of finding out its casuistry, she hurled this faith of hers to heaven – but without pausing in it was swept on to where, in human terms, her great guilt lay. Against Marie-Rose. Yes – against the beloved, pretty sister whom she had once loved above all living things, whom still in essence she loved like that, or even in her torment, more than that, against Marie-Rose, the flippant and untrusting, who would trust her soul to her, her sin, long hidden even from herself, had grown in these ten weeks into an offence which the shoddiest morality could tilt at. The common sin against the ninth commandment, enhanced by all the pitiful complications of sister love.

That brought her to the last section of the examination of conscience. Against herself.

She was sitting upright now, for the sermon had started. The Rector of the Jesuits was preaching. He had a quiet, holy voice, and after the swinging tide of prayer its unbroken flow was tranquilising. Agnes did not bother to take in the words, which seemed to be such as she had heard a hundred times, but she let herself assent contentedly to their tone of steady faith. Thus she might legitimately postpone the real business of this preparation for Confession. There was plenty of time yet before she need ring the bell and ask for a priest. Really, she might rest and listen to these blessed platitudes about the Queen of Saints.

For her final fear was of words. When she was a schoolgirl, once or twice she had had to accuse herself of vague curiosities and stirrings of her sensual imagination – matters which she had not understood, but which she knew to wear the look of sins against the sixth commandment. The problem of how to frame these shapeless things for confession so as neither to exaggerate nor minimise them had been an agony – but to her great peace the chaplain had accepted her half-breathed phrase, "immodest thoughts," with an incurious calm. From then until now the sins of the senses had not over-troubled her confessions. And whereas in relation to her neighbour, her sister, Marie-Rose, her sin could be described as an abstraction, an idea, against herself, in its recurrent visions, its suggestions, its seductive day-and-night dreams, it took on a particularly and harmfulness which could not be shirked.

The voice of the preacher thinned away from her, and she lent an elbow on her knee, bending her face to the shelter of her hand.

Must she then say that since she had last seen him her defences had grown less and less against definite adulterous longing? Must she tell of nights when sleep would not come, however she sought it, because of his mad haunting – or of other nights when she would hold sleep off, the longer to delight in him? What words were there that would be honest and yet utterable, in which to describe fool-fantasies of being his wife, or even, in secret, in treachery, his mistress? Oh, god! Must she say even that? Must all her hoard of miserly be sloughed away?

It was too much, this shame, this pitiless exaction. She had fought her dark imaginings, and if they had defeated her, were they not only dreams, and senseless, hers alone, safe in the shame of her heart? Safe maybe – her disciplined spirit answered – except from God. It is that for what He accounts your sin against yourself that you are searching now, and here it is. You answer to Him for your own soul as for every other. And as to shame - you have merited it. Without it, what would confession be?

She surrendered to the training that was at least half herself. Surrendered into a sudden prayer for contrition and honesty.

The preacher left the pulpit. Young acolytes, moving softly about the sanctuary, had lighted more than a hundred candles. The atmosphere of the church was hot and still. There was a breath of incense and the soft clink of a thurible, then as the organ emitted a familiar chord of music, a procession of boys poured out from the sacristy and led a gold-coped priest to the altar steps.

"O salutaris hostia-"

Contrition, which for her characteristically was self-contempt, in the relation of personal pomposity to a ritual and a mystery which overwhelmed, contrition flooded her, cooling her shame as effectively as it did her heart-ache. Desires of the flesh, it told her, were not only as unimportant and transient as gnat-bites in summer, but quite as common, so that a confessor must be sick to death of little dreary tales of them – and hardly able to listen to another. To stage one's miserable narration in terms of distress and tragic uniqueness was nothing short of idiotic, a schoolgirl conceit so green and silly as to insult the whole purpose of the soul. Surely one must ask God to forgive that sort of idiocy as much as the idiocy of specific sin? Our absurdity must be more of a wound to the Eternal, Agnes thought, than our guilt. To have sinned was only too nauseatingly ordinary; not to see that and to make a self-inflating drama of sin was not so ordinary, but more despicable.

That was her contrition – to deny her own awareness of the agony which this confession was to be. Her contrition and her safeguard.

So, resolutely cold and still, resolutely contemplating, for its effect of levelling the ego, the beautiful pattern of Benediction, she took her place in that pattern, and refused herself to agitation. She was not herself. She was, much more fortunately, part of a formula. What was required of her was to be accurate in moving with that formula. Accurate, regular, and cold. So conforming she would reach her own small objective, which was part of the whole, and thus important.

They sang the Litany of Our Lady, and Agnes listened, concurring in the list of glories. They sang the "Tantum Ergo," and a little alarmed by the assault which the great words made on that personal anguish which she was here to kill with coldness, she snatched at two lines: "Praestet fides supplementum. Sensum defectui –" and roughly adapting them to her own need, she took their message that faith was her supply, her sufficiency, the senses yielding nothing. Faith a cold thing, a fact – that was what she must use to destroy fantasy.

The monstrance was raised. God's blessing spread above bowed heads, and Agnes, feeling it, was afraid of everything she felt. She only wanted to know even this – that God blessed her. Not to feel it. Feelings, amorphous things, pressed on each other, merged, disturbed – and were of their very nature stained by human life.

But – "Blessed be God, blessed be His Holy Name –" the divine praises were pure, and to be raised up without anxiety. Agnes's voice joined in them, coolly triumphant. Blessed be God, who extracted self-forgetfulness. Blessed be God, who made so absurd a thing as human love.

". . . Laudate Dominum omnes gentes . . . sicut erat in principio . . . "

Benediction was over.

The crowd surged down the aisles, bearing on it those cousinly hats and bonnets which Agnes had marked down to be avoided. Her corner was dark and it sheltered her. One by one the candles were extinguished in the sanctuary; quickly, once doors were opened, the atmosphere of heat and incense thinned.

She rose and walked to a door in a shadowy part of the centre aisle. She pulled the bell beside it. Far away she heard it jangle coldly. The aftermath of silence seemed very long before it was broken by the shuffling of old feet on tiles. Brother Fahy opened the door and peered into the shades. She made her request, which he took in silence. Then, dropping into a bench, she waited, kneeling.

She must keep herself cold and quiet. This was a matter-of-fact and necessary transaction, an excellent means to an excellent end. In ten minutes it would be over, and she would be loosed from sin. How good an expression, cool and invigorating!

"Since my last confession I accuse myself of – oh, Vincent!" Her heart contracted in pain, and simultaneously she thought this calm which she was enforcing upon agitation was probably very like the calm a murderer would assume. She was going to murder the only thing which could be said to live in her heart.

She twisted about, her body unable to keep still. There was a curious twitching in her fingertips. "Oh, I wish he'd be quick," she whispered into her hands, almost sobbing suddenly; "I can't bear this waiting. Oh God, make him be quick."

She heard the door open, and lifting her head saw a priest advance across the aisle to a confessional box. His Jesuit "wings" flapped as he moved; he carried his stole in his hands. Something both familiar and mystical in his aspect steadied her. She rose and followed him.

"Bless me, Father, for I have sinned."

Beyond the lattice, as she grew accustomed to the darkness, she could trace the grave, averted outline of his profile, could see his hand move slowly in the blessing as he spoke it.

"It is ten weeks since my last confession." She paused on that, but the confessor did not move, holding himself detachedly in listening attitude.

"Since then . . . " The tale of venial sins came out accurately and simply. Sometimes when she paused, the priest inclined his head to indicate attention. At last there was a longer silence.

"Is that everything my child?"

"No, Father. The chief thing I have to confess – the chief thing - "

"Yes, my child?"

Steady, steady. Remember how cheap and commonplace the whole thing is. Hysteria and self-indulgence. Remember that it is God who hears us in confession – God, to whom time is not, and who knows the end as the beginning of this triviality.

"For three years, Father, I have – I have cared more than I should for someone – who is married. Married to a near relation of mine – a sister. At first it was all right. I could control myself, and didn't think about it. But lately it has been more in my head, and in the last ten weeks – it has been an occasion of sin. I have committed sins."

"You have spoken to him of it, do you mean? He to you?"

"No, Father."

"There has been no expression of feeling between you – no indication?"

"Oh, no. I have only sinned in my thoughts."

"How often?"

"These last weeks I have thought of very little else."

"You have prayed against it?"

"Not enough. I have said my routine prayers. But I have not really prayed – I couldn't – and I didn't want to."

"You were afraid of the power of prayer – that it might kill this thing?"

"Yes."

"You have faith?"

"I haven't used it. I took a middle way. I accuse myself of having been mean and cautious in my prayers – half afraid to give them up, in case all decency would leave me, but afraid to use them honestly too."

"At least you do not deceive yourself."

"I pity myself – isn't that the same thing? I have often pretended there is something tragic in my case."

"That is a human thing to do."

"Oh, human – yes."

The priest moved a little, then resumed his immobility.

"After ten weeks of more or less surrender to yourself, this decision to confess and repent is impulsive?"

"Yes. Two things made me come to confession today. There is a special family intention for which I felt I must make this effort. And – and I shall be seeing him again this evening. I want help, Father. Oh, I want courage."

She bowed her head.

"God will assuredly grant you both, my child. It is your honest intention to give this thing no further licence in your mind – to keep it out of your imagination at any cost?"

"Yes, Father."

"Since that is so, and if, with prayer, real prayer, you stick to it – have no fear. It will die."

"Yes. It will die."

Her voice was desolate.

"That is in any case the fate of earthly love, my child. Whereas in the search for God, in the idea of God, there is matter for eternity."

"Ah – for saints, or philisophers."

"Why should you not be either or both?"

Agnes smiled in the darkness.

"I am a frivolous kind of person, Father."

He seemed to smile a little at that.

"That would not have struck me," he said. "But these imaginings then, these illicit thoughts – were they only frivolous perhaps?"

"No." She paused and when she spoke again her voice was less distinct. "They were serious and – and wicked. I can't explain them."

"There is no need to. I only feared that you were perhaps making a mountain out of a mole-hill – though it did not seem as if you would. Do not distress yourself. I repeat that with prayer and courage you can kill this thing. You are disciplined in your mind and you do not deceive yourself. Have courage. What you want to do cannot be done without struggle, and perhaps frequent failure, but God will by no means refuse you the help you are striving for. For your penance you will say the Litany of the Saints once a day for three days. And I advise you to return to what was probaly your former practice of frequent confession. Now compose yourself, child, to make a fervent act of contrition –and God will absolve you."

She saw him, still sitting in profile, lift his head and hand as his voice dropped mystically into the Latin absolution. Then she bent her own head into her hands and began her act of contrition. How simple! How formal and civilised was the method of the Church and its exactions. As she prayed and allowed the priest's words to flow into her mind, she was aware of coolness in herself, that her heart was only beating normally now, that the tiny twitchings had ceased under the flesh of her fingertips. She had done that which her belief exacted, and here, without fuss or probing, was the immediate award – the cold comfort which assured her with gentle contempt that everything dies except the idea of God – even sin itself, being more mortal than the sinner. No need to distress herself. Self would thin away if one pursued the idea of God. Oh, blessed absolution, which can absolve us not only of our sin, but of its occasions, by making out of it own tranquillity nothing of them and of our confusion in them. She felt, most blessedly, of no importance to herself now, and Vincent of still less. It was strange, her mind asserted, to be able to say that without a quiver, and without a suspicion of hypocrisy, but her body gave her none. She was cold all through, and coldness, she was now aware, was the perfect state. Goodbye to vagueness, pain and restlessness, goodbye to heat and fidgeting and to fear of Marie-Rose's eyes. God had absolved her from all that. She was loosed from sin. What was that nonsense she had talked with Dr. Curran this morning? A maggot in her brain? And he had said he'd cure it. Well, she had found a quicker doctor. "Oh God," she prayed with gaiety, "Oh God, that folly's over. And with all I am I thank you. With all my strength I thank you for this strange thing you have done. Lamb of God that takest away the sins of the world –"

"Go in peace, my child – and pray for me."

From *The Ante-Room*, Virago Press, 1988.

The Soup Kitchen
J. M. O'Neill

THE noise alerted him. He saw the approach of marching men: young men, some of them in Sunday best, some of them striving, with little, for respectability, some ragged. They had taken the centre of the road. Rosary beads were evident, and some carried small crucifixes. An enemy would call them a mob, but the zealotry of set faces and eyes would leave him in doubt. These were crusaders, purifiers, the street was crammed. As they halted before the soup kitchen, Edward was crowded, isolated. They dragged a table from inside and blocked the doorway, raised up a lion-hearted champion to stand surveying his believers and the faint-hearted on-lookers of the streets.

The man was in his thirties, maybe older, a navy blue suit, a shirt and tie, polished shoes. His cap was pulled low; he wore glasses and a scarf. He held out his hands, waited until there was almost silence.

'You are Catholics,' he thundered; a great rousing metallic voice. 'First we pray.'

He held up glittering rosary beads, made the sign of the cross, recited the Pater Noster while he looked up at the rooftops and the black low-lying clouds that shielded earth from heaven. He called out the Ave Maria ten times and orchestrated the volume of their response. He paused for stillness; the road was blocked, the small traffic detouring.

He held up his rosary chain of glass beads, and shiny crucifix that had been dipped in pinchbeck.

'Good friends were in Rome last year,' he began, 'and Christ's Vicar on Earth walked among them, raising his hand in blessing. He blessed these holy beads that are a hymn of prayer to the Mother of God. We call out, 'Hail Mary, full of grace, the Lord is with thee.' Our humble words of homage. Our faith has survived dungeon, fire and sword. This land, our land, newly recaptured from repression and slavery, is still the Island of Saints and Scholars; and it has been decided, I'm told on good authority, that within a short span of three or four years His Holiness, Pius XI, will come and walk among us. He will walk on the same Irish ground as we, poor banished children of Eve, have walked.

'He will say mass and sanctify the Host, and ask God to bless our nation, to make us worthy of the blessings he has showered on us.'

He was silent and the crowd was silent. He was gathering breath and power for his attack. He flung up his hands as if he had been stricken, shouted at heaven beyond the blackness. He was a raging, hysterical demagogue.

'Are we worthy? Do we deserve the Vicar of Christ should come to visit us? Do we? Answer me! You stand there like cattle. But cattle have dignity. Answer, answer! Are we worthy? Are we worthy that Christ's Vicar on Earth should come to walk among us? Are we worthy of God's love, or deserving of his contempt?'

Silence again.

Now his voice was heavy with sadness. 'I am waiting.' He kissed the pinchbeck cross of his rosary beads, held up his hands.

A great shout from his little army. 'No!'

'We are not worthy.'

'No!'

The entire gathering was enmeshed now; they were chanting, beating their hands together. He stood before them, head bowed, the rosary beads wound about his hands. The voice, Edward thought, a hammer on steel.

Suddenly he was upright, a hand raised for silence. It came slowly, unevenly, possessed them.

'Why are we not worthy?'

A shuffling uneasiness everywhere.

'Will I tell you?'

'Yes!'

'Louder!'

'Yes!'

He rolled his words at them like great crushing orbs of stone; he paused, studied them, was unhurried.

'You have allowed your city, a tabernacle of Christ, to be invaded, desecrated, by *apostates*! Those who forsook the infallibility of Rome to proclaim a lewd, sensuous, diseased, lustful, royal dissolute to be head of our Church! Who spurned the holy commands of the papacy. Who live only awaiting eternal damnation.'

Silence.

'Who are they? Where are they?'

Silence.

'They are here behind me feeding soup and bread to your brothers and sisters in Christ. And for what? I ask you, why are they feeding your brothers and sisters in Christ?'

A great pause for silence again.

Then almost a whisper. 'To take hold of their immoral souls! To win them over. To cast them into damnation.' He waited. 'Apostates must be crushed, destroyed, driven out!'

There was a thunderous cheer; he was lifted down from his humble rostrum.

Edward Burke watched. He didn't fear for himself; he was a person of courage, caught in the crowd, tossed about in the heave and sway. The thin glass shattered, the crude peeling mullions snapped. He was trapped tight on the crushes. The vanguard was already at the work of clearance. War cries were in the air, and the hungry were bloodied, beaten and pummelled, chastised for their sinful greed. There was the crash of cast-iron. The pendant paraffin lamps were flung against the walls and there was smoke and licks of flame. The crowd was tossed like gravel in a sieve. Edward, in the alleyway, caught a small boy, gave him a shilling and sent for fire brigade and ambulance.

There were residents and small shopkeepers, and the passing few, too, trapped, crushed, left to stand and stare.

A place buying souls for soup. It would be sinful to touch it. Charity was only for the *very* poor, the totally incompetent, the wretches of society who came down through every generation. The Church and Catholic people, their committees and societies, looked after them.

Edward Bourke roared at them. 'There are people in there!' He was fighting his way through, past little groups that might be in shock as they stood in gaping wonder at the sudden explosion of violence. Now they were coming to life, moving again.

He saw Lillian, his wife, and the younger supervisor from the tables. They had tied wet towels to cover mouths and noses and were dragging the few remaining staggering bodies to the space outside the doorway where the air was clearing. Lucy Langford, the dispenser of soup, was lying on the floor, blood smearing her face, distressed with smoke inhalation.

Then everything was clear: bodies on the pavement breathing air again, being tended. Lillian Burke and her helper wiped away the blood from the face of Lucy Langford, propped her to sit up and breathe. But she was ill. The bell of the fire brigade was only a block away.

The gathering flames lit up the smoky room and kitchen; tables had been ripped asunder; the legs used to beat the ragged clientele, the huge soup cauldrons were toppled, the chest of coal scattered.

The fire brigade had arrived. The ambulance, old-fashioned but clean, efficient, functional, was a legacy from the British army garrison that had left hardly seven years ago. Both were manned by city crews who had learnt their trade in the days of military occupation.

Lillian Burke came to Edward, gripped his hand. 'You're safe and sound?' she asked.

'You?' was all he could say.

'I'm fine, not a scratch,' she told him, 'but Lucy Langford is shaken. The window and the table that smashed it, caught her. The bleeding is nothing much, but she may have fallen heavily, and her legs were scalded when the cauldron was toppled.'

The ambulance men passed carrying Lucy Langford loosely strapped to a stretcher, and covered in a red blanket.

Lillian Burke said, 'I must go with her to the hospital.'

'Barrington's?'

'Yes. Taddy will be there, and the matron is a good friend of mine.'

. . . .

The head of the procession, more than a mile long, pushed into the broad crescent, passing the patriot statue. Acolytes in soutanes and surpluses carried a crucifix mounted on a tall brass tube, and behind it, the little black and white retinue with joined hands and bowed heads seemed to glide. Following them was a cleric in flowing cassock and biretta. They were the outriders.

The pavements, in a few minutes, had become crowded, a waiting congregation whom age or profusion of children had forced to the sidelines. There were the wheelchairs and crutches of the stooped, the lame and the halt. Rosary beads hung from hand everywhere.

The sound of a brass band, playing church music in slow march, reached them; a fine melodious sound from practised bandsmen. It grew louder.

Alexandra Bennett called to them, 'What is that?'

'The procession is arriving.'

'Isn't standing at the window a bit rude, Arnold?'

The heavy lined curtains had been thrown open since morning. Arnie had drawn across the lace-panelled drapes against the window.

'We're out of sight,' he said.

John Bennett, who had found his newspaper again, looked up. 'Who are we hiding from?' he asked.

Lillian said, 'Not hiding. Just peeping from their coign of vantage.' She brought him a new measure of malt.

Thaddeus slept soundly in his armchair.

The city was a city of churches, each with its platoon of clergy from monsignor or canon to the lowliest curate. Churches had confraternities and sodalities of men and women and waiting lists of young communicants with God.

A serried block of clergy led the way, their vestments moving like an iridescent slab catching the light and shadow of the day, their lips moving silently in prayer.

An ageing monsignor carried the monstrance, a sunburst of gold-washed metal, studded with semi-precious stones; and its orb, the Light of the World, was a consecrated wafer of unleavened bread that had become the body of Christ, the Son of God.

Four canons walked with him to constantly relieve him of his burden. Nearing the end of this march through the city, he was growing unsteady beneath a great ornate canopy held aloft by pillars of the church, men of substance and property if possible. An endless army of confraternities, men's and women's, carried banners to announce themselves. The faces of the marchers were as solemn as funeral mourners; they wore badges and sashes over their Sunday-best clothing. White and pale gold of papal flags fluttered everywhere, and national tricolours, blessed by anointed hands, mingled with them. Bands, in the distance, played their own music, and visiting clergy led their congregations in prayer or singing.

Finally, the statue of the Mother of God came, held aloft by chosen men of dedication to the faith of their fathers. Her canopy was a rich magnificent baldaquin, portable, carried by clerics in white albs and girdles. Her raiment was gleaming white satin, and a web of diaphanous fabric floated down from her head. A banner, wide as a country roadway, proclaimed: 'Hail Queen of Heaven.' The mitred bishop, in his open carriage, held up and fluttered his hand in blessing. He was surrounded by men of importance, clergy and laity.

The procession took an hour to pass beneath the Bennett windows. So many bands, so much music, so many hymns, so much booming recitation of prayer; it should have made a great cacophony, but the procession passed by with an almost frightening dignity.

As the blessed statue passed blow them, Edward said, 'There's a guard of honour for Our Lady of Deliverance from Disease. A line on each side?'

Arnie said, 'Yes, I see them.'

A leading member on one line, in a sharp penetrating voice, called out the First Joyful Mystery of the Rosary of Our Holy Mother. When the time of response came, he raised up his hands in exhortation, urging them to shout their prayers to heaven. It was a great roar.

John Bennett lowered his newspaper. 'Is there trouble out there?'

'Just prayers,' Edward said.

'Sounded like a battle-cry.' John Bennett was deep in his newspaper again.

Lillian was smiling.

Edward said to Arnie, 'The leader of the prayers down there . . .'

'The loud fellow?'

'Yes, the loud fellow. It could be Carmody. He's a high prefect in his confraternity, too, it seems.'

Arnie gazed down on him, the solid build of him, his face twisted in a distortion of sanctity.

'He knows this is my house. The crescendo or prayer was for us, I imagine. For the Bennett family.'

'Probably,' Edward said.

'Not for our salvation.'

'No.'

Edward said: 'I remember his voice, the trembling praying voice down there. That's all.'

'Thaddeus might remember his face.'

'Thaddeus is a worn-out man. He needs rest. Let him sleep. We've met Carmody face to face. Mulvey will get to know him better.'

At the top of the hill, the procession had been turning, out of vision, to the church and its acres of paved and consecrated grounds.

The magnificent statue in regal attire, a great potent fetish of holiness, had passed below them; in minutes it would be gone from sight. The pavement was dispersing. Quite Sunday was returning.

From *Bennett & Company*, Mount Eagle Publications, 1998.

FICTION

Some critical notes on Kate O'Brien
Paddy Lysaght

FOR all I know, there might well be a deeply researched thesis by an assiduous student, gathering dust in a pigeon-hole in some American university or other, on Kate O'Brien and her place in Anglo-Irish literature. Somehow I doubt it. She has never been the target for students in search of a thesis. It is not easy to understand why this writer's work has received so little critical assessment. Has it, I wonder, something to do with the profoundly Catholic dimension of most of her work, a dimension now out of favour with writers and critics? Whatever it is, even in Ireland she has not received the attention she deserves. Praised yes, and often lauded to the skies, but as far as I am aware, apart from *The Stony Thursday Book No. 7* (an issue devoted to her and which gives us some excellent sidelights on her work), anything approaching a critical study of her novels is not available.

True, you will find a paragraph or two devoted to her work in most studies of Anglo-Irish literature, but the impression still persists that even those who have made a study of such literature have, at best, only skipped through her novels. It soon becomes clear that most of the writers have not read her in depth, and thus we can be pardoned if we find their critical assessments often suspect, sometimes shallow and never quite satisfying.

For instance, when a distinguished English critic wrote: 'Genius is the lightening rod of the mind and Miss Kate O'Brien has it'; and when another stated that 'her style is one of the most distinguished possessed by any living novelist', we might well ask ourselves if such sweeping statements should be taken seriously or with a grain of salt.

Genius is a word which critics should keep under lock and key for most of their lives. It is even doubtful if it could be used to describe any of the women novelists in this century. There is no doubt in deluding ourselves: *Without My Cloak* is not another *Wuthering Heights*. Kate O'Brien is one of the few accomplished Irish women novelists, a stylist who will delight anyone in search of this rare commodity, one who gives a leisured chronicle rich in detail, but who finds it difficult to paint a picture with a few quick strokes, which is another way of saying that she has her limitations and is not a genius.

From a close reading of one or two of her novels it is possible to see where her strength lies and to suggest a weakness common to most of them.

Take, for instance, *Without My Cloak*. Essentially the story of an Irish middle-class family through three generations, it paints a vivid picture, often an alarming one, of Irish society of the time, its rigidity, its religious solidarity and the constraints under which some of its people suffered. The main characters, Honest John, Anthony, Molly, Denis and Christina, are as alive as our own acquaintances. We can see them; they are full human beings of flesh and blood with whom we can identify and sympathise. The Considines are a solid family, as solid as the house in which they live outside Mellick (Limerick).

But it is a novel which requires careful reading, and only when it is re-read is one not surprised to learn that it won the pretigious Hawthornden Memorial Prize, as well as the James Tait Memoiral Prize, when it was published. But I think we can note its faults as well, faults which reappear in many of her novels. She is so pre-occupied with main characters that many of the minor ones, who come and go in the course of the novel, are somewhat wooden. We cannot visualise them clearly, because they have not been delineated with enough care.

It appears that she is not too interested in them herself. She is in such a hurry to examine her principal characters' motives and emotions that she has not the time to sketch in thoroughly all the minor ones. Her Freudian pre-occupation with her major characters means that she views them as one might view a precious stone – from every conceivable angle so as to reveal every subtle nuance of their personalities.

This constant, probing search for minute details in the make-up of her heroes and heroines often mars the flow of her narrative. While an author may legitimately pause to analyse a character's intentions or motives, the undue use of this device can often lead to boredom. It is a weakness and a serious one; it constantly retards her novels and confuses and often irritates the reader. It is, I suggest, one of the reasons why her novels are not as popular as they deserve.

From *The Old Limerick Journal,* Spring, 1983.

Crossing the Line: The School Inspector
John McGahern

HE told me his father had been a teacher. 'My poor father had to go to the back door of the presbytery every month for his pay. The priest's housekeeper gave it to him. It was four pounds in those days. I'll never forget my mother's face when he came back from the presbytery one night with three pounds instead of four. The housekeeper had held back a pound because the priest had decided to paint the church that month. One of the great early things the INTO got for the teacher was for the salary to be paid directly into his own hands – to get it through the post instead of from the priest or his housekeeper.

'All that was changed by my time. The inspectors, the dear inspectors, were our hairshirts. A recurring nightmare I have is walking up and down in front of a class with an inspector sitting at the back quietly taking notes. Some were the roaring boys. One rode the bucking mule in Duffy's Circus in Ballinasloe, got badly thrown, but was still out before nine the next morning to check if the particular teacher he'd been drinking with was on time. They were lords or judges. Full-grown men trembled in front of them at the annual inspections. Women were often in tears. The best hams and fruit cakes were brought out at lunchtime. For some there had to be the whiskey bottle and stout in the schoolhouse after school.

'Then, during the Emergency, we had an inspector in Limerick called Deasy, a fairly young man. I was teaching in his area at the time, he was a real rat. In Newcastle West there was an old landed family, a racehorse and gambling crowd, down on their luck. An uncle was the Bishop of Cashel. One of the sons was a failed medical student, and God knows what else, and as part of a rehabilitation scheme didn't the Bishop get him a temporary teaching job.

Deasy was his inspector. I'm sure the teaching was choice, and what Deasy didn't say to his man wasn't worth saying. This crowd wasn't used to being talked to like that. He just walked out of the school without saying a word. Deasy sat down to this tea and ham sandwiches and fruit cake with the schoolmistress. They were still having lunch when your man arrived back. He sat down with them, opened his coat nice and quietly, produced the shotgun and gave Deasy both barrels. He wasn't even offered the Act of Contrition. I was in the Cathedral in Limerick the night Deasy's body was brought in. It was a sad sight, the widow and seven children behind the coffin. Every inspector in the country was at the funeral. Things were noticeably easier afterwards.

'What happened to your man?'

'He was up for murder. He'd have swung at the time but for the Bishop, who got him certified. They say that after a few years he was spirited away to Australia. He was as sane as I was.'

'It seems to be a more decent time now,' I said.

'It's by no means great, but it's certainly better than it was' . . . . .

From *Creatures of the Earth, New and Selected Stories,* Faber and Faber Ltd., 1992.

After Father Cletus
Michael Curtin

ALL the things that ordinary fathers used to do with ordinary sons overtook him. The first manifestation took the shape of his decision to take Jackie to a rugby match. He stopped outside the gate of the house with his hand held out from his side. Jackie thought he was pointing to something on the ground. Then Jackie realised, Timmie Droney wanted to hold his hand. They went down the road and around the corner. Timmie Droney said, 'I spy with my little eye something beginning with C.' The C was the clock in a butcher's window. Before they got to the match he switched to O'Grady Says. 'O'Grady says count to three.' Jackie went along. 'One two three.' 'Count to six.' 'Four five six.' Ha! O'Grady didn't say it.

He brought Jackie to Kilkee, not now on a Finucane's excursion when Jackie wouldn't see his father all day because of the pubs. Timmie Droney borrowed the Holo truck. Mrs. Droney stayed at home. It was a day out for the men of the family, they would swim in the nude in the men-only Pollock Holes.

At Christmas Jackie was forced to draw the line under his co-operation when his father said *à la* Mr. Hassett: 'Jackie, I'll take you down to Woolworth's to get your photo taken with Santa.' The last photo Jackie had with Santa was four years earlier and there was a smell of porter off that Santa.

Jackie's father mentioned the circus. Jackie thought trapeze. But it was only clowns and star spangled ladies on ponies and old elephants.

Timmie Droney brought him to see De Valera at the O'Connell Monument. He lifted Jackie over the railings of a Georgian building so that Jackie could stand on the window ledge and see over the crowd. He took Jackie to the championship hurling matches. Jackie saw the legendary Christy Ring play.

Timmie Droney joined the library. He encouraged Jackie to take out books that he would read himself. He taught Jackie how to handle a cue in Burton's.

All this time Timmie Droney put on the Oberammergau in Finucane's. Mr. O'Donoghue was the William Howard Russell on the spot. Timmie Droney didn't go to the pub now until half-nine instead of seven. He was a model customer. With Timmie retired from all offices the Finucanes had to run their own pub. At home while reading his library books waiting for the new pub departure time Timmie Droney would look up at Jackie doing his homework: 'If there's anything you don't understand ask me.'

Little Blackie McDonald made his first communion. He had his photograph taken outside the house with the whole road gawking. Mrs. McDonald asked Jackie and his mother and Timmie Droney to stand in. Tommie Droney put his arm around Jackie and pulled him close.

That Saturday night Jackie was up late listening to Radio Luxemburg. Timmie Droney came home from the pub while Jackie was having his cocoa. When Jackie stood up to go to bed Timmie Droney put his arm a round him again. And kissed Jackie on the forehead. Taking aim so that he would miss the port wine stain. But he did that as though the port wine stain was something he didn't want to hurt. Something he respected.

Every Thursday, on his half-day, Timmie Droney gave Jackie the money to go to the pictures after school because Mrs. Droney would be having visitors and Jackie might be only in the way. Jackie had to grow older to understand that Timmie Droney had rediscovered his wife and the Thursday half-day was when they made love and not just when Timmie Droney came home from the pub on Saturday nights.

The benefits of the port wine stain began to gallop in all directions. In primary school Jackie had only been given token slaps. Now in secondary, with exams and the Brothers wanting to maintain their reputation, Jackie's face alone would not have saved him. But the visit of Father Cletus had reached the school. Jackie was seen as a sort of Joseph of Cupertino. He was never picked on except to go on messages.

Jackie – and his mother – were still obliged to go to Mass. Women and children could not share in this burden. But Jackie no longer had to serve. Mr Spencer knocked on the doors of those who thought they had outgrown the altar. Mr Spencer stopped children in the street and gave them an inspection and told them to be sure and stay out of trouble. But now when Mr Spencer saw Jackie he discovered a reason to cross the road and if he didn't see Jackie in time he said hello Jackie with fondness.

Timmie Droney had given everyone a lead.

Mr Hassett stood stricken outside the coal yard. He tried the game on Jackie just once more. Jackie, will we go to Dublin and see the GPO. Jackie said, I can't. I haven't time. I have to do my exercise. Mr Hassett said, pity. He didn't say he had a magic carpet. He saw a defeated Mr Hassett. Mr Hassett was a spare father to all the children with his whistle and his sweets.

All of them, Mr Hassett, Mr Spencer, Dodo, my aunt, the neighbours, the Brothers, and the other boys around the road, they all took what happened to Jackie as part of their lot the way they had been instructed from pulpits all their lives. So nothing cataclysmic happened that you could point your finger at. It was a drip-drip process. Droney the adult philosopher, today everyone is free but you can't leave the key in the front door anymore.

For three and a half years after Father Cletus called to the house Jackie was smothered by the man trying to be his father. Timmie Droney tried hard. But it didn't work. It couldn't work. He'd started too late.

From *Sing!* 2002, Fourth Estate, 2001.

Angela in New York
Frank McCourt

MALACHY'S Bar is so successful he provides passage for my mother and my brother, Alphie, on the *SS Sylvania* which arrives in New York on December 21st, 1959.

When they emerge from the customs shed there's a piece of broken leather flapping from Mam's right shoe so that you can see the small toe of a foot that was always swollen. Does it ever end? Is this the family of the broken shoe? We embrace and Alphie smiles with broken blackened teeth.

The family of broken shoes and teeth destroyed. Will this be our coat of arms?

Mam looks past me to the street beyond. Where's Malachy?

I don't know. He should be here in a minute.

She tells me I look fine, that it didn't do me any harm to put on a bit of weight though I should do something about my eyes they're that red. That irritates me because if I even think of my eyes or anyone mentions them I can feel them flush red and of course she notices.

See, she says. You're a bit old to be having bad eyes.

I want to snap at her that I'm twenty-nine and I don't know the proper age for not having bad eyes and is this what she wants to talk about the minute she arrives in New York? But Malachy arrives in a taxi with his wife, Linda. More smiles and embraces. Malachy keeps the taxi while we retrieve the suitcases.

Alphie says, will we put these in the boot?

Linda smiles. Oh no, we put them in the trunk.

Trunk? We didn't bring a trunk.

No, no, she says, we put your bags in the trunk of the taxi.

Isn't there a boot in the taxi?

No, that's the trunk.

Alphie scratches his head and smiles again, a young man understanding lesson number one in American English....

For the first time in ten years we are all together, Mam and her four sons. Malachy has his wife, Linda, and his baby, Siobhain, the first of a new generation. Michael has a girlfriend, Jan, and Alphie will soon find one too. I'm reconciled with Alberta and living with her in Brooklyn.

Malachy is the life of the party in New York and no party can start without him. If he doesn't appear there's restlessness and whimpering, where's Malachy? Where's your brother? And when he roars in they're happy. He sings and drinks and passes his glass for more drink and sings again till he rushes off to the next party.

Mam loves the life, the excitement of it. She loves having a highball at Malachy's Bar and being introduced as Malachy's mother. Her eyes twinkle and her cheeks glow and she dazzles the world with a flash of false teeth. She follows Malachy to the parties, the oul' hoolies, she calls them, basks in the mother spotlight and tries to join in Malachy's songs till she runs out of breath with the first signs of emphysema. After all the years sitting by the fire in Limerick wondering where the next loaf of bread was coming from she's having a lovely time and isn't this a grand country altogether. Ah, maybe she'll stay a little longer. Sure, what's the use of going back to Limerick in the middle of the winter with nothing to do but sit by the fire warming her poor shins? She'll go back when the weather warms up, Easter maybe, and Alphie can get a job here to keep them going.

Malachy has to tell her if she wants to stay in New York even for a short time she can't stay with him in his small apartment with Linda and the baby, four months old.

She calls me at Alberta's and tells me, I'm hurted, so I am. Four sons in New York and no place for me to lay my head.

But we all have small apartments, Mam. No room.

Well, one would wonder what ye're all doing with the money ye're making. Ye should have told me this before ye dragged me from my own comfortable fireplace.

No one dragged you. Didn't you say over and over you wanted to come for Christmas and didn't Malachy pay your fare?

I came because I wanted to see my first grandchild and, don't worry, I'll pay Malachy back if I have to get down on my knees and scrub floors. If I knew the way I was going to be treated here I would have stayed in Limerick and had a nice goose for myself and a roof over my head.

Alberta whispers I should invite Mam and Alphie for dinner on Saturday night. There's a silence at the other end and then a sniffle.

Well, I don't know what I'll be doing on Saturday night. Malachy said there might be a party.

All right. We invited you to dinner, but if you want to go to another party with Malachy, go.

You don't have to sound so huffy. It's an awful long distance to Brooklyn. I know because I used to live there.

It's less than half an hour.

She whispers something to Alphie and he takes the phone. Francis? We'll come.

When I open the door she brings her own chill along with the January chill. She acknowledges Alberta's existence with a nod and asks if I have a match for her cigarette. Alberta offers her a cigarette but she says no, she has her own and these American cigarettes barely have any taste anyway. Alberta offers her a drink and she'll have a highball. Alphie says he'll have a beer and Mam says, Oh, you're starting, are you?

I tell her it's only a beer.

Well, that's how it starts. One beer and the next thing ye're roaring and singing and waking the child.

There's no child here.

There is in Malachy's house and the roaring and singing too.

Alberta calls us into dinner, tuna casserole with green salad. Mam takes her time coming to the table. She has to finish her cigarette and what's the hurry anyway.

Alberta says it's nice to eat casserole when it's good and hot.

Mam says she hates hot food that burns the roof of your mouth.

I tell her, for Christ's sake, finish your cigarette and come to the table.

She comes with her offended look. She pulls her chair in and pushes the salad away. I ask her what the hell is the difference between the lettuce in this country and the lettuce in Ireland. She says there's a big difference, that the lettuce in this country is tasteless.

Alberta says, Oh, never mind. Not everyone likes lettuce anyway.

Mam stares at her casserole and forks noodles and tuna aside while she hunts for peas. She says she loves peas though these are not as good as the ones in Limerick. Alberta asks if she'd like more peas.

No, thank you.

After which she probes the noodles for bits of tuna.

I ask her, don't you like the noodles?

What?

The noodles, don't you like them?

I don't know what they are but I'm not fond of 'em.

I want to lean into her face and tell her she's acting like a savage, that Alberta went to great lengths thinking of something that might please her and all she can do now is to sit with her nose in the air as if someone had done something to her and if she doesn't like it she can put on her damn coat and go back to Manhattan to the party she's missing and I'll never bother her again with an invitation to dinner.

I want to say all this but Alberta makes peace. Oh, that's all right. Maybe Mam is tired with the excitement of coming to New York and if we have a nice cup of tea and piece of cake we'll all relax.

Mam says, No, thank you to the cake, she couldn't eat another morsel but she would like a cup of tea till, again, she sees the tea bag in her cup and tell us this isn't a proper cup of tea at all.

I tell her that's what we have and that's what she's getting though what I don't tell her is that I'd like to throw the tea bag between her eyes.

She said no to the cake but here she is pushing it into her mouth and swallowing with hardly a chew and then picking up and eating the crumbs from around her plate, the woman who didn't want the cake.

She glances at the tea cup. Well, if that's the only tea ye have I suppose I'll have to drink it. She lifts the tea bag on her spoon and squeezes it till the water turns brown and wants to know why there's a lemon on her saucer.

Alberta says people like lemon with their tea.

Mam says she never heard the likes of that, it's disgusting

Alberta removes the lemon and Mam say's she'd like milk and sugar, if you don't mind. She asks for a match for her cigarette and smokes whiles she drinks only half the tea to show she doesn't care for it.

Alberta asks if she and Alphie would like to see a movie in the neighbourhood but Mam says no, they have to be getting back to Manhattan and it's too late.

Alberta says it isn't that late and Mam says it's late enough.

I walk with my mother and Alphie up Henry Street and over to the subway at Borough Hall. It's a bright January night and all along the street there are still Christmas lights glowing and flickering in the windows. Alphie talks about the elegance of the houses and says thanks for the dinner. Mam says she doesn't know why people can't put the dinner in a bowl and give it to you without a plate under it. She thinks that kind of thing is putting on airs.

When the train comes in I shake hands with Alphie and I bend over to kiss my mother and hands her a twenty-dollar bill but she pulls her face away and sits in the train with her back to me and I walk away with the money back in my pocket.

From *'Tis, A Memoir,* Flamingo, HarperCollins, 1999.

Death in Claughaun
Helena Close

WE all followed Dodge up the Bloodmill and we knew we were nearly home when we smelt the slaughter house, a sickly, clinging smell in the warm morning sun. Jesse was still glued to Pinhead's heels and nobody talked.

Pinhead saw it first just as we passed by Claughaun.

'What's that?' he asked, looking over the hedge towards the playing fields. He shaded his eyes from the sun. I couldn't see a thing, just spots in front of my eyes from the blinding glare of the sunshine.

'Nothing there, come on lads, I could drop down dead the minute from the hunger, let's go,' said Dodge.

I blinked and then I saw it too, swaying gently on the goalpost, and my mouth did a little flip. Pinhead was over the hedge like a shot, still clutching the bags of mushrooms. Jesse sat in the middle of the road howling. I ran after Pinhead, mushrooms flying everywhere as I tried to catch up with him. I could hear him saying 'Jesus fuckin' Jesus' over and over as we raced towards the goalpost. The others were behind us. I could hear them but they seemed very far away, like they were in another part of the day altogether. Jesse's howls sounded far away too.

I was just behind Pinhead now and if I'd reached out my hand, I'd have been able to touch him. Someone was swinging from the goalpost, we couldn't make out who it was but I could see blue jeans and a red T-shirt and I could hear Pinhead saying, 'It's a fuckin' joke, this is a joke, what bastard would think this was funny?'

and we stopped then and I made myself look straight at the goalpost. Pinhead dropped his mushrooms, I could hear the bags rustling as they hit the ground.

There was a body hanging there. Adidas sneakers with a red stripe, blue jeans, red T-shirt, hair falling down, covering the face, orange rope around the neck, like the rope on our clothesline. It was swinging slowly from side to side and I thought I saw the hands twitching. It was a joke, the head would rise in a second the hair would fall back from the face and the face would smile a fooled-ye smile.

I stood perfectly still, unable to move. Then Pinhead let out a roar and lunged towards the goalpost, screaming and roaring. 'You fuckin' bastard, Enda, you bollocks, get the fuck down.' My legs wouldn't move and I stood like a statue watching Pinhead screaming and belting the body with his fists. He could only reach to the top of the legs and as he beat and shook them the head fell to one side, and I could see him then, Enda, but not Enda, more a Hallowe'en Enda, with bulging eyes and a huge tongue. The skin on his face was purple.

I could hear the other lads right behind me and I turned to look. Dodge had this awful smile on his face and Eyebrows was talking rubbish, like baby talk, and all the time Pinhead's voice shouting, 'Bastard bastard fuckin' bastard.' Then he started to climb the goalpost and I made my legs move. I forced them to, and I ran to Pinhead and said, 'We need help, Pin, get the fuck down.' And I grabbed his leg and tore him down and he landed on the brown earth where the grass was worn from the goalies standing there.

A swaying Adidas sneaker was inches from his face. He was crying and held his penknife in his hand, grasping the bone handle in a tight grip. I took it off him and said, 'Get Dodge away, get up and get him the fuck away from here. I'm going for help, get up.' And he did and wiped his face with his jumper and he stood for a second there in front of the goalpost with Enda swinging behind him and then he said, 'Dodge,' but Dodge didn't hear, he just stood there with a big frozen grin on his face, smiling at his brother. Eyebrows was still jabbering, but now he was running around in circles like a dog. Pinhead screamed, 'Dodge, we're going now,' like it was an order or a command, but Dodge didn't move, so Pinhead grabbed him by the arm and made him turn his back on Enda.

I ran across the field towards the road. My heart was thumping in my chest and I had a bad stitch in my side. I couldn't think over the roaring noise in my ears, so I stopped at the gate of Claughaun and hung over it just for a second, and when I looked up I knew what I had to do and I talked to myself out loud as I did it to stop the pictures in my head, stop the pictures of swaying shoes and bright red T-shirts and orange rope. Out loud, I said, 'Walk don't run to the railway house they have a phone over minding the railway gates walk there and knock on the door and say there's something wrong in Claughaun call the guards and then go back and find Dodge poor Dodge stop thinking about Dodge there's the door now knock.'

A man opened the door in his vest and long johns and said, 'Jesus Christ' when he saw me, 'Jesus Christ, what's wrong, what happened to you?' A woman stood behind him in a pink dressing gown like my mother's. I wanted my mother.

'I . . . there's something . . . in the field . . . the goalpost . . . we need the guards . . . will they save him?'

'Where? What field? Claughaun is it? Jesus, get me shoes, Mags. Jesus, what happened? Save who? Was there an accident?'

'On the . . . goalpost . . . the hands twitched though . . . so it could be fine if they hurry . . .'

'Mags, ring 999, tell them, go on, it's not a trick. Look at the state of the lad, he pissed himself and everything.'

The man flew past me on a black bike, his shirt open and flying behind him like a white shroud. I didn't run, I walked and talked out loud again. 'Go back now go back and find the lads and pick up the mushrooms.' The woman's voice was calling me. 'Come back, the guards are coming, stay with me and Paddy will sort it out.' But I kept walking, the sound of my own voice filling my ears and my head, repeating over and over the things I needed to do.

The man was with them when I got back to Claughaun. He had them halfway up the field with their back to the goalpost. He had his arms around Eyebrows and Dodge. I walked towards them without looking at the goalpost, with my head turned sideways.

There was vomit on the ground near Eyebrows. Pinhead stood a little bit away from the others, head down, his hands in his pockets. I could hear the man saying, 'it's all right, take it easy now, lads, the guards will be here in a minute.' And then he made all of us, even Pinhead, sit on the grass with our backs to the goalpost and he talked and talked about hurling and telly and fishing and I couldn't follow the half of it but the sound of his voice made everything stop in my head and that was good.

The guards came over and crouched down in front of us. 'I know this is awful lads,' he said, 'but we . . . I need to find out who . . . the boy . . . do ye know him?'

'Is he . . . will he be alright?' I asked.

'Enda O'Riordan, 22 Lilac Court, St Patrick's Road, that's his brother there,' said Pinhead in a low, tight voice. The voice he used when he was really mad.

'Ah Christ, no, ah Jesus, is there any God at all?' said the guard and he covered his face with his hands.

Dodge started to laugh. A weird, high, girl's laugh that caught in his throat and turned to crying.

Pinhead got up and walked towards the goalpost, his head still bent and his shoulders hunched. I followed him and so did one of the guards.

'Come back here, now, you've no business going over there again, come on . . .'

'Fuck off,' said Pinhead, and he kept walking. 'Fuck off and leave me alone, just fuck off, do you hear me?'

The guard grabbed him by the arm and then he lost it. Pinhead did. I knew it was coming because his face was red and he was all wound up and tight like a spring. He just lashed out at the guard, kicking, head-butting, belting. The guard put his two arms around him from the back but it was like trying to hold down a wild animal or something. I just stood and watched.

Pinhead stopped all of a sudden when he caught sight of me, of my face. 'Don't cry, stop it, will you? Don't, Nod, don't,' he said. He was completely still now and the guard held him tightly by the shoulders.

I put my hand to my face and felt wet tears. The salt taste was in my mouth and nose and I could feel my trousers wet and clammy between my legs. I started to sob, long, shuddering sobs that came up from right inside me and made my body shake.

Pinhead shook his head at me. 'You fuckin' eejit, shut up, will you? Shut the fuck up,' he said. He tried to hold me with a stare but I looked away. I wasn't able not to cry. He came towards me then and when he put his hand on my shoulder, and I fell into him, into his body, rigid still with anger. 'Stop it, d'you hear me, you fuckin; ghoul? Stop it and cop yourself on,' he said, but he put his arms around me, not tight like I wanted but around me all the same. I let my head rest on his shoulder and my breath slowed down until it matched his.

I heard the guard behind Pinhead saying, 'that's it lads, it's OK,' but he was crying too. I could hear tears caught in his voice.

Then I thought I heard my dad's voice: 'Séanie, Séanie, are you alright? Ah Séanie,' and I lifted my head from Pinhead's shoulder and there he was right in front of me. I threw myself at him and he scooped me into his arms and hugged me and kissed the top of my head, and I started sobbing all over again . . . .

They laid him out in the parlour, the Sacred Heart scowling down at him. This was the first time it happened in our estate. The first time a body didn't go to the dead house but stayed at home until it was time for the burial Mass. Everybody talked about it, on the street corners, in Mac's shop, whether it was right or wrong to keep a body in the house. I asked my dad what he thought about it, and he said that people always did it in the past, and he thought it was right if Enda's family wanted it. But Pinhead said Dodge wouldn't be too happy with a dead body in his parlour, even if it was his brother.

We all gathered outside the house on the evening of the wake. Nobody planned to do this, to gather in silence outside the house, it just kind of happened that way. First Eyebrows and Pinhead and me, then some of the Claughaun team and towards the end the Garryowners and all were there. A big gang of us, talking in whispers, wanting to show Enda how much we liked him. I was mad to see Dodge. I hadn't seen him since it happened, but my mam had said not to call, to give him time.

O'Riordan opened the door when it was time for the viewing, that's what they called it, looking at the dead body, they called it a viewing. I didn't want to go in but I knew I had to, like this was the end part of all the stuff with Enda.

We saw Angela Walsh going into the house with her father. She was crying. All dressed in black and tears streaming down her face ruining her make-up and making her eyes black too. Her father held her tightly around the waist. Everybody was dead silent when she walked up the path, no-one even sniggered when she stumbled in platform shoes as they climbed the steps to the front door.

Crowds came then and there was a queue going in the front door and I wanted to go home. To go home and watch *The Man from Uncle* and have nan to tea and play with the small brothers.

My dad came then and said, 'Come on now, lads, we'll go in together. I'll go first, so ye'll know what to do. Come on, it'll be grand.'

So we followed him in. Pinhead first, then me, then poor Eyebrows, his face white and haunted. He wasn't able for this, looking at dead people in houses. The hallway was crowded but there was just the low murmur of voices. I could smell roast chicken.

We followed the queue into the parlour. The men stood at the side of the coffin and the women were sitting down in a row. I couldn't see the women but I knew it was them in the corner because of the crying. I searched for Dodge but the men standing in the black suits blocked my view. As we got near them I watched to see what my dad was saying and doing, so I could copy him when it was my turn. My dad shook hands with a row of men and then he stopped at the last one.

It was O'Riordan, standing tall and straight, his eyes fixed on my dad. I waited for dad to shake his hand and move on to the women, but he stood there just looking at O'Riordan. Then he nodded at him, and shook his hand fast, and walked over to Dodge's mother. He bent and whispered in her ear, his hand on her shoulder. She wiped her eyes with a pale, yellow hanky.

O'Riordan stared at my dad, still talking softly to Dodge's mother. Then it was Pinhead's turn.

They stood there looking at each other. I was standing next to Pinhead and I could feel all the anger in him, waiting to escape. He finally stuck out his hand and O'Riordan hesitated like he expected a head in the face instead of a handshake, but then he took Pinhead's hand and shook it. Pinhead leaned in close to him and whispered something. I nearly died when I heard it.

'Fuckin' steamer.' Only a whisper, a breath, but I heard it. Pinhead walked away and let me there with O'Riordan who looked like he couldn't decide if he'd heard it or not.

'I'm sorry for . . . you know . . . it,' I said then and caught his hand and shook it like a madman.

He nodded at me but his eyes followed Pinhead.

I looked back and there was poor Eyebrows turning tail and running out the door before he even got a glimpse of the coffin. I followed my dad and circled the coffin. I tried to keep my eyes on the picture of the Sacred Heart on the wall above the crying women but I looked when my father bent into the coffin and kissed Enda. Jesus, poor Enda, his face covered in make-up, and he said, 'God bless you son.' I stared at Enda's face then and it was all right because it wasn't really Enda, just something left over from Enda.

Dodge was standing next to a little table covered with pictures of Enda. Enda as a baby. Enda as toddler with fat legs in cowboy suit, Enda making his First Communion, Enda making his Confirmation, Enda smiling in the Claughaun jersey, with the League cup held over his head.

And that's what made me cry. Not Dodge's stricken face, not the cute baby pictures or the body in the coffin. It was the picture of Enda in his glory, because that made you see how sad it really was. Tears ran down my face and I looked at Dodge and looked back down at the picture and sobs were coming and my dad steered me out the door.

In the hallway and the kitchen other people were crying too, so I didn't feel bad about it. Angela Walsh came over to me and put her arms around me and hugged me tightly. So tight I could feel her chest right up against mine, and when I opened by eyes, Pinhead was there winking and grinning at me and giving me the thumbs up. I was laughing and crying all at once then, and knew I'd remember this for a long time. The feel of her chest pressed up against me.

We hung around outside the house while the grown-ups drank tea and whiskey and stuff in the kitchen. Someone brought out a crate of lemonade for us and bags of crisps and we sat on the wall watching people going in, with Pinhead giving a running commentary.

'There's oul prick face Burke. Jesus, I didn't realise how fuckin' small he is. I'm bigger than him, so I am. And Balls of Flour. His wife is a fine thing, nice arse,' he said.

Libby was with him now, leaning her body into his and laughing at everything he said. Karen was there too, with Deirdre, and they came and stood next to me.

'Hi Nod, you OK?' asked Deirdre, her dark slitty eyes searching my face. Karen said nothing, just examined me as well.

'Fine, I'm grand. Why wouldn't I be grand?' I asked, looking straight at them.

They dropped their eyes but nudged each other.

'Well, if you . . . you know . . . if you ever want to talk about it or anything, I'll . . . we'll be there for you,' said Karen, shaking her blonde ponytail.

I got it now. They couldn't help Enda, so they were going to save me instead. Fuckin' girls, all concern when there was a big drama. I hated every last one of them. Except for Angela Walsh. I felt sorry for her.

'Thanks, girls. I'll call ye so. One of ye can hold the goalpost for me and the other one can hand me the rope, thanks a lot,' I said, my voice low and steady and mean. Pinhead was laughing softly on the wall.

'Prick,' said Deirdre, and she walked away with Karen. They were like the terrible twins now and I could imagine the talks they had about me and what a bad kisser I was and what a ghoul I was. They deserved each other.

Pinhead was laughing out loud, shaking his head and saying, 'You mad bastard Nod,' but the minute I said the thing about the goalpost I was sorry. It wasn't funny at all.

It was late when Pinhead's parents came. Diet was with them and Uncle Pat. He hadn't a clue what was happening. Uncle Pat. He was rubbing his hands together and asking people were they going to Kelly's for a jar, like he was at a hurling match or something. They came just as the coffin was being closed and the priest was saying prayers. We'd all piled back into the house for this.

Mr Duffy's voice sounded loud and happy in the quiet parlour. His face was bright red, like it had been in the pub in Salthill the time of the pound. Pinhead moved away, almost to the front door, and I wanted to tell Mr. Duffy to shut up and keep his voice down, but I gave him a stare instead. He just smiled and waved when he saw me.

Enda's mam cried as they put the lid on the coffin. Long hoarse cries that filled the house and gave you a pain in your heart. The crying drowned the priest's blessing. When they brought the coffin out, the Claughaun team stood guard of honour outside the door. Some of the senior team shouldered it, and all the girls were crying now, and the women. Black funeral cars were waiting at the kerb and the women climbed into them. We all lined up behind the hearse. O'Riordan was right in front of us, his hand tight on Dodge's shoulder.

So we walked behind the hearse, all the men and the boys, and when Diet asked could he walk with us, Pinhead said, "'Course you can, no need to even ask.' That was a first for Pinhead.

I slept badly that night. Dreams came up but I couldn't remember them. I just woke up trying to scream but no sound came out of my mouth. When I told my mam, she said, 'Sleep in our side, you dream more if you sleep on your back.'

It rained for the funeral the next day. Wet rain in non-stop sheets and we had to search the house for umbrellas. I found a Harp one but my mam said black was best. We walked behind the coffin after the Mass, and rain beating down on a sea of black umbrellas. We made our way slowly to Mount St Laurence's graveyard. Dodge and O'Rirodan were at the front, just the two of them, his big hand on Dodge's shoulder again. As we made our way through the graveyard, I read the headstones. 'In Loving Memory of Lily Byrne who died 17th November, 1962, aged 2 years.' 'In Loving Memory of John Higgins, who died 6th July, 1967, aged 13 years.' My age, that boy died at my age. I wanted to know what happened to him, but the headstone didn't tell you that.

We came to Enda's grave all of a sudden. There it was in front of us, a freshly dug hole, the earth wet and dark. No headstone. I never took my eyes off the hole, all though the priest's prayers and the crowd's mumbled answers, and I watched as they slowly laid the coffin into the black earth. That made my heart do a somersault. I watched as they shovelled earth into the hole. I heard it drop on the coffin. I heard the hollow sound it made and the sound of rain dripping onto umbrellas and trees. Our feet crunched on the wet gravel as the crowd drifted away and I took one look back at the grave. His grave. It looked lonely.

From *Pinhead Duffy*, Helena Close, 2005, Blackstaff Press.

Happy days in Laurel Hill
Lorna Reynolds

KATE O'Brien's mother died in 1903 of cancer. Her youngest brother was still a baby and she herself only a little over five. Her elder sisters had been sent to Laurel Hill, the convent of a French Order, The Faithful Companions of Jesus, known in Limerick as the 'French School.' Her father decided that it would be less lonely for the little girl to be with her sisters than to remain at home with the baby brothers, and so, at the unusually early age of five and a half years she became a boarder at Laurel Hill Convent.

She tells us in an article in *La France Libre* (December 1947) that she made a fearful scene when her father first took her to the convent, screaming and kicking and almost reducing her sisters to the same state of hysteria. But the Reverend Mother – English and considered to be very cold – told her that since they had never so small a pupil in Laurel Hill, they had to order a special chair for her: three of them had been sent on approval and were in the parlour, waiting for her to choose which one she would prefer. By this clever move Reverend Mother overcame the child's natural fear of her new surroundings, and Kate O'Brien began her long and happy association with the nuns of the Faithful Companions of Jesus, who from 1903 to 1916 ruled not only for her spiritual life but also the thousand and one details of her ordinary life.

The pupils at Laurel Hill were astonishingly well fed she tells us – and even moderately good food in an Irish Convent would be surprising enough – perhaps because the Foundress of the Order had come from Lyons, but more probably because the lay sisters in charge of the kitchen were still French.

Discipline was strict and scholastic standards were high at Laurel Hill, but inevitably so young a child as Kate O'Brien became something of a school pet. To be singled out in any way as a child gives one a sense of being special. This happens to every intelligent child, but to be special because of several reasons is to have one's identity and importance highlighted to no small degree. Kate O'Brien was 'spoiled' as we say in Ireland, in this way, however austere she may have found life in other respects. When she went to live in England, she was regarded as an Irish charmer, and the 'spoiling' continued. A natural imperiousness of temperament was not discouraged by this treatment.

In *Presentation Parlour* (1963) she tell us how much she learnt from visiting her aunts in their convent, from watching as a 'mere and small and uninformed crowd-actor' the play and affection and rivalry, expectation and disappointment, the intricacies and involutions of human feeling that were revealed when the whole family gathered in the parlour of the convent where two of her mother's sisters were nuns. We may deduce that her own boarding school offered a similar, though more extended theatre for the sensibilities of the small watching child. To be for so long the youngest at school gave her an unrivalled opportunity for studying her elders at leisure.

The aunts in their convent were all the more demanding of and anxious about these children, because their mother was dead. However conscientious a mother is, there are long spells when she takes her children for granted. Theses aunts, Aunt Mary and Aunt Fanny, it seems were in a constant sate of anxiety about the motherless children, who were always expected to look well and happy and physically unblemished. A sprinkling of freckles on the white skin caused consternation. 'The child is destroyed,' her Aunt Fanny would say. No wonder the child, grown-up, remembered the mood of the convent parlour, where sensibility so clearly got the upper hand of sense. Nuns who have themselves renounced the vanities of the world can expect the most assiduous attention to them from those remaining 'outside.'

From *Kate O'Brien, A Literary Portrait*, Colin Smythe, 1987.

The First Day
Patrick J. Carroll, C.S.C.

FAN was back from a two week holiday the Sunday following Assumption. Monday morning at half past eight we set out for Askeaton school. We took our lunches but no books, as the books we used in Cappa might not serve us there. Fan looked lovely in a new dress and hat. I was all right too, except that the right side of my eye was covered with plaster strips.

The day was calm and cool, with here and there signs of departing summer. All the hay was gathered home, and the Stokes were stacking their wheat. Wisps of meadow grass and rushes clung to bushes growing beside the borheen, plucked from hay loads by the teeth of outstretched brambles. I could hear Pad Lane driving his mule behind us on his way to Rathkeale. O'Brien's cows were on the cut meadows, and Mikie O'Brien was ordering his calves through a gap in the borheen ditch, aiming a stone at one for not obeying him. Pad Lane caught up with us at the road.

"So ye're off to the new school-g'wan our' that!" (to the mule)

"What time is it?" I asked. I knew well enough he had no watch, but wanted to say something.

He closed one eye and cocked the other at the sun. "Tis early – maybe eight"

"Tis nearer to half eight," Fan said with a sureness that went with her like a shadow.

"Is it then! Well, I hope you like the new school. Patch and don't get more batings than Burke gave you."

His roar of laughter maddened me, but I said nothing, I hadn't the heart. With his long legs almost brushing the road from the rider (corner seat) of the car he drove on south. Fan and myself went north. And who do you think came galloping along behind us in a flurry, but the Demon! He looked up at Fan respectfully, his tongue out, his tail wagging.

"Isn't it nice of him to come and say goodbye!" Fan said, patting his brown head.

Seeing myself as dead as a flag from a tall pole on a still day, he leaped up, set a paw on each of my shoulders and began to lick my face.

"Get down, Demon!" Fan said as if she were the school mistress. That quited him. He hunched back and looked at me.

"Good bye," I couldn't think of anything else. I was very depressed. He turned, trotted on for a bit, stopped and looked back. I looked at him, waved and walked on. Ah, dear!

"Fan," I said. "I wonder will we ever be through school? I don't think I ever remember when I wasn't getting an education."

"But won't we be glad later on - when we're grown up?"

"Ah, now you're talking like the mother."

"Yes, but the mother is right."

"Why can't I be a smith, or a carpenter, or a cooper, or a porter up at Ballingrane or a –"

"Tinker," she finished.

"Tinkers have a fine life, Fan. They have grand times on the road."

"Patch, you'll be sorry if you stop school too soon. Maybe then you'll want to go on, and won't be able."

I couldn't imagine such a thing. We met the Ive's below Hunt's gate- Paddy and Bridgie. We met the Madigans at the Cross- Paddy, Jim and Bridgie. I knew the boys, but not so well: the girls I don't know at all, but Fan did. So we followed our kind - boys with boys, girls with girls.

Of the two Madigans, Paddy was wiry and swift: Jim stocky, slow, goodnatured. A crop of freckles on his cheeks and nose made him better looking than he was. Paddy Ives was a butty who didn't like school any better than myself. His brother

FICTION

Con was a butty too, but so young that I did not pay much attention to him. We walked slowly enough down the side path running below Hunts' estate. The talk was mostly about school, which is always a sad subject at the end of the holidays.

"What kind of a man is the teacher?" I asked.

"Kind! He isn't kind at all!" Paddy Madigan pretended he misunderstood me.

"Ah, he's not so bad," Jim, his brother assured me. "He's short and thick. He must weigh fourteen stone anyhow."

"He's alright if you know the lessons," brother Paddy thought. "That's the great trouble - the lessons," Butty Ives said in a very sober voice.

Up the road came a blind man led by a dog. He held one end of a chain, and the other end went around the dog's neck. I was amazed, and at any other time would have stopped to watch the pair of them. Then at the Four Cross roads came John Hogan mounted on the bridge of his sidecar with four peelers behind him. They were going to Rathkeale. I thought at the time what a fine life the Askeaton peelers had looking down the Deel from the bridge, or spending one day a month at the fair of Rathkeale. But then, I couldn't be a peeler, because I heard Dan Sheehan reading out of the paper to Mick Hacket that any Irish taking service under the British government was welding another rivet in Ireland's chains. I could never put another rivet on Ireland.

Askeaton is a very quiet town almost any time. There is an east side and a west side, with the river Deel between them. I used always think - and do yet – that there is no place in the world so motionless with sleep as the east side. But when I went to the west side I became doubtful.

Everything was hum-buzz, hum-buzz that morning in the Askeaton school. The boys were in a school below, the girls in a school above, the infants in a room by themselves just back of the boys' room. There was a band room in the same storey with the girls which I will mention again. The boys were all seated at desks stretched across the room, or on forms that went along the walls. Mr. Conway was standing behind his desk, one of his feet resting on a support. Jim Madigan's description of him fitted like a new glove, except that I would not call him thick. He was a bit above butty height, though he might be a butty's width. I went up to him, but everybody was so busy talking about the finished holidays they didn't notice. And you may be sure I was glad of that.

"You're the boy from the Crags, aren't you? Cappa, is it?"

"No, sir. Nantenan is my district."

"Yes. Well, the district don't matter much. Not nearly so much as other things. What happened to your eye?"

"A horse bit me, Sir."

"My! My! A horse bite is unusual. You've had it looked after? Good. You are in first fifth aren't you? Good. Well. We'll see if you can maintain it."

I paid my tuition and that softened him.

"Work hard and keep up with the best. Hard work is the only road to learning."

I went back and took a seat beside a boy I got to like very much as the days went on. And I think he liked me too. Everybody called him "Mikie" Kennedy but I always called him "Mike" because I liked it better. We got to know each other by instinct rather than by introduction - like dogs and donkeys.

"How do you like the boss?" he asked first thing.

"I don't know very much about him yet," I answered.

"Ah, but you will though - before the year is out. So you were hit with a hurley. So was I - last June. But I got my lick on the chin. Had four stitches. Did you get a bad crack.?"

"It would have to be to make the cut I got."

"You should keep on your own side - that's the safe way."

"Well, if you get a chance to make a goal that will win the game, you don't think much about staying on your own side."

Well, Mike Kennedy told all his crowd how I got the cut from the slash of a hurley in a game which I won by making the final goal. Of course, I didn't tell him anything of the kind, but he thought I did. So I was marked from the start as the fellow from the Crags below Nantenan, that had his right temple slashed in a hurling match in which he drove home the winning goal.

The day went quietly enough as first days after holidays do. I met a great many boys for whom I had a liking, all the years I was in Askeaton. Paddy Hough was one. His father kept a big shop in the Square, west of the bridge. Then there was Tommy Sheehan, who lived up the lane, and Jack Lynch who came from below the town, and Paddy Cahill from beyond the Four Cross roads, who had a bigger brother Tom and a bigger brother Mick going to school also: and Terry Feeheny, and the Shaughnesseys, and Pat Joe Hanley. Then there was Danny Conway the master's son, whom I got to like very much, in spite of the handicap that he belonged to the teacher's family. Jack Kett was also a likeable boy, although his father was a peeler and a noted rogue for discovering unlicensed dogs.

I liked them all. And I think they liked me. Although I was from the Crags, they never limited their liking.

I bought what books I needed and paid for them, which also pleased Mr. Conway, because a bird in the hand is worth two in the bush. And then at half three school was out. I walked behind a crowd of boys who were gabbing away about things, places and people I knew nothing of. Tommy Sheehan eased back and walked beside me. He was small, hardy and a great fighter.

"Don't mind Conway," he said after he had taken a look at my new books. "He's easy enough some days: and he is always easy if you know the lessons."

"How long will you go to school?" I asked him.

"Oh…. After I get through second stage of sixth, I'll …. maybe join the soldiers."

"I'd like to be a carpenter," I said in confidence.

"Mike Morrissey is your man. His shop is across the river on your way to the crossroads."

How often after that I stopped at Morriseys, and watched Mike and his brother making cars and tables and doors and window frames and coffins! That day I stopped on the hump of the bridge with the two Madigans and Paddy Ives, and watched the river Deel. Collins' shop was at one end, Hallahans' pub at the other. It was nearly four o clock, peaceful and cool. The tide was out: and so the stream of water that ran down the river bed over moss-covered stones looked like a little band of silver patterned into curves of different sizes. Desmond castle was behind me on the other side of the bridge. "A lonely ruin out of an earlier day," an Askeaton curate called it in a sermon at a pilgrimage to the Abbey.

From the square opposite Fitzgibbons' shop, I saw the police barracks beside the avenue going up to Hunt's great house. A girl was pounding a piano in at Collins' and Mr. Casey was walking up and down the elevated side walk in front of Fitzgibbons' humming. "Dumbledee-dumbledee-dumbledee."

Fan and myself were together again after the two Ives left us at their own gate. She had grown very lovely. She was taller and stronger: and you would not think of her now when you saw a daisy.

"O my! You got your new books. Miss Riordan won't have mine till Thursday."

She took my reader and eyed it: balanced it and weighed it: and looked at it page after page with as much joy as if it were a new hurley. And then she stopped walking too.

"O Patch, this is grand; This is lovely! I heard it spoken once at a concert in Cappa."

"If it's Ninety- Eight, I won't care to hear it."

"I know you don't like Ninety- Eight, but this is something else. Listen, dear."

I have been sad about many things; things I lost which would have made me happy had I found; things I found which would have made me happy had I not found. But there is nothing from now to then I miss so much as that sweet bit of writing Fan read for me that evening on the road below the trees just above Deely's gate. I can see her white, gentle face, her lips moving up and down, her teeth shining below the movements of her lips. Just when she had finished Jack Prenderville in the field beyond began shouting at the mouse-gray donkey. I could have thrown himself and the old ass into the Deel, I was so mad at them.

"Say it again, Fan! Never mind him."

I meant Jack Prenderville.

"Some other time, Let's go on." She put her hand on my arm and kept it there as we walked up the road to the borheen gate. She never again recited the forgotten poem; for in my stupid way I never asked her to; nor read it myself. If only I knew it now, I could say it to myself; and saying it I would see and hear again my comrade and my sister.

Going in the borheen, I opened up my heart. "Fan, I think I'm way behind the class. I've learned nothing at Cappa."

"Listen, Patch. Let's both start to work. It will please the mother - oh, so much.!"

"Fan, I'm the one that must start. You've always studied; and, signs on, you're smart."

"In six months you can make up for the lost time. I know what you can do."

She said that just to give me a lift, for Fan was miles smarter than I was.

"I'm going to try, anyhow," I said, kicking up a small stone from a wheel track with the tip of my shoe. Mick met us at the gate, his shoelace untied.

"Fan, put a knot in this - I've a pain in my back."

She bent over and did it without a word, though she could well have told Mick he was lazy enough to tie a knot in his own shoelaces. The mother saw us coming in and waved a welcome.

From *Patch of Askeaton Days*, the Ave Maria Press, 1943.

Daddy is Dying
Roisin Meaney

DADDY has cancer. Daddy is dying. Lizzie sits beside Mammy, holding her hand. Mammy's hand is cold and rough. It's twenty past midnight, and they've just been told that Daddy has enough cancer in his body to make sure he's dead within weeks.

Daddy's bad leg. For the past year and a half they've called it *Daddy's bad leg*, in the same tone of voice they'd use to talk about *Daddy's best suit* or *Daddy's gardening gloves.* Daddy limping around the house, wincing if he banged his knee against anything, saying, 'It's at me today a bit.' Mammy and Lizzie taking turns to rub Deep Heat into Daddy's bad leg. And all time it was filling him up with poison, spreading the poison around his body till he was eaten up with it. Trying to cure cancer with Deep Heat. Like trying to put out a blazing building with a watering can.

How could they not have known? How could they not have noticed that Daddy's bad leg was slowly killing him? Why there was there no sign, no warning that in the middle of one night they'd be sitting close together in a doctor's office, holding hands and trying not to hear the words coming out of the doctor's mouth?

Lizzie can't remember the last time she held Mammy's hand. The skin is rougher than she thought it would be - all that scrubbing and polishing and scouring. Mammy stares straight ahead - she hasn't said a word since they sat down - and her empty face doesn't change as tears start to pour slowly down her cheeks.

She makes no effort to wipe them away; it's as if she doesn't know they're there. They fall off her chin one by one onto the handbag in her lap. The sound they make is tiny, a little, gentle *plup.* Lizzie watches them and thinks: *Daddy is dying. Daddy has cancer.* She lets the words fall like the tears; but they're heavy and black.

They're taking Daddy home tomorrow. The hospital will arrange for a nurse to visit the house each day and inject him with enough morphine that he won't be in pain. Or not in too much pain.

'I'm so sorry; it's quite clear from the X-rays that we can do nothing for him.' The doctor looks too young and too tired to have to do this terrible thing. Lizzie looks at him and wonders how often he has to smash people's lives with a few sentences. Does it get easier every time he does it? After a few years, will he be able to break hearts and then go home and eat his dinner? She wants to hate him, but she can't. All she can do is hold Mammy's hand and watch the tears leaving dark splotches on the cracked brown leather. *Daddy has cancer. Daddy is dying.*

Daddy is sixty-nine.

They go to sit with him in his room. He's sleeping, his mouth slightly open. His false teeth are sitting in a glass on the locker, giving his face a defenceless look that makes Lizzie want to wail out loud. He's wearing his own pyjamas, which their neighbour Claire brought to the hospital at some stage. Lizzie wonders who put them on him. There's a needle attached to the back of his hand - Were his fingers always that thin - with a tube going into it from a see-through bag of clear liquid. Something is beeping. The room is warm and smells of medicine.

They sit on either side of the bed and look at him. Lizzie feels wide awake. She watches Daddy's chest rising and falling under his pyjama top. She imagines him not being around any more, and has to push the thought away quickly because it makes her feel like getting sick.

She remembers a one-man show she saw once, years ago, in Dublin. She and a pal were up for a few days, staying in a B&B near the theatre, and they decided to check out the show for the laugh. The actor was an Australian, and he pranced about the stage and spoke in rhyme about his speckled life. One line stuck in Lizzie's head: 'He dragged me from happy and pushed me to sad.'

Now she knows what he meant. She feels as if some brutal hand has reached out and wrenched her from the happy place she lived in until this morning, and someplace dark and cold . . . .

Over the next few days, they accumulate enough casseroles and apple tarts and fruitcakes to last a month. Hardly half an hour goes by without someone calling to see how Daddy is - neighbours, friends, people from his work, even though he retired four years ago. It's exhausting, but Lizzie is glad of it; it keeps the darkness away for a while.

She's terrified at how quickly Daddy has deteriorated since he came home. Now she understands what people mean when they talk about someone 'going downhill.' It's as if Daddy was teetering at the top of a steep slope for the past eighteen months, and one day someone came along and nudged him gently in the back with a finger, and off he went.

He sleeps a lot; there must be some kind of sedative in the injection he gets from the nurse who calls in the afternoons. He doesn't seem to be in pain – not that he'd say if he were - but he eats very little; a slice of Lizzie's lemon sponge, one of his favourites, comes downstairs barely touched. He takes Complan, and a little stewed apple sometimes, and occasionally one of Mammy's egg flips, dolloped with sherry.

They take it in turns to sit with him when he's awake, and when it's Lizzie's turn she reads him bits of the paper - the main news, the sports, anything she thinks will appeal to him. He lies there and listens, smiling gently now and again. Sometimes they do the crossword. Sometimes she just sits in the room with him listening to the rain outside . . . .

One night, when Mammy has gone to bed, Lizzie goes out into the back garden and walks down to the end. She sniffs: the saltiness of the Merway air is missing. No waves rattling the pebbles. The moon out, though - she can make out the shapes of shrubs, the shiny leaves of the red robin catching the cool white light, the last of the clematis draped over the stone wall.

The garden was always Daddy's territory. Lizzie can see him, in his old blue shirt and grass-stained trousers, trowel in hand as he squats beside flowerbeds, digging out weeds and slinging them into a green plastic bucket. On his head is an ancient white baseball hat that Mammy hates - 'If you see how ridiculous you look' - but that he quietly insists on keeping. He found it on a golf course years ago and has worn it for gardening ever since. Lizzie wonders where it is now.

She looks at the sky and ignores God. She's ignoring Him since she came home. The stars go blurry, and she puts up her hand and wipes her eyes. She wonders where people go when they die, and hopes Daddy will be happy when he gets there. More tears flow and she feels them sliding down the sides of her upturned face and into her ears.

After a while her neck starts to hurt, and she stops looking at the stars and pulls her head back up. She stands at the bottom of the garden, hands in the pocket of her jacket, and wishes again that she'd brought Jones home with her. She wants to hug his furry warmth and bury her face in him.

Or Joe would do instead. He could hold her and tell her everything will be all right, and she'd close her eyes and lean against him and believe him.

She goes back to the house and locks the door for the night, and goes upstairs to lie in bed and stare at the bedroom ceiling until it's time to get up again.

It takes Daddy nineteen days to die. He does it quietly, like he did most things, in his own bedroom, in the middle of a sunny afternoon in June, when Lizzie is in town shopping for groceries and Mammy is hanging out the washing. The only person with him is Gary O'Rourke from the end of the road. Gary is studying to be a nurse and has been sitting with Daddy for a couple of hours a day. He hears the change in Daddy's breathing and calls to Mammy out the window, and she drops the sheet she's holding and runs in with two clothespegs still in her hand, and by the time she gets up to the room Daddy is dead.

From *The Daisy Picker*, Tivoli.

One Funeral and a Weddin'
Pat Shortt

CAMILLA and Charles postponed their weddin' for the Pope's funeral but not Superquinn and Dixie Ryan. 'Twould take more than the pontiff's obsequies to stop those nuptials.

The mother and myself spent the mornin' of the weddin' glued to the telly lookin' at the papal funeral. I was bowled over by the pomp and ceremony. The heavenly strains of the Sistine Choir were no preparation for what I had to endure in Honetyne church that afternoon.

I arrived at the church around two o'clock to find Dixie pacin' the yard and smokin' three fags at the one time. He looked like a man facin' the electric chair. His cousin and best man, Jimmy 'The Stick' Ryan, wasn't doin' much to help. The

Stick is a hungry-lookin', cantankerous scarecrow of a man. When he isn't pullin' on a fag he's wipin' the non-stop drip from the end of his nose. As I passed he was stampin' out a fag and shakin' his head at Dixie sayin', 'hadn't you a grand life till you met her?'

I went into the church and sat beside Pa Cantillon, Pa Quirke and their wives. The women were of the opinion that Superquinn wouldn't be a minute late. 'Breda Quinn will be here at half-two on the button,' predicted Trisha Cantillon.

By three o'clock there was still no sign of the bride and the crowd was gettin' fidgety. Another fifteen minute passed before we heard the clippa cloppa of a horse and the sound of excited conversation echoin' up the aisle. The best man wasn't too impressed with Superquinn's punctuality.

'What kept you?' he barked. 'Only for me, Dixie would have done a runner.'

'Listen here, you gobdaw,' snapped the beautiful bride, 'the only one doin' a runner this mornin' was this lunatic of a horse. As soon as we left the house he bolted. I've been up and down the main street of Killdicken fourteen times. 'Twas like the feckin' Grand National.'

'Well,' says The Stick, ''tis time now to straighten yourself and face Becher's Brook.' He turned to Dixie.' 'Now, Dix,' says he, 'either you head to the altar or you let the mad hoor of a horse take you off in the sunset.' With an air of resignation Dixie made his way up the aisle and the musicians got the nod to strike up.

Pee Hogan and the Blue Boys were organised to play the music in the church and in the hotel. Superquinn had obviously negotiated an all-in deal. 'Twas a good job the bishop wasn't listenin.' I go to enough weddin's to know what's allowed and what isn't and to my ears there was no difference between what Pee and the boys played in the church and what they play in Walshe's on Friday nights. Obviously Canon McGrath decided not to interfere with the choice of music and gambled on there bein' no Vatican spies around.

As the shadow of Superquinn appeared at the church the first few bars of Tammy Wynette's 'Stand by Your Man' rang out from the gallery. Hogan was at his melodramatic best as his voice quivered at all the right moments. I had to take a look back to make sure that he wasn't in drag for the performance. He certainly sounded like someone in a blonde wig and a sparkly dress.

Superquinn was given away by an uncle from Fethard, the owner and pilot of the runaway horse and trap. The poor man looked as if he had just come through downtown Baghdad. He got her to the altar and made his escape just as 'Stand by Your Man' climaxed with a big finish. Pee held the last note for five minutes while the drummer walloped the bejapers out of the drum kit. Poor Moll Gleeson's hearin' aid was screechin' like a siren at the last crash of the cymbal.

Everyone breathed a sigh of relief when the song finished. Canon McGrath welcomed the people and asked Dixie and Breda to light the candles. At that point Pee and the boys launched into a loud and ropey rendition of 'Come On, Baby, Light My Fire.' There wasn't a dry eye in the church – for all the wrong reasons. The ceremony continued with no major hiccup until the music started again. Just after the vows and the exchange of rings, Canon McGrath invited the congregation to give the newly-married couple a round of applause. From the gallery we heard

Pee count in the band with 'A wan, a-two, a wan, two three,' and they proceeded to belt out a few choruses of Cliff Richard's 'Congratulations.'

For incidental music Pee had brought along a local box player, The Ticker Wickham. Now, Ticker has a repertoire of three tunes: 'Slievenamon', 'The Galtee Mountain Boy' and 'The Boys from the County Armagh.' Whenever there was a lull in proceedin's you'd hear a husky Pee callin,' 'Ticker, Ticker, a few tunes.' Ticker grew in confidence as the ceremony went on. Durin' the signin' of the register he decided to have a second run at 'The Boys from the County Armagh' and threw in a few words of encouragement: 'Keep your partners for a last round of the house. Look into her eyes, hold on to her hips and you'd never know your luck. 'Tis my own Irish home, far across de fooooam.' Even Canon McGrath shook uncontrollably.

Just before the final song the main fuse blew, renderin' Pee and the band soundless. Ticker was about to step into the breach but Superquinn had had enough. 'Ticker,' she shouted, 'if you play one more note on that mellojun I'll tear you to pieces and make you ate it.' The weddin party went down the aisle in silence. A dignified end to a most unceremonious event.

From *I Will In Me Politics – The Maurice Hickey Diaries*, The O'Brien Press, 2007.

Broken Bread
Joan McDonnell

LIKE almost everyone I know, I dread the winter because of the cold and damp. When it's raining and cold, it's hard to keep warm. The beds are piled with coats and this makes them very uncomfortable. But this had to be endured along with the hairy blanket which itches something terrible, and causes me to wake at night, terrified and breathless. One night the breathlessness is worse than usual. As I struggle to suck the air down into my lungs, it is Pat who runs downstairs and brings up his bottle of orange that he was worked so hard for. He gives it to me and I manage to gulp down some of it. With its fizzy tang and bite, the relief I feel as it slips down my throat will remain with me always.

We then get sheets when my mother obtains flour bags. She sews a number of bags together and makes a coarse type of sheet that ranks amongst the best of them. I hope that the sheets will prevent the hairy blanket from not only scratching me, but making me breathless as well, yet it turns out to be a forlorn hope. Over the years the breathlessness will only get worse.

There is still the bitter cold though, and when we complain about it, my mother advises us to put our feet into our jumper or cardigan. It will be warm straight from our bodies and we, in turn, will be nice and cosy. It works well and is a real treat.

There are three of us sharing the one bed and that too helps to keep warm, except, of course, when one of the others drags the bedclothes off me. There is more room for the three of us if two sleep at the head of the bed and one at the foot. Yet sleeping at the foot, there is always the danger of having one of the other two occupants' smelly toes stuck in your mouth.

But if keeping warm at night is a major problem, doing so during the day is a real nightmare. We don't have any warm coats – despite the piles on the beds – and no scarves, gloves or warm shoes. So for the most part it is the extremities – the hands, feet and face – that bears the brunt of the cold. We all suffer, but none more so than my older sister, Kathleen.

Kathleen attends St. Mary's school because our new local national Girls' School had not yet been built when she left the infants' school. Once she had started in St. Mary's, she didn't want to leave and return to the new school when it was built. I suppose she had her friends there and didn't want to leave them.

St. Mary's is more than a mile from home and it is a long, cold walk on a wet winter's morning or evening. But the fact that Kathleen goes there has one great advantage. Tubridy's bakery is quite near the school and on her way home, Kathleen's job is to get bread there. We cannot afford proper loaves so we get the broken bread there. A bag costs one shilling and sixpence and we depend on it for a major part of our diet.

Sometimes there is no broken bread left, but we don't go hungry. A man who works there and who knows our situation, deliberately breaks the fresh bread for Kathleen. It is simple act of true Christian charity, and so often the poor survive because of such acts of kindness. This man is probably risking his own livelihood in doing what he does and perhaps one might claim that it is sinful or wrong, or even illegal, but I prefer to see it as genuine Christian charity.

The fresh bread is always a rare treat because it tastes so nice. Normally we would get the old stale bread. So, day after day, Kathleen carries the bread home. In winter time she is often frozen to the marrow as she carries the bag and her school bag on the long journey home to Killeely.

One Saturday, on the way home with the bread, she meets my father. Because it's Saturday, and there is no school, she has our baby brother Buddy, with her and her bare hands are frozen from the steel handle of the pram. Dad places his own hands over hers and together they wheel the pram home. And the warmth she feels creeping over her hands is precious, because it is warmth generated by love. It must have been intense because to this day she can still feel the warmth of his hands on hers . . . .

Mostly Celia runs off with her friends. Even she does not want to be seen with me. I am too slow, too timid, too afraid and too goody good. I never get into trouble. But then, I don't need to get into trouble. Trouble usually finds me.

I have no one to talk to or no one to understand my predicament. I am a child who is different – a so-called special child, only the special child is usually special because of her inability to stand up for herself. The very act provokes such a backlash that she learns quickly that she may as well do nothing. But I do something. I become moody, which doesn't endear people or family to me. I become silent when hurt, but they don't understand – they will never understand.

Often I am the innocent caught in the crossfire of someone else's misbehaviour, and one such occasion happens this school year. To add insult to injury, I wasn't even at school when the terrible deed which was to affect me so much, was done.

It was so bad that the children didn't even speak of it among themselves, no doubt terror stricken by the anger of the head nun, which is sufficiently potent to curdle the blood. And the reason for all this, is the pristine banister, that even I am not allowed to hold either going upstairs or down, has been scratched.

Someone in the school – it has to be a pupil for no one else would be capable of such wickedness – has dragged something like a hair clip from the top of the banister right to the very bottom. It is along deep scratch and stands out like a meandering river on a brown map. The whole school is suspect and everyone is asked if they have seen anyone do it.

The conclusion is that it had to be done when someone went to the toilet. All the children have to raise their hands and request in Irish: *Bhfuil cead agam dul amach, ma se do hoille* which translated means: 'May I go out please?' I am too scared to ever raise my hand for anything except to answer a question, so there is no possibility that I can be responsible for this act of wanton vandalism.

The school has a policy that children with weak bladders or kidney problems don't even have to ask permission to go to the toilet. Having to listen to *Bhfuil cead agam dul amach . . .* dozens of times a day is more than enough for any teacher to bear, never mind having to listen to it dozens of times from those regularly short taken. So the policy is to grant those pupils absence without leave.

There is a girl in my class who is allowed out at anytime and my sister Celia, who is in a lower class than me, is also in this situation. When the head nun gets to Celia's class on her round of interrogation, she orders them to all kneel before a statue of Our Lady and to swear to tell the truth. Hellfire, she tells them, is beneath the floorboards. Any girl who doesn't tell the truth will fall into the fire when the boards part beneath her and down there she will burn forever with the devil and all the fallen angels.

Under this threat, Celia tells the nun that she saw the girl from my class with the weak bladder dragging the clip down the banister. And so while Celia saves herself from the fires of hell, unknowingly, she inadvertently drops me right into them. But I know nothing of this. So when the culprit is punished for the terrible deed, we think that should be an end of the matter. And by the start of the new week it should be forgotten.

On Sunday my father sends for the paper. I am happy as I begin my return journey home, the newspaper tucked firmly under my arm. If I am lucky I may get a halfpenny for bringing back the paper and will be able to return to the shop where I will be able to buy three carmel sweets. They will last me a long while.

As I approach the top of the hill leading home, I meet the banister-scratching girl's older brother. He is with another boy and this gives him courage. He grabs me by the arm and says menacingly: 'You told on my sister, didn't you.'

I am terror stricken as I answer in a quivering voice: 'I . . . I didn't.' He raises his hand to strike me, but somehow I twist away from his grasp and run as fast as I can, which really isn't very fast.

I am running for my life as a rock is sent tumbling down the hill after me. This is

FICTION

the reality of life in Limerick in the early 1960's. This is life and it is rough and tough.

It isn't long before the rock catches up with me. Well, it would have caught up with anyone, even an Olympic sprinter, never mind me. It hits me on the back of my bad left leg.

Enormous pain hits me. I ignore the pain and run on. Sheer terror now keeps me moving. As my left foot only lifts very slightly from the ground, the rock is like a terrier worrying my ankle, gashing it with his teeth. My poor leg is no match for it.

I can't escape the rock without leaving the footpath and running onto the road. Then knowing my luck, I will probably be chased by a car. But as I round the corner, the rock, having no sense of direction, does not follow me. I stop running. I catch my breath and continue the rest of the way home, walking slowly, silently and grievously wounded.

When I arrive home, I hand my father the paper without a word. He offers me a halfpenny, but I do not take it. Halfpennies are scarce and one does not refuse them lightly. He does not accuse me of being moody. He knows there is something wrong and he asks. 'What's wrong love?'

This show of concern for me is something I welcome. Everyone else would assume that I am just in a mood. But not Dad. He is different. He knows there is something wrong.

And with those caring words of his, I can no longer remain silent. I become hysterical as I try to tell him what has happened. He lifts me up onto his lap and very gently removes my shoe and my blood-stained sock. He looks at my heel, tiny, purple, and oozing with the little blood there is left in that leg.

He is white with anger as he says to my mother: 'Mary, that boy is not going to get away with this.' With that my mother puts pen to paper, her answer to everything, and writes to the head nun, telling her what has happened to me because of the damage to the banister.

I will not take the note to school. It is Celia who takes it to the nun, who in turn reports the boy to the boys' school where he is punished. But the matter is far from over.

Because I fear the schoolyard and being bullied going to and from school I am always late back from lunch. That way I think I am safe. Only I haven't reckoned on boys mitching, or mooching as we called it. And, of course, with my luck I meet them, though as my rock thrower is with them, I think they might have been waiting for me.

This time rock thrower does not attack me himself. Instead he has his pal to do it for him. It's like something out of the *Godfather* long before Marlon Brando stuffed his cheeks with cotton wool and began making offers no one could refuse:

'Is this the one, Don Corleone?' Luca Brazzi asks.

'Yeah. That's her.'

And then Lucca Brazzi proceeds to choke me. He places his hands tightly around my neck and squeezes, tighter and tighter until tears break from my eyes which surely must be bulging right out of their sockets. I begin to gag and because they are not the real Mafia, but mean, nasty cowards, they get frightened and let me go, and run off.

But where do I go? Do I go home and complain again. If I do, the brutality will never stop. So do I continue onto school as if nothing's happened. I settle for the latter, never telling a soul about this murder attempt which has been made on me. But it is not the first secret I have kept and it will not be the last.

So, despite this attempt to murder me, and as to make up for the terrible disappointment of failing as a ballerina, I make my stage debut at my very first Feile Lumini concert. I am one of the four smallest children in the class and because of this we are put in the front row. Our class is reciting poetry. There are three benches on which we must stand: small girls in front; bigger girls behind us and the giants at the back.

My big worry isn't stage fright, but how I am going to get up on the bench. I don't think it will look very professional if I put my hands on the bench to help myself get up on it. But I can't step up on it, left leg first, because the leg wouldn't hold my weight. Neither can I place it on the ground and lead with me right leg. Same problem applies. I just hope no-one wishes me luck by saying 'break a leg' because I might just do so.

I needn't have worried though because we got into our positions behind the curtain, and I am able to get onto the bench with a helping hand – my own to be exact. But now, all during the *Battle of Fontenoy*, I worry about how I am going to get down gracefully.

The *Battle of Fontenoy* ends without any casualties. But there is no relief for me and I watch helplessly as the curtain remains open and each girl gets gracefully down from the bench. As I agonise over what I should do, fate intervenes and takes the decision out of my hands. As the last girl gets down from my bench it begins to wobble. Self-preservation takes over and I jump for dear life. But my heel gets caught and the bench topples over with a loud crash.

I blush with embarrassment, but console myself with the thought that at least I won't be shot. It isn't as if I'd deserted the battlefield in the midst of the action. So I compose myself and go backstage, glad that the ordeal is over. Well, the battle is over but there is one sniper in a gymslip waiting for me. 'It was you who knocked over the bench, wasn't it?' she says scornfully, taking away what little self-confidence I possessed. Should I have wanted to be an actress, destiny in a gymslip has decided for me at this moment that I shan't succeed. Stage fright takes a new and terrible meaning. It now means not failing on the stage, but falling off it.

From *A Spring in my Step*, The Collins Press, 2004.

FIVE

HISTORY

The Funerals
Des Fogerty

SEAN South's remains had left Monaghan early that morning the 5th January to begin the long journey to Limerick. There had been earlier a Requiem Mass in the Cathedral celebrated by Rev. T. Mohan, St. Macartan's Seminary. There was a huge congregation and the coffin was draped with a tricolour.

At Dundalk a large number of Great Northern Railway workers and employees of other factories stopped work as the cortege passed through the town. Many shops and businesses closed as a mark of respect. Hundreds of people lined the streets of Drogheda. The coffin was accompanied by a guard of honour of six young men and about a hundred or so walked behind.

When the remains reached Dublin at about 2 pm they were met at Clonliffe Road by a number of young men wearing black armbands and escorted to Parnell Square where the hearse drew up in front of Charlemont House. The escort provided a guard of honour. These men were from the Dublin Brigade of the IRA.

Along the route from Clonlilffe Road to Parnell Square several thousand people had joined the procession and by the time it reached the Square a very large crowd had gathered. A young man stepped forward and recited the Rosary in Irish. Several wreaths were then placed on the coffin, which was draped with the tricolour. The crowd grew even further as more prayers were said before the hearse moved off at 3 pm.

It travelled through O'Connell Street, Dame Street and Thomas Street and out to Inchicore where it halted. The people on foot, who numbered several thousand, then stopped and the cortege moved to Portlaoise escorted by several Garda patrol cars. Sean's two brothers had accompanied the remains from Monaghan and their mother and the rest of the family met the cortege at Roscrea. Steve Coughlan, Mayor of Limerick 1951-52, an old comrade of Sean's from his days in Clann na Poblachta, had driven Sean's mother to meet the funeral. In every town and village that they passed through large crowds had gathered, and the Rosary was recited as the remains passed. The larger towns of Portlaoise and Roscrea provided guards of honour of local IRA men and detachments of the old IRA.

A scene quite without parallel was observed as the cortege reached the Borough Boundary of Limerick at Pennywell at about 9.00 pm. An estimated 20,000 people had gathered in the pouring rain to welcome home to Limerick a man they considered a true hero of Ireland. It took an hour and half to reach St. Michael's Church in Denmark Street, a distance of only a mile, the crowd was so dense.

In the church local IRA men placed a guard of honour around the tri-colour-draped coffin. The vigil was maintained until 1.00 am and renewed again at 7.00 am the following morning. The coffin was surrounded by hundreds of wreaths from various organisations, local business firms and ordinary people.

The church was crowded to capacity next morning when solemn Requiem Mass was celebrated by Rev. P. Lyons of St. Michael's. There were numerous other clergy present, many of them personal friends of Sean.

Throughout the day thousands of people passed in an unending stream by the tricolour draped coffin which was piled high with Mass cards. The bier was surrounded by magnificent wreaths. An estimated fifty thousand people lined the route from St. Michael's Church to Mount St. Lawrence cemetery where Sean was to be buried in the Republican Plot.

Sean's comrades in the local IRA had gone to the Mayor of Limerick, Alderman Ted Russell, and asked that Sean be given a civic funeral by the city of Limerick. Even though Sean was an old political ally of Ted Russell, it was reluctantly refused. Alderman Russell pointed out that not all of the Corporation would agree and he suggested that members of the city council could if they so desired go in their official robes, which most of them did.

Bohemians Rugby Club played a match in Thomond Park on the day of the funeral and refused to lower the National flag to half mast even though Sean's younger brother Gerard was the club's senior captain.

As the funeral bell pealed, blinds were drawn, business establishments closed and people stood in silence to watch the cortege wind its way through a corridor, four deep, of men, women and children, many of them weeping and praying as the horse-drawn hearse passed through the streets.

Gardai on duty stood to attention and saluted while tricolours flew at half-mast from many business and private houses. It seemed Limerick had come to a complete stop to mourn and at the same time honour its dead son. A guard of honour of young Fianna Eireann boy scouts marched with the hearse and they were flanked by local IRA men with black armbands with tricolour flash. There were contingents from all over Ireland represented. The cortege was headed by the Cork Volunteers' Pipe Band. People from every walk of life in Limerick including the Mayor, Ald. Ted Russell, were present.

At the graveside Brian Mac Lughadha from Ennis recited the Rosary in Irish. A friend of Sean's, Diarmaid O'Donnchadha, stood at the head of the grave and gave an oration in Irish.

He said he would like to say a few words on what Sean South had done for Ireland. Everyone knew why he died. The huge throng about him in the cemetery knew, as did the crowds in Dublin and on the roadsides from the time the body left British possession and came back to Limerick.

'His death was a source of sorrow to me and to all of us, but his deeds and the honour he earned were a cause of joy and pride. His sacrifice on the altar of freedom is encouraging to us.

'He cherished his freedom and his Irish heritage. He died for freedom, for my sake and yours, and for the generations that are to come. Not only did he follow in the footsteps of Pearse and Emmet and Tone, but he made a study of his Irish heritage from the beginning.'

In conclusion, Tomás Mac Curtain from Cork, whose father had died for Ireland in the War of Independence, stood to attention beside Sean's brother Jim and delivered commands to the bugler and drummer from the Cork branch of Fianna Eireann and the Last Post and Reveille were sounded. At about eight o'clock that night, three volleys of shot rang out in the darkness of the cemetery as Sean's comrades paid their final salute to their fallen hero.

As the cortege passed through the country on its final journey, many people came forward and asked to be armed so they could go and fight for the liberation of the Six Counties from British oppression. It was the moment for the IRA to exploit the situation, but they were not organised on a large enough scale to undertake a countrywide recruiting. But the older statesmen De Valera saw the signs coming and after an RUC man was killed in the North in July, he used it as an excuse to introduce internment.

Sinn Fein did, however, get four of its members, including Fergal O'Hanlon's brother, elected to the Dail. An old interment camp in the Curragh was hastily prepared and several hundred suspected IRA volunteers and Sinn Fein supporters were rounded up, thus nipping any chance of further sympathy being utilised.

From *Sean South of Garryowen*, Copper Reed Studio, Limerick. 2006.

Feeling hard done by
Michael McCarthy

PERHAPS one of the more celebrated compensation cases in the Shannon Scheme was that of Mrs Catherine Davidson who lived just below the tailrace bridge at Parteen. Her home and licensed premises were within the danger zone affected by the extensive blasting operation of the canal. In fact, the house and pub were very close to the centre line of the rock cut making it extremely vulnerable to vibrations and flying rock.

On 8 June 1927 Mrs Davidson wrote to the Resident Engineer at the Strand Barracks asking about protective measures for her property against the blasting operations:

> I trust that some protection will be afforded me without delay as already the premises have been subject to some damage as a result of the explosions. I am also informed that the road passing by my premises where I carry on a licensed trade will be closed during the period of the construction of the tailrace. This will, as you can understand, materially damage my trade owing to the fact that the public will then no longer use the said road.

As a result of her request, the contractors shored up the premises with props, put up window guards and covered the slate roof with a wooden roof. Apparently these measures proved ineffective and, in spite of the timber covering, flying rocks damaged the roof and large cracks appeared in the walls.

A tragic occurrence took place on 17 July, when eighty-six-year-old Mrs. Flynn, Mrs Davidson's mother, was opening one of the timber window shutters. It fell from its place crushing her against the parapet wall at the front of the building. She died shortly afterwards. The inquest, at which the minister was present, expressed the opinion that there was gross negligence in the putting up of the window shutter. Her accident caused all blasting in the area to cease temporarily. Once her body was removed for inquest, however, blasting operations were resumed again.

The death of her mother, the continuing damage to her house and the effect of the excessive explosions, all combined to affect Mrs Davidson's nerves. It was imperative that Mrs. Davidson and her son and daughter should vacate the house immediately.

Even though a temporary footbridge to facilitate those who wished to travel to the village was erected, the closure of the road had badly affected her trade in the pub thereby eliminating any residual reason for her to stay.

Mrs Davidson's solicitors, Connolly and Co. of Limerick, then wrote to the Minister of Industry and Commerce, shortly after the accident to her mother, in order to expedite matters. Interestingly enough, they mentioned that their client kept occasional lodgers and supplied lunches to the Irish engineering staff who were engaged in supervising the work of the contractors. All that was now finished, the letter went on, and of late people are prevented from passing along owing to the danger of being struck by flying rocks. Apparently, Mrs Davidson had to leave the house on two occasions recently because of the proximity of the blasting.

Arthur Taylor, the assessor, was then called in and he confirmed that:

since the death of her mother, Mrs. Davidson is in an extremely nervous condition. The blasting is on a colossal scale and every now and then Mrs. Davidson has to leave her home and go down to a place of safety together with any customers that may be in the bar at the time . . . . I suggest that it would be advisable to close the premises and to offer her compensation for finding accommodation elsewhere until such time as no further damage is likely to arise from the blasting operations.

Taylor's corroboratory report was enough to move matters forward and he was instructed to enter into negotiations with Mrs Davidson with a view towards settlement. By early October he reported that he had reached a most satisfactory outcome from the point of view of the Department of Industry and Commerce. He had examined Mrs. Davidson's trading books and concluded that her net profit for a week was £6. Considering that she would have to secure accommodation for herself and her two children in Limerick and to travel by car to inspect the property regularly, he would recommend that she be paid compensation of £6 per week.

The Department of Finance sanctioned this proposal, but not before checking with the assessor as to whether Mrs Davidson's tax returns were in order! J. J. McElligott suggested that the local inspector of taxes would be willing to furnish this information if Mrs Davidson gave her permission. This exercise took four weeks, which is a long time for someone in a highly nervous condition, whose house was being literally bombarded on a daily basis and who had a business to run and two young children to care for. At any rate, Mrs Davidson's tax affairs were in order, also the payments were made from January 1928, even though she was forced to vacate the house in early December because of its dangerous conditions. These payments would last for a period of twelve to eighteen months.

Work continued on the tailrace and by early summer 1928 J. K. Prendergast, the Resident Engineer, was of the opinion that unless Mrs Davidson's house was properly shored up that it was liable to collapse at any moment. The fact that all of her furniture and effects were still in the house, some of which had been damaged by rain pouring through extensive holes in the roof, could lead to a very expensive claim.

Further devaluation of Mrs Davidson's property took place when it was decided to build the tailrace bridge at its present location, and not farther down the road towards Limerick. This meant that part of her car-parking area in the front of the house was truncated, bringing her considerably closer to the road. At the back of the house, the railway line to Ardnacrusha cut through an accommodation paddock that she and her predecessors had rented from the Glosters for eighty years. All in all, with the top floor of the house having to be rebuilt completely and with the general despoliation of the property outside, Mrs Davidson was entitled to some compensation.

In mid-1929 she and her engineer W.J. Holmes submitted plans to Siemens Bauunion for the rebuilding and general refurbishment of the house with an estimate of £750. The contractors stalled immediately and said that refurbishment was not their responsibility as the damage was caused by vibrations. They were now using the House of Lords agreement that the government had used against John Browne. 'We could only acknowledge liability if the decision were made in court', they emphasized. However, they did concede that while they did not have a legal liability, they would be prepared to pay, without prejudice, half the sum in question, i.e. £375 in settlement of their liabilities.

It would have been interesting to see what the government would have done had the Germans played hardball and not made the part-payment concession. There would have been a protracted stand-off involving lengthy legal proceedings. The contractors' contention was that they were responsible for such damage done by blasting as could be proved to be due to negligence. The government, on the other hand, relied on a clause in the Conditions of Contract that placed liability on the contractor for all damage to property arising out of the blasting operations. The House of Lords judgment though effectively modified this clause somewhat.

A summary of Mrs Davidson's case for the Chief State Solicitor contained one very interesting and little known fact:

> It is understood that the contractor is insured against all compensation claims arising out of the blasting operations and that in repudiating responsibility he is acting on the advice of the insurance company which is located in Germany. There is, however, no official knowledge of this.

In the meantime, Mrs Davidson's claim had risen to £1000 because of interest costs, architects' fees, etc. Arthur Taylor reported that the claim was reasonable in the circumstances. 'However, I queried the claim and fought it on at least six occasions with Mrs Davidson and her Valuer and Engineer. Eventually I am happy to report I succeeded in reaching a most satisfactory settlement, namely £800 in full satisfaction of the claim . . . .'

On 17 July 1930 the Department of Finance finally signed off on Mrs Davidson's claim, allowing her £800 in compensation, 25 guineas Valuer's fee, £6 per week for accommodation until the end of June, and a final lump sum of £54 for alternative accommodation, as her house would not be completed until 30th August. This brought to a close what must have been a nightmare for Mrs Davidson and her young family. The engagement with the various government departments was a veritable war of attrition, on top of the trauma of being blasted out of one's home and losing a loved one in the process. Happily, Mrs Davidson and her family lived in their house for many years after that and provided a welcome service for all bona fides and even for those who may not have been as eminently qualified!

While the issues involved in compensation cases were complex thereby delaying an outcome, there were some instances when matters were decided relatively quickly. William O'Grady's case was one of those. His farm was in Blackwater, where nearly thirty acres of land were flooded by the contractors in 1925 as a result of the canal cutting. For four years the land was covered in water preventing him from sowing crops or making hay on it. In February 1929 a claim was made in the courts for £200 19s. 3d. and costs against Siemens Bauunion. It quickly transpired that the contractors were not responsible for the damage so that it was up to the government to settle the matter. Arthur Taylor then got involved and a conference was arranged between the various parties. After intensive arguments he got the claimants to accept a sum of £130 in full satisfaction of their claim including costs. Taylor recommended to the Department of Industry and Commerce that it should accept this settlement and pay up immediately. By early August Finance had approved the payment. The whole process had taken only six months, which was comparatively speedy, but there were no great complications in the case.

There were many people adversely affected by the construction works who could not afford to travel the legal route to progress their grievances. There were many others who, as we know from the numerous inquests, could not write or even sign their names so that they could not correspond with the government or state their case. Their stories will never be known, which, unfortunately, is our loss. For those people, unrecorded and now forgotten, as well as those of whom there is some evidence of what they went through, the cost of progress was high. The minimalist awards were of little comfort for what they and their families suffered and lost. For them it was a huge investment in the future and in the next generation.

From *High Tension: Life on the Shannon Scheme*, The Lilliput Press Ltd., 2004.

Limerick's Fighting Women in the Siege of 1690
Maurice Lenihan

IT must be added that the moment the retreat of the Irish soldiery was discerned by their comrades in the streets, and above all by the women, it is impossible to describe the sudden, overwhelming reaction which at once took place. Every feeling that could arm citizens and soldiers, with vengeance, and brave, defiant, death-scorning women, was aroused within their souls. Grenades flew thick and heavy about them, shot and shell swept the walls, but they faltered not; the Grenadiers followed now by several detachments, were fighting within the very streets.

John Street, Broad Street, Mungret Street, every street of the Irishtown down to Baal's Bridge, were crowded with those detested freebooters and vagabonds – the ruffian rabble soldiers of the bloody-minded massacre of Glencoe! Burning with insatiable revenge, the women, forgetting their nature, called aloud on husbands, sons and daughters to rally – and showed the example themselves. The ranks that had been broken were re-formed in order to beat back with irresistible force the tide of sanguinary foreign cut-throats which poured across the walls, and which even the battery at Curry's Lane was not able sufficiently to resist, though it continued to make lanes in the legions of the Dutchmen and to strew the pavement with their bodies.

The brave Wauchop, a Scottish soldier of considerable ability, commanded 1,700 Irish soldiers chosen for the duty. The contest was the fiercest yet remembered. The fight raged, the women in front and centre urged on the soldiers by word and example. Half the Earl of Drogheda's Grenadiers were actually on the rampart, says Harris, while others, still more eager, pushed into the very town. Captain Cadogan, of William's army, raised his sword in triumph as his men were on the breach. Sarsfield, lion-like, went through the streets, ascended the walls – was everywhere. By an exhibition of personal courage and daring never yet surpassed, he proclaimed aloud the imperative duty which every Irishman owed to his country in the crisis.

Elated with this success, the Irish ventured again upon the breach, and the resolution of the women was so great, they pelted the besiegers with stones, and so inspired the men by their example, that after three hours unequal fighting, the Williamites were forced to retire to their trenches. In the assault, the women used whatever weapons came first to hand – stones not the least useful. Dr. Davies, Dean of Cork, then present in William's army, states in his journal, 27th August, 1690 – after describing the assault he says; 'it was a very hot service, both great and small shot firing continually on both sides – we lost many men, and had more wounded, and of them the Lord Charlemont was bruised with stones. The Earl of Meath was bruised with a stone on the shoulder.'

Here the fact is proclaimed, trumpet-tongued to the entire world, that it was the heroines of Limerick who nobly repelled the savage invaders that endeavoured to obtain a firm footing within the walls! Let us picture to ourselves the heterogeneous battalions of William bristling with all the latest appliances and weapons of aggressive war – stung by the miseries of a protracted siege; resolved on 'death or glory' – making their way blindly over the counterscarp, through the breach, enfiladed by the fire from the ambuscade, from which the Irish soldiers had not been driven at any time – like famished wolves, hungry for their prey – and at length, within the precincts of the coveted city, the capture of which was to place the crown permanently on the head of William, who in person commanded the besieging host! Picture the garrison – worn out by constant watching – pinched by irremediable hunger – the victim to every species of privation; subject to treachery within – swayed, however, by the never flinching courage of Sarsfield, and holding out against all odds!

Imagine the wan and wasted figures of those maids and matrons who, forgetful of the gentler influences which reign predominant in the female breast, lost for the moment the amenities of their nature, wild with the excitement of battle – and nerving their arms to hurl death on the heads of the most odious foemen that ever challenged an outraged people to combat.

On, on the crowds rushed from every contiguous lane and alley – from Palmerstown, from Mungret Lane, from Curry's Lane, across Baal's Bridge from all the streets and lanes; from Emly Lane, Barrack Street, Tumbling Lane, &c. of the English Town, which had never, even in Ireton's cruel time, been witness to a scene so bloody and awful as that which was enacted on the very memorable evening of the 27th of August, 1690. Creagh lane, Fish Lane and Churchyard Lane, the 'Great Street' and every other street, gave out their crowds of enraged heroines, who, armed with whatever weapon fury supplied, swelled the ranks of the Irish soldiers who now fully restored to nerve and vigour, and with the cry, which in a few years afterwards, made the English pale in the fields of Fontenoy and Cremona, of Steenkirke and Dettington, they drove terror into the coward hearts of the retreating Dutchmen, Hugenots and Danes, as they endeavoured to run from the streets over the walls, through the breach back to their trenches!

Broken bottles was a favourite weapon with the women. But few, comparatively few of William's army lived to make their escape from the city. William, all the time, was viewing from Cromwell's fort the events of that, to him, most disastrous evening. The afternoon had cleared up, the sun, in the west, invested with a crimson glory, gave a delightful tinge to the foliage of the old woods of Cratloe. The scene beyond the city was one calculated to challenge the admiration of the painter, whilst the ruin and havoc of war blended with those elements of tranquil rural attractions which nature profusely shed over the more distant outlines of the landscape, constituting a picture to which Claude Lorraine could only do justice. A shout of victory arose from the besieged, as they hurled from the walls the last remnant of the beaten Dutch battalions.

But there was still more work to be done Those mines which Sarsfield had planned had not as yet been set to work – but the opportunity was speedily to arrive! Dr. Molleneux says that 'they sprung a mine in the Ditch with but little effect.' Dean storey does not say a syllable about the Ditch or anywhere else. Harris more truthful – tells us that 'during the heat of the engagement a detachment of the Branderburgh regiment got on the enemy's Black Battery, the powder of which by accident took fire, and blew up numbers.'

No. There was no accident! It was all intended in the well-weighed and artistically planned calculations of Sarsfield. Molleneux admits that there was a 'mine in the ditch': no doubt of it; and there were mines, in numbers, wherever it was imagined that one could be of use.

From *Limerick, its History and Antiquities*, Hodges, Smith & Co., 1866.

The Fighting Women of Limerick: fact or fiction?
Kevin Hannan

VALUABLE accounts of the Siege of Limerick (1690) have been left by Dean Story. He came to Ireland in 1689 as chaplain to Sir Thomas Gowar's regiment, and was attached to this regiment until after the surrender of Limerick. He remained on in the city, and married Margaret Water, a Co. Limerick lady. His *True and Impartial History of the Wars in Ireland* is a sound and reliable work that has remained a basic source document for historians, though the word 'impartial' might well have been left out of the title, for his views are sometimes coloured by his Protestant faith, and his allegiance to his sovereign. He will be forever remembered as the author of the account of the fighting women of Limerick.

Story was not a combatant, and we are told that he was 'at the camp' which may have been a temporary camp nearer the city, and thus he may have been afforded an opportunity of close observation of the conflict during the fighting at the breach. He started a long-running controversy when he referred to '. . . broken bottles from the very women, who boldly stood in the breach, and were nearer our men than their own.' It is significant that not one of the Jacobite combatants or observers mentions the presence of a woman anywhere near the scene of battle. In his second account of the fighting at the breach Story makes no mention of the women.

Dalrymple, who also left an account of the siege, latched on to Story's dramatic descriptions and gave it further credence '. . . the inhabitants of Limerick, eager to give that defeat to King William which those of Londonderry had given to King James, animated the garrison. Even the women, from the same emulation, filled the places which the solders had quitted.' The word 'quitted' sets us a poser; did the soldiers quit because of injury, or even death, or did they run away in terror?

Another account of the Limerick women's involvement in the battle is given in a letter from Limerick to King Christian V of Denmark, by Jean Fouleresse, but this account is also based on hearsay: 'The very women, prone as they are to violent passions, have since then become furious. It was noticed that during that attack on the counterscarp they caused as much, indeed, more damage than the garrison by throwing huge stones on the assailants, of which a great number thus perished.' Unfortunately, he did not say who 'noticed' the fighting women. This statement must be seriously questioned. Surely, a few women could not possibly cause more damage than the garrison by throwing 'huge' stones with such prowess and velocity that 'a great number perished.'

It is significant that none of the other people who took part in the engagement and wrote about it afterwards noticed the presence of a woman during the conflict. Boisseleau and Stevens described the action in close detail, and the authenticity of the pictures they paint is established in their similarity, even in the most unimportant details.

The account of the fighting women reminds me of one of those rumours that often spread like wildfire throughout a city. It was Story who set the ball rolling, right up to nineteenth century historians like Fitzgerald and McGregor, who, in their 1827 *History of Limerick*, sympathise with the Williamites. 'Those brave men were assailed at the same time by showers of stones, broken bottles and other destructive missiles from a mixed multitude of men and women.'

Leland, in his *History of Ireland* (1727) was content to rely on the imaginative writings of previous writers, but varies the legend, adding some trimmings of his own. 'Even the women of Limerick mingled with the men, advanced in front, defied the besiegers and assaulted them with stones.' John Ferrar, in the history (1787) cites Leland's contribution to the controversy and advances no personal opinion.

Rev. James Dows passed away without leaving us a hint as to where he learned of the women 'advancing into the vacant space between the two opposing armies, so that they were sometimes nearer the English regiments than their own countrymen, and when all the missiles failed, attacked them with their tongues.' The inventiveness and latitude of this description makes for some degree of fantasy.

However, the palm for the most vivid imagination must go to Maurice Lenihan, whose eager pen leaps into a merry dance of dramatic fiction:

Burning with insatiable revenge, the women, forgetting their nature, called aloud on husbands, sons and daughters to rally – and showed the example themselves . . . the fight raged, the women, in front and centre urged on the soldiers by word and example . . . . Imagine the wan and wasted figures of those maids and matrons who, forgetful of the gentler influences which reign predominant in the female breast, lost for the moment the amenities of their nature, wild with the excitement of battle – and nerving their arms to hurl death on the heads of the most odious foe men that ever challenged an outraged people to combat.

Indeed, Lenihan's whole description of the climax of the first siege is pure, unadulterated invention.

The survival of the belief in the fighting women has for long depended on the powerful and unremittant claims of writers, who, through a refinement of the art of varnishing a stubborn and litigious tale, have left us a heritage of which so many generations of our citizens have been so proud. The few words on which this contention has subsisted for the past 300 years have, in the meantime, stirred the imagination of those writers who were so delighted with the rare opportunity of enlarging on the tale of a few women equipped with broken bottles and stones attacking a battle-hardened army.

The legend has given the women of Limerick a special place in our folk-memory, even if they never handled a stone or a broken bottle 300 years ago. Human nature being what it is, to enlarge on the report of a really dramatic incident is one of the most common dispositions of most people. Even the historical sagacity that should manifest itself in reporting accurately on one's own experience, the experiences of eye-witnesses and the writings of indirect commentators is often pushed into the background, as has been done with the nineteenth century accounts of the fighting during the attempted invasion of the city by the Williamites.

From *Fact and Fancy: Story and Storytellers of 1690, The Old Limerick Journal, 1690 Siege Edition*, Winter, 1990. No. 28.

1916: A Stupendous Piece of Folly
Limerick Leader Editorial

THE public mind of Ireland is but slowly recovering from the stunning blow of horror inflicted upon it by the insurrection which broke out in Dublin on Easter Monday. That wholly insane enterprise had in it every element of sadness and tragedy, and there is not a man of the Irish race the world over capable of reasoning facts but abhors and condemns with vehemence the "mad campaign" as the Most Rev. Dr. Kelly, Bishop of Ross, aptly described it.

The solitary redeeming feature in connection with the whole uprising is that the outbreak was the work of a small minority, most of whom were themselves mere innocent if well-meaning dupes of others, and that it is denounced by none more loudly or more vigorously than by the vastly overwhelming majority of the Irish people themselves both at home and abroad.

The actions of public bodies and Nationalist organisations all over Ireland, as well as the messages received beyond the seas, make it clear beyond question that the insurgents had not the sanction of approval of the Irish race, and that, in the words of Mr T. P. O'Connor, "the overwhelming majority of the people of Ireland condemned, reprobated and sorrowed over what had taken place."

There is no need now to sell on the fatuity and shortsightedness of the men who embarked upon and encouraged this utterly hopeless and chimerical undertaking of setting up an Irish Republic by force of arms. The survivors amongst those who carried out or allowed themselves to be made the instruments of such a stupendous piece of folly are today sadder and wiser men, and now that the revolt has been crushed and extinguished it would be unwise and unjust on the part of the responsible authorities to persist in any action that might be looked upon as vindictiveness on their part.

Enough examples have been made in all conscience in the shooting of the twelve who have already paid the extreme penalty and to any ordinary mind it is evident that there is no necessity for any further blood-spilling over the regrettable happenings. Further executions as a deterrent are wholly unnecessary, for apart altogether from the disastrous failure of the insane attempt made by the insurgents the feeling and opinion of Irishmen at home and abroad may safely be relied upon to prevent any repetition of the madness that marked Easter week of 1916.

In the course of an able article showing the unwisdom of what it describes as the "drastic severity" of the Military Tribunal in Dublin and appealing for clemency towards the insurgents, the *Freeman* says: "Everywhere one turns, among all classes of the population and especially among the Nationalists of Ireland who for the past two years have been fighting and circumscribing the evil influences that have produced such tragic results, there is one universal argument being used. Men are pointing the contrast with South Africa, where the victorious General who put down the rebellion, to the great good fortune of South Africa and its enduring union, loyalty and peace happened also to be a wise and prudent statesman.

"There when the King's Arms were triumphant only one rebel was shot. People are asking, why the difference? There would be some explanation of the severity if the mass of the Irish people were in sympathy with the revolt, if the young Irish reserve battalions had been false to their trust, if anywhere in Ireland there was anything but an impotent minority that approved the insanity of the insurrection. Then the executions might be explained as intimidatory and preventative. But the conditions in Ireland are the reverse of all that. Everywhere in England and in Ireland there is acknowledgment of the excellent spirit displayed by the masses of the people in the tragic crisis . . . .

Limerick Leader, May 10, 1916.

Queen Elizabeth I and Limerick
Matthew Potter

DURING the reign of Queen Elizabeth I (1558-1603), the whole of Ireland was brought under effective English rule for the first time. An important aspect of this process was the establishment of provincial governments in the outlying parts of Ireland. While it had been originally intended that Munster, Connaught and Ulster would each be ruled by a governor called a lord president, appointed by the Queen, Ulster was eventually excluded from the scheme and it was implemented in Connaught in 1569 and in Munster in 1571. The lord president of Munster was to play a major role in extending English rule and was to prove to be a formidable enemy of Limerick's municipal autonomy on a number of occasions.

Throughout her reign, Elizabeth I also tried to impose the Reformation on Ireland, though she usually lacked the means to do so effectively. All of the principal civil and religious office holders were supposed to take the Oath of Supremacy to the Protestant Church of Ireland while attendance at divine service was made compulsory, on pain of a substantial fine. In the towns and cities, the mayors were given the task of enforcing this legislation. As before, passive conformity continued to be the norm and the mayor and city councillors of Limerick circumvented the legislation.

On 9 June, 1564, the Mayor and the recorder of Limerick were among the commissioners appointed by the queen 'with power to correct heresies and other offences . . . and to administer to all persons there, as may seem good to them, the Oath of Supremacy' in the counties of Carlow, Waterford, Kilkenny, Cork, Kerry, Limerick and Tipperary. This policy was a total failure and when the staunchly Protestant Lord Deputy Sir Henry Sidney paid an official visit to Limerick in March 1567, he was disgusted to have to endure Catholic ceremonial including a Te Deum in St. Mary's Cathedral. Things did not change much in the next quarter of a century. On 23 May, 1594, the Mayor of Limerick was again appointed as one of the commissioners to enforce the Acts of Supremacy and Uniformity, this time in the dioceses of Limerick, Cork, Cloyne and Ross, but seven months later, the Anglican bishop John Thornburgh wrote to the English Privy council, urging them to force the mayor and aldermen of Limerick to bring their families and servants to his church services.

However, the government's contradictory policies towards the towns were to hinder more vigorous enforcement of the Reformation legislation. The queen and her advisors wanted to promote the Church of Ireland but simultaneously, continued to promote the autonomy of the boroughs. This produced two major absurdities. Firstly, responsibility for enforcement of the legislation lay with the mayors of the town, who were themselves usually at the forefront in disregarding the Oath of Supremacy. Secondly, a successful prosecution for any breaches of the Reformation legislation by the citizens including the mayor and city councillors would result in a fine being paid to the corporation, not to central government. The prospect of the corporation paying a fine to itself was not a serious deterrent to the flouting of the law, and not surprisingly, the Reformation made little headway in Limerick city until the 1650s.

Limerick's tenth charter (dated 28 October 1575) included the grant of a sword of state to be carried before the mayor on ceremonial occasions. Sir Henry Sidney himself made an official visit to Limerick in 1575 and presented the sword to the mayor, Richard Everard. The civic sword signified that the mayor possessed the power of life and deaths over his citizenry and thus symbolically reinforced his authority. It is both the oldest surviving item of the city insignia, and the oldest Irish civic sword in existence and is kept in Limerick's Jim Kemmy Municipal Museum. The charter further stipulated that the mayor, bailiffs and recorder in their legal capacity could now try felonies, which was a power that they had not previously possessed. All fines and forfeitures or other financial penalties arising from any act of parliament could now be retained by the corporation for its own use. The mayor and bailiffs could not be summoned to appear before any court of law, except in cases of contempt, felony or treason.

On the 24 April, 1578, Queen Elizabeth I granted Limerick Corporation jurisdiction over Scattery Island (which has an area of 166 acres and is situated in the Shannon Estuary about sixty miles from Limerick city) at an annual rent to the crown of £3-12s-12d. While it may be a far-fetched comparison, it can be argued that in an age of colonial expansion, the 'local kingdom' of Limerick, headed by its quasi-monarchical mayor, acquired an overseas possession like Spain, Portugal and other contemporary kingdoms.

Since the creation of the title in 1329, successive Earls of Desmond had been traditional enemies of Limerick Corporation and the city's mayors usually looked to the government to protect them from this danger. In the reign of Elizabeth I, the thirteenth Earl of Desmond rebelled against the government twice: in 1569-73 (when the rebellion was actually led by his cousin James Fitzmaurice Fitzgerald) and 1579-83. The outbreak of the second Desmond Rebellion in 1579 precipitated one of the most terrible wars in Irish history. Limerick city remained loyal to the Queen, and served as a major base for operations against the rebels as well as providing municipal troops for the government's army. The Mayor of Limerick, Nicholas Stritch, presented a force of 1,000 armed citizens against Desmond. Limerick's municipal army fought with the government forces until the rebellion was finally crushed in 1583.

Limerick did not have to wait long for its loyalty to be rewarded as the city's eleventh charter was granted on 19 March, 1583. Under its most important provision, 'our city of Limerick shall be, and remain forever hereafter shall remain one body corporate and politic, in deed, fact and name by the name of Mayor, Bailiffs, and Citizens of the City of Limerick.' This granting of corporate status made of Limerick's civic authority a separate legal entity, distinct from its members, so that it is only from 1583 that we can correctly refer to the government of the city as 'Limerick Corporation.'

The dogged loyalty of Limerick's staunchly Catholic and Old English mayoral elite to the Protestant English crown may seem puzzling, but it was grounded in a coherent political ideology. Since the 1530's, the Reformation had created a gulf between the Old English on the one hand and the Dublin government and the New English settlers on the other. In response, the Old English developed a coherent ideology which informed their actions until their final overthrow in the 1650's. Firstly, they considered themselves to be the English nation in Ireland, a middle nation between the native Irish and the Protestant New English, and that the kingdom of Ireland was a separate sister kingdom, equal in status to England while sharing the same monarch. Secondly, the Old English wanted a sort of 'Home Rule' centred on the Irish parliament and wanted to be actively involved in governing the country in partnership with the government. Thirdly, and most controversially, they believed that they could combine loyalty to the crown in civil matters with loyalty to the Pope and the Catholic Church in matters of religion. This contention was anathema in the sixteenth and seventeenth centuries and was never accepted by the English authorities in Ireland, although they were unable to do much to suppress it until the 1650's.

Following the conclusion of the second Desmond Rebellion, the plantation of Munster and the activities of the lord presidency transformed the province, placing it more firmly under English rule than at any previous time in its history. Despite the increasingly Protestant nature of the crown's administration, Limerick remained stubbornly loyal to both queen and pope. England and Spain were at war from 1585 to 1604, and although Spain claimed to be champion of the Catholic Church, the mayoral elite remained loyal to the English connection. Successive mayors of Limerick gathered intelligence from merchants newly arrived from Spain and its dominions (trade was continued throughout the war) and passed it on to the authorities. The civic elite was afraid that the Spanish Armada might succeed in conquering England and in the autumn of 1588, they were horrified when seven Spanish ships anchored within their territory at Scattery Island. After they left, Mayor George Fanning of Limerick wrote to his Waterford counterpart describing 'the happy news of the departure of the Spaniards.'

From *First Citizens of the Treaty City*, a Limerick City Council Publication.

ANONYMOUS

Death in Mount St. Vincent

EARLY in November, 1908, a dreadful calamity befell the orphanage. To our human way of thinking such it seemed, but, no doubt, in the inscrutable designs of providence it was a "Celestial Benediction that assumed the dark disguise."

To us it is not given to penetrate the secrets of the Divine Mind, but we know "that all things work together unto good to them that love God"; and it may be that the good, darkly veiled in the sombre shadow of the great cross, was the salvation of the young souls taken in their youth and innocence, who, perhaps, would have suffered defeat in the hard battle of life on which they must shortly have entered had they been spared.

As a calm and smiling landscape becomes overcast, and the storm clouds breaking overhead suddenly change the whole face of nature, so swiftly was the happy scene of childish life and merriment changed into one of the deepest gloom and sadness.

It was the evening of November 3rd. About 5 o'clock one or two of the children complained of sickness and headache and were sent to bed; others followed suffering in the same way, until between 9 and 10 o'clock those ill numbered twenty. Vomiting attended the severe headache and all cases were alike. The doctor was summoned and considered the illness due to some form of poisoning, but as there were no alarming symptoms; he went away, having given directions as to treatment which he expected would counteract the attack. But as the night wore on, child after child took ill, so that by morning sixty or more were affected.

As the gravity of the situation did not appear until some time after the Sisters had retired, Mother M. Joseph, then in charge of the orphanage, not wishing to disturb or alarm them, remained up all night with only one Sister and the resident trained nurse.

Who can picture the consternation among them all next morning when at about 7 a.m. death claimed its first victim. The priest was with the poor child just before community Mass.

Soon all the medical men in the city were in attendance, and several trained nurses, each doing all in the power of medical skill to allay the sufferings of the poor stricken ones, and taking preventive measures with those not yet attacked. The scenes in the dormitories – now changed into wards - can better be imagined than described.

Sisters accustomed to hospital duty said they never witnessed such suffering. The poor children were writhing in the agony of excruciating pain. The intensity of the suffering rendered them unconscious of what was going on around them. Many of the city priests visited the scene, anxious to give all the help and comfort they could, both to the Sisters and the children.

On the 4th, the situation was so alarming that it was deemed better to administer the Last Sacraments; two priests went round from bed to bed and anointed the sixty-five. Ere the dawn of the 5th seven young souls had passed to God. All had been to Confession and Holy Communion for the Feast of All Souls the day previous to the sad occurrence. Extra Sisters were sent from St. Mary's to help. And one and all worked day and night in a spirit of heroic sacrifice in constant attendance to the poor little sufferers.

About 6 o'clock on the evening of the 5th, Fr. N, Dillon, OFM, visited the dormitories. He was taken to several bad cases and prayed by the bedside of each. Then he knelt in the middle of the dormitory and prayed aloud. He was considered by everyone to be a Saint, and the Sisters believed it was owing to his prayers that several whom they thought could not possibly survive were spared. Later another child passed away. This brought the death roll to nine; then the hand of "Death" was stayed.

Professor McWeeney, the eminent bacteriologist, was sent by the Local Government Board to investigate the case and arrived from Dublin about 10 pm on the 6th. He was conducted through the orphanage by the doctors and was highly pleased with the efficient method in which everything connected with the sick children was carried out.

A Protestant military doctor, who kindly proffered his services, remarked that in the twinkling of an eye the whole place was turned into a hospital as perfect as any of their military hospitals. Nurses all commented on the wonderful order and discipline that prevailed throughout, and that anything and everything called for was provided on the spot. The nine bodies were laid out in pale blue habits, and a more touching scene could scarce be witnessed.

There were two funerals – five bodies were interred first, the remainder later on. Letters of heartfelt sympathy poured in from all quarters. A telegram was received from Rome conveying to the community and children the blessing of our Holy Father, the Pope.

The Verdict was: "Died from 'Cholera Nostra,' due to meat poisoning and we are further of opinion that at the time of cooking the unsoundness of the meat could not be detected."

From *St. Mary's Convent of Mercy Centenary Booklet*, 1938.

The lighter side of Patrick Sarsfield
Paddy Lysaght

PATRICK Sarsfield was born in Lucan where the ice cream comes from. Being of Anglo-Irish stock he was superior to the plain people of Ireland, though he loved them greatly. If he wished he could quite easily have received a commission in the British army, and have ended his days in some officers' mess in India, playing cricket with the natives, riding about on elephants or crushing the Kurds. But he did none of these things. Instead, he joined the Irish irregulars, became a great general, and then a wild goose; but as he was Anglo-Irish naturally he was not as wild as most of the wild geese were.

Sarsfield was a fine cut of an Anglo-Irishman, tall and with a noble stance, and long hair in ringlets cascading down his manly chest. All is evident from his noble statue, now tucked away near the cathedral, which tourists should visit. However, a word of warning here. At the cathedral, pigeons, jackdaws and starlings show a decided preference for the venerable general's head, at certain times his physiognomy is clouded over. Thus the most opportune time to view this magnificent statue is after a good downpour, when the features in all their noble manliness are distinguishable.

The ordinary people of Ireland called Sarsfield 'Patrick', his wife called him 'Pat', his children 'Da', and the French under St Ruth called him 'Paddy'. Since Sarsfield disliked being called 'Paddy the Irishman', he mistrusted St Ruth. So there you had it - the old sad story over again, one general mistrusting his chief officer, thereby giving the enemy the opportunity of driving a wedge between them, and conquering them in battle.

When Sarsfield was a young man in Lucan, James II, the wisest fool in Christendom, and William the Orangeman came over to Ireland to do battle. William brought a big train with him to transport himself easily through the country. He also erected statues at Kilkenny, thereinafter known as the Statutes of Kilkenny. He erected these in honour of one Poyning whom he admired greatly for the famous laws he promulgated. Why, you might well ask, did two English kings come to Ireland to do battle? Well, since battles, usually mess up the countryside in which they are fought, and since English kings are understandably loathe to mess up their own country, they formed the habit of coming over to Ireland every time they wished to fight.

Thus it was that James confronted William at the Boyne. Sarsfield was on James's side, but since he was not able to run as quickly as James, he bumped into William on the battlefield, and told him bluntly that if he wished to change sides he would fight the battle all over again. As William would not agree to this reasonable proposal, Sarsfield sulked and returned to Limerick, via Athlone, where he busied himself building walls and making friends with a jockey called Galloping Hogan. When William heard all this he sat into his train and headed for Limerick, ran out of coal at Ballyneety, and walked the remainder of the journey, where he met with stout resistance. Meanwhile Sarsfield and Galloping Hogan blew up the train, forcing William to make a treaty with them.

Whether the famous Treaty of Limerick was actually signed on the equally famous Treaty Stone is a question which has been debated for ages past. Professor P. Shogue has studied the problem in depth, and as one would expect from such an eminent authority, his conclusions are interesting and all but conclusive. While he himself admits that these conclusions contain a slight element of doubt, the balance of evidence seems to point to the fact that both protagonists were actually sitting on the Treaty Stone when they were actually signing the treaty. Thus it is not incorrect to state that the Treaty of Limerick was signed on the Treaty Stone. In one sense it was thus signed. The professor has, by careful examination of the contours of the stone and by measuring its greatest length, proved conclusively that both Sarsfield and William the Orangeman could have sat on the stone at the same time, preparatory to and immediately after the signing of the treaty. Furthermore (and this is important) since one half of the stone is higher than the other half, and since protocol would have demanded William be that shade higher than Sarsfield, the stone, because of this inequality in height, would have been most suitable for the said signing, William sitting on the higher portion, Sarsfield that inch below him. But, in pursuit of truth, the professor has researched still more deeply. By measuring the waist of Sarsfield's kilt, now in the museum at Landen, he has been able to prove that Sarsfield's buttocks were x inches wide. Research on William's buttocks has revealed that his were x plus 2 inches wide. Now add both and you get 2x plus 2 inches. Even allowing for an expansion of one inch per buttock when both were seated preparatory to signing the treaty, you get 2x plus 4 inches overall. But since the Treaty Stone is in reality 2x plus 10 inches wide, there remains a comfortable 6 inches on which both could manoeuvre preparatory to and immediately after the signing.

From *The Comic History of Limerick*, Mercier Press, 1979.

It's a long way from the Markets Field
(To my Father, who answered The Call)

Remembering John Redmond's call in the Markets Field, Limerick, for Irishmen to fight for Ireland's freedom on the battlefields of France:

By Tess Guerin-Letendre

It's a long way from the Markets Field, John!
About our necks, grey thread of Somme
Is hung with stones of Abbeville and Maiens:
'Save Petain, Verdun and France!' We stand for them.

It's a long way from the Markets Field, John!
A long way from the Shannon and the Liffey and the Lee!
We are young and with some shred of innocence
We still believe Night's promise of silence and of peace.
But here our peace is murdered
By whining shell and gangrenous Verey light . . .
While we, canopied by arching flight of steel,
Tread out, with thousand thousand feet,
Pavane for the watching, waiting dead.

It's a long way from Markets Field, John!
From the smiles and cheers and flowers,
On the day we marched like children,
With wooden sticks, to fight and set them free.
The flowers are dead, the cheers are turned to curses,
And we are outcasts in the Potter's Field.

Our ears are rent and deafened, John!
We read each other's words, by lips alone.
And what do our lips soundless say, John?
'God save Ireland'?
Yes, let God save Ireland
While we die for France.

From *The Old Limerick Journal*, Winter 1992. No.29.

Bishop O'Dwyer and Maxwell
Anon.

(The British General, Sir John Maxwell, called on Dr. O'Dwyer, Bishop of Limerick, to punish certain priests who had helped the I.R.A.)

Will you join me in my dirty work,
Wrote England's butcher bold;
"You've rebel priests within your See
That love us not, I'm told.
Remove these men where never more,
They'll threaten England's sway,
And England's love and gratitude,
Shall be your own for aye."

Then answer made the brave O'Dwyer:
"My laws are not as thine,
For yours condemn in ruthless haste,
It is not so with mine.
Ere I'll accuse I'll know the charge,
The witness, place and time,
And ere I'll punish I'll have proof
That there has been a crime."

And quickly came the bogus charge,

In humble accents formed;
"Me thought it needed not to prove
The guilt of those I named,
They've hearkened to the rebels' word –
They've blessed the rebels' cause –
By voice and pen they've taught their flocks
To spurn the Empire's laws."

Our Bishop true no longer now
His anger can restrain:
His words are cutting as the scythe
That reaps the harvest grain:
"These men you name are godly men,
In act and thought guilt free –
They serve their God and love their Land,
And that's no crime to me.

"And were their guilt as black as night,
Don't think at your behest,
I'd join with those whose hands are dyed
In blood of Ireland's best.
Full many a ruthless English churl
Has held our land in thrall,
But history sure will write you down
The blackest of them all.

"And do you think that I forget
My country's martyr dead;
The brave, the pure, the high-souled lads
Whose blood you foully shed?
Then here's your answer I may share
The fate of those who died.
But I'll not be the first O'Dwyer
To take the tyrant's side."

Descendant of a noble clan,
May you be left us long –
Fearless and true to uphold our cause
'Gainst tyrants cruel and strong,
The thought that every voice was stilled,
That hearts were cold with fear;
No coward threats your heart could chill
Nor make your voice less clear.

And oh! thank God that there are men

To speak with love and pride
Of those who lie in prison cells
And those who nobly died.
And where the glorious tale is told
Of Ireland's latest fight,
In letters golden shall be writ:
O'DWYER UPHELD THE RIGHT!

King William in Limerick
Henri and Barbara van der Zee

BEFORE he left Dublin for Limerick, he made an effort to settle Irish affairs by peaceful means. He had already issued a declaration in which he promised mercy in exchange for obedience. Now, in a second Declaration of 1 August, 1690, he demanded the surrender of the last rebels and promised an amnesty to those who submitted to him, 'as we abhor all manner of violence done to our loving subjects of what religion whatsoever...'Leading citizens were ordered to go to certain towns and remain there until their future was considered, and foreigners were to be allowed a passport to return to their own countries.'

He reached Limerick a few days later. This port at the mouth of the Shannon was the second largest in Ireland and the key to the whole of the south-west. It could be easily supplied from the sea and as long as it remained in Jacobite hands it would be a rallying point for rebellion. Hopes that the town would fall easily into English hands rose when it was known that the French troops had pulled out, leaving it to the Irish to defend it – since the Battle of the Boyne respect for the Irishman as a fighter was non-existent. As the town's fortifications were not more impressive than the defenders, the English troops were surprised by the determined resistance that met them. When William joined his armies in rain soaked swamps before the city, he sent a trumpeter to the governor of the town, Boiseleau, demanding his surrender. Back came the messenger with a guinea 'to drink the health' of King William and defiant message from Boiseleau: 'Since King James had entrusted him with that garrison, he would recommend himself to the Prince of Orange by a vigorous defence.'

The English army found the siege of Limerick a miserable and depressing business. The rain poured steadily down day after day and the Irish gave them not a moment of rest, constantly harassing them with skirmishing parties. They sometimes came so near, 'that we could hear them talk with their damn'd Irish brogue on their tongues,' complained an Englishman bitterly.

The Irish efforts were not confined to skirmishes; knowing that the King's troops were short of ammunition, the one commander of brilliancy on the Irish side, General Sarsfield, took out on 12 August a raiding party to intercept the reinforcements that he had learned were on their way from Kilkenny. The English now paid for their contempt of their Irish opponents: this train of wagons loaded with the urgently needed powder and several large guns was so lightly guarded that when Sarsfield swooped on it at dead of night he met almost no resistance. Both guns and powder were blown up and sixty of the English escort were killed.

The siege dragged on for weeks, and ammunition ran low. On 27 August William, whose health was amazingly good, made a last desperate attempt to take Limerick, but after terrible fighting on the walls and in the streets, where the people of Limerick – even women and children – defended their town with murderous courage, the attackers were driven back. Three days later William decided to raise the siege. It was his first defeat in this campaign.

From *William and Mary*, Macmillan London Ltd., 1973.

Death in Brookeborough: Seán South's last hours
Kevin Haddick Flynn

THE IRA unit involved had been lying low in Fermanagh for several days beforehand and was led by Sean Garland. It was his decision to hit the barracks, but he had only an old town-planner's map of the village and was unaware that the post provided security for the Coolebrook estate, home of the Northern Ireland prime minister, Sir Basil Brooke, a few miles away.

It was thus strongly armed and guarded. Garland had over a dozen men and before the raid had requisitioned a lorry owned by a Lisnaskea building firm. Its driver, Leo Morton, was forced to drive towards Brookeborough; afer a few miles he was bound, gagged and left lying in a field.

Garland's ordnance included mines that he had primed and batteries to provide current to detonate them. The strategy was to park the lorry by the barracks and make a direct assault. The unit was split in two: an assault party to lay the mines and a fire party to provide cover. Two lookouts, Mick Kelly and Mick O'Brien, were dropped at the outskirts and instructed to give signals should RUC patrols or reinforcements approach. This arrangement was problematic; neither had much knowledge of the area nor of the side-roads that led into the village.

Moving up the main street, the driver, Vince Conlon, had difficulty locating the barracks; its only identifying features were the sandbags on its windowsills. It resembled an old schoolhouse, with one gable abutting the street and a central porch. He pulled up beyond the gable, but too close in to give the firing party sufficient sweep to cover the upper windows.

The assault team ran to the front wall to lay a mine. At this moment, RUC sergeant Kenneth Cordner came out to investigate. His saw the mine being laid and ran back inside, slamming the door. A heavy fusillade spattered the building. He sprinted upstairs to fetch an automatic. Outside, Seán South was letting off his Bren gun, which stood on a tripod, while Paddy O'Regan fed him the magazine. South was stymied, however, because he was too cramped to properly direct his weapon at the higher windows. And it was from one of these that Cordner now returned fire. Behind the lorry, Daithi O Conaill turned on the juice to set off the mine, but nothing happened.

With the unit coming under heavy fire from the barracks, and particularly from its upper windows, Ó Conaill was forced to make a suicidal dash to lay a second mine. In frustration, he fired his Thompson gun into both mines, still they failed. They had been incorrectly wired.

When Cordner reached the upper room, he had difficulty in finding his Sten gun as the lights had been shot out. On his knees, he crept towards the gun rack and edged towards the window. He could see the lorry below, the IRA men milling around and firing at the building. He poked his weapon out and squeezed off a few rounds in a wide arc. Garland and Ó Conaill returned fire, and someone – possibly Fergal O'Hanlon – tossed a hand grenade at the window. It hit the sill and bounced harmlessly into the street.

Cordner now acquired a second magazine, while bullets rained through the window, showering him with glass. He poked his gun out again and this time could see the assailants more clearly. He let off a well-directed burst that had a deadly effect on the attackers. When he looked again, South lay slumped on his Bren gun, O'Hanlon (who had been throwing Molotov cocktails) was bleeding on the ground and O'Regan was lying face downwards after being shot. Garland was limping, having taken a bullet in the leg. It was now obvious that the game was up. Garland shouted to the men to pull out.

Pulling out was easier said than done. In the lorry's cab, Conlon had been hit in the foot and Phil O'Donovan, sitting beside him, was grazed. The lorry resembled a sieve: the cab was riddled, the sideboards peppered with holes, two tyres were burst and the tip-gear had been perforated. The latter mishap meant that the tailpiece bobbed up and down – to the discomfort of the injured – when the driver accelerated. After a few false starts, the vehicle made off down the street, wobbling crazily and only stopping to pick up the lookouts.

The rear of the lorry looked like an abattoir. There was little doubt that South was dying and that O'Hanlon was almost gone too. Somehow, Conlon drove on for five miles. He stopped at a place called Altawark (also known as Baxter's Cross) and those who were able stumbled out. It was realised that the RUC would be in pursuit and that the barracks at Roslea, which lay ahead, would be alerted.

The men had to make a quick decision about South and O'Hanlon, who plainly could go no further. The rest of the journey would be on foot, over rough terrain towards the border. A deserted farmhouse and cowshed were spotted; it was decided to leave the wounded men in the shed and request local people to call a doctor and a priest. This was done, but Garland became reluctant to leave. He wanted to stay in the shed with a gun, so that he could make a fight of it with the oncoming RUC and gain time for the rest to get away. With difficulty he was dissuaded, and with the rest retreated up a hill in the direction of the border.

Ten minutes later, the RUC drove up in two Land Rovers and moved in on the abandoned lorry. From the hill, the men could see the RUC raking the vehicle with machine-guns. A few minutes later they heard a long burst of gunfire from the direction of the cowshed. Afterwards some said that this was the *coup de grace* being administered to South and O'Hanlon. But the bullet holes in the shed were waist high and could not have hit the wounded men, except by ricochet.

It was conceded that firing on the shed constituted a standard military tactic, employed when an oncoming force approached cover held by an enemy. This explanation was not, however, accepted by the IRA activists, who have held, with great bitterness, that South and O'Hanlon were 'finished off' by the RUC.

At the subsequent inquest in Enniskillen, RUC Inspector W. D. Wolesley said that John South (sic) was past medical help when found but that if O'Hanlon had received first aid he would have been saved. A search had revealed that the raiders had a first-aid kit with them, 'but far from helping the unfortunate man, his comrades abandoned him and left him to die' – a claim repudiated by the IRA.

The survivors successfully evaded pursuit by getting into the Slieve Beagh Mountains; on taking a compass bearing they headed for Monaghan. It was a long and hard slog; the RUC set off flares over the area and helicopters hovered overhead. Some of the wounded had to be carried and they often had to lie on the bracken to avoid being spotted. The ordeal lasted six hours before an advance scout reported that they had crossed into the Republic. They had successfully avoided 500 RUC and B-Specials who has scoured the mountains with baying hounds and airborne units.

The men's luck ran out, however, when they crossed the border. On leaving the wounded in a friendly house, the remaining eight were picked up by a Garda patrol, but not before they had dumped their arms. The wounded were taken to hospital to recover and await trial, the others to the Bridewell in Dublin. All twelve refused to recognise the court and got six months in prison under the Offences Against the State Act.

The raid made immediate headlines and within days South and O'Hanlon were seen as martyrs. In true Irish tradition, the ballad-makers set to work. Like Father Murphy of Boolavogue in 1798, and Kevin Barry during the Tan War of 1920, the names of South and O'Hanlon were added to the national repertoire. This was not surprising, as no tradition runs deeper in Irish history than the turning of physical defeat into spiritual victory.

The following week was almost an occasion of national mourning as the coffins – draped in tricolours – were taken across the border. As South was carried to Limerick the hearse was stopped *en route* as Mass cards piled up and overflowed the breastplate. On arrival at midnight the cortege was met by the mayor and 20,000 people. Next day more than double that number were present at the interment in Mount St. Lawrence cemetery, where a Last Post was sounded and a volley fired by men in black berets.

In the week that followed, the characters of the dead were scrutinised. Nineteen-year-old Fergal O'Hanlon from Park Street, Monahan, a draughtsman with the local county council and the subject of another well-known ballad by Dominic Behan, was seen as a fine young fellow who had played senior football for Monaghan and had a host of friends. He had impressed all who knew him as a solid young man.

South, a 27-year-old clerk in a timber importing firm in Limerick, was seen as something special. In many ways he resembled Patrick Pearse, whom he had admired. Deeply religious, dedicated to the revival of the Irish language and to traditional music, he was well liked by all shades of opinion. He was also highly talented: he painted in oils and drew cartoons for local newspapers; he ran his own magazine, *An Gath* (The Sting), and played the violin with professional competence. In the last issue of his paper he penned a piece entitled 'Jacta alea est!' ('the die is cast!'), in which he said: '. . . there is an end to foolishness; the time for talk is ended.' Then he left Limerick for the border. Today his memory is embalmed in the famous ballad.

Big claims were made for the IRA's attacks, not least by Moscow's Pravda, which on January 4 disputed Downing Street's dismissal of them as isolated incidents without popular support. It saw the raids as part of a bigger picture: 'Irish patriots' it declared with Cold War testiness, 'cannot agree with Britain in transforming the Six Counties into a military base for the Atlantic Alliance.'

Once the initial attacks were launched, de Valera was quick to call upon Taoiseach Costello for firm measures against the IRA. This was politically difficult for Costello, given his government's dependence upon Clann na Poblachta. His government did, in fact, fall shortly afterwards on a related issue. A fresh general election was called for March 1957. Sinn Fein candidates, despite their pledge not to enter the Dáil, won four seats, and nearly 70,000 votes. This was proof positive of a significant measure of support for republicanism, heightened no doubt by the emotions generated by the funerals of South and O'Hanlon.

After the Brookeborough raid, the IRA's campaign became increasingly sporadic and only limited manpower was committed. Each operation had to be judged against Stormont's superior forces and the resources it could deploy. These included 4,000 full-time RUC men, plus a B-Special reserve of 13,000 and a substantial British army back-up. The campaign was finally abandoned on 26 February, 1962.

From *History Ireland*, January/February 2007. Volume 15, No. 1.

Death on the Irish Sea: The tragedy of the Goulds
Michael J. McNamara

ON the morning of the 10th October, 1918, at 9.45 am, the mail-boat *Leinster* (2,646 tons gross) belonging to the City of Dublin Steam Packet Company, left Kingstown Pier (now Dun Laoghaire) bound for Hollyhead. She carried 771 men, women and children, including crew, civilian passengers and 492 individual soldiers and sailors going on leave or returning. She had been attacked already on the 27th December, 1917, by a German submarine whose torpedo missed its mark, and since then she had been defensively armed.

About an hour after leaving Kingstown the *Leinster* was 11 miles east south of the

Kish Light Vessel. Lying in wait was the German submarine U 123 under the command of Kapitan Robert Ramm. At that point, without warning, she was struck by a torpedo; a second torpedo struck her some minutes later. The engine room was blown out, and she sank in 13 minutes from the first impact. The lifeboats were launched and SOS messages were sent; after about an hour, two old destroyers and other vessels arrived from Kingstown and Holyhead and combined in the work of saving life.

But in spite of the energy of the rescuers and the heroism of individuals from the Leinster, 501 persons lost their lives. Of these, 145 officers and men including members of the Royal Navy and Mercantile Marine, whose bodies were recovered, are buried in Grangegorman Military Cemetery, Dublin. 142 officers and men of the Army, one nurse and one civilian messenger are commemorated at Hollybrook cemetery, Southampton; 39 of the crew, including the Master, William Birch, are commemorated on the Merchant Navy Tower Hill Memorial, London.

From a Limerick viewpoint, the sinking of the *Leinster* brought great tragedy. Catherine Gould, 3 Creagh Lane, Mary Street, together with her five daughters and only son were on their way to join her husband, who was working in a munitions factory in England when the ship went down. Only one survived, Essie Gould, and only one body was recovered, that of the mother, who is buried in Mount St Lawrence Cemetery.

The other Limerick victims on board the *Leinster* that morning included: Private Honan, Royal Defence Corps; he is buried in Mount St. Lawrence Cemetery; Private Michel Barry, Royal Garrison Artillery; his body was not recovered and is commemorated on the Hollybrook Memorial, Southampton. Private Joseph Cronin, Cappamore, is buried in Grangegorman Military Cemetery; Corporal Timothy Hennan, South Irish Horse; his body was not recovered and is commemorated on the Hollybrook Memorial; Ms Anne Maude Barry, youngest daughter of James Grene Barry, Sandville House, Ballyneety; she is buried in Rockstown Churchyard, Ballyneety. Ms. Louis Frend, Boher, Caherconlish; her body was not recovered and is commemorated in Abingtron C of I.

No complete passenger list is available for the last voyage of the *Leinster*. It was only when the bodies began to come ashore, that people realized the scale of the disaster. The view expressed at the time was that the loss of a mail steamer travelling between Ireland and England would be a national disaster, considering the amount of civilian passengers ferried on them.

The sinking of the *Leinster* was to be Ireland's worst ever maritime disaster, and the greatest single loss in the sinking of the *Leinster* was the loss of the Gould family of Limerick.

The wreck is located at a depth of 100 feet, 12 miles from shore and is virtually intact with the bow pointing South. During the 1990's the wreck's owner, Desmond Brannigan, and several sub aqua divers from the locality of Dun Laoghaire arranged for the recovery of one of the *Leinster's* anchors. With financial assistance from Stena Sealink, Irish Lights and others, they raised one. It was brought to Dun Laoghaire and placed on the seafront; a stark reminder of man's inhumanity to man.

The *Limerick Chronicle* of October 12, 1918, carried the following report of the sinking:

> The sinking of the Royal Mail steamer 'Leinster' on Thursday has very cogently brought home to the people of Ireland the fiendish and inhuman methods of warfare waged by the Germans. That the crime has been strongly condemned by every section of the public was more than half evident yesterday, and in Limerick, which has shared in the mourning brought to Dublin and other parts of the country, the greatest indignation was expressed at the latest act of Hunnish devilry. Enquiries instituted go to show that one Limerick family, humble, decent people, have been practically wiped out by the torpedoing of the steamer. The name is Gould, and the circumstances are particularly sad and poignant.
>
> The father, who is a retired Army man, has been at munitions work in England for some considerable time past, and on Wednesday last the family, who live in Creagh Lane, Mary Street, left to join him. They consisted of the mother, five daughters, and one son, ranging in age from twenty years to twelve months. They travelled by the 'Leinster' from Kingstown, and, as result of the disaster, all, with the exception of the second eldest, Essie Gould, were lost.
>
> This little girl arrived in Limerick last night by the 8.55 train and was met at the station by a number of her friends. On the train also was Alderman Joyce, MP, who was the recipient of congratulations from many on his providential escape from death. The Alderman, who looked none the worse for his experience, has given a graphic description of the disaster as it presented itself to him. The names of the Gould victims are: the mother, May; Alice, Michael, Angela and Olive.

From *The Widow's Penny*, Patrick J. McNamara, 2000.

Limerick in 1916
Mannix Joyce

THE Irish Volunteers came into being at a meeting held in Dublin on November 25, 1913. The first volunteer company to be formed outside of Dublin was in Athlone, the second was in Dromcollogher, Co. Limerick. The prompt formation of a company in Dromcollogher was due to Fr. Tom Wall, then a curate in the place. Charlie Wall, no relation of Fr. Wall, was appointed Captain of the company.

The first meeting for the enrolment of the volunteers in Limerick city was held in the Athenaeum Hall on Sunday, January 25, 1914. It was addressed by Padraig Pearse and Roger Casement, and practically every man of the large crowd joined. Further enrolments took place nightly, and soon the numbers were sufficient to allow for the formation of eight companies.

The new spirit, a combination of the Fenian and the Gaelic traditions, was abroad in Limerick; and Limerick people are proud to recall that that highly successful operation – the Howth gun running – was carried out to the plans of a patriotic West Limerick woman, the Honourable Mary Spring Rice, who, with her friends, Erskine Childers and his wife, was on board the Asgard, the yacht that brought the guns to Howth, that famous July 26th, 1914.

At the time of the Redmondite 'split' in the autumn of 1914, the strength of the Limerick City volunteers was about 1,240 men. Of these, approximatley 1,000 declared for Redmond and his policy of aiding Britain in her war against Germany. On November 14, 1914, Captain Robert Monteith of 'A' company of the Dublin Brigade of the Irish Volunteers, arrived in Limerick city. Dismissed from his post in the Ordnance Survey because of his nationalist activities, and deported from Dublin, Monteith, a man with military experience, was a decided acquisition as far as Limerick was concerned. He had begun work with the 250 or so volunteers who had remained loyal to the original objectives of the founders of the volunteers and had high words of praise for them.

Ernest Blythe had already been active organising companies of Volunteers in Co. Limerick, and now Monteith assisted him in his work, travelling to such places as Dromcollogher, Ballylanders and Galbally. When Battt Laffan, John MacCormack and David Hennessy of the Ballysimon National (Redmondite) Volunteers came over to the Irish Volunteers, it was a fortunate day for the Limerick City Volunteers, for now they had Batt Laffan's extensive farm at their disposal any time they wanted to carry out field exercises or manoeuvres.

The inspiration and driving force of the Volunteers in Limerick city were concentrated mainly in three men: Michael Colivet, Commandant of the Limerick Brigade of the Volunteers; Seoirse Clancy, his Vice-Commandant; and James Leddin, Hon. Colonel. Comdt. Colivet had eight battalions in his Brigade area; one in Limerick city, three in Co. Limerick and four in Co. Clare.

Capt. Monteith left Limerick on August 24th, 1915, and began his perilous wartime journey to Germany, where he was to meet his friend, Roger Casement, who was there engaged in endeavouring to obtain German aid for the coming fight in Ireland.

Limerick was to have been a pivotal point in the nation-wide Rising which the Military Council of the volunteers had planned. According to the general plan of the Rising, the Cork Volunteers would move towards Macroom, and link up with the Kerry Brigade, which in turn, would be in communication with the volunteers in Clare, Limerick and Galway. Ultimately, a line would be held from the Shannon through Limerick and Galway, and East Kerry to Macroom. Volunteers from Ulster would occupy positions from the Shannon to south of Ulster. The Rising would begin with the declaration of the Republic and the seizing of Dublin, with action against the British troops in adjoining counties, whole moves would be made by country Volunteer forces towards the capital to relieve the ring of positions inside. One of the chief duties of the Limerick Volunteers would be to hold the line of the Shannon from the Clare side.

That the volunteers in Munster and Connacht would have sufficient arms to carry out their tasks depended on the safe arrival of a German arms ship that was to come to Tralee Bay. In fact, the whole plan was based on the assumption that the guns would be safely landed.

As an tAthair Padriag de Brun wrote:

Their eye were straining for the help to come
Over the seas, as in a far-off day
Men waited for the ships of Spain or France
Bearing on Bantry or Killalla Bay.

On the Sunday prior to Easter Sunday, 1916, Charlie Wall, Captain of the Dromcollogher Volunteers, was told the date of the Rising, and was appointed commandant of the West Limerick volunteers, who were to be mobilised by him at Glenquin Castle. Part of their duty would be the all-important ask of ensuring the safe passage of the train carrying the German arms from Fenit to Limerick.

But the German arms ship, the Aud, came – and was lost, 'through force of evil chance.' On Good Friday, two Limerick cars, one driven by Sam Windrim, the other by Tommy MacInerney, conveyed from Killarney five Volunteers from Dublin who had hoped to make radio contact with the German ship. Tommy MacInerney's car took a wrong turning in the darkness and plunged into the sea at Ballykissane. MacInerney himself escaped, but the three Volunteers with him were drowned. They included Donal Sheehan of Rollison's Bridge, Templeglantine.

With the arms ship gone, the foundations were pulled from under the plans for a general Rising. Disappointment and confusion spread through Munster. On Holy Saturday, Comdt. Colivet sent Lieut. Seamus Gubbins to Dublin for instructions. A few hours later he despatched Captain Liam Forde on a similar mission. Lieut. Gubbins met Sean Mac Diarmada, and saw the preparations going on for the Rising. Capt. Forde spent the night with Mac Diarmada and was seen off the following afternoon by a very solemn and very kindly Pearse.

The Limerick officers mobilised their men on Easter Sunday as had been arranged. Colivet marched 130 of the Limerick City Battalion out to Batt Laffan's farm at Killonan; Comdt. Liam Manahan mobilised the Galtee Battalion; and Comdt. Charlie Wall saw 150 of the West Limerick Batt. assemble at Glenquin Castle. Then to all three centres there came in due course Eoin Mac Neill's countermanding order calling off the Easter 'manoeuvres' – in reality calling off the Rising.

In no centre did the men disperse immediately; instead, they carried out some field exercises. Fr. Tom Wall and Fr. Michael Hayes were at Glenquin, and blessed the men before they dispersed. On Easter Monday, Comdt. Colivet received a message from Pearse which said: 'the Dublin Brigade goes into action today. Carry out your orders.'

In all the circumstances, it was impossible for Colivet to do so. Comdt. Manahan was grimly determined that his Galtee men would strike a blow to aid the gallant men in Dublin, and was strengthened in his resolve by the arrival in Ballylanders from Tipperary on Wednesday night of the 20-year-old Sean Treacy. But everything was against Manahan, and so no fight was made in Limerick in Easter Week, 1916.

But good men and true from Limerick took part in the fighting in Dublin: Ned Daly from Limerick city, and Con Colbert from Athea, both of whom were executed after the Rising; Eamon de Valera from Bruree; Geroid MacAuliffe from Newcastle West; Eamonn Dore of Glin; Jim Flanagan and his cousin, Matt Flanagan of

Killougheen; Pat and Jim Collins of Tully, Templeglantine; Pat Mulcahy of Rathcahill. And, of course, there was Donal Sheehan of Rollison's Bridge, Templeglantine, who was drowned at Ballykissane on Good Friday. Laura and Nora Daly, sisters of Ned Daly, went to Dublin and served with the Dublin Cumann na mBan in the GPO.

Of such men and women was the Easer Week Rising made. They changed the course of our history forever. *Dia go deo leo.*

Our Catholic Life, Summer, 1961.

Letters of John FitzGibbon, Earl of Clare, 1798
D. Fleming / A.P.W. Malcomson

Clare, Dublin, to Auckland, 21 May 1798 (about arrests of United Irish leaders and state of the country): 'We have done much towards disconcerting the Irish rebels in the last fortnight. A man who had given us private information on the express condition of never being desired to come forward publicly, was betrayed by some of his subalterns in the county of Kildare and arrested in consequence by General Dundas who commands in that district, without communication with government, and sent up to Dublin in custody. In this dilemma the gentleman's scruples have vanished, and he will, I think, enable us to bring many of the leading traitors to justice, and at their head Lord Edward Fitzgerald. This reprobate was arrested on Saturday, after a severe struggle in which he was wounded from a pistol-shot in the arm, after having wounded two of the constables who were employed to arrest him, most desperately. None of the parties, however, are hurt mortally, and I think Lord Edward bids fair to make his exit on the scaffold.

His arrest determined the rest of the gang to make a desperate effort on this night or tommorrow (sic); of which also we had full information and two very leading members were taken up this morning, against whom we have the fullest evidence. They are brothers of the name of Shears, and worthy members of my profession. In the desk of one of them was found a manifesto ready drawn, penned in the genuine style of Marat and Robespierre, to be issued by the new government on its establishment.

We have been obliged to proclaim the city of Dublin under the Insurrection Act, and shall proceed early tomorrow to a general search for arms. More than two thousand pikes have been already been seized in this town, and I have no doubt there are considerably more than ten thousand still concealed in the city and its environs. Scarcely a day passes without a discovery of pikes, either finished or in a state of manufacture.

The county of Kildare is nearly disarmed, and in that district alone more than four thousand pikes, and fifteen hundred stand of firearms, have been already seized. Their plan was to attack the park of artillery at Chapelizod, the magazine in the Phoenix Park, a small camp at Laughlinstown, about seven miles from Dublin at the same time, and by way of diversion to have detached small chosen parties to the houses of obnoxious individuals, with order to murder them all, and at the head of this proscribed list I had the honour to stand.

I think we have now a fair prospect of crushing this rebellion. Its nature and extent have been so completely developed that no man will now venture to condemn the necessary acts of vigour which have been, and will, I trust, continue to be exerted for its suppression. Tomorrow a special commission will issue for the trail of the principal traitors; but although we have not the misfortune to be hampered by the laws passed in England at the Revolution for the encouragement of treason, it will not, I fear, be possible to bring them to trial much sooner than a month hence, I have a lively hope that by this time Messrs O'Connor and Co. have been disposed of according to their desserts.

If anything can open the eyes of that perverse and sulky mule Abercromby to his misdeeds, what has passed since his departure from hence ought to induce him to bury himself in obscurity in the Highlands. Surely he will not be employed in England. Many thanks to you for Mr Stone's correspondence with Doctor Priestly. I have sent the pamphlet to Lees.'

Clare, Dublin, to Auckland, Wednesday, May 25, 1798: 'We have now been at issue with the rebels in the county of Kildare for more than ten days, and I am sorry to say that they are not as yet subdued. General Ralph Dundas commands in that district, and his conduct seems to be inexplicable.

On Thursday last they attacked him at Kilcullen bridge, where he routed them completely, without the loss of a man; he retreated immediately six miles to Naas, and suffered the rebels to take possession of the town of Kildare and of Kilcullen, where they broke down the bridge over the Liffey, and thus cut off all communications between the province of Munster and Dublin. On Saturday last a deputation from the principal rebel camp, consisting of 3,000 men, waited on Mr Dundas, at Nass, with a proposition in writing. I have not seen it, but the import was 'that the rebels had taken up arms for the redress of their wrongs, to which they were fully competent; however, they were willing to forgive and forget what had passed, and to lay down their arms. on condition of indemnity to them and their friends, but especially on condition that Lord Edward Fitzgerald and their other leaders who are now in custody, were immediately set at liberty.'

You will scarcely credit me in stating that Mr. Dundas, at the head of 1,500 men, who were with difficulty kept back by their officers, and with a sufficient train of artillery, sent up this defiance to Lord Camden, with a recommendation to yield to it. Lord Camden immediately sent an aide-de-camp to him with orders not to accept of any terms short of unconditional submission by the rebels, and the surrender of their leaders to be punished as they deserve. The aide-de-camp, Colonel (Horatio) Walpole, opened up a new negotiation with the rebels, and came up to town on Sunday with the result, for the approbation of Lord Camden; and on the evening of Sunday, General Lake went down to Naas to attack the rebel camp immediately, unless they surrendered at discretion. But, on his arrival at Naas, he found that Mr Dundas had agreed to an armistice, and had solemnly engaged not to march against the rebels till 2 o'clock the next day (Monday).

Clare, Dublin., to Auckland, 3 September 1798: I send you two copies of our report, and will by the post tomorrow send you some more. You will agree with me that it ought to be put into general circulation in England.

I took the hint which you gave me, and moved an address of the House of Lords to the Lord-Lieutenant to lay it before the King; and the Commons have followed our example. The examinations of the leading traitors are also much more full in our appendix than in that of the Commons, which has been, of course, sent to you. I would send a copy of our report directly to Mr Pitt, but I know that one of those which I send you will immediately find its way to him. I do not see a chance of adjourning our parliament for more than a week to come. We must allow more than a fortnight for the return of bills before a prorogation, so that I have no possible chance of being allowed to quit Ireland before the latter end of this month or the beginning of the next.

If Pitt wishes I should then go over the England, he knows that I shall be at his command. The bill of attainder against Lord Edward Fitzgerald, after a most peevish and vexatious opposition, very much fomented by Lord Yelverton, in the Commons, has at length been sent up to us. It passed the committee this day, and his Lordship has announced his intention of opposing it on the report tomorrow. As I may probably very soon see you, I shall not say any more on the subject.

What a country this is, that can be thrown into confusion by a force not exceeding at most fifteen hundred men, who have been thrown upon our coasts! Nothing can be more disgraceful and alarming than the conduct of two militia regiments who were opposed to them at Castlebar. If these villains had stood their ground but ten minutes, the enemy would have been repulsed, as our artillery (all Irish) was most admirably served, and had made sensible impression on the French line. Lord Cornwallis has marched a very great force against them and if they wait for him, means to attack them tomorrow morning.

Our last accounts are that they had not advanced beyond Castlebar, and, as our force exceeds 10,000 men, a great proportion of them British, there cannot be a doubt of the event, whenever Lord Cornwallis comes up with the enemy. I fear that the natives have flocked in crowds to the French standard. However, we have no symptoms of insurrection in any other district, and I understand that the savages who have joined the enemy are already sick of the experiment, as some of them have already been flogged, and some more hanged, by the French officers, who are equally sick of the Irish auxiliaries.

The explanation which you seek of the manuscript copy of the confessions by O'Connor and Company, you will find, I hope, very ample in our report and the appendix for it. Our bill for preventing the return of these villains into the King's dominions is so framed as to leave it very much to the conditions of their pardon, to be hereafter settled by the crown, to secure the Empire against it, If they shall violate the conditions of their pardon, they stand attainted; and much caution will be necessary hereafter in arranging this subject.

From *A Volley of Execrations, the Letter of Papers of John FitzGibbon, Earl of Clare*, Irish Manuscripts Commission, 2005.

BOB RYAN

The Orphans

MENTION had been made in these annals of the monthly collection in aid of the Sick Poor and towards the support of the Young Women in the House of Mercy. At this period it was carried on by two orphan children – inmates of the House of Mercy – they were dressed alike with little bonnets, etc. and each morning were provided with a list of places at which to call. The contributors were numerous for the population was then large; one child had a box made of tin, locked with an opening in it to admit the money to slip into it – suspended round her neck inside her outer covering. The other had a basket on her arm, in which there were books in which the donors inscribed their names and the amount given by each. The money bought back should thus correspond with the entries. It was amusing to listen to the accuracy which these little ones would tell the sister in charge who were the persons – the previous day – who told them to call again when they had change, etc.

Being so young and intelligent, their whole appearance was calculated to excite benevolence and sympathy in the hearts of those to whom they appealed, but to guard against their acquiring unprincipled habits, they were strictly prohibited to partake of anything offered to themselves when out collecting. They had also to observe silence in the street, unless it was merely useful and necessary. Though there might be grown children the smaller ones were mostly selected as companions, and looked most interesting. When a new child had to be trained into the duty, she on whom it devolved did so with as much precision as possible, and would be very sensitive if any deviation from their usual practice happened while out, which might show to Seculars a little covetous trait in the newly initiated.

From *Annals Sisters of Mercy*, Limerick, 1842.

More wretched than any other town
Bob Ryan

IN 1840 Limerick Corporation sent a petition to the parliament at Westminster stating that it had been the opinion of many notable visitors to the city, who included Thackery, Ingles and Kohl, that: 'There were more wretched men among the poor of Limerick than in any town of equal population in Ireland and that this was due mainly to a lack of regular employment.' It is also interesting to note that the Commission that conducted the national Poor Inquiry of 1835 estimated that 9,500 people in Limerick lived in pauperism. It was common to find six or even ten families crammed into one house.

HISTORY

Rev. O'Grady in his report to the Poor Inquiry wrote:

'I have seen whole families with no other covering than an old broken blanket and a torn rush mat to lie on, and the children perfectly naked – the rain coming in though the roof, not a spark of fire, nor any article of food in the room. The windows were without glass and the wind kept out by an old mat – every indication of the most abject poverty. The smell and filth is so shocking that I think not only a human being but a pig could not endure it.'

During the height of the famine, seventy-two deaths were recorded in Limerick in the week ending 20th March, 1847, and by April an average of 15 deaths per day were being recorded. One of the saddest scenes witnessed in Limerick during the famine occurred on St. Patrick's Day, 1847, in Rutland Street, and the tragic event was described in the Limerick Reporter on the following day:

'Opposite the Town Hall was stretched a dead child, a little girl of about ten or eleven years of age upon a little straw, thus being waked in the open street, while on the body lay a plate for the purpose of collecting pence to purchase a coffin, and the unfortunate father stood by with famine depicted all over his face in characters that told the spectator that he should soon follow the child. At the desire of Mr. E. Costelloe, the body was removed to a shed at the rear of the Town Hall. A coffin was afterwards supplied by the Mayor.'

The Society of St. Vincent de Paul came to Limerick in November, 1846, during this, one of the most traumatic periods in Irish History: the Great Famine, which began in 1845 and lasted until 1849. The members were faced with an enormous challenge. The winter of 1846-47 was very severe, and the famine was about to enter a critical phase. The members applied themselves as best they could to relieving the poor and destitute, performing great works of charity as did other charitable organisations. £215 was raised by the Society from a bazaar held in the Philosophical Building in Glentworth Street. This was a substantial amount of money and reflects the generosity of the local citizens. The members of the Society gave aid to any poor families in distress, and fulfilled a critical need especially for those who were not entitled to government relief.

From *The History of the St. Vincent de Paul Society in Limerick*, 1846-1996.

Published by the Society of St Vincent de Paul, Mid -West Region, 1996.

Some City and Liberty Place-names
Gearóid MacSpealáin, M.A. (F. G. Spencer)
(a condensed version)

Annacotty: The Ford of the Little Boat.

Ballinacurra: The first part was known as Béal Átha; the second part Ballynagalleagh (otherwise Farrannagallagh, now Rosbrien) in the south of Curry. Curry is An Currach, the marshland (adjoining Catholic Institute Athletic Grounds). Thus we get the full name Béal Áth an Curraigh.

Ballyclough: Baile na Cloiche, the place of the castle.

Ballykeefe: Baile Ui Chaoimh, O'Keeffe's Place.

Ballynantymore (Beg), Baile Uí Neachtain Mór (Beag), ONeachtain's land.

Ballysimon: Béal Áth Síomoinn.

Black Boy: An Bealach Buidhe, the yellow road. From the turnpike arose the name Black Boy Pike.

Boherbuoy is another yellow road in the city: an Bóthar Buidhe – part of the Pilgrims' Road to Mungret in the Middle Ages.

Ballysheedy: Baile Shioda, the land of the branch of the MacNamaras with whom Sioda was a favourite Christian name.

Caherdavin: Several versions including Caherdavy, Caherdavyne, and Caherdavine, impossible to say with any degree of certainty what the Irish name was.

Castletroy: Caladh Uí Throighthigh. Caladh could be a ferry or riverside meadow, Troy was O Troighthigh. The castle was erected by Dermot O'Brien in the reign of Henry VIII.

Clarina: Clár Aidhne: The ffoorde of Clare Iny.

Claughaun: An Clóghan. See Killalee.

Clondrinagh: an Chluain Draighneach, the meadow full of sloe bushes.

Clonlong: Cluain an Longaigh, Long's meadow-land.

Conigar: Coinigéar, a place of rabbits.

Coonagh: Cuanach, a place indented with inlets.

Corbally: An Corrbhaile. May owe its name to the fact that it stretches away from its neighbours into the bend of the Shannon.

Corkanree: The King's Corkis.

Curraghower: Cora Chobhair, water weir.

Derryknockane: Cailseán Doire, the castle of Derryknockane.

Dooradoyle: Túr an Daill or Blind Man's Tower, or the Blind Man's Bleach Green.

Farranshone: Farrann Seoin, John's land.

Friarstown: Baile na Mbráthar. An old Franciacan monastery stood here, the ruined church of which can still be seen.

Gallows Green: the Gallows were situated about the site of the present Good Shepherd Convent.

Garryowen is Garrdha Eoin, not Owen's Garden, as Joyce and others have it, but rather St. John's Garden, the garth or precinct of St. John's old church, which occupied the site of the present Protestant church.

Gouldavoher, the V-shaped patch between Patrickswell and Mungret roads, is Gabhal Dá Bhóthar, the fork of the two roads.

Greenhills: Cnoc na Bualie Glaise, the hill of the green 'booley' or milking field.

Illaunaroan: Oileán na Rón, the island of the seals.

Killalee: Cill Fheidhlimidh: Killalee adjoins An Clochán (Claughaun, the ford of stepping stones) and the causeway was also the church ford or the ford of Feilim.

Killeely: Cill Liadhaine: The Church of Lelia.

Kilmurry: Kylmohorok or Kilmehurroc. The Munster saint, Mochuarog, is believed to have been its first patron. The later name, Kilmurry, evidently came into into use after the church had been dedicated to St. Mary Magdalen, c. 1440.

King's Island: has been identified with Inis Siobhtan. The king who first claimed it as his own was the English King John.

Knockea: Mullach Chae, Cae's Height. It was here St. Patrick met the youth Nessan for whom he founded the church of Mungret.

Lax Weir: a name of Danish origin, meaning salmon weir, known to the Irish as Cora na mBradán. The old ruined Weir Castle is Cashlanenacorran, Cailsean na Corann.

Lemonfield is a corruption of the Irish Leim na Fhiadh, the deer's leap.

Liberties: From such examples of sanctuary (on church estates) all lands that gave shelter or protection took the name of termon lands, as, for instance, the Liberties of Limerick. So, Tearmann Chathair Luimnigh.

From *North Munster Antiquarian Journal*, Spring, 1942.

Hell is an emigrant ship
Eitienne Ryan

STEPHEN de Vere, a brother of the poet Audrey, in 1847 bravely decided to join an emigrant ship to America in order to highlight the desperate conditions then pertaining on board. His damning report was read out in the Commons afterwards. The following are some excerpts from the report:

'The fearful state of disease and debility in which the Irish emigrants have reached Canada, must undoubtedly be attributed in a great degree to the destitution and consequent sickness prevailing in Ireland; but has been much aggravated by the neglect of cleanliness, ventilation, and a generally good state of social economy during the passage, and has afterwards been increased and disseminated throughout the whole country by the mal-arrangements of the Government system of emigrant relief. Having myself submitted to the privation of a steerage passage in an emigrant ship for nearly two months, in order to make myself acquainted with the condition of the emigrant from the beginning, I can state from experience that the present regulations for ensuring health and comparative comfort to passengers are wholly insufficient.

'Before the emigrant has been at sea a week, he is an altered man. How can it be otherwise? Hundreds of poor people, men, women and children, of all ages from the drivelling idiot of 90 to the babe just born, huddled together, without light, without air, wallowing in filth and breathing a fetid atmosphere, sick in body, dispirited in heart; the fevered patients lying between the sound, in sleeping places so narrow as almost to deny them the power of indulging, by a change of position, the natural restlessness of the disease; by their agonized ravings disturbing those around and pre-disposing them, through the effects of the imagination, to imbibe the contagion; living without food or medicine except as administered by the hand of casual charity; dying without the voice of spiritual consolation and buried in the deep without the rites of the Church.

'The food is generally ill-selected and seldom sufficiently cooked, in consequence of the insufficiency and bad construction of the cooking places. The supply of water, hardly enough for cooking and drinking, does not allow washing. In many ships the filthy beds, teeming with all abominations, are never required to be brought on deck and aired: the narrow space between the sleeping berths and the piles of boxes is never washed or scraped, but breathes up a damp and fetid stench, until the day before arrival at quarantine, when all hands are required to 'scrub up' and put on a fair face for the doctor and Government inspector. No moral restraint is attempted; the voice of prayer is never heard; drunkeness, with its consequent train of ruffianly debasement, is not discouraged, because it is profitable to the captain, who traffics in the grog.

'In the ship which brought me out from London last April, the passengers were found in provisions by the owners according to a contract, and a furnished scale of dietary. The meat was of the worst quality. The supply of water shipped on board was abundant, but the quantity served out to the passengers was so scanty that they were frequently obliged to throw overboard their salt provisions and rice (a most important article of their food) because they had not water enough both for the necessary cooking and the satisfying of their raging thirst afterwards. They could only afford water for washing by withdrawing it from the cooking of their food.

'I have known persons to remain for days together in their dark close berths, because they thus suffered less from hunger, though compelled at the same time, by want of water to heave overboard their salt provisions and rice. No cleanliness was enforced; the beds never aired; the master during the whole voyage never entered the steerage, and would listen to no complaints; the dietary contracted for was, with some exceptions, nominally supplied, though at irregular periods; but false measures were used (in which the water and several articles of dry food were served), the gallon measure containing but three quarts, which fact I proved in Quebec, and had the captain fined for; once or twice a week, ardent spirits were sold indiscriminately to the passengers, producing scenes of unchecked blackguardism beyond description; and lights were prohibited, because the ship, with her open fire-grates upon deck, with lucifer matches and lighted pipes used secretly in the sleeping berths, was freighted with Government powder for the garrison of Quebec.

'The case of this ship was not one of peculiar misconduct, on the contrary, I have the strongest reason to know from information which I have received from very many emigrants well-known to me who came over this year in different vessels, that this ship was better regulated and more comfortable than many that reached Canada.

'Some of these evils might be prevented by a more careful inspection of the ship and her stores, before leaving port; but the provisions of the Passenger Act are insufficient to procure cleanliness and ventilation, and the machinery of the emigration agencies at the landing ports is insufficient to enforce those provisions and to detect frauds. It is true that a clerk sometimes comes on board at the ship's arrival in port: questions the captain or mate, and ends by asking whether any passenger means to make a complaint; but this is a mere farce, for the captain takes care to 'keep away the crowd from the gentleman'. Even were all to hear the question, few would venture to commence a prosecution; ignorant, friendless, pennyless, disheartened, and anxious to proceed to the place of their ultimate destination ....

Stephen de Vere had much more to relate of the difficulties of the emigrants in Canada but it is important to consider what effect his letter had on the Atlantic traffic. Dr. McDonagh has no doubt that the Commissioners took serious note of Stephen de Vere's letter and considers that it was an important source for new legislation. He writes: 'This was the first occasion on which an educated observer had made the Atlantic voyage between-decks, and described exactly what he saw. The letter made a profound impression on the commissioners. It is scarcely too much to regard it as the basis of most of their future legislation for ship life. Attempts were soon made sooner or later to achieve every one of de Vere's projected reforms except for the provision of chaplains, and even this subject was to some extent explored.

What sort of a man was Stephen de Vere? Wilfrid Ward who wrote a Memoir of Aubrey de Vere, mentions him on page 183: 'Aubrey's elder brother Stephen had joined the Roman Catholic Church not long after his father's death. The change-over was not due primarily to intellectual causes. He was dissatisfied with the Church of his birth. He was deeply impressed by the goodness of the Irish Catholic peasantry to whom he devoted his life.'

Ward also quotes a note by Aubrey on his brother as follows: 'From his early youth Stephen's life has been one of labour for Ireland. He has saved sons of hers from the gallows - laboured in their schools - abstained from wine for twenty years that he might encourage temperance among the poor, brought dying men into his house that they might have more comfort in death, pleaded their cause in public and private life, and during thirty years, he has reduced the rental of the property by about a fourth below what would have been considered the fair value. You know about his going to America as a steerage passenger that he might speak as a witness respecting the suffering of emigrants. He has always been a Liberal as he is now: and (unlike me) he approved of Gladstone's recent Land Act, having himself recommended nearly the same thing to the Government in 1870.'

One must surely conclude from these facts that Stephen de Vere was a brave and good man, and one whose memory should not be forgotten in County Limerick.

From *North Munster Studies*, Thomond Archaeological Society, 1967.

MacAdam the Traitor
Maurice Lenihan

TRADITION states the ford or pass through which the Williamite Army crossed over to the Clare side of the river in the 1690 Siege was betrayed by one MacAdam, who is said to have lived by fishing on the Shannon, and that his knowledge of the fords of the river was consequently very good. As the army approached, a block and hatchet and a keg of gold were placed outside the door of the betrayer. The rich lands adjoining were pointed out to him. He was asked which he selected – the gold and the lands, or the hatchet and death. The tradition goes on to say that as he had already determined, he at once proceeded to point out to the enquirers the only place in that apportion of the river which they could pass in the manner they desired.

A rock was near the river bank, some few perches above the old churchyard of Kilquane, and to this rock, ever since called Carrig-a-Clouragh, or Chain-rock, were attached chains which are said to have crossed the river from Corbally, nearly opposite Corbally House on the Limerick side. A bridge of boats, or a pontoon bridge, was thus constructed by the engineers. The rock appears to have been cut umbrella-like, or of mushroom shape, in order the more securely to hold the chains. For many years, it was an object of singular curiosity: men of science, archaeologists, historians, enquirers, and patriots from all parts of Europe were in the habit of visiting it in the course of their tours of Limerick; there were shallow holes in the top of the rock and when rain fell, the holes, thus filled with water, appeared as if saturated with blood, the stone being of a reddish colour. About twenty years ago Captain Hamilton Jackson, the then proprietor of this land, ordered a servant, Connell, to blast the rock, but the act was but partly accomplished, and Carrig-a-Clouragh yet remains to fix the spot where William made his successful passage. Townsfolk for a long period, and up to the last few years, were in the habit of going out to Kilquane on Sundays and heaping every indignity on the grave of the alleged traitor. A couplet was also cut on the tombstone, and, as a specimen of the spirit of the poet and of the times, it deserves to be recorded:

Here lies the body of Phillip the Traitor,
Lived a fisherman and died a deceiver.

It is but justice to state that the highly respectable family of MacAdam, of Blackwater House, near the scene of the pass, utterly deny the truth of this tradition, which, as an impartial historian, I am bound to give. Major Thomas MacAdam,. JP,

HISTORY

of Blackwater House, has shown the author documents which go to establish the fact that his ancestors were in possession of land which they now have, some years before the events here detailed; that they rented them from the Earl of Thomond, and that they did not obtain them by any act of treachery.

From *Limerick, its History and Antiquities*, Hodges, Smith & Co., 1866.

SIX
THE COUNTY

The Dog Hoaxes of West Limerick

A CORRESPONDNENT writes: There was very little new to be discerned in the latest idea of the mysterious West Limerick hoaxer who got the local bellman to announce on Sunday last, to all whom it may concern, that Mr. B, some well-known Cross-Channel buyer of greyhounds, would attend Abbeyfeale Market on Monday to buy all sorts and breeds of greyhounds.

It was not an original idea, because a similar announcement was made at Newcastle West some time during the Boer War, when mules and donkeys having been sent to the Velt as invulnerables against the "Rinderpast", there was every reason to believe that dogs would come in there handy too. So when the day dawned on the day appointed by the announcement hundreds of dogs voicing their protests against such unreasonable travelling, assisted the traders of the old town of the "Templars" to rise from their beds a great deal earlier than was comfortable. It is on record, however, that shop assistants found many a window guard serving a new purpose that morning, holding a new sort of livestock, to which their cattle fairs had previously been strangers. Numerous dogs, of low and no degree, were whiling away the early hours of the morning barking for a purchaser, but there appeared to be nothing doing.

Later things became more active in the queues, and some whirling contests developed. These were generally of the one-round species, which made a ring of some of the shop counters and sometimes wound up inside them, where the shop assistants appeared to referee with a pike instead of a sponge.

When, as no buyers turned up, and it became obvious later in the day that the whole thing was a hoax, the most amusing situations arose. Most of the would-be sellers retired to licensed premises to console themselves while little boys busied themselves tying saucepans and other such utensils to the dogs' tails, so that towards the evening almost every public-house in the town was in a state of pandemonium from the leashed canines struggling and snarling and fighting each other. Many of the poor dogs got a watery grave on their way home that evening but their fate was mild by comparison to which the practical joker would be subjected were he found by those whom he had duped.

It was not until time was stealing its way into the afternoon of that memorable day, as we learned at the time, and no dog jobber had put in an appearance, that the weary owners, who were part responsible for the greatest concentration of undesirable curs and mongrels in the history of West Limerick, laid their plans for as dignified a retreat from the "Dog Fair" as was possible under the circumstances. Retreats are usually difficult affairs. Hannibal, Alexander and Napoleon conducted a few of them with more or less success in their days, but it would be interesting to know how any of the trio would have extricated his dignity under similar circumstances to those that faced the innocent canine vendors at Abbeyfeale or Newcastle West.

One would have thought the news of the hoax would have reached Abbeyfeale, and that the dog owners there in later years would have been on their guard. But no. Humbugging smiles and comments raked the retreat of the victims of the heartless joke as they struggled homewards. At the latest fair, one such victim innocently admitted that he did not mind so much "coming in"; it was the going out that was killing him.

The retreat from Abbeyfeale was only a repetition of Newcastle West. Like seasoned Generals, some of the would-be sellers withdrew under cover of the night. Others departed as the shadows were lengthening, leaving some old friends of theirs behind. One or two of the latter still tugged at the ropes that held them to the window guards of the pub, from which their owners were last seen to depart.

It was a cruel sort of joke all round, not so much for the greyhound, which is still worth at least the licence money, but for many days subsequent to the Abbeyfeale Fair, hungry dogs ranging the plains, neglected and unclaimed. It may be assumed, however, that Dog Fairs are a dead institution in West Limerick for at least another generation.

From *Limerick Leader*, April 4, 1931.

A Glenstal Boyhood
Fitzwilliam Barrington

'WELL, Master Croker, this was the way of it. The coachman, Mr. Whelan, was driving the pony and trap by Cappernuke bog one winter night and heard a baby crying under a clump of heather. So he just put you into the trap and brought you up to the castle.'

This was the answer to a child's question given by one of the staff.

The real event had already taken place in November, 1909, and although I was christened Alexander Fitzwilliam Croker, the last was the family name most familiar to the local people during my early days. My parents always called me 'Fitz,' and only Fitzwilliam, full out, if I was being reproved for bad behaviour.

My brother, Charles, had always been known as 'Pat,' since the Limerick horse, Ardpatrick, won the derby on the day he was born.

I was an afterthought in the family, my sister, Winifred, being eleven years older, and my brother seven years older than myself. So I was to some extent left without playmates, since the age gaps tend to become exaggerated at that early stage.

In those days, there was a large indoor staff at Glenstal, consisting of butler, footman, odd-job man, cook/housekeeper, housemaids, nanny, nursery-maid, my mother's lady's maid, and the laundry maids, which made up a total of twelve. The most unenviable job was that of the junior kitchen – or scullery maid – who had to be up around six o'clock in the morning to get the bathwater hot.

The cook/housekeeper, the lady's maid and the butler took their meals in the housekeepers' room, and the others in the servants' hall. Nursery meals were sent up on a tray.

Outside in the stable yard were the coachman, who looked after the horses, and the chauffeur, who also ran and maintained the electric light engine.

In the garden there were Mr. MacBean, the head gardener, who had his house close by, and about nine other men, who came up from Murroe. This staff not only tended the gardens and glasshouses, but also the ornamental paths and shrub plantings etc. around the inner part of the estate.

The gardens were laid out in an Italian terraced style, said to be the earliest of this kind in Ireland. I well remember that daily, at twelve noon and six, in the evening, when the Angelus rang in Murroe, all the men took off their hats and said a prayer. The gardens supplied flowers, fruit, vegetables and honey for the house, and every evening a bunch of cut flowers and ferns were sent up to decorate the dinner table.

Mr. Gow was the steward at the home farm, about a mile from the house, where he lived with his family. The milk, cream, eggs and other supplies were sent up every morning to the Castle, whilst the main bulk of the milk went to the creamery at Abington. Mrs. Gow was an expert cook of Scottish scones and cakes, so I greatly looked forward to being invited to tea, when there was always a lavish spread of good things.

My father was a keen sportsman, and on the estate there was good shooting of woodcock, pheasant, duck and snipe. Mr. Verrant, the keeper, had several foresters who worked under him. The pheasant population was maintained by rearing the chicks under a turkey, before they were released into the wild.

In the earlier days, there were large shooting parties, with some guests staying in the house. With the advance of World War I, these were less frequent, and were finally discontinued in the early 1920s when sporting guns were prohibited.

My mother was also a good shot, as well as being a keen fisherwoman. There were several lakes in the park at Glenstal, which were well stocked with trout, and there was good trout fishing also in the river up at Vancluse. The mayfly season on Lough Derg was an important seasonal event.

Prior to 1914, my parents took a grouse moor and fishing in Scotland for August and September. In subsequent years, we all went to a house near Moyard in Co. Galway where there was good sea and lough fishing.

During the Great War years, we took in a Belgian refugee family, who occupied a spare cottage in the grounds. The husband, a hard worker, was employed in the gardens, and the children attended school in Murroe. We used visit them every Sunday afternoon, taking supplies of tasty extras, etc. When the time came for their repatriation, many tears were shed. They took back a lasting memory of Ireland, as Monsignor Dwan in Murroe christened their younger son Charles Albert Patrick.

In nursery days, I was brought down to the dining room at breakfast time by my nanny and sat down beside my mother to be taught to read and write. After the lesson had finished, I was allowed to draw trains in the exercise book, except on Sundays when only churches were permitted. My father taught me Latin tags, which I had to recite parrot-wise for the amusement of any guests who reckoned I must be rather a bright child.

After breakfast, I was returned to the nursery and did not see my parents again until I was brought down to the drawing-room in the evening at six o'clock. Then my mother might read stories to me, or often we sang songs at the piano, but on

Sundays only bible stories and hymns were allowed.

On Sunday mornings, any tenants, or others, wishing to consult my father would come to the stable yard to state their problems. After that, we drove down to morning service at Abington in a horse-drawn covered waggonette. When this was required to come to the hall door, my father blew on a bugle; this signal also applied when a motor car was needed to take us to Limerick or elsewhere.

In those days, there was no television so we made our own entertainment: playing cards or other paper games and listening to the gramophone. I was very attached also to my clockwork model railway. Sometimes I was able to go to the staff quarters to dance 'sets' and reels to accordion accompaniment.

In late spring, I was sometimes sent with my nurse to a hotel at Lahinch for some sea air. This meant the excitement of travelling on the West Clare Railway, immortalised by Perch French.

On the subject of acoustic gramophones, a relation of my mother's – who had invented the turbine engine – gave us a machine which somehow amplified sound under air pressure produced by an electric motor; it had a copper horn six foot in length, and when Caruso records were played out through the window, the sound could be heard two miles away.

On Christmas Eve there was the annual 'giving out of the meat.' A suitable animal had been killed and butchered at the home farm, so the beef came up to the Castle in easily divisible form. The family assembled at 6 p.m. in the gun-room and my father, assisted by help from the home farm, presided at a big table to divide up the meat. All the estate tenants waited their turn outside in the yard and my father called their names which were relayed by a linkman at the door. They were then asked 'how many are you?' and a suitable joint of beef was accordingly handed over. Then came thanks and Christmas greetings to my parents and the family as each recipient took his leave.

When my sister was twenty-one, there was a ball in the house. At the supper table I was offered 'tipsy cake.' As a ten year old, not being used to strong drink, I got quite a shock and have never cared for trifle laced with wine ever since!

Out in the park there were deer, red, fallow and japs; as a small child I remember two emus, as well as swans on the lakes. My father was very keen on golf, and there was a nine hole course laid out in the park, whilst on the lawn, up at the house, he practiced shots with a woollen ball, fashioned with a crochet hook.

Saturday was the day for motoring ten miles to the shops in Limerick. It was a slow journey as the Ballyarra road was in poor state in those days. The first visit would be to Mr. Woodhouse the grocer, then to Mr. O'Malley the butcher, and then probably on to Todd's department store. After that, my father retired to the County Club and my mother to the Ladies Club – in Bedford Row I think – to play bridge. I was sent off with nanny to Miss Smith's tea room, and in later years occasionally to the Coliseum or Gaiety cinemas.

I very much wanted to see a silent film, the *Four Horsemen of the Apocalypse*, but sadly it could not be shown, as a permit to obtain the explosive sound effects would not be granted.

The first time I went to a theatre was to the pantomime *Cinderella* at the old

Theatre Royal. There were some catchy songs and local riddles like 'Why did Barrington Pier'? – 'To Cedar View,' and 'Why was Bunratty?' - 'Because Cratloe Wood looked down on her.'

In 1915, my father, aged sixty-seven, went off to drive an ambulance in France. He carried the rank of a colonel in the Limerick Militia.

When I was seven years old, the nanny was replaced by a governess, who extended my education to French, geography, arithmetic, history and so on. When I was nine and half, I was sent away to board at a preparatory school, Castle Park, at Dalkey, Co. Dublin, where my education was extended further to take in Latin, geometry and algebra. There was also team games like, soccer, rugger, hockey and croquet.

Great was the excitement on coming home for the holidays by the 9.15 a.m. train from the then Kingsbridge Station in Dublin; after that, a change at Limerick Junction and on to Boher Station where I would be met by the coachman. At Abington, there was always a friendly stop at Mr. Power's bar, where I was regaled with lemonade and the coachman with porter. My mother could never make out why the drive up from the station took so long!

When I was eleven my sister died; it was very sad for me as we were just beginning to become friends. Leave, to come home for the funeral, was not requested either for my brother at Eton College or myself at Castle Park. My parents believed it would be too upsetting for us.

In 1922 the country became very unsettled, and we received columns of 'visitors', both regular and irregular. They all behaved correctly and I found them all friendly. At that time, we were all advised to sleep with our bags packed in case of an emergency, but my luggage only consisted of my stamp album, my precious model trains being too big.

By autumn, 1923, I was approaching fourteen and the time came to go to a public school in England: Shrewsbury School had previously been selected being easily accessible from Ireland. However, by the Christmas holidays of 1923, my parents had already started to move to England, and I was to spend only one more school holidays at home in the summer of 1924. Thereafter I did not see Glenstal again until 1939.

From *The Old Limerick Journal*, Barringtons Edition, 1988.

Angling in Castleconnell
Kevin Hannan

WOULD the castle and the spa have been enough to make the name of Castleconell an enduring household word if its salmon and trout fishing was not the most sought after all over Europe? I think not. Every Waltonian's dream of paradise was surely Castleconnell.

Up to the completion of the Shannon hydro-electric scheme, salmon catches were touching on the phenomenal, both in quantity and size of fish. 'Big water – big fish', a rule well known to every angler, was borne out here. The stories of giant salmon, some taken, and others (the bigger ones of course) 'lost at the gaff' mostly represent tales of the imagination. The farther back one goes in search of records of outstanding catches, the more fantastic the results. An ancient document, the *Cronicon Scotorum*, sets out details of a rare monster: "A salmon was caught in Luimneac this year (1109) which was twelve feet in length, twelve hands in breadth, without being spilt open; and the length of its neck fin was three hands and two fingers.' This story illustrates the angler's gift of being able to see his catch gain enormous weight after it is hooked and landed.

On the realistic side, however, there are many well authenticated records of giant salmon of more than 50lbs. taken in the river between Castleconnell and the head of the estuary at Limerick city. A 54 pounder caught by John Milburn at Castleconnell in 1903 remains the record rod-caught salmon for the Shannon. This fine fish was just three pounds short of the Irish record, one of 57 lbs. taken in the River Suir by a Mr Maher in 1874. In April, 1879, the *Limerick Chronicle* records:

'The finest fish both in contour and quality, which perhaps has ever been taken from the prolific waters of the Shannon, was exhibited yesterday at the stall of Mrs. Lyons of Bedford Row. This lordly salmon weighed 53 lbs. and was caught by an angler of piscatorial notoriety.' The no-punches pulled description of the angler suggest one of those colourful characters who was known to every generation of anglers as a poacher, and one who would snatch a fish whenever the opportunity presented itself. At the time, this was one of the heaviest salmon taken in the British Isles, and it seems extraordinary that it should end up on a fish-monger's slab in Bedford Row.

All through the last century and well into the present one, great salmon have been taken here; its popularity was universal. Millionaires trod the banks and delighted in the splendid scenery; they fished in the sparkling pools, drank ale and whiskey in the friendly taverns and found solace in the old-world atmosphere of the village. Needless to mention, the wealthy visitors were a boon to the local people, almost all of whom enjoyed a reasonable standard of living at a time when other less favourable placed communities were only struggling along.

Experienced gillies, with their expertise and local knowledge of the fisheries, were indispensable; every visiting angler had to have one; it was a badge of respectability and to venture onto to the river bank without one was unthinkable.

Some gillies were employed to fish commercially by fishery owners and lessees, as can be noted from the many press reports of catches made in this manner. A snippet from the *Limerick Chronicle* of May, 1913, tells us that . . . 'the men employed by Mr Wm Enright, at the Newgarden Fishery, took several fine salmon of up to 40 lbs. in weight. These were on display by a Limerick fishmonger.' Hundreds of such news items appeared from time to time in our local papers and helped to enhance the reputation of Castleconnell among those had no other contact with the place.

Up to the decline of fishery, which started in the early 1930's, hardly a week passed without reports of outstanding catches. A report of March, 1879, goes on:

'Some fine salmon have been landed this week on the Castleconnell waters. On Tuesday, 11th Inst., Capt. F. C. Lester Kay (Queen's Bays, now quartered in Dublin), accompanied by Mr. M. J. Byrne, County Inspector RIC, Galway District, attended by the redoubtable Patsy Hickey and Maurice Johnson, fished on the preserve of Mr. E. J. Ingham with much success; Capt. Kay, having killed two to his rod, took salmon weighing 37 lbs. and 19 lbs. Capt. H. B. Rhodes, who holds the Newgarden salmon fishery, caught two salmon of 13 and 30 lbs. The fishermen, Hickey and Bourke, on the Erinas or World's End fisheries caught two salmon of 25 and 30 lbs. the fishermen, Enright and Dwyer on the Landscape Salmon rod fishery, on the 24th inst., landed one beauty of 37 lbs., and Capt. Vansittart, 3 salmon at the Hermitage. Mr Henry Hodges arrived on Wednesday afternoon at his usual fishing quarters, the Shannon Hotel. Several other English gentlemen are expected next week.

The social cleavage that existed in those days between the gillies and the privileged sportsmen they assisted is clearly evident in this report. It is notable that Johnson, Hickey and Dwyer are given no title whatsoever, while even those 'expected' from England are referred to as 'gentlemen.'

From Limerick: *Historical Reflections*, Oireacht Publications, 1996.

Pigkilling
Michael Hartnett

Like a knife cutting a knife
his last plea for life
echoes joyfully in Camas.
An egg floats like a navel
in the pickling-barrel:
before he sinks,
his smiling head
sees a delicate girl
up to her elbows
in a tub of blood
while the avalanche
of his offal steams
among the snapping dogs
and mud
and porksteaks
coil in basins
like bright snakes
and buckets of boiling water hiss
to soften his bristles
for the blade.

I kick his golden bladder
in the air.
It lands like a moon
among the damsons.
Like a knife cutting a knife
his last plea for life
echoes joyfully in Camas.

From *A Farewell to English*, 1975 Gallery Books, 19 Oakdown Road, Dublin 14.

Men of Annaholty: their measure taken
Denis O'Shaughnessy

FOR generations, the men of Annaholty were privileged drinkers, cocking a snoop at their fellow imbibers in nearby Castleconnell. Living three miles outside the village gave them drinking privileges afforded to travellers only, bona-fide's they were called and this happy state of affairs lasted many years until the fateful afternoon of Sunday, October 7th, 1951. Guard Flanagan, stationed locally, decided to pay a visit to Winifred Fitzgerald's pub in the village to make sure that the law was being complied with and that no wayward drinking was taking place. It was 4.45 pm, a quarter of an hour before the pub was legally due to open, and to his amazement the front door was open. He immediately decided to raid the pub, which was then the term used for Gardai entering pubs suspected of serving outside the allotted hours.

In the court case that followed, (reported in the *Limerick Leader*) Guard Flanagan said he found five men drinking in the bar and a sixth escaped through the back-door but he (Guard Flanagan) followed him and brought him back. 'I only came in for a box of matches' claimed the one who had made the aborted dash for freedom. Guard Flanagan then began to take names. The men from Annaholty, in number four, smiled benignly. 'Bona-fide men Guard, pass on,' they said.

Guard Flanagan, obviously a highly conscious upholder of the law, and possibly piqued at finding nearly all of the apprehendees bona-fide, decided to test the Annaholty men's claims for immunity.

Soon afterwards, armed with his measuring tape, he set off on his bicycle and measured the distance from the men's homes to Fitzgerald's and triumph was his when all four were found to be inside the three miles limit. It didn't matter that one of them was only a mere 300 yards short of the three miles, being measured at 2 miles, 1,213 yard from the pub, and the rest not much further off the mark either. Not bona-fide. All were charged with breaking the law.

Justice Gleeson was somewhat sympathetic. 'They nearly made it. They were only a few hundred yards short of being bona-fide,' he said.

Replying to a question by Mr. T.E. O'Donnell, solr., Guard Flanagan said the sensible way for anybody from Annaholty to cycle or drive to Castleconnell would be Daly's Cross, which would be slightly longer than via the Bog Road: it was the distance over the Bog Road that he measured.

Justice: 'The sensible thing would be to wait at home when the premises are shut legally to them.'

John Kinevane, barman, said all the men told him they were travellers. He thought he was entitled to serve them. The licensee was ill at the time.

Three of the Annaholty four claimed they honestly believed they were bona fide travellers in Mrs. Fitzgerald's Bar. One of them said he had believed this for the past twenty years.

Justice Gleeson: 'Well you know differently now.'

So ended the good times for the Annaholty men and from then on, like their fellow Castleconnell imbibers, they had to meekly leave the village hostelry when the barman gave the time-worn call: 'Time, gentleman, please.'

From *Limerick: 100 Stories of the Century*, 2000.

Burning of Mansions and the Friendly Ghosts of Curragh Chase House
Joan Wynne Jones

ONE of the tragic by-products of the 'Troubles' in this country was undoubtedly the wanton destruction of a number of fine old houses which formed the focal point of large, private estates.

In some instances, it is possible to understand how this happened, as a downtrodden people rose up in anger against those who they saw to be the oppressors.

Unfortunately, they were misguided on two major counts.

First, they did not realise then that they were destroying part of the Irish heritage which had been painstakingly built, even by those thought of as aliens, and much of which would eventually come back to the native Irish.

Secondly, not all landlords were bad, indeed many of them went to some pains to care for those whom they considered to be their responsibility.

Patriarchal the system may have been, but there were many instances of real concern and kindness, not to mention some element of nationalism, among those landlords.

Happily, in the majority of such cases, their concern was rewarded and the fine old houses were spared.

One such house was Curragh Chase which although having been spared one form of destruction, was unhappily to come to grief by fire in 1941.

Its attendant estate, together with the ruined shell, is now in the hands of the nation, to be enjoyed not by the privileged classes of the past, but by all the people.

Not so well known perhaps, as some of the other great houses, and certainly rather smaller, it nevertheless had under its roof some famous personalities and its importance in the historical scheme of things should not be minimised.

Nobody, perhaps, is more qualified to write about it that Joan Wynne-Jones, who lived there as a child and who developed for it a love that I know to be still undimmed....

When as a small child I carried my flickering candle up the winding staircase to bed, I would feel, like the man in 'The Ancient Mariner', that a presence was following me. I would rush into the Green Room where I slept and pile the chaise longue and other furniture against the door. Then I would swiftly bury myself in the depths of the large four poster.

As soon as my head touched the pillow, three sharp knocks would occur against my bedroom door. These were not rats or mice, but distinct imperative knockings. I would sit up and say: 'Come in' and the knocking would stop. This pantomime would be repeated every night several times, as if someone outside was observing my movements in the dark.

On one occasion I also heard most desolate moans and sobbings coming apparently from a blocked-up doorway. Curiously enough, when as an adult I also slept in this room, I never experienced anything, though a visitor, a hard-headed doctor, when sleeping in the same room, woke up one night to see a female figure leaning over him. He packed his bag the next morning and departed with all possible speed.

In the dressing room next door many years earlier a very strange thing happened. A young boy, who with his mother was on a visit, was put to sleep there. He said to his mother one morning, 'A strange little boy came to play with me last night,' and he described the old-fashioned way in which this child had been dressed. 'We played together but he left in the morning.'

The mother said to her son, 'If he comes again tell him that I do not care for you to play with strange children.' The following morning her son said to her, 'I told the other little boy what you said and he looked very sad but went away.' Many years later when alterations were being made to the house, the coffin of a child with a skeleton inside was found underneath the floorboards of this particular dressing room.

The housekeeper in my time remarked how on many occasions from her bedroom right down in the basement she would be awakened by the most fearful noise as if all the coal scuttles and fire irons in the house were being thrown downstairs. When she rushed up there was nothing whatever to be seen or heard. It was remarked by some that this was probably like the sound of knights in armour clattering up and down the stairs.

Another curious phenomenon was that, periodically, all the umbrellas and walking sticks in the hall stand would disappear, and be recovered eventually in a remote corner upstairs.

In spite of these curious happenings there was nothing sinister about the house. There was no feeling of evil or atmosphere of cold such as sometimes occurs in a haunted premises. Rather did there seem to be a pervading ambience and a timeless presence of those who had loved the place in other days.

In the Pleasure Ground in the vicinity of the dwelling certain apparitions were spoken of with bated breath and the locals would not remain there after sunset.

One day when I was a child of about seven years old I was sitting on the little hillocky spot which is still there and which was commonly known as 'Little Heaven'. Behind this spot there was a shady walk which in more class-conscious days had been known as the 'Servants' Walk.' Suddenly before me there appeared a man and woman of short stature and to my youthful eyes fairly old. The man was dressed in which I now realise must have been livery of a dark green material with brass buttons. I cannot remember what the woman wore. I took to my heels and ran but was told by the housekeeper's daughter, 'if you had seen what I saw there, you'd never have gone near the place,' but she did not elucidate.

In the middle of the wood along the overgrown path which we used to take when going by foot to visit our neighbours at Holly Park, there was an isolated and rather picturesque cottage. It had been uninhabited for a long time. One day when passing it with my governess an old woman came out of the door and proceeded to gather sticks. She curtsied to us in a completely outmoded manner but when, a few yards further on, I looked back in astonishment having never seen the woman before, she had entirely disappeared. This cottage had been used by Lady de Vere in the Famine years as a lace-school to train girls in the productive craft of Limerick lace-making. I never saw here again but when, as frequently occurred, I took this isolated walk alone I made extra haste when passing the cottage.

With the passing of the house any 'spookiness' connected with it or the grounds seemed to have disappeared. Perhaps the spirits have found rest and ceased to be earthbound. Those who stood around the last 'holocaust' of the old house recall that, as they looked towards the lake lit up by the raging inferno, a shadowy figure was seen to move beside its surface. The cry went up, 'The Lady walks.' Had she left those shadowy corners of the building for good? I believe so.

It is easy to believe in fairies in that leafy, sheltered part of the country and a curious event occurred to me in my early days. Out for a walk with two of the household staff we came to what was known as a 'fairy ring' (or circle) in the grounds. This is now known to be caused by a fungus but popular superstition still links it with the 'little people.' One of the girls said to me, 'say nothing about fairies while you are here or they will lead us astray.' Out of mischief, I jumped inside and proceeded to shout, 'There are no such thing as fairies.' We were comparatively near home but it took us hours to find our way back and we were all in trouble for being late. In the distance Knock Fearna (The Fairy Mountain) seemed to say to us, 'That'll teach you.'

The house was never wired for electric light as there was no pylon nearby. In my early days there were a number of acetylene fittings and lights and a plant for making gas in the yard, but the pipes became unsafe and we fell back on those large brass paraffin standard lamps which fetch such a price nowadays in antique shops, and silver carrying candle sticks with snuffers like witches' hats attached. There was a lamproom in the house and it was quite a job in the winter to clean and prepare the lamps.

The roof of the house was flat and inclined at the time to give trouble. There was always a damp patch in one of the bedrooms. It was possible to climb up on the roof. When the battle of Adare took place during the period of the Civil War we stood on the roof and watched it proceed. Eighteen pounder guns were used and could be clearly heard from where we were some five miles away. For all the commotion very little actual damage was done, but the cook from the Hotel unwisely put her head out of a window to observe what was gong on and had it blown off. People rushed out of Adare in fear but soon returned again. Some of them turned up at Curragh Chase with garbled accounts of the happenings.

When the house caught fire in December 1941, a few days before Christmas, my mother was alone in the house except for two maids sleeping downstairs. They were alerted by the library bell ringing downstairs due to the action of the fire. When the girls got upstairs there was very little that could be done as the fire had gained a hold starting in the library. There was no telephone anywhere near by and by the time the Limerick fire brigade arrived the roof was practically falling in.

An inadequate water supply was also part of the trouble. Unfortunately, some of the many connecting doors already mentioned were opened by people wishing to escape from the smoke and fumes. It was really a chapter of disasters as rabbit trappers had been camping in the yard until just before this catastrophe but, when it happened, everyone had gone home for Christmas. The big yard bell was rung to very little avail.

People going along past the cross outside the main gate quite some distance away from which the house was in no way visible, remember seeing smoke and flames. I think I have already mentioned that it was held by some that there was a curse on the house, for what reason, I do not know, and someone seeing the house finally disintegrating, remarked, 'Now the curse is gone!'

From *The Abiding Enchantment of Curragh Chase*, Clo Duanaire.

Play
James Kennedy

I WALKED the bank of the river that twisted its way by the water meadow and kept glancing into the pools where the trout lay. I came to my favourite spot. A black sally hung over a bend where the water was two feet deep. When I waved my arms the trout took off and darted under the hairy roots of the black sally, leaving faint trails of muddy water behind. I went upstream, stripped to my shirt (we never wore underpants then) and muddied the water with my feet so that the trout would not see me. I began groping, foot after foot, downstream under the bank, my fringe touching the muddied water. I felt four fish. One was worth taking and I cupped one hand over its mouth and gills and the other around its tail. It floated gently and unafraid against my fingers. A gentle squeeze and I'd got my supper.

Had I a diary for the summers of 1948-52 I could have written this regularly. In later years my brother and I became fly-fishing addicts but walking the bed of the river in our bare feet was enough then.

That and the swimming hole which we made by damming the cold water of our little river which had no name. Cows sheltered from the July sun upstream under the railway bridge. When we swam in the early afternoon, rather than with the men, after milking time, the water was sometimes yellowish with cow-shit and urine.

My sisters Breda and Mary and their friend Josie Byrnes got us to make a smaller dam for them a few hundred yards downstream. It was not that they were fastidious about bathing in the 'Yellow River', it was just that they felt that our swimming hole, at three feet, was too deep for them.

Harry and I worked for a few hours and completed a dam with rocks, mud and *feileastraim* (yellow flags) until the water was about a foot and a half deep. Come afternoon the three girls appeared, wearing white vests which my mother had stitched at the crotch to make one-piece swim-suits. They giggled and shivered and oohed and aahed but refused to put a foot in the eighteen inches of water. They settled for the downriver side of the dam where there was an inch of water, small rocks and skeins of green scummy moss. There, crouched down and with sharp intakes of breath, and squeals, they were happy that, at long last, they were swimming.

But fishing and swimming and hunting played second fiddle to the great passion of our lives – hurling. It ran in the family. Half the Pallas hurling team sometime previously was made up of the Ryans of Cross (who lived less than a quarter-mile away) and my father and his brothers. There were so many broken hurleys about the place that many of our tools, such as hammers and hatchets, had the end of a hurley as a handle. I never used a bought hurley. My father made them all and gave me my first one when I was about six.

It became my constant companion like the assegai of a young Masai. I learned to wield it against daisies and piss-a-beds. I drove the cows with it. It served as a Sharps rifle in cowboys and Indians. Few days passed without a puck-around in the paddock or on the road in front of the house. We would be sent to pull *geosadáns* and the hurleys would be hidden so that when my father went in we would puck around again.

The time came for my first competitive hurling match. It was for Doon CBS (called St. Fintan's) against Cashel and I was fifteen. All the years of pucking around in the paddock and on the road would be tested. My mother sewed up a pair of knicks for me out of a flour bag. I think the ANK of RANKS FLOUR was up near the elastic and I could cover it with the appalling white-brown jersey of St. Fintan's. I played left full back. My opponent got two goals off me. I never forgot that. It was a great humiliation. My father had held the great Tipperary full forward Hughie Shelley, scoreless in the few matches they played against one another.

There was plenty of time for all sorts of other play in Brackile. I think my parents were wise in encouraging us to do so because many of our contemporaries were inducted into farming responsibilities at too early an age and missed out on many of the hectic hours and adventures which we enjoyed, running wild.

THE COUNTY

We lived on a quarter-mile straight, two thirds of the way up a steep hill. We built go-cars, tricycles, toboggans to take advantage of the gradient. These were our toys. We were good at hammering, sawing, chiselling, clinching, boring because we saw our father at it. He allowed us his tools (all but his wood chisels) but never helped us make anything, nor praised our workmanship. It seems to me now that it was believed that the greatest disaster that could befall an Irish father's son was that he might get a swelled head from a modicum of affirmation.

They tell the story of a middle-aged man and a youth in his early twenties sitting at a bar. The man was laying into the younger one over something and a stranger who was drinking by himself intervened:

'Why are you insulting that young man?' he asked.

'What's wrong with insulting him?' the elder man responded. 'He's my son.'

My father certainly observed the custom that you should not be seen to praise your own child. If we played well in a hurling or football match he'd say nothing. If we made mistakes he'd pounce on us.

One day during a football match in Caherconlish I got a kick in the ribs when I tried to block down a ball being kicked by Timmy Reardon of Knockane. I headed for the sideline. My father shouted:

'Where are you going?'

'There's something wrong with me.' I answered. 'I can't breathe.'

'There's nothing wrong with you. Get back in there, again!'

I turned around and went back in and at the first tackle fell down again and had to come off.

I had three broken ribs, not cracked or fractured, but broken.

I took it as perfectly normal that you didn't give up anything until you were incapable of going on. It wasn't a bad principle, and in my life, I've never regretted it nor blamed my father for being a hard taskmaster. Anyway, there was another side to him. He was the one, who, very gently, took thorns out of our feet in summer, checked that we always had dry feet in wet conditions. (He mended our boots and shoes on days in which it would be too wet to work outside). He responded immediately with cuts of bread and jam if any of us were hungry and went to great lengths to warn us of all the dangers (from poisonous berries to sharp instruments) that were inherent in rural life.

There was a day, though when his no-praise syndrome misfired. For five minutes at half time in a football semi-final against Claughaun, in Hospital, I and in particular my brother, were affirmed and supported publicly by him and Uncle Jim. And the shock of it, for both of us, led to great melodrama.

I was playing in goal and Harry, aged seventeen, was getting his first outing in the senior team as a corner forward. I believe the coach intended giving Harry a run in the first half and replacing him by another youngster at half time but Harry threw a spanner in the works by playing well, scoring a goal and a few points and laying on more.

My father and uncle Jamesey, as usual, stood out on the fringe of the crowd on the sideline. They were big men and wore wide, soft hats. I was saying to myself this looks like being one of the days we'll get no criticism from Pop. (We called my father

Pop in his latter years).

At half time the two of them sauntered on to the pitch where our team were standing or lying on the ground, talking among themselves and to supporters and well-wishers. Some of us took a few drags of a cigarette. One or two I know had a slug out of a Baby Power. We were all in high spirits at having secured a very surprising lead over Claughaun.

Then Harry was told by the coach that he was being replaced and he accepted it without murmur. When he announced this to Pop and Jamesey, their faces got red and Harry couldn't believe it when he heard them saying: 'but that's ridiculous. You're playing well. Why should you go off?'

He was being praised!

'Because so-and-so said so,' answered Harry.

'What does he know about football!' said the two.

Suddenly it flashed to Harry that he was now the victim of a bad decision and he got red-faced too. When the Kennedys get heated they do so with the speed of lightning!

Next thing there were 'words' between Harry and the coach. A fracas developed and restraining hands and words had to be laid on both. In high dudgeon, Pop stalked off to the sideline, Harry with him. I had never seen him so angry.

He had wanted me to abandon the game with Harry but I wouldn't. I couldn't. But I did make some verbal contribution during the melodrama – and in very unclerical language. I was reported to Dalgan Park by the curate for using the word 'shit.' I was nearly expelled. Harry got the worst of it. The club suspended him for a year.

When I think of it now it was Pop and Jamesey who should have been suspended. To support and affirm us out of the blue like that was just too much!

From *The People who Drank Water from the River*, Poolbeg Press Ltd., 1991.

Gold rush in Bulgaden

A LONG, disjointed but interesting headline in the *Limerick Leader* of Monday, April 24, 1924, must have attracted immediate attention. It said: 'Treasure Hunt. In East Limerick. A Dream of Gold Supposed. 'Klondyke' in Bulgaden.'

Elaborating on this exciting intimation of hidden treasure, the Kilmallock correspondent of the *Leader*, having discoursed wisely about the lure of gold in general, returned to the story of the moment, to wit, the gold rush then taking place in Bulgaden.

'For days,' said he, 'the roads leading to Bulgaden were utilised by cyclists, pedestrians, and vehicles, all bent on one objective, and if you should stand by the way and be not impressed or enthusiastic about the idea, you were hailed with a cry, 'Are you not going up to Klondyke?' as they sped on at as quick a pace as possible betokening the urgency of their mission . . .

The correspondent continued: 'And for days and nights men delved into the soil where the treasure was supposed to lie, but chiefly by night, aided by the moon's pale beams, or, when occasions required, by artificial light, indeed the night is considered the most propitious time for such an enterprise.

'But what,' asked the Kilmallock correspondent, 'was the origin of the project?' 'It was no more or less, he tells us, 'than that two or three men had dreamt that gold lay concealed near Bulgaden Hill, the residency of the first Lord Carbery,'

It would appear that in their wild quest for gold the 'prospectors' may have damaged or destroyed an archaeological site. For the place of the digging was, according to the Kilmallock correspondent, a circular mound about twelve feet in diameter and about two feet high. A stone alignment, consisting of three standing stones, about three feet high and a like distance apart, projected outwards from the mound in a westerly direction.

The gold diggers had not dug too deeply when they came to a very large flagstone about 9 feet long, 4 feet wide, and 2 feet thick. Other large stones lay beside it. Since there was no way of lifting the central stone the diggers reluctantly abandoned their quest.

From *Souvenir Issue, Centenary of the Limerick Leader*, September 30, 1989.

The Hiring Fair at Kilmallock
John Gallahue

WHEN Danny came to 11 years of age, he left school and was available for service, that is being hired out to a local farmer for 11 pounds for eleven months. This was conducted on a bargaining basis: the farmer would offer a fee and Dad would haggle. Eventually a deal was struck and Danny found himself a servant boy to Mrs Dunne of Shraharla.

Danny recalls life in the Dunne household as being like home from home. They were wonderful kind people to work with. He actually got no money himself, since his earnings had to go toward the upkeep of the rest of the family. He was to walk home every second Sunday to collect clean clothes, and Dad would give him a few pence, usually a threepenny bit or a sixpenny bit. While the work was hard and the hours were long, 6.30 am to 7.00 pm, all the experience Danny had gained while working with his Dad was invaluable to him.

After two years with Mrs Dunne, he was hired by Tom Carthy of Kilglass and increased wages up to 12 pounds for 11 months. The only form of entertainment was to assemble at the crossroads in the evening playing skittles, duck and granny, throwing a 28 pound and 56 pound weight, jumping the river in season, raiding local orchards for blackcurrants, gooseberries and apples.

It was a time when the hiring fairs were in vogue and Danny recalls that

Kilmallock was by far the biggest in South East Limerick/North Cork area. He says that most of the servant boys and girls would have come from Kerry. They would assemble near the railway station and prospective employers would eye them up and down, and question them on what skills they possessed. After some banter, a bargain would be struck, and the Kerries as they were called, would travel to a new home for the next eleven months. Danny feels it was degrading and had many similarities to former slave markets. There was a popular mythology that many a Kerry girl returned home at Christmas with more than their wages, however, he hastens to add that he had no definite information on any such happenings.

He recalls, with a twinkle in his eye, the tale of two Galbally lads going to Kilmallock fair pretending they were available for hiring. Their plan was that they would hire with a farmer who would take the two of them. Eventually a deal was struck with a prosperous farmer from East Limerick. He took them to an eating-house (restaurant) for a feed and escorted them to his pony and trap, and told them to wait for a while, as he had a bit more business to attend to. As soon as he was out of sight, the two boyos took off with the pony and trap, pulled into the pub in Garryspillane, left the pony off back towards Kilmallock and had a good few pints before returning to Galbally. As they arrived in the Square, Jack shook hands with Mike and left for the Unites States of America the following morning. Danny says, I expect the farmer was none too pleased.

Later, his neighbour Morgan O'Brien approached Danny's Dad and asked if Danny would like a job at Mitchelstown Co-op. He was delighted, as work at the fledgling co-op was better paid, with regular hours. Morgan put his name down at the committee meeting but another member, a local farmer stated: 'Young O'Brien has plenty of work on local farms.' Not to be outdone, his Dad approached Con O'Brien of Killacane, a distant relative and then chairman of the co-op.

Unfortunately, he said he could not reverse the decision of the previous committee meeting. The co-operative movement was brought about by farmers joining together, pooling their meagre financial resources, and in conjunction with banks, either buying or building creameries to separate the milk. This process involved removing the cream and giving back to the farmer almost eighty per cent of the whole milk as skimmed milk. Danny says this was an excellent food for pigs, calves and even for making home-made bread. The price paid at that time varied between five pence and seven pence per gallon depending on the butterfat content. This was established by a simple test sample analysis taken by the creamery manager. The cream was then converted to butter and dairy products. Mitchelstown Creamery was the first to establish a cheese-making facility and traded under the brand name 'Mitchelstown the home of good cheese.' The creamery was always a source of great banter, a little devilment and all sorts of yarns.

Many a local shop or pub enjoyed spin-off business from the creamery. Danny recalls one character of note who approached the Manager Ryan in Angelesboro Creamery for a loan.

Mister Ryan was a little dubious about our friend's ability to repay and he told him that he did not have the authority to give a loan, but he would give him a note recommending him to the General Manager, Mister Brickley of Garryspillane. Our friend was a bit doubtful of the manager's support so he took the note and on his way to the head office he inspected its contents. Just as he had suspected, Manager Ryan had advised against the loan. Needless to say, he never mentioned the note to Mister Brickley, who advanced a small sum of money. The following morning Mister Ryan found our friend very pleasant to him, which he could not quite understand, so he enquired: 'How did you get on with Mister Brickley?' 'I got on very well, no thanks to you, you so ---', came the instant reply.

The chapel was an important focal point during that era also, and Danny vividly recalls such big occasions as christenings, communions, confirmations, weddings, funerals, the mission and the confraternity. That was an era when he said there was no such thing as funeral homes or hospices. When someone died they were waked in the family home, which during that period would be known as the corpse house. As soon as one breathed his or her last, all mirrors would be faced towards the wall and the kitchen clock would be stopped. It was the job of a local man or woman to lay out the corpse in their own room with a crucifix and two blessed candles, and the holy water by the side of the bed.

Close relatives would sit around the room, and usually old friends and near neighbours would stay with them. If rigour mortis had not set in full, old people would say: There is another one to follow. It was also the custom for the bereaved family to provide refreshment food, snuff, clay pipes and drink during the wake. In fact, the bigger the do was, Danny said, the more standing the family would have and the usual comment in the area would be: They gave him or her a decent send-off. Removal from the house and procession to the chapel would be slow and dignified, and he well remembers the horse-drawn hearse.

Should the journey be a short one, the coffin would be shouldered by family, friends and neighbours. As the cortege came within sight of the chapel, the funeral bell would resonate in mournful tones. Three strokes on the bell and a short interval indicated a male death, two strokes a female and one stroke for a child.

Requiem mass for a deceased at that time was either low mass with the celebrant usually the local priest, or a high mass with several priests from neighbouring parishes drafted in for the occasion on the invitation of the bereaved family.

Such ceremony, plus the number attending, was taken to reflect the status or standing the family enjoyed in the community. Indeed, many a time a local wag was heard to comment: low mass for low money, high mass for high money and no mass for no money. Although I must state, says Danny, I have never seen anyone in civilian life being buried without the sacrifice of the mass being celebrated. The grave was dug by close family friends, a custom which sadly no longer exists, he said.

Danny's next job was at John O'Donnell's at the Boro Road, Anglesboro, whom he recalled was a wonderful person, a farmer and a businessman. O'Donnell was operating a creamery on his own premises, making butter and taking it to Clonmel to the market.

Danny also says he was an expert at 'brewing the juice of the barley' and his best customers at the time were the police. He would be well tipped-off about any impending raid.

As a result, he rarely lost very much of this very special elixir of life. This was an era long before electricity, or indeed the motor car in Ireland and tales of ghosts and the fairies and 'Jackie the Lantern' abounded. People were very superstitious of red-haired women, black cats, robins, magpies, lios's or fairy forts.

The horse and common car was the most popular for small farmers, and the donkey and car for poor people, with a form seat suspended between the two cripples which protected one from the wheels of the car. The trap car and back to back were the most common amongst the better off.

There were always rumours of ghostly sightings at certain locations, and balls of light seen going from fairy fort to fairy fort. Danny still thinks that these were wonderful times, and as he says, wasn't there a certain degree of innocence when someone fervently believed that should a black cat or red-haired woman cross one's path during a journey, the really superstitious person would turn back, as they felt such occurrences were the harbinger of bad luck or even worse still. For a robin redbreast to alight on a windowsill, or enter a house, or even appear close to a person, many people believed that there was going to be imminent death in the family. He says that one would not dare to interfere with even a twig from a lios and one would be even very slow to walk past one late at night.

In some instances where an infant might develop some rare disease, or it was discovered to have some form of hereditary illness, or to be wasting away, it would be said that the fairies had taken the original baby and left a changeling in its place. While the belief in witches and witchcraft were consigned to the history books in the early 1900s, there was belief that certain individuals were practicing a black art of pisheogery. This was allegedly done by actions of the use of dead animals or eggs to cast an evil spirit on whomsoever was targeted by the person with evil intent.

He said it would happen regularly enough in some districts where one would find a number of eggs in haystacks, corn stacks, potato pits and in some instances actually in the ridges or drills before they were dug. The idea was to cast an evil spell on one's neighbours using the eggs, or even dead bonhams, as instruments of evil and the devil as their accomplice.

Immediately anything like this happened, the priest would be called and he would say special prayers to exorcise the evil spirit and shake holy water on the spot where the items were found.

Another belief was that if the woman of the house was in the process of churning butter and a neighbour or stranger called, they would have to turn the churn a few times, and in some homes the practice was to put a cover over the churn while they remained in the house. Should they be inclined to delay, the woman of the house would explain what she was doing and ask them to leave. The reason for this was that people honestly believed that the butterfat could be reduced from the milk, or taken away completely by weaving an evil spirit. Another method used for this purpose was to put a lump of butter on the door to the cow byre or the diary, and wish evil on the people. Danny says the people had absolute belief in the power of religion to counteract such practices, and it was very rare not to find some kind of religious icon or blessed candle or a bottle of holy water in a crevice in the cow house, or fixed to the rafters to ward off evil.

As he says, maybe all this was a bit over the top, but unfortunately we have lost all these practices and seem to have no respect for authority or the clergy. He says that statistics worldwide clearly show that where there are strong religious beliefs, there are less suicides, and people are better able to cope with the stress of modern living. In other words, in olden times, no matter what grief, the response was: 'welcome be the holy will of God.' Without faith, there is nothing to hang onto, Danny maintains.

On the day before the first of May many farmers would sprinkle holy water all along the bounds ditch that is the boundary of one's holding. Another tale he heard so many times was of going for the priest for someone who was dying in the middle of the night.

The route to the sick person's house involved crossing a ford on a stream, and lo and behold, when they came to the water's edge, the horse snorted with fear and refused to cross the river.

The priest took out a crucifix and raised it aloft praying fervently; eventually, the horse calmed down and carried onto the house where the last rites were administered. As the final blessing was given to the person, they were called to God, and there was a sound like the rattling of chains heard leaving the doorway. This was believed to be the devil having failed in his quest to commandeer a soul, as indeed the prayers of the holy priest repelled him at the river crossing.

Another old custom at the time of the year was to bathe our skin in the May morning dew. Old people would say: 'Wash your face with water that is without rain, or run and dry it with a towel that is not woven or spun.'

This morning dew was supposed to be very good for your complexion and skin care, and was alleged to have many curative properties.

Danny said the method used by people who believed in this practice was to rise early in the morning of the 1st of May and spread a sheet out on the grass to absorb the dew. They would then squeeze out the dew into an enamel bucket and repeat the procedure. He has no recollection, nor is there any reference in folklore to suggest that the dew would be used in phisogues or for evil intent.

Danny says there was even a story told of a very good-looking girl dancing in the club one night with a real handsome man. In the course of an old time waltz, she noticed the person had cloven feet, and the following day she was struck down with a strange illness and wasted away. True or false, Danny says, whether the devil ever danced in the club, this story was told at many a fireside by the Galtees by older people and storytellers. Strangely enough, there was never a mention of who the musicians were on that fateful night, nor was the name of the unfortunate young lady or her family were revealed.

Another superstition he recalls was that it was unlucky to pass out a funeral, and if one was going in the opposite direction, one would remove their cap or hat and make the sign of the cross and utter a prayer.

It was deemed to be very unlucky if one did not turn around and walk with the funeral for at least three steps. 'Tri cois ceim leis an trocaire', and as he says, what a lovely practice, and what respect it showed for the dead.

From *Knockadae to Mandaly, a Biography of Sgt. Major Danny O'Brien*, Councillor John Gallahue, Ballylanders, 2007.

Memories of Crecora
Canon Punch, P.P.

THE late Canon Tom Wall often urged me to write about the things that happened in or near Crecora in the old days. I would be recalling my own memories or telling him the things my father used to speak of. The most remarkable and certainly the most sensational event, in not so distant times, was the hanging of Scanlan for the murder of Ellen Hanly (the Colleen Bawn). Scanlan belonged to the landlord class which in those days, at least in the country places, could be described as being above the law. Scanlan apparently did not dream that he was in much danger and did not go on the run as has been suggested but returned to his mother's house.

However, an intrepid J.P., Mr. Lyons of Croom House, forced the authorities to take action, with the result that the Light Horse were sent to arrest Scanlan. They were evidently in no great hurry as Tomsy Higgins had plenty of time to run across the fields to warn Scanlan. He had plenty of time to go away but chose instead to hide in the stable (which incidentally still exists) and where one of his men threw some straw over him.

Mrs. Scanlan entertained the officer in charge, whilst his men made a perfunctory search, but as they were leaving, one of the soldiers prodded the straw with his bayonet and pricked the murderer, who was promptly arrested. Scanlan was hanged in Gallows Green and buried in Crecora Cemetery.

The churches in the present parish of Mungret and Crecora were burned in 1641. There were three of them, at Mungret, Lemonfield and Crecora. Kilpeacon Church was also burned at that time but was re-built as a Protestant Church in 1691. The present church at Crecora was built by Father Casey in 1864. Its immediate predecessor was the building used as a school house for many years.

Before that a thatched cabin situated at Dooneen near the gate leading to the farmhouse now occupied by Mr. James O'Donoghue, did service as a chapel. There is still a chalice in the parish with the inscription, Dooneen. Father Casey must have been a remarkable man. In addition to building the church at Crecora, he roofed the church at Raheen, put monuments over the graves of three of his predecessors in Mungret cemetery and cleared the whole debt. Old people who remembered him told me in my youth that he was the most eloquent preacher they had ever heard.

Kilpeacon must have been a fairly important place in the old days. My father told me that he often saw twelve four-in-hand on a Sunday outside Kilpeacon Protestant Church. Alas, he had other memories too. He saw eighty families evicted from their homes. These poor people built huts at the top of Woodcock Hill in the parishes of Cratloe and Meelick and from there scattered all over the world, many of them dying of hardship.

Joe Minihan remembered, and often told me, that he found a man dead in the field near Kilpeacon House. Villiers, the landlord, sent a servant with a tumbling cart to bury this poor fellow, much as we would bury an animal nowadays, without inquest or ceremony.

Kilpeacon House was built by Edward Cripps Villiers at a cost, according to

Linehan, the historian, of £12,000. Though he had a rent roll of £3,139 4s. 4d., he got into financial difficulty and sold his house at Kilpeacon and his lands in Co. Limerick to Major Gavin, who was the first Catholic member of Parliament for Limerick. The sale took place on Wednesday, November 20, 1850.

In the early days of the GAA, Crecora claimed to be one of the best if not the very best in the county, and local bards celebrated their victories in song. In modern times, owing to the parish rule, it has to take a lowly place as the majority of those attending Mass at Crecora or going to school in Crecora school are from the parishes of Fedamore and Patrickswell. Some of the best hurlers who ever donned the green and white went to school at Crecora in my time. Paddy Buskin, who played at full-back with Kilfinane when they won the All-Ireland in 1897, is still hale and hearty. Martin Hayes and his brother Tom, played for Limerick and Dublin. Martin must surely rank as one of the greatest in the hurling world, playing in nine All-Ireland finals with four victories. Their cousin, Tom Hayes of Young Irelands, and Limerick, also went to school at Crecora.

Manister, nearby Crecora, has the distinction of producing Jerry M, one of the greatest of race horses. Strange to relate, Jerry M happened to be a 'whistler.' He won the five-furlong Paris Steeplechase in a canter and the Grand National carrying 12 st. 8 lbs. The leading trainer of his day, Michael Dawson, told me around 1918 that Jerry M was undoubtedly a 'whistler', and when I asked how then he could have won the hardest races in the world, Michael Dawson replied: 'Jerry M was such a great horse that he could beat any horse in the world without being asked do his best.'

Our Catholic Life, Summer, 1961.

A Comic Look at Adare
Paddy Lysaght

ADARE is a corruption of "Ah, there", an Elizabethan salutation (see Shakespeare). It is not a corruption in the usual sense, simply the normal way Limerick people drop their aiches. Go to the confraternity any night and listen to that exemplary body of men sing, "Since they like them would die for thee", and you will note that it comes over as, "Since day like dem would die for dee". The nearest modern equivalent to the Elizabethan "Ah, there" is perhaps "How Dee?" or "How ya?" When Gertrude Stein visited Adare she maintained that Adare is Adare is Adare - however her witticism is not really here nor there. It was bad taste on her part, really.

"Oh, sweet Adare, oh, sylvan vale." For centuries Adare has prided itself on its trees, especially its elms, huge magnificent specimens which tourists, plain people from other parts of the country, viewed with wonder and delight. Aesthetically beautiful, their fame spread far beyond our hallowed shores, to England, the USA and finally to the other members states of the EEC. Unfortunately, the Dutch Elm Bugs heard about these magnificent trees and, as there was a shortage of elm trees in their own country, they decided to emigrate to Adare to feast on the succulent elm barks to be found there. They became enamoured with their new found home, settled down extremely well, worked hard as the Dutch always do, married and produced progeny galore.

The people of Adare, being intelligent, soon realised what was afoot in their beloved elms, and when it dawned on them that there was no point in having all the elms in one basket, they decided to search about for something else to hang their fame on. At first they thought of Clounanna, where the Irish Cup is held, but when they realised that the Anti- Blood Sports coterie would write nasty letters to the papers about them, calling them cruel, inhuman and unchristian, they had no option but to look further afield.

And so these intelligent people put their heads together once more. They wrote to Bord Failte telling them that they had a very tidy town which they were certain was tidier than any other town in Ireland. Of course, Bord Failte did not really believe that this was so - they are an incredulous lot. In due course, they sent their spies (incognito) to Adare to see for themselves whether Adare was as tidy as the people themselves claimed. When they returned to their head office, they too put their heads together and, after much deliberation, they, in fact, agreed with the Adare contention that their town was the tidiest in the country.

As was to be expected, the honour of being Ireland's tidiest town brought Adare great publicity. Tourists and common people flocked to see this unusual phenomenon, a tidy Irish town. However, since most of these people came from very untidy towns themselves, and were thus uneducated in the art of tidiness, they brought their litter with them, and as often as not left it in Adare when they departed. And so on Sunday evenings, when these people returned to their own untidy towns, empty cola tins, bottles, papers, apple cores, orange skins, banana peels, soggy chips, yes, and even chicken carcasses were often to be seen desecrating the immaculate streets of tidy Adare. Unfortunately, one of Bord Failte's spies, on his way to Puck Fair, saw this sorry mess, duly reported it to the proper authorities, and Adare was relegated to the Untidy Town category. This was a great blow to Adare and its intelligent people.

On a fine day the Galtee mountains are visible from the Dunraven Arms. Sometimes a gurgling sound can be heard in Adare - the waters of the Maigue stealing over its limestone bed on its way to the Shannon. It is well, however, not to confuse this gurgling sound with a similar sound made by those on the dole as they refresh themselves after the rigours of having signed for same.

Places of interest: the old ruins of the elm trees.

From *The Comic History of Limerick*, The Mercier Press, 1979.

Despair in West Limerick
Gerard Curtin

DURING the spring of 1848 hopes were high of a repeal of the Union with Britain. West Limerick was the home of William Smith O'Brien, MP, of Cahermoyle, Ardagh, one of the leaders of the repeal movement. The success of the French Revolution in Paris in the spring of 1848 caught the imagination of the public in the county. On 6 March an Irish tri-colour flag was displayed on Limerick for the first time, at Rathkeale. Bands played in the streets and pistol shots were fired in celebration of the French Republic.

At Shanagolden on 19 March, during St. Patrick's Day celebrations, an alleged 4,000 Repealers from the parishes of Loghill and Shanagolden had gathered calling for the repeal of the union. Fearful for their safety, seventy-five soldiers stationed at Shanagolden had been withdrawn beforehand by stealth unknown to the people.

The Limerick newspapers from the 15 to 22 July reported that the early potato crop was affected by blight from the third time in four years. A week later, William Smith O'Brien was out trying to raise the country at Ballingarry, in Tipperary. The people were not interested in rebellion, as their potato crops rotted before their eyes. Alarmed at the failed rebellion at Ballingarry, the authorities in County Limerick ordered all police stations in the rural villages to be closed and the police concentrated at the Desmond hall at Newcastle West. With no-one to enforce the law in large areas of the county, much unrest followed all of it apparently economic rather than political in nature. On 4 August the Limerick to Tralee mail train was robbed near Abbeyfeale by what were described as '400 wretched creatures armed with old firearms and sticks.'

Authority was gradually restored, not least by the stationing of the fifty-six gun warship the *H.M.S. Blenheim* between Tarbert and Foynes, for the purposes of putting down any disturbances on the coast of the river Shannon. In the aftermath of the disturbances, the *Limerick Chronicle* of 16 September reported that in the west part of the county the late crop of potatoes was totally lost and unfit even to feed pigs. The failure of the crop in 1848 was as complete as 1846 and coming as it did on a people already impoverished and enfeebled by distress, the results were disastrous. On 21 October 1848 it was reported from Shangolden that 'hundreds were starving around the neighbourhood.'

Labourers and small holders found that after three years of famine, they were unable to pay the rent and feed their families. Evictions followed. The incentive to farmers and landlords to evict was considerable, because all relief was channelled through the workhouses and the insistence on local financial support led to high rates for the support of the poor.

For all local holdings valued at less than £4, the rate had been paid by the immediate lessor. Frequently no rent had been paid by the tenant during famine conditions. This led to a net financial loss and an incentive to evict the occupier and destroy his dwelling. At Ballyane, half a mile south of Shanagolden during the month of November 1848 six families were evicted. Their houses were knocked to the ground by the authority of the Sheriff. Those evicted huddled together in the ruins of one hovel, where 'the starved and famine stricken appearance of the children' was described as 'a haunting experience.'

Despair and ruin spread throughout the land. At a Board of Guardians meeting at Rathkeale, in late November, upwards of 300 starving people from Glin and Shanagolden crowded around the workhouse in an effort to gain admission. For the want of accommodation, they were unable to obtain admission and were obliged to retrace their footsteps back to their homes. The starving people became violent. At Shanagolden, on 3 November 1848, despite an armed police presence, an excited mob of paupers attempted to break into a house where a Board of Guardians meeting was taking place. Unrest was widespread, the focus of the outrages had by now shifted to the stealing of food. Armed parties transversed the countryside between Shanagolden, Loghill and Foynes.

From *A Pauper Warren, West Limerick*, 1845-49. Sliabh Luachra Books, 2000.

When the Limerick people came to Castleconnell
Joe Carroll

THE licensing laws covering Sunday drinking then were such that local residents couldn't enter a public house in their own place, but anyone who had travelled a distance of three miles or more was free to drink in any of the bars. But laws are made to be broken, it is said, and ways were found around the problem. I remember my father and Joe Kershaw, Pat Ryan, Frankie Rose, John Byrnes and the men from Gooig could get into Hartigan's via the back gate and back door and would have their few drinks at their ease, happy in the knowledge that Lizzie Hartigan was on the lookout.

Every Sunday Lizzie's duty was to position herself at an upstairs window that afforded a perfect view of the Mall right up to the Island gate. The guards then would be on foot patrol and were easily spotted by Lizzie the instant they appeared on the horizon.

'The guards are coming, the guards are coming,' she would shout down the stairs. There would be an immediate scattering of the ones who shouldn't be there. Drinks left unfinished would be hidden under the bar counter. When the guards arrived on the premises they found only drinkers from the city or other places, but not a sign of a local law-breaker.

There is a story told of a new Guard, just out of training depot and posted to Castleconnell, far from his West of Ireland home town. Anxious to make an impression on the Sergeant, and at the same time let the locals see that he meant business, he raided a public house in the village on his first Sunday night of duty. It was the perfect start for the young rookie policeman and he came away with a broad smile on his face and along list of names in his notebook.

Next morning he presented the list to the sergeant at the barracks. The sergeant ran his eye down the list and studied it for a few minutes.

'You found all these men on this licensed premises last night?' he enquired.

'Yes, Sergeant, all the names and addresses are there, as you can see.'

'Oh, indeed they are surely, Guard, a good night's work I must say.'

'Thank you sir,' the young Guard beamed.

'There's just a couple of things about this list I think you should know,' the sergeant told him.

'But surely there's nothing wrong with the list, Sergeant, all the names and addresses are there.'

'Indeed they all there, every one of them, but the trouble is that half of those on your list have been dead for years and the other half have gone to England.'

During the long summers of the 1940s Castleconnell held a big attraction for people from Limerick City and they came in droves by various methods of transport, jarvey cars, long cars, carriages, bicycles, in fact every means of travel except the motor car, off the roads for most of that decade because of the scarcity of petrol during and after the war.

I remember on one particular Sunday evening seeing five or six older women being driven through the village in what was known then as a mourning carriage. These horse-drawn carriages were normally used for funerals and were common only to the city. Judging by the singing and laugher from this group of ladies, they weren't going to a funeral. Then sometimes CIE put on an excursion train to Castleconnell on Sundays during the summer and this would usually bring at least a hundred people into the place. Inevitably, some of the revellers would miss the return train in the late evening and would end up having to walk the seven miles back to Limerick.

One Sunday two young women visitors from the city came to our door and asked my mother if they could use the toilet. My mother ushered them through the house and out the back door to the shed at the end of the yard where the toilet was and left them to themselves.

What she forgot was that Spot was in the shed, more wicked than ever because she was raising pups at the time. When my mother heard all the screams and curses she suddenly realised what was happening. She found the pair desperately trying to fight off old Spot who was hell bent on protecting her litter from these invaders. Eventually my mother rescued the women and spent the rest of the evening tending to the bites on their legs and arms. After tea, sympathy and repeated apologies, the two women left not much the worse after their ordeal.

Some time later in the year my mother was coming down William Street one Saturday, when she saw the two women at the other side of the street. One of them shouted at her, 'have ye still got that ould hoor of a dog out there in Castleconnell?' But they became great friends after that and the pair came regularly to Castleconnell and our house. They worked together in Cleeves Factory and we were glad to see them coming as they always brought us Cleeves Toffee.

One of my lasting memories of Limerick crowds was the number of fine singers they brought with them. Most of them – men and women – had good singing voices and could do justice to any song. They also brought to the place many of the well known and popular songs in the city at that time. We got to know the airs and words of many of them from listening to the weekly rendition emitting from Hartigan's next door. The ones I remember best were 'Happy Moments', 'Charmaine,' and the song that seemed to be the big favourite with most 'Juanita:'

> Up o'er the fountain lingering falls the southern moon,
> Far o'er the mountain breaks the day too soon.
> In thy dark-eyed splendour where the warm lights love to dwell,
> Weary looks yet tender, speaks their fond farewell.
> Nita, Juanita, ask they soul if we should part,
> Nita, Juanita, lead thou on my heart.

In memory I hear those old songs again and the voices joining in harmony, voices from those days of simplicity and innocent gaiety when the Limerick people came to Castleconnell.

From *No Lock on the Door, Childhood in a Shannonside Village*, Stradbally Books, 2004.

A distinguished Co. Limerickman
Liam Irwin

THE name of Thomas Johnson Westropp is rarely mentioned in any list of distinguished County Limerick men yet he arguably contributed more to the history and heritage of his native county and to Ireland in general than many whose contributions are better remembered and honoured. He devoted his entire life to researching, publishing and campaigning for the preservation of the archaeology and history of medieval Ireland. He was born in 1860 at Attyflin, near Patrickwell, Co. Limerick, the youngest child of a local landlord, John Westropp. He was educated at home by private tutors until he went to Trinity College in 1879, where he qualified as a civil engineer. He only worked briefly in this profession as his private income allowed him the freedom to devote himself full time to the work of studying, recording and helping to preserve the monuments and sites of the Irish past. These activities were pursued with vigour and dedication and in spite of increasing ill-health right up until his death on 9 April 1922 at the relatively early age of sixty-one.

In May 1878 he made his first tour of the Burren, an area to which he was to devote a major portion of his working life. The drawing, sketches and notes that he took on this visit formed the basis of the extensive survey that he was to complete over a twenty-year period. From his first publication in 1887 until his death he maintained a prodigious output. Virtually every volume of the *Journal of the Royal Society of Antiquaries of Ireland* had a major article by him as well as numerous notes and observations. He published important papers in the *Transactions and Proceedings of the Royal Irish Academy* and in local journals such as the *Journal of the Limerick Field Club, North Munster Archaeological Society Journal, Cork Historical and Archaeological Society Journal, Galway Historical and Archaeological Society Journal*. Articles were also written for the *Irish Monthly* and *Folklore*.

Much of his work was on his native county of Limerick. He produced comprehensive surveys of all its castles and ancient church sites and published detailed papers on Askeaton, Newcastle West, Carrigogunnell, Monasternenagh and St. Mary's Cathedral. He described the structures in detail which provides important information for sites which have since been damaged or destroyed. He consulted a wide range of documentary sources for each site, most of these from the Public Record Office in Dublin which was destroyed in 1922. In addition to his vast output of major publications he regularly contributed miscellanea on an enormous range of topics. These show the impressive breadth of his interests and erudition. He drew attention to and summarised neglected historical source material, published corrections of place name derivations, recorded stray archaeological finds and elucidated heraldic devices. He offered informed comments and comparisons on architecture, corrected errors and unwarranted assumptions relating to folklore and oral history. He provided descriptions of dog wheels, fish ponds and bullaun wells. He discussed witchcraft in Co. Limerick, cow legends in Co. Clare and weasel folklore in Munster.

Westropp deserves to be remembered for his remarkable achievements. He had an amazing capacity for work, done in days when transport facilities were limited and uncomfortable. He used his own private income and received no official financial support or even formal encouragement for his dedicated work. To this day scholars, local historians and the general public rely on his work as a vital foundation for their own investigations into the Irish past which he did so much to preserve, protect and record. He was a man of which County Limerick can be, and should be, justly proud.

Growing up in Newcastle West
Lindie Naughton

IMMEDIATEY AFTER the tragic death of her mother, Sophie was brought to the house of her grandfather, Dr George Peirce, in Newcastle West. While his wife did her best, she was neither young nor capable and the day-to-day job of looking after the infant girl soon fell to her aunts, in particular Ann Maria, usually called 'Cis', and Sophia Louisa, called 'Lou'.

Sophie was to spend her childhood in the prosperous and busy market town, twenty miles south-west of the city of Limerick. Dominated by the Earl of Devon's estate, society in the Newcastle West of Sophie's youth was still strictly divided. While the Protestants and planters, the landlord's support class, were neighbours of the Peirces in The Square, the poor of the parish, mostly Catholic, were kept remote and out of sight, though not entirely neglected, with the Earl of Devon contributing generously to the local Catholic church and to a school for all the poor children of the neighbourhood.

Through marriage, the Peirces were related to the owners of many of the big houses in the locality. Heathfield belonged to Edward Locke Lloyd and Castleview to Thomas Locke, and later to Sophie's grand-uncle, Robert Peirce. Perhaps the best known of the big houses was Cahirmoyle, where the artist Dermod O'Brien, a son of the Irish rebel William Smith O'Brien, lived until the 1920; he was an acquaintance of the Peirce family.

In 1910, the fabric and character of Newcastle West changed forever when the town was sold off by the Earl of Devon, who was experiencing financial difficulties. In the prospectus for the auction, it was stated that Thomas E. Lloyd, a cousin of George Peirce's and the executor of his Will, was paying the ground rent for the Peirce house on The Square.

Time was running out for the landlord class in Ireland. The disestablishment of the Church of Ireland in 1869, followed by the Irish Land Act a year later, allowing tenants to buy out their landlords, heralded the beginning of the end for the Protestant ascendancy. As Roman Catholicism and Irishness became synonymous, it cannot have been easy for ordinary Protestant families like the Peirces, who, simply because of their religion, were associated with all that had been bad about English rule; many simply left the country they had lived in for centuries. Ironically, the impetus for a Gaelic cultural and social revival had come from well-educated, middleclass citizens just like them, such as Douglas Hyde, John Millington Synge and William Butler Yeats.

Others, especially those deeply rooted in their rural communities, refused to leave a country they saw as their own. But they lived in fear, especially in the volatile early 1920's, when gangs of excitable youths, stoked up on alcohol and Republican ideology, considered anyone living in a big house to be the enemy and roamed the countryside looking for trouble.

This was the background to Sophie's childhood and adolescence, though there is no evidence that she ever took any interest in Irish politics and the cataclysmic events that were to alter the country's political landscape forever during those years. All her life, she believed unthinkingly, like so many of her class, that the British Empire brought civilisation and improved prosperity to its dominions and subject nations. She never had any difficulty describing herself as both Irish and British.

In Newcastle West, she was brought up in the same stiflingly strict manner as her four aunts before her. None of the girls had attended local schools and since they were not allowed on the streets of the town alone, their only experience of the outdoors was in a special play area behind the house, accessible by a private gate. The arrival of a baby in the house must have been cheering for the remaining aunts, but as the years went by, money was increasingly a problem, especially after the murder trial, with a broken-hearted Dr Peirce unable to maintain his medical practice. At the turn of the century, the family had two servants, few enough for a family of its status; a decade later, they had just one. By the time Knockaderry House was sold off to the Hannon family in 1907, Dr Peirce's health was failing and later that year, on 20 October, he died of senile dementia. Despite his failing faculties, he is said to have instructed Cis and Lou, the two daughters remaining in Newcastle West, to look after young Sophie, then almost ten years old. He left £4,712 in his will to be administered by his wife and his cousin Thomas E. Lloyd, all of it going to his wife and daughters.

Cis, then in her early thirties, was the eldest of the aunts. She was Sophie's favourite - 'my mother aunt' she called her in her letters home as an adult, signing herself 'Baby'. Remembered as a small, busy woman with a shock of dark hair that she attempted to control with a large floppy hat, Cis was well-liked locally and Sophie was lucky to have her, according to those around then. Cis occupied her time with painting, including portraits of local children, some of which still exist. She particularly loved dogs; at one time she owned one so small, it could fit in a teacup, her distant relative Helen Allott remembered.

Sophia Louisa ('Lou') was altogether a more fragile character and the only other sister still living in Ireland. By the early part of the century, Frances Thomasina and Margaret had both moved to England, while Aphra Jane married a man called Pepper and moved to Canada. After the sale of the house in 1915, Lou finally found the courage to leave Newcastle West for England, a move Sophie approved of. She appears to have settled in the Isle of Man, but later on would meet Sophie on regular trips to London. Both Lou and Aphra suffered from depression all their lives.

For a vivacious child like Sophie, the atmosphere in the house on The Square was suffocating, especially while her grandfather was still alive. Even before the dreadful murder case, the Peirce family had little contact with the world outside, despite their father's continuing involvement with the local workhouse. Their names do not appear in the lists of guests for the hunt balls and other glittering social occasions, despite their family connections to several of the local 'big house' families. As she grew into a lively child, the aunts did their best to keep Sophie protected from taunts or insults, but she did not always understand this and all her life aspired to be part of the 'county' set she was excluded from when young.

According to local anecdote, the young Sophie was occasionally seen in the town; once rescuing a kitten, or 'pusheen' in the local dialect, from the river. When asked what she would call it, she replied, 'Moses - because I found him on the banks of the river.' By her own account, she could not play games and was permitted only a half hour's walk each day. As a result, before she was sent away to school in Dublin at the age of twelve, she weighed twelve stone, very heavy even for a tall child like herself. 'My childhood has made me love freedom of every kind today,' she was to say.

She claimed that her aunts disapproved of sport for girls and moved her from one school to another when hockey or athletics figured too prominently on the timetable: 'I was taken away from one school...on account of the fact that not only was hockey played there, but one match in the term was played against a boys' school! I was at once transferred to another school where the girls went out, two and two, every day for a nice long walk in galoshes!'

Judging from photographs taken at the time, Sophie's childhood included regular outings to Ballybunion, where she could visit either her Uncle Robert's cottage at

Doon Bay or another called 'Raven Cliff', which belonged to her D'Arcy cousins. Ballybunion, with its cliffs, caves, long beaches and the crumbling ruin of the Fitzmaurice castle, was not only breathtakingly beautiful but designed to enthral any child and she always remembered Kerry with delight:

This delicate fairy grass, with seeds all shrouded and shaking.
I used to gather it, quaking, where the Kerry highroads pass.

she writes in a poem after spotting similar grass on a visit to Africa in the 1920s.

From *Lady Icarus, the Life of Irish Aviator Lady Mary Heath*, by Lindie Naughton, Ashfield Press, 2004.

The First Trans-Atlantic Flying-Boat Passenger Flight
Valerie Sweeney

ON 30 June 1939 the first transatlantic passenger flight took off from Foynes. The flight took Ireland's first half-ton of airmail to America. Capt. Harold Grey again had the honour of captaining that first passenger flying-boat, the famous 50-passenger seaplane *Yankee Clipper*. The aircraft had arrived at Foynes early that morning, carrying the first passengers and mail to cross the Atlantic from America.

Among the passengers on board was Mr. Juan Tripp, President of Pan American Airlines, who was greeted by Mr. de Valera. The oldest passenger on board was an 81 year old Judge, Mr. Walton Moore, Counsellor of the State Department in Washington, who brought greetings to Mr. de Valera from President Roosevelt.

An American news network sent a broadcasting crew to Foynes. Its mission was to relay a live radio transmission to the American people, detailing the historic departure of the first passenger flying-boat to cross the Atlantic from Ireland.

The first passenger on board was John Cuddihy, an American businessman, who was understandably very excited about embarking on such a unique journey. "I can't tell you how thrilled I am to be the first passenger on board this beautiful flying-boat," he told the listeners "Here we are in this little village of Foynes in Ireland, surrounded by the Clare hills, on this beautiful summer's evening. And to think that soon I'll be crossing the Atlantic Ocean on this wonderful craft is truly awesome. I'm really proud and delighted to be the first passenger on board this historic flight."

That live broadcast relayed from Foynes to America, placed the little village of Foynes firmly on the world aviation map.

On 7 August 1939 *The Caribou*, a giant flying-boat owned by British Imperial Airways, inaugurated the first official transatlantic airmail service from Britain to America. The flight of *The Caribou*, piloted by Capt. J.C. Kelly-Rogers, was also a historic occasion. It marked the second stage of experiments being conducted to decide the best type of aircraft for future transatlantic flying-boat flights. The experiment was to see whether it was possible to refuel a flying-boat in mid-air. The experiment provided an amazing spectacle, which was witnessed by the Taoiseach, Eamon de Valera, as well as the people of Foynes and the surrounding areas. A special train brought hundreds of spectators from Limerick.

The Caribou, took off from Foynes at 7 p.m. en route to America, with a comparatively light load of fuel. At the same time, a converted Handley-Page Harrow bomber took off from the newly completed grass runway at Rineanna. While both machines were in flight over the River Shannon, the spectators watched with bated breath and hearts as the tanker shot a grappling line across *The Caribou*, and a hose was quickly lowered to the flying-boat. 800 gallons of fuel was then passed through the hosepipe, which was flushed with nitrogen, to avoid the danger of a possible electrical discharge while the refuelling took place. An electrical discharge would have resulted in an immediate explosion with disastrous consequences. The fuel flowed from one machine to the other at a rate of 80 gallons a minute. According to those people lucky enough to be present, the spectacle was amazing.

"It was a wonderful sight which I'll never forget," said John Finucane. "The spectacle of those two aircraft refuelling just above our heads, with the sun going down in the background, was an awesome sight that I and everyone else will remember until the day we die."

As soon as the mid-air refuelling was completed *The Caribou* set off for America. It was carrying 1,000 lbs. of mail from Britain. Capt. Kelly-Rogers later told how the flying-boat battled with severe head-winds on the way, reducing its ground-speed to a mere 89 knots. It arrived in Botwood 19 hours and 25 minutes after departure from Foynes.

Such a novel refuelling system meant that an aircraft could fly with a far greater load of fuel than it could carry at lift off, making it possible to stay in the air for a much longer period. Several more flights were refuelled by this method over the few years at Foynes.

Flying boats were soon a regular feature of life in the little village of Foynes. By 1939 Pan American Airways were operating 12 Boeing 314 flying-boats in out of the small airport on a regular basis. They each weighed 40 tons and were capable of carrying 39 passengers on long-haul journeys. They also carried a crew of eleven. Most of the passengers were wealthy Americans, although British and Irish people also used the service. The fare was $375 single and $675 return, which was very expensive in those days. The flying-boats were luxurious and beautifully fitted out on the inside.

High-level civil and military personnel all had to travel in civilian clothes because of Ireland's declared neutrality. Government Ministers travelled incognito. Because of this, the identities of the majority of passengers remained unknown to the general workforce at the airport. On two occasions Capt. J.C. Kelly-Rogers flew Winston Churchill from Foynes to America for crucial war talks with President Roosevelt.

Some very well known film-stars also travelled into Foynes. They were engaged to entertain the American troops based in Britain. People still fondly remember

Gracie Fields singing a few impromptu songs as she arrived at Foynes harbour.

Other famous people who flew into Foynes included Ernest Hemingway, Sir Anthony Eden, Senator John F. Kennedy, Lord Louis Mountbatten, Yehudi Menuhin, Mrs. Eleanor Roosevelt, Bob Hope, Humphrey Bogart and Douglas Fairbanks Snr. The arrival of famous film stars in Foynes naturally made headlines in newspapers around the globe . . . .

The spin-off from the flying-boats landing at Foynes gave much employment to the local fishermen, mechanics, shopkeepers and bar people in the area. The arrival of the flying-boats also heralded the first idea of bed and breakfast accommodation in Ireland, as many of the enterprising villagers turned their homes into guesthouses to accommodate the growing work force.

The population of Foynes almost doubled from 600 to over 1,000 in the years of the flying-boat operations. The nearest large town, Newcastle West, was 25 kilometres away. Dances there were advertised as all-night functions. The dances went on till the early hours of the morning, at which time the local farming youths had to go home to milk the cows! The highlight of the year was the annual dress dance in Newcastlewest. The fashion for men was tails and black tie, with the ladies resplendent in long dresses. As the aviation staff set off on their bikes for the grand occasion, the locals gathered to cheer them off. The men were a special sight with their coat tails flapping in the wind. They carried their ladies on the handlebars of their bikes. The women modestly hitched their long skirts up around their knees, to avoid them getting tangled in the spokes of the bike's wheels.

From *Shannon Airport, a Unique Story of Survival*, published by Valerie Sweeney, 2004.

Bruree in World War II
Mainchín Seoighe

WORLD War Two World broke out on 1st September, 1939 with the German invasion of Poland. On 3 September Britain and France declared war on Germany. On the same date Ireland declared its neutrality in the conflict. On 10 May, 1940, Germany, having occupied Denmark and Norway the previous month, invaded Holland, Belgium and Luxembourg, its soldiers sweeping through them in their *Blitzkrieg* - lightning war - and into which France capitulated on 25 June. All British forces on the continent were, with great difficulty, evacuated through the port of Dunkirk.

There was alarm in Ireland. Would Germany now invade Ireland and use it as a launching pad against Britain? Or would Britain, in order to forestall such an attack on its territory become the invader? The government, and all political parties in the Dail, were of one mind that the best way to deter any would-be invader was to have a large, well trained, well armed, defence force, that would offer the stiffest resistance, and contest every yard of Irish territory, against any invader.

And so a call went out to all men of military age to join the defence forces, either the regular army, or a new part-time force to be called the Local Security Force (L.S.F.). The L.S.F. was to be divided into two groups, which would act as an auxiliary to the regular army, and Group B, which would undertake police duties. In September 1940 Group A became the Local Defence Force (L.D.F.) - later still to be known as An Fórsa Áitiúil (F.C.A.) - and Group B became simply the L.S.F. Initial recruitment for both groups had taken place in Bruree hall on 28 June, 1940. More than 200 enrolled.

On 18 September, 1940, quite a stir was created in Bruree when a large military force arrived there and took over Bruree House (now Cuan Mhuire), which had been purchased from David Browning by T.J. Sheehan, of Mallow, only five months previously. The military were to remain in occupation all during the World War Emergency period.

Each Sunday morning the soldiers marched to a special Mass in Bruree church, headed by a band. Mick Mackey, the legendary Limerick hurler, was one of the soldiers. Pádraig Ó Loinsigh, of Rathcannon, tells how on many a Sunday morning he and some school companions would go to Bruree to see the soldiers of the 12th Battalion parade to Mass with their pipe band, but especially to see Mick Mackey marching among them. And he says: "We'd be pointing him out to one another, and we proud as peacocks having seen him".

And stone cutter Jack Byrnes, of Clogher, was another admirer who used go to Bruree on Sunday mornings to see the great Mackey. He wrote a song about these trips, in which he tells us how he would cross back to Howardstown bridge and up the railway line to Bruree, and stand at the church gate:

We went to see our hero, Mick Mackey was his name,
Sure he brought honour to his county, to Limerick he brought fame;
Then we'd stand outside the chapel gate, to attention we would stand
For the marching of the soldiers and the playing of the band.

Another well known personality to be stationed in Bruree House was Colonel Eoghan Ó Néill, who later served in the Congo, and later still was in charge of the Military College in the Curragh.

The first Group Leader of the Bruree L.D.F. was Mick Dunworth, a former army sergeant; and when he left the district local postman, Jack Murphy, succeeded him. After a little while members of the L.D.F. were supplied with brown uniforms, resembling overalls or dungarees; but these were replaced by regular army-style green uniforms. Boots and groundsheets were also supplied. The part-time soldiers of the L.D.F. met once a week in what had been a vacant house, down near the bridge, in Water Street. Sergeant Joe Ryan was instructor, and was popular with everybody.

Rifles and ammunition supplied to the Bruree L.D.F. were, at first, as the case of all rural centres, kept in the local garda station, being guarded each night by two armed L.D.F. men. This arrangement ended 25 May, 1941, when each individual

L.D.F. man was given custody of one of the rifles (Winhchesters), and sixty rounds of ammunition and thereafter kept gun and ammunition in his own home.

There was great unity among the people, and the divisions remaining since the Civil War began to be pushed more and into the background. A never-to-be-forgotten night in the history of the Bruree L.D.F. was the night of the big manoeuvres. The manoeuvres commenced early on the afternoon of Saturday, 27 September, 1941, and continued for 24 hours. In Bruree armed soldiers stood on guard at the garda station and the Maigue and railway bridges. Groups of L.D.F. men went from post to post. Dispatch riders, arriving on motor cycles, rushed here and there with messages. As evening fell, people coming into the village brought accounts of roads swarming with military, lorries, motor cycles armoured cars. At times it was hard to credit that it all was only make-believe and not the real thing. The action continued all day Sunday, until evening, when the exercise came to an end. Exhausted and bleary eyed, the Bruree L.D.F. men made their way home and to bed!

Another notable occasion was on Sunday, 30 November, 1941, two lorry loads of the L.D.F. left Bruree for Limerick to take part in a monster parade of the defence forces and voluntary organisations: Participating in the parade were several units of the army; L.D.F. members from Clare, Limerick and Tipperary; members of the L.S.F., Red Cross, A.F.S., A.R.P. and St. John's Ambulance Brigade. In all, some 10,000 marched past the platform at the junction of William Street and O'Connell Street, where An Taoiseach, Eamon de Valera, took the salute. The L.D.F. gave many of their Sundays to field exercises, shooting competitions, etc. Several members did courses in army training camps,

They never knew when they might be called on to defend their country's neutrality. Several times between the summer of 1940 and the summer of 1944 there were well - founded fears of invasion by one or other of the opposing sides in the war. On meeting nights the Bruree group was regularly visited by the District Leader, Liam Purcell, of Uregare, who was sometimes accompanied by Commdt. Liam Fraher, of Ballynanty, Bruff. Like Joe Ryan, the group's instructor, both men were Old I.R.A. veterans; and again, like Joe, both were very popular, were men of gentle disposition and were highly respected.

Not all the activities of the Bruree L.D.F. were serious ones. They organised concerts in the village hall to raise funds. And there was one year when they learned and staged two plays, "Billy Joe" and "Blitz in the Kitchen", both very much altered and adapted versions of two fairly well known plays, normally presented under different names! The hall was packed for the occasion.

During the war years, or the Emergency period, as they were known in Ireland, several commodities became very scarce, or were completely unobtainable. Fruit such as oranges, lemons, grapes and bananas disappeared from the shops. Tea and sugar were rationed, as were flour, bread, clothes and petrol (eventually, private motorists ceased to get any petrol allocation). Items such as cigarettes, bicycle tyres and dry batteries for wirelesses (radios) were in chronic short supply. Coal became very scarce, and people came more and more to depend on turf. In order to supplement food supplies, especially flour supplies, the government introduced compulsory tillage. Evidence of the effect this had locally is seen in a news item in the Bruree Notes in the *Limerick Leader* of 19 April, 1941. Said the Bruree correspondent of the paper: "In this district, I am pleased to state, the slogan 'Grow more wheat', had been lived up to. No matter what way you turn you will scarcely see anything but gardens of wheat, oats, barley, potatoes or beet".

How different is the story today!

From *Bruree to Corcomohide*, Bruree/Rockhill Development Association, 2000.

Sad Day in the Manor
Ann Morrow

A STIR as the owner, the seventh Earl of Dunraven, arrives. Thady Wyndham-Quin has been in a wheelchair since he was sixteen, a marvelous handsome head, a body shriveled by polio. He moves about and rewards the gawpers. Yet the big blue eyes restrain them too, his is a rare presence. A couple of housewives push their catalogues at him, and this gentle man, a descendant of Lord Mayo, signs his name.

Then contents of his home, Adare Manor, which has been in the family for 300 years, are up for sale today. Soon all that will be left will be the indestructible shamrock-girt Kilkenny marble and the Gothic doorcases.

'We had to sell. You can be trapped by pride.' Dunraven succeeded to the title in 1965 and as a realist, philosophical too with all the dignity and gritty reasonableness of a last heir to this distinguished title. 'Hanging on, paying heating bills at ten pounds a day, maintenance £300,000 a year and insurance another £10,000 was too much.'

But Lady Dunraven takes it very badly. When they were married in 1969, Ascendancy friends of the family wondered about this girl called Geraldine, 'daughter of an Air Commodore McLeer from Tyrone and Sheila Byrne of Ailesbury Road, Dublin,' marrying their 'Thady,' an earl's son who had been educated at le Rosey in Switzerland. However they would grow to admire her for her energy and devotion to him and were delighted when a daughter Ana - the Russian version of the name – was born in 1972.

The sale hums on through the day; it has a fashionable buzz, and those who have driven from Dublin for this day out with 'the county' enjoy rubbing shoulders with commercial aesthetes, sharp eyed 'private' academics, librarians and fine art dealers from Italy, Paris and New York. Others get a tiny vicarious thrill and link themselves with the Dunraven family, women in silk dresses are overheard saying to each other: 'Oh no, I don't think so, mahogany doesn't grow in Ireland' as they admire some rare Irish mahogany chairs; others sink gratefully into squashy old sofas or sit on button-back chairs and slip off their unsuitable high-heeled shoes.

Geraldine Dunraven's hazel eyes still mist over at the mention of Adare Manor and she seems to grieve more than her husband over the old house as if it had been hers all her life: 'It's still my home, my daughter feels the same, she is very emotional like me.'

The sale has been masterminded by the engaging Knight of Glin who represents Christie's in Ireland. There are those who call him the 'Shite of Glin' because of his shrewd eye and ability to outwit even the gypsies, but on this traumatic day he is protecting his Dunraven cousin's interests. The Knight says: 'If I am going to be the undertaker, I'd like to do it in the glossiest hat possible.'

As always, certain important valuable things have been spirited away ahead, wrapped in green cloth and put up in fine art sales for the cognoscenti in London and Geneva. An important Georgian silver teapot made in Dublin by Archdall in 1717 once held gracefully in unrivalled hospitality at tennis and croquet parties, pale pink of Albertine rose petals reflected in the polished silver, '£27,500, going, going.' It has gone.

There is no gloating today; the Dunravens never attracted unkindness. Any landed or Ascendancy is label is resented for they claim to have arrived in Ireland in 607 long before Cromwell. The Wyndhams made money, farmed in Wales and, thorough marriage, changed their name to Wyndham-Quin, taking their title from a Glamorganshire castle owned by Thomas Wyndham.

Adare village was created around the seventeenth century with a benevolent stipulation that the villagers could walk through the estate and clamber round the ruins of the Franciscan Abbey and Desmond Castle whenever they desired – a right of way that would prove just a slight deterrent to potential buyers.

Lord Dunraven, the present Earl's grandfather, was slightly unusual in being a member of the Free State Senate that was headed, under the new Constitution of 1922, by a Governor-General rather than a Viceroy. During the Republican campaign to burn down the homes of 'Senators and Imperialists', Adare Manor somehow escaped, perhaps because it had been a model village with a good landlord and Catholicism had been important in the family.

The droning voice of the auctioneer lulls even the most curious. Paintings fetch £17,000 each and a George III Langlois marquetry bureau, a precious family wedding present, goes for £5,000. Now the crowd has grown tired of staring at the Dunravens and the house is stripped bare. Guns, sabers, swords and armour are next, women lose interest; then a final flurry of excitement; tapestries and rugs, until the swallows fly low over the river Maigue and people begin to slink away.

From *Picnic in a Foreign Land*, Grafton Books, 1990.

SEVEN

SONGS AND POEMS

Thirty-two Bob!
(anon)

Thirty-two Bob! Thirty-two Bob!
Come and we'll give you a beautiful job!
Come and enjoy some light recreation
Down on the Shannon electrification!

Sit down at once and send in your name,
And start in at playing an elegant game;
All you've to do is spend a few hours
Admiring the sun as it shines through the showers,
While you're up to your waist in mud and in stink,
Wielding a shovel or staking quick lime,
Shoving a barrow or lifting a load,
Digging a channel or making a road.

We don't want to strain you,
And so we won't detain you
For more that a mere fifty hours on the job,
And for that we'll pay you thirty-two bob!

Even that's not the might of our generous care,
We've taken great pains to ensure your share
Of good things to eat –
A whole half-pound of meat
And some scones at mid-day
And morning and night bread and jam with your tea;

For this we will charge you no more than twelve bob,
Sure everything's cheap on this wonderful job!
If you want any supper all you've to do
Is ask for it nicely and pay for it too.

After that you can roll yourself up in a cot,
In a nice wooden cabin set up on the spot.
You won't have to worry about paying rent,
For a rig and a stretch we won't charge you a cent.

Now isn't that a really beautiful job?
And don't forget a whole thirty-two bob!
Why don't you jump at the chance of your life?
Did I hear you say something about having wife?
And kiddies at home who will want to be fed?

What's wrong with you is, you've got a swelled head,
You shouldn't have children, your wife should be dead.
Didn't you know that the new Irish nation
Is only to last for one generation?
How dare you be married when your rate for the job
Is thirty-two bob! Thirty-two bob!

Death of an Irishwoman
Michel Hartnett

Ignorant, in the sense
she ate monotonous food
and thought the world was flat,
and pagan, in the sense
she knew the things that moved
at night were neither dogs nor cats
but púcas and darkfaced men
she nevertheless had fierce pride.
But sentenced in the end
to eat thin diminishing porridge
in a stone-cold kitchen
she clenched her brittle hands
around a world
she could not understand.
I loved her from the day she died.
She was a summer dance at the crossroads.
She was a cardgame where a nose was broken.
She was a song that nobody sings.
She was a house ransacked by soldiers.
She was a language seldom spoken.
She was a child's purse, full of useless things.

From *A Farewell to English*, 1975, 1978, The Gallery Press.

Why?
By Paddy Lysaght

Why is the buttercup yellow,
The lichen dun?
Roses – why have they thorns,
Lilacs none.

Why at the break of dawn
Should birds sing?
Bats – why at twilight
Take to the wing?

Why so much hate towards our fellow men,
Why keep our loving furled?
That's an unravelled paradox
Just one in this complex world.

Rubbish

Quite right:
Our dump is renamed
A landfill site.

Yet, methinks
Our rechristened dump
Still stinks.

From *A Torrent of Versatile Verses*, O'Brien Publications, 2001.

Portrait of an Old Woman
Frances Condell

Old Mayneen's back is double bent;
She's stopped, as if the days she spent
In picking praties, held her there;
Or sweeping earthen cabins where
Her children played, or hens picked up
The scattered crumbs, and the spilt sup
Of milky gruel, or praiseach husk,
As gathered by the turf-fire dusk.
She gropes and lights the candle-wick

And time stands still tho' seconds tick . . .
I wonder what her life has been,
What worldly things those eyes have seen . . .
Her hands were gnarled as a bough,
That saw the new, now rusted plough
With stiffened limbs attend the sod.
To mould those fists sent us by God.

Her wrinkled skin is creased with care,
While laughter adds its jovial share,
Her eyes, alive and keenly true,
Were they grey, once, or deeper blue?
Her 'Yankee' head-scarf hides her hair,
I wonder was she dark or fair?
Her calloused feet hug the green earth
Or nimbly thread the sodded hearth,
Her clothes are tattered, old as Time,
Her dudeen rank with handled grime.

She speaks with music in her voice,
And Gaelic is her envied choice.
I look at Mayneen, nodding low,
And feel a radiating glow
Of peace, contentment, love and God,
And truth, affirmed in every nod.

From *The Old Limerick Journal*, No. 38, 2002.

A rural sing-song
Constantine Fitzgibbon

IN the pub in O'Brien's Bridge, I told them I had come from Limerick. Their disapproval was instantaneous and overwhelming. Limerick, it seems, was the very last place in which to find out anything about Mount Shannon. The Limerick people, I gathered, not only knew nothing whatever about Mount Shannon but precious little about anything else either. (Irish patriotism is solidly based on local pride. The Clare people dislike the people of the County of Limerick – they're mean and too shrewd about money, they say. The Limerick people look down on their Tipperary neighbours as rough savages, stone-throwers they call them. In County Tipp they say that the men and women of Clare are intolerably stuck-up, and devil if they can see what reason the Clare folk can have for being so conceited. And so on. The rivalry between next-door villages is also often very acute).

They told me the man I was looking for would probably, on this particular afternoon, be in a pub in a particular village some five miles away. With many thanks my friend and I got into his car and drove off.

We soon found the pub and indeed, if it had no sign we should have recognised it for what it was, since it was crammed with men, women and children, and the hum of conversation, the occasional laughter and the chink of glasses were clearly audible a hundred yards or so away. No doubt, all these people were as boner feed* as ourselves, but they certainly knew each other very well, and at once, with a quite conscious courtesy, set out to make the strangers feel at home, to entertain us.

The bar, as I say, was crammed and so was the bar parlour and the yard out the back. The publican and his lady were fully occupied pouring stout and a Mr. McGinney had more or less taken charge of the customers. He was a powerfully built man in his fifties, wearing a green shirt with purple braces, a natural leader of men as he sat on his hard chair, his knees far apart, in the centre of the crowded room. He had one of those brick-coloured faces which are rightly said to be like the map of Ireland. I asked him if he knew the old man. He said that he did and that he would be in directly. Meanwhile, he went on, how about a song? Did we care for songs? We did. In that case Timmy should sing. Two men were dispatched to find Timmy.

And Timmy sang. He sang with extreme and unselfconscious concentration, assuming those grimaces which for many singers seem to be inseparable from the practice of their art. He had a very fine, light tenor voice and he sang beautifully. Another man had produced a flute from his pocket and on this he accompanied Timmy in those haunting, elegant songs of dear Tom Moore's. The whole pub had, of course, fallen silent. There were no choruses, no bawling and banging of pots, though at the end of each song they would clap and applaud. They enjoyed listening to Timmy as much as he enjoyed singing, and he put his whole heart into it. After perhaps five or six songs he was done. The sweat was pouring down his cheeks and he could sing no more.

'I can't sing any more, Mr. McGinney. I'm dry as a bone.'

It was a sort of apology as he leaned over and picked up his jar of stout.

'Thank you Tommy,' said Mr. McGinney, 'you sang very nicely. And now I'll call on Mrs. Ryan for a song.'

Poor Mrs. Ryan! There was considerable giggling and flustering in the corner where the ladies were mostly grouped and then, without getting to her feet, Mrs. Ryan began her song. It was a dull and sickly sentimental dance tune of 1946 and the emphasis with which Mrs. Ryan sang the poor thin melody and the idiotic words only served to underline the dullness of her choice. The man had put his flute away and she sang unaccompanied. She did as best she could, but her high notes broke and squawked. It was a pathetic performance. Yet when she had finished she received as much applause as had Timmy. Was this gallant courtesy, or was it that the audience had absolutely no taste whatever? I like to think that it was the former.

And so they sang on, under Mr. McGinney's supervision, none quite as bad as Mrs. Ryan but none ever approaching Timmy's virtuosity.

*Editor's note: should be read as *bona fide*

From *Miss Finnigan's Fault*, Cassell & Co. Ltd., 1953.

ANONYMOUS

The Fág a Balla Hall
(anon)

When our hard days work was over to the rockery we strayed,
We dug out the ould foundation with our shovel, pick and spade,
We got finished in October when the leaves began to fall
Oh may god bless the young men who built the Fág a Balla Hall.

Here's luck to the woman sure that gave us the land.
And likewise to the young men who brought the stones and sand,
A word of praise is also due to the young lads big and small
Who lent and bared a willing hand to build the Fág a Balla Hall.

(Chorus)
Fare thee well Ballysimon, fare thee well for a while,
It's all around the border of sweet Bother Coyle.
When Ireland gets her freedom we'll rally one and all,
And we'll dance our Irish reels and jigs in Fág a Balla Hall.

Now our hall sure it is finished we can sit down at our ease,
The door is always open you can walk in as you please,
If ever you feel weary you need only give a call,
And you'll always find welcome in the Fág a Balla Hall.

(Chrous)
Now there's one advice I'm giving to the young and the old
Keep up the reputation of the black and green and gold
And when this present generation have answered their last call
We'll leave the boys and girls behind us in the Fág a Balla Hall.

We got a grand name printed and we put it o'er the door
Some cowards there by midnight came and down that name they tore.
But if ever we find out their names they'll surely get a fall.
And they'll curse the night they meddled with the Fág a Balla Hall.

We went up sure to Morrisons for to have a social drop
We were scarcely sure inside the door when in the old sergeant popped,
We asked him not to summons us 'twas Christmas time and all
We were marched to Ballyneety from the Fág a Balla Hall.
(Chorus)

From *Remember Limerick, Ballads, Poems and Songs of County Limerick,*
edited by Sean Murphy.

Johnny Come Lately
Jonath Dillon

Johnny come lately by chance not choice
Will capture your notice by his action and voice
Expressing his views word by word
Of course there's no doubt, he is always heard.
Forms his opinion, takes his stand
He is ready to move forward and give command.
In places of interest he will be there
To act as chairman without a chair.
He quotes Bible without flaw
And becomes an authority on canon law.
Always available at his own request
To give his lecture and feel impressed.
Prides himself on sincerity
In his newly adopted locality.
In that townsland bar he is the likely one
That the popular Barsman will hastily shun.
He rejects his chat, ignores his passes
Despite his 'collecting' of empty glasses.
If up for election he would head the poll
With promises of less working hours and extra dole.
Would give extra welfare and no work for all
No need for Ministers, just a one man Dail.
For him reality is close to the ground
He has ambitions but may feel unsound.
Alas, he is 'Gifted' - akin to his tribe
He will yet achieve fame as a Poet and a Scribe.
Acquire riches and have a home that is stately
By choice, not chance – Good Luck to Johnny Come Lately.

From *S-S-Stammers For Now*.

Poem for a Local Historian
in memory of Jim Kemmy 1936 -1997
Keith Armstrong

Old people mumbling
low in the night of change and of ageing
when they think you asleep and not listening -
and we wide awake in the dark,
as when we were children.'
              Desmond O'Grady

'It was poignant,
when walking away from the graveyard
that very warm midday,
that the only sound which could be heard
after he was buried
was that of a member of his trade, a stonemason,
simply chipping away
at a monument.'
              Mary Jackman

In this city, in every town, in every village,
there is this man
dusty with archives
and old snapshots;
this deep fellow
who digs out truths from scraps,
who drinks from a bowl of swirling voices
and makes sense of things,
makes sense
when all else
lies in chaos.

In his dreams,
wars are not dead.
They scream
from his books.
He will not let
the suffering go -
he owes the children that.
There is something noble

in his calling,
in his bearing.
His work is beautiful.
In this particular place,
you can call him 'Jim'.
You can see his face forever
in the autumn leaves,
the leaves of books,
and the dance of history,
a local historian
and carver of tales

so memorable
that every street must value his love:
the love of our people though the ages,
the love of learning,
the search for dignity
that underpins these lanes.

In Limerick,
Jim's imagination still blossoms
and keeps us rooted
in the drift of memory.
He teaches us lessons.
Listen to his spirit breathe
deep as the Shannon.
His voice forever flies
with the power of knowledge.

'Beautiful dreamer wake unto me,
Starlight and dewdrops are waiting for Thee.'

Revival Poetry Journal **Issue 10 Jan 2009**

Shanagolden
Sean McCarthy

The cold winds from the mountains are calling soft to me,
The smell of scented heather brings bitter memories:
A wild and lonely eagle up in the summer sky,
Flies high o'er Shanagolden, where my love Willie lies.

I met him in the winter time when snow was on the ground
The Irish hills were peaceful and love was all around.
Scarcely twenty years old, a young man in his prime.
We were married, darling Willie by the eve of Christmas time.

Do you remember Willie, we walked the moonlit road
I held you in my arms, love, I would never let you go.
Our hands they were entwined, my love, all in the pale moonlight,
By the fields of Shanagolden on a lonely winter's night.

Then came the call to arms, love, the heather was aflame.
Down from the silent mountains, the Saxon strangers came.
I held you in my arms then, my young heart wild with fear,
In the fields by Shanagolden, in the springtime of the year.

You fought them, darling Willie, all through the summer days.
I heard the rifles firing in the mountains far away
I held you in my arms then, your blood ran free and bright,
And you died in Shanagolden, on a lonely summer's night.

But that was long ago, love, now our son grows fine and tall;
The hills they are at peace again: the Saxon strangers gone.
There's roses growing on your grave, there's an eagle in the sky
Flying high o'er Shanagolden, where my love Willie lies.

Rumour Has It
Maureen Sparling

HAVE you ever blown a bubble
And watched it grow in size,
A tiny, little circle
Grows huge before your eyes.

The same with nasty rumours
That start as tiny acorns,
Expanding and growing,
Tongues wagging and stinging,
Busily creating their crown of thorns.

Ostracising the innocent
And covertly looking askance,
'Till rumour becomes accepted fact,
And its victim doesn't stand a chance.

From *A Gem in Wasteland*, Insignia Publications, 2002.

An Muince Dreoilíní
Micheal Hartnett / Micheál Ó hAirtnéide
(do Mhícheál Ó Ciarmhaic, file)

I mo bhuachaill óg, fadó fadó,
    d'aimsíos nead.
Bhí na gearrcaigh clúmhtha, fásta,
    is iad ag scread.

D'éirigh siad – is thuirling
    aris ar m'ucht
Ormsa bhím muince clúimh
    sa mhóinéar fluich.

Níor dhuine mé ach géach crainn
    nó carn cloch
ach bhí iontas crua nár braith siad
    ag bualadh faoi m'ucht.

B'in an lá ar thuirling ceird
    a éilíonn ómós:
is d'fhág a n-ingne forba orm
    nár leigheasadh fós.

From *Adharca Broic*, The Gallery Press, 1978.

Mission Week
Tim Cunningham

They turned up once a year like Duffy's
Circus, the two Redemptorists:
One with blowlamp tongue stripping
Paint from the city's peeling soul,

The other's brushes dipped in tins
Of beatific light. Keen
As Pentecostal wind, they stormed
The pulpit steps in black birettas

And soutanes, rosaries dangling
From their belts like rope ladders
To heaven. One stoked embers of fear,
Made words glow like burning coals

Indelibly searing his picture
Of hell and fanning its flames
With eternity's huge bellows.
The other squeezed words to diamonds:

Jewels in the Virgin's tiara,
A celestial treasure hoard.
Their leaving was the folding of tents.
Amen to trapeze, strong man,

The chair and whip in the Daniel cage.
Back then to the tip-toe, soot-soft
Words of the curate at St. Michael's:
His index finger writing on sand

The secrets of heaven and hell,
His passport stamped at both borders.

From *Kyrie* (Revival Press) 2008

Abbey Fishermen Elegy
Arthur Lysaght

No more their small boats move up that clear stream
At the rising or the ebb of tide.
Their agile black brocauns no more are seen.
For they are gone now from the Abbeyside.

We do not see them paddle past the tall reeds
To join the mother Shannon up above,
Or troll their snap nets where clear waters swirl
For silvery salmon by the Sallygrove.

They do not pass Lax Weir in early springtime,
To fish the draws at lovely Corribalawn,
Or go by the old Mill at night's diffusion
Nor see the river mists rise at dawn.

They knew the moods of the winding waterways
And dark pools where the salmon stopped to rest,
Their paddles dipped with practised skill and ease
From home-made craft the Parish Priest had blessed.

Oft' times they met the barges on the tide
Waving the water on their journey down
And swapped a friendly word with these good men
Who ferried porter to a thirsty town.

And coming tired homewards in the evening
Their boats to moor beside their own Sandmall
Where swayed unladen sand-cots on the river,
And kin awaited by the limestone wall.

But no more their small boats shadow Abbey's stream
As crying sea-gulls circle overhead.
Their agile black brocauns no more are seen,
For years have passed, and most of them are dead.

The Miser's Grave
Michael Hogan

In silence I gaze on the dust where you lie,
But my breast feels no throb, and my heart heaves no sigh;
"In memoriam" above you appears the cold stone,
Sure, while living, your heart was as cold as its own!

You might be 'below' or you may be 'above',
But I'm sorry you died, without no one to love!
Tho' your gold, in a shower, on your gravestone would glare,
'Twould not purchase one tear to your memory there!

You were cold to the poor, to the sick, and distress'd,
But why you were so, your Creator knows best;
You spurn'd the friendship that links man to man,
Alas! that too many are following your plan!

Cold moans the bleak wind o'er the grass and the dew
On your grave – yet I know 'tis not moaning for you;
Tho', like your drear life, 'tis unfeeling and cold,
Yet it sighs not, with pity, for you and your gold!

On the side of your mound, a young daisy appears,
Its pure snowy fringe is besilver'd with tears;
I'll kiss off those sun-gems – from Nature they grew –
For I know the sweet flower is not weeping for you!

A wild bee's weird hum, 'mid the silence, I hear,
He's gone – for a moment he only came near –
To some sweeter part of earth's bosom he flew,
For he knows that he'd gather no honey from you!

From yonder hawthorn's white vest in the sun,
A red-breasted bird all the morning sings on;
You cared not for song while life's throbbings you knew,
Then the sweet thing is singing for Nature, not you!

A grass-spider has woven his web at your head,
To entangle some poor, winged victim 'tis spread;
He has just merely done what you often did do,
For many a victim was tangled by you!

If the treasures of earth were all circling your brow,
You'd not open your cold eyes to look on them now;
While travelling through life little mercy you knew;
Yet I hope our dear Saviour has mercy on you!

You lived for yourself and for no one you cared,
You saw friends in want while your money you spared;
You left if behind you – what more could you do?
Then no one – ay, nothing! should mourn for you!

McNamara's Band
W. W. Gleeson

My name is McNamara, I'm the Leader of the Band,
And tho' we're few in numbers we're the best in the land.
We play at wakes and weddings and at ev'ry fancy ball,
And when we play to funerals we play the march from Saul.

Oh! the drums go bang, the cymbals clang, the horns they blaze away,
McCarthy puffs the ould bassoon while I the pipes will play;
Hennessy Tennessy tootles the flute, and the music tis something grand,
A credit to Ould Ireland, boys, is McNamara's Band!

Whenever an election's on, we play on either side-
The way we play our fine ould airs fills Irish hearts with pride.
Oh! if poor Tom Moore was living now, he'd make yez understand
That none could do him justice like ould McNamara's Band.

Oh! the drums go bang, etc.

We play at wakes and weddings, and at every county ball,
And at any great man's funeral we play the "Dead March in Saul,"
When the Prince of Wales to Ireland came, he shook me by the hand,
And said he'd never heard the like of "McNamara's Band."

Oh! the drums go bang, etc.

Tra - la la lah, etc.

THERE are few of us who are not familiar with the above lines from the well-known song 'McNamara's Band'. But how many know that the world-wide celebrated musical ensemble got its name from the four Limerick brothers: Patrick, Michael, John and Thomas McNamara, all of whom were born at Meat Market Place, Old Thomas Street, off Athlunkard Street, in St. Mary's Parish, Limerick, in the latter part of the nineteenth century.

Thomas – the last of the quartette – paid his second, and last, visit in 64 years to the spot where he was born and reared, on July 18, 1965. He died in May, being the last survivor of the combination that won the All-Ireland Championship for St. Mary's Prize Band in 1895. His brother, Patrick, was the bandmaster on the occasion, when they 'stole the show' from 26 other groups . . . something rarely heard of nowadays.

Patrick was a musician and composer, and there were few who could claim to be his peer, with the honourable exception of his good friend and neighbour, Patrick Salmon of Church Street.

He played throughout the 32 Counties, at balls, Pattern Day celebrations, weddings, St. Patrick's Day parades; all the time with banner proclaiming 'McNamara's Band' of which he was leader and arranger.

When he emigrated to the United States in 1905, he carried with him this great musical tradition, and his orchestra there continued to be known as McNamara's Band. Reunited with his brother Thomas, who had arrived in the States in 1901, the combination soon caught the imagination of a Tin Pan Alley song writer, and so the famous tune was born.

In later years discs were cut for the Voralion Records by the McNamara trio: Thomas on the piccolo; Patrick the violin, and Patrick's daughter Eileen, on the piano. A number of other records were cut by the Aeolean Company in 1921, and some – set tunes, reel medleys, Irish waltz medleys and old classics – are treasured family possessions in the home of Mrs. Isobella McCarthy, Long Range, St. Francis Abbey – a niece of the McNamara's.

Patrick who did much to popularise Irish music in the States, visited Limerick with his wife and children in 1912. The return trip was to be made on the Titanic, but after some muddling, providentially for the McMamara's, the arrangement misfired.

All four brothers played in one row with St. Mary's Fife and Drum Band. Michael, A Boer War veteran, was an instructor and sergeant in the Royal Munster Fusiliers. He died in Devon in 1962. John was also attached to a regimental band, but was transferred to an ambulance corps during the Great War he was killed in France in 1916 while attending the wounded.

Thomas saw service with the British Navy; later with the army where he was awarded the 1914 Mons Star and British War medal, while also gaining the Merchant Marine medal and the Victory Medal 1914-18. Subsequently he was one of the crew that smuggled de Valera from Liverpool to the United States in 1920. He spent most of his chequered career with the American Navy, and for 23 years, after leaving the Merchant Marine, worked on the boats for the New York Fire Department.

When I organised the Old Limerick Historical Society's flight to New York for the World's Fair, in 1964, I tried to contact my old friend, but failed. Little did I think then that a year later I would bang into him in Nicholas Street, around the corner from where I lived in Exchange Street.

A month later I was to meet the grand veteran again – for the last time- as he accompanied this old band to St. Mary's Church for a feast-day celebration. It was to be his final parade and performance in the 'parish.'

It was a day of many memories for Thomas. He told me that all the old places that he knew were gone, and there was little left to remind him of the old days when he was a child. But it brought back the happy past when he met his bosom friend, Christopher 'Ducker' Nash, with whom he joined St. Mary's Band 75 years ago.

And so ends the McNamara's Band saga.

Those who gave it the name and musical life have passed over to the Great Majority; still in its ancient records the band plays on. And though the McMamara's and their band are gone their name will live forever in the words of the very popular song:

> *A credit to old Ireland*
> *Is McNamara's Band.*

From *The Old Limerick Journal*, No. 9, Winter 1981.

A Farewell to English
Michel Hartnett
(for Brendan Kennelly)

Her eyes were coins of porter and her West
Limerick voice talked velvet in the house:
her hair was black as the glossy fireplace
wearing with grace her Sunday-night-dance best.
She cut the froth from glasses with a knife
and hammered golden whiskies on the bar
and her mountainy body tripped the gentle
mechanism of verse: the minute interlock
of word and word began, the rhythm formed.
I sunk my hands into tradition
sifting the centuries for words. This quiet
excitement was not new; emotion challenged me
to make it sayable. The clichés came
at first, like matchsticks snapping from the world
of work: mánla, séimh, dubhfholtach, álainn, caoin:
they came like grey slabs of slate breaking from
an ancient quarry: mánla, séimh, dubhfholtach,

álainn, caoin, slowly vaulting down the dark
unused escarpments, mánla, séimh, dubhfholtach,
álainn, caoin, crashing on the cogs, splinters
like axeheads damaging the wheels, clogging
the intricate machine, mánla, séimh,
dubhfholtach, álainn, caoin. Then Pegasus
pulled up, the girth broke and I was flung back
on the gravel of Anglo-Saxon.
What was I doing with these foreign words?
I, the polisher of the complex clause,
wizard of grasses and warlock of birds
midnight-oiled in the metric laws?

dubhfholtach: blacklocked. álainn: beautiful. mánla, séimh and caoin: words whose meaning hover about the English adjectives graceful, gentle.

From *A Farewell to English*, The Gallery Press, 1975, 1978.

To an Infant
Aubrey de Vere

Familiar Spirit! that so graciously
Dost take whatever fortune may befall,
Trusting they fragile form to the arms of all,
And never counting it indignity
To sit caressed upon the humblest knee;
Thou, having yet no words, aloud dost call
Upon our hearts; the fever and the gall
Of our dark bosoms are reproved in thee.

From selfish fears and lawless wishes free,
Thou hast no painful feeling of thy weakness;
From shafts malign and pride's base agony
Protected by the pillows of thy meekness;
Thou hast thy little loves which do not grieve thee,
Unquiet make thee, or unhappy leave thee.

From *Poems of Aubrey de Vere*, McMillan & Co., 1894.

On the One-day-dead Face of my Father
Richard Harris

Can you touch me
now
With your marble lips
and increase your love?

Can you touch me
with your dead hand
and direct me in my path?

Now you can see me
in your dead
and say 'What is right?'
Though you know the answer now
Now in your stillness
Pave the way of my doing

Cold thoughts in your give
creep away
and stay
in your marble walk
and cold tombstone of your stare

Rise
now
above your mound and wound
and see your son in your eye
Touch again
the fond fountain of his
flow;
Grow
in the dead and deadly of your going

From *I, In The Membership Of My Days*, Michael Joseph Ltd., 1975.

EIGHT
SPORT

Limerick My Lady!
Tony Ward/John Scally

"SOCCER had been my game up to that match (Garryowen v. Wanderers) but I was immediately struck by the camaraderie of rugby. In the club house afterwards I remember our scrum-half, Liam Hall, getting up on the table and leading a sing-song. It was all so enjoyable and I remember that feeling of kinship and, at that moment, thinking this is the game for me. That weekend was the start of my demise in soccer and my rise in rugby. I never lost my love for soccer, even though I decided rugby was my number one. Throughout my career I always regretted that the rugby and soccer seasons coincided. Had they run at different times I would have combined both."

Ward feels a particular debt to Frank Hogan who nursed him along in the early days.

"He was in so many ways the father I never had."

The following week Ward was selected for his first Senior Cup game for the 'Light Blues' against Sunday's Well in Cork. Ironically, Garryowen were coached by a Cork man, Pat O'Riordan, that season:

"I had never heard of the 'Well'. I didn't know which teams were from Cork and which were from Limerick apart from the fact that Garryowen were obviously from Limerick and Cork Con was from Cork. Mind you, I wasn't long in learning I can assure you and the history and traditions attached to each.

"That cup game was a totally new experience for me as I had only been used to Leinster schools rugby. The passion and commitment of the players in my first taste of Munster competitive rugby will always remain in my mind. It was unbelievable. there were boots and fists flying everywhere. I was taken aback at the time but I learned subsequently that was a typical Munster Cup match.

(Garryowen went on to win the cup and Ward recalled):

"I really didn't appreciate the significance of the occasion at the time. In later years I came to appreciate that winning the Munster Cup was the ambition of every player in Munster and when you think of great players like Tom Clifford, Phil O'Callaghan, etc., who never won a Senior Cup medal, you began to appreciate its significance. It was all new to me and even today Leinster players cannot appreciate the passion that Limerick rugby arouses.

"I remember after the Old Crescent game walking down by the flats in Watergate, off William Street, and a couple of corporation workers, literally surveying the roads, shouted over the me: 'all the best in the Cup final Wardy.' This would never happen in a million years in Dublin as I was then a complete unknown. I found the experience very strange and very moving.

"I also recall O'Shaughnessy's florists alongside the Franciscan church with a full window display of white and blue flowers for Garryowen. Dublin rugby fans think I am exaggerating when I mention these happenings but they are part and parcel of every day life in that rugby daft city. Similarly, there was a big extension being built at the time in the college and I was amazed at the fact that so many of the construction workers knew so much about rugby. This to me was alien to what

I was used to in Dublin where your parents' choice of education decides what game you should play."

. . . .

"I was travelling with Mick Sherry to pay in the Blake Sevens, which is an annual event on Easter Monday run by Galwegians' rugby club. We stopped for petrol at Martin Bradshaw's service station on the Ennis Road. The pump attendant was John 'Fox' O'Halloran, the former president of Shannon rugby club – a great rugby gentleman. That epitomises Limerick rugby. You would never get anything like that in Dublin. Can you imagine driving into a petrol station in Dublin and being served by the president of Lansdowne or Wanderers? 'Fox' was one of the many great characters of Shannon with people like Michael Noel Ryan, Micky Yelverton, the late Enda McNamara, Gus O'Driscoll (a former Mayor or Limerick), Thady Coughlan (the youngest ever Mayor of Limerick), the late Willie 'Whack' Gleeson, the renowned Limerick historian, and Bob McConkey, Frankie Flynn and Tommy Creamer.

"Whenever Shannon won the Munster Cup final Frankie and Tommy would take turns to sing 'The Isle' which is the traditional Limerick ballad and rugby song, particularly of the Shannon rugby club. One of my own saddest memories is of sitting in the dressing room in both 1977 and '78 when Shannon defeated us in the Cup finals in Thomond, because, believe me, there is nothing worse than losing a Munster final, particularly to another Limerick team, and then having to listen to the Shannon fans singing 'their' song and virtually lifting the roof off the stand.

"I can still hear it to this day. It was an eerie sound. Nonetheless I could still appreciate their passion for all the despair and self-pity I was feeling. 1977 was the start of Shannon's glory years and nobody did more to bring them to their current high state in the Irish game that their coach, Brian O'Brien, their first Irish international and a former Ireland and Lions selector.

"The big song at the time was 'Don't Cry For Me Argentina' but they adapted it and came up with 'Don't Cry For Me Garryowen.' Of course their other great club song is 'Roll Along Shannon Forwards, Roll Along.' Forward play has been the traditional strength of both Shannon and Young Munster. Nowhere do they know their forward play better than in Limerick . . . .

"Another great memory I have is of the local pirate stations which were a huge novelty in Limerick at the time, The great Limerick institution then was the late John 'The Man' Frawley – star of Radio Luimní. He as one of the great pioneers of local radio and everyone was glued in when he read out the local obituaries. He would read out Mass times and also times of the Novena when it was on which was and is always a big thing in Limerick. He had his own pet names for the weather like 'Billy Breeze' and 'Sammy Sunshine.' Everyone knew his old Volkswagen car which he called 'The Galloping Maggot.' All he had in front of him was a copy of the *Cork Examiner*. He worked in the most primitive conditions but he was way ahead of his time." . . . . .

"Another thing about Limerick clubs and Munster rugby clubs generally, is that they regard beating Leinster clubs not as the be all and end all but pretty close to it because they perceive Leinster clubs to be arrogant. This is why Munster teams raise their game so much against Leinster sides and why a team from Munster has won the All-Ireland League every year so far and will win many more in the future." A classic story about the passion of Limerick teams' intense desire to beat Dublin teams goes back to a visit of Lansdowne to the Shannonside city to play Shannon. The dressing-room was being renovated at the time and there was a six inch gap in the wall which allowed the visiting side to listen in to the Shannon team talk. Their captain was exhorting the team to beat these 'pansies from Dublin.' His concluding remark, much to the mirth of the Dublin players, was: "I'll finish with just two words for you – (there was a pregnant pause) - A Tack!"

Ward's friend, Ken Ging, has a very special memory of travelling down to play Shannon in Ward's first match with the Wicklow club. He was coach at the time and had to suffer the frustration of seeing his side annihilated. After the game he got a bit worried when he saw a man, no more than five feet tall but seemingly the width, wearing a black beret approaching him with a menacing look. The stranger barked out at him: "Are you that team's coach?" Ging knew instinctively that it was not one of the times when honesty was the best policy and said: "No. I'm their coach driver!"

Ward attributes the success of Limerick clubs to three main characteristics: their passion for the game, their competitive spirit and their great personalities on and off the field:

"When you think about it, it's extraordinary that a city with a relatively small population has five senior clubs, including four in the top divisions of the AIL, not to mention the junior sides. When we would play Dublin clubs in friendly games, for example, it was approached almost like a Cup tie. It's going to take a huge effort for either Dublin or Ulster teams to win the AIL because of this attitude in Limerick and Munster in general – mind you the others are beginning to learn how to adapt and cope with it better.

"Young Munster's achievement in winning the All-Ireland League was extraordinary considering they have such a small geographical base and no old boys network to feed them new talent. In Dublin, clubs depend on schools but in Limerick they get boys from the age of under-10 and work with them all the way up . . . .

"It goes without saying that my love-affair with Limerick will be eternal. But one thing disappointed me greatly was when I was accused of bias when Young Munster beat St. Mary's in the decisive match of the AIL and of not giving Munsters a fair crack of the whip, as it were, in my analysis. Because of Fred Cogley's connections and indeed mine with St. Mary's he was considered, most unfairly, to be 'less than totally objective' in some of his comments. In my case it was guilt by association. I attribute the slur on me to a few local media people trying to stir things up in Limerick (they know themselves who they are). I was there at the match to do a job which I did honestly and objectively as possible. Those who said I was biased that day could not have been much more wrong and I was hurt by some of the comments and innuendoes. The irony is that on my Christmas mailing list for clubs St. Mary's would be a very, very long way from the top – and quite a way behind Young Munster at that."

From *The Good the Bad and the Rugby*,
the Official Biography of Tony Ward, Blackwater Press, 1993.

SPORT

A journey to an All Ireland - by lorry!
C. B. McKernan

IT was in the early thirties, Limerick had reached the All Ireland Final. Money was scarce and the prospect of getting to Dublin for the match remote, until word got round that Sweeney could provide a lorry and driver for a modest ten shillings a head. There would be a canvas cover in the event of rain. After much scrimping and scrounging, we got the money together and a few bob to spare. We were off to see Limerick play Dublin.

The lorry arrived at eight-thirty a.m., that Sunday. What a thrill we got as we scrambled aboard and secured seats on the forms provided! The more senior passengers were given first preference for the comfortable positions. The very young made cushions of their coats on the floor. The entire avenue turned out to wish us luck. The green flag was raised to resounding cheers.

It was 9 o'clock when we sallied forth. We had been to early Mass and packed a few sandwiches. There would be nothing to eat until after the match. The driver was cautious. He had a heavy load, so he decided to take the quieter roads. We went through Cashel. We met the Archbishop on the road, walking back from Mass. He blessed the passing lorry. Shortly after, disaster struck. We came to a sudden stop as a tyre exploded. We looked at one another in awe – surely it wasn't his Lordship. There were comments about the ancient rivalry between Tipperary and Limerick. Paddy Mick Ryan, whose origins were inside the Tipperary border, laughed and said that of course his county had enlisted supernatural support against our team. The driver hustled us off the lorry to stretch our legs while he changed the wheel. He told us to exercise our tongues too and start pleading with St. Christopher for his support.

Soon we were on our way again. The sun appeared and our spirits rose. On entering the square of the next town, our soaring spirits once again sank into our boots; we had two more flat tyres! It was 1 pm. We were still forty miles from Dublin. Our dream match was only two hours away. The driver, with the authority of a sergeant-major, marshalled his troops and buckets of water. Those past the age of strenuous work joined the locals in the nearby pub. They supped pints and peered through the windows while the repairs were being carried out and we took turns to pump up the tyres. Our elders, two pints later, were placed aboard and we were off again, with the hearty cheers of the locals ringing in our ears.

The next few bad patches of road were treated with respect. Only the elderly were allowed stay on board while the driver steered though cut stone chippings. He shouted encouragement at us. We kept up with that lorry as if she was a stage coach carrying bullions of gold.

The last few miles of our journey seemed to grow longer, the seconds ticked ever faster. Each pothole hurt not only our posteriors as frayed tempers snapped with each toppled poise. Ned Ryan, who was known as 'The Curser', hurled maledictions on the lorry, the roads and the driver. He, in turn, blamed 'the bunch of magpies' he had taken aboard.

We arrived in Dublin's city centre with four instead of six wheels intact. There was a frantic scramble off the lorry and a mad rush for the 'Park.' One man, who had taken an extra pint, jumped on a tram. He later said he listened to the match on the radio in the comfort of a pub near the Phoenix Park. Another, less fortunate, caught his trouser turn-up on the lorry, struck his head on the pavement and spent the evening in Jervis Street Hospital. He got seven stitches.

With a companion, who knew the way, I ran like hell to the grounds. We arrived panting brandishing our banner. It was half-time. The attendant let us in for half-price; we had to jump over the stile. The match was restarted. Breathless though we were, we opened our throats and let out the roar. 'Come on Limerick.'

Nearby spectators jumped with shock. There had been a lull in play. They said we brought the excitement back. The result was in doubt until the final whistle. It was a draw. I was relieved. The excitement of the match was instantly replaced with the anticipation of the replay.

Flat tyres were not a feature of the journey home, but rain and sudden gusts of wind were. We huddled together. Outbursts of song took our minds off all the drips and trickles. Our chorus rose to a grand crescendo when we reached home. It was after mid-night. Neighbours spilled out to hear our account of the day.

Over our midnight feast of cold meat, bread and butter and pots of tea, we filled them in on the long journey and the match. The Dublin team had had a father and son playing; the father was in goal. But it was the deeds of Mick Mackey, Paddy Clohessy, Paddy Scanlan and Mick Cross that brought the smiles to their faces and the shrill of excitement to our voices.

Our dreams of going to the replay never materialised. Sweeney just shook his head when he surveyed his tyres. Instead, we listened to it on the best radio in the neighbourhood. And Limerick won next time round!

The Old Limerick Journal, 1987. No. 21.

The Munster Monster
Pat Shortt

LET me out from under this never-endin' Munster rugby scrum. Now, don't get me wrong, I'm as proud a Munsterman as the next fella, but I've had an overdose of rugby and rugby experts lately. I am delighted when they win. The best win of all time, of course, was that one against Biarritz in Cardiff and, like everyone in the province, I nearly had heart failure durin' the match. I walked the backyard for the last ten minutes in fear and trepidation that, like the Battle of Kinsale, the '98 Risin' and the Civil War, the misfortunate Gael would once again snatch defeat from the jaws of victory.

In fact, without any great knowledge of the sport I had come to the conclusion that Limerick hurlin', and Munster rugby have a lot in common: great entertainment, great heroics and little silverware. I was beginnin' to believe that the Munster team was the teaser pony of the Heineken cup: it created a bit of excitement before the real stallions took over. I'm relieved I was proved wrong.

Aside from all the mopin,' I know nothin' about rugby except that a try gets you five points, a conversion adds two to it and a penalty gets you three. For all I know, when it comes to rucks, mauls, scrum halfs, lock forwards and hookers, you could be talkin' about the internal workin's of a JCB or someone makin' a livin' on the streets of Amsterdam.

I'm afraid not everyone is as frank as myself about their knowledge of this rough sport for young gentlemen. I'm worn from listenin' to eejits who have transmogrified into clones of George Hook over the last two weeks. There are fellas who have been watchin' junior football and hurlin' for a generation and still know nothin.' The intricacies of rules governin' the square ball is beyond them – they're the clowns who call for the referee to be lynched for disallowin' a goal even when the full forward has been sittin' on the goalie for ten minutes before the ball comes near the square.

Years ago, people weren't a bit shy about displayin' their ignorance. The day Ireland won the Triple Crown in 1985 Tom Cantwell's father was in Walshe's pub holdin' on to the counter with one hand and to the remnants of his life with the other. When asked what he thought of the match, he declared: 'Twould be a grand game if they would only pump up the auld ball. Sure, by the end of the match, 'tis gone into a duck egg from them big lazy hoors lyin' down on it.' God be with the days of the honest man.

The Cardiff match and its aftermath have left me with serious questions about the mental state of the people of this country. The notions some people have got has to be seen to be believed. Some fellas are turnin' up to GAA matches in sheepskin coats and carryin' noggins of brandy, while others have developed the flattest Limerick accents you ever heard.

But what bates Banagher is the rash of rugby-style pet-names people have taken to givin' one another. The rugby crowd loves to rechristen their buddies with names you wouldn't give a pom dog. I went into the pub the other night and discovered the infection had spread to my own intimate circle of friends. Cantillon had become 'Canty', Quirke had become 'Quirky', Walshe had become 'Walshie' and Cantwell was now referred to as 'Wellie.' At first I chose to ignore this rugbification of titles until Tom Walshe addressed me as 'Hicksie.' I told him if he didn't ban these pet-names, I'd bar myself from his premises.

I can't take much more of this Munster live-in. Thanks be to St. Jude for the return of the Munster championship when Cork, Tipperary, Limerick, Clare, Waterford and Kerry revert to the natural state of mutual hatred that has existed between them since Adam was a gorsoon. As it was in the beginnin' . . . .

From *I Will In Me Politics – The Maurice Hickey Diaries*, The O'Brien Press, 2007.

My Beloved Bohemians
Sean J. Fielding / Aidan Corr

SEAN Fielding always had a deep love of Bohemians Rugby football club. Ever since his late father, Pat, took him on his first Bohs game as a very young boy in Limerick, he had held an affinity to the 'Reds' and he has held many posts within the club over a period of over sixty years.

"In 1930, during the Christmas holiday period of that year, Freddie Lawlor from Ballinacurra and myself decided that we would play at schoolboy level with Bohemians RFC. We were both playing for Sexton Street CBS at the time. I needed little persuasion. From the time I was seven it was my ambition to wear the red jersey.

"Bohs had been formed some years earlier and according to legend, the club came into being when a group consisting of the O'Sullivan's, the McMahons, the Ryans and the Stokes brothers joined 'Tishy' Auchmuty in Geary's Hotel in Thomas Street, held a formal meeting and registered the club with the Munster Branch.

"And thereby hangs a tale - about the red jersey, I mean! A long and argumentative meeting took place at the first Bohemians meeting as to what colours they would wear. They failed to reach an agreement so it was decided that a few committee members would go to Nestors in O'Connell Street and see what colours were available.

"But like Old Mother Hubbard, when they got there the cupboard was bare. The only jerseys available at the particular time were red ones. So the decision was made for the boys. Like Henry Ford and his model T cars, "you can have any colour you want as long it was black! Bohemians were told they could have any colour as long as it was red! Bohs have worn it with pride ever since.

"Our first competition was a Junior Medal Competition organised by the Pioneer Total Abstinence Association. How very appropriate – or maybe they were trying to tell us something! Be that as it may, Bohs were not long in finding their feet on the rugby fields of Munster. We won the Munster Senior Cup in 1927, having lost in the final to Garryowen in 1926. We were on our way.

"Our headquarters in those early days were in the Catholic Institute Grounds at Rosbrien. The grounds were mostly used by the Catholic Institute members for hockey, cricket and tennis but there was space for a rugby pitch there also. The initials for the Catholic Institute were of course CI, and the same held good for the Church of Ireland. A little confusion raised its head at times and we were sometimes labelled a Protestant club. The name Fielding seemed to fit that bill.

"Our 'pavilion' at the grounds was a small galvanised shed where the groundsman Peter Crowley (a legend in his own lifetime), who lived with his family in a cottage on the grounds, stored all his needs. The grounds were always immaculate so he needed a lot of equipment. As a result, he togged out amidst a collection of lawnmowers, tennis court machines, rakes, shovels, buckets and bags of lime and whitewash brushes.

"The showers were something else. We washed while straddling the small but freezing cold stream that flowed past the pavilion. I remember my father and Ted Russell and others coming out by car to the training sessions. They would sometimes use their car lights to throw more light onto the pitch during the winter training nights. There were no alternators in the cars in those days so car batteries never lasted too long when they were being used to train Bohs.

"Those were not great days and nights, but hope was at hand. In 1938 Bohemians moved to Thomond Park. Our first game there was against Young Munster. In 1955 we opened our new pavilion there and extended it in 1962. We moved into our present fine complex in 1990 when the new stand was completed.

"Our glory years, if such a name is appropriate, were between 1958 and 1962. We won the Munster Senior Cup in 1958, '59 and '62; the Munster Senior League in 1959 and the Limerick Charity Cup in 1957, '59 and '60.

"J P Mullane from West Limerick, and some of whose relatives now are big in the tourist business in Chicago and maintain constant contact with this country, was the first Bohemian to wear the green of Ireland. That was in 1928. Des Torrens, M. E. Bardon, Mick English, Bill Mulcahy and Brian Spillane brought the same honour to the club. Many others who had worn the red jersey subsequently played for Ireland. Maurice Mortell, and Sean McHale readily come to mind. Then there is Tommy Lenihan, an under 25 international; J. Barry, Ireland B; T. Shire, O. Moran (also of Limerick hurling fame), Martin Cahill and Tom Clifford, all Ireland youth internationals.

"There have been famous names associated with Bohemians RFC. I remember the first coach, 'Petty' O'Neill. He had been a chief petty officer in the Royal Navy in the 1914-18 war. There were the Stokes brothers. There was the greatest character of all, 'Tishy' Auchmuty, who hated Garryowen and if and when Bohs defeated the 'light blues', which was not often, he would celebrate for days.

"Dave Barry is sadly no longer around but his name is remembered each year when we meet Dolphin for the cup that is named after him. 'Maxi' Hogan, for years another staunch Bohs and Dolphin man, is thankfully still with us though living in Cork. And so are Gerry Dixon, 'Mebs' Bardon and our well known playwright and author, Ged Galvin. Donie Dononvan was a captain in a bracket of his own. Mick English was, in my opinion, the most under-rated out-half ever to play for Ireland. His partner at scrum-half, the late Tommy Cleary, a substitute for Ireland on fourteen occasions, was the best scrum-half never to have been capped.

"Ted Russell retired at an early age when he was on the brink of being named for the international side. He turned his attentions to politics, became mayor of the city and was a member of the Limerick City council for a thousand years! Thankfully, he is still with Bohs where on occasions when the boat is foundering, he is called upon to pour oil on troubled waters and keep it afloat. His son, George, is now in line to become president of the club in succession to John Reidy."

From *A Horse With Good Handwriting: Sean J. Fielding's Memories of Limerick* by Aidan Corr, 1998.

A Shattered Dream
Thomas Toomey

AT the beginning of 1936 hopes were extremely high within the circles of the Irish Army Equitation team that that year would see them fulfil the destiny that they believed was rightfully theirs. The winning of the Olympic gold medal for show jumping had been the goal which the team had set for itself at the beginning of the 1934 season and now, as the 1936 season opened, it looked to be well within their capability. The winning of the gold medal, they felt, would set the seal on their claim to be the foremost equestrian team in the world.

At the Olympia show on Tuesday June 22nd, 1936, Gerard O'Dywer was to annex one of the most prestigious individual prizes in the world of showjumping when he won the King's Cup on *Limerick Lace*. In doing so he was furthering the bond between himself and Colonel Rodzianko, who had won the event twice before the outbreak of the First World War. Ironically the competition had started, rather disastrously, when *Limerick Lace* refused at the first jump. However, O'Dwyer then really got down to work and they cleared the rest of the fences with plenty to spare. To further emphasise the mood and form of the Irish in the competition, Captain Jack Lewis and Captain Fred Ahern were joint second on Tramore Bay and Blarney Castle, respectively. Major Joe Dudgeon and the French Captain, Bizard, also claimed a share of second place. All the second placed horses had recorded four faults for having one fence down. Following his victory the King's Trophy was presented to the winning Irishman by Sir Anthony Eden, Secretary of State for Foreign Affairs. It was an extremely proud moment for the Irish as the 'Soldiers Song' ran out throughout the arena.

In the Prince of Wales Cup, which was Britain's Nation's Cup, the Irish finished in second place to the French. It was a measure of how the Irish team had evolved, that finishing second, in such a prestigious event, was regarded as a disappointing result.

In the Nations Cup at Amsterdam, held in beautiful weather conditions before a packed arena, which included Queen Wilhelmina, the Irish again swept to victory. Commandant O'Dwyer also won the individual award for the outstanding rider in the Nations Cup with two faultless rounds. In addition, he also won the award for the outstanding rider of the show. A note in the files, in the Military Archives, commented on the tremendous reception accorded to the team by the Amsterdam crowds. On a slightly different note however, a communication from the Secretary of the Department of Defence, Mr. M.J. Bery, to the Secretary of External Affairs, Mr. Sean Murphy, complains about the fact that at the official Horse Show dinner Commandant O'Dwyer, who was the head of the Irish party and also O/C of the Irish Cavalry School, was placed very far down in the order of dignitaries, notwithstanding the fact that he was the most senior Irish person present.

On Sunday July 12th, at Lucerne, the Irish wrote themselves into the record books when they won the Swiss Nations Cup for the third successive year and as a consequence they won the trophy outright.

SPORT

Sometime after their arrival back from Lucerne, Gerard O'Dwyer received the devastating news that the team had been withdrawn from the Olympics. Commandant O'Dwyer, even years later, was not too clear as to how he was given the news. He believes that he would have been informed verbally by Colonel O'Carroll and then been given the decision in writing. However, there is no record in the Military Archives relating to that order or decision to withdraw the team. Indeed, there is no reference to the teams participation or non-participation in the Olympics, whatsoever. The decision about withdrawing the team remains, even to the present day, one of the most – if not *the* most, controversial in Irish sport.

Apparently there had been a major dispute about the representation of Irish athletics in the international sphere. In the 1928 and the 1932 Olympics athletes from the N.A.C.A.I. (National Athletics and Cycling Association of Ireland) had represented Ireland with outstanding success. The N.A.C.A.I. was however a body which legislated for athletes north and south of the border and it was this point which was to bring it into conflict with the International Athletics Federation. The N.A.C.A.I.'s claim to legislate north and south was contested by the British and the international body took the side of the British. Negotiations on the matter between the N.A.C.A.I. and the International Federation broke down and this led to the N.A.C.A.I. being excluded from competing abroad. The N.A.C.A.I. were believed to have put a lot of pressure on the Fianna Fail administration of Mr. de Valera to withdraw all Irish teams from the Olympics.

It seems that it was on the foot of this pressure that a decision was taken to withdraw the team. Indeed the controversy did not even end there as, initially, it was believed that the decision was made at a cabinet meeting. However, some of the ministers, primarily Frank Aiken and Sean McEntee, stated in later years that no one in the cabinet was consulted and that Mr. de Valera had made the decision without reference to anyone. Indeed, both McEntee and Aiken stated that if they had been consulted they would have been against the withdrawal of the team.

For Gerard O'Dwyer and indeed for the rest of the team members and their close advisors and friends, the decision was a devastating blow. All the struggle, sweat, effort and hardship had been in vain and the great dream of Olympic glory was now a tarnished memory. As no record now remains in the Military Records as to the exact timing of the decision it would appear that the decision was made and relayed sometime between the 28th of July and the commencement of the RDS Show on August 4th.

Indeed, in a private letter to Gerard O'Dwyer, dated July 13th, 1936, Colonel O'Carroll, who was then holidaying in County Monaghan, was extremely upbeat on account of the success of the team at Lucerne and there is no intimation of anything untoward in the contents of the letter. On this basis it would appear that no decision had been made at that stage to withdraw or if it had it does not appear to have been relayed to Colonel O'Carroll.

Commandant O'Dwyer was extremely close to tendering his resignation in disgust, at what he felt was a cynical political stroke and which he felt smacked of Civil War opportunism. The decision to withdraw the team was to fester with him over the next number of years and indeed it was to be at the root of his eventual decision to leave the army. It is probable that, were it not for the tactful handling of Colonel O'Carroll, Gerard O'Dwyer would have resigned from the army soon after the announcement of the withdrawal

To exacerbate matters even further, O'Dwyer was informed that he was to travel to the Olympics as a non participating, token emissary. This decision, which was possibly an even more insensitive and pointless gesture, was intended as an appeasing sop to the Germans. It was also to remove any illusion that the Irish team had withdrawn for idealistic reasons such as abhorrence of fascism. Ultimately, the question would have to be posed that if there were two strong chances of gold medals in athletics and there was a similar rift within equestrian circles, would the Irish athletics team be withdrawn to appease persons within the equestrian world. The issue of the withdrawal was to continue to haunt the team members ever afterwards and Gerard O'Dwyer would say that as a group, or even individually, they never discussed the matter. The hurt feelings and bitter disappointment were too great. To compound the bitterness and their sense of frustration was the fact that no word of explanation, consolation or apology was ever received. It was a very clear and harsh reminder that those in the public service are but pawns at the behest of their political masters.

Prior to the Olympics, the matter of the RDS Show had to be taken care of. If it can ever be said that the Royal Dublin Horse show was a total anticlimax, even before the event was held, then such was the case in August 1936. Ostensibly, five nations were to participate at Ballsbridge, England, France, Belgium, Holland the host nation, Ireland. On the surface it would appear that there was a strong an international presence as in previous years but the underlying fact that the foreign nations had only entered second string horses, as all their first choice mounts were being held for the Olympics. The Irish trio of Gerard O'Dwyer, Jack Lewis and Dan Corry achieved a narrow victory over England in the Aga Khan Cup.

Immediately following the completion of the horseshow at Ballsbridge Commandant Gerard O'Dwyer set out on a very depressing visit to the Olympic Games which were being held in Berlin. It was a very bitter and frustrating experience for the thirty seven year old County Limerick man. He attended all events in the full uniform of an Irish Officer. The betting within equestrian circles, prior to the Irish team having been pulled out, was 6 to 4 against, that the Irish would win the gold and Germany were at odds of 4 to 1 against. One could virtually have any odds on the rest of the teams.

On the morning of the show-jumping, he walked the course and tried to gauge how the Irish team would have performed. He reckoned that, at worst, the Irish would have incurred sixteen, maybe twenty, faults. In the event, Germany won the gold with forty four faults. Holland were placed second with fifty one and Portugal picked up the bronze medals with a total of fifty six faults.

In the individual medals, Oberleutenant Kurt Hasse of Germany won the gold with the Romanian Henri Rang, taking silver and the Hungarian, Josef Von Platthy, taking the bronze. It was especially galling for O'Dwyer to know that Germany took the gold without even jumping well, and the Dutch, who had never finished ahead of the Irish in any Nation's Cup in the previous four years, picked up the silver medals. In the individual contest, any of the four Irishmen, O'Dwyer, Ahern, Lewis or Corry, was capable of lifting the medals. Certainly, O'Dwyer and Ahern would have been extremely fancied and it was well within the bounds of possibility that any three of the four might have made a clean sweep of the individual awards. One memory that O'Dwyer did bring back from Berlin in 1936 was the noticeable increase in militarism in the country.

From *Forgotten Dreams, the Life and Times of Major J.G. "Ged" O'Dwyer*, O'Brien-Toomey publishers, 1995.

A reunion of the heart
John Scally

AS Tony Ward's rugby star ascended in Limerick he decided to make a return to soccer.

"Up to joining Garryowen I had been playing nothing only soccer with Rovers and nothing else. The travelling though was killing me and that was why I had to leave Miltown. I had spent two years at Glenmalure Park and it was a troubled period for Rovers. The slump was beginning to bite and after my first season, the man who signed me, Liam Tuohy, resigned. That's when everything went really downhill. We had a number of managers then including Shay Noonan, Dickie Giles (Johnny's dad), Mick Meegan, and Sean Thomas. Sean asked me back in '77 when I played about half-a-dozen matches for them.

"John Herrick, then Limerick manager, had come to me on a few occasions after that but I was solely concentrating on rugby then. When Eoin Hand and Dave Mahedy came along they got me at the right time."

On 10 August, 1981, Ward played his first soccer game for Limerick – a friendly against Spurs with Glen Hoddle putting on an exhibition of football at its very best. A few weeks later he played against Southampton in the UEFA Cup. Thrown in at the deep end, Ward did more than just play, he set the soccer public agog with his performance. Although Limerick lost 3-0, Ward's display caught the eye of Kevin Keegan who was sufficiently impressed to remark:

"Some players have the ability to generate excitement by running onto the pitch. Tony Ward would appear to be one of them. It was a fine performance from a man who could have made a name for himself in top class soccer. He could probably make a lot of money for himself . . . money is not everything but it makes life a lot easier..."

Lawrie McMenemey was generous in his praise for Limerick: "They certainly hit us with everything in the first half and Tony Ward buzzed around like he was at Twickenham. For a while I was half expecting Terry Wogan to come on."

He was also impressed by Ward's tremendous display of wing play and expressed the view that Ward had what it takes to make it in the big time. "With fulltime coaching it would not take much to play him in higher company."

For his part Ward was very impressed by Keegan:

"Soccer and rugby have at least one thing in common – the higher you go in class, the easier it is to play. Sharing the same pitch with Kevin Keegan, Mike Channon, Dave Watson and Alan Ball, was a marvellous experience. And of these, Keegan was easily the greatest."

"Soccer has always meant a lot to me, but when it came to priorities, it was no contest – it has got to be rugby. When it comes to playing nothing could compare to the involvement of rugby. And to me, sport is all about enjoyment.

"Young people who work hard all week, crave the satisfaction of playing at the weekend. In that I was no different from anybody else. Put another way, representative honours came low down the list, when I was asked to explain my motivation in sport."

Ward became particularly close to Eoin Hand in those years.

"Eoin was brought to Limerick by my dear old friend, the late, great Harry Gibson Steele, a great character, friend and indeed Peter Clohessy's father-in-law. Eoin was far and away the best soccer manager I ever played under. He was a brilliant organiser, as honest as the day is long and he played with total commitment. His success in Limerick is unparalleled. In his three years there they qualified for Europe each season and they won both the League and Cup. To be a successful manager you must have a ruthless streak, perhaps that was Eoin's weakness, but there was nothing he liked better than a night with the lads. Eoin was a great singer and he became very close friends with Frank Hogan. They were inseparable during Eoin's time in Limerick.

"I was a bit annoyed to see the way Eoin was portrayed in the media towards the end of his reign with the Irish team. Perhaps he did allow himself to be excessively influenced by the star players on the team like Liam Brady and Frank Stapleton but one thing he brought to every job in which he was involved was total professionalism down to the smallest of details. He was a very good manager and Limerick will never forget him.

"One thing about playing for Limerick which I always had some misgivings about, was that I only played at the start of the season, usually in the glamour friendlies against teams like Tottenham and Manchester United and at the end of the season in Cup matches. The result was that I missed much of the hard toil in the winter months on muddy pitches and dreadful weather. I feared some people might resent that I was only around for the big games because I missed so many 'bread and butter' matches during the rugby season but Eoin was happy, Limerick were happy and so was I. 'We had great players and marvellous characters in the squad like Muckels' O'Donnell, Kevin Fitzpatrick, Johnny Walsh, Al Finucane, Joe O'Mahony, Pat Nolan, Des Kennedy and Tony Meaney to name but a few and great supporters in people like Michael Crowe, Mick Webb and Willie Flaherty.'

Sunday 2, 1982, May saw Ward play for Limerick in the FAI Cup final at Dalymount Park against Bohemians before a crowd of 12,000 people who paid £25,000 to watch a memorable match. He had a significant impact on the match by being involved in a move with Garry Hulmes and man-of-the-match Johnny Walsh to force a corner in the 33rd minute. Ward took a low corner for Brendan Storan to get a touch and stroke the ball home though a tangle of legs for the only goal of the game. In the second half Ward tortured the Boh's defence with a dazzling display of old-fashioned wing play. It's a game he remembers with understandable affection.

"You can't compare the two sports. As regards rugby internationals there is nothing on the domestic football scene to compare with them. Naturally, I was more nervous before such occasions but I admit I was edgy before playing in the FAI Cup final. It's good to have butterflies and I always like to get them. I was always a worrier anyway."

"After we won the Cup in '82 we had a fabulous session in the Burlington arranged by Eoin Hand. Shaun Connors was MC and Luke Kelly, the Dublin City Ramblers and the Wolfe Tones performed for us.

"I played for Limerick because I enjoyed it. The Cup medal was a bonus. I'll never forget though the reception we got when we arrived home to Limerick the Monday after the final and parading through the city on an open-deck bus. It was a really special occasion and memory.

"My one regret was that I was forced to miss the celebratory dinner to mark Garryowen's first Munster League win since 1954 which was on the night before we played Bohs. My cup final appearance deprived me of opportunity to play for a team I had selected myself, to play against Thomond rugby club, arguably the best junior club in the country, at the request of Seamus Kiely and Declan Cusack to celebrate the opening of their new pitch at Woodview. I had organised my back row to be Shay, David and Kevin Deering. It was one thing both Kevin and David thanked me for subsequently – for giving them their only opportunity to play with their brother Shay.

"A few months later on 2 August 1982 I played my last competitive game of 11-a-side soccer in a friendly match between Limerick and Manchester United. It was a lovely way to finish though it was not planned that way. It was the day that the Leaving Cert results came out. Kevin Moran, Bryan Robson, Ray Wilkins, who is one of the most charming people I've met in any sport, and I ended up in the Parkway Hotel. There was a marvellous atmosphere because of the exam elation.

"I never accepted a penny for playing for Limerick even when we won the Cup, despite the fact that they were one of the wealthiest clubs in the country at the time. Pat Grace was at the helm and he put a lot of money into Limerick soccer and to the League of Ireland in general. I was being so careful in avoiding anything which would antagonise the IRFU, particularly in relation to my amateur status, even though they were two totally separate sports!"

From *The Good the Bad and the Rugby, the Official Biography of Tony Ward*, Blackwater Press, 1993.

How Tom Clifford Became a Forward
(and other sporting memories)
Sean J. Fielding

IT was the rugby season of 1937/38. It was Munster Senior Schools cup time and in a first round encounter Christian Brothers, Sexton Street, were matched against Rockwell College away from home.

I had been full back on the team for this and the previous season. Then Tom Clifford arrived at Sexton Street. He began playing rugby and by the time that we were to play Rockwell, he had established himself in the side. Brother O'Dea and Mr Malone were our mentors and there were no managers or coaches in those long-ago days. In their limitless wisdom they picked the team and, surprise, surprise, Tom Clifford was the new full-back and I was switched from the number 15 shirt to the centre.

The game was played in Clonmel and I do not remember at which particular rugby ground. Rockwell won by 27 (or was it 37) points to nil and as the late great Tom Reid once said, "we were lucky to get the nil"! They gobbled us up. None of us were any good but it was more than obvious that poor Tom Clifford was completely out of his place at full-back.

Nothing went right for him and to crown it all one of the Maddens from Rathkeale laid him low in the second half with an uppercut that would have done justice to Mike Tyson. There were no substitutes allowed the, so when Tom was carried off, Fielding (yours truly) reverted to his usual position at full-back. Wasn't Fielding a great name for a full-back? "He'd catch taws for you." "A great pair of hands." "Fielding by name and never by nature." They had a million such sayings in those days.

Tom Clifford never played full back again. He tried the forwards and there he found his true vocation. He became arguably one of the greatest forwards to ever wear the green jersey and I often wonder had he been a successful full-back that day in Clonmel would he have gone on to be as successful in that lonely position.

And what about Fielding? He went on to become a fairly useful full-back with a big, long drive of a ball with either foot. He played in the centre too and out-half. Nothing more!

. . . .

THERE are stories told of Limerick rugby, true or apocryphal, they are still doing the rounds with little change from when I first heard them many years ago.

There was the forward, a member of the Arch confraternity and a pious man, who could not resist kicking opponents in the head when the opportunity arose, during a game. When they writhed in pain on the ground following the indiscretion, he would kneel over them and say an act of Contrition in their ear.

The same guy was accused of going over to a fallen opponent, kneeling down beside him and putting his mouth to the stricken player's ear and telling him in no uncertain terms and "if you ever kick me in the scrum again I'll kick the effin' head

SPORT

off you!"

The crowd, of course, considered this player to be a true gentleman as all they saw was his apparent care and sympathy for the injured party. If they only knew the truth, then it would have been a different story.

Bohemians and Garryowen were meeting in a 'needle' cup match about which much hype had been generated. The Markets Field was the venue and both sides had made a 'hard man' available especially for the occasion in case the game took a robust turn.

Bohemians kicked off and there was the usual ruck and maul. Inevitably, a few fists flew and the referee's shrill whistle was heard half way down Mulgrave Street. The two 'hard men' were singled out and sent to the sideline, shaking hand with each other graciously as they left the field after only seconds of action.

The game went on in perfect peace and harmony, or as near to those as was possible.

....

WE were all members of a fourball in Adare Golf Club. There was Aidan Walsh, Des Tighe, Joe Hanrahan and myself and it was Walsh and Tighe versus Hanrahan and Fielding who played every week-end and on some summer evenings for half a crown a man over eighteen holes. If the light hadn't faded we would play what we called 'the short circuit' which consisted of four holes near the clubhouse.

The second of these holes was a par three. I was last to play but while the others were on the green I mis-hit my shot and it fell half way. As I prepared to play my second shot, Aidan Walsh, who was on the green, shouted: "Would you like me to hold the flag Sean?" "Please, Adian," I replied as it was getting dark and even then the old eyes were not too good.

So Aidan held the flag but when I wasn't looking he moved it about ten yards to the left. I lined up my shot and played it. The distance was perfect but to my chagrin and disappointment the direction was all awry. The ball hopped once and then rolled on. I was ten yards to the right of the flag, held by Walsh.

Then, suddenly, the ball disappeared into the hole. Aidan threw the flag at me in disgust. It was one of the worst golf shots I had ever played but with one of the best results. And a half crown was not to be laughed at – particularly when it was I who did all the laughing!

From *A Horse With Good Handwriting: Sean J. Fielding's Memories of Limerick* by Aidan Corr, 1998.

Limerick v. Wexford
Con Houlihan

I WASN'T in Dublin on the eve of Clontarf and I haven't an inkling of the mood on that day; perhaps the atmosphere was little different from the usual. Perhaps the fishermen down below in Ringsend were following the ancient profession adorned by Peter and his brethren and perhaps Molly's ancestors were busier than usual because a day of abstinence was imminent – all I know is that the peasants of Brabant milked their cows on the morning of Waterloo.

I suppose it is fair to say that this afternoon's showdown is awaited as eagerly as any Hurling All-Ireland ever; it isn't too long since you could stroll up to Croke Park after the pubs closed and be sure of getting into one terrace or another. The long absence of Limerick and Wexford from the crock of gold under the rainbow has added to the ferment. A fair proportion of the lads and lasses whose hearts will rise and sink this afternoon have never known their counties win September glory. To me is seems only a few years ago since Limerick took gold – in fact, twenty-three years have gone by; Wexford haven't been in the winners' enclosure since 1968.

I should be more excited about today's game than about any hurling final ever because both forces are dear to my heart. I need hardly add that in our part of Kerry we follow the green and white.

I grieved especially after the All-Ireland semi-final between Galway and Limerick in 1981. That was the occasion when Sean Foley was harshly sent off. Sean wrote me a long letter about his trauma; he felt that his dismissal had cost Limerick the game and probably the All-Ireland. I never showed the letter to anybody – Sean's sorrow was intensely private. Limerick folk will tell you that the loss of that semi-final cast a gloom from which it has taken a long time to recover.

How can I make a forecast for today? My heart says Limerick. My head says Wexford. My head is in confusion, I have seen Limerick only once this season – that is, apart from on television. I have seen Wexford three times – they excelled against Offaly and Galway.

I have no doubts about Limerick's defenders and mid-fielders. Unless their forwards make a great leap upward, my neighbours in the hills north of Castleisland will not see the glow from the bonfires in Abbeyfeale and Broadford and Templeglantine and Castlemahon and beyond.

Sunday World, 1 September, 1996. From *In So Many Words*, Mercier Press, 2002.

Be a Proud Shannon Man
Maureen Sparling

AN old man on his death-bed lay,
His body weak, his cheeks so dim,
A strong man once, he played the field,
His virile strength, alas, worn thin.

His grandson by his beside sat,
Sad tears rolled down his cheeks so red,
The old man eyed the youthful frame,
And to him these words of wisdom said:

As you go through life, my dear young lad,
Stand tall and be truthful, if you can,
But win or lose, you must always remember,
To be a proud Shannon rugby man.

The boy's lips quivered, his young hands shook,
He had loved this old man all his life,
He had shared with him his joys and sorrows,
His happy moments and those of strife.

Then, all of a sudden, the old man rose,
A former strength he did assume,
Two socks he rolled up altogether,
Which he kicked like a ball about the room.

The young lad's eyes then all alight
Took in the action swift and fast,
He saw a man who loved the game,
Trying to relive his rugby past.

The sock-ball rolled on and on,
He reached to grab it and on it lie,
See that! He roared with vibrancy,
I've just now scored my very last try.

Back to his death-bed he then hobbled,
His breath was short, his strength had waned,
Yet, he felt good and knew it well,
For, a victory over self he'd gained.

The young boy rose, his crying ceased,

No longer an old man he viewed,
He left that bedside much altered then,
His mind in gear, his strength renewed.

And, as that steep stairs descended,
These wise words through his young head ran,
But, win or lose, you must always remember,
To be a proud Shannon rugby man.

From a *Gem in the Wasteland*, Insignia Publications, 2002.

My Early Hurling Days
Séamus Ó Cinnéide

WITH Limerick doing battle on the field of Thurles last Sunday, the emotional epidemic diagnosable as Munster Hurling Championship fever gripped our citizens and country folk.

This peculiar fever heightens as the home county team graduates victoriously up to the Munster Final. If they take the Munster Championship beating whoever has the temerity to oppose them in the All-Ireland is only an unavoidable formality.

Like in my own young days – the golden 1930s of Mick Mackey's era – it's a certainty that every Limerick young fellow that wields a caman dreams of getting at least one all-Ireland medal pinned proudly on his chest.

The Golden Thirties were exhilarating years for aspiring young hurlers. Our heroes were home produced and accessible. My pals then and myself can proudly reminisce that not only did we see Mickey Mackey and his men play superbly – but we often got hurleys that suffered damage in the Homeric battles of those times from them.

How is it, given all the glorious hurling heroes, you never made the hurling scene?

It all had to do with a Kilkenny-born Christian Brother who was our mentor when we were novice hurlers at Sexton Street CBS. He was a whimsical class of a tyrant where hurling was concerned. From the first Autumn days we were in his class, he conscripted the whole lot of us up to the Claughaun field, near Ballysimon. A few of what he scathingly called 'sissies' and two or three from snob suburbia – whose families never had a hurler in them – tried to dodge the draft by coming back at lunchtime without camans– as sternly ordered.

He fixed them. The school maintenance man (from the Pike, Claughaun territory, where boys used to be born with a caman clutched in their infant hands) ran some extra hurleys into the classroom.

The conscientious objectors were armed with these and marched with the rest up to Claughaun field straight from school that afternoon. The Kilkenny brother –

SPORT

by a kind of lottery – picked two teams.

They fielded and did battle. He constituted himself referee, selector and commentator.

At religious instruction, he taught us that one of the cardinal virtues was to speak only good of your neighbour. As a commentator the Kilkenny brother had that virtue (or commandment) well and truly broken to smithereens during this and subsequent trial games. When one fumbled a puck or missed the solitary, he would roar derisively: 'god help us, so-and-so, couldn't hit a haybarn.'

We noticed – as the trial continued – that he had favourites and non-favourites – whom he called gluggers – and recommended a method of getting shut of the gluggers.

When one of his favourites (a classy hurler) tried for possession of the sliotar against a glugger, the Kilkenny brother would draconically urge: 'don't mind hitting the ball – hit the glugger and smather his contents all over the place.' Most unchristian brotherlike sentiments.

For a fortnight before the selection of the class's A and B teams to represent third year in the schools' hurling league, he carried out another form of psychological warfare against us – before we got on the pitch at all.

He would line us up – like a most inquisitorial sergeant major – and examine our camans. If your caman was not shapely or strong enough, he snorted that it was only a sawn off chunk of a tree.

You were suspended and told to give up spending money on sweets or immoral American films, save up, get a proper caman and you might be re-instated. The best camans that time were made by man called Billy Slattery. Billy lived at Crossagalla, up the old Cork Road. Ordinary Slattery camans were 9d and de-luxe 2/6 – half a crown.

In those years of economic depression – further aggravated by Mr. De Valera's Economic War against the ancient enemy – you'd be lucky to get 2/6 from your (if you had one) benevolent Yankee uncle (or aunt) and at Christmas only.

After about a month of agonising trial games in Claughaun the Kilkenny Christian Brother selected the A and B teams. He published their names on two blackboards, which were situated in a strategic place in the school playground for a week before the league's start.

The captain of the A team was a lad called Frank O'Neill. A really robust hurling maestro – with an unerring air for scoring points whether marked or not. Only, the Kilkenny Christian Brother didn't nominate the captain as Frank O'Neill. What appeared was 'Franko' captaining.

Asked about this odd appellation by mentors of the rival teams at peak viewing time, the Kikenny Brother replied: 'General Franco – and his men – are making Aligigots of the Communists in the Spanish Civil War, Franko and his men on my A team will make Aligigots of all the molly-coddle hurlers ye'll put out.'

My good aspiring self didn't get on either the A or B side – I had to be content to be a sub, who never saw one bit of hurling active service under Captain Franko.

In a way, I was greatly relieved, my nerves were in tatters after the trial games and the off-the-pitch psychological warfare. In fact, so bad was my nervous state, a kindly doctor at a local hospital clinic put me off tea and coca.

I took to reading about hurling from 'Thomond's' Games of the Gael column in the weekend *Limerick Leader*. From the 'Thomond's' weekly column, I got a grand eloquent hurling vocabulary – it somehow impressed the Kilkenny Brother.

My admiration for 'Thomond' as one who gave stirring accounts of the great doings of the Gaels of the 1930's was unmitigable.

From *Last Word by the Listener*, Séamus Ó Cinnéide's Journalism and Local History, selected and edited by Eoin Devereux, University of Limerick Press, 1999.

Munster and the All Blacks 1978
Moss Keane

TOMMY Kiernan was the Munster coach. He was meticulous but not in an annoying way – there's nothing worse than a coach who concentrates on small things that don't really matter. Tommy organised squad training in Fermoy, Co. Cork. We were a very scattered squad (and not just geographically): six of the team were Limerick based – Moloney, Dennison, McLoughlin, Whelan, Foley and Tucker; four lived in Dublin – Keane, Ward, Caniffe and Spring; four came from Cork – Bowen, Finn, Barrett and Cantillon – and then there was Les White who hailed from somewhere in England; at that time nobody knew exactly where.

There were no floodlights in Fermoy so the selectors had to turn on the headlights of their cars instead. I'm sure Kiernan did this deliberately, though he will never admit it. The thought of preparing to take on the greatest rugby team in the world by training under floodlights from Cortinas and Ford Escorts gave us a real lift. It made for a lot of fun, too. Brendan Foley would pass remarks like: 'Tommy, can you switch to dims? Mossy is having a 'gawk' or 'turn on the indicators, Mossy is about to turn', which had us laughing as we worked out. We worked hard, too; the regime was tough. Nothing scientific, just hard running, but Kiernan had an eye for players and could tell at a glance if you were carrying a knock or had a touch of flu or, worst of all, if you had been out drinking the night before. There was one area of the pitch where the lights did not reach, which provided us with an escape from his all-seeing eye.

One night I headed for the dark of this black hole, totally knackered, and met full back Larry Moloney lying down on the grass.

'Are you alright Larry?' I asked.

'No, Moss,' he said. 'I'm going to die.'

Kiernan must have known we were there but he knew when to allow a bit of slack. He also knew how to push us. He had something of the gift of his fellow Corkman, the great racehorse trainer Vincent O'Brien, and knew instinctively how to train rugby players. Then he brought us to London for a preparatory race – we played Middlesex and they thrashed us soundly. It was no surprise; most of the team had been out on the piss the night before. Ill-disciplined as that might sound, Kiernan had his reasons for allowing it.

One was that the All Blacks spies would report that we were useless. Middlesex had an All Blacks coach and he would be bound to pass on the word that we were no-hopers. Secondly, there was the group dynamics of a bunch of young lads hitting London and having a good time, breaking down the barriers between them. The yarns that follow keep you going through the hard slogs of training, and thirdly, Tommy could assess exactly where we were in terms of fitness at that stage of the season.

We went on to play London Irish two days later, a club side, and barely scraped a draw, and had a final trial sometime in October. Afterwards, Pat Whelan, Captain of the Probables, was called out of the dressing room. He was back five minutes later, and beckoned me over.

'There's been a coup,' he said, pronouncing the 'p' at the end. Donal Canniffe, our scrum-half, and yet another Lansdowne clubmate, had been appointed captain. He went on to play a hugely important role, both in the build-up and in the match itself.

Pat accepted the decision without complaint. He was a team player and just got on with it. And the captaincy wasn't as big a deal then as it is now.

The All Blacks were in Britain at that stage. They hammered the London Counties. Middlesex was one of the London counties, so by that measure the All Blacks would eat us without salt.

We went into a squad session a few days before the game. Kiernan told us we would win. Olan Kelleher, the sub scrum-half and the most photographed non-playing member of the squad was certain we would win. The rest of us just wanted to perform to our optimum and take it from there. We made no provisos of any kind.

Instead, the day before the game we went for a boat trip on the Shannon and threw Kiernan into the cold water. We all ended up soaked to the skin in the end. Wardy always makes out that we gelled that afternoon and he was right; it was the making of us. I believe really successful teams must have the utmost respect for each other, and we all got on very well. There isn't a single player on the squad I ever want to avoid.

Kiernan organised a man by the name of Vincent O'Connor to look after physiotherapy on the morning of the game. He pulled every one of our toes and fingers and the cracking and clicking of bones nearly drove me to distraction, but I felt free and loose afterwards.

There was no need for a big speech. We all knew who we were playing and what was expected of us.

The All Blacks lined up and performed the Haka with the usual menace and threat. I whispered to Foley, 'will we ask them to dance?' He just smiled.

Thomond Park was packed to the rafters, with 12,000 plus inside. Years later many multiples of that number claimed to have been there. The atmosphere and support of the crowd was incredible from the off. Maybe they sensed history was about to be made, though I was concentrating so hard I barely heard them. *The Fields* of Athenry hadn't yet been written so there was no unifying song on the terraces. If someone sang The Banks of My Own Lovely Lee the Limerick lads would have been offended, and if the Rose of Tralee was sung that wouldn't satisfy the Cork people and so on. Maybe that's why the new breed of Munster supporters chose The Fields of Athenry as their signature tune – Athenry is safely situated in Connacht.

The Blacks took control early on. Then Christy Cantillon, a gusty, open-side wing forward with a real turn of foot, backed up Jimmy Bowen's brilliant first-half break and we scored near the posts. Wardy was in his element. He was a confident player and he just looked a class apart. Seamus Dennison hit Stu Wilson with the hardest tackle I have ever seen and this lifted the whole team. I think that, rather than the try, was the moment we knew we could win the game.

For my part, I spent the day trying to disrupt Frank Oliver, who had cleaned me out in the first test with the Lions the year before. Andy Haden was another lineout expert and I shouldered him Gaelic football style every chance I got. I struck no blow during the game. The only incident was when Les White was hit and it was all my fault. I'd instructed Les to stand on Haden's toe when he was jumping for the ball; we called it a toe-job. But the all Blacks gave us plenty to do in the line-outs and after a while Les had enough of it. 'That's me finished with the toes, Moss,' he said, 'You'll have to jump higher.'

Brendan Foley consigned me to playing behind my very good friend Ginger McLoughlin. 'But why?' I asked, 'Aren't ye both Shannon men. It's only natural that ye play on the same side,'

'No, you're better then me,' he answered. 'Keane, I hate to say it, but you're the best scrummager I've ever seen, and Ginger has very high standards. He's a kind of a scrummaging perfectionist.' I thought he was going to cry if I didn't agree.

My head swelled to the size of a watermelon to hear a Limerickman praising me; it was like winning an Oscar. I should, of course, have known better – Foley knew from experience that his clubmate's diet was causing him to produce too much gas. I discovered that in the scrum, and learned quickly to scrummage low – methane gas is lighter than air, a fact I knew from the bit of science I picked up at UCC. Moreover, if you scrummage low enough you will avoid being crushed between the prop and the hooker's hips. My new technique helped me to avoid the cauliflower ears most second rows pick up from constant friction in the scrum. I have Ginger and Foley to thank for this development and my beautiful ears.

But I still picked up a dose of the dreaded herpes. The All Blacks prop, Gary Knight, played with a bandage around his head. He picked up the virus a few weeks before and, in the days before very much was known about herpes, passed it on to Ginger and me. My head was so low to avoid the farts that I was in constant friction with other players' heads, and herpes spreads with contact. In November of every year I get a major flare-up on the top of my head. It is a constant reminder of a memorable day.

We had the better of the All Blacks in the scrum, where Ginger proved he was as good as anyone in the world. That day was the making of his international career. And outside the scrum it was our tackling allied to their poor use of the ball that won us the match.

SPORT

It was a famous victory, 12-0, perhaps too famous: I get embarrassed when people talk of how we humiliated the All Blacks at Thomond Park. We didn't. We beat them, that was all. They were the best rugby team in the world and went on to achieve the Grand Slam in the course of that tour. I believe it's the only time the All Blacks were held to a scoreless defeat.

It was reported that towards the end of the game a bit of argy bargy broke out and I said to Andy Haden, 'You've lost the match. Do you want to lose the fight as well?' Maybe I did, but it doesn't sound like me, and I have no recollection of saying it. There was no chatting with the All Blacks. If you wanted to do one of them you did it at your peril. And they were very sporting on the day. In fact, I thought we were lucky more penalties weren't given against us. Believe it or not, there were no penalty kicks at goal that day.

From *Rucks, Mauls and Gaelic Football*, Moss Keane with Billy Keane.

Limerick Boating Song
(adapted from the Eaton Boat Song)

Jolly fine boating weather,
Jolly fine crew are we;
All on the feather,
Steady from stroke to bow.

Chorus:
And we'll all swing together,
With our bodies between our knees,
And we'll all swing together,
With our bodies between our knees.

Down by the glen and the bushes,
Down by Barrington's Pier,
'Tis there the crowds will gather,
To give Athlunkard/Shannon a cheer.

Chorus

Shannon may have great oarsmen,
Athlunkard and Michael's too,
But for sheer guts and courage,
Give me a Boat Club crew.

Chorus

Trinity are in the lead boys,
National are running them tight,
But what's this on the South Shore,
It's the jolly old Blue and Gold.

Chorus

When we are old and grey boys,
And bent up with old age,
We'll go and teach the young ones
And teach them all we know.

Chorus

The Great John Burke
By Ivan Morris

LONG before I took up golf, my Dad told me – with great reverence – colourful stories about a man whom he always referred to as "the great John Burke." When I began playing at Lahinch, this mystery man's reputation seemed to grow and grow. At Lahinch, Burke was called The King of the Links. This was slightly ironic, because John was a proud Old Irish Republican Army man who had served during the difficult times of the 1920's, when Ireland was struggling to secure its independence from British rule. Naturally, in the circumstances, he had little time for royalty of any sort. In fact, John's association with the IRA cost him his place on the Walker Cup team when his freedom-fighting past accidentally became known to the British golf establishment. He told me this himself, more with pride than bitterness. It was the era of Eric Fiddian and Cyril Tolley, but John was by far the best player in these islands. Apart from his single appearance in 1932, the Walker Cup selectors ignored him. It was a complete travesty of justice.

How the British found out about John's politics was interesting. During a raid on a British Army Encampment in County Cork, John's brigade "purloined" a fine pair of brown military boots belonging to an enemy officer, amongst other goodies. The boots had the initials "JB" displayed prominently on them, so they were given to John as a matter of course. Some weeks later John and a few colleagues were detained for questioning in County Clare. Gradually it dawned on him that the Interrogating Officer was the owner of the very boots he was wearing. It could have been disastrous if it had been discovered.

Exactly ten years later John was playing for Ireland against England at Sandwich, south of London. During one of his rounds, he became aware of a familiar face in the crowd but could not place it. After the game he approached the gentleman who had aroused his curiosity only to find that it was the officer whose boots has been "captured", and who had questioned him about his IRA membership. When the secret of the boots was revealed, the officer fell about the laughing and "forgave" John with alacrity.

Soon afterward, John was selected to play for Great Britain and Ireland in the Walker Cup matches in America. The team was to sail on the "Queen Mary" from Southampton, with the Irish contingent joining the boat at Cobh, County Cork, en route. John's new friend, not realizing this, drove to Southampton to wish him bon voyage. But of course, John was not there. Instead, the former officer told one of the GB&I officials about his and John's unusual friendship and gave him a handwritten "best of luck" note for John. When the notice was being handed over, John was told in no uncertain terms that it would be his last Walker Cup because there was "no place on a British team for IRA terrorists."

Treated as *persona non grata* by his colleagues throughout the trip, John decided, for a bit of devilment, to play up his Irish Nationalism by refusing to honour "God Save the King". He also insisted on his separate Irish identity being recognized at every opportunity. Having been told he was never going to be selected again, he got as much enjoyment as he could tweaking British tails in his harmless way. But it cost him.

At Lahinch, John's royal status was fully justified on account of his record of winning the annual South of Ireland Championship on eleven occasions, and indeed he was "discouraged" from entering the championship for a number of years because his presence was affecting the size and quality of the field. The revenue was badly needed by the club. Being a local boy, born close to the Village of Lahinch in 1899, John was well aware of the importance of "the South" competition to the well being of the golf club and the developing economy of the village, so he complied. Only Joe Carr has won more Irish and Provincial Championships than John Burke. It should be remembered, though, that World War II interfered with John's run of victories. No wonder the locals are still proud of their great champion long after his death in 1974.

As a young man, John spent some time as a caddie. but when he showed promise and talent for the game, a far-seeing member who had observed his magnificent, flowing action when playing illegally on the links in the evenings with his pal, local butcher Mick O'Loughlin, kindly championed a campaign to have them both invited to join the club. They were the first locals to be so honoured. The two friends set about taking full advantage of the compliment and were determined to master the game. Together they undertook methodical and scientific approach. Burke's stated credo, which he passed on to me years later, was "Good, better, best. Do not rest until your good is better than your best."

It should also be remembered that John played during the Bobby Jones era, a time when amateur golf was considered more important than the professional game. When I asked him why he never turned professional, he said he could make more money and have a better life by remaining amateur. That would not be so today, but back then it was the case.

A master of improvisation, John learned the game by experimenting with every shot and situation imaginable with a limited arsenal of implements, just like Ballesteros many years later at Pedrena. John worked hard and eventually thought he might be ready to begin competing, so he applied for a handicap. Straight away he was given scratch, and he maintained that standard for all of his golfing life. Even after he acquired a full set of clubs, John continued to play a game that featured all sorts of make-up shots. The famous trick shot artist Joe Kirkwood wanted John to join him on one of his World Tours when he saw what John could do during his visit to Limerick in 1937.

John was a character and a loveable rogue. Long before the balata ball was ever heard of, he talked me into having what he termed a "soft" ball available for use at short holes. He suggested I tee the ball a little higher than usual so that the weaker top section of the blade would make contact. One could then play a much stronger club than was really needed, deliberately show the club to one's opponent, putting on a show of throwing grass in the air to gauge the wind and discussing the shot out loud in an effort to mislead the gullible!

When I tried this tactic myself, it achieved inconsistent results and I was not long abandoning it, preferring to play my own game and not become too embroiled with the opposition. Another trick he told me was to throw the ball down onto the ground, spurning the use of a peg. If the ball sat up nicely for a brassie, as he called it, fire away, but if the ball rolled into a poor lie, not to be too proud to pick it up and tee it properly. Such "one-upmanships" were designed to unsettle the enemy in the middle of a match. John also told me that whenever I was in a tight situation, to walk to the shorter ball at some stage and claim it and hope that my opponent would go to the longer ball only to have the humbling experience of having to walk back. John was full of such roguery. He played that way all of his life; for him it was all part of the enjoyment.

Father Enright told me two stories about John that emphasise his impish attitude. Once, John bet the Reverend a "half a crown" that he would not get down in two putts. When my friend one putted, Burke claimed that Father Enright had lost the bet. On another occasion, John threw a coin into a bunker beside Father Enright's ball. When Father Gerry stopped to pick up the money, a penalty was called for touching the sand! In spite of this carry one, Father Gerry thought the world of John Burke and was in awe of his ability.

One of John's favourite stories concerned Henry Cotton when he came to Ireland on one of his coaching tours for the GUI. As usual, an elite squad of players was sent to the great man.

"Try a swing," Cotton said to one of the hopefuls.

The player obliged.

"Try again." The player obliged.

"And again." The player did it again.

"Now," Cotton said, "I want you to swing as if you were about to hit the ball."

The player did as he was told.

"What is your handicap?" Cotton asked.

"Scratch at a seaside links in the West of Ireland." was the proud reply.

Cotton was surprised. "You must be a hell of a great putter!" he said.

John always enjoyed telling that tale.

From *Only Golf Spoken Here*, Sleeping Bear Press, 2001.

SPORT

Crimson and Blue
Hugh Flannery

Oh sweet A.B.C. you're there as of yore,
When we shouted your name from out every shore,
And we cheered every man of that gallant crew,
Who brought victory and fame to the Crimson and Blue.

As the boat cuts the water your oars make a flash,
When you reach for your stroke and your slides they do crash,
And the cox hoarsely shouts 'it's all up to you,'
To add further laurels to the Crimson and Blue.

Our Union record they'll find hard to beat,
The Senior, the Junior and our Maidens so neat,
The Inter-pro Press Cup, it was something new,
But they all found a home with the Crimson and Blue.

From Galway to Dublin, from the Lee to Coolraine,
We beat all before us, and can do it again!
New Ross and Clonmel, and Waterford too,
Sure they can't stop those heroes in Crimson and Blue.

And those exiled oarsmen, far from the sea,
Who loved the old Slip and the old A.B.C.,
Let's keep their memory always in view,
They'll always be welcome to the Crimson and Blue.

And let's say a prayer to the men who passed on,
They fought to a finish for their club they loved so strong,
May we all meeting in heaven, and there's we'll review,
And victories and glories of the Crimson and Blue.

Limerick Rugby full of Heroes
Richard Harris

HOW do you explain a love affair? It belongs to the heart, not the head. Something to be embraced or spurned – there can be no middle ground. There are those who stare blank-faced when I talk of rugby but others instantly understand my breathless enthusiasm and stomach-churning anxiety. We are the lucky ones.

Munster rugby, Limerick rugby. Through gritted teeth, as we approach Saturday's historic occasion at the Millennium Stadium – Munster v. Leicester in the Heineken Cup final – I must also acknowledge Cork's wonderful contribution to Munster rugby over the years, but the essence of the game I know and love is to be found in Limerick.

The heroes of Limerick rugby are my heroes, Gladiator, square-jawed warriors who represent us on the battle field. They are also heroes off the field – men who can drink, sing and talk of great deeds. I am intensely proud of Peter Clohessy, Mick Galwey, Anthony Foley and all the boys. Keith Wood, whose father (Gordon) I used to play alongside, is another hero. He lives the rugby life we all dream of.

It was a bittersweet day two years ago at Twickenham when we lost to Northampton, but the sweet lingers longest. There must have been 30,000 Munster fans in red – an unforgettable and moving sight – they conducted themselves beautifully. Supporting his rugby team is almost the only way a Munsterman can display his allegiance; we have no other comparable sporting or cultural outlet.

Rugby has always been there for me, even if I have occasionally gone AWO. I have enjoyed its many pleasures, as a player and spectator. Perhaps it is the sociability or possibly it's just the sheer physical pleasure that appeals. Very little on this earth can beat soaking your body back to life in a warm bath after an afternoon of cold rain, mud and pain with the prospect of pints and high jinks ahead. A warm glow envelopes you.

Or maybe rugby simply brings out the best in people. It's a chicken and egg situation. Does rugby simply attract the sort of person those friendship and qualities I enjoy or does the game itself – the actual physical confrontation and challenges it presents – help mould and create those people? Answers on a postcard please. There is an instant recognition and understanding between rugby people. Would that it be so easy in the 'showbiz' world where, you may have noticed, I am not universally popular.

I remember phoning Sir John Gielgud on his 90th birthday. I didn't know him really but admired the man tremendously from afar.

'Happy birthday, Sir John,' I bellowed down the line. 'This is Richard Harris phoning from the Bahamas, just to wish you Happy Birthday and thank you for everything you have done for British theatre. We are hugely in your debt.'

'Harris you say,' replied Sir John. 'I don't know a Harris. Of course there is that very loud, vulgar chap from Ireland. Did the Camelot thing. Very bad reputation with drink and women. I believe. Very bad indeed. Rugby chap. Anyway, thank you very much for phoning from Bermuda. So sweet.' 'Bahamas Sir John.' 'Yes, yes, yes, yes. The sun shines there as well I believe.'

I was a second-row at school but seriously miscast. I should have been a flanker. I loved roving, snaffling tries, putting in big hits though we called them tackles in those days. I attended Crescent College, played in two Munster School finals and represented Munster Schools and Munster Under 20 – I still wear that very red shirt and intend to be buried in it, I have left instructions – before TB struck and I discovered books, women and a hitherto unsuspected, or submerged, desire to act and show off.

SPORT

God they were great days. To play rugby and glory in your fitness. To feel invincible. If you could bottle the moment. Rugby was life in Limerick. It was a love of sport and also a parish thing. The junior teams were based around parishes and local pride was always at stake. We were tribes and you needed visas to move safely between parishes. Inter-marriage was almost unthinkable. Garryowen man /Shannon girl? Scandalous.

The rugby was intense and bloody hard – savage in fact – but, because we were neighbours, people were respectful and forgiving. Sometimes it was 'them' against us – touring sides, the inter-provincial champs – and the competing parishes became a tight-knit diocese. We could be quite parochial. The players and supporters in far-flung Cork – the Posh – hated us and the feeling was reciprocated. Deep down – so buried as not to be ordinarily visible – we also respected each other as fellow Munstermen, but such solidarity was only rarely displayed or articulated.

I have spoken before about my hatred of Frank McCourt's book *Angela's Ashes* and the film adaptation by Alan Parker – a highly selective, misleading and unbalanced look at life in Limerick. Let's put the record straight, Limerick is one of the most progressive cities in Ireland, an industrial powerhouse and home to one of our great universities. Of course, it has known hard times, but it is a city in harmony with itself, a city that has never climbed above its station, yet will reach the pinnacle of its aspirations. It has history, culture and humour. Above all, it has rugby.

Not that we are above a little sporting chicanery. So you remember those horrible quartered leather balls we used in the old days at school? Well, when the opposition were awarded a penalty in a kickable position two things happened, almost simultaneously. One of us would absentmindedly kick the ball to the touchline, while our captain was protesting to the referee or perhaps one of the forwards was receiving a lecture for over-vigorous play.

In the meantime, our reserves had been 'preparing' a second ball on the touchline, soaking it in a bucket of water until it weighed two or three pounds heavier than regulation. This was the ball that would be returned to play, totally unkickable. Happy days. I adore Thomond Park, which I could see and hear from my bedroom in our home on the Ennis Road. It is the citadel of Munster rugby; we have never lost a European Cup game there in seven years. If Ireland played there we would never lose. Did I ever tell you I scored 19 tries and one dropped goal on the hallowed turf in various schools and junior games? I can recall every score in intimate detail. My proudest achievements – that and playing alongside Keith Wood's dad Gordon, the Ireland and Lions prop – the day he scored four tries, appearing on the wing, in a cup match against Mungret.

I would give up all the accolades – people have occasionally written and said nice things – of my showbiz career to play just once for the senior Munster team. I will never win an Oscar now but even if I did I would swap it instantly for one sip of champagne from the Heineken Cup. Good luck boys.

From *The Daily Telegraph*, May 22, 2002.

Munster v Biarritz 2006
Gerard Nix

"They were there before the Huns", George said,
In that Basque country between the sea and the Pyrenees.
The pride of French rugby,
Munster men, you'll take your hat off to these!
He forgot to mention the ten million sum,
And that ours were the boys from down the road
And are they not the descendants of Brian Boru
And Art O'Leary too!
We had Clontarf, they had Waterloo.
Peter Stringer was our Patrick Sarsfield
Who stole a march behind enemy lines,
Only this time we had the power to see it through.
Ronan O'Gara was our Cuchulain,
Who silenced the hounds of prey.
This is ours
You out there can have another day.
The rest were Caesars in their own right
And like true Romans to a man
They can look at the Cup with pride and say
Vene Vidi Vichi...

From *Revival Poetry Journal* Issue 2 Jan 2007

It all goes back to Thurles: when Mick Mackey was still King
Raymond Smith

MANY old-timers I know will contend that the tremendous battles between Limerick and Cork in the early forties – when Mick Mackey was still King – started it all and left an aura over this pitch and over the town itself that could never fade. These were the games that cemented it certainly and gave it an even deeper dimension.

Remember 1940 and envy those who were there and who can recall for us what it was like to experience the rare flavour added to Munster championship hurling by the Cork and Limerick rivalry at Thurles. See the teams come out of the town end and walk past the wooden stand and take their places behind the band in front of the old covered stand, now replaced by the imposing concrete structure that runs the whole length of that side of the field. Conjure in the mind's eye the momentum when Mick Mackey appeared at the head of his men – the buzz that arose around the ground, fathers pointing him out to their sons and the rising sense of expectation among those on the embankments, ordinary sons of the soil, mostly, who never aspired to a seat in the stands; they would never know what it was to eat a prawn cocktail or smoked salmon or duck á l'orange or drink a chateau wine or head for the sun on the Costa del Sol or the Canary Islands.

But in lean days of food rationing in the war years, when men were satisfied with much less than is demanded today, and the avoidance of cholesterol in the daily diet was not a phrase in vogue with our fathers – happy if they could get a box of butter somewhere and exchange clothing coupons for tea! – Mackey lit a flame in the drabness of that period that was never to die for those who saw him at the peak of his powers in the thirties, in the last grand title winning flourish of 1940 or even in the twilight seasons of 1944, 1945 or 1946.

Mick Mackey may be just a name today for a whole generation of young GAA followers – and for many grown-ups also – but through most of the thirties and well into the forties he was not just an ordinary mortal to those of his own generation but a legend in his own life-time.

He created horizons beyond which ordinary men – you might even say the obscure Willie Lomans of our society – felt they could never venture, limited as they were by the fact that they did not have cars and even those with cars were totally restricted by petrol rationing. You headed for Thurles either in a turf-burning train or on your bike or even got there by shank's mare.

Mick Mackey called the South as Napoleon summoned his men to his flag. He broke through all the accepted barriers of what seemed possible on the field of play. He made man dreams in an era when television had not yet arrived in Irish homes and there were no international standards by which to judge in sport; and what spectators saw before them on the field of battle or conjured up in the mind's eye, as they listened to a radio commentary by Michael O'Hehir, sufficed to give a depth of satisfaction that young television addicts cannot comprehend today.

Thus it was that Mick Mackey was more than just a great hurler. He was a God to those who worshipped at the shrine of his greatness in an age when men needed to look to the heavens beyond daily grind, beyond much poverty and insecurity and say with Joxer Daly – 'What is the stars, Captain, what is the stars.'

Mackey ranging through the centre on a defence-splitting solo-run, culminating in the green or white flag waving at the town end or Killinan end in Thurles, representing the fulfilment of the secret ambitions of the poor, of all who knew they would never climb to the top of the ladder in life itself.

They saw him born to the stardom they could never hope to achieve. They were fated to live through the bitter, struggling days of the Economic War of the thirties - when men made personal sacrifices beyond our understanding today – or the War years themselves when a man's parish was an entire world and it was necessary to create symbols to cherish. For hurling men Mick Mackey was the greatest symbol of all. And those who saw him in his prime will tell you it was impossible to forget him. There was only one Mick Mackey, as for a later generation there could only be one Christy Ring.

Christy Ring was as yet just another name in the Cork side in the golden season of 1940. Recall the galaxy of famous names that clashed in that superb meeting of old rivals for the Munster crown. Cork, set to start their four-in-a-row run the following season, were led by Jack Lynch and boasted Alan Lotty, Willie (Long Puck) Murphy, Jim Young, John Quirke, Ted O'Sullivan, Micka Brennan, Sean Barrett and Batt Thornhill.

And Limerick, led by Mick Mackey, with his brother John beside him in attack, had Dick Stokes, Jackie Power, Paddy McMahon, Jim Roche, Paddy Scanlan, Jim McCarthy, Mick Kennedy, Paddy Clohessy, Paddy Cregan, Timmy Ryan and Tony Herbert, later to play with Dublin.

It was a draw the first day – a memorable draw. And the replay was even more hectic. The crowd encroaching the pitch after Micka Brennan was injured. Limerick two points ahead at half-time – and in front by the same margin at the final whistle. And this was the margin Cork had beaten them the previous year. Always it seemed to be no more than two points.

Jackie Power made the piercing thrusts that beat Cork in the replay but they hailed Dick Stokes that day too – and Mackey himself had the last word with a point, after Cork had cut back the Shannonsiders lead to a single point.

Sometimes Mick Mackey would come down from the field and would show the scars of battle to the aficionados gathering in Jim Maher's. He seldom escaped unscathed. Did he not play against Tipperary at Thurles in 1939 with special headgear to protect an injury sustained in a tournament match a week previously that necessitated eleven stitches? And played a hero's part in victory.

I suppose Jimmy Langton was remembering all this when he said to me one evening in his home in Kilkenny with no qualification whatsoever: 'Mick Mackey was the greatest man ever to catch a hurley in his hand.'

High praise indeed from one who was himself one of the most classical sticksmen to don the Black and Amber of Kilkenny.

Langton put it this way: 'Mackey could go from one end of the field to the other with the ball on his stick, hitting men off him as they went in to tackle him – and he would come laughing through it all. He was the laughing cavalier of the game and, like the great player he was, he had the ability to play in any position if the occasion demanded. Yes, I would put him before Christy Ring. Ring may have been a fine artist with his caman and a magnificent striker into the bargain but Mackey had it every way – we will probably never see his likes again.'

Mackey belonged to an era when in possession of the ball you could hit a man with the full power of your shoulders going through the centre – and the big defenders of the day did not stand on ceremony in their efforts to stop him. Take the Tipperary defence of 1937 and you see what I mean: Jim Lanigan, Ger Cornally, Dinny Gorman, Johnny Ryan, John Maher and Willie Wall.

Mick Mackey talking in his home in Ardnacrusha to Val Dorgan of the *Cork Examiner* when Val was researching his book 'Christy Ring' and scoffing at some of the rules that in his opinion had spoilt the modern game: 'If you run at a back now, it's a free . . . in my time you could hit a man with a frontal charge.' And then he recalled going to Nowlan Park to play Kilkenny in the National League after the Shannonsiders had won the 1940 All-Ireland crown: 'Blanchfield came out to take me and the two of us collided. We went down but I got up. I broke his collarbone. He was a great bit of stuff. I had great respect for that kind of hurler.'

Jimmy Langton made the point that every day he went out, Mick Mackey was meeting top-notch centre-backs in inter-county hurling – John Maher (Tipperary), Jim Regan (Cork), John Keane (Waterford), Padge Byrne (Kilkenny).

What the crowds liked most of all about Mackey was that he played with a sense of the old glory of the game. He gloried in victory, but he realised that you couldn't win them all. All games came alike to him. As he told me himself one time, he was out almost every Sunday of the year – challenge, tournament, championship, club and inter-county and he played Gaelic football too. And if All Irelands were lost through trying to disappoint no one, then he must have given an infinite amount of pleasure to eager crowds at out of the way venues.

He brought a sense of colour, of excitement, above all daring to his play. He hurled with a *joie de vivre* that is so often missing today. In a mercenary age, our hurlers seem to be more serious now and lack the panache that made one feel mercury tingle in the veins in other days.

From *The Hurling Immortals*, Aherlow Publishers, 1984.

Don't Cry for me Garryowen
Tommy Creamer
(to the air of Don't Cry for me Argentina)

It won't be easy!
You'll think it strange
When we try to explain what we feel
How we still need your love
After all that we have done.

You won't believe us!
All you will see is a team you once knew
When things were going fine
At sixes and sevens with us.

It simply had to happen
It had to change
Couldn't spend all our lives down at heel
Looking at Garryowen winning the Cup!

So we choose freedom
Running around trying everything new
But nothing impressed us at all

We never expected it too!
We love you and hope you love us.

CHORUS
Don't cry for us Garryowen
The truth is we never left you
All through your wildest days
Our mad existence
You kept Tradition!

And as for Sherry and as for Shay,
We never invited them in
Though it seemed to the world
They were all we desired

For we had Colm, and Johnny and Eddie too
The answer was with us all the time
We love you and hope you love us.

CHORUS

Have I said too much!
There is nothing more I have to say to you
All you have to do is look at us
And believe every word is true.

CHORUS

(Garryowen were the dominant team in the Munster Senior Cup through the 1970's, as Shannon, to their cost, only knew too well. Revenge came in 1977, however, when the Parish team were triumphant over the old enemy, and Tommy Creamer penned the above lines).

NINE
THE CITY

Memories of Limerick
Sean J. Fielding

She is old but to me she is beautiful
In her own sort of bedraggled way,
And she was there long before the other one
Had ever seen the light of day.
They may talk about millenniums
And wheelbarrows in the 'rare ould times,'
But there's never a song they can ever sing
That for me can beat 'the Fathers' chimes.'

For Limerick is my only jewel,
My river and my rose,
She's the People's Park
And Mungret Street, she's Garryowen and Bohs,
And 'Up and Under Munsters',
And Claughaun and Treaty stars,
And Sexton Street and the 'Brothers,'
And thornybacks in jars.

For me she's Patrick Sarsfield
And Dan O'Connell in the Crescent,
And St. Mary's old Cathedral
And King John's Castle ever present;
And the Treaty Stone and the Leader,
With the Chronicle on Tuesdays,
And Thomondgate and Soda Cakes
And St. Munchin's curse on blue days.

She's the Yellow Road and Cannock's Clock,
And Treacy's Tripe with onions,
And a cure in Widdess chemists
That would do away with bunions;
The Markets Field and 'There is an Isle,'
And fish and chips wrapped in the "Indo,'
And 'Confraternity Men to the Fight,'
And a bike in Nestor's window.

She is Tait's Clock and the Lyric
And the Stella and the Rink
And the 'Colla' and O'Connell Street
And Christmas street lights on the blink,
She is Barrington's and the Abbey,

> She's 'The Station' and 'The Pike'
> She is 'Balla' and 'Cappanty'
> And the Clare Hills on a bike.
>
> She is Prospect and the 'Bombin,'
> And the 'Mount' and Laurel Hill,
> And the Windmill and proud Thomond Park,
> And Sarsfield Barracks on the Hill;
> She's all these and many others,
> Though a lot have ceased to be,
> But to me she's home and with all her family,
> That's what Limerick means to me.

From *A Horse with Good Handwriting*, Sean J. Fielding's Memories of Limerick, by Aidan Corr, 1998.

A pint for the stevedore: hard times in Limerick Docks
Pat Doran

WORKING in the docks in the 1950's was very hard work and a very degrading experience in some respects. You went to the dock gate in the morning at 7.30 am and stood in a line, often three deep, with hundreds of other men hoping to get a day's work. We stood there, including my Dad and myself, and if there was a ship or two in port, or any other work in the warehouses, but only work for forty or fifty men, a lot of pushing and shoving went on to get a good position in the front of the line.

At 8 o'clock sharp the stevedores would approach the 'jobbing gate.' Some wouldn't even call your name; just nod in your direction. He might call the man alongside you and you'd often think that it was you he was calling and you would walk from the line only to be told by the stevedore 'Not you! go back in line.' The entire thing was a very degrading practice.

The work was certainly hard. A typical job would involve working in the hold of a ship manually filling coal into a wooden tub with a large shovel. It would take three days to get to the floor of the hold. I also filled bags with salt or coal and carried 10-stone bags of coal and often 16-stone bags of salt on my back for eight to ten hours a day. When the heavy bags of salt got wet you would have an extra half-stone on your back. I was only 10½ stone in weight and I have seen men weighing 12 or 13 stone falling to the ground with 16½-stone of wet salt on their back. The stevedore would say to them 'Don't bother standing out for a job again: you are not fit for this work.' It was very degrading the way some stevedores treated dockers who were getting on in years; their pet dogs were treated better. That was a terrible way to be treated after slaving all their lives and some dockers looking like old men at 50 years of age.

Some stevedores had a system of paying the poor misfortunate men in a public house and most of the dockers getting paid would leave a drink for the stevedores. Some men were practically forced to leave a drink for fear of not getting a day's work the next time. The young dockers were not going to put up with the pub-paying system. We saw the way the older dockers were treated and that was the start of the change in Limerick Docks. I never drank until I was 29 and still at the age of 66 do not class myself as a drinker. Paddy Benson, our chairman, was one of the first dockers to own a car and I was the second or third. Later on so did a lot of the young dockers, and later on again they bought taxi plates and fuel trucks. Some even purchased their own pubs – what a big change in a very short few years.

Some of the stevedores' lieutenants were worse than the stevedores. They were dockers like ourselves and did not get any extra pay for working directly with the stevedores but they tried even harder to get the work done so as to impress the stevedores at the expense of the ordinary docker. These lieutenants were informed by our Chairman and some of the younger dockers to stop this practice of treating other dockers like slaves. These few individuals soon got the message and came back to the fold.

The dock was a very dangerous place to work in. I didn't do too badly out of it; but I had a couple of near misses and a few stitches. I saw legs broken and fingers nearly ripped off. I remember one particular ship that docked with a cargo of net nitrate fertiliser and I was one of over forty dockers unloading the cargo. Whatever substance was in the nitrate, it affected all our hands. they got raw and red and later the skin started to peel off. It took a week or two for our hands to heal. At the time fertiliser was shipped in strong paper and plastic bags, each bag holding 8-stone in weight. Breakage was inevitable and we were handling nitrate with our bare hands. However, not one of the over forty dockers working on that ship ever put in an insurance claim or demanded any kind of compensation. The year was 1958. Today if a person fell and got a slight injury they would claim a few thousands euros.

Life was very rough on some of the dockers' wives as they would have to bring down the tea for their menfolk at the 10 o'clock break. This break lasted only ten minutes and the wives would walk down with their husbands' tea in a tin container that had a handle and was called a canister. The poor women would often walk two miles in all weathers from the different housing estates of Limerick with an old stocking wrapped around the can in an attempt to keep it warm. Even so, it was often stone cold when they reached the docks, especially in winter time. The wives would go into the docks, go to the ship where their husband was working on and he would have his break sitting down on a bag of coal or a plank of wood. Looking back on it, it was a very degrading experience all round. Some wives would make a second trip for the 1 o'clock lunch break. Many of these women had six to seven children to look after; how they managed I do not know.

Dockers in general were very witty people. Two dockers were walking home with dirty clothes and black faces after unloading a fertilizer ship and a man passing said 'Where were ye working today?' and the reply was: 'We got a day's work on the stage.' Incidentally, the wooden platform was called a 'stage' because dockers were a jolly gang and often danced and sang on the platform between loads.

From *A Clune's Lane Fisherman*, Pat Doran, 2008.

O'Rahilly strongly opposes University

IN connection with Limerick's claim for a Constituent College of the National University, an important meeting was held in the Limerick County Council offices on Wednesday night last. The proceedings were not open to the Press, but the following official report has been supplied:

The members of the Executive Committee assembled at the County Council offices on Wednesday 11th December, 1946, when Professor O'Rahilly, President of University College, Cork, was in attendance in connection with the proposed Constituent College for Limerick. His Worship the Mayor, Mr. J. C. Hickey, presided. In connection with the establishment of a University college in Limerick as a separate entity, Professor O'Rahilly strongly opposed the project as it would involve the amendment of the Charter and such procedure would have eventually very serious repercussion on the autonomy of not alone University College Cork but the other Universities in Ireland and may eventually promote State interference, which would have very disastrous consequences as regards the liberties that were bequeathed to the University Authorities in the existing Charter. Not alone would the project be strenuously opposed by the Authority of University College, Cork, but the Senate and the other Universities would be very determined in their opposition to the proposal since it would involve the amendment of the Charter.

After a lengthy discussion, it was decided, having regard to Professor O'Rahilly's observations and review of the position, that it would be absolutely impracticable to proceed with the project of the establishment of a separate University for the City of Limerick.

The question of the provision of courses in arts, commerce, science, and engineering to cover a period of two years to meet the requirements of potential undergraduates, was considered and Professor O'Rahilly stated that he was very sympathetic to this procedure and would gladly place his services at the committee's disposal to advise, examine and analyse any proposals to render effective the establishment of facilities to provide courses in the faculties of art, commerce, science, engineering, to embrace the University curriculum of the first and second years as well as the possibility of the provision of courses for the Diploma in Education, Social Science and Public Administration.

It was eventually agreed that a further meeting of the Executive committee be convened and make arrangements for a public meeting of the citizens at a later date.

From *Limerick Leader*, Saturday, December 14, 1946.

Limerick Bells
Finbarr Crowe

Limerick City, river wedded,
City of the pealing bells.
Booming out the Christian message,
Filling Clareside's hills and dells.
Sweet the sound of Mount Alphonsus
Sweeping down on Shannonside,
Old St. Mary's mellow pealing,
Mingling with the rushing tide.

Down the years their sounds have echoed
Crisp-clear in the frosty night,
As the ringers in their belfries
Practice through the fading light.
Tunefully their notes resounding
Flooding Thomond, Garryowen,
Chime an ageless theme for lovers
Strolling by the Strand, alone.

Sad then my lot, forced to wander,
Haunted by those Limerick bells.
In London, New York, Perth they echoed,
Exile reawoke their spells.
Then the joy when sailing homeward,
Past Kilrush, by Glin and Foynes,
Hearing faintly on the full tide,
Limerick's welcome in her chimes.

Let them ring out, fill the city,
Swell her proud breast with sweet sounds,
Keep them swinging, bell-ropes dancing,
Let them ring their happy rounds.
And when Time calls let me hear them
Softly, though the dim twilight,
Plaintive tones that bid 'bon-voyage,'
As I sail into the night.

From *Old Limerick Journal, Winter Edition*, 1998.

The Parish
By Willie W. Gleeson

OF the fifty-seven parishes that comprise the Limerick Diocese, one – and only one – St. Mary's. "The Parish", would seem to be of any consequence at least in the minds of those who inhabit that historic and hallowed spot, surrounded by water, which they love to call their island home - There is an Isle!

And how, the inquiring mind will fathom, did that once battle-scarred, beloved wasteland acquire so romantic a name which as well as being famed in song and story, racy of the soil, become a household word in far-distant places – stretching from Garryowen to the USA and the land of the Southern Cross!

According to local ecclesiastical records, the first parochial church in Ireland dedicated to the Mother of God, later raised to the dignity of the Cathedral of the Diocese, took place at the national Synod of Rathbresail in 1110 AD over which Gillebert, Bishop of Limerick, presided. This event took place many years previous to the fictitious donations attributed to King Donald O'Brien. There are many enduring memorials of the splendour of worship within its hallowed walls to this day.

Whilst it is true to say that from the 11th century, kings, queens, princes and countesses of Thomond had their palaces in the Parish – Kincora albeit (the remains of O'Brien's palace may still be seen in Athlunkard Street), it is equally true also to point out that the parish houses many of the Religious orders, e.g. Dominican, Augustinian (3 branches), Franciscan, Jesuit, Vincentian, Nicoletian, as well as the Poor Clares, Canonesses of St. Augustine, Knights Hospitallers of St. John, until the "Virgin Queen", Cromwell, Ireton, etc., laid waste to what was good and holy.

The glory that was once St. Marus can be gleaned, even though briefly, when it possessed the undermentioned priceless treasure, including the finest examples of medieval post-Conquest art remaining in Ireland.

The O'Dea Mitre and Cross (1418) belonging to Cornelius O'Dea, Bishop of Limerick, had only one equal, that of the Mitre and Crozier of William of Wykeham in England. It is the treasured possession of Most Rev. Jeremiah Newman, our own beloved Bishop.

The Terence Albert O'Brien Cross (1648) was presented to the Dominican Fathers in 1927, on the occasion of the Sep-Centenary of their coming among us to Old Dominic Street.

The Ferral Chalice (1619) and Rice Chalice (1626) in the Franciscan Church, was originally made for the use of the Friars in St. Francis Abbey.

The Rinnucini and O'Keeffe specimens are now deposited in the Jesuit church. The first-named was used in St. Mary's Cathedral by the Papal Nuncio, in thanksgiving for Owen Roe's victory at Benburb in June, 1646.

After the Restoration, the gold and silver Lacy Chalice (1662) fashioned by hand, was presented to St. Mary's where it is in daily use in the present church. Other chalices with it are: Meagher (1645), Meade (1652), Creagh (1724), O'Casey (1783), O'Farrell (1904), O'Farrell (1909), a solid silver ciborium and silver chalice belonging to Father O'Keefe, and a monstrance, the gift of John, Archdeacon of Rotterdam, which has an historical significance with the rising under Charles Edward Stuart, the young Pretender, which makes it all the more valuable.

A silver chalice, stolen by two drunken British soldiers stationed in Castle Barracks, was found damaged on the Island Bank in 1873 by a young boy who was fishing for thorny-backs in a nearby stream. It was later restored by Father Casey.

Among the church plate is a solid silver ciborium, presented by the CYMS of Ireland, to mark the centenary of its founding (1849). Regretfully, the house bearing the commemorative plaque was blocked up recently by Corporation Order. Five others in the same range suffered a similar fate, and all in the name of progress . . . to make way for the proposed ring Road in 1984.

The Parish claims, and rightly so, to be the repository, if not the archive, of the city's religious history. For this the credit must go to one of its outstanding sons, Father White, author of the famous manuscripts, bearing his name and written in copperplate, now a fastly-disappearing art.

Another great priest was dean Richard Baptist O'Brien, P.P., who founded the CYMS (already mentioned). And who hasn't heard, at some time or place, the name of Gerald Griffin, poet, playwright, reporter, Christian Brother. Born at Old Dominic Street (1803), later moved to Bow Gate - now St. Augustine Place, rear of St. Mary's Cathedral. Catherine Hayes, born at No. 5 Sheep Street (off Athlunkard Street) 1825. World famous prima donna, also affectionately claimed "Pearl of La Scala", "Swan of Erin", "Irish Nightingale."

That every city or parish has its celebrities – grave, gay and otherwise, goes without saying. The Parish can hold its own with the best, as the Baptismal Register shows . . . and here under are five who come to mind.

Andrew Cherry, actor, playwright, songwriter. Born Crosby Row, 1762; Cherry Villas named after him. Best remembered for his "The Dear Little Shamrock."

The McNamara Brothers (4), born at River Place, towards close of last century. World famous musical ensemble that gave their name to the well-known song "McNamara's Band."

Rev. Robert Nash,. SJ, celebrated preacher, newspaper columnist. Born at Mill View Terrace, Sir Harry's Mall, in the early part of this century.

Patrick O'Donovan-Reid, one of Limerick's outstanding tenors in his day. Recorded "Bird Songs at Eventide" for 2RN (now RTE), over 50 years ago. Born at 16 Athlunkard Street.

From *St. Mary's Church Golden Jubilee (1932-1982) Booklet*, 1982

Franco says thanks

IN reply to a recent resolution passed by the Limerick Corporation, congratulating General Franco on his victory at Barcelona, the Mayor of Limerick, Ald. D. Bourke,

TD, on Saturday received the following letter from the National Government's Minister for Foreign Affairs, dated February 3rd:

"Dear Sir – On behalf of Generalissimo Franco, through his Minister for Foreign Affairs, I am to convey to you the lively gratification of his Excellency for the enthusiastic message of congratulations which you sent him on learning of the magnificent victory at Barcelona. I take this opportunity of extending to you my most friendly greetings."

The letter was written in Spanish and signed by the Foreign Minister.

From *Limerick Leader*, 20th February, 1939.

Che Guevara in Hanrattys Hotel
Keith Armstrong

All the beer mats turned red in Limerick
the night that rebel Doctor Che Lynch took a wander
along Glentworth Street,
pouring
the jingling city
down his throat
on this island of his ancestors.
With a beard
as dark as the comforting Guinness,
he slaked his ruggerman's thirst,
his well-shaken mix of Irish and Galician roots,
by the night-soaked Shannon.

Thirty months later, he was dead in Bolivia;
smashed bones,
splintered beads
of a revolutionary's sweat
rolling down the gutter.

Now, I am sending this green poem
to your own heaven, old Che;
for your spirited lapel,
a singing sprig of shamrock
to light up the culture shock
of your long wild hair.

You chanced it in Hanratty's 'Gluepot' bar,
you plunged from the leaden sky

to chat up all this local talent
in the eloquent lilt of a roaring evening.

Mighty 'Red Bird',
icon at the bar,
no better or worse
than the barman
who served you
a pint or two of Irish love,
to make your heart
grow even bigger;
to set you up
for your flight
from Limerick,
'three sheets to the wind',
rocking across the mighty expanse
of the rolling drunk Atlantic to Havana,
to a certain
martyr's death.

And, amid the glorious beauty
of trees,
in the murderous jungle
of brutal dreams,
we soaks
will remember you
and celebrate the night
you fell in with us.

From *Revival Poetry Journal*, Issue 5, Oct 2007.

"My Dear Native Place"
Michael O'Toole

IN 1962, her creative talents largely spent, Kate O'Brien wrote a strange dedication to her travel book *My Ireland*. She had given up the practice of dedicating her books after 1934 when she inscribed her second novel, *The Ante Room*, to her sister Nance, and her brother-on-law, Stephen O'Mara. Now, three decades later on, she took up the practice again and wrote: "With warmest love, as my father Tom O'Brien would have thought proper, I humbly dedicate this little book to Limerick, my dear native place."

That Kate O'Brien should have written these lines in dedication of what was anything but a "little" book may itself be an indication of the detachment and generosity of that formidable lady. She was – and still is – Limerick's finest writer. The years in which her creative talents flowered coincided with the worst fevers of the great censorship and, along with practically every other Irish writer of worth, her work was banned.

In the city that she had presented to the world as Mellick, the odium of the official censorship was backed by rumour, innuendo and misrepresentation. Didn't everyone of the Limerick of the 1950's know that Reverend Mother FCJ had written from Laurel Hill to its former student asking why she was disgracing the convent by writing salacious books and that Miss O'Brien, the hussy, had replied with a mere postcard bearing an English stamp and containing only the words: "pounds, shillings and pence." And so when it was suggested to the Limerick city council that the author of *Without My Cloak* and *The Land of Spices* should be given the freedom of the city the idea was promptly abandoned on the grounds that the clergy might make trouble.

Miss O'Brien kept her head in the air and refused to join that band of writers and journalists who down the years ensured that poor old Limerick got a consistently bad press. She would have none of this. It was in Limerick, she declared, that she "began to view the world and to develop the necessary passion by which to judge it. I know that wherever I am it is still from Limerick that I look out and make my surmises."

That's one thing I have in common with her. The other, as she took pains to point out on the one and only time I met her, is that she was a journalist. But her journalism was very different to mine – in her heyday she was the principal reviewer of fiction for *The Spectator* – and I doubt if she ever saw the inside of a police court. Her critical journalism, though, was both serious and generous and its philosophy is expressed in a couple of lines from her review of Elizabeth Coxhead's biography of Lady Gregory:

Let us return for our own sakes to the lady of Coole and study her again – learn from her to be serious in art, to be humble, and to be generous towards talent as she always was – generous, instead of eternally malicious as it is often our curse to be.

Limerick was the first city I knew and its stern streets will always be magic places to me. Unlike Kate O'Brien, who was born in an imposing if ugly villa on the outskirts of the city, my own infinitely more humble birthplace was seventeen miles south east in the Golden Vale past Ballyneety where – or so we Limerick folk like to think – Patrick Sarsfield delivered that great stroppy line to the Williamites: "Sarsfield is the word – and Sarsfield is the man."

This is important territory. Close by is Lough Gur, where men lived and farmed in the Neolithic period, say around 3000 BC. A little to the south again is Knockainey ("the land sacred to Aine") and my own village of Hospital is one of its suburbs, having being named after a thirteenth century foundation of the Kings Hospitallers of St John of Jerusalem known as "the hospital at Any." On the way to Limerick you pass the ruins of Ballinagarde House where the squire, John Croker, terminally ill but still with hunting horn in hand and his hounds around him, had the answer pat for his clergyman son when he suggested that he resign himself to

abandoning the chase as greater joys soon a waited him:
He tried to persuade him to make him resigned,
On heavenly mansions to fasten his mind;
"There's a land that is fairer than this you'll regard" –
"I doubt it," said Croker of Ballinagarde."

And then, on to leafy stretch, the spire of St. John's Cathedral – still the tallest church spire in Ireland – comes into view and soon the sounds and the smells of the city are all around you.

The opportunity of returning to practise my craft in "my dear native place" was immensely attractive. The new and youthful editor of the *Limerick Leader*, Pat Comyn, had been supportive when I was trying to break into journalism and I had written two regular columns for him on a freelance basis. He was now, he told me, assembling a team which would transform the stodgy old *Leader* and establish it as a modern day version of the Manchester Guardian . . . .

The influence of the Redemptorists on the entire culture of Limerick has been enormous and will, I hope, provide some young social historian of the new University of Limerick, with a fascinating PhD thesis. Founded in Naples in the mid-eighteenth century with the specific objective of caring for "the most abandoned souls," the Redemptorists arrived in Limerick in 1852 as part of Cardinal Cullen's "devotional revolution" to re-evangelise the Irish. Limerick had not been their first choice – the Redemptorists superiors had hoped for a foundation in Dublin – but Cullen craftily diverted them to Limerick where he rightly assumed that the competition provided by a body of zealous, no-nonsense pulpit thumpers would put manners on the established and relaxed Dominicans and Franciscans who were now seen to have become lax. As underdogs are wont to do, the Redemptorists eagerly set themselves to the task of establishing themselves as the dominant men in their field – in their case, the hell, fire and brimstone business. And they succeeded brilliantly.

The Redemptorists concentrated their Methodist-style evangelism largely on the working classes, leaving the salvation of the bourgeoisie to the Jesuits down the road at the Crescent.

In Kate O'Brien's fictional works it is the Jesuit Fathers and the nuns of Compagnie de la Sainte Famille (the model for the FCJ's) whom we meet rather than the Redemptorists and the sisters of the Presentation. In *The Ante Room*, when on the Eve of All Saints Agnes Mulqueen presents herself to be shriven of the sin of coveting her sister's husband, it is to the Crescent rather than to Mount St. Alphonsus that she is driven and the letters after the confessor's name are SJ rather than CSsR.

From *More Kicks Than Pence – A Life in Irish Journalism*. Poolbeg Press, 1992

I can remember
Mrs. Manning

I CAME to live here with my husband in 1932 but I can remember it when the King's Island was a cul de sac. There was a big arch down at the bottom of the road, which was knocked down when the 'Field' houses were being built. When people moved down there first, they came down in shawls. That time it was during the war, they were all going over to London and their sons too. When they all came back they were all dressed up.

It was very quiet here, because it was a cul de sac. Clohessy's owned the shop across the road, Miss Ryan was in the other. Mr. Clohessy sold it then to the O'Donoghue's. The children used to play outside on the doorstep or in the O'Dells Lodge, or on the bank. There was no fear of them. I remember my second son he was very bold and he went into Mrs. O'Dell's for a drink of water, and Mrs. O'Dell had fallen into a weakness. She was lying in font of the fire – he was very young at the time, he fixed her up and came into me and I got her a cup of tea and she was grand.

I remember when I was filling the whole town with bags of soap. It was illegal at the time because soap was scarce but I'd make it out the back. We had a bin and we'd put sawdust into it and we'd put in the six lbs. of fat, that I'd get from the butcher, and when it'd come to the boil, I'd put in six gallons of water (I think), but I'd throw in the lb. of resin and when that'd melt, I'd throw in the caustic. I'd buy that every day off Jack Murray. There were two other people – Harts I think and somebody else that started making it. They put it into a shop in Nicholas Street and they were fined a shilling and had to go to court and pay it.

My son then would turn out the soap and cut it into bars. I remember Jack was going out one day to bring it up to O'Riordan's at the top of William Street and he got the lend of a box to carry it. When he got there, there was a queue waiting for it and he went and asked the man working inside for a hand – a low sized chap. "Lift it yourself" says the man. Jack went to walk away to go over to the other shop across the road, "Stretches" I think it was called and the queue followed him, and he sold the lot. I got a letter from Mr. O'Riordan wondering what had happened so I went and explained to him and we sorted it out.

I used to make canvas shopping bags here; it was like a little factory in the house. I was making a canvas rug and I going up to Cannocks to buy some Hession Canvas – 1 and 4 pence for the half yard and I said to myself "Sure you don't bag a hand made rug so I am looking at it and at that time you had to bring your own bag to the shop, everything was so scarce you see. So I made a shopping bag and my husband went down and put half a dozen into the shop below. I put a four leaf clover onto it afterwards. Then he went up to Peacocks and O'Riordans and all the shops in Nicholas Street. They went all over the country and a place out near the railway used to come down every Monday morning and they'd take away a gross.

I used to be up until two or three every morning. I made more money than my husband did at that time. T'wasn't planned, it just happened that way.

From *A Day in the Life*, stories complied by the residents of St. Mary's Parish, 1998.

The Local Defence Force
Séamus Ó Cinnéide

HERE are some of my eminence's comical military memoirs. We in the Limerick city Local Defence Forces (LDF) carried on through the summer, autumn and early winter of 1940 with a bizarre assortment of guns.

We had a ridiculously small amount of Lee Enfield 303 rifles – British made, and the most dependable. About 5 to every 50 men. These doubtful weapons were said to have been impouned from gun licence defaulters by the Gardai and disinterred after years of disuse to equip the Limerick LDF to repel either invading Brits or Jerries.

In December 1940 (thanks to a legal gun-running USA mission by Mr. Frank Aiken, then Minister for the Co-ordination of Defence Measures in Dev's Cabinet) we got a Christmas present of plenty of Springfield 300 rifles.

We were soon disenchanted with these Uncle Sam rifles. They were murderously heavy to march with, certain wags cracked that we should get covered wagons to carry them.

An Old IRA and Connolly Socialist LDF-er expressed a suspicious theory about the Uncle Sam guns. 'Of course they'll kill us all, marching around with them. Them's the guns used by standing still American National Guards to break workers' strikes,' he informed us all.

As the summer of 1941 went on, we were eagerly looking forward to our first LDF summer camp in Lahinch, on the Costa de Clare. By then, we were the 49th Battalion FCA, Gaelic for Local Defence Force. But, initials that got us nicknamed the Free Clothes Association.

The Lahinch summer camp was a hilarious experience. It was run on regular army lines by a regular army commandant, a sergeant major and other n.c.o's – of ditto category.

While most of the regular army personnel were okay, the camp commandant and the sergeant-major would have been okay in the French Foreign Legion.

'Twas woe betide any LDF-er who, in the slightest, messed drill movement on parade. The 'Foreign Legion' S.M. would menacingly spot the delinquent and keep the whole 49th Battalion there all day in the sea-blown deluge until everyone got the drill movement perfectly right.

We went one afternoon for live ammunition rifle target tests on the local beach. A party of LDF-ers were detailed to fill sandbags for rifle-rests for the test.

Somehow, the army buckchaser (a sort of jeep) with the requisite spades didn't make it to the beach firing range. The sandbags details were standing idly round. The camp commandant spotted them and asked them the reason for their idleness. 'We've no spades,' they replied. 'Get on with it. Spades is it? Use the spades Adam and Eve used,' thundered the camp commandant with authority.

So, as the victims of that kind of ferocious military discipline, it wasn't any wonder that most of the 49th LDF-ers sped into Lahinch town to whoop it up in the pubs, like Foreign Legionnaires after years in the burning deserts.

The nightly therapeutic atmosphere of the Lahinch taverns was such, one young LDF-er, uninformed about alcoholic beverages, drank too much and too unwisely draughts of cider one night.

He got obviously blotto drunk. His less stocious pals smuggled him in commando style under the barbed wire entanglements at the far end of the camp. The cider blotto LDF-er was deposited on to his bed in a marquee, where he fell sound asleep instantly. That, we thought relievedly, was the end of that.

Until, about half an hour before parade next morning, he climbed up one of the marquee poles, shouting out loud that he was a monkey and get him nuts for breakfast.

The sergeant major heard the cider-blotto LDF-er's roars. When (with the aid of other n.c.o.'s) the s.m. got the delinquent grounded, he told him: 'As there's a war on, we want no monkey tricks in this here camp – we've a few long trenches for you to dig for the rest of your stay.'

If and when the next big war starts, my eminence is resolved to be a conscientious objector!

From *Last Word by the Listener, Séamus Ó Cinnéide's Journalism and Local History*, University of Limerick Press, 1999.

Recovery
John Liddy

THE annual summer visit to Limerick this year was marked by the turn of the key in the door of the house that is now the family home without my mother. I wrote about that feeling of absence many years ago, in a poem called Emptynest, on the death of my father, when we children

> Jumped for those impossible bites
> Or raced round the room
> In search of the silver sixpence
> That was my father's eye.

And I tried to imagine how my mother felt, in the lines

> Such energy she doubts existed.
> Now that the piano's shut tight
> As a coffin lid, the room
> Where she sits full of absence.
> (from *The Angling Cot*)

Mother had now become the absence and would not be sitting, waiting for us. To alleviate this confrontation with one of life's sorrows, was my brother Mark and sister Miriam, standing on the platform of Colbert station, that monument to 'Chivalrous Con Colbert of Athea', in the words of Madge Daly. Over a drink with my brother in the Railway Hotel I recounted a detail of the journey from Dublin. My wife, Pilar, and two sons, Marcus and Seán sat across the isle from me as I joined in the easy flow of chat between a retired teacher from Clonmel and two elderly women, who might have been sisters, from Thurles. I noticed the man reading The Little Prince in Spanish and soon the talk turned to Spain and language learning with my eldest joining in. We were treated to an invited reading of a chapter by Marcus to the amusement of fellow travellers and then the talk turned to sons and daughters living abroad and married to Austrians, French and Italians. "It's great", said one of the ladies, "I can visit whenever I want and I am now trying to pick up some of the language." The retired teacher, who was learning Spanish, mentioned the need for a bilingual approach to Irish and so we then had the cúpla focal agus rud a rá i mbeagán until the train reached Thurles. I mused on the range of our chat and thought how the time must surely be right for a national push towards a bilingual Ireland. Multicultural, cosmopolitan Dublin, that Tir na nÓg of the third millennium, was living proof of another kind of absence, the absence of the Irish language amidst the sounds of foreign words wafting in the Grafton Street air. Perhaps in some near future, as Irish people grow accustomed to other nationalities speaking their languages with uninhibited pride, there will be a national willingness to converse in Irish as there is in English. A widespread, bilingual Ireland, or do I dream?

This I recounted in the place where we had our farewell drink amidst 'that sing-song at a wedding before departure', shortly after my mother's funeral. Before leaving for home I quoted the closing lines for my brother from a recent poem

Recalling Mother

No further revelation could make the journey without you
More acceptable, or fill my eyes with the goodness
I have known despite this empty pain.
(*The Stony Thursday Book*, Vol 2, 2.)

It was time to partake of the welcoming warmth of my sister and my brother. The orphanage was still a home and a happy place to be. My mother's absence was everywhere in the presence of a benevolent spirit. The road to recovery had been taken.

Sightings

WALKING around Limerick I glimpsed from different angles, the new hotel by the river. Shaped like a towering ship's bridge, or as the wits will have it, a phallic edifice, vying for supremacy of the skyline with the Cathedral spire where, as the poet O' Grady recalls, in his poem Homecoming:

THE CITY

> Feathereye Mykey my uncle told me a soldier
> Once shot down a hawk dead from the cross
> With a telescope fixed to his rifle.
> (from *The Road Taken*). Poems 1956-1996).

Prosperous looking buildings and bustling streets have now replaced the silence of the cannonballed ruins that seemed to belong to the time of the sieges. But, thankfully, there is still the feel of a country town about the place, inspite of the glitz and the gloss. This is the great challenge of modern architecture: to blend the old with the new in the harmonious flow from generation to generation. The critical eye will have much to praise and, perhaps, bemoan. Whenever I pass where Cruises Hotel used to be, I decry the loss of at least the façade, and recall the shiny, brass circular bar, the meeting of country people in the foyer, a wedding party of four, and my own wedding dinner, the last (supper) to be served by waitresses who joined us for a glass of champagne before the big lead ball swung into action.

In the centre of this strollable quarter the bronze sculpture of the woman with the tambourine plays us along towards, what we used to call, Joe Malone's Lane, where The Corner Stone guided carriages safely off Todds Row onto Denmark Street, and was, as I remember it

> Chipped by centuries of safe homecoming,
> Along tight streets where no lamp shone,
>
> That polished granite-resting place
> Steadfast, tenacious, almost forgotten.
> (from *Wine and Hope/Vino y Esperanza*)

or sometimes guided me up to my flat overhead Clunes after a night of revelry in the bohemian 70's of Malone's (formerly O' Briens'), and Dinny O' Malley's. Often those nights would sneak into morning with talk of politics, art and local gossip in the American-style kitchen that was home to many a vagrant soul and broken spirit. Some of us survived those live performances of private hells and are reminded that, perhaps, regrettably, youthful concerns have less a future than the power of Mammon. For the flat is now in the hands of a certain bank, and the walls have only ears for the sound of money-talk.

Yet there is solace in memory. Whenever I walk along Denmark Street I can hear myself again playing the bodhrán with Tommy "spoons" and Danny Hynes on the banjo. And imagine us busking outside the Augustinians with my sister tugging the sleeve of my mother, trying to get her to cross the street in order to avoid the spectacle. But, maybe, they are the notes of the accordion-playing poet on Chapel Street, opening the way to the Milk Market. This oasis of colour and character has never lost its appeal for me and seems to improve with the years as new blood peddle their cheeses and spiced patés, copper works and wood carvings, alongside the older breed of sellers with their shocking bunches of carrots and earth-caked potatoes. I wonder about the photographs taken by Gerry Andrews of the Market in 1979 for Joe Taylor's newspaper *The Limerick People on Sunday.*

But it is time now for respite in one of the cobblestoned cafes or join a 'tertulia' of Limerickites in O Blathmhaic, where talk turns on a whim of fancy over coffee and Sweet Afton. One could roam around the world without leaving your seat. Meet Nelson Eddy and Veronica Lake, get off at the station of Inishfree and have Barry Fitzgerald waiting or imagine yourself buying a newspaper again from Fonsie, or hear his pen-pal Gigli when he came to town to sing Ponchielli's La Gioconda. Here is another watering hole where stories are hatched to be read in the novels of one of Ireland's gifted and much neglected writers, Michael Curtin, who has accepted the baton from writers like Kate O Brien and become Limerick's answer to Madrid's Galdos. Raconteurs, poets and painters might drop in to mull over the conversation, check the day's racing card or settle a line of translation before catching the train to Cork enroute to Kinsale, for it is still morning in early July and this year's visit has only begun.

Limerick.com, 2005.

The Magdalene Asylum
Kevin Hannan

WHEN the Good Shepherd sisters settled in Clare Street in 1848 – during the height of the great famine – there was already a home for girls on the Clare Street site. This was established through the energies of Rev. James Houlihan, C.C., St. John's, who had it removed from a congested site in Newgate Lane where it had been first established by Rev. Fr. Fitzgibbon of St. Michael's.

This home was conducted by a dedicated and charitable lady, popularly known as Miss Reddan, who handed over her little institution to the Good Shepherd sisters on their arrival from the mother house of the order at Angers, in France. She then left the city for Kinsale, where she entered a convent of the Sisters of Mercy. We are left with no explanation for this radical change in her career.

Today one might wonder as to the need for such a home in the past. Did not all girls have a home of their own, with their parents? But if one bothers to study the revolution which has occurred in the social order during the past forty years, the question will answer itself.

Up to the mid-forties, or thereabouts, young girls who found themselves in difficulties were, in many cases, treated as pariahs, and even their own families were disenchanted at the prospect of sharing a disgrace with an errant daughter.

Thus, institutions like the Good Shepherd Home catered for a situation that would not just go away, or would not be dealt with satisfactorily elsewhere. In their time, the Good Shepherd Sisters were the subjects of much unjustified criticism, mainly by those who were too ignorant to understand a situation where young girls were forced to undergo the harsh discipline of a closed institution because the authorities and the people failed to come up with a more desirable alternative.

Harsh and all that it was, it was the only refuge open to the young girls who were regarded as having fallen by the wayside. It was a cruel and barbaric system that died in a more enlightened and liberal age.

For more than a hundred years there was need for the *services* of the Good Shepherd sisters, if not for the penitents, certainly for the orphanage which catered so well for the victims of domestic misfortune. Today people simply laugh at the reality of a situation that once required the services of the sisters of the Good Shepherd.

On arrival in Limerick, the sisters were welcomed by Dr. Ryan and the clergy of St. John's. They set up house in a small building in Clare Street at the rear of the old brewery, and a short time afterwards the redundant lace factory of Messrs. Walker was taken over and in the course of a few years a number of other adjoining sites were acquired, including the brewery, the Christian Brothers' School, a number of houses in Pennywell Road and two complete thoroughfares, Magdalene Lane and Buckley's Lane. These two lanes joined Pennywell Road with Clare Street. The splendid community church – erected in 1931 – stands on the site of the first Christian Brothers' school in the city. Thus the well-known complex came into being.

The authorities took full advantage of the community, and the space was availed of to accommodate an Industrial School (1873), Reformatory for Girls (1859) and a Laundry (1886). The new convent was completed in 1900.

Limerick Lace, clerical vestments and other such articles requiring much operations, together with their laundry work, went a long way towards the cost of running the institution.

The sisters also purchased twenty acres of pasture – part in poor heart – at Monamuck, adjoining the old canal. This is still known as the *nuns' field*. Winter and summer cows were pastured here, and were herded into the complex twice a day in the summer to be milked by the penitents. This operation ceased with the modern advances in the preparation of milk.

Fortunately, the institution has outlived its usefulness. This is a situation to be welcomed, as it indicates a more humane and helpful approach to domestic problems which were formerly left to the sisters.

From *Limerick: Historical Reflections*, Oireacht Publications, 1996.

Duffy's Circus Limerick
Desmond O'Grady

That's what left
of all the magic
was our Duffy's Circus:
that child laying his toy

trumpet, stamping barefoot
at the Fair Green alone.
But to that staccato lyric note
and the golden noisy band was able,
now departed too far elsewhere,
dance brightly coloured clowns; could
swing trapeze artists, balance tightrope walkers . . .

I recall those magic days ago
when school gave us the afternoon free
and we scruffy headed children marched
up one side madhouse Mulgrave Street to the circus
and the madmen, and mad women too,
from our local lunatic asylum,
were marched up to the mad side
with their gray abandoned faces, lost eyes.

And there we crouched in the Big Top – we
the children on one side, they the lunatics
on their facing other, laughing our lungs out;
grasping for terror of a fall, wide eyed, open mouthed
at the highwire walkers surefooted as flies.

I remember best the saddest of anonymous clowns
blowing his wailing lament on this trumpet while,
unseen by him, his big toe ballooned larger
and larger the more heartfully he blew his lyric cry.
And then the ballooned balloon of his toe exploded: Bang!
to the delighted shrieks of children and lunatics alike.

From *The Old Limerick Journal*, No. 14, Spring 1983.

Memories of St. John's
Ciarán MacMathúna

MY first appearance in St. John's Cathedral I do not remember; it was the day I was baptised in 1925. I was born in a nursing home run by a Nurse Cullen and her sister in St. John's Square, a few doors from the present museum. Even though we lived in St. John's Avenue in Mulgrave Street, the great meeting place of the clan was at 2 Church Street just off St. John's Square where my mother's family grew up and my cousins, the Powers, then lived. Sadly, that row of houses was demolished and replaced by new buildings – the end of an era for me.

I made my First Communion not in St. John's but in St. Michael's because my first school was the Presentation Convent which was in that parish. These good nuns I still meet from time to time and remember with great affection.

My Confirmation day I remember well, when I was made a true and perfect Christian with a gentle stroke on the cheek from a gentle person, old Bishop Keane. This perfection did not last, I'm afraid; perhaps he should have slapped me with greater force. By the way, for this occasion I was wearing a boy-scout uniform of St. John's Troop, also known as the Bishop's own troop.

I also recall being called on parade as a scout very late at night outside St. John's Pavilion to welcome the Limerick members of General O'Duffy's Brigade coming home from the Spanish Civil War. Looking back now, this case would not have brought me out of my bed; at the time we had no choice and indeed no understanding of what was going on.

Looking back now, with hindsight, there was one rather sad and disturbing scene at Confirmation – disturbing today, perhaps, but not then. The boys and girls of the schools filled the top seats of the Cathedral. Way down at the back but completely segregated from us settled folk, were a few rows of travelling people of all ages who were Confirmed when the likes of us had returned to our seats.

As far as I remember, some of the Masses in the Cathedral seemed to be at odd times like ten past nine. My father went every morning of the year to half past seven Mass and we went during Lent. Confession queues were long and slow but nobody seemed to mind. Fr. O'Grady was my favourite confessor and Fr. Moran.

The music in the Cathedral was dominated by the tall and rather haughty figure of the organist and choirmaster, professor 'King' Griffin, who wore gloves all the time to protect his hands. I always thought he came from some mid-European musical city but was delighted when I found out later that he was a native of one of my favourite places, Miltown Malbay in Co. Clare.

In my secondary school days there was a strong liturgical revival in Limerick and the monks of Glenstal were very much involved. We learned the Plain Chant very well and remember the Cathedral filled with boys and girls with the singing conducted by Dom Winoc Mertens, O.S.B. Even today, at gatherings of old friends like Fr. Tom Stack or Sean MacReamoinn I can still join in some of the great plain chant songs, the Credo, the Pange Lingua or the Salve Regina.

Funerals from the Cathedral were fascinating with horse drawn hearse and carriages. There is an old Irish saying 'an cóngar chun na bainise agus tímpeall chun na reilige (the short-cut to a wedding, the long way round to the churchyard). And sure enough, funerals instead of coming up Cathedral Place and straight to the cemetery, went all around the city through Patrick Street and up William Street.

We lived in Mulgrave Street and all the funerals passed that way. We stopped our street hurling or handball to let the funeral pass and when we saw a white horse in the procession we wet our fingers with the tongue and touched our right heel. This was, I imagine, a survival of some old folk custom and had nothing to do with Christianity.

At the funerals from St. John's the priests walked ahead on the footpath and wore folded lengths of white linen across one shoulder and tied diagonally under the other arm. What these were for I never found out but I understand they were donated by the family of the deceased. The number of priests present was also a measure of status in the community.

As a student in Dublin in the 1940s travelling back to Limerick was not as easy or as frequent as it is today and so there was a certain excitement when the first landmark of the city, the spire of St. John's, came into view. I still feel a little of this excitement but unfortunately I don't get to visit the Cathedral all that often.

From *In the Shadow of the Spire – a Profile of St. John's Parish*, 1991.

Some Limerick Characters
Thomas Ryan

THE Ball's Bridge Lavatory: I was painting a picture of St. Mary's Cathedral and Mathew Bridge from the quay wall near the neo-Georgian red brick lavatory when a man came up behind me for a look at the unusual sight.

He said: "Very good, isn't it – did you do that yourself sir?"

This I took to be a conventional phrase of approbation rather than a disturbing question. It turned out that he was a most interesting person with a peculiar sense of humour. In his earlier life he had worked for a snuff manufacturing firm and described the preparation of the powder from the tobacco twigs and the blending – I remember he told me of having to stand on the heap and crush with his bare feet like in vine-crushing.

I commented on the useful proximity of the nearby lavatory; he agreed and told me that there had been an earlier erection near Baal's Bridge, opposite Quilligan's public house. It had been a cast-iron structure without a roof and was much used by men who frequented the numerous pubs in the Irishtown.

Mr. Quilligan did not approve of the location of this convenience for family reasons – his daughters could not avoid seeing the goings-on inside from the windows of their home overhead the pub which overlooked the lavatory. He warned the Corporation that if it did not remove the structure he would. The Corporation ignored him. One night Quilligan, enraged at the comings and goings across the road, "came out with a sledgehammer and battered the whole thing down and fur it into the Abbey River ." Some bits of it are probably still there.

Dan the Monkey's: While on the subject of departed conveniences mention should be made of another. Up to about ten years ago there was an impressive public lavatory at the top of Upper William Street – it was removed on the claim that it constituted a traffic hazard.

It was also a much used and appreciated convenience, especially by farmers who came to the nearby markets and fairs and who did their shopping in the street. A water-trough beside the gable wall of the lavatory was an extra attraction. The site of these conveniences has now been made into a mid-street car park.

The lavatory was unusual of its kind because of the poetic injunctions to holy purity it displayed at eye level, framed under glass, directly above the urinals. The work of a local joiner, Jack Reddan, the rhyming couplets were briefly to the point, as befits a transient, but compulsorily immobile, readership. One verse began, "Little boys be careful of your eyes."

The place was known as 'Dan the Monkey's', the unflattering sobriquet of its custodian. In his younger days 'Dan' had been a conscientious and hardworking caretaker of the lavatory. Indeed, the building was something of a model and was one of the best-kept public conveniences in Limerick. 'Dan' took a personal pride in keeping the place spic-and-span and clean-smelling, with its copper and brass fittings glittering.

But he became enfeebled and finally crippled with old age and was forced into reluctant retirement away from his beloved lavatory. The Corporation no longer provided a full-time caretaker and the vandals had a field-day. The inside became run-down and dirty and, inexplicably, the Corporation took off the roof. The neglected, roofless structure became a sorry sight and the Corporation eventually shed its responsibility by demolishing the building.

Up to its very end the lavatory was most useful socially, not only for its relieving function, but because it allowed hard-pressed mourners marching behind the funeral hearse to fall out with grace; then they waited until the procession had moved on its way to Mount St. Laurence's cemetery.

Alas, poor Mr. Reddan, for all his rhyming reverence, was referred to, inelegantly but not surprisingly, as 'the lavatory poet.'

Father Taheny: Father Taheny was a Dominican priest attached to the priory in Glentworth Street. He was known, not only for his eccentricity of behaviour, but for his unusual appearance. He had no neck! Some form of nervous disorder to which he was prone had directed that he carry his head inclined downwards and at an angle to the right. He looked as though he might play the fiddle any minute . . . .

The opening of the white cape and cowl, worn in the priory and church, was wide enough to allow him to do this in comfort, though it looked odd. But the restrictions of the black walking-out suit, which its stiff white collar, was another matter. Fr. Taheny got over this difficulty by wearing his collar just below his mouth.

The poor man was obliged to look under his eyes to see where he was going and his mannerism gave him a suspicious appearance – which was unfair – as he was affable, though somewhat nervous.

Fr. Taheny was reputed to be an historian of distinction. He once told me that if the Reformation had not happened when it did it would have to be invented.

Mary Ann Walsh: Mary Ann Walsh was what is now called an alcoholic, but we knew her as a drunkard. She was famous for her uninhibited behaviour in public, letting fly in all directions – in every sense of that term.

Apparently, she came of a respectable background and had a grown-up family: drink was her undoing. She could be violent when drunk, broke windows and had a fierce tongue. The local district justices, J.M. Flood and Dermot Gleeson, kept a benevolent eye on her and sentenced her to periods of incarceration in inclement weather. But as often as not they left her off scot-free.

On one such occasion, on the eve of a Munster senior rugby cup final, the delighted Mary stood up in the dock of the court and, having thanked the justice for releasing her, concluded her remarks to him with the celebrated phrase: 'Up Guinness and back Garryowen tomorrow!'

Mary Ann always wore a hat and coat, not a shawl, in attestation of superior social status, though the impressiveness of the ensemble was considerably modified by her face of flaming addiction.

Penny Bun was a quiet person. A tall, well-built country woman, more than 6 feet in height, with soft, sad face, she was soberly dressed in a heavy overcoat, and had her hair piled on her head in an Edwardian bun. She bothered no-one, paid her way and was regarded for her independence and fortitude in the face of a 'come-down' in the world. She always carried a laden bag in either hand and lived in a little shack inclined against a wall on the 'Long Avenue.'

Jack: 'Damn de Valera that got me out of my fine house in Mungret,' was the raucous cry of an elderly man called Jack. He had a tongue and (to our delight) used it to the full. It was said that the Redemptorist Fathers gave him his dinner every day. 'Jack' was a dependable 'rise'. We would shout: 'Up Dev!' to start him off. He never failed to respond to the well-tried bait.

Johnny Raw: Garryowen seemed to have a disproportionate quota of eccentrics: no doubt the proximity of the Mulgrave Street Asylum supplied a large number of these. Many inmates, harmless people, were allowed out for walks, and to buy a twist of tobacco. One such was 'Johnny Raw', a tall, burly man who walked with both hands held stiffly in his overcoat pockets. It gave him the look of a farmer-gangster. We used to call out: 'Take the guns out of your pockets, Johnny.'

Ryan Bulleen was a much more formidable person who owned lands in Garryowen and Singland. A man with strong proprietorial instincts, he strenuously resisted any trespass on his lands and hotly pursued – often on horseback – marauding boys: sometimes he caught them and physically punished them, occasionally inflicting damages that required medial attention. He was a powerful, patriarchal figure and greatly feared.

Alice Duck Egg: Another famous rise. She was a fiery little woman who lived in the Garryowen district and rarely moved outside that area. She terrified all the small children attending St. John's Convent School.

Mick the Ghost: Mick Moore was a Parkman who lived near the Dublin Road, beside the Groody river. He was a hardy fellow whose peculiarity was that of swimming all the year round. Mick was undisturbed by social conventions. He was never known to wear swimming togs or to use a towel for covering or drying himself. He dived daily, and vigorously, into the Groody and walked along its banks to dry himself.

Mad Mary walked up and down O'Connell Street all day. She was a tall, very thin person, with a long neck and small, pinched head on top of it. She wore the same gabardine all year round, a little too short at the knees for the time. Mary always carried a handbag held tightly under her arm. Judging from her loud mutterings some Guard had let her down. She often recited poems, many of a

religious nature, such as this one:
Holy Moses and the rod
Holy Trinity, one God.
Mary stopped every few yards, said something loudly and then moved on.

Cough No More operated in churches. This fellow was irritated by coughing, particularly during sermons. His method of silencing an offender was to leave his own place and move to that part of the aisle nearest the cougher and stare at him. It usually worked.

The Little Red Hen: A minor celebrity was The Little Red Hen. One of three sisters, she lived in a little lane off our street. She was a tiny person with big eyes like a marmoset. She wore a draped shawl from which thin-like legs, encased in dirty stockings, emerged. The Little Red Hen drank a colourless liquid from a bottle concealed under her shawl. Judging from her torrid complexion, it was unlikely to have been holy water.

Thumbs Up: An odd sight was presented by Thumbs Up and his wife. He was a small man, an ex-jockey. His wife was a large woman with a florid face. Unbelievable as it may now seem, they lived much of their middle age in a tomb. After a day in town the pair retired, drunk, to their churchyard chamber (see Stage and Screen section, 'Memoirs of a Savoy Pageboy' by Joe Malone).

Josie was a woman and is not to be confused with her better known male counterpart of the same name (see *Old Limerick Journal*, June 1980). She carried a stick and used it if she got a chance. The trick was to shout 'Mad Josie' and run, Josie in hot pursuit.

Marconi – The Iron Man. A spectacular eccentric was 'Wires' or 'China Dong.' Many readers will remember him. He was known in different parts of the city, by various other names, including 'The Iron Man' and 'Marconi'. Two descriptions of his extraordinary aspect were given in the March edition (1980) of the Journal but hundreds of other people could give their own memories of perhaps the most exotic character in the Limerick of his day.

From *The Old Limerick Journal*, No. 5, Dec., 1980.

The Park
Dominic Taylor

In the Peoples Park in Pery Square
we forged our first beginnings.
Like Eden it was our paradise -
a haven of harmony and tranquillity.

Both relief and sanctuary from the
tenemented room it became a balance

for our lives. It's well-set earth and
feet-worn grass gave form to our
existence and in this God
given nature, we measured
and compared our lives
against every new experience.

We walked its footpaths, tramped
incessantly its grass, louched by plants
and trees. Played ball through those green
grass days and wandered by the soulful
silent bandstand. While mothers
chatted children played by the man
made monument springing forth from
this piece of nature perfected.

Unbounded from any given course
we milled where we willed, safe and secure
with no anxiety for the future.
As the evening came we reluctantly bade
farewell and the Park reverted to an empty
stage in anticipation of a new day.

From *Revival Poetry* Journal Issue 1 Oct 2006

Paradise Lost
Criostoir O'Flynn

WHEN the Corporation of Limerick decided in the mid-1930's to make a drastic clearance of some of the worst slum areas in the city, they looked around for a site where they could build about five hundred houses and they decided on the Island Field. This low-lying part of our island Parish was hemmed in on one side by the Shannon and part of the Abbey River. It had been a training ground for the British Garrison in King John's Castle for centuries, and when the castle was abandoned in 1922 it became a natural playground for the children of the area, especially in summer. In winter, much of it became a swamp because of the overflow from the trench below the Island Bank, a high grassy causeway which separated the Island Field from the river. In the summer evenings, apart from other activities, we used to ride the donkeys left by traders to graze in the extensive field, but if any of the owners came on the scene, we had to wade through the trench and clamber up on to the Island Bank to escape.

I should mention that we had a resident donkey in our own street, an animal which my father said was surely the best-fed donkey in Ireland! It belonged to two poor women named Weldon, an elderly silver-haired mother and her middle-aged daughter, who lived in one of the old cottered houses and who made a meagre living by purchasing 'seconds' or slightly damaged kitchenware and other items at the city's stores and then hawking them around the countryside with their donkey and cart to sell to the farmers' wives in County Clare. The boys on our street provided the Weldon's donkey with the finest of hay by blatant robbery which in our innocence we considered an act of great charity. While playing in Castle Street, if we saw a hayfloat coming in across Thomond Bridge, we hid behind the corner house of our own street. As soon as the hayfloat passed by, we ran out and pulled fistfuls of hay from the back of the load. The Weldon ladies showered blessings from God and his Blessed Mother on us, but many a farmer must have scratched his head on arrival at Cantrell's store on Charlotte's Quay – where my father had to pay hard-earned cash for the hay and straw and oats for his own horse – and found that some thieving horse or donkey, as it seemed, had made a large cavity in the back of his load of hay. In their trips around the villages and farms the Weldons were able to supplement our hay donations with other food, but how the donkey survived the winter I don't know. It was hard enough on the poor women to feed themselves.

Like many another mother of a large family, mine would have been glad to be allocated one of the houses that were to be built in the Island Field, but my father and many of our neighbours were convinced that building houses there at all was madness. Not only was the land swampy, but the winter fog from the river, they said, would cause the people to die like flies from consumption and pneumonia.

We listened in wonder at the stupidity of the Corporation, not realising the cataclysmic change that was about to disrupt our own lives. When the preparatory work began, we were chased out of the Island Field one day by a foreman, and ordered to crouch down behind the wall beside the entrance – the old firing ranges of the soldiers were being blasted. We heard the bang and imagined ourselves to be under shell fire in France with the Munster Fusiliers. And when they began to dig miles of trenches to lay the foundations of the houses, we had even more stimulation for our imagination in wide-ranging war games every evening when the workers had knocked off, with tons of mud available to make 'hand grenades' as we charged the enemy trenches or defended our own.

But already our street was resounding to the clatter of the builders' lorries, and our street games of hurling and rugby, as well as the girls' games, were being interrupted with increasing frequency every day, not only by the trundling lorries but by the hundreds of men walking or cycling to and from the building work. Even the wider Castle Street leading from the corner of our Old Church Street down to Thomond Bridge, became less safe. When opening the new bridge in 1840, Daniel O'Connell recalled having seen, after the rebellion of 1798, the gruesome sight of corpses hanging from the lamp-pots on the previous centuries-old structure; but for us – apart from the night terror of the Bishop Lady's Ghost – the bridge and Castle Street had always been an extension of our own street, the more open and sunny part of our tranquil playing area.

Rolling hoops, spinning or pegging tops, playing conkers or dobbers (marbles) or taws in season (certain pastimes mysteriously came into seasonal fashion), throwing our slang-bangs (a small metal object into which a 'cap' was inserted to explode when the 'slang-bang' hit the ground), sometimes having rides in a homemade go-cart, the children were always under the watchful eye of mothers from the open doorways of the houses or of the men who used to gather in the evening for a chat at the corner of the castellated little tollhouse near the bridge.

As soon as the first section of the Island Field houses was ready, we knew that not only was our playground in the field itself gone forever, but our street games – and eventually even our annual bonefire – would become impossible to continue. And it was not just traffic that bought disruption; after our ball had been snatched on several occasions by young ruffians passing by, we realised that only by building high walls at each end of our street could we ever hope to use it as a playground. The completion of the nearly five hundred houses was a long drawn-out process, but from the time when the new residents began to move in, our street was like something out of the war films showing the refugees streaming along the roads in France.

The people from the tenements and other areas had to transport their goods and chattels by any and every means – a horse, donkey and cart, handcart, box-car, pram and human shoulders – and this traffic went on from early morning to late at night. Even when all the houses were eventually occupied, there were now some thousands of new residents packed into that small area between our street and the river, and the great majority of these, going to work or shopping in the city, had to pass along our street that had hitherto been practically a cul-de-sac (except for a short street beyond the bend in the road and leading to the Island Field itself).

A further interesting light on the way planners plan is the fact for what it was, in effect, the equivalent of a small town, there were only six small shops provided, all in one row at the very entrance to the estate. This gave rise to the story about 'Gurky' McMahon – one of the new residents who was to become well known as a much loved character in our parish – on the first occasion that his wife sent him off to the new shop with a jug to buy milk. On the way back he was unable to locate his own house in the maze of identical yellow-washed and red-roofed streets of houses with their little gardens. After wandering around for a while, he asked one of the girls skipping in a street, 'Tell me, little girl, did you happen to see e'er a man comin' out of a house with a jug in his hand?'

Such yarns did nothing to lessen the hardship imposed on the residents in the new estate, not only by the failure to provide a church, school, medical centre or even a pub in such a comparatively huge centre of population packed into an area that was in effect isolated in a dead-end from the rest of the city. Their problems became our problems when the two schools in our Island Parish, The Sisters of Mercy School and the Christian Brothers' school at Quay Lane, were being asked to add the children from five hundred new houses to their already full classes. The Brothers divided the four big classrooms in the old school with partitions and packed as many pupils as they could into the school. Teachers in those days just had to accept that the size of the class was the number of pupils that could be fitted into the available space. The nuns also took in as many as they could but most of the children of school-going age in the new estate had to continue at their old schools, with the consequent hardship of a very long walk twice a day. In the churches, too, St. Mary's in the Parish and St. Munchin's across Thomond Bridge, there were soon almost as many people standing outside the door as there were seated, especially at the later Masses on Sunday. (There was no evening Mass on Saturday or Sunday then).

Our summer playground on the riverside Island Bank was also doomed. In the old days, when we enjoyed 'Home Rule' in the Island, as my mother would put it (by extension, she would call a big sandwich or any other such item 'a real Home-Ruler'), there would be only the children from a few families paddling at the Fairy Steps under the watchful eyes of our mothers; but as the houses mushroomed in the Island Field beside our Island Bank, there suddenly came swarming across from the new estate hordes of children who had every bit as much right as we, the Island natives, to enjoy the pleasures of the Shannon with its sandy coves and grassy bank. We couldn't even swim now there was such a crowd jumping and splashing and pushing.

And what about our clothes that we used to just throw there on the grass banks? We were all from the same few streets, and even if we had not been raised with very strict standards of honesty we could hardly have appeared in public wearing clothes stolen from a neighbour. Not only were our clothes unsafe now but even our swimming togs could no longer by left on the grass to dry. And when winter came, we found that our traditional slide in the New Walk which led down to the big double gates of the convent grounds, was also invaded by strangers. Our cry as we ran to commence our slide, 'offa dee ice, mag-gie!' must often have penetrated the conventual silence. That too was silenced when we natives realised that there was no point in pouring water on the road on frosty nights and then not being able to enjoy ourselves with some semblance of order and control.

Here is must be firmly stated that the knackers and robbers among the thousands of people who came to live in the Island Field (officially renamed St. Mary's Park) were only in the same proportion as in any other area of Limerick or Dublin or any other town or city. Just as happened in Dublin when the people in the city tenements were moved to estates similar to St. Mary's Park, the few vandals and blaguards soon earned a bad name for the entire estate, with the consequent unfortunate discrimination in employment and social life.

My father and mother were vehement in their opinions on this kind of snobbery. Some of the men who had played with my father in the Sarsfield Band and had lived near his own family in the Mungret Street and Watergate areas, were among the new residents of the Island Field, as were some of my mother's friends, both from her childhood in Athur's Quay and her teenage working years in the caramel factory. She went to visit them and admire enviously their lovely new houses, and they sometimes dropped by for a chat when going up the town or on their way home. And in our class in school we had new pupils who were same mixture as ourselves, 'good, bad and middling,' whether academically or at games or in general behaviour. But after my father had repaired our window three times – at least we learned how to do it by watching him – and the midnight rowdiness of rolling-home drunkards (the small pub at the corner of our street, Halpin's, as the nearest pub for the five hundred new houses) had often made us children think the Bishop's Lady was on the rampage again, even he began to add his prayers to my mother's that the promised new house on the site of the old distillery out in Thomondgate would soon become a reality.

Whether coincidentally or as a result of the traffic and population problems in our street, we noticed also that the casual traders and characters whom we had known for years gradually disappeared. Even 'Annie the Cabbage-Woman' from Park came no more. The call of 'rags, bones and bottles' from the tall foreign-looking man who gave us a balloon or a plastic windmill in exchange, was heard no more. The street-singer who cupped his hand to his ear would not have been able to hear himself with that natural echo-chamber.

And most of all we missed the man who used to come along pushing an old bicycle which was loaded down with coils of wire and old batteries. He was dressed in the dirtiest clothes we ever saw, with a big cap of the same quality around which there were more wires, and his face was greased with Vaseline and grit, causing his eyes to gleam like little blue stars (an appropriate image, as will be seen). He used park his bicycle and stand on a tin box, doing strange movements with the wires. He never spoke to us except to answer our greetings in a gentle voice and he even responded with a polite shake of the head when we inquired if there was any news from Mars today. We had seen the film serial (or follin-up one' in our dialect) Flash Gordon's Trip to Mars, and so when we gathered to watch this poor man 'communicating with Mars' were able to suspend our disbelief and even the cruel mockery with which, like all children, sometimes added to the misery of other such afflicted people.

The only recompense the new estate afforded us for the loss of all these old characters was the arrival of one new character, the aforementioned 'Gurky' McMahon about whom there many stories to add to the incident of the jug of milk. He too became a patron of Halpin's pub, but he was no rowdy, rather a genial and convivial man, and a man my father had known long before he came to be one of our new neighbours in he Island field. 'Gurky' won his way into the hearts of us children the very first time he came strolling along the street from Halpin's, with his cap on his ear and his benign smile taking in the scene where we were playing.

He stopped and called us to gather round him. Then he produced a penny and offered it to anyone would could sing 'The Legion of the Rearguard,' a rallying song of the Republican side during the civil war. Money, like death, is a great leveller, and there was a serious fight in our street after the benevolent 'Gurky' had ambled on down to his new house – because (would you believe) didn't some of he Free Staters join in with us genuine Republicans as we sang:

> *Soldiers of the Rearguard, answering Ireland's call,*
> *Hark, the martial tramp is heard from Cork to Donegal;*
> *Tone and Emmet guide you, though your task be hard;*
> *De Valera lead you, soldiers of the Legion of the rearguard.*

Our subsequent fight had as much to do with the money as with that Treaty: Gurky had only three coppers in his pocket, and faced with the impossible task of selecting three from about ten; he decided to throw the pennies 'up for a rawk'. The civil war after the signing of the Treaty, was only a bigger and more violent version of the hostilities on our street for a week after that night.

A lot of Shannon water has flowed along by the Island Bank and Thomond Bridge since then, and in the three score years that have gone by since it was developed, St Mary's Park has become an integral part of the island parish in Limerick. And what we considered to be its isolated position, is now nearer to the centre and amenities of the city than many of the big housing estates that were built in subsequent years far beyond what were the urban boundaries of the 1930's.

From *There is an Isle, a Limerick Boyhood*, Mercier Press, 1998.

Limerick Bands and the Parnellite Split
John McGrath

THE CIVILIAN BANDS OF Limerick city were extremely politicised in the nineteenth century and this was to be the cause of tension between them, and between the communities they represented, in the early to mid-nineties. The first signs of a schism between the city bands was in January 1891 when Parnell visited Limerick, an event that was attended by most of the bands but with the Victuallers' Band conspicuous by their absence. Following this the Victuallers' Band were abused and threatened in a letter from the Sarsfield Band, this incident marking the beginning of a tumultuous time in the history of the city's bands.

To understand the riots in Limerick in the early 1890s, one had to understand the average mind-set of the time. One of the most important qualities a person could have in Limerick during this period was to be a 'local,' in other words to have been born in Limerick, or even better to belong to a family that had a long affinity with Limerick, or best of all to have been born and raised in a particular parish, and to belong to a family that had a long history in that parish. As a result of this very strong parochialism that existed, Limerick consisted of a number of different communities, some parish-based, others not, that stood like islands in an archipelago. To list some of these working class communities and their traditional names, there was St. Mary's parish, which actually was an island in the Shannon river and was referred to simply as 'The Parish.'; St. Munchin's parish/Thomondgate, whose populace were referred to as 'Soda Cakes'; there was St. John's parish/Irishtown, where people were said to be living 'under the steeple'; there was the Boherbouy area, referred to as the old yellow road; St. Joseph's parish, or the 'Back of the monument' and many more. These communities were not always homogenous however, and they were often split into even smaller micro-communities polarised and the borders between them starkly highlighted.

Tension between the Victuallers' Band and the Sarsfield Band was further emphasised in February 1892 following a parade through the city by the Victuallers' Band. The Victuallers' Band and the Sarsfield Band both hailed from roughly the same area, the Sarsfield Band clubhouse in Mungret Street at the heart of the Irishtown district, and the Victuallers in Gerald Griffin Street (then known as Cornwallis Street) just on the edge of the Irishtown district. They both had their own 'turf,' however, defined by certain parameters, and the Sarsfield Band took exception when the Victuallers' Band decided to pass by the Sarsfield clubhouse during their parade. This route was allegedly one not normally taken by the Victuallers' Band and the locals in the Mungret Street area responded by firing stones at the band, an incident that was followed later by a melee outside the Victuallers' Bandroom. The incident was unlikely to have happened in the years preceding the Parnellite Split; clubs were proud of the community they represented then as much as they were after 1890 but the split exacerbated the situation to such a point that communities became hostile to one another.

As the aftermath of the scandal enfolded the people of Ireland were forced to choose a side. Most of the people of St. Mary's Parish soon declared themselves as being anti-Parnellite, or as being 'Federation' supporters. St. Mary's Band joined the Victuallers in support of the Federation and the island parish of St. Mary's soon became enemy territory for any Parnellite Bands. The violence between the two communities escalated in July 1892 around the time of the General Election. After the victory of the Federation candidate a large crowd of Parnellites gathered near the train station and from there marched, led by the Boherbouy Band (playing the tune of the 'the Boys of Wexford') through the town until they came to Mathew Bridge where intense stone-throwing occurred in which a St. Mary's man was severely injured and 'from this up to a late hour, several parts of the city were in a state of absolute riot.' The bands leading the Parnellite mob had actually contravened an order from the magistrates banning them from parading the city streets. Rioting again erupted later on in July when Parnellites and anti-Parnellites clashed in Mungret Street at the heart of the Irishtown, this was followed again by yet more arrests and hospitalisations. This was the start of a pattern of conflicts in the vicinity of the main bridges leading to St. Mary's parish, namely the Mathew Bridge and Ball's Bridge. These bridges marked the contact zone between the politically opposed communities.

August, September and October of that year were relatively calm but November saw more politically fuelled violence, triggered by Municipal elections for five Town Council seats. St. Mary's Band and the Boherbouy Band paraded the city following the elections; each band followed by large entourage. The two bands met in Patrick Street where, predictably, a riot quickly ensued. The police quickly scattered the crowds who returned to their respective enclaves, the St. Mary's mob smashing windows of the offices of the Parnellite *Limerick Leader* newspaper on their way home and the Boherbouy mob damaging the premises of the anti-Parnellite M.P., Francis O'Keeffe during their return journey.

The split had an effect on the nationalist processions in the city; the Manchester Martyrs commemoration, which normally united all nationalists, saw more rioting, and the Federation supporters boycotted the oration and parade itself. Many nationalist bodies in the city, such as the Amnesty Committee and the national league, were taken over by Parnellites, and Federationists either abstained or were excluded.

A year of relative quiet followed, helped by the fact that there were no elections of any sort. However, Parnellites in St. Mary's parish were certainly active during this time. They were eager to show that the Federation did not have a complete hegemony in the parish and, with bands being extremely important emblems for working class communities in Limerick, formed their own Parnellite St. Mary's band in late 1893. According to the urban traditions of St. Mary's parish, dissenters in the St. Mary's Band formed the Parnellite band. Traditional accounts of the split in the band allege that this Parnellite band consisted mainly of men from the Crosbie Row vicinity; and cross-referencing the 1901 and 1911 census with newspaper reports of membership can confirm that a large section of the Parnellite band came from Newgate Lane, Crosbie Row, Nicholas Street, and lanes close by. It might just have easily been the case however that the Parnellite band was formed almost completely independently of the St. Mary's Band but as no list survives of the membership of the pre-1892 St. Mary's Band to cross reference with the membership of the Parnellite band, the origins of the band remain obscure. The Parnellite band seem to have attempted at first to wrest the name 'St. Mary's Band' from the original band of that name and the first reference to the band in the city newspapers titles it the 'St. Mary's Independent Band.' However, it was eventually to become known as the No. 9 Band, signifying their allegiance to the nine members of the Irish Home Rule Party who sided with Parnell during the initial split.

From a Thesis: *Sociability and Socio-economic conditions in St. Mary's Parish, Limerick, 1890-1950.* 2006.

Origins of some Limerick City Street Names
Gerry Joyce

Athlunkard Street, in Gaelic, Sráid Áth an Longphuirt, the st. of the camp ford. The ancient ford crossed the Shannon at, or near, the place where Athlunkard Bridge was erected about 120 years ago.

Baker Place, in front of the Dominican Church, was named after Richard Baker, the builder of the houses in Baker Place. Taits Clock, located in the centre of Baker Place, was erected in honour of Alderman Peter Tait, owner of the Army Clothing Factory, who was Mayor of Limerick in 1866, 1867, and 1868.

Boherbuoy, Boherbee and **Boherglass** are mentioned in some old Pery Leases. Boherbee (or Bóthair Buí), which means yellow road and still exists as Boherbuoy, between Parnell Street and Lord Edward Street, was apparently known as such because of the yellow clay under the road, or perhaps from the yellow gorse which grew beside the road. On the other hand, however, there is no explanation for the word Boherglas (Green Road) except to speculate that it was a passage which ran originally through fields of open green areas.

Brunswick Street (now Sarsfield Street) was named after the British Royal Family at that time. After the death of Queen Anne (a Stuart) in 1714 the crown passed by Act of Settlement to George the First, who was Elector of Hanover. When he ascended to the throne he was styled 'King of Great Britain, France and Ireland, Duke of Brunswick- Luneburg and Defender of the Faith.'

Carey's Road, named after Joseph Carey, a 19th century Limerick doctor, who was noted for his charitable work for the poor of Limerick City.

Catherine Street is reputed to be named after Catherine Uthank, a member of a prominent Limerick merchant family.

Cecil Street is named after the Right Rev. William Cecil Pery, Bishop of Limerick. He was brother of Edmund Sexton Pery.

Collooney Street (now Wolfe Tone Street) was named after a military engagement near Collooney, Co. Sligo, in 1798, during which the Limerick militia fought under the command of Colonel Vereker.

Cornwallis Street (now Gerald Griffin Street) was named after Charles Lord Cornwallis, who was Lord Lieutenant of Ireland in 1798. During the American War of Independence, Cornwallis' surrender to George Washington at Yorktown in 1781 virtually ended the war with victory for the Americans.

Crosbie Row (also known as Cherry Place), was named after the distinguished Limerick clergyman, Dean Crosbie.

Denmark Street: The origin of this street name is not documented but Maurice Lenihan in his History of Limerick states that the street was named in 1870. A number of suggestions have been put forward, one being that it was named because of our ancient connections with that country.

Downey Street, named after Michael Downey who was killed at the Fairgreen by Crown forces after attending the funeral of Henry Clancy who had also been shot by Crown forces.

Ellen Street, named after Ellen Arthur, a member of the famous Limerick family.

Flood Street, named after Joseph Mary Flood, a popular District Justice and local historian, who was made a Freeman of Limerick in 1948.

Glentworth Street, named after the Right Reverend William Cecil Pery, Bishop of Limerick, who was created Baron Glentworth of Mallow, 1790.

Hartstonge Street, named after the Hartstonge family who resided in this street. A member of the family, Sir Harry Harstonge, was MP of County Limerick from 1776 to 1789 (see Sir Harry's Mall).

O'Connell Street (formerly George's Street) and **O'Connell Avenue** (formerly Military Road) were named after Daniel O'Connell, known as The Liberator, because of his initiation of Catholic Emancipation.

Patrick Street, named after Patrick Arthur, a member of the famous Limerick family.

Playhouse Lane (now Little Gerald Griffin Street) named after the Theatre or Playhouse that used to exist at its junction with Lower Gerald Griffin Street).

Richmond Street (now St. Joseph's Street) and Richmond Place (now The Crescent) were named after Charles Lennox, 4th Duke of Richmond, who was appointed Lord Lieutenant of Ireland in 1807.

Rutland Street, named after Charles Manners, 4th Duke of Rutland, who was appointed Lord Lieutenant of Ireland in 1784 and who visited Limerick in 1785. He died in office in 1786.

Shelbourne Road, the name derives from the original landowner in the area, William Petty, who was 2nd Earl of Shelbourne and 1st Marquis of Lansdowne, after whom Lansdowne Park is named.

Sir Harry's Mall was named after Sir Henry (Harry) Hartstonge around the year 1760. He built the Mall after reclaiming the foreshore. He lived in the corner house close to Baals' bridge. It has also been called the Sandmall, because sand dredged from the river was deposited in piles along the Mall.

Thomas Street is reputed to be named after Thomas Uthank, who was a prominent Limerick City merchant, but there is no documentary evidence to support this.

Wellesley Bridge (now Sarsfield Bridge) and Wellesley Place (now Clontarf Place) were named after Richard, Marquis of Wellesley (a brother of the Duke of Wellington), who was Lord Lieutenant of Ireland in 1823 when the act for the building of the Bridge was passed. It was officially opened in 1835 by the then Lord Lieutenant, the Earl of Mulgrave.

William Street is reputed to be named after one of the King Williams and if so would be one of the few royal names retained in Limerick as a city street. The dates of the reigns of these kings do not support this theory as Maurice Lenihan states that the street was named in 1789. In view of the fact that it was the principal street in the New Town Pery development, it is more likely to have been named after William Cecil Pery.

From *Limerick City Street Names*, published by Limerick Corporation, 1995.

Limerick City
Desmond O'Grady
(for Jack Donovan, Michael Cunneen and Richard Harris)

All night in a room on the road to Kilkee,
where Europe stumbles to stop at the sea,
surrounded by empty family furniture
and the fierce presence of those absent
crowding the room like the Court of King Arthur,
we talked fairly straight the bent
years of our tangled past
and clinched off the chances we'd taken and missed.

Between going and coming, time makes no
matter – gets clobbered. All value
lies in the effort to return, recognition,
continuity of the original temper intensified.
My fifteen years on the open road between
the school of priests and the school of hard
knocks finds you, like a thoroughbred, leaner
but recognisable as my own front door.

Here there's small chance to explain
or examine the whole pain
in its very detail like a stained glass
window – barely time to observe,
and love, what carves from the face
the equine jaw and starts the nerve
to jig the throat. For survival we grip
the desired, endurable gut in personal torment

and count ourselves damned well-to-do
if we hack out a crossed stick will measure
the dung in each day we are faced with.
Older now, wiser and much weaker,
our strength in a *Modus Vivendi* almost monastic –
silent survival in the stone hard cell of our meeker

THE CITY

selves – our bargains the one hand, our error
the other, both clenched in desperate prayer.

This wide whacky world's just one small town
with its watchers and watched and genius unsung
and a marble of meaning may be quarried quite simply
right where you stand. The town's young
painter, actor, poet may make Mayakovsky
Square, London's Chelsea, Paris or mad Manhattan
reel in his head from his own village air
and sit in his pub as though in the Latin Quarter.

And those gone elsewhere, gone cosmopolitan,
in time remould in the long left town
for self safety. We once saw our Shannon
and Seine – now the Seine flows back our Shannon. All
public image (stuff the punk publicity man
thrives on) does not mean personal
survival – playacting the king before you're a knight,
high-priest before you're an acolyte.

In between it's the daily routine
persistent reality, repetition,
the mutual hardship of the merely physical,
geographical isolation,
hammering away at the wall
until we break free
from our state's severity.

Once, in this small town,
in the beginning, untravelled, young –
painter, actor, poet – we were daring , gay
visionaries full of blind virtuosity; blind too
of machine making men and their methods. Older today
we are tamer, timid even, terrified – but know
there's a provincial power in the weakest heart helps take on
all alien slaughter and keeps us unchanged for our own.

The few in the end remain –
step from behind the barricades of their ruin;
return in caravans of one at a time from the sea
of the soulless desert
where the gulls molest and mute without mercy;
return in that single, sacred effort
to drink together at the common oasis
where no one is best or better or worse.

From *The Road Taken*, University of Salzburg Press, 1996.

Remembering Professor King-Griffin
Eoin Devereux

PROFESSOR Michael King-Griffin began life as Michael Griffin on January 26, 1909 in Miltown-Malbay, Co. Clare. Having attended school at the local national school and later the Christian Brothers' in Ennistymon, he studied piano with Miss Mary Burke Vaughan and he subsequently taught music to boys and girls in the local area.

He furthered his studies in music under the guide of Professor Earnest de Regge – a Belgian who was organist in St. Flannan's College in Ennis – who was tragically killed with seven others when a floor collapsed at a furniture auction at Carmody's Hotel in Ennis in 1958. The Professor's connection with De Regge may have been a strong influencing factor in his decision to leave Ireland in order to further his studies in continental Europe. Although the details of his travels at this time are rather sketchy, we know that he studied in Bonn and that he met Fr. W.J. O'Grady (who would later become Administrator of St. John's Cathedral) at the Irish College in Paris, a fact that no doubt influenced his decision to return to Ireland.

The Professor arrived in Limerick in the late 1930's and took an appointment as organist in St. John's. He also taught music in the old St. Munchin's Diocesan College and supplemented his earnings by teaching elocution and music in the variety of places in which he lived in Limerick.

In sartorial terms, he appears to have 'cut quite a dash' by wearing a cape tied at the neck with a sapphire and was said to wear a Dexter (frock-like) coat and bowler hat. The RTE broadcaster, Ciaran MacMathuna, commented upon his dress-sense and recalled that 'the music in the Cathedral [St. John's] was dominated by the tall and rather haughty figure of the organist and choirmaster Professor 'King' Griffin who wore gloves all the time to protect his hands. I always thought he came from some mid-European musical city but was delighted when I found out that he was a native of one of my favourite places, Miltown Malbay in Co. Clare.'

The Professor made an immense contribution to city life as an expert musician, and was instrumental with Fr. O'Grady in organising the annual Gregorian or 'Plain Chant' festival between school choirs. He also acted as a critic and contributed colourful reviews of the musicals, and other occasional pieces, to the local press. He was also a prime mover in the local Trees for Ireland campaign, and donated some cedar trees for planting at King John's Castle in 1959.

Professor King-Griffin died in London on March 22, 1981, aged 72 years. He is buried in Ballard Cemetery in his coastal home town of Miltown-Malbay, Co. Clare – itself renowned for its traditional Irish music. A simple limestone headstone erected by his sister Minnie marks his last resting place.

From *The Old Limerick Journal*, Winter Edition, 2004.

TEN
POLITICS

The Poor Hoor Was Killed
P. J. Browne

IN a Dail debate, Donogh O'Malley, when Minister for Education, and Deputy Oliver J. Flanagan engaged in a heated debate over the suitability of an anthology of short stories prescribed by the Department of Education for Intermediate Certificate English. Flanagan found two stories objectionable: 'Guest of the Nation' by Frank O'Connor, and 'The Trout' by Sean O'Faolain – because of inappropriate language:

'This type of language might be expected in a low class pitch-and-toss school but should not be contained in a book for young children, many of whom are in their first years or preparation for, perhaps, a religious life, or to take their place in whatever profession they are going to follow.... Maybe we are reaching the stage of modern teaching when everything is being modernised, but if this type of language is to be used in our textbooks, I am sorry we did not remain old-fashioned. 'On page 198, one sees the expression 'Ah for Christ's sake.' There are numerous parents who would not allow their children to use that expression. It would be wrong and improper.'

The Minister's response was somewhat mischievous but it was highly effective, delivered with flair and humour. In reference to 'The Trout' O'Malley suggested that the deputy had not read the story in its entirety.

Flanagan: 'The Trout?'

O'Malley: Yes.

Flanagan: From cover to cover. Very suggestive. I did not like it.

O'Malley: Does the Deputy, if he has read the story, realise that it is his own vivid and excitable imagination-

Flanagan: No. Parents have written to me.

O'Malley: I would be pointing out to the Deputy that if he had read the story he would see this young girl is going into the tunnel to catch a trout and not to catch anything else. If these ideas which the Deputy is putting into Irish minds which no doubt, will be widely published in tomorrow's papers are all he can find in Sean O' Faolain's 'The Trout', which has been described also as the finest story of O'Faolain, then I can only say 'God help us,' and it is a very lucky thing that O'Faolain and O'Connor cannot combine to write a story on the proceedings here tonight and on the last day.

It is safe to say that five or ten years hence world television, to which nothing will be sacred, will be thrown open to us from many stations in the sky. It may have seemed to the committee that the responsible milieu of the classroom is, next to the home, the best place to prepare the pupils for what we must expect in a world of such open communication which is coming, if indeed it is not already upon us ...
It should be said that the words concerned, apart from their legal sense, do not carry, at least in Ireland, a connotation other than mild, vulgar, opprobrium. Curiously enough, if preceded by the adjective 'poor', they would express sympathy. I think the Deputy will agree with that. In the south of Ireland, if he said: 'John fell down a cliff, and the poor hoor was killed –

Flanagan: If he is a poor bastard or a poor hoor, he is still a bastard or hoor.

O'Malley: If Deputy Flanagan went down to the south of Ireland at a by-election, pulled up at the side of the road and was told: 'John fell down a cliff and the poor hoor was killed-

Flanagan: I would say 'Lord have mercy on him.

O'Malley: The Deputy would say rightly: 'The Lord have mercy on him. He would not start slagging him for using that type of language. He would say: 'The poor hoor, Lord have mercy on him.

Flanagan: I would not; I would leave out 'poor hoor.' I do not care for that type of language.

O'Malley: I think the ordinary reasonably-minded person appreciates the fact that we are doing a good service in the teaching of English literature to our children. Anyone who has read this story would not have the slightest qualms of conscience about letting a child read it, it fits so aptly into the whole trend of the story. If the mentality of Deputy Flanagan is like that of the unfortunate girl who went into the tunnel to catch a trout, and not to catch anything else, the Lord have mercy on us all.

From *Unfilled Promise: Memories of Donogh O'Malley*, Currach Press, 2008.

The Night de Valera Came to Town
Mae Clancy-Leonard

I REMEMBER it well. Well enough that is. I must have been about six years old and there was a General Election in the offing. My mother was a political animal but my father was non-committal.

Someone in the school yard at lunch time invented a great game. We marched round and round following the leader shouting "Up McBride" and neither the nun nor lay teacher put a stop to it. Later at home, I introduced my brother to the same game in our backyard and got an unexplained clout on the ear from my mother.

Who was Sean McBride anyway? "The next king of Ireland," my best friend informed me. She knew because she was going with her parents to hear him speak at the O'Connell Monument at the Crescent in Limerick. I could come, too, she assured me. All I needed was my mother's permission. I can still see the look on my mother's face. Puce. She turned puce and I did not get to see the next king of Ireland.

The following Saturday as we played rounders outside her house everyone remarked on the awful smell of burning cloth in the air. My father came home late from work with the news that Roches Stores was on fire. Of course we wanted to rush uptown to see it but we were grounded and had to be content to watch from an upstairs window.

On Monday morning as I made my way to school, the burning smell still hung on the air. Our nun bemoaned the thousands of pounds worth of damage done and the number of jobs lost. "Nothing left but an empty shell," she sighed and the made us all aware of the danger of fire and its consequences. She made us feel so depressed that day it was a great relief when the three o'clock bell rang.

At home my mother was in a state of euphoria. Someone called Dev was coming to Limerick. She said he was The Chief and I had an instant vision of Sitting Bull with a full feathered head-dress. My father did not want to know. He refused the invitation to accompany her and she turned to us saying – "You'll come to see The Chief with me, won't you?" What could we do only nod?

There were thousands of people gathered at The Crescent. I couldn't see a thing and was in danger of being squashed against an iron railing. I complained to my Mam and she tore herself away from the booming voice to lift me and then I saw him.

"That's my Granpa up there. Is he The Chief?"

"No," she smiled, "your Grandpa is the Mayor and he's welcoming The Chief to Limerick."

But there was nobody else on the platform. There wasn't hide nor hair of a feathered head-dress. Not an Indian in sight. And what was this about my Granda being a horse?

Any question died on my lips and my mother joined in the chant. "Up Dev. Up Dev." and I thought how adults get away with stuff like that when I got a clout for the same thing a couple of days previously. Then foul smelling paraffined torches lit up an avenue towards the high platform. I began to tremble with pure fright. Would we all be burnt down like Roches Stores?

My mother thought I was cold and she bent down and pulled my woollen stockings up over my knees securing them with my white elastic garters. I hated that, but it was cosy and warm.

Someone in the crowd shouted "Up McBride" and my mother made an annoying clucking sound. The speaker began and his words boomed over my head but the crowd cheered and clapped at intervals through his speech.

And what seemed like hours later the voice eventually halted to an almighty cheer. Could we go home now? No. My mother had another of her great ideas. Full of excitement, she dragged us to the opposite side of the Crescent where, right outside the Jesuit Church, was a large black car. "The Princess," my mother breathed, "the only one in Ireland."

Before we had any say in the matter, she tackled the huge man in the trench coat. "Could they sit on de Valera's seat?" Oh the mortification of it. "Something to tell your grandchildren," she told us on her way home afterwards.

"Did you feel the detective's gun under his arm?" my brother asked. I didn't. All I felt was embarrassment when my skirt rode up as he lifted me into the car to reveal to the whole world and de Valera, the knotted elastic garters holding up my thick-knit stockings.

From *My Home Is There*, Isle Publications, 1996.

POLITICS

Stevie Coughlan and the IRA
as told to John Liddy

IT was a ha'penny a game and a penny a jink and usually, after prayers, there was nothing but talk of politics and religion. Steve Coughlan remembers those evenings as a child growing up around the card table, where arguments over Parnell and Healy, Davitt and Fenianism, de Valera and Cosgrave, were zealously aired, sure and certain on a table of trumps.

His parents were deeply religious. They were both members of the Confraternities in Limerick. His father, a quiet, politically subdued man, belonged to the Arch Confraternity for fifty years, while his mother, more outspoken, attended the Holy Family Confraternity in St. John's Cathedral. They both shared an allegiance to Parnell and the Fenian movement.

Young Steve Coughlan absorbed the political ideologies of his parents and as he grew older, began to read such books as A. M. Sullivan's 'New Ireland,' 'Political Sketches and Personal Reminiscences' and 'Recollections and Fenianism' by John O'Leary.

Ireland, at this time, was still preoccupied with Parnell's downfall and Healy's 'unenviable success.' The Civil War, fought in 1922-1923 between those who supported the Treaty with England, which involved the partition of Ireland, and those who wanted a thirty two county republic, was only 'over on paper.' The country was more politically divided than at any other time.

Cumann na Gael was the elected Government after the Treaty was signed on December 6, 1921. It was founded by W. T. Cosgrave and Kevin O'Higgins and Paddy McGilligan. de Valera had ordered the IRA to cease fire and tackle the issues in a political rather than in a military fashion.

But groups of IRA men continued to bear arms with Sean McBride as Chief of Staff. McBride was later to leave the IRA when de Valera introduced, in 1937, the Constitution of Ireland. McBride felt then, that the Constitution provided the necessary freedom to achieve the unification of Ireland by peaceful means.

Against this backdrop of political and social upheaval, Steve Coughlan's own political loyalties were now being shaped. Parental influence was obvious. He was young, immature, and believed that the whole slanderous attitude shown towards Parnell was not in keeping with the Fenian tradition or the Wolfe Tone tradition, a tradition which was deeply concerned with the unification of Ireland and its people – whether they be Catholic, Protestant or Dissenter. 'Parnell wanted to unite the country as did Tone. I made up my mind that their answer was the right one in dealing with the British intelligence and the British Government, at the time.'

As an insurance clerk with Prudential Insurance Company, an English firm with offices in Ireland, twenty year old Steve Coughlan was transferred from Limerick to Tralee in 1931. In Tralee, he 'met men of outstanding honour who were associated with the Republican movement,' and he associated himself with them.

Among those men were John Joe Sheehy, who died recently in Tralee, and the late Johnny O'Connor, former Clann na Poblachta TD for Kerry who later died in a car accident. Other members of the IRA whom Steve Coughlan met were Moss

Toomey, Sean Russell and Sean McBride.

'I knew them well and believed as they did, in a united thirty-two county republic.' As an intelligence officer in the IRA he had to gather information on members of Cumann na Gael and the Detective Force. Weekly meetings were held in Tralee and training in the use of arms provided at these meetings. The IRA at that time were forbidden to take part in an agrarian or industrial disputes as their only concern was with the unification of the country.

'But we were aware that physical force could not be ruled out. We knew that we had to be prepared to take on the enemy who were the British in Kaki. There were thousands in the country at the time who felt like we did.'

Prior to the General Election of 1932, contested between Cumann na Gael, Fianna Fail and Labour. Frank Aiken, who succeeded General Liam Lynch as commander of Republican forces, came to Tralee to discuss the election with members of the IRA. The meeting took place in Farmers Bridge in the house of John O'Connor. Cumann na Gael had introduced a Public Safety Act, which meant that a person could be brought in for questioning and held for twenty four hours and then released.

'Frank Aiken felt strongly about the fact that there were men held in the Currragh without any time limit on their imprisonment and his main priority was to defeat Cumann na nGael. de Valera was leader of the Fianna Fail party then and the behaviour of the Cosgrave regime was totally unacceptable.'

Steve Coughlan remembers voting fourteen times in that particular election, even though he was not yet eligible to vote. He never voted again until the general election of 1948.

A week before the election, Cumann na Gael organised a public meeting in Tralee in support of their candidate. Con Brosnahan. The leader of the Government, W. T. Cosgrave, was to address the meeting. Throughout the country, the IRA were united in their wish to put the Government out of office, at any cost. In Tralee they decided the meeting would not take place and it was agreed that W. T. Cosgrave would be shot.

'I was detailed to shoot W. T. Cosgrave and thankfully it never happened. But at the time I was a member of the IRA and did what I was told. We succeeded in disrupting the meeting and a Fr. Molyneaux of St. John's Church appealed to the crowd to go home. But nobody stirred until the Guards, under Supt. Kelleher, broke loose and batoned everybody in sight. Cosgrave was travelling in a Black Maria and as the car passed me at Moyderwell Cross I jumped onto the running board and shouted 'you're for it.' But the driver elbowed me onto the ground and the course of history remained unaltered.'

The Cumann na nGael candidate, Con Brosnan, was defeated and Fianna Fail won five seats. Fianna Fail's outstanding victory in the '32 election was due mainly to the fact that Labour party voted with Fianna Fail against Cumann na Gael. Professor Marcus O'Sullivan of Killarney won a seat for the Government. The IRA claimed a victory with the election of Stephen Fuller, a survivor of the Ballyseedy bomb attack. He was one of the five men taken from Ballymullen barracks by Free State troops, who brought the men to Ballyseedy and tied a land mine to their bodies and blew them up. Fuller crawled on his hands and knees to the nearest house, a half mile away, and was taken to hospital.

After the '32 election, many members of the IRA gave up their arms and joined Fianna Fail. It was a time for change and de Valera had made his point in favour of pursuing republican goals by peaceful and democratic means. Still, there were groups of IRA men in Tralee and elsewhere, clinging to the gun and refusing to row in with de Valera. Arms continued to be bought back from America by visiting All Ireland teams and there was the question of the Blue Shirt Movement to be tackled. Shortly after General Eoin O'Duffy was sacked from his position as Commissioner of the Guards by de Valera, he formed the Blue Shirt Movement. Though offered an alternative job, he declined, preferring instead to succeed in his boast that the 'Blue Shirts would be victorious in Ireland, as the Brown Shirts were victorious in England and the Black Shirts victorious in Germany!'

When he announced his intention of addressing a meeting in Tralee the IRA planned to shoot him. They were opposed to O'Duffy and the Blue Shirt Movement as they felt he was impeding the national aspiration towards unity. O'Duffy, at that time, was seen as a traitor and his sacking helped to fuel that belief. The Government felt that he was using his office for personal motives which lay outside Government policy.

The meeting was held privately, as Cumann na Gael, of which Duffy was a member, was very weak after the election. Nevertheless, the meeting did take place in the Forestors Hall in Stauntons Place. 'We got a message by phone from a man in Cruises Hotel in Limerick, saying that O'Duffy was on his way to Tralee. He was travelling in one of three cars and my job was to signal which car O'Duffy was in. A few miles outside Tralee I saw three cars approaching but I couldn't tell O'Duffy's car from the others. So we never fired and he reached Tralee and held this meeting. But as O'Duffy addressed the meeting in Forestors Hall, a second attempt was made on his life. 'A bomb was dropped through a glass domed ceiling into the hall but it never went off. There were crowds on the street and the army was called in from Cork. They used tear gas on the crowd and O'Duffy made his escape out of Tralee.' Although there were former Cumann na Gael government ministers one hundred per cent behind the Blue Shirt Movement, O'Duffy and his dream, faded from the Irish political scene around 1934-35.

After the '32 Election, Sean McBride and Liam and George Gilmore came to Tralee to enlist support for a new party called Saor Eire (Ireland Free). The party were more extreme than Fianna Fail and was in fact banned by de Valera and the Catholic Church, However, Saor Eire only lasted for two or three years. But because of that meeting in Tralee, a life-long friendship developed between Sean McBride and Steve Coughlan. McBride later stood as god-father to Steve's daughter, Nellie.

Another friendship that developed out of those IRA days in Tralee was with Frank Ryan, a member of the IRA command and later Republican soldier in the Spanish Civil War. They met during an Easter Week commemoration ceremony in Rath Cemetery, Tralee. Frank Ryan delivered the oration over the Republican plot. Steve Coughlan was a member of the guard of honour.

Around 1933-34 Steve Coughlan returned to Limerick and attended a dance, organised by the Blue Shirt movement, in the Lyric Ballroom. He went with friends to protest against the organisers of this dance. They were advised at the door by the late Mossy Reidy not to go in as their lives were in danger. But Coughlan and friends persisted and during the playing of the National Anthem, everybody in the hall, except Steve and company gave the Facist salute.

'On our way home after the dance, a couple of Blue Shirts attacked us with iron bars and I received sixteen stitches as a result. But it is interesting to note that at the dance there were people present who are now closely associated with Fianna Fail.'

From an interview published in the *Limerick People on Sunday*, December, 1980. Vol. 1, No. 3.

Carry-on at the 'Monament'
David Lee

IT is popularly assumed that the Georgian district of Limerick has no history worth speaking of, unlike the old mediaeval quarters of Englishtown and Irishtown which can boast of King John's Castle, the Williamite sieges and all that stuff; and while Georgian Limerick may have some worthy buildings that worthy people want to preserve, it is otherwise seen as a rather dull place, devoid of all historical interest. It's just a place to shop, visit the doctor and become obese on fast food. However, the streets of Georgian Limerick do have their own fascinating little stories to tell – stories that give much needed human dimensions to the brick and mortar we see all round us.

Take the Crescent for example – There was a time when the Daniel O'Connell Monument on this elegant Georgian thoroughfare was a traditional meeting place for open-air political rallies and election meetings from the nineteenth century until the 1950's; and there are people today who can still recall the hurly-burly of the political hustings at the Crescent and the slanging matches that went on between politicians. Limerickman and Labour Party supporter, Bob Kelly, recalls that in the late 1950's the Crescent, or the 'Monament' as it was referred to by the locals, was the place to be for all the fun and excitement at election times; and while there was no shortage of personalities at the time, the two main political protagonists in Limerick were Donogh O'Malley (Fianna Fáil) and Steve Coughlan (Labour).

'Steve Coughlan was a very colourful character,' says Bob Kelly. 'I remember one occasion when Donogh was on the platform at the 'Monament' and Steve seemed to lose his cool and began to hurl very offensive remarks at Donogh concerning his personal and private life.'

Hecklers also played a considerable part in these proceedings, for more often than not they had been planted by the opposition to disrupt the orator's flow. Bob recalls that there was very little political analysis in those days, for Civil War antagonisms were still very much alive; television had not yet arrived and there was no forum to listen to reasoned political debate between the political parties. Whenever 'political debate' took place at the Crescent it invariably ended up in 'uproar and bedlam', people allowing their hearts to rule their heads. As a generalisation, many people of that era were less well informed and less educated than today's electorate and they sometimes let their emotions run away with them. 'Despite all this, I found the evenings spent at the political gatherings at the Crescent well spent,' says Bob. 'I well remember the buzz and excitement generated by these meetings at the 'Monament' and they also proved to be my introduction to politics.'

Another Limerickman who remembers the theatrical nature of street politics in days gone-by is Michael Donnellan who vividly recalls seeing Eamon de Valera being driven up O'Connell Street in a motor car one evening on the late 1940s to a Fianna Fáil rally at the Crescent. 'He was seated in the car with the windows rolled down, waving to the crowds as of he were Royalty,' says Michael. 'A throng of people were following him up the street and he was being escorted by a line of supporters marching in single file on either side of the car, each man holding a torch made of a burning sod of turf, soaked in paraffin and held aloft on a pitchfork. I was only a boy at the time, but it seemed quite spectacular.'

The O'Connell Monument itself was a great place for patriots to hang a flag or two to display their political passions. When Queen Victoria celebrated her Diamond Jubilee on 12 June, 1897, the 'Liberator' was draped in black flags by nationalists eager to recall to public memory the 'Famine Queen' and on 12 October, 1912, the statue in the Crescent is decorated with mottoes of FAITH AND FATHERLAND and a dozen or so young men dressed in saffron coloured kilts and stockings appeared in along procession which with many bands marched through the chief streets, representing the Home Rule demonstration.'

In the days before television civilised us, political passions ran high in southern Ireland, especially during the early 1930s when Republicans and Blueshirts bashed each other with gay abandon in a match replay of the 1922-23 Civil War. It was a political rally organised by the United Ireland party at the Crescent on Saturday 23 September 1933 that sparked off one of the worst political riots Limerick had seen for years.

According to media reports 10,000 Blueshirts assembled in the city on that day to hear William T. Cosgrave, the former Cumann na nGaedheal President of the Free State Executive Council, General Eoin O'Duffy and James Dillon speak at the Crescent. Supporters, many of them wearing their blue uniforms, poured into the city in buses and lorries to assemble at Cruise's Hotel in Lower O'Connell Street and march from there to the platform at the Crescent. However, the day would not be allowed to pass peacefully if the large numbers of anti-Blueshirt demonstrators who had also assembled in the city were to have their way.

The first indications that trouble was brewing occurred outside Cruise's Hotel when general O'Duffy, Cosgrave and Dillon arrived at the hotel. A crowd of demonstrators, shouting 'Up Dev' and 'Up the Republic' surged forward to get to grips with the Blueshirts, but the protestors were held back by a cordon of gardai and batons drawn. The first blood was spilt when the Collins Pipe Band was leading a group of United Ireland Party supporters down O'Connell Street to the assembly point at Cruise's. As the pipe band passed the Bedford Row junction they were ambushed by a group of republicans who charged out of the side street and attacked the bandsmen. A short, sharp struggle broke out during which one of the drummers received an ugly gash on the head. It was said at the time that he had been battered by his own drum.

Following these clashes, the Blueshirts formed up outside Cruise's Hotel and marched up O'Connell Street. As they did so, determined efforts were made by their republican opponents to halt the march and deny the United Irelanders the right to free speech. Baton-wielding Civic Guards had to clear a way through the protestors, who included women and girls in their ranks. All along the route of the march stones and bottles were thrown at the Blueshirts from sidewalks and street corners and many Blueshirts were hit by flying missiles.

Eventually, the procession reached the Crescent and the Blueshirts rally got under way, but the chairman's opening remarks were lost in a deafening din of shouting and booing. To allow the meeting to proceed, gardai chased the boisterous protestors down Hartstonge Street and Mallow Street, pursuing their quarry into Catherine Street and Glentworth Street. The meeting then passed off peacefully except for a few minor scuffles. Other parts of Georgian Limerick, however, were in uproar as gardai made repeated baton charges in an attempt to disperse the hostile crowds. According to the *Irish Times*, during the rally, 'and for a considerable time after it had ended, O'Connell Street and the numerous side streets were the stage for fierce faction fights, in which sticks, stones and bottles were freely used, whilst baton charges by the Civic Guards occurred every other minute in an effort by the police to drive off the opponents of the O'Duffy party. Casualties were numerous.'

The most serious incident of the riot took place when shots were allegedly fired at a group of gardai who were chasing stone-throwers along Mallow Street into Upper Mallow street. According to a garda statement, gunmen fired on the police from positions near the Lyric Cinema in Glentworth Street. But, as often occurs in cases such as this, a different version of events emerged. Local Fianna Fáil Alderman Dan Burke, T.D. claimed to have witnessed the shooting himself, and in a public statement made several days later at a public rally, also held at the Crescent, he alleged: "I went down Glentworth Street and saw a party of guards running up firing shots. I ran in front of them and said, 'For God's sake, are you gone mad? What are you firing at? Innocent men, women and children.' To which the police replied that they were shooting because they had been 'fired at with stones.' Alderman Burke also accused the gardai of indiscriminately batoning defenceless people during the disturbances and he alleged that he himself had been assaulted by gardai.

When the Blueshirt rally in the Crescent had ended the United Irelanders again had to brave the gauntlet of O'Connell Street as liberal quantities of stones, bottles and abuse rained down on to of them. One man, who became separated from the parade, was beaten to the ground and kicked. Outside Cruise's Hotel there were wild scenes as the visiting Blueshirts fled to the safety of their transport. Attempts were made by republicans to set fire to three motor vehicles parked outside the hotel and, as buses inched forward through the crowd, they were sent on their way with volleys of bottles, stones and republican slogans. The Blueshirts had to be escorted by gardai out of Limerick while street skirmishing continued until midnight. Thirty-three people were reported to have been treated in Barrington's Hospital, mostly for head wounds. Given the scale of the violence it was lucky that no lives were lost.

From *Georgian Limerick*, Vol, II (Limerick's Historic Georgian Quarter)
Limerick Civic Trust Publication, 2000.

The O'Malley Dynasty
Dick Walsh

DES O'Malley shrugs off the suggestion of a dynasty; but before he ever thought of entering politics his family had reached an uncommonly powerful position in Limerick. His father, also called Des, and two of his uncles, Michael and Donogh, had served as mayors of the city. Des senior, in particular, was a highly valued member of Fianna Fáil, although long after his death stories persisted about how he could as easily have stood for Fine Gael. Both Eamonn de Valera and Sean Lemass pressed him to accept the nomination when the patriarchal Limerick Republican, Dan Bourke, who had been in the Dáil since the Twenties, died in 1952. When he refused, the offer passed after a short delay to Donogh. Des was to remain Fianna Fáil's anchor man in the constituency, while Donogh became one of Lemass' mohair-suited men and, in time, one of the most adventurous and innovative Ministers in the history of the State.

Some politicians find themselves stretching a tenuous line of kinship to make a connection with the constituency they hope to represent. Des O'Malley bore the indelible stamp of his family; and the O'Malley's were quintessentially Limerick.

The first thing that most Limerick people will tell you about their city is that it is not as outsiders see it: ultra-conservative, pious and poor. O'Malley is no exception. To him, the city is – outside Dublin – the most cosmopolitan place in the country. And there's no denying that from the settlement of the 17th century to the development of Shannon in the 1950s, Limerick has been exposed to regular, if sometimes unwelcome, doses of outside influence. It was here, after the cruel sieges of 1690 and 1691, that the Wild Geese spread their wings; and the garrison that replaced them, with a broken army and wounded pride, stood guard over a new order. Gaelic Ireland died in Limerick, Irish troops went to fight on 'far foreign fields' and the Williamite forces consolidated their success, which, as the English historian, G. M. Trevelyan, noted, marked a turning point in European history.

In Limerick the new settlers – and, indeed, many of the old as well – welcomed the garrison and felt grateful for its protection. Merchants and tradespeople took the living that it provided and asked no questions. But others saw in it a bitter reminder of the old betrayal, a humiliating memorial to a cause that seemed forever lost, in one of the fiercest struggles of the War of Independence, the garrison was dispatched in 1922. Limerick was, and still is, to a great extent, a city of layers.

Even in the centuries after the broken treaty, its prosperity grew. Not that everyone enjoyed it: in the 1770's for example, the poor of the city laid siege to its flour mills and had to be fought off by the militia. But for the settlers and merchants life was full of delights. They made the most of what the poet Spencer called 'the spacious Shannon spreading like the sea'. Upriver they took the air by the falls of Doonass or across the weir at Castleconnell, where they built a discreet and elegant resort. They ventured downstream on boats owned by an ancestor of Richard Harris, that plied between the city, Foynes, Tarbert and Kilrush, from where it was a short, overland spin to the seaside at Kilkee.

On their journey they passed the scene of that recent ghastly drowning of a young girl by a paid murderer. Gerald Griffin, a reporter on the *Chronicle*, had made a book of it called *The Collegians*. The book was to be turned into a melodrama, *The Colleen Bawn* (ah dear Mr. Boucciccault) and an opera, *The Lily of Killarney*. They had theatres and music-halls on their doorsteps. That, at least, was something the rest of the citizens could enjoy; when O'Meara, the tenor, returned to the city from a triumphant European tour, thousands turned up to stand beneath the balcony of his hotel in Bedford Row to hear him sing. Everyone could recite *Drunken Thady and the Bishop's Lady* by their own Bard of Thomond, Michael Hogan, though few enough probably knew of the works of Brian Merriman of Clare who completed his masterly satire, *The Midnight Court*, while teaching mathematics in the city.

A city of layers, indeed. To this day, the huddled streets and lanes of The Parish (St. Mary's) are a world away from the spreading lawns of Castletroy or the solid brick of the Ennis Road. And there are lines of local geography which the outsider will pass without noticing; a corner turned, a bridge crossed and there is a new inflexion, a new tone which only the most finely tuned ear in a musically inclined city will detect.

The change of tone if often more than musical: tuppence-ha'penny looking down on tuppence is one local version of the many social distinctions which are entwined in the barely perceptible boundaries. 'Old stock' is a commendation that money can't buy. Lineage and schools are important to the status-conscious. And games, or at any rate rugby: Limerick is one of the few cities in Ireland where rugby has a strong working class following. This, however, does not mean that the working class players join the professional and propertied men who, elsewhere, are most commonly associated with the game. The working classes have their own clubs, Shannon and Young Munster; the middle-classes play with Garryowen; the well-to-do join Bohemians and Old Crescent. Each group has its meeting places; members rarely break into each other's territory.

The O'Malley's fit comfortably into this urban maze. Not in the top layer, but near enough. They are long enough resident to be considered 'old stock.' Des O'Malley's paternal grandfather was an architect; his maternal grandfather owned a hotel. Their children were educated by the Jesuits at the Crescent or by the Faithful Companions of Jesus at Laurel Hill. Donogh played his rugby with Bohemians and, if it hadn't been for the war, might have been capped for Ireland. Given the circumstances that prevailed once independence had been achieved, they were the kind of people that might naturally be expected to a have a hand in running the affairs of the new State.

Des O'Malley was born in Eden Terrace in the North Circular road in 1939. He was three when his parents moved back to his father's old home where Corbally slopes gently towards the river. It may not have been the city's most exclusive area, but they had the Catholic Bishop of Limerick for a neighbour. For Des, his sister Denise and brothers Joseph and Peter, school lay on the other side of the city. To get there they passed through the Parish and the city centre; and there were five Catholic churches along the way. Through the Forties and the Fifties, neither the city's poverty nor its piety could be ignored.

'It was only 15 years earlier that the first slum clearances took place,' O'Malley now recalls. 'Slums were still very visible around the centre of the city. I think everyone had to be conscious of them. And remember, welfare levels were very low, not just by comparison with what they are now, but in absolute terms.' As for religion, it was a dominant influence in everyone's lives. These were the heydays of the Arch Confraternity of the Holy Family which claimed a membership of 10,000 men and boys. O'Malley himself never joined but served Mass regularly at the Jesuit church just down the road from the Redemptorists' where the Arch Confraternity met to wage war on the devil with all his works and pomps. It was about this time that a group of Jehovah's Witnesses was set upon by a gang of men near Killaloe in Co. Clare, and when the case was heard in Limerick it was the Witnesses who were bound to the peace.

At home in Corbally, however, the talk was of politics and books. It was a busy house. O'Malley senior was the eldest of a family of twelve and considered himself responsible for his brothers and sisters as well as for his own children. Donogh, whether in college or later in politics, often brought his troubles to be sorted out. A brother-in-law, Stan Stewart, and his wife Nora, brought news of the world of art and literature. Occasionally they were accompanied by a tall grey-haired man called O'Donovan; he turned out to be the writer, Frank O'Connor. And there were frequent visits from Gerry O'Brien whose sister Kate O'Brien, had lately been banned for half a sentence in an otherwise irreproachable novel. The family kept a look out for the works of Sean O'Faolain, Liam O'Flaherty and others lest all of Frank O'Mahony's copies be snapped up before he was forced to remove them from the shelves of his bookshop in O'Connell Street.

Lemass phoned regularly, probably about once a month, to seek advice. Dev also called, especially when he was trying to convince O'Malley senior that he should stand in the by-election. To Lemass he was a valuable sounding board, one of several throughout the country who could be relied upon to give a straightforward answer to a straightforward question. An observer who had watched him during the last years of his career in local government said: 'It night take him some time to make up his mind, but when his mind was made up, he didn't mince his words. You knew all about it.'

Perhaps because his father had already suffered a heart attack and had a big legal practice to look after, it was taken for granted that Des should follow on his professional footsteps. He came to take it for granted earlier on. Certainly, no thought of an active career in politics entered his head; Donogh, after all, was the full-time politician in the family. Indeed, the only political event that seems to have impinged deeply on his consciousness at the time – the end of the Fifties – was the funeral of Sean South, a Limerick man shot during the IRA campaign. He had become something of a folk hero almost before his body had been brought home to Limerick. O'Malley was among the thousands who attended the funeral. They had known each other slightly, since South was a regular communicant at the Jesuit church:

> It had quite an effect. He was someone, however misguided he may have been, that you couldn't but help feel was in the same tradition as, perhaps, those of 1916 and 1921. He was a gentleman, very much a Christian in the true sense of the word and, in the proper sense, he was a soldier – he had the kind of qualities one would look for in a real soldier as opposed to a terrorist or a gangster. That explains the different attitude that could have been taken then to South and some of the other people involved in their very limited campaign by comparison with the present set-up where you don't have people of that calibre or quality at all but, by and large, thugs who engage in atrocities by any standard. Yes, I was aware of the type of man that he was, a dignified man and a Christian type of man.

These sentiments, however qualified, must sound surprising, especially to those who viewed O'Malley simply in the light of his performance as Minister for Justice – the youngest and arguably the toughest since Kevin O'Higgins. But Irish politics are never simple as they seem and O'Malley's family, too, had its share of wartime tragedy. On 19 April, 1921, his mother's father, Denis O'Donovan, was shot dead by British Auxiliaries in his hotel at Castleconnell. It appears that IRA from Clare and Limerick were using the weir to cross the river and meeting in the hotel bar. The incident is described by Charles Townsend in his book *The British Campaign in Ireland, 1919-1921.*

The raiding force, commanded by Capt./2nd D.I. Wood, was divided into two parties. Two officers and twelve cadets in plain clothes were ordered to filter unobtrusively into the hotel bar to look for suspects, while a uniformed party of an officer and twenty cadets with two Lewis guns surrounded the area. As they drove up to Castleconnell, however, a number of men were seen running across the fields, and the Auxiliaries promptly forgot their plans.

The plainclothes party, on reaching the hotel, rushed straight into the bar, shouting 'hands up'! In the bar were three off duty RIC men, who took the intruders to be rebels, opened fire on them, and drove them out. A brisk exchange followed in which an RIC sergeant in the bar and a cadet in the courtyard outside were killed. Eventually the arrival of the uniformed party led the two remaining RIC men to realise their mistake and they, together with the landlord, Denis O'Donovan, ran out to surrender. The Auxiliaries continued to fire, wounding one of the RIC and killing O'Donovan, who was hit by six bullets. Capt. Wood then ordered fire to cease. This, at least, was the official story. But the incident was witnessed by an eminent surgeon named Cripps, whose brother, Lord Parmoor, and nephew, Stafford Cripps, were in turn members of the British labour administrations. Cripps reported that the Auxiliaries rampaged around the hotel 'like demented Red Indians.' And his account was supported by members of the hotel staff who said that O'Donovan had been put up against a wall and shot. A week later, Lord Parmoor presented the evidence and a dum-dum cartridge to the House of Lords. An official enquiry produced the predictable whitewash, but the event helped to convince the military authorities that auxiliaries should no longer be used as part of a police force.

His family history pushed O'Malley inevitably in the direction of Fianna Fáil. It was not even that his grandfather had been shot by the British or that, like many others, he admired South's courage and dedication. With a father and two uncles so deeply and so publicly involved, he must necessarily be of the party if not in it. Following in the family's footsteps was taken for granted in political as in professional matters; you were born into Fianna Fáil and that was that . . . . . .

From *Des O'Malley – A Political Profile*, Brandon Book Publishing Ltd., 1986.

'The Liberator'
Edward O'Dwyer

The discernment and decorum
of a poetry reading
at The Whitehouse
we shed easily as inhibitions
with a drink or two,
by 3a.m.
soaked to the skin
dancing, kissing and splashing
in Daniel O'Connell's fountain.

"Get me a coin," you said.
You must have seen my suspicions
when a moment later
you'd added "please,
I want to make a wish."

How could I refuse?
As I leaned,
tentatively reaching in
and down through the inky dark
for that shining copper moon

at the bottom,
farther than it seemed,
you pushed me –
how could you not?
I went over face first.

But I don't remember you now
as the brazen bitch
I thought there and then.
Rather as a liberator;
returning to me what I'd lost –

freedom,
and like all freedoms,
this was wings with which to fly;
to fly high enough,
bring back
even the shining copper moon.

From *Revival Poetry Journal*, Issue 5 Oct 2007

Dev's train journey to Limerick
Eamon de Valera, 1885

WE landed at Queenstown (Cobh) and then went by train to Kilmallock. At the station we were met – my uncle Ed was with me – by his brother, my uncle Pat. He had, probably, a donkey and cart to take the luggage . . .

My first night there, curiously enough, was the last night that anybody slept in what we called 'the old house.' The old house was of mud and clay and they were fairly substantial – I remember using a pickaxe and crowbar in later years to try and break them up and they were about three feet at the base.

My first night, anyhow, was in that old house and I wakened up in the morning and there was nobody about. I suppose I was frightened and I shouted and screamed. At any rate my aunt, who would have been about fifteen years of age at the time, came in to soothe me and I asked her where Uncle Ed was and she told me that he was up at the new house. I remember wondering what the new house could be. 'Twas a cottage – I remember it well. I was always interested in the fact that my first night in Ireland was the last night that anybody slept in the old house . . .

I think it was when my aunt was about to go to America and they were anxious to send my photograph to my mother. So I had a grand journey by train to Limerick. Of course I was dolled up before I started out! One of the problems was the boots: apparently they didn't pass muster. A solution was found – they found that my

aunt's button boots would fit me. At least they thought so!
I didn't like the idea at all! I would have preferred my old boots. However, they fitted on my aunt's boots and I was taken to O'Shea's of Limerick and I remember seeing the man behind the cover which he put on his head when he was taking the photograph and he was trying to attract my attention so that I would look straight at him. I have a copy of that photograph still . . . .

I can't say that I remember exactly coming into the school or what happened on that first day, but I do remember the schoolroom very well. It has been divided since, unfortunately. It was a fine room as it was and there would be about sixty pupils. One half would be, as a rule, standing up and the other half would be sitting down in the desks. Those who would be in the desks would be writing or doing some arithmetical exercises, or, perhaps, learning grammar. Those who were standing were being questioned or taught directly by the teachers. I remember well in the winter time, on one occasion, anyway, we had to bring one shilling each to buy coal, so that even if half the class bought it, it would bring us through the winter . . . .

There was a slight slope in the school yard and sometimes we used to get geosadáns (ragweed). Now, you can easily pull it and the geosadán has a good healthy root to it. So we used to have battles. Those who went down Howardstown way at the Cross of the Pumps were in one batch, against those who went over towards Joyce's country, that's in the Tankardstown direction.

We arranged to have a fight in the school yard on this particular day at lunchtime and we all armed ourselves in Roche's field with geosadáns. I was at the lower end, defending against the hill. I wasn't by any means a leader! There was a charge and in the charge I was thrown back and a fellow put a broken tip of a shoe through the palm of my hand, I have the mark to this present day.

From *The Grand Tour of Limerick* complied by Cornelius Kelly. Cailleach Books, 2004. Adapted from *Voices of Ireland*.

The Bishop and the Poor
Thomas J. Morrissey, SJ

THERE was another issue during his years at St Michael's, which moved O'Dwyer to emphatic, and even precipitous action, namely, the housing conditions of many of the working population. He instituted a campaign for better housing, founding for the purpose the Artisans' Dwelling Company. The more he experienced the misery and health hazards endured by so many, the more his anger grew against the wealthy employers of the city, who showed no signs of compassion or of practical intent to remedy conditions. Consequently, when he obtained permission to address the members of the Limerick Harbour Board, composed mainly of wealthy merchants, he was not in a conciliatory mood. He told them that, with the possible exception of Dr W.T. O'Sullivan, they had no 'adequate idea of the miserable way in which their workers were housed.' then, singling out one member, he declared vehemently that when he went one morning to the house of a poor working man in the employment of that merchant, the man's 'poor wife and children were sitting crouched around a meagre fire, the roof was broken in and the snow was falling through. The poor children were trying to warm themselves as best they could . . . and the poor wife was shivering . . . and cried to him, 'Oh Father, the cold is going through me.'

'That,' O'Dwyer added, 'was only one out of hundreds of cases' of the working man of the city in the employment of the gentlemen who constituted the Board. He then proceeded to lecture them and quoted the section of the government act that, in his view, empowered the Harbour board to erect labourers' dwellings. Not surprisingly, the board's reaction was hostile. When he had withdrawn, his words and manner were vigorously criticised.

O'Dwyer himself realised that he had been offensive and tactless. In the *Limerick Chronicle* of 5 April, 1881, he had the grace and common sense to apologise. 'I should consider it a great misfortune', he wrote, 'if by mistaken zeal I should have weakened the force of my own advocacy.' He did not intend, he explained, to rebuke the members of the Harbour Board, whose generosity and genuine desire to promote the well being of the people he well knew. He finished, nevertheless, with the reminder that 'a master is not a mere task-maker, and his workman is not a beast of burden. They are both men – made in the image of God, and are bound to love one another.' And to take the 'lowest view' of the matter, he added, just as 'a man makes a stable comfortable for his horse that he may get more work out of him,' so an employer 'ought to make a fairly decent home for his men, to keep them in health, to withdraw them from the public house and to give them the self-respect which is a strong stimulant of honesty and energy.'

At this time, 1880-1, the *Limerick Chronicle* was testifying to the inadequate wages of many workmen in the city, some of them with large families. Largely through O'Dwyer's social concern, and his political and social influence with the corporation and wealthy classes, first as a priest, and then as bishop, hundreds of working families were provided with better housing, though the problem remained far from solved. Thirty years later, some 31.7 per cent of the population of Limerick city were said to be still living in overcrowded, unhealthy conditions.

In the light of this evident concern for the welfare of youth and of the less well-off members of society, and his readiness on their behalf to face down local authorities and the wealthy, O'Dwyer became a revered and popular figure to a large section of the population of the city and in parts of the county. Even those he challenged could not but respect his zeal and whole-hearted solicitude for those in need, and they were conditioned to accept even his lectures and abuse by the fact that he was a hardworking priest, who spoke in a cultured accent and came from a respectable family. His very genuineness and forthrightness earned him admirers.

'Never . . . hesitate to impress me with your opinions,' his friend Richard O'Shaughnessy, MP. requested on 1 January 1877. 'They are of high and valuable [sic], because they come from an honest man that understands thoroughly what he desires.'

From *Bishop Edward Thomas O'Dwyer of Limerick, 1842-1917*, Four Courts Press, 2003.

POLITICS

The night Che Guevara came to Limerick
Martin Hannan

IT WAS a throwaway line in a pub in Limerick some 24 years ago, but I never forgot it: 'We had that Che Guevara in here, you know.' On Halloween, 1979, on a tour of Ireland, I had walked into several pubs and hotels in Limerick where the entire city seemed to be getting drunk. They take their drink and their rugby seriously in Limerick, and they were celebrating the first anniversary of the victory of Munster over the All Blacks.

I can't swear to it, on account of joining in the celebrations, but I think I was in the famous poet's pub, the White Horse, on the corner of O'Connell Street and Glentworth Street, when I was told about Che - then, as now, a figure of fascination for me. I dismissed it as a fantasy, the result of too much drink, and I almost forgot about it.

Researching Guevara's life in more detail earlier this year for a play I'm writing, I discovered that I had maligned my forgotten informant. Guevara did indeed go 'on the batter' in Limerick. The story is true.

Let's put Guevara in context first. To most people he is just a handsome face on a poster, and even those who know he was an Argentine can get confused about his life as a revolutionary. It was Cuba he freed along with Fidel Castro wasn't it, they may ask, so why did he end up being shot in Bolivia in 1967?

It was the CIA who did him in of course. And his martyrdom in the cause of revolution sparked all those riots and protests in 1968, didn't it? Subsequently he has become an icon thanks to the most famous poster of all time. And that's about it really. Except that Ernesto Guevara de la Serna was much more than a picture on the wall. He was one of the most fascinating and complex people of the 20th century. Guevara was a rugby-playing doctor of medicine who became a killer of the revolution's enemies; a lifelong asthmatic who often needed injections just to stay alive, but could track through jungle and mountains for days; a writer of genuine power; a revolutionary Marxist who turned his back on the only successful communist state in the western world to lead guerrilla insurgents in often hopeless battles against their oppressors; a man who loved women, a good party, a Havana cigar, and a pint of Guinness; who loved life yet gave it up for a cause which hopefully will never be lost - changing the world.

Guevara was one of the most famous people of his time, so it is a fair bet that when he walked into Hanratty's Hotel in Limerick on the evening of March 13, 1965, at least a few people there recognised him. It's not every day the world's most renowned revolutionary orders a pint of the black stuff in an Irish hostelry - and you would think his unannounced visit might have made the front pages of every paper in Ireland. Indeed, more than 30 years later, the Dublin-based Sunday Tribune would describe Guevara's visit to Limerick as 'one of the great missed scoops of Irish journalism.' It was wrong. The story was just one of the many exclusives garnered in six decades of remarkable journalism by Arthur Quinlan.

I had thought that since it was all of 38 years ago, no one would be around who could remember Guevara's visit to Limerick. Fortunately I was wrong. Quinlan will be 83 next month, and he is still contributing to the *Irish Times*. His memory is as sharp as a tack, and his claim to have scooped the world with his story of Guevara's night on the tiles is easily proved. The front page of the venerable *Limerick Leader*, on March 15, 1965, contains Quinlan's account of how Guevara eschewed the delights of bingo and ballad singing in order to sample the local brew.

'He was three sheets to the wind when he got back to the airport,' said Quinlan as we talked in Jury's Inn on the banks of the Shannon last week. Dapper and looking at least a dozen years younger than his age, Quinlan has that old-fashioned courtesy and love of the craic that make Irish journalists such a pleasure to meet. He had refreshed his memory by consulting the meticulous diaries he has kept throughout his career. 'Dr Guevara was also festooned in shamrock, as it was coming up for St Patrick's Day,' said Quinlan. 'So you can take it that he enjoyed himself in Limerick.'

Guevara had been aboard a Bristol Britannia aircraft of the Cuban national airline which developed mechanical trouble en route from Prague to Havana. It was one of the most important weekends of the Comandante de la Revolucion's life. At a conference in Algiers, he had just denounced the Soviet Union for failing revolutionaries across the globe. He knew that Fidel Castro, by now aligned with the Soviets, would not be pleased, to put it mildly. Quinlan had made it his speciality to cover the activities at Shannon Airport. The last runway in Europe had been the stopping-off point for airliners for many years. Long after Guevara's visit he scored a notable double by interviewing Castro.

'His guards weren't going to let me near him until I mentioned that I had interviewed Dr Guevara,' said Quinlan, who showed his respect for the man by referring to Che as doctor throughout our conversation. 'That did the trick and we ended up showing President Castro how to make Irish coffee.'

Guevara's arrival was sudden and unexpected, but his contacts did the trick for Quinlan. A public relations officer at Shannon, who might just have been a CIA agent, tipped off the journalist about the imminent arrival of an important visitor who was going to be detained in the airport overnight while his aircraft was fixed. Rushing to the airport, Quinlan found Guevara accompanied by his fellow revolutionary, Dr Osmani Cienfuegos, the Cuban minister for construction, and some other Cuban friends and government officials.

'Dr Guevara indicated that he did not speak English, but I knew something about him,' said Quinlan. That something was the fact of Guevara's Irish roots - his grandmother was Ana Isabel Lynch, and the Lynches of Argentina had become notable citizens of that country after emigrating from famine-ravaged Ireland. They most likely hailed from the west coast around Galway, and only last year Che's daughter, Dr Aleida Guevara, spoke of her family's pride in their Irish ancestry when she visited Ireland. Quinlan recalls playing his ace card: 'I told Dr Guevara, anybody whose maternal grandparents were Lynches either speaks Gaelic or English. Which is it to be?' We went outside and began to talk in English. He spoke it quite well, and I found him charming but I didn't learn very much from him as he would not speak about politics.

'He talked of his Irish connections through the name Lynch, and after a good chat he told me he wanted to go with a few friends to 'see the nightlife'. I recommended that he should visit Hanratty's Hotel on Glentworth Street. I knew he would be welcomed there.' We do not know who Guevara met or what exactly happened in the Gluepot, as Hanratty's bar was nicknamed. Suffice to say Guevara enjoyed himself. Quinlan filed his copy and saw the Cubans off next day.

On his return to Cuba, Guevara met Castro and declared his intention to become a roaming revolutionary, even if it meant death in the cause. As he put it himself: 'We cannot be sure of having something to live for unless we are willing to die for it.' A little more than two years later Guevara was captured by the Bolivian army after his small platoon of guerrillas was almost wiped out in an ambush. He was not killed by the CIA - the Bolivian government ordered his immediate execution. Guevara once wrote: 'I have a wish. It is a fear as well - that in my end will be my beginning.'

After his death, photographer Alberto Korda's famous image of Che became the symbol of a generation and Guevara was many times more famous dead than alive. Yet there is so much more to him that has largely been ignored. Thanks to Arthur Quinlan, however, we know at least one small and surprising element of his story.

From *The Scotsman*, December, 2003.

ELEVEN
TRAVELLERS

A peek at 1950's Limerick and its beautiful, chaste women
Constantine FitzGibbon

MY motive in visiting Limerick was primarily to find out what I could about my great-grandmother, Lady Louisa FitzGibbon, the last member of my family to own Mount Shannon House and, I gather, a remarkable woman in her own right. What I knew of her before my arrival in Limerick was slight: she was the daughter of the third and last Earl of Clare; her brother, Viscount FitzGibbon, was missing presumed killed in the notorious charge of the Light Brigade at Balaclava; she therefore inherited Mount Shannon and her husband took her name, as is not uncommon in Ireland when property is involved: she spent a great deal of money, was forced to sell Mount Shannon, after her first husband's death married a Sicilian nobleman, and finally died and was buried in a convent in the Isle of Wight. She had left Ireland in 1887.

I arrived in Limerick by bus and went at once to what had been described to me as a charming, old-fashioned and comfortable hotel. My informant was well out of date. The charm and the comfort had been very thoroughly torn away, to be replaced by fake marble, neon strips and some sort of machinery in the walls, an air-conditioning unit perhaps, which hummed insidiously, a malignant irritant. These improvements had been carried out in order that American visitors, held up overnight at Shannon airport, might feel thoroughly at home during their brief stay. The architect or decorator or whatever he is called must have cherished some curious ideas about American homes. The transients, standing in hopeless knots or sitting in the ugly armchairs and gazing ahead of them with the blank and bovine expression which is common to all stranded travellers, certainly looked anything but happy among all this bleak and shoddy modernity. I moved my bags to the Royal George Hotel which has not been improved and where all is as it should be. I then set forth to explore Limerick.

The atmosphere at Limerick, on this warm evening, was surprisingly different from what I had expected. O'Connell Street, the main thoroughfare, and shopping centre, was humming with activity. There seemed to be a purposefulness, a determination, in the people I passed which contrasted strikingly with the apparent lethargy of Cork, a city I had left that morning. Such impressions are misleading, perhaps, but in this case I think they were correct. Limerick, Ireland's third city if you don't count Belfast, is growing fast. The airport and the big hydro-electric installation that they call the Shannon Scheme have brought it considerable prosperity, and industrially it is also expanding.

The Limerickman, allegedly pushing and aggressive, is not popular with his fellow Irishmen, a fact which worries him not at all. He is proud of his city and wishes to make it into a great industrial and communications centre. There seems no reason why he should not do so, particularly if present political tendencies continue and the Atlantic community assumes greater reality, for Limerick is geographically well suited to be the hub of an air network linking the old World to the New. A tremendous expansion in the next few decades seems not at all unlikely.

TRAVELLERS

There are fortunes to be made in Limerick and no doubt, the Limerickmen will make them for they are, I am told, very hard-headed businessmen.

O'Connell Street, at its top end a dignified and Georgian sort of place, degenerates into a mass of untidy shops of the chain store variety before petering out near the bridge that leads to the old town, or English Town, as it is called, though there is little English about it anymore. Here the atmosphere is very different, aged and grey and restful. King John's Castle, with its satisfactory round towers, stands four square on the left bank of the Shannon, Behind it is St. Mary's Cathedral . . . . .

It is wise to keep off the subject of religion in Limerick, for I am told that the Limerickmen are the only bigoted Catholics in the south. In Limerick, it seems, a discussion of dogma can degenerate into a rumpus almost as easily as Belfast. Whether this is a malicious slander or not I cannot say for I did not discuss such matters, but certainly the Limerickman is a violent sort of fellow, as was proved during the Anglo-Irish wars. And certainly that violence still lingers on. I was told a story of an Englishmen who last year was in conversation with an Irish acquaintance in these parts. The Englishman, it seems, was one of those fatuous, red-faced, military men with loud and braying voices and an acute insensibility to the fact that they are not invariably taken at their own valuation when abroad. The Irishman was a softly spoken gentleman who had played a fairly conspicuous part in the Irish Republican Army and whose brother was shot by the British during the troubles. The Englishman, slapping his acquaintance on the shoulder, had asked loudly and cheerfully:

'Do you get any decent rough shooting up around Castleconnell?'

The Irishman replied with a smile:

'Well, thirty years ago, anyone who looked like you in or about Castleconnell was shot on sight.'

The Englishman gave his usual hearty laugh. What a capital joke! The Irishman went on smiling. They tell me that a number of the English who have settled in Ireland since 1945 do not really feel at home here, despite the fact that they all, like myself, have Irish great-grand-mothers, despite the fact that, unlike myself, they often find the natives so quaint . . . .

On Sarsfield Bridge there is a rather gloomy statue commemorating the I.R.A., a schoolmasterly figure in bronze. He is flanked incongruously by two small Russian cannons captured in the Crimean War. For here stood McDowall's fine statue of Viscount FitzGibbon. It was blown up in the troubles, a senseless act of vandalism. The young man seems to have been popular in the neighbourhood and certainly did no one any harm. It was no doubt intended as an act of petty revenge against his grandfather, the hated architect of the Union of whom I shall have more to say elsewhere. But it was Limerick's loss.

Of this young officer a curious tales is told, for the truth, of which I cannot vouch. As I have said, he was missing believed killed in the charge of the Light Brigade. A quarter of a century later, during the second Afghan War, his regiment, the 8th Hussars, was stationed in India, near the Northwest Frontier. One evening a bowed and tattered figure was brought by the sergeant of the guard into the officers' mess.

He spoke a halting, rusty English. No office knew him and yet, since he was apparently a gentleman of their own race in this distant place, he was invited to dine.

Since he did not say who he was, no one asked him his name – manners were better in those days – though he mentioned Siberia. He was plainly at home and knew the various regimental customs. After dinner he thanked his hosts and disappeared into the night. An examination of regimental records showed that the only ex-officer of the 8th Hussars who would be the stranger's approximate age, and whose whereabouts could not be accounted for, was Lord FitzGibbon, Kipling based a short story on this strange anecdote, which he entitled The Man Who Was. So far as I know, this unfortunate young man's only other appearance in literature are the following impolite lines by Hogan, the Bard of Thomond, who emigrated to America from which land he was brought back by popular subscription. No doubt his style appealed to the Limerick temperament.

> *There stands in the open air,*
> *The bastard son of the late Lord Clare.*
> *They call him FitzGibbon, but his name was Moore,*
> *Cause his father was cuckold and his mother was a whore.*

Effective, but I am glad to say, untrue. The real story is slightly less disreputable. The third Earl, when he was Mr. FitzGibbon and M.P. for Limerick, became enamoured of a Mrs. Moore, with whom he eloped and lived openly in sin, as they say. Mr Crosbie Moore sued him in 1824, and a Dublin jury awarded the unfortunate husband the considerable sum of £6,000 damages. An Act of Parliament was necessary to obtain divorce, a lengthy business, with the result that when their first child, a son, was born, his name was Moore. Before their other children arrived Mrs. Moore had become Mrs FitzGibbon. Thus the younger son was the legitimate heir, a confusing state of affairs. The elder became some sort of colonel and died a bachelor. An old gentleman I met told me he remembered seeing him in the streets of Limerick and described him as a melancholy sort of fellow. He might well have been.

That evening I was driven to a party in a large house some ten miles or so outside the city. My host and hostess were young people who had recently bought this property, which they were farming. Odd farmers, I thought, to give a party that started at midnight. But they assured me that theirs was the latest milk-round hereabouts and that there were many people who preferred to have the milk arrive at about ten rather than to be awakened by the clatter of pails at half-past six. Furthermore, they struck me as strange farmers in that he was a man of wide culture and knowledge in fields far removed from food while she was a lady of striking beauty. Their home was a sort of gigantic cottage, fifty small rooms perhaps, of which a quarter, I reckon, was barely furnished. The place was candle-lit, and this accentuated the magnificent looks of the women present – most of whom, like their hostess, were the wives of farmers.

And here I must stop to comment on the beauty of the Limerick women. I have been in Arles, I have lived in Rome, I have frequently walked down Fifth Avenue, but never, anywhere, have I seen so many handsome girls as in or about Limerick. At this candle-lit party, and without benefit of John Jameson, half the female guests could easily have replaced Lady Lavery on the Irish banknotes. Indeed, perhaps advantageously, for they quite lacked that famous beauty's insipidity of expression. Gorgeous, tall, slender, swan-like creatures they were, proud of carriage and with that easy, open smile which comes of assurance and the knowledge that their men both love and respect them.

In the streets of Limerick, too, the girls were startlingly beautiful and seemed, if anything, more self-assured than the men. I think that the ideal rhythm of life for men and for women is not quite the same, and that the rhythm which prevails in a devoutly Catholic community makes for feminine happiness. Certainly, in the vast majority of cases, promiscuity does not, and here there is none of that. To keep her boy-friend a Limerick girl does not have to go too far with him. Indeed, she would get a tremendous wigging from her father-confessor should she do so, as would the boy.

Thus they can be beautiful, flirtatious, gay and honest without any fear that they may be misunderstood. And a community where the women are happy must be, by definition, a happy society. The few who cannot manage to or do not like a life of chastity can always move, to Dublin or London. This accounts for the fact that the Irish women in England have a reputation which is grotesque if applied to Irish women in Ireland. In this connection I heard an anecdote about some American politicians.

It seems that these gentlemen, returning to their native shore after one of their junkets about Europe, were stranded overnight at a hotel near Shannon Airport. The local head of the airline did his best to make them comfortable with bottle and glass. After a while one of the politicians remarked that since this seemed to be an impromptu party it would be as well to invite some girls. Who ever heard of a party without girls? The airline official, slightly worried, said that he could invite some of the air hostesses from the field. At this point another Irishman who happened to be present carefully pointed out that in Western Ireland the girls insisted on marriage, as a *sine qua nihil* (though no doubt he said it in English). That party never took place.

One day, when I was talking to a shop-keeper at a village some miles from Limerick, I had occasion to comment on the beauty of the Limerick women.

'They are beautiful,' he agreed, 'and they can fight too.'

He knew how they had fought, side by side with their men, during the siege. So did I, for was not an ancestress of mine killed while helping to repel a Williamite assault?

They were not fighting that night in this huge, candle-lit cottage, nor was anyone else. Indeed the only person who nearly did was myself, after a glass of poteen which some thoughtless person thrust upon me. I saw a gentleman wearing the tie of my old school and, being utterly befuddled by the home-made spirit, my dislike for the school became transformed into a dislike for the wearer of the tie. However, I had sufficient self-control to avert my eyes from the object of my displeasure and then, in order to be entirely on the safe side, made my way down a long, dark, flagged corridor to the vast kitchen where I found a splendid gentleman seated in solitary grandeur with a glass of stout in his hand.

Tipsy though I was, I could easily see that he was tipsier still, if so flippant a word may be applied to his sombre melancholy. He informed me that he advised my host on the matter of pigs. He told me his name, a fine old Irish name, and that if he had his rights this house and all its land would belong to him, for had it not been stolen from his great-great-great-great-grandfather by some Cromwellian scallywag? Then, with a courtly phrase he invited me to join him in a glass of our host's beer. I was delighted to accept.

The extraordinarily dignified manners of the country people are a never-ending source of wonderment to me. The only way in which I can account for it is that when the old Gaelic aristocracy was dispossessed and that portion of it which was not driven abroad to France or Spain or Austria was forced down to the economic level of its peasantry, it clung to its manners with a jealous and honourable pride and spread them across the land. But perhaps this is fanciful.

From *Miss Finnigin's Fault*, Cassell and Company Ltd., London, 1953.

Dickens: a very odd place
Limerick, 1858

THIS is the oddest place – of which nobody in any other part of Ireland seems to know anything. Nobody could answer a single question we asked about it. There is no large room, and I read in the Theatre – a charming Theatre. The best I ever saw, to see and hear in. Arthur says that when he opened the doors last night, there was a rush of – three Ducks! We expect a Pig in tonight. We had only £40; but they seemed to think that, amazing! If the two nights bring £100, it will be as much as we expected. I am bound to say that they are an admirable audience. As hearty and demonstrative as it is possible. It is a very odd place in its lower-order aspects, and I am very glad we came – though we could have made heaps of money by going to Dublin instead . . .

Letter from Dickens to his friend W. H. Wills, from *Charles Dickens's Ireland*.
From *The Grand Tour of Limerick* complied by Cornelius Kelly. Cailleach Books, 2004

Visit of the Marquis of Lansdowne to his Limerick Estate
Liam Irwin

THE following account of the first visit of the 5th Marquis of Lansdowne to his extensive Limerick estates 30 September 1868 was printed in the *Cork Examiner* on the following day. This twenty-three year old descendant of the two famous families with strong Irish connections was Sir Henry Charles Keith Petty FitzMaurice. He held in addition to his marquisette, the titles of Early Wycombe of Chipping Wycombe, Bucks, Viscount Caln and Calnstone, Wilts, and Lord Wycombe, Baron of Chipping, Wycombe, Bucks, in the peerage of Great Britain. He was Baron Nairn county Perth in Scotland and Earl of Kerry and Earl of Shelbourne, Viscount Clanmaurice and Fitzmaurice, Baron of Kerry, Lixnaw and Dunkerron in the peerage of Ireland . . . . .

The Marquis of Lansdowne owned 1,526 acres in Limerick, valued in 1876 at £2,701. His Kerry estates were however more extensive totalling 94,983 acres to the value of £9,553. He owned all the land on which the roads and housing estates on the north side of the city which bear his name or titles, such as Lansdowne, Shelbourne and Clanmaurice were erected in the last century.

> LIMERICK: Wednesday: The Marquis of Lansdowne and suite arrived at Cleary's Royal Hotel, Limerick, yesterday; and this day his Lordship, accompanied by his relative, the Hon. Mr. Howard and his agent, Mr. Harvey Todhunter, proceeded to pay a first and formal visit to his large property in the immediate neighbourhood of this city; on the Clare side of the river and in the north liberties of Limerick. The marquis, who has not very long attained his majority, had not until today made personal acquaintance with his Limerick estate and its occupiers, and the occasion was availed of by the tenantry to present his lordship with an address of welcome. A deputation of some 40 or 50 tenants, headed by Rev. D. Kennedy, P.P. of St. Munchin's, accordingly met their noble landlord at the Crossroads of Cahirdavin, as he was on his rounds to the several holdings, and as the car drove up from the Thomondgate side, they respectfully uncovered and received the marquis with a cheer which his Lordship courteously acknowledged. The car was stopped, the deputation gathered around, his Lordship and his friend got down in the gutter, and there and then, upon the public highway, at the meeting of four crossroads, and immediately in front of the Cahirdavin police barracks, the address was duly read by Rev. Mr. Kennedy (who was first introduced to the Marquis), presented and replied to.

The address, which was tastefully engrossed in illuminated text hand upon a large sheet of velum, set forth the feelings of the tenantry for the noble house of Lansdowne, and bid cordial welcome to its present representative, whom it trusted, would follow in the footsteps of his lamented ancestors, and be, if possible, a frequent visitor among them. It also referred in terms of gratitude to the kindness of the agent (Mr. Todhunter) and touched upon other topics of general or special interest in connection with the event. Father Kennedy, in presenting the address, begged to assure the Marquis of the industry, honesty, and worth of the subscribers to the document, and said he felt delighted in having an opportunity of bearing testimony to their respectability.

His Lordship replied in a brief speech, in which he expressed his pleasure at the reception they gave him and the welcome they accorded him, which was only similar to what he had experienced in his other Irish properties. He hoped he would deserve their good opinion, and he would endeavour to follow in the footsteps of his father (hear, hear), to whom their address made such kindly reference. He had much pleasure in finding that although he had not been amongst them before, he was well represented in Mr. Todhunter (hear, hear). His Lordship warmly thanked the deputation, remounted his car amid a hearty cheer or two, and drove off in the direction of Cratloe, to continue his round of farm and domiciliary visits.

From the *North Munster Antiquarian Journal*, 2003. Vol. 43.

Charlotte Bronte's Kilkee Honeymoon
Thomas J. Byrne

ON the evening of their wedding day, Charlotte and her husband journeyed to Conway, near Llandudno in Wales, and stayed overnight. She wrote: '. . . . The evening is wet and wild, though the day was fair chiefly with some gleams of sunshine. From Conway they planned to travel to Bangor on Friday, June 30th, or Saturday, 1st July, sailing from Holyhead to Dublin on the steampacket on the night of Monday July 3rd. They arrived in the Irish capital on July 4th (Tuesday).

In Dublin the newly-weds were met by Arthur's brother Alan, who was manager of the Grand Canal from Dublin to Banagher, and two first cousins, Joseph Bell, a student TCD who had just gained three premiums, and his sister Mary Anne Bell, then aged 24 years, whom Charlotte described 'as a pretty lady-like girl with gentle English manners.' What they thought of the famous English authoress, who had so predictively chosen their family name for her nom-de-guerre, is not recorded.

After touring the main sights of Dublin, especially Nicholls' old university, its library and museum and chapel – 'and should have seen much more – had not my bad cold been a restraint upon us.' They travelled with Arthur's cousins by train (surprisingly, considering Arthur's brother's position) to Banagher. Here they spent one week (probably from Friday July 7th to Wednesday July 12th). At Cuba House, Banagher, they met other Bell cousins including the Rev. James Adamson Bell. Charlotte described Cuba House as 'very large and looks externally like a gentleman's country-seat – within most of the rooms are lofty and spacious and commodiously furnished.'

Why did Charlotte and her husband choose Kilkee for the greater part of their honeymoon? It is clear from a letter written by Charlotte at Banagher to Miss Wooler that Kilkee was to be the intended destination: 'We go in a few days to Kilkee, a watering place on the South-West Coast. The letters may be addressed, Mrs. Arthur Nicholls, Post-Office, Kilkee, County Clare, Ireland.' I suggest the following: In August 1846 the names J. Bell, Esq. and Mrs. Bell appear among a list of visitors to Mrs. Shannon's West End Hotel. I suggest that these were Mrs. Harriet Lucinda Bell and her son, James Adamson Bell, then aged 20 years.

We know that Mrs. Bell kindly nursed Charlotte back to health – 'Fatigue and excitement had nearly knocked me up – and my cough had become very bad' – and it seems more than likely that Arthur's aunt and cousin would have enthused about their earlier visit to Kilkee and would have recommended the very hotel where they had been only 8 years before. It is highly unlikely that either Charlotte or her husband would have seen the following advertisement which appeared in the Limerick Chronicle, 5 July 1854 (Wed.):

> WEST END HOTEL, Kilkee
> MRS. SHANNON *begs leave to acquaint her friends and the Public, that she has fitted up her Hotel, in very superior Style for the accommodation of Tourists and Visitors to that beautiful watering place.*
> *From the long patronage Mrs. S. has received from her Friends, she expects a continuance of their support. Families requiring private apartments can be accommodated by application at Cruise's Royal Hotel, Limerick, or at the West End Hotel, Kilkee.*
> *This hotel commands a magnificent view of the Cliffs, Bay, and surrounding scenery.*

After spending about a week in Banagher, the newly-weds travelled along the banks of the Shannon and Lough Derg to Limerick, where they took a boat – either the *Erin-go-Brath* or the *Garryowen* – to Kilkee. The *Koh-i-noor* steamer was then out of commission, having met with an accident near Foynes. From Kilkee on Tuesday, July 18th, 1854, Charlotte wrote to Catherine Wooler, her former teacher:

'My Dear Miss Catherine, - Your kind letter reached me in a wild and remote spot – a little watering-place in the South West Coast of Ireland' and she gave her a synopsis of her honeymoon tour in Wales and Ireland, adding: 'I had heard a great deal about Irish negligence &c. I own that till I came to Kilkee – I saw little of it here. Here at our Inn – splendidly designated 'The West End Hotel' – there is a good deal to carp at if one were in a carping humour – but we laugh instead of grumbling – for out of doors there is much indeed to compensate for any indoor shortcomings, so magnificent an ocean – so bold and grand a coast – I never yet saw. My husband calls me -.'

Dr. Barker remarks of this letter: 'It was a very long time since Charlotte had written anything so light-hearted as this careless valediction or, indeed, enjoyed the intimacy of shared humour'. The air at Kilkee adds to humour a quality of its own. Later in the same month, Charlotte wrote again about her Kilkee experience, which had greatly impressed her, in a letter to her friend, Catherine Winkworth. In her enthusiasm for Kilkee, Charlotte gave only the briefest account possible of her honeymoon (and strangely omits all reference to Banagher): 'after a short sojourn in the capital – went to the coast – such a wild iron-bound coast – with such an ocean-view as I had not yet seen and such battling of waves with rocks as I had never imagined.

'My husband is not a poet or a poetical man – and one of my grand doubts before marriage was about 'congenial tastes' and so on. The first morning we went out on to the cliffs and saw the Atlantic coming in all white foam, I did do not know whether I should get leave or time to take the matter in my own way. I did not want to talk – but I did want to look and be silent. Having hinted a petition, licence was not refused – covered with a rug to keep off the spray I was allowed to sit where I choose – and he only interrupted me when he thought I crept too near the edge of the cliff. So far he is always good in this way – and this protection which does not interfere or pretend is I believe a thousand times better that any half sort of pseudo sympathy . . .'

I like to think that Arthur and Charlotte stood or sat near the Amphitheatre watching the great rollers of the Atlantic coming in, in wild white fury with their foam caps iridescent with a green colour not to be found elsewhere, and a light spray blowing landwards, tasting of salt.

Nor was Arthur the unpoetic soul that Charlotte wrote of. In a letter to the cleric who had married them (Rev. George Sowden) Arthur wrote on his return to Haworth: 'We had a delightful tour over nearly the same ground as you and your brother travelled, only we took the Shannon in our progress to Limerick: we also diverged to Kilkee, a glorious watering place, with the finest shore I ever saw - completely girded with stupendous cliffs – it was most refreshing to sit on a rock and look out on the broad Atlantic boiling and foaming at our feet.'

Kilkee, as Winfred Gérin has pointed out, was the longest stop during a fortnight's tour through the south-west of Ireland and from Kilkee they went to Tarbert, from Tarbert to Tralee and Killarney, which Charlotte decided 'I will not describe it one bit.' At a dangerous point in the Gap of Dunloe she had a near intimation with death when her horse seemed to go mad 'reared, plunged' and threw Charlotte on the stones right under her. 'I was lifted off the stones neither bruised by the fall nor touched by the mare's hoofs.' Charlotte added gratefully.

From Killarney they travelled to Glengarriff, and then turned eastwards to Cork, and finally returned to Dublin from which place Charlotte wrote to Martha Brown, the house-keeper at Haworth, that 'we shall come home on Tuesday' (1st August, 1854).

Eight months later, Charlotte Bronte died, on Easter Eve, Saturday 31st March, 1855, 'of Exhaustion', and was buried on the following Wednesday, April 4th. Her husband continued as curate at Haworth caring for his father-in-law, as he promised his wife on her deathbed – carrying out to the letter his promise to be the support and consolation of the Rev. Patrick.

From *Old Limerick Journal*, Winter Edition, 1998.

TRAVELLERS

Belgian Refugees in Limerick during the First World War
Tadhg Moloney

From 1914 to 1919 Belgian citizens who had fled their homes due to the German occupation of their country were accommodated in Ireland and some of these found temporary refuge and work in Limerick city and county where they were given a warm welcome and support.

REFUGEES are an inevitable consequence of the disruption caused by war. When Belgium was invaded by Germany on the outbreak of the First World War in 1914 many of its citizenry left and sought refuge in other countries. As Ireland was one of these countries, preparations had to be made for their welfare. The responsibility for looking after these refugees was vested in the Local Government Board (LGB) and it established a central Belgian Refugees Committee (Ireland) on October 1914, at 62 Upper Mount Street, Dublin. The committee emphasised from the beginning that its main role was to alleviate the sufferings of these Belgians whose life was made unbearable by the German occupation and that it was not in existence as a mechanism for the supply of workers. This suggests a fear that employers might exploit the situation, which would appear from the evidence, certainly in Limerick, to have been groundless.

When the idea of accommodating some refugees in Limerick was suggested, the Mayor, Alderman P. O'Donovan, convened a meeting in the Town Hall on 27 October, 1914. An enormous crowd representative of every social class in the city attended it. Arising from this meeting in which 'a subscription list was opened and the sum of sixty pounds received,' it was decided that the provision of accommodation for these refugees was of the utmost priority, and a committee was established to oversee both. This was not the first sum of money to be collected, nor the first indication of the generous attitude of Limerick people towards providing for the refugees. Some weeks previously a flag day collection had proved to be very successful.

By the time accommodation had been obtained for them in Mount Kennet House, Henry Street, the fund had received over £125. Among the more generous contributors were Colonel O'Grady, C.B., High Sheriff, Co. Limerick, and William Nolan, Town Clerk of the City Corporation, who was also the Belgian Consul for Limerick, Clare and Tipperary. The Bishop of Limerick, Dr Edward O'Dwyer, offered his support to the efforts, as would be expected given that the Catholic dimension of Belgian suffering received much contemporary emphasis in Ireland. Speaking at the annual general meeting of the Limerick District Nursing Association held at St. Munchin's College, Henry Street, on 11 November 1914 he called upon the people of Limerick, rich and poor, to help 'the poor refugees from Belgium' and 'to make their stay amongst us if not happy – that is impossible – at least tolerable and as far as you can by kindness to draw the sting of their exile.'

The first refugees, numbering thirty-six in all, had arrived in Limerick that day by train and they were met at the Railway station by the Mayor and other prominent citizens and 'an escort of National Volunteers accompanied them to their lodgings in Mount Kennet House.' They were greeted enthusiastically by the people who gave them 'a wholehearted and thoroughly Irish welcome and created a visible impression on the recipients.' Although the refugees included labourers, hawkers and the blind beggar, they also included members of the aristocracy, the professional classes, the artistic world, shopkeepers and tradesmen, and citizens who may have belonged to the Belgian Civic Guard. Many of these had lost their worldly possessions, or, as one correspondent put it, 'all that was left to them after years of toil was the clothes they stood up in.' It is unclear if Dr. O'Dwyer used the term 'poor refugees' for these initial arrivals in a literal sense or more as a sympathetic comment on their suffering. However during the subsequent year 1915 the 'hawker and blind beggar' certainly disappeared, for the refugees who came to Ireland were now chiefly of the commercial or semi-professional class, and included some families of high standing in the country (Belgium).

While Mount Kennet House was the initial place of accommodation for the refugees on their arrival, people came forward and offered them homes in the city and county. One offer came from an unusual source, the War Office, which was prepared to allow them the use of the married quarters at the Strand Barracks. A house was provided at Castleconnell to facilitate six refugees; a Mrs. Harding of Patrickswell gave three cottages for such families, and a Mrs Maunsell had agreed to provide one.

One family was housed at Furnittestown, Adare, and Mr. David Dwane, Post Office, Kilmallock, offered a cottage with a garden to the refugees. Others offered their services by holding concerts and football matches and forwarded the money collected to the relief fund. A lecture entitled, 'Belgium, the Battlefield of Europe', was given by Mr Alfred Dobbs, FRGS, and was followed by a concert after which the funds collected were donated to the relief fund. Two concerts were held in Newcastle West and were very successful, and Garryowen Rugby Football Club played two games and donated the proceeds of £12 10s. to the fund.

Dioceses held collections at churches throughout the country and published a list of the amounts collected. No record exists for the Diocese of Limerick and the reasons remains unclear. No collection may have been held, as was the case in some dioceses. The spokesmen for the bishops, Robert Browne, Bishop of Cloyne, explained that 'owing to local circumstances some Bishops have had to postpone the collection in very many parishes . . .' Although the Caherconlish Branch of the Teachers' Association decided against making any contribution on the basis that teachers had already donated in the area where they lived, those would appear to have been the exception rather than the rule for members of the Limerick Teachers' Association gave a grant of £5 for the assistance of the refugees.

One woman, Mrs McNamara, Springfield House, Kilmallock, decided that instead of sending the amount of money she had collected for almost thirty weeks at 1s each week to the Limerick Fund, she would retain it for the maintenance of a Belgian family in Kilmallock. With such generosity from local people and nationally it was not surprising that the LGB could claim that out of the 3,000 refugees who came to Ireland in the first year two hundred or '70 to 80 per cent were maintained in private or local hospitality, and without cost to local funds.' Great credit was given to the refugees for their desire to be self-supporting and independent in that many who had never occupied themselves in work of a physical nature did not hesitate to undertake such work when it as deemed necessary.

A number of the refugees who came to Limerick were from a farming background and were accordingly offered work on farms in the county, and gave great satisfaction wherever they were employed. Again the fear that some farmers might be tempted to use them as sources of cheap labour is evident in the comments of the Chairman of Limerick County Council, Mr. W.R. Gubbins, JP, who warned 'that it must be distinctly understood that the refugees must not be utilised as a means of obtaining underpaid labour.' There is, in fact, no evidence of any such exploitation either intended or attempted. In Limerick, as elsewhere throughout the country, the Belgians were warmly welcomed and well treated. Apart from farm work, employment was obtained for them in the munitions factories established for those who had skills to contribute such as metal workers, fitters, turners, etc. Throughout the four years of the war the number of families who came and went varied and many seem to have only remained for a relatively short period. One of the refugees, Madame Vlamynck, died while staying with her husband and some of her children in Limerick. She had her family had been accommodated at Mount Kennet House.

By 31 March 1915 the number of Belgian refugees being catered for by committees was 1,1426 and on the same date the following year there were 938, which meant that 829 refugees left the country and 341 had arrived. There was a reduction in the number of refugees by 31 March 1917 of approximately 400, giving a total of 600 still being accommodated in Ireland. At the same date the following year 527 refugees remained in the care of the LGB committee. On 15 February 1919, just three months after the termination of the war, the remainder of the refugees, numbering 414, including those left in Limerick, numbering 15 in total, left Ireland for their homes in Belgium. During the four years and three months that the war had lasted, some 2,300 Belgian refugees 'were at one time or another in receipt of hospitality in Ireland.' Many of those were catered for in Limerick, and all the evidence suggest that people of all social classes were welcoming and generous to the Belgian war refugees.

From *North Munster Antiquarian Journal*, 1988/99, Vol. 39.

Stop-start journey to Limerick in an old car
John B. Keane

OLD cars are like old people: they need to be rested occasionally. They need sympathy and understanding, for great age is often the breeding ground of great bitterness. But if a car is looked after with great care and love it will grow old gracefully and give as good as it gets.

Recently I went to Limerick city with a friend of mine. It was a fresh, frosty morning as we set out and it was decided that we should travel by the coast road, since my friend and I both like a bit of scenery.

The light wind on the Shannon was like a young girl whispering and my friend whistled happily while we sped over the tree-lined roadway at 25 miles an hour. "She's in good order this morning," he said, "and what harm but she had had a hard week of it."

The doors rattled merrily at this unexpected compliment and from various places in the back came a succession of clanking noises. As we neared Foynes, she stopped, for no reason at all.

"That's all right," my friend said. "We'll give her a rest until she gets her wind back."

Ten minutes passed and he started her again. All went well until we reached Askeaton, when our noses were assailed by three distinct burning odours.

"All she wants is a drop of oil," my friend explained reassuringly. "We'll have a drop ourselves, too," he said, "but a good cowboy always waters his horse first."

At the petrol pump the attendant looked the car over without change of expression.

"Throw a pint of oil into her," my friend said.

The attendant returned with a pint of oil and when the bottle was empty he shook his head with the least sign of emotion. "She'd take more than a pint! he announced.

"She would not."

"She would!" the attendant said, as if it was none of his business.

"She would if she got it!" my friend said and we drove off, a defiant cloud of blue smoke rising behind us. Several uneventful miles passed and finally my friend announced that we were near Limerick.

"How do you make that out" I asked.

"There's smoke from the cement factory in front of us."

"That's not the cement factory," I said. "That's the carburettor."

We pulled up at a labourer's cottage and a small, curious man hurried out to inspect us.

"Is she on fire?" he enquired.

"Is there any chance you'd oblige us with a gallon of water?" my friend asked, ignoring the question.

When the gallon was empty, we thanked the kindly cottier, who was still regarding our conveyance with a mixture of amusement and ridicule. "She takes a share of water," he laughed.

My friend sat behind the wheel again and looked as his benefactor straight in the eye. "If you were after running from Listowel you might like a sup of water too," he pointed out.

That night, as we were leaving the city, I was a little apprehensive. Mr friend sensed my worry. "You won't hear a word out of her now," he said. "She knows we're on the road home."

As we neared home she seemed to grow younger. Now and then she lurched a little to the left and right.

"If I give her her head now," my friend boasted, "you wouldn't catch her with a jet. But it wouldn't be fair to her and besides, I want her tomorrow."

"Did you ever think of trading her in?" I asked.

He looked at me with unconcealed astonishment.

"A new car is no good to anyone," he said defensively. "It's no good to the garages because it doesn't need repairs, it's no good to the owner because he's afraid he'll tarnish her, and it's not good to a man looking for a lift because new cars are in such a hurry they haven't the time to stop and pick up a person.

"This ould car gave me the best years of her life. I courted in her, and I proposed in her, and I was accepted in her. I took her on my honeymoon with me and I drove my five children to be christened in her. She never let me down. I know her weaknesses and she know mine. She knows my pubs and she'll pull up outside them without my having to touch a clutch or a brake.'

"There's no fear she'll be stolen because she'd frighten the life out of a car thief. But I suppose I'll have to get a new car soon, because my sons are growing up to me and there's no one could handle her but myself. But I'd better shut up," he concluded, "because all this praise isn't good for her, and she'll probably sulk like a racehorse in the morning."

Limerick Leader, December 22, 1962.

An unhappy experience in Cruise's Hotel
Liam Irwin

CRUISE'S Hotel attracted a lot of favourable notices from nineteenth century travellers. William Makepiece Thackery in 1843 referred to 'the excellence of Mr. Cruise's hotel which every traveller knows.' This 'large, neat and prosperous' establishment was, he asserted, 'one of the best inns in Ireland.' This excellence he put down to the care and attention of the owner: 'Mr. Cruise is the only landlord of an inn I have had the honour to see in Ireland. I believe these gentlemen commonly (and very naturally) prefer riding to the hounds or many sports, to attendance on their guests; and the landladies, if they prefer to play the piano, or have a game of cards, in the parlour, only show a taste at which no one can wonder; for who can expect a lady to be troubling herself with vulgar chance-customers, or looking after Molly in the bed-room or waiter-Tim in the cellar?'

Mrs. West, a Quaker traveller in 1846, found on her arrival that the hotel was full. 'However, the very civil landlord seeing a lady, and as he said, 'a very tired one too,' would not run us away, but got two young barristers to vacate their rooms in which we were installed with all possible speed.' Regrettably, the peremptorily expelled barristers did not record their feelings for posterity. J.H. Ashworth was equally rhapsodic in 1853. 'I found myself most delightfully located in Cruise's hotel, an establishment that is not excelled even in Dublin.' Towards the end of the century favourable comments were still being made. S. Reynolds Hole in 1892 praised 'Mr. Cruise's very excellent and extensive hotel.'

It is of interest then to find a very different view expressed in 1860. Julius Rodenberg, a distinguished German author and traveller, presents a picture so at variance with other accounts, that it is difficult to believe he was describing the same hotel. Rodenburg, who was born in 1833, abandoned his initial career as a lawyer to travel and write. Having lived for a time in London, he settled in Berlin in 1859 where he achieved a distinguished literary reputation. On his death in 1914 such was his fame that a street in Berlin was named after him. Among the books he produced was an account of his travels in Ireland, *Island of the Saints*, published in 1861. This work is a fascinating, intelligent, sympathetic and insightful of the country and its people. His comments on Cruise's hotel are therefore of particular interest:

> I reached my inn and it was a perfect Colossus of a building, displaying on its broad forehead in golden letters the name 'Cruise's Royal Hotel.' The royal glory sank considerably, however, as soon as I entered it and climbed up a labyrinth of steps. On gazing at the glistening gold letters and mighty front of my hotel, what expectations were aroused! But inside everything was as badly managed as possible, uncomfortable and disagreeable. The tall windows had not been cleaned for an eternity. Dust lay on the torn velvet of the furniture, the damask beds were disgustingly filthy, while silver teapots and cups with broken handles, knives with the points missing and bent forks formed the service. The perfect indifference and want of sympathy for everything that makes existence not only endurable but pleasant rose before the new arrival at every step and produced a depressing effect upon him. I did not feel so desolate on the most gloomy shebeen-houses of the farthest west. There it was my free choice to share whisky and oatmeal with the most unhappy and poorest portion of the poor people; and their stories and songs spiced with the meal and made the scene full of painfulness and poesy; but here, wedged in between pretension and insufficiency, between the white chokers of the waitresses and the dirty chairs and tables, a great fear fell upon me.
>
> Cruise's coffee-room was arranged on the English model. The waiters were very stiff and grand although the green island peeped out at times at their elbows or through some treacherous holes. Gas-lights were burning and striving to display their brilliancy through dusty globes as well as they could. Wearied travellers were seated at tables, like myself, and shouting for newspapers. Very few of which were to be seen. My dinner was in the mean while brought in under covers as in England; but the peculiar tricks the cook plays in this way, both with the hunger and imagination of the diner, were not so pleasantly terminated as in the case here. The fish was half raw and red; the joint – mutton of course – was uneatable from the opposite fault. The mutton patriotism becomes, from this point westward, always more and more opposed to the demand a well regulated stomach

must take for a reasonable variety. At last, you rise with mutton and go to bed with mutton and the whole world seems to exhale a smell of mutton. Wherever I looked and felt, the same discomfort; the porter bottles were badly corked, the cheese was utterly decayed and the butter was ornamented with breadcrumbs; the plates and dishes were strongly plated, on the other hand, and the waiters' cravats of the most aristocratic stiffness. Fortunately my appetite was not alarming and I was soon out again with a cigar between my lips.

The Sunday bells awoke me next morning. It was a rainy day, cold and uncomfortable. I shivered all over the dark, gloomy bedroom allotted to me. I had put on my over-coat and yet I shivered. My window offered a prospect of the Arthur quay and the Shannon. In spite of the piercing cold of the autumn morning the river was crowded with men and horses bathing together and that took place in front of the most fashionable and lively streets in Limerick and on the quay stones the men performed their toilet while the horses coolly shook off the water drops.

And, yes, it *did* rain continuously during his time here.

From *North Munster Antiquarian Journal*, 2000, Vol. 40.

A Frenchman's Experiences on his Walk through Limerick 1796
Chevalier de La Tocnaye

LA Tocnaye was 27 years old when he arrived in Ireland. He set off on foot from Dublin, and usually travelled about 22 Irish (28 English) miles per day. At the end of nearly every day's journey he was able to rest in comfortable accommodation, because of the many letters of introduction he carried.

But not all of his perambulations were pleasant. La Tocnaye was most unfortunate when he entered the County Limerick village of Glin, on the road from Kerry. He was so badly bitten by fleas in a miserable eating house – which had been recommended by a priest – that he was forced to run to the Shannon early next morning to secure relief. On another occasion, after leaving the house of a marquis, who could or would not find him a bed, he spent the night in a beggar-woman's cabin, with six nearly naked children, a pig, a dog, a cat, two hens and a duck. He suffered a variety of other trials and tribulations.

Fatigued by the long walk of the day before, and by the great heat, I thought it well to stop at the village of Glin, which gives the title of Knight to its proprietor. There are but four places in the whole of Ireland which have this privilege, and all are in this part of the county. It is not a title of English origin. It was given by the sovereign to four brave men of the country before or at the time of the conquest, and those who bear the titles at present are their descendants.

I asked a big priest whom I met where I could find lodging, and he led me to a miserable eating-house, assuring me that it was very good. I passed the night defending myself from the monsters who regarded me as their lawful prey, and when the sun rose it was on a bloody scene. I had the appearance of having taken part in a battle, as really I had.

Happily, the sea was not far off, to it I fled quickly to drown unwelcome guests, and that operation finished, I was with my friend the priest going, himself, to the water. I told him of my miserable hap, but this he took merely as an everyday matter and made light of it – in fact he laughed very heartily. I felt inclined to wish him a warm place, but calmed myself and only wished him, for the good of his soul, several nights such as the one I had just passed.

I went on my way, and finding at the entry of the village, a beautiful inn, the sight made me so angry with the priest that I could hardly resist turning to seek him and administer to him some well-deserved chastisement. However, I resisted the impulse and proceeded on my way. I saw on a height the ruins of an old castle, which sustained a siege by the forces of Queen Elizabeth. It is still surrounded by its ancient fortifications and outworks; there are also in the neighbourhood some ancient raths. I had already walked ten miles and I had been on foot since three o'clock in the morning, and began to hear the wailings of my stomach; there was no inn to be seen, but I saw on the heights a pleasant-looking house, and made inquiry also the name of the owner. The answer was John Evans.

I had observed several times that while the poor are very hospitable and offer to the tired strangers according to his needs, yet if this same traveller presented himself at the house of well-to-do people, he could get no more than a glass of water. The occasion seemed to be fit for making an experiment, and presented myself at the door.

The owner, Mr. John Even, appeared. 'Monsieur,' I said, 'I have not the honour of your acquaintance, and I have no letter of recommendation to you, but I declare to you that I am extremely hungry and if you will give me something to eat, I shall be extremely obliged. 'Faith,' said he, 'you could not have come at a better time for breakfast is ready.'

He brought me into his house, where I found everything I could desire. I was charmed to find myself wrong in my conjecture, but promised to myself that I would not try such an experiment again, lest I should find my first opinion to be justified.

Making a little zigzag of ten or twelve miles I came to Newcastle, where I was received by Mr. Locke, and his brother, who is the minister of the place. This town is situated in a long, fertile valley, which is only separated from that of the Blackwater by a little range of heights. This castle formerly belonged to the Templars, and must have been at one time of very considerable size. It is now in the possession of Lord Courtenay.

If the great English proprietors had the wit to place on their estates men of the type found here, the country would have no occasion to complain about their absence. Mr. Locke has founded, at his own charge, a manufactory of linen, in which children can be employed from a very early age. There is no doubt that such establishments cannot make a profit at present, they are useful for the country, and cannot be too much encouraged. The proprietor will find himself amply rewarded for his trouble and cost by the new spirit of industry which will be fostered among the peasants . . . .

From Newcastle to Limerick the country is superb. This is, without doubt, the most fertile stretch of land in Ireland. Near Rathkeale, I had occasion to visit three or four villages inhabited by the descendants of a German colony from the Palatinate, established by the owner of the soil nearly eighty years ago. Until now they have always remarried among themselves, and have preserved the custom of their country.

At the time of my visit, there was only one man living of the original members of the colony. There is no doubt that they were received on very advantageous conditions, each family receiving, in perpetuity, ground for house and garden, as well as several acres of farm land at a very moderate rate. The rich and fertile country on which they were established was uncultivated before their arrival. Their industry is still very remarkable. Their farms are certainly better cultivated than others near, and their houses, built after the fashion of their former country, are of a comfortable character and so clean that they look like palaces in comparison with the poor cabins of the Irish. The women still wear the large straw hats and short petticoat as worn by the Palatinat.

The natives hated them cordially at the beginning, and do not love them much better now, as they are very jealous of their successes, and such feelings do not tend to make them attempt to imitate the foreigners with intention to equal, or even surpass them in results. Naturally, I suppose, the Palatines will finish by becoming like their neighbours.

Passing through the long town of Rathkeale, I directed my steps to Adare, where I was received by Sir Richard Quin. The town was formerly full of colleges and ecclesiastical establishments. The ruins of several well-preserved buildings are still to be seen, and four or five miles away, at Selton, are ruins of abbeys, which are perhaps the largest I have seen in this country . . . .

I took the road to Limerick and saw on the way a 'wake' in the house of a dead man. It was Sunday, and the women did not cry so loudly on that day but the scene was, nevertheless, a rather singular one. The dead lay on a table, and the house was full of women sitting on their heels that a bullet dropped among them would not have touched the ground. The men were outside on the road, to the number of about two hundred, on foot or on horseback, and a great number prudently waiting at a neighbouring inn until it would please the dead to move.

It was the time of the horse races at Limerick, and also it was the duelling season. The confusion everywhere was extreme. The town was full of people coming and going. The workers were doing nothing. Everything had given way to the desire to see some breakneck performances on horseback; there were on the course more than twenty thousand persons. What made the people anxious to see was that three of the jockeys were peers. Or was it that three of the peers were jockeys? The one as bad as the other.

There came to the races some bullies from Cork and Youhgal, with the laudable intention of putting lead into the brains of the Limerick folk. They were about saying to anyone they met: 'Do you want powder and ball? for we can give it.' During the eight days of the races there were ten or twelve duels – an officer of the Irish brigade was killed. Then it occurred to the Chancellor to put an end to these quarrels by proceedings for criminal acts, and the warlike gentlemen took their departure.

The races finished at last, and happily for the country, for had they lasted three weeks longer, the inhabitants were so given over to sport that the harvest would have lain in the fields ungathered.

The city of Limerick is famous in history for having sustained a long siege by the troops of King William, holding out for the cause of his unfortunate father-in-law; famous also for the capitulation which the besieged troops made in the name of all Ireland. The terms of this capitulation were most scrupulously observed during the lifetime of King William, but, with assignments of reason other than the desire to discourage the religion of the inhabitants, and force these to adopt the established form, they were most cruelly violated in the reign of Queen Anne. Priests were condemned to be hung for saying mass, and any person convicted of hearing it said, suffered severe penalties.

I must add that the excessive severity of these laws was its own antidote, for judges often sought pretexts for acquitting the accused. These laws were rarely, if indeed, it may be said, never put into execution; but the son, the brother, or even the distant relation of a Catholic could make himself possessor of his friend's property by becoming Protestant.

These cruel laws existed for nearly eighty years, and it is only fourteen or fifteen years since they were abrogated, and that necessity was felt to make the laws supportable to the inhabitants. In this short space of time Ireland has attained to an extraordinary degree of prosperity, giving occasion to hope that, with a continuance of the present system of moderation and kindness, Ireland will soon rival the country that held her in bondage, and this will mean good fortune for both.

The new city of Limerick is very pretty and very regular, and just to as great degree is the old disgusting. One can hardly believe that there are here fifty thousand inhabitants . . .

I travelled to Castle Connell, a charming spot situated on the banks of the Shannon which flows there like a torrent through stones and rocks. The beauty of the place and the mineral waters draw here a great number of Limerick idlers, who pass the summer in the village and drink, every morning of their stay, a glass of the water. The rich strangers attract beggars from afar, and there are already more here than elsewhere in Ireland. It may seem a strange remark, but it is true, that the richer the country in Ireland, the poorer are the people, and the lower the labourer's daily wage . . .

Several persons near Castle Connell (among others the Lord Chancellor) and Mr. Bruce) in multiplying industries have increased the rate of wages – there can be no better way for the rich man to employ his money. Often I have heard the peasant reproached for his idleness and drunkenness, but when one is reduced to danger of dying from hunger, is it not a better thing to do nothing, since the most assiduous work will not hinder the evil from arriving? In such a situation also, is it not natural to drink when one can, a drop from the waters of Lethe, in order to forget one's misery? If the poor man could really feel that work would ameliorate his situation, he would quickly abandon the apathy and indifference which are born of despair. The inhabitants of Castle Connell were assessed with a rate to provide means to build a Catholic chapel. I do not know what fault had been committed by the priest of the parish, but the Catholic bishop of Killaloe interdicted the work, and the church remained half built, and without a roof. Mass, however, was celebrated in a corner covered by a few planks, and the people continued to come as before, but resolutely resolved not to finish the church unless or until the favourite priest should be recalled ...

I went to O'Brien's Bridge and after having taken a plunge into the Shannon in order to put him in good temper with me, I ascended the river with Mr. Waller in a little boat, for which my umbrella served as a sail. The river was charming, beautiful, calm, and it seemed to be deep, but soon were came to a waterfall and were obliged to land. They are here digging a little canal of about one hundred paces long to join the two navigable parts of the river.

The lake beyond Killaloe is an immense one, of thirty miles long by twelve or fifteen wide, and although it offers, at different parts, interesting and pleasing views, like the greater part of the lakes of Ireland, it has rather the look of a great inundation, and the islands through it give *vraisemblance* to the appearance.

A company offered to drain nearly the whole of this lake, provided that the riverside proprietors would give them half the newly-formed land. Difficulties arose, and the matter has not been carried though. The company had calculated that, in lowering the bed of the river at Killaloe, by twelve feet, they would drain fourteen thousand acres. The cost of the works would have amounted to over twenty thousand pounds sterling. It would not have been a great deal to pay for seven thousand acres of land, but is to be presumed that this would not produce very much in the early years, and perhaps one-third of it would be sandy or unfit for cultivation.

The proprietors are usually very jealous about companies executing such works. Often they oppose the designs and prefer to have their land under water than divided with the interfering company, but it should be possible to find a way of arranging the matter to the satisfaction of both parties. A proprietor might be persuaded to pay four or five pounds sterling for every acre of land, good or bad that the company should drain for him at its risk and expense.

The little town of Killaloe is very ugly; the cathedral is large and appears to be fairly well built. The stone bridge which crosses the Shannon here has eighteen arches, but they are very small, and the bridge will have to be rebuilt – a modern one need not have more than nine or ten arches. I paid a visit to the minister of the parish, who has a superb house at a little distance from the town, on a height dominating Lough Derg. From there is to be had a really magnificent view of this vast sheet of water, whose banks are also everywhere high, and cultivated with care. There is a bay of seven or eight miles, which cannot be seen without climbing to the summit of a fairly high mountain in the neighbourhood. From this height the Shannon can be seen winding through the plane as far as Limerick, with all the little towns which are on its banks, the principal of these being Nenagh.

It is disappointing that there is nowhere to be seen any appearance of industry. There are no manufactures. Beyond the labouring of the soil there is nothing to do, but patience – a certain time must be allowed to a nation to come out of its stupor of seven hundred years. It is only fourteen years since its genius made effort to fly, and already thought is being taken to find means to surmount the immense difficulties which the navigation of the Shannon presents. A certain measure of success had followed through the use of communications canals. The Grand Canal is proceeding very slowly, but it will be finished in a few years, where interiors communications will be opened across Ireland from Dublin to Limerick, and industry will grow in proportion as the means are being provided for the disposal of its product . . .

I followed the western course of Lough Derg, and on the way met an honest attorney going gaily to put the surrounding countryside under contribution. He pointed out to me, at some distance from the shore, a square tower situated on a rock. Some determined contraband bandits had there established a distillery, with intention to pay no duties. They barricaded the place, and being provided with firearms, no customs officer dare hazard his life in approaching these friends of the 'creature.'

To dislodge them, it was necessary to send troops with cannon, but the distance from the bank being considerable, and there being a wish not to proceed to extremes, they proceeded to starve our illicit distillers, who did not surrender until the fifteenth day, and then only after having effected an honourable capitulation.

From *The Old Limerick Journal*, French Edition, No. 25, Summer, 1980.

A Swede in Limerick
By Mikael Fernström

THIS is a story about some of my experiences when moving from Sweden to Ireland. We all have ideas about what life is like in other countries and we can all get access to official information and statistics, but I have found it more interesting to note the small things in life – linguistic, social, etc., that are part of everyday life.

The month of March, in western Sweden, is normally cold, wintry and often with icy slush, all over the place. I first visited Ireland in March 1991, as a tourist. Arriving in Dun Laoghaire the day after St. Patrick's Day, I followed the southern coast road from Dublin to Galway. I had a fantastic week in the village of Carrigaholt in County Clare, with a flowing green landscape, blue skies and sunshine, +15°c. degrees plus. After some day trips to Limerick, we knew we had found the place to move to. Everybody was very nice to us and the infra-structure with the University of

Limerick, Plassey Technologcial Park and Shannon Airport was very appealing.

In September the same year I arrived in Dublin airport, picked up a rental car and drove to Limerick to get the keys for the house we had decided to rent. The sky was blue, birds were singing and it was about +30°c. I thought, 'This is a wonderful climate . . . . Mediterranean'. Later on in the year, probably December, we discovered that to keep an acceptable indoor climate, several bags of coal and bales of peat briquettes were necessary. We had assumed that with houses with only single glazing and no real thermal insulation, the climate must be really nice.

If there was the slightest breeze through Elm Park on a winter's night, it would take at least half a bag of coal to keep the indoor temperature up, and often a couple of woolly sweaters to keep warm. While trying to operate the fireplace, I found myself, on several occasions, cursing the Irish heating and plumbing trade, as the whole heating system started to a boil. Trying to understand how it worked, I traced all the pipes in the house and made a drawing of the system. When looking at the drawing, I realised that Irish heating and plumbing is psychedelic. The diagram looked like one of those pictures by Esher where the laws of perspective and gravity are violated.

We knew that the Republic of Ireland is a peaceful and neutral country with a low crime rate. You get these figures from the official statistics. Over the first few months in Ireland, we were often surprised by the strong language used by mothers (I think Brendan Grace has illustrated this as well). Irish mothers would seldom say 'you have to do this now' or 'stop that.' The standard phrase we often heard was 'do this now or I'll kill you.' As this something that the official statistics hadn't covered, or . . .? Another social-linguistic observation was 'I'm starving.' Nobody ever said 'I'm hungry.' or 'I'd like a bite to eat' – everybody was starving. Perhaps this reflects back to famine in the 19th century? (Sweden also had a famine at the same time as Ireland because of the same potato blight. Many surviving Swedes went to Minnesota).

How long are you here for? Initially when asked this question, I would explain that I'm planning to stay here for good. This might seem strange to a native English speaker, but when you're not, it translates into most European languages as a possible future tense. After a couple of months, many smiles and a lot of confusion, I started to produce the correct answer – for how long we had been here.

How are you? This, of course, is one of the most common greetings in Ireland. When first coming to this country, I often gave a full account of my health, and if the person asking the question still looked confused I would tell about the health and well-being of my wife, brother, parents, etc. When I eventually got the message, I realised that in Swedish, the corresponding phase would normally result in an (often exaggerated) all positive response, while in Ireland it's 'not too bad . . . ' A closely related query is 'Are you OK', but our first guidebook informed us about the intent of that question.

Pubs: There are no pubs in Sweden, or, there wasn't any when we left, seven years ago. It took some time to understand the full scope of the Irish pub – as an institution. It's not only for drinking, it's for meetings, gatherings, company, and, from a Swedish blow-in's viewpoint, the glue that keeps society together. In Sweden people would normally invite people to their homes when celebrating a birthday or any other significant event. The Swedes would clean, polish, hoover and tidy their homes until presentable. My observation in Ireland, is that whenever you want to go social, there's always the local pub, and this solves the problem without any excessive homework.

So, where do the Swedes drink in Sweden? They can either visit the state-owned off-licence and buy beverages by the bottle for consumption at home, or if they are living in a city, visit one of the few copies of an Irish pub. One significant difference is that in Sweden it's only a very limited age group that goes to the pub, perhaps between 20 and 30 years of age. You'll never find a family or a senior citizen there. Another problem is that a pint in Sweden is often around £5.

Go for one. This is an interesting concept. It can be interpreted as an invitation to go for one singular drink. Over the last seven years the only working metaphor I have developed is what happens when you add one pile of sand to another. You still have just one pile of sand.

This brings us to the next topic: *The round . . . .*

In Irish pubs (in Ireland) I have learnt that if you're in good company, there's an ad hoc organisation for buying the next round of drinks. This can be quite difficult to understand for foreigners. In Sweden and many other European Countries, everybody buys for themselves. Luckily, I quickly developed an understanding of these principles of social organisation, but I have seen European friends and colleagues having great difficulty to understand and keep up with the Rounds.

Even when you get to understand the concept, it is strategically difficult to 'make the move' at the right time. Any small gesture, wink or nod at the right time in the direction of the bartender might initiate another Round. Eventually, foreigners develop either a feeling of guilt, not being able to reciprocate; spasms, or severe drunkenness.

One day in September 1993, Basil Cosgrave told the locals in the Hurlers Bar that he had seen a planning application in the paper to remove Kilmurry Church from its original site. Over the next few months, residents in the area and relatives of the people buried in the graveyard opposed the application and a committee was formed. The activities that followed, such as door to door collection, auctions, quizzes, raffles and concerts and this very magazine, were extraordinary experiences to me.

In similar situations in Sweden, the locals wouldn't have had a chance to take charge due to both planning laws and lack of tradition in such ventures. The Swedish planning system is different to the Irish system insofar that it isn't announced in local papers what the planning authorities are up to, hence most developments go ahead as long as they comply with the overall plans devised by civil servants and local politicians that seldom have any interest in the real public opinion, due to the Swedish electoral system.

Looking back over the last few years, I think that the Kilmurry Church Restoration project has been one of my most important experiences in Ireland. It has been an outstanding opportunity to make many new friends and getting to know the local history and landscape. And this is just the start . . .

Kilmurry Review, 1998.

I wish we were out of it
The Letters of William and Dorothy Wordsworth, 1829

LIMERICK, September, 17. My dearest Friends: I received your letter (Mary's and Dorothy's) at Killarney. I thought that in a letter sent from Dublin the day we left it, I had directed you to write to Cork; but as I have no such letter, I suppose I have been mistaken. I am truly thankful dearest Sister that you are so well; and glad to hear such a good account of Dora; but poor dear Willie I am almost alarmed about him – how is he [to] stand the winter yonder.

I fear the climate does not agree with him. Does he speak of a cough; and have you charged him again on no account to injure himself in the least degree by application. I long to hear more of him and wish I had directed you to this place where we are just arrived – Mr. Marshall and his Son are gone out; and here are six Letters on the table for him at his return, but not a line written for me – alas – alas. I wish I could have heard from you at least twice a week. But our movements and rate of travelling are so uncertain – hindrances from weather and want of post-horses so often occurring – We are now travelling northward direct having left Killarney yesterday, slept at Askeaton and reached this place, after visiting the ruins of Adair – where there are three abbeys, and a castle within less than a quarter of a mile of each other . . . .

But upon the whole I reckon the weather has favoured us though it is raining hard now, and has done so all day. Mr. Marshall has just come in – and has opened his Letters, - none for me how could there be [a sorry] blockhead as I am. I beg therefore that you will not fail to write by return of post, directing to Coleraine and 4 days to Lurgan – Lurgan I have written the word twice, the first letter is an L. Tomorrow we go to Nenagh, next day we hope to reach Edgeworth Town where we shall meet the Professor, thence to Londonderry and so forth. I shall despatch this from Limerick though it tells you little.

Limerick is a large uninteresting town – and I wish we were out of it; but this morning we were much pleased with the ruins at Adair, and also though in a less degree with those of Askeaton.

On our way we met a characteristic sight today – a [hearse] bedizened with white plumes; the Driver with a white hat-band – and by his side sat on the box a beggarly woman, her elderly cheeks streaming with tears and her countenance looking the genuine Irish howl or ululation. At the back of the hearse sat aloft, precisely as people do with us behind a coach, two ragged people with countenance nearly as ludicrously woeful. I should scarcely have mentioned this but that similar contrasts are so common everywhere in Ireland. Yesterday we met on the high road a Lady upon a Donkey, the Rider most flauntingly overdressed – by her side walked a Gentlemen carrying on his arm a huge lap Dog, as Frenchmen do – he too was wondrous fine and with them walked three or four young ladies all in full feather - it was quite a continental exhibition with something in it nevertheless peculiar to this strange country. – We do not in future expect interesting scenery; so that we must depend mainly on what we can collect concerning the people.

From *The Grand Tour of Limerick complied* by Cornelius Kelly. Cailleach Books, 2004.

A Frenchman's view of the Clergy
Paschal Grousset

AT the large hotel in Limerick I meet again three of my ecclesiastical fellow travellers. They evidently know what is good for them, and would on no account stop at second-rate inns. One cannot blame them for it. But this is a sign of prosperity, added to all the others; a hotel at fifteen shillings a day, without counting the wine, seems at first sight suited to prelates rather than to humble clergymen. Yet these are only village and parish priests, as I gather from the book on which I sign my name after theirs. At dinner, where we sit side by side, I am compelled to see that the appetite of the reverend fathers is excellent, and that the *carte* of the wines is a familiar object to them. They each have their favourite claret, and they drain the cup to the last drop. After dessert they remain last in the dining-room, in company with a bottle of port. At 10 o'clock that night, entering it to get a cup of tea, I find the three seated round glasses of smoking toddy.

Everywhere, in visiting this island, one meets with this typical pair of abbots, well dressed and well groomed, the general impression left by the Irish clergy – that of a corporation greatly enamoured of its comforts endowed by good incomes, and whose sleekness forms a striking contrast with the general emaciation of their parishioners. It is startling in this realm of poverty, the more startling because the Catholic clergy have no official means of existence, no salary paid them by the State. They owe all the money they spend to the private contributions of their admirers.

Where does their income come from? This is a question doubly interesting to us Frenchmen, who every year pay out two million sterling for the budget of public worship. A placard seen everywhere in Limerick, and presenting a marked resemblance to the advertisement of a theatre, will help to tell us. This placard is to the effect that on the day after tomorrow a general ordination of young priests will take place in the Cathedral of St. John, by the hands of the Right Rev. X. O'Dyer, archbishop of the town. It proceeds to state that excursion trains have been established for the occasion, and that tickets for the ceremony my be procured, at the price of half-a-crown and one shilling, at No. 98 George Street. One has only to choose one's place, to pay the price down, and to take away the ticket. Evidently the receipt will be good. The cathedral of St. John must be able to accommodate at least three or four thousand spectators. At 1s. 9d. per head on the average, that gives already a total of two or three hundred pounds. To this must be added the product of the collections and that of the money-boxes, that open everywhere to receive the generosity of the faithful. It is true that an ordination is not an every-day event, and that it must be an expensive affair to put on stage. We must therefore suppose the ordinary income to be raised by way of semestrial and direct contribution.

This is how the thing is done; each parish priest has two Sundays in the year devoted to the taking of his dues, as he calls it. On these days, instead of preaching, he exhibits a manuscript list upon which are inscribed by name all his tributaries, that is to say, all his parishioners, with the sums they have paid into his hands; this he reads publicly. As a rule he adds a running commentary to each name, either to praise the generosity of the donor, or, on the contrary, to complain of his stinginess. In the country, especially, the scene is not wanting in humour.

'Daniel McCarthy, four shillings and six-pence,' says the priest, 'that's not much for a farmer who keeps three cows and sold two calves this year. I will hope for him that he only meant that as a preliminary gift.'

'Simon Redmond, seven shillings, he might have given ten shillings, as he did last year.'

'Henry Townsend, Esq., of Townsend Manor, three pounds sterling. That's what I call a subscriber! And he is a Protestant. You ought to be ashamed of yourselves to let a Protestant be more generous to your own church than you are.'

'Harriet O'Connor, one shilling and nine-pence. I will be bound she liked buying a new bonnet better that doing her duty. That is between her and her conscience. But I am afraid that at the Day of Judgment she won't find it such a good investment . . . .'

From *Ireland's Disease; the English in Ireland*, George Routledge and Sons, 1887.

TWELVE
MISCELLANY

First published in the 'Limerick Socialist' in February, 1977, Sean Bourke's (author of 'The Springing of George Blake') account of his sentencing to Daingean Reformatory School for three years (as a twelve year old, he admitted under duress in court that he stole a bunch of bananas), Part 1 was reprinted in the 'Limerick Compendium' 1997. The following are Parts 2, 3 and 4:

The Hell that was Daingean
Sean Bourke

IF only the night watch-man hadn't been late coming on duty in the dormitory that night, it might never have happened. But he was late, a whole hour late. There had been some breakdown in communications and Brother Stack had left the dormitory at half past eight, expecting Mr. Donegan, a local villager, to arrive at any minute and take over his vigil for the night.

We had said our prayers in the chapel at night and had then been marched across the dark, wintry quadrangle towards the junior boys' dormitory where the junior boys, from twelve to fifteen, slept in two long rows of iron beds spaced evenly along the full length of the green-painted walls. The senior boys, from sixteen to twenty, had their dormitory at the opposite end of the school and where watched over for the night by yet another civilian night watchman.

There was no supper at Daingean. The last meal of the day was tea at five o'clock which consisted of a plate of porridge and two slices of bread and dripping, washed down by lukewarm, unsweetened tea contained in a rusty tin mug. The porridge and tea were poured out on all the tables about ten minutes before the boys were marched into the refectory and so were barely lukewarm when the boys finally sat down after a prolonged grace-before-meals. The grace itself might have to be repeated two or three or four times until the Brother on duty was satisfied that it had been said in perfect unison by the ravenously hungry mob.

Iron discipline was the rule at Daingean, and God help any boy who stepped out of line. The only rules in Daingean were the Ten Commandments. A boy who did wrong did not commit a breach of discipline: he committed a sin. And sin had to be punished far more severely than purely temporal misdeeds. To remove a crust of bread from the swill-bin, as many of the starving boys were wont to do, was to break the Seventh Commandment. This merited a flogging. To say 'Christ' or 'Jesus' unless you happened to be on your bended knees in the chapel, was to break the Second Commandment. A boy who was rash enough not to comply instantly with an order given by a Brother broke the fourth Commandment.

Rude and vulgar language, which by its very nature is bound to have some sexual overtones, was only one step short of the ultimate sin in the eyes of the priests and brothers: undue familiarity with another boy. For both these sins the brothers invoked the Sixth Commandment. The penalty was a severe flogging followed by a diet of bread and water kneeling on the concrete floor of the refectory for a week.

I suppose it was a combination of hunger and the pent-up frustrations of the harsh discipline that made some of the junior boys go a bit wild that night in the hour between Brother Stack's departure and the arrival of Mr. Donegan at nine-thirty. Not that anything very serious happened. There were a few innocent pillow fights, a certain amount of mock wrestling which I remember, involved at least two Limerick boys, whom I still meet in the street today, and a great deal of shouting. There was one boy, Mick Houlihan from Cahirciveen in the County Kerry, who did a little more swearing than the others. If a priest or brother walked in all the Ten Commandments would have been invoked and half the dormitory of a hundred boys would have been flogged.

But tragically one brother did see and hear. And that brother was the most savagely sadistic member of the Order in Daingean. Brother Fitzpatrick was from Co. Clare, and on that dark wintry night in October 1949 he was standing on an upturned box in the grass verge outside the dormitory wall peeping through one of the uncurtained windows, invisible in his black habit to the unsuspecting boys inside and to the other brothers and priests who might be passing on the outside.

Equally tragic was the fact that Mick Houlihan worked in the priests' and brothers' kitchen with four other boys and myself. And the man in charge of the kitchen was Brother Fitzpatrick.

The principle that an accused be punished only once for his crime did not apply to Daingean. Apart from the punishment meted out by the Prefect of Discipline, there were other beatings administered by the brother in charge of the boys' working party and by any other brother who just happened to be on duty when the accused came in sight. And Brother Fitzpatrick was in charge of Mick Houlihan's party in the kitchen.

Brother Fitzpatrick had a ritual which he had carefully developed and perfected over the years. A boy must not be punished too quickly; he must be made to suffer the mental torture of knowing that he is going to be beaten without knowing when or for what reason. And so when the five of us arrived for work in the kitchen at nine o'clock that morning exchanging a little cheerful banter, Brother Fitzpatrick carried out the first move of his sadistic ritual.

'Keep quiet and get on with yeer work!' He looked Mick Houlihan straight in the face and scowled. 'and that goes for you too, Houlihan. Get on with your washing-up.'

And so the ritual began. It was familiar to all of us. In exactly two hours, as the clock struck eleven, Mick would be beaten. And between now and then none of us would utter one word to each other lest we be made to join our wretched comrade on the sacrificial altar of Brother Fitzpatrick's sadistic lust.

The soup was made. The roast was in the oven for the priests and brothers. The breakfast pots and pans and cups and saucers were washed and shined. I myself as a senior boy had laid out the cutlery and the various items of delph on the crisp white linen in the priests' refectory. Brother Fitzpatrick sat on a chair next to the work-table against the kitchen wall opposite the long anthracite range reading his breviary, his pale lips moving silently in an ashen face. Mick Houlihan was over at the sink washing a plate for the tenth time, afraid to look up, visibly trembling. The silence was almost physical in its oppressiveness.

The kitchen clock struck eleven. Brother Fitzpatrick slowly closed his breviary, kissed it, and placed it on the shelf above the table. He reached in and pulled out a stick about three feet long and an inch across. Nicholas O'Grady from Kilkenny picked up a sweeping brush and started towards the scullery in a desperate effort to escape what was to follow.

'Put that brush down and stay where you are!' Brother Fitzpatrick growled. It was part of the ritual that when a boy was to be beaten the others must watch. The fear in their young faces was something Brother Fitzpatrick seemed to get great satisfaction from.

Mick Houlihan was still washing the same plate, afraid to stop, afraid to be idle and add to his guilt. 'Put that plate down and turn round!' he did as he was told.

'You are the dirtiest little scut it has ever been my misfortune to meet. You are dirty and filthy and evil minded. Well, I'm going to teach you a lesson that you will never forget. Hold out your hand!'

Mick Houlihan held out his right hand. He thrust it forward fully and firmly, as if to show Brother Fitzpatrick that whatever he had done wrong he was sorry for it and was prepared to take his punishment like a man and maybe Brother Fitzpatrick in his mercy would take this into account. But this bold and frightened gesture was wasted and Mick Houlihan, at fourteen and a half years, was to receive the most vicious beating I have ever seen inflicted on another human being.

Brother Fitzpatrick reduced Mick Houlihan's right hand to a black and blue pulp of bleeding flesh from the finger tips to the elbow, and then ordered him to hold out his left hand. He did the same to this, bringing the stick back over his head and then down with all his physical might on the boy's trembling flesh. By this time, Mick Houlihan was begging for mercy. 'Pease sir, oh please sir, I won't do it any more. I won't sir, I won't sir . . . .'

'Shut up your whimpering, you cowardly little wretch.' Brother Fitzpatrick's face was by now a sickly white in colour and his lips a trembled visibly. He looked almost epileptic. 'You are filthy and disgusting. You have a foul mouth. You have a dirty mind. You are totally obscene. You are a dirty little coward who cannot take his punishment. And you are a robber and a Daingean boy. That is the testimonial you will take out into the world with you when you go. And I hope you are proud of it, you filthy wretch!'

'Oh, please sir, please sir, I won't do it anymore, sir. It was a slip of the tongue sir . . .' By this time Mick Houlihan's knees were giving way under the sheer agony of his ordeal and his torrential tears were forming small pool at his feet. 'Please sir, please sir . . . .' He looked like he was on the point of fainting. Surely Brother Fitzpatrick must stop now.

'Roll up your sleeves to your shoulders.'

Mick Houlihan looked at him in horror. 'Oh, Please sir, please.'

Brother Fitzpatrick delivered three rapid blows to the boy's upper left arm, then three more to the right causing the shirt sleeves to sink into the sweat-soaked flesh with the force. 'When I tell you to do something, you do it!'

'Yes sir, yes sir . . .' Mick Houlihan's fingers were now twice their normal size and he could not bend them at the joints. His hands and forearms looked like joints of raw meat that had been left hanging in a butcher's shop too long and had putrefied.

He made a feeble gesture at forcing his sleeves up at the elbows but could not do so. His elbow joints, as well as his fingers, were beyond use. 'I c-c-can't sir. I c-c-ant . . .' The sweat was pouring down his forehead in large beads. 'I'm sorry, sir, I'm, sorry sir . . .'

'You filthy wretch!' Brother Fitzpatrick leaned the stick against the wall and grabbed hold of the boy. He forced both his sleeves up to the shoulders and picked up the stick once more. The contrast between the lower half of Mick Houlihan's arms and the upper was quite frightening and sickening. The broken black and blue flesh gave way at the elbows to the smooth, white skin of the upper arms and biceps so characteristic of the Daingean boy deprived of the sun. I felt myself trembling with fear and impotent rage and a deep loving compassion for my comrade in his terrible agony. The other three boys, from Longford, Wicklow and Cork stood transfixed at their respective places of labour, afraid to make a sound or a movement.

Realising that the boy was no longer physically capable of actively co-operating in the obscene ritual, Brother Fitzpatrick no longer told him to extend his hands. Instead he proceeded to lash him on the upper arms with all his force and continued for at least another five minutes unto Mick's entire arms, from the fingers to the shoulders, were no longer recognisable as human limbs.

'Oh God, oh God, please Brother Fitzpatrick, please sir, please . . .'

Mick Houlihan fell to his knees at last, his young boy's strength and endurance finally spent. Sitting on his haunches, he eased his body forward and rested his forehead on the ground, his chin touching his knees. His arms hung loosely by his side, completely out of control, and the blood, trickling down his broken flesh, paused for a second at the finger-tips, and then fell to the floor to mingle with his sweat. He had finished pleading and he just moaned softly to himself.

'Dirty cowardly filthy wretch!' With all his might, Brother Fitzpatrick delivered three final blows to the boy's quivering back. The stick made a sickening thud as it fell and Mick Houlihan eased over on his side and lay still.

Brother Fitzpatrick looked across at me and then at the other three boys in turn. His face was contorted almost beyond recognition and he seemed to be shaking all over. When he spoke his breath came in short gasps.

'Let that be a lesson to all of ye. There is enough filth and dirt in this world without ye people starting. Even to think an impure thought is a mortal sin, If ye haven't got the strength to avoid temptation and sin, then by God I'll give ye that strength to – with this!' He held the stick tightly in his right hand until the knuckles were white and jabbed it rhythmically at each one of us in turn. 'With this,' he repeated, 'with this.'

He looked down at Mick Houlihan again with hatred in his eyes. 'Get up, you devil incarnate, get up, before I give you the same gain. Get up, you filthy, foul-mouthed wretch! And for the rest of the week you will wash up all the greasy plates in cold water. Do you hear me – you filthy, cowardly little wretch!'

With what must have been a superhuman effort, Mick Houlihan slowly got to his feet. He turned his back to his sink, and, by raising the right side of his body as high as he could, and then the left, he managed to get both his dead arms into the by now cold, greasy water. Lowering his head, he pulled at the plug stopper chain with his teeth and then somehow managed to turn on the cold tap in the same manner. He let the water flow over his broken flesh as he sobbed quietly to himself.

Brother Fitzpatrick walked across the gap between the table and the dresser and replaced his blood-stained stick. Then he turned his attention to the four of us once more.

'Let that be a lesson to all of ye, do ye hear? If I hear any of ye using dirty language, that's what ye'll get. Foul, dirty, sinful language. Evil, that's what it is. Foul and evil. An insult to God. Just one word of foul language out of any of ye and ye won't be able to walk for a month!'

It was then I noticed that the crucifix, which was the badge of the Oblates of Mary Immaculate, had worked its way loose from the belt of Brother Fitzpatrick's black habit during the ritualistic torture of Mick Houlihan and now hung loosely from the cord around his neck, swinging gently to and fro as he spoke. The crucifix had the figure of Christ in brass on a black wooden cross. Brother Fitzpatrick seemed to notice it at the same time and hastily tucked it into his belt.

'Alright, get back to yeer work, all of ye,' he said, dismissing us. 'And I repeat for the last time, don't ever let me hear any of ye using a foul word, for if ye do, then may God help ye because I won't.'

I made my way across the hall to the priests' and the brothers' rectory. I took a bundle of rags from the press and went down on my knees to shine the linoleum floor. I couldn't get the thought of Mick Houlihan's mutilated young arms out of my mind and the terrible agony and despair of his tortured face. I didn't realise it then, but that day was to be the turning point of my life. It was the day I lost my innocence. Hardly a day was to go by from that day to this without my recalling the obscenity of Mick Houlihan's desperate sufferings and total degradation.

It was all done for the greater glory of God and with the acquiescence of the Civil Authority. And I have never respected either concept since. And never will as long as I live.

In praise of a reformatory

'THE scene outside the courthouse, as the lads were being driven away, was pitiable. The mothers and friends of the youthful offenders kept up a continuous cry and followed the car for a good distance.'

This was a *Leader* report of the sad culmination of a court case in 1900, when two young defendants were sent to a reformatory for five years after being found loitering in an enclosed premises in Robert Street for unlawful purposes. The boys had previously been apprehended for stealing tins of condensed milk from a nearby factory.

The boys cried bitterly in court on hearing the sentence and asked to be forgiven this time. But the magistrate refused to alter the decision. The youngsters were evidently devoted play-goers and they admitted that their attempted larceny was designed to provide money to gain admittance into the National Theatre in Charlotte Quay.

After sentence was passed, the chairman spoke eloquently of the advantages of a reformatory, saying 'in this institution, which is decidedly less objectionable than the poorhouse, they will be taught trades, and this advantage could with the strict moral supervision exercised in such institutions, fit them to take an honourable and independent position in society when their period of detention has passed.'

The *Limerick Leader*, commenting on the case, said 'the pangs of separation are as keen in the case of the poor as in that of the rich, but the distracted parents can, at all events, console themselves with the reflection that the youngsters themselves will be removed from the influence which tempted them to criminal paths at such an early age in life.'

Around the same time, three other boys, having been charged with taking a purse from a shop, it was suggested by the prosecution that they be whipped for their crime, and their parents, who were present, assented to the suggestion.

Judge Adams, however, who was presiding, said this punishment was old fashioned and barbaric. He did not believe the Irish people would like to see this archaic discipline used any more. The boys were sentenced to terms in a reformatory.

The use of the birch to punish young offenders was the cause of discussion in a city court case in 1916. There was divided opinion as to the use of this form of punishment, usually twelve strokes, with some advocating its introduction. It was still used in England as a deterrent but there was no power to do so here.

A *Leader* editorial said where fines on parents for their children's misdemeanours would cause hardship, the use of the birch in these cases should be considered. 'If that could be done with success, youthful offenders will be thankful in after years to the magistrates and others that they will grow up not as criminals but as decent boys and men respected by all.'

From *Limerick - 100 Stories of the Century*, 2000.

Skipping
Jim McInerney

Mother, mother, I am sick,
Send for the doctor, quick, quick, quick.
And if I die before he comes,
How many carriages will I have,
One, two, three, four . . . .

This was one of the best known skipping chants that were sung on the avenue near our house. Though the words might seem morbid, they had a message, since the number of carriages that attended a funeral indicated the status of the deceased.

Skipping was a favoured pastime on the avenue, since it was a cul de sac, and therefore carried very little traffic. It was confined almost entirely to the girls, and we, as boys, considered it to be a bit sissy. It was anything but that, as to run in and out of a rapidly turning rope required a degree of mental and physical co-ordination that we, as amateurs might not have, and maybe if we tried it would be shown up as lesser than mere girls. We would, on occasion, have a go at turning the rope, as that was easy enough. One chant that I also remember was . . .

> *Turn the rope, turn the rope,*
> *Never leave it empty.*

This was sung when the skipping was in full swing, and there would be a number of girls waiting to go through, which they did, give the required amount of skips, and them jump out, ready to start again. Yet another chant began . . . . .

> *All in together,*
> *This fine weather,*
> *I hear a lark,*
> *Singing in the dark.*

This could go on until everybody got tired, both of skipping and turning the rope, and they would think of something less strenuous to do.

The games that the girls played were more varied and imaginative than anything that the boys could think up. One of these was when some of the girls linked hands to form an arch, and the others had to file through the arch in their turn. While I cannot remember how the game was played, I can still hear the first lines of the sad little verses that were sung for it:

> *Oh, wallflower, oh wallflower,*
> *Growing up so high,*
> *Just like children,*
> *Growing up to die.*

The words and the air puzzled me, and I wondered where they had come from, and it was not until years later that I found that the air had been taken from a passage in Beethoven's Pastoral Symphony. So I was still non the wiser. Another change, sung for a similar game, went something like this . . .

> *Oliver Twist, couldn't do this,*
> *What's the use of trying so,*
> *Tip my toe, under I go,*
> *Oliver, Oliver Twistio.*

In this game, two girls faced each other and clasped hands across the intervening space. The other players ran under their outstretched hands, which were held progressively lower for each round, until eventually the players had to wriggle through at knee level. This was reminiscent of the Fianna war games, where a warrior had to run at full tilt under a knee-high obstruction without breaking his stride. Many of the children that used to play on the avenue had been born in the area, and it became accepted as almost an official playground. So, after school hours, and during holiday time, it was usually a busy place. Perhaps a little too noisy, in fact, for some people.

We used play a game called High Strong Horse against Cusack's low garden wall, opposite a shop at the bottom of our garden. Nobody knew where this game came from, or who introduced it to our area. It usually took six to play it, although four would do at a pinch. One boy would fold his arms on the top of the wall, and put his head down on them. The next would grasp him around the hips in a manner of a rugby scrum, and the third would do likewise to the second.

The first one of the second group would then vault as far up as he could on to the backs of the underlings, and then the other pair would follow suit. The vaulters would not be too particular as to where their boots, knees or elbows landed while they were scrambling into position. The top team were not to utter a sound of any description while in position, and the underdogs would do their best to goad them into doing so, and therefore disqualify them. This game could go on for a long time, or at least until the shop light went out, when everybody went home.

From *Farranshone, A Memoir*, Ryan Printers, 2003.

Milford House – its owners and occupiers
Tony Browne

MILFORD House is situated in the townland of Srelane in the modern day parish of Milford. The present house was built as a dower house by the Monsell family in 1780. Dower houses were residences where the widow of the former lord or owner, of the main seat, took up residence upon the title or possession of the main inheritance falling to the heir or heiress.

The history of Milford House is tied very closely to the fortunes of three families: the Monsells, the Widenhams and the Russells. The relationships between the three families, especially the Widenhams and the Monsells, is so closely interlinked that at times it is difficult to unravel the various generations. All three families had one thing in common. They were all descended from families of Cromwellian origin. The Russells were descended from one Nathaniel Russell, 'Officer of the Troops', who was killed at the Siege of Limerick in 1651. Monsells would claim to be descended from a cup bearer to William the Conqueror. The original Widenham was a Lieutenant Colonel John Widenham, who was originally in charge of the Royalist garrison at Youghal but in an act of crass opportunism he betrayed the town of Youghal to the Cromwellian forces. Widenham was rewarded with a generous grant of land, for his newly found allegiance, at Castletownroche in Co. Cork. This land was confiscated from the family of Lord Fermoy, the direct ancestor of the late Princess Diana. Today this house at Castletownroche has been converted into a luxury hotel.

As indicative of the early links between the Monsells and the Widenhams, Colonel John Widenham, probably a son of the betrayer of Youghal, married

Margaret Monsell in 1692 and they had a family of five children. From this early union many other marriages were forged between the Monsells and the Widenhams, in particular, and the Russells to a lesser extent.

The local connection between the Monsells and the Milford/Plassy area is given a further twist by virtue of the fact that Monsells were also heavily involved with Clive in the East India Company. When Clive came to Ireland among the lands that he acquired were those of Ballykilty which soon had its title changed to Plassey after the decisive battle of Plassy, in which he conquered India for the British.

In 1728 a Thomas Monsell of Ballybrood near Caherconlish married Alice Widenham of Ballinamona, near Hosptial. Their son John Monsell married Catherine Widenham of Milford and Plassy in 1753. From this record it is apparent that Widenhams were resident at Milford in the middle of the 18th century. This is further reinforced when the Rev. Walter Widenham is listed in Taylor & Skinner's coach map of Ireland dated 1777. Widenham was also listed among the sponsors for the publication. An interesting point about the Widenhams is that although they first appeared in Ireland as Cromwellian soldiers, by the 18th century they had very much become associated with the church ministry. Forsaking the sword for the pulpit one might say.

In 1798 Thomas Monsell MP of Plassy married a Dorothea Monsell. To further increase the propensity of intermarriage a daughter of that union, Elizabeth Dorothea married Robert Hedges Eyre Monsell. Thomas Monsell was one of the directors of Monsell's Bank which was the leading banking institution in Limerick City until it collapsed on 'Black Monday,' 29th of May 1820.

In 1837 Milford house had come into the possession of one Thomas Fitzgerald who is listed as being in possession in Lewis's Topographical History. By 1840, however, a Captain Stacpoole was in occupation. In the 1850's it was purchased by Thompson Russell. Thompson Russell was a son of John Norris Russell and Maria Thompson of Cork. John Norris Russell was easily the most dynamic businessman in the Limerick region and he established a very extensive milling and shipping network which was among the greatest in the British Isles.

Lady Massy was the next occupier of Milford House but in 1883 it was purchased by Edward Maughlin Russell. At the time of purchasing it, Maughlin Russell was forty years of age. He was married to Maria Fitzgerald-Blood. The connection to the Bloods is interesting because at different times different branches of the Blood family were resident in both Rose Lawn House and Willow Bank House. Edward Maughlin Russell sold the house to the Little Company of Mary in 1923. He died a couple of years later in his 83rd year.

Since its purchase by the Little Company of Mary, Milford House has been used both as a nursing home and a hospice and it still continues to make a very vital contribution to health care in the Limerick region.

From *Kilmurry Review*, 1998.

A bountiful salmon harvest
Pat Doran

SADLY, salmon drift net fishing, which has been a major part of my living over the last fifty years, and also my passion and hobby, is no more as it has been outlawed on the (Shannon) estuary. Salmon stocks have been in serious decline for many years and action has at long last been taken to rectify the situation, but it is a case of too little too late. I can still remember vividly the times when salmon was plentiful and able to support fishermen and their families. The best years of summer salmon fishing were from 1974 to 1978 and the very best year was 1975 – my father said that it was the best season he could ever recall. My brother John fished with me most of the years of that decade.

Some fishermen, when asked how many salmon they caught, would inflate the amount – but that was often out of embarrassment because other experienced fishermen may have caught double the amount they actually caught. It was the opposite with the Doran fishing family. We would tell lies and say that the fishing was poor and that we did not do too well. We would never give a correct amount for obvious reasons; also, if you did tell people the amount that you had caught they could easily make up what you had earned for a week's fishing.

Net salmon fishing on the estuary is history now, so there is no point in keeping secrets any longer. I kept detailed records of salmon catches for every season since 1965 and the worst year for me was 1970, a total of 410 salmon. The best seasons were taken from 1974 to 1978, and the two best in the history of the estuary were 1974-75. Looking back on my records, 1975 was, without a doubt, the better of the two and in one week alone, 16-21 June, I caught 254 salmon and in the following week, 23-28 June, 159 salmon. In that two week period I actually caught three salmon more that I did for the entire 1970 season. My total catch for 1975 was 811. My Dad, although he had retired from fishing in 1971, came out of retirement for the 1974 season and that year I fished all days with my brother while my Dad fished the evening tides. We were 'double-banking' and our total catch for that year between the two fishing crews was 1,362 salmon.

From 1981 there was a drastic decline in wild salmon stocks in conjunction with a fall in the price we received due to salmon farming. This was the start of a downward trend concerning salmon stocks on the estuary and from 1994 to 2006 I did most of my fishing with members of my own family, my sons and daughter because the fishing had gone so bad it was a problem to acquire crew members. Only twenty years previously crewmen would be lined up at our door to get a berth with my Dad or myself, but those days were long gone. In 1999 I built a special small gandloe boat and fished completely on my own. I operated the oars and net in often very windy conditions and still competed for the best fishing positions with other fishermen, some of them were still operating with a tree-man crew, I had no outboard engine on board so I relied totally on my expertise and physical strength, rowing and fishing for a full day or twelve of fourteen hours.

From *A Clune's Lane Fisherman*, Pat Doran, 2008.

Keeping the lid on things
Michael McCarthy

WHILE there were a few celebrated cases associated with the Shannon Scheme, most of the crime was of a petty nature, frequently associated with drink. There were twenty-six pubs within a two-mile radius of the works, not counting the clubs in the camps and the various shebeens that did a roaring trade in poitin.

One of the earliest reported cases concerned a group of eighteen German engineers, scientists, electricians, servants, and, of course, Dr. Myles MacSwiney, the camp doctor, living in Doonass House. The majority of the Germans working on the various building sites lived in nearby wooden houses and huts. They had their own club. They also had their own school for their children, run by Herr Stumer, and their religious needs were looked after by Rev. Jupp from Roscrea.

Those in Doonass House were perceived as the aristocratic grandees of the German contractors and had rather exclusive arrangements for themselves, so much so, that Doonass House was looked on as the epitome of up-market hauteur. It is difficult to imagine what must have been for them a heady cocktail of genuine culture shock and outrage when they received a summons under the Shebeening Act from the local gardai on 26 June 1926, as a result of which their fine cellar of wine, totalling 1500 bottles and valued at £700, was seized.

A month later the case came up for hearing at Limerick County District Court. Baron Gravenitz, a senior executive of Siemens Schucker, gave evidence. He stated that all of the drink belonged to the company, which had taken over Doonass House for its use. He told the court that in fact there were two cellars, one for residents and one for visitors, who were mostly German callers. Acting District Justice Conroy did not have much mercy on the Germans as he ordered that all the drink be confiscated. He imposed a fine of £10 on Ernest Fiege, the mess steward, for selling liquor without a licence on 1 March and on the day of the raid.

Another case that caused a certain amount of amusement and revelry among the navvies on the works concerned a consignment of Murphy's stout that went astray. The consignment, meant for Anselm Taylor, a caterer in one of the canteens at Ardnacrusha and subsequently the owner of a pub at O'Brien's Bridge, disappeared from the Longpavement Station, having been collected in a lorry by someone other than Taylor. The latter then brought an action against Great Southern Railways and was awarded £25 compensation by Judge McElligott in Limerick Circuit Court. Reportedly, it was one of the 'wettest' summers ever in the area.

While these cases may have brought a certain amount of hilarity into workers' lives, the increased rate of traffic in the courts did not amuse the judges. The increase in crime was putting a lot of pressure on the system. At Killaloe District Sessions, Justice Gleeson declared that he was determined to put an end to the scandal of drunkeness at O'Briens Bridge, which had become notorious, there being more cases then that in the whole of Clare. He accused the Shannon Scheme workers of being mostly responsible.

Curiously enough, it was predominantly Germans who were making the headlines in this regard. For example, during the lead-in to Christmas 1927, two of their mechanics tried to get into Sadlier's pub in Catherine Street, Limerick, just after midnight. They were refused entry, but being already somewhat 'tired and emotional' after a serious crawl, they began to create trouble on the street outside. Inevitably, the guards were called. On arrival the Germans assaulted them and one poor guard had to face Christmas without his two front teeth.

The season of goodwill was still in full swing when another group of Germans left a pub in the city late at night. 'Feeling no pain', one of them decided to entertain the locals with a rendition of The Watch on the Rhine. One of his countrymen took grave exception to this and a vicious fracas ensured. Again, the posse of guards duly arrived and after firing a few shots they managed to break up the row and arrest five Germans – but not before one of their number, a detective, sustained a bad gash over the eye.

While the Shannon Scheme was looked on by many at the time as a 'Free Stater' project, making the government extremely sensitive about security matters, there was little direct threat to the project itself. Even when the enormous stores at Ardnacrusha went up in flames in September, 1927, and subsequently the same thing happened to the massive storage depot at the railhead at Longpavement in May 1928, there was no major stepping up of security as a result. The paranoia of the authorities never really translated itself in a commensurate show of force on the ground, even though it was discussed ad nauseam in certain quarters.

The larceny of food, clothes, was by far the most common crime on the Scheme but occa: MICHAEL McCARTHYore serious proportions. For example, in November 1928, John Hogan, John O'Neill and Ed Toomey appeared at Ennis District Court for attempting to rob £2000 from the pay office at Ardnataggle, O'Brien's Bridge. The robbery had been planned in the disused Blackwater Mill, but the men were captured before they had completed the job. Another hold-up that ended in failure was that conducted by Terence Connolly and James Kelly, employees on the Scheme. Armed and masked, they held up the mail motorcar at Kilmore, Broadford, on November, 1927, robbing £100 and the car that they later abandoned it Hassett's Cross, near Killeely. Subsequently, they were captured and brought to trial.

Some appearances in court were the direct result of the economic conditions under which the workers lived. Great Southern Railways brought Daniel Flynn of Tipperary, a labourer at Ardnacrusha, before Justice Troy at Tipperary District Court for travelling from Oola to Limerick on October, 1927, without a ticket worth 2s. 8d. He explained to the court that while working on the Scheme he did not earn enough to buy a ticket. He made £1 from a three-day week in bad weather. He sent 5s. a week to his mother. After paying for his digs, he had nothing left. He was given a 5s. fine with 20s. costs.

The 'want of money' got the better of two entrepreneurial types in Clonlara in January 1929. A coiners' den was discovered in a hut there and two men were charged with producing and passing counterfeit coins. One has to admire not just their ingenuity but also their sense of timing, as the new Irish coinage had just been introduced after a protracted and passionate controversy. As yet, people would not be all that familiar with the new coins and mistakes could easily be made. The coiners were making Irish and English coins and the newspaper reported that the 2s. 6d. piece was very popular.

With the 800-odd Germans controlling the 5000-strong Irish workforce, it was inevitable that racial friction would surface, but very little of it appeared in the courts. There was the odd case of German foremen being assaulted by Irish navvies and of misunderstandings arising from relatively thin communication because of language difficulties, but a case in Killaloe District Court in April 1928 showed admirably how to play the dumb foreigner when it was to your own advantage. The case concerned three Germans, one charged with being drunk and the other two representing themselves as bona fide travellers. One admitted to having 'a leedle English', but he managed to translate for the other two. The justice asked if the summonses were translated in German before being served. Superintendent Mooney replied that all aliens were supposed to know either Irish or English once they were admitted to the Free State and they had to sign their names in Irish or English on admission. How the proud owner of a name like Adolf Burkhardt or better still, Waldemar Czapiewski would attempt to do that is a real test of anyone's imagination. The gentleman charged with being drunk conveyed to the court that he only had taken 'a leedle' and that he had less English. By all accounts he did seem to have tremendous difficulty in following proceedings and kept repeating 'trunkenheit nein'. When the judge fined him 5s, he produced two half-crowns immediately without the slightest hint from his amateur interpreter.'

Language was a problem not only for the Germans, but for the Irish. The men from west Galway and from the Aran Islands stuck to themselves and conducted their business through the first language, much to the annoyance of some other workmen. The first Connemaraman to be brought to court was Edward O'Loughlin who was charged with stealing 30s. from a colleague and for assaulting him. The judge commented on the fact that O'Loughlin was the first Irish speaker to come before him and asked the garda to translate from the Irish. O'Loughlin was fined £4 for stealing and 5s. for assault.

The fact that the Connemaramen did not mix much and were unable to speak English made them the butt of many jokes. Eventually the men from the west got tired of being ridiculed, so, on Sunday night, 4 September, 1927, they decided to put manners on their English-speaking colleagues by taking the law into their own hands. Being well fortified after some serious drinking in Clonlara and led by John MacDonagh of Lettermore, about forty of them went on the rampage. A bottle was sent flying through a window and that signalled the start of the proceedings.

The MacDonagh brothers, the Flahertys and the Mannions, armed with sticks, stones and other missiles, attacked the occupants of the huts. They smashed everything before them and when the dust settled two people had to be hospitalized and a large number were treated for minor injuries. The gardaí from Clonlara were unable to restore order on their own, so their colleagues from O'Brien's Bridge were drafted in as reinforcements. Peace was eventually restored, but not before fourteen men had been arrested and transported to Limerick County jail in an open truck reminiscent of the Black and Tan times. When the case subsequently came to court evidence was given by other workers against the attackers, to the effect that the Connemaramen did a lot of overtime and that this caused jealously. Others stated that they were an uncivilized lot, not just because of their lack of English, but because they were a dirty crowd as they never washed! Both MacDonaghs were fined £2 and the others were fined £1 each for causing bodily injury and damage to property.

Another Galwayman, with a German-sounding name, Josef Bulistron, was in the wars in January 1929 for slashing the faces of two gardaí with a razor outside of Stritch's pub in Clonlara. He worked on the Scheme and had been discharged from a mental institution in the United States, but was deported from there when he was discovered to be insane. Strains of Ellis Island, but how times have changed.

The various bus companies bringing men from and to the city were also frequent visitors to the courts. The most common charge was that of over-crowding. For example, a fine of 7s. 6d. was imposed on Denis Humphreys, a conductor with the Irish Omnibus Company for having 40 passengers on a 26-seater bus. Michael Leo, a conductor with Flannery buses, appeared in court on the same occasion in January 1929, for two similar offences.

All news was pushed into second place by an horrific murder that took place in the days leading up to Christmas 1928. This became known as The Parteen Murder and it cast a dreadful pall over the whole area for the festive season and for the early months of the New Year. A German foreman, Jacob Kunz from Bavaria, was struck by an assailant with an iron bar at Parteen-a-lax while returning to Limerick. He died a short time afterwards. John Cox, an ex-soldier from Limerick, who formerly worked with Kunz, was later charged with the murder and robbery of £80 10s. from the Bavarian's pocket and of £409 10s. that he had sewn on his vest. The accused was charged in Limerick District Court on Saturday, 29 December and was remanded until 15 January 1929. In the meantime the money was found under a stone in Corbally. The case was heard in Dublin Central Criminal Court on 11 March. The trial lasted four days and the jury returned a guilty verdict. He was sentenced to hang on 11 April. The sentence was appealed and at the same time his family conducted a strenuous campaign to have him reprieved, but it was all to no avail and the sentence was made to stand. Cox was hanged on 25 April, 1929, just two months before the official opening of the Scheme.

From *High Tension: Life on the Shannon Scheme*, The Lilliput Press Ltd., 2004.

The Korean War
Michael Browner
(formerly O'Dwyer Villas)

WE spent the first month in Korea in reserve guarding POW's on the island of Koje – Koje Do in Korean. There had been a prisoner "disturbance" that summer where they had even held a Colonel hostage for a while. It was easy duty and mostly boring. Four hours in a sentry tower standing behind a 30 calibre machine gun staring into an empty compound can be that way, especially at night, especially when it was freezing. Then we were put "on line", manning bunkers along the MLR – the Main Line of Resistance. We were issued parkas and "Mickey Mouse" boots. They were clumsy for walking in but they were so well insulated that our feet would sweat on all but the coldest nights.

There was not much action on our part; an occasional patrol, maybe a fight around Pork Chop Hill, an exposed, morbid mound of mud which there was a movie made with Gregory Peck. Small arms were fired, mortars lobbed, grenades tossed, casualties inflicted, and screams heard. All of it was viciously noisy, but it didn't last long. No ground was given or taken. There was no movement on the 38th Parallel the whole ten months. I was there with the 17th Infantry. I can't say I was afraid, but you had to develop a healthy fear, not only from the enemy, but from our own too. The whole place was riddled with minefields.

My most memorable two days were spent with Sergeant 1st Class Smith, a combat engineer, whose job it was to check these minefields. The first day I was ordered to report to him for duty and he informed me that he would be inspecting an anti-tank minefield. He showed me how to read maps of the minefields; how to find the base mines that lead to other mines, and how to find the safe path, with the warning, "Nothing's safe out there." He talked with passion about booby traps and anti-tank and anti-personnel mines, which he referred to as 'Little Bastards.' But his efficiency and expertise made me yearn for his approval. At the end of the day he questioned me on what I had learnt and I told him what I knew about AP's (anti-personnel) and flares.

The anti-personnel mines consisted of two cylinders, one inside the other, buried so that the top is level with the surface. A little dirt was thrown over it so it was camouflaged, difficult to see. It was awakened by stepping directly on it or by tripping a wire so fine you could search on hands and knees and not find it. Either method blows the inner can 10-12 feet into the air where it explodes into god-knows-how-many pieces of shrapnel, each one capable of killing or maiming. "Cost effective," said the Sergeant. The flare is almost identical, except it doesn't explode. Instead the inner can shoots maybe 100 feet into the air before it ignites a brilliant white light that illuminates the area below as it floats down under a small, white parachute. It was not designed to kill. But it could.

I was prepared to tell him more how front line troops scatter illicit AP mines and flares in front of their positions as protection, as warning, so they feel a bit more secure. I'd tell him how they kill the unwary GI who takes a misstep, perhaps an unarmed young man wearing a red-cross armband answering to the cry, "Medic. Medic." I'd tell him that we call them Bouncing Betty's. "What else?" He interrupted me before alighting into his truck, I wanted to shine my boots on the spot, anything to please him. "Always be prepared," I said. He nods. "Always tell someone you're going out there. Always move slowly. Speed kills."

I'm on a roll now. "Overconfidence kills." He started up the vehicle. "Kill one, it happens; kill two, it shouldn't." I paused, expecting some friendly farewell. The gears crunched and he drove away. "Good job." He shouted back at me. Private 1st Class Browner was just praised by the most remarkable soldier I would ever meet. The next day after a few hours sleep I'm told Sergeant Smith wanted me again. A surge of elation swept through me, as I knew I had approval. We are to inspect more minefields, but not the same as the previous day, as "It's never the same." I was told. We climbed up an access trench to reach the MLR. Sergeant Smith warned the Infantry C.O. that we were going "out there." We left the safety of the main trench and cautiously made our way down a hill. We moved step by careful step. The ground was rough and covered with the remains of the previous summer's growth. Dead leaves, broken twigs and bare shrubs slowed our descent. All of it provided cover for stray tripwires and for the mines. Even with the Sergeant leading, this was still a tension filled process. My neck was stiff, I paused to rotate my head when I noticed a vague, residual image to my left. It was a pair of boots, or more accurately, a pair of soles, minus the boots, and beside them a long formation of bones, bleached white, I alerted the Sergeant. We found a skeleton.

The boots and the bones were about twenty yards away from us, the boots precisely arranged, heels and toes together as if at attention, as if this unknown soldier had grown jaded of war and wanted to sleep it off. It was a lonely scene, but now he had company. While the Sergeant went to get help, I sat and chatted with my new friend. I lit a Pall Mall and reached for a small bone, a finger perhaps, and it resisted. I pried it loose from the frozen ground and cleaned it with my bayonet. As I cleared some of the mud away I discovered bits of rotting fabric, some rusted with blood, and then something else. It was an arm band, tattered and dirty, but with the Medic's Red Cross, faded but clear. He was one of our own. A second trove turned out to be his wallet, which contained an army ID, his rank was Corporal, a driver's license from Minnesota, pictures of his family and girlfriend in front of a sturdy, red-bricked house, and a letter I did not read. The impersonal pile of bones was now a person.

I wondered how long it would be before Mom and Dad would learn that their son was no longer MIA, but KIA; that their hope was hopeless, their prayers wasted. How long before the phone call, "the Army regrets." I nod at the skeleton. "Corporal," I said, "You've created a heap of harm just because you didn't watch out for the bastard mines." But how was he to know. He'd never gone mining with Sergeant First Class Smith, Combat Engineer. The Sergeant returned with a ROK soldier carrying a folded stretcher, I helped him drag the stretcher back up the hill while the bones bounced and Sergeant Smith cleared the way.

I had always especially admired the medics because they were never afraid of danger, always ready to run when help was called for. I could imagine my medic, for he was mine then, heeding the screams for help and stumbling and crashing his way down the hill, no thoughts for mines. Did he hear the explosions? Did he die instantly? Or did he linger, fatally wounded, calling, "Medic, Medic," as if talking to himself? We dropped him at Battalion Headquarters and Sergeant Smith took me for dinner in the sergeant's dining room. As he drove away from me later, he looked back, "You're a strange one at times, a bit weird, but you're OK in my book." He smiled. "I hope you make rank." He waved and was gone and I never saw him again. I hope he was glad when I did make rank. Before I left Korea, I too was a Sergeant First Class.

As Sergeant First Class Browner, I watched one of my own men being killed by a friendly fire. It hit him in the head and ripped his eyes and brains out. Sergeant Smith had been right, deadly right – "You never know what's out there." The following week, July 27, 1953, the truce was signed and the war ended. For years I couldn't get this man out of my mind until I finally visited his grave in Kentucky. I left a note, which was found by his aunt, and his wife later contacted me. I have since been to visit her and finally found a sense of peace.

Some morning on sentry duty I would gaze over the valley, at the hills all covered in icy white-blue frost, so silent, so peaceful, nothing was stirring. It was like a Christmas scene, not a killing field. And I would wonder, "Why don't we lay down arms and leave the trenches? Why don't we walk across the valley to meet in the rising mist? Share cigarettes? Swap souvenirs? Admire family photographs? Maybe in the mystery of the mist we'd find a common language. Why don't we walk away together, disappear into the field of mists; go home or wherever our hearts takes us, so when the call to arms sounds over the battlefields, there's no one there to hear it? I'm reminded now of a Vietnam era, pacifist fantasy: "suppose they gave a war and nobody came?" Suppose.

From *While Mem'ry Brings us Back Again:* A Collection of Memories produced by the Aisling Community Center, New York, 2006.

Jane Austen's Limerick Romance
Harriet O'Carroll

WHEN Jane Austen was twenty-one, she lived with her rector father; her mother and her sister Cassandra in Steventon, Hampshire. It was here that she had a brief romance with the son of an Army officer from Limerick. It was a pivotal time in Jane's life. Cassandra had become engaged, all her brothers had left home to become clergymen or officers in the Royal Navy. It was expected that Jane would either marry one of the eligible young men of the locality or stay at home to care for her hypochondriac mother. Jane had already been writing for some time, she considered that her early scribblings were amusements for the family. However, a first draft of *Sense and Sensibility* had been completed and it seems she considered the possibility that she could earn money from her writing.

But at Christmas 1795 Cassandra went to stay with her prospective in-laws and Jane was left free to enjoy the weekly dances of the neighbourhood without any sobering warnings from an elder sister. One of her best friends at the time was the wife of a neighbouring rector, Isaac Peter George Lefroy. Anne Lefroy was twenty-six years older than Jane and Ashe Rectory, her home, was within easy walk of Jane's home. This Christmas, Anne had been asked to invite her husband's nephew,

Thomas Langlis Lefroy, to spend Christmas in Steventon. Tom was tall, fair, a good dancer and but one month younger than Jane.

Tom's father, Anthony Peter Lefroy, was an army officer who had settled in Limerick and married an Irish squire's daughter, Anne Gardiner from Co. Clare – the couple being blessed with five daughters and five sons. The Lefroys were Huguenots, descendants of Antoine Loffroy from Cambrai in Flanders, who had sought refuge in England in the sixteenth century and settled at Canterbury about 1587. Tom's grandfather, Anthony, born in 1703, had gone to Tuscany, joined the banking firm of Peter Langlois and wisely married the boss's daughter. They sent their two sons to England to be educated, Isaac becoming a clergyman while Anthony chose a military career, joining the 33rd Regiment of Foot at Limerick as an ensign. He subsequently transferred to the 9th Light Dragoons, becoming Colonel of the regiment. In 1792 Col. Lefroy, now retired, and his family took over occupancy of a newly built house in George's Street, Limerick – the house subsequently becoming No. 108 George's (O'Connell) Street. It remained the family home until 1820 when the lease was offered for sale in March that year following Col. Lefroy's death in 1819.

Early on in Anthony's military career disaster struck the family fortune when his father's bank in Tuscany crashed, causing problems for the young officer. In those days advancement in the army depended on the support of an independent income and this was now compromised because Anthony's marriage to Anne Gardiner had been performed in secret by the regimental chaplain, a union considered irregular by Anthony's wealthy uncles. To placate the relatives, the couple went through a second, public wedding ceremony in 1774 in St. Mary's Cathedral, Limerick. Five sons blessed this second marriage.

The eldest, Tom, who had been born on 8 January 1776 in Co. Limerick, attracted the attention of great-uncle Benjamin Longlois. Since Tom appeared intelligent, likeable and compliant and had the advantage of being male, Uncle Benjamin agreed to pay for this education. This kind offer though, was accompanied by the injunction that if Tom did not give satisfaction, neither his brothers nor his sisters, nor his cousins, would be similarly helped. So the family's fortunes depended heavily on Tom's behaviour.

At the age of fourteen he went to Trinity College, Dublin, to study law (making a three day journey from Limerick to Dublin). Studious and popular, he debated against Robert Emmet and was contemporaneous with Tom Moore (of the Melodies). In his final year, 1795, he won three gold medals for debating and awarded a B.A. But the effort proved too much, his health was affected and he suffered from sore eyes. That Christmas he was sent to his uncle at Ashe Rectory in Hampshire for a holiday. The parish had been bought for Isaac (who was more generally known as George) by benevolent Uncle Benjamin as a way of ensuring a living for him. The web of family responsibility and financial obligation was tightly spun around Tom Lefroy.

So the young Irishman, who was described as serious, intelligent and shy, arrived in the small English village of Steventon just in time for the Christmas dancing season. When Jane met him there at a ball in Manydown Manor he impressed her as a 'very good looking, good humoured, pleasant young man' and they were drawn to each other. Jane freely admits in a letter to Cassandra, dated 9 January, that her behaviour had attracted attention to herself in local society. 'I am almost afraid to tell you how my Irish friend and I behaved', she writes with typical good humour. 'Imagine to yourself everything most profligate and shocking in the way of dancing and sitting down together.' That Tom Lefroy had made a favourable impression on her is indicated by the fact that although she mentions a number of other young gentlemen during the course of her letter, she opens with, 'in the first place I hope you will live twenty-three years longer. Tom Lefroy's birthday was yesterday, so that you are very near of age.'

The level of teasing directed at Tom by his cousins over his fondness for Jane was so severe, it seems, that when Jane and her mother called at Ashe to visit the Lefroys the young Limerickman made himself scarce. However, he did call to see her at Steventon and Jane records that he wore a light coloured coat and that they discussed the novel *Tom Jones* by Henry Fielding. But Jane saw that the romance might be short-lived, for she informs her sister that 'I can expose myself however, only once more, because he leaves the country soon after next Friday, on which we are to have a dance at Ashe after all.' Shortly before his departure, the Limerickman, as token of his esteem for Jane and as a momento, allowed his likeness to be drawn by a young man by the name of John Warren, a friend of Jane's, who delivered the sketch to her on Tom's behalf.

Jane Austen's next letter to Cassandra, written Thursday 16 January, shows Jane eagerly awaiting the following night's dance. 'I look forward with great impatience to it, as I rather expect to receive an offer from my friend in the course of the evening. I shall refuse him, however, unless he promises to give away his white coat.' However, Jane seems simultaneously to try to reassure Cassandra about her feelings for Tom, to both declare and to deny that she cares about him. 'Tell Mary (a friend) she writes, 'that I make over Mr. Heartley and all his estate for her sole use and benefit in future, and not only him, but all my other admirers into the bargain wherever she can find them, even the kiss which C. Powlett wanted to give me, as I mean to confine myself in future to Mr. Tom Leffroy, for whom I do not care sixpence.'

The following day, however, Jane's mood had changed. Emotionally upset, she writes in a postscript, 'Friday – at length the day is come on which I am to flirt my last with Tom Lefroy, and when you receive this it will be over. My tears flow as I write of the melancholy idea.'

Anne Lefroy had become extremely dismayed by the friendship that had arisen between Jane and her nephew. They had known each other a little less than a month, but at the time alliances were frequently formed very rapidly and Jane's expectation of 'an offer' showed a relationship that was fast developing. Anne was well aware that a clergyman's daughter with no connections in the legal profession, or dowry of consequence, was not at all the sort of bride that Uncle Benjamin would welcome for Tom. She blamed Tom, believing that he was flirting with Jane and might break her heart. The Irish Lefroys later took the opposite attitude and blamed Jane for distracting the sober Tom. It seems clear that there was an attraction between the two young people but the circumstances of his responsibilities to his family, and her 'unsuitability', forced them part. It was apparently Anne Lefroy who was instrumental in sending Tom away, for her sons said later that their mother had taken this action so 'that no more mischief might be done.' She probably believed that she was acting in the best interests of both Jane, her friend, and her nephew, who, if left to their own passions, might end up a penniless pair.

Tom finished his studies in London, at great-uncle Benjamin's command and returned to Ireland and was called to the Bar in 1797. That same year he became engaged to Mary Paul, only daughter and heiress of Jeffrey Paul of Silver Spring, County Wexford. They were married in Abergavenny, Ghent, in 1799, and had four sons, three daughters and numerous grandchildren. His legal career was distinguished and prosperous and he is described in the Dictionary of National Biography as a 'typical Irish protestant tory' of the period and opposed Catholic Emancipation. He became King's Counsel in 1806, King's Serjeant (a barrister of the highest rank) in 1808, and was elected Member of Parliament for Trinity College in 1831, a seat he held until 1841. The pinnacle of his career came in 1852 when he was appointed Lord Chief Justice of Ireland, a post he held until his retirement in 1866. He built Carrigglass Manor in Co. Longford, a Tudor-Gothic Revival house, designed by Kilkenny architect Daniel Robertson and built 1837-40; prior to that, Lefroy lived in his own house in Leeson Street, Dublin.

The story of his relationship with Jane Austen was known within the family. Shortly before he died in 1869, at the age of 93, a nephew, Edward Preston Lefroy, asked him had he been in love with Jane Austen and according to a letter the nephew wrote to James Edward Austen-Leigh on 16 August, 1870, Tom 'said in so many words that he was in love with her, although he qualifies his confession by saying it was boyish love. As this occurred in a friendly and private conversation, I feel some doubt whether I ought to make it public.'

This comment was occasioned by the fact that James Austen-Leigh, a nephew of Jane Austen, was writing a book about his famous aunt, publishing *A Memoir of Jane Austen* in 1870; a title that appeared the following year in a second, enlarged edition. Accordingly, Austen-Leigh adulterated this intriguing insight into his aunt's private life by saying that Tom Lefroy in his extreme old age did sometimes speak of Jane, 'as one to be much admired, and not easily forgotten by those who had ever known her.' Tom Lefroy's fond memories of Jane, and his confession of 'boyish love' made some seventy years after the event, clearly indicates that the young woman had made a very strong impression on him – so who knows what might have happened if Tom had not been sent away from Jane's company.

Jane's feelings for Tom seem to have run much deeper. Two years after he had left Hampshire she mentions him in a letter to Cassandra. She says that Mrs. Anne Lefroy, who had been away visiting relatives, had visited her in November, 1798. At first, Jane found out nothing about Tom, as Anne would not mention him and she writes, 'I was too proud to make any enquiries but on my father's afterwards asking where he was, I learnt that he had gone back to London on his way to Ireland where he is called to the Bar and means to practice.' The fact that Tom Lefroy was called to the Bar in 1797 and Jane only learnt of this in late 1798, indicates the extent to which the Lefroys had kept Jane ignorant of Tom's whereabouts. In recent years it has emerged that after his departure, Jane copied out Irish love songs and kept that up when too proud to enquire about him.

Tom left Steventon in January 1796, and Jane started writing *Pride and Prejudice* in August of that year. It's tempting to see the shy intelligent young Irishman in the reserved Mr. Darcy and to imagine that she gave her hero the one item her Irish friend lacked, that is, a large independent fortune. The heroine of *Pride and Prejudice* has a favourite aunt who is ready with comfort and good advice. Her name is Gardiner, which, by coincidence, was Tom's mother's maiden name. One can also wonder if the fact that Tom's family had contained five sisters in a row suggested a fictional possibility to Jane, which she realised in the five husband hunting Bennet sisters.

There are no personal comments in her letters to indicate that she ever felt betrayed or bitter about Tom. There are a few references to Ireland in her novels, all but one is positive. In *Watsons*, the unfinished novel she worked on before her father died, an older lady with 8-9,000£ to her name, is seduced into marriage by a flattering, fortune hunting Irishman by the name of Captain O'Brien. But in *Emma*, Jane Fairfax's best friend marries Mr. Dixon and goes to Ireland to be 'happy and settled' at Mr. Dickson's country seat at Ballycraig. Mr. Dickson does not actually appear in the novel, he is a very, very minor character off-stage somewhere in Ireland, but he is described by the author as a 'most amiable, charming young man . . . Jane was quite longing to go to Ireland from his account of things.'

Also in *Emma*, when Frank Churchill sends a present of a pianoforte as an offering of love to Jane Fairfax, to whom he is secretly engaged, he also sends a music sheet of new Irish melodies. This, as part of his elaborate 'cover story' to Highbury society that the instrument had come from a Col. Campbell who had recently travelled to Ireland; but the introduction of 'Irish melodies' into the love story is perhaps further evidence of the author's romantic memories of Tom Lefroy. As Frank Churchill says of the music sent with the gift, 'I honour that part of the attention particularly; it shows it to have been so thoroughly from the heart. Nothing hastily done, nothing incomplete. True affection only could have prompted it.' *Emma* was written between January 1814 and March 1815, almost 20 years since Jane had last seen Tom.

Persuasion was Jane's last novel, when she knew she was seriously ill. In it an older woman with the best of intentions breaks up a romance between Anne Elliot, the heroine, and a young man who had nothing to recommend him but himself. Anne regrets the influence of her friend and the novel gives her the chance to retrieve her youthful mistake. Her lover is drawn back on overhearing her defend the constancy of a woman's love. Anne Elliot says, 'All the privilege I claim for my own sex (it is not a very enviable one; you need not covet it) is that of loving longest, when existence or when hope is gone. In the same novel Anne Elliot is gratified to hear someone say of her loved one in passing, 'a very fine young man! Irish I dare say.' It's quite an unexpected line considering that there are no other references to Ireland in the novel.

Cassandra and Jane both remained single, they lived together with their mother and a family friend, Martha Lloyd. (Cassandra's fiancée had died in the West Indies of yellow fever in 1797). Cassandra told a niece of another gentleman who fell in love with Jane, but who died before he could propose. Jane herself died at the age of forty-two. She was not forced to remain single. She received another proposal from Harris Bigg-Wither, the brother of a friend, which would have made her and her family rich. She accepted it in the evening, but the following morning she changed her mind. It looks as if she believed her own advice to a niece: 'Anything is to be preferred to marriage without love.'

From *Georgian Limerick, 1714-1845*, Vol. II. A Limerick Civic Trust Publication, 2000.

The Brave Shannon Pilots

PILOTING vessels between Limerick City and the sea is a highly skilled operation. Long before Limerick Harbour Commissioners installed navigational aids, the intrepid Shannon pilots demonstrated their intimate knowledge of tides and currents in the winding channel to Limerick City. Pilots on the Shannon have a long family tradition with four to five generations providing a continuing link as river pilots right up to the present day. Over the years, Shannon pilots have been celebrated in song and story and in 1978 featured in the world famous National Geographical Magazine. Many romantic stories are told of the lives of pilots in the nineteenth century, whose work was hard and dangerous as they braved the changing moods of the Shannon Estuary to make a part-time living from piloting sailing ships and the early steam ships to and from Limerick.

Since 1823, The Limerick Harbour Commissioners have been the Pilotage Authority for the entire Shannon Estuary from Limerick City to Loop Head/Kerry Head including the navigable waters of all tributaries and inlets. The renowned *Scattery men* who provided pilotage service inward to Limerick City settled on Scattery Island in the 1830's. Some pilots from Kilbaha salvaged *Windsor Castle* and with the proceeds from their efforts purchased Scattery Island. With two families already settled on the island – the Morans and the Hehirs – the population was increased significantly by the addition of the Brennans, Griffins, McMahons, Melicans and Scanlons. A teacher was brought from the mainland to tutor children in homes prior to the building of a school in 1895. In the 1920's there was twenty-seven pilots on Scattery with more than sixty-five children attending the school.

The Scattery Pilots were hardy, rugged seafarers, who ventured out as far west as the Blasket Islands in currachs (locally called canoes) which were generally built at Kilrush or Crusheen and were preferred to ketch rigged pilot boats formerly stationed at Carrigaholt. Frequently there was more risk to life and limb in boarding or disembarking from a vessel than in the sea trip out to the ship.

When boarding a vessel a pilot had to be hoisted onto the deck of a vessel by means of a rope tied around his body and in some conditions could find himself being dragged through the sea prior to boarding. On disembarking and landing in the canoe, there was risk too of serious damage to the skin of the small craft. To minimise the risk of serious accidents of this type, the canoe was heavily layered with hay to cushion the impact of the pilot on landing.

The Scattery men had their own special ritual of dedication when initiating a new canoe. The crafts were taken clockwise around the island and at a certain point went in a full circle ten times when traditional prayers were recited. Canoes were used up to the 1920's. Records show that of a pilotage charge of £4.10s. on a vessel, 10 shillings was for the canoe.

It was nothing unusual for a pilot to maintain a watch for a particular vessel for several days in order to ensure he got the job. Prior to the introduction of tugs in the 1890's, pilots could sometimes spend three weeks aboard a sailing ship before arriving in Limerick. Pilots also supplemented their income by crewing for short periods on vessels trading in and out of the Shannon.

Pilots operate a type of co-operative; their earnings are pooled and subsequently divided in accordance with the arrangements laid down in the bye-laws. However, anomalies have occurred from time to time as is recorded in the 1930 report of the Port and Harbour Tribunal. The Tribunal reported that an arrangement had existed for a considerable time which resulted in an inequitable sharing out of pilotage earnings. Under procedures then pertaining, a vessel which failed to obtain a pilot at Scattery Island picked up a stand-by at Tarbert. The pilots in Tarbert, having no guarantee of regular work, had negotiated an arrangement whereby a fixed amount from all pilotage charges paid by vessels was set aside to pay them. The Ports Tribunal pointed out that the arrangement which had been in place for three generations was providing the Tarbert pilots with incomes which were almost three times greater than those of the regular pilots, whose average earnings at that time amounted to £112.7s.2d. per year. The anomaly of course had to be rectified and new arrangements were drawn up for division of earnings.

Social and political change swept through Irish society in the later years of the nineteenth century and in the opening decades of the twentieth century leading up to the Great War of 1914-1918. Reflecting these changing times and trends, one of the pilots licensed by the Limerick Harbour Commissioners, decided to leave his regular, hazardous employment and carve out a new career for himself in local and national politics. Michael Joyce was a third generation Shannon pilot, shipwrecked four times in his five years of seafaring before becoming a Shannon pilot at the age of 26 in March 1878. He built up his political base in Limerick on a variety of fronts. The chairman of the meeting which founded Garryowen Ruby Club, he played for the first fifteen as well as with the Limerick County selection.

With Rev. Robert Ambrose, he was one of the founders of the Sarsfield Branch of the National League and was also prominent in St. Michael's Temperance Society which fostered one of Limerick famous rowing clubs. His popularity had grown steadily in the community by the time the 1899 local elections took place. Arising from legislation passed in the previous year, when voting rights were extended to a wider section of the populace, Michel Joyce headed the poll in the Customs House Ward. His large vote helped Labour to sweep eight candidates on to the Limerick

Corporation in what the *Limerick Leader* dubbed a *people's parliament*.

In the General Election of the following year, Michael Joyce caused a huge upset when winning 2521 votes against the 474 votes for Francis Kearney (solicitor), taking a Westminster seat for the Irish Parliamentary Party. He held his seat for twenty years, became Mayor of Limerick for two terms in 1905/6. Elected a Harbour Commissioner in 1899, he resided over meetings of the Commissioners, on many occasions particularly during his term as Mayor.

In 1913 Joyce became President of the UK Pilots Association. At the age of 67, the Limerick Member or Parliament was shipwrecked and rescued yet again when he was a passenger on the S.S. *Leinster* which was torpedoed and sunk in the Irish Sea in 1918. He had intended contesting his parliamentary seat in the 1918 General Election but having regard to the emergence of Sinn Fein, he decided to stand down in favour of P. Colivett (Sinn Fein) who was returned unopposed. He died in his home *The Moorings*, O'Connell Avenue on January 9th, 1941, in his ninetieth year.

The seafaring expertise of the Shannon Pilots was accorded historic recognition when a mariner from one of the pilot families of West Clare attained distinction as a key member of Admiral Byrd's expedition to the North Pole in 1926. Michael Brennan, known as *Michael Ruadh* in his native Carrigaholt, started his seafaring career at the age of 15 in 1901. At the age of 24 he was he was a Master mariner, in charge of his own vessel and settled in New York. He became a US citizen and switched from sailing vessels to steamships when he served in the US Navy in World War I.

At the conclusion of hostilities he joined the American Republic Line, trading between the US and South America. As Port Captain of New York, he was involved with every vessel of the company fleet and its crewing. In 1926 Admiral Byrd selected Captain Brennan to manage the marine side of the Polar expedition, which involved handling delicate equipment, including the aircraft used in the first air crossing of the North Pole. Under the command of Captain Brennan, the *Chantieforde* sailed from New York in 1926, carrying the Fokker aircraft *Josephine Forde* to King's Bay, Spitzbergen, from whence Pilot Floyd Bennett flew Admiral Byrd to the North Pole and back on May 9th, 1926.

Captain Brennan was a member of the Byrd party, which was accorded a ticker tape reception in a parade down Broadway on their triumphant return to New York. He was one of the last survivors of the expedition party on his death in July 1976.

From *A Rising Tide, the Story of Limerick Harbour*,
published by Limerick Harbour Commissioners, 1994.

The Bonny Baby Competition
Fergal Keane

ON my first afternoon at the *Leader* I was taken on a tour of the 'stone' – the lair of printers which sat at the back of the building, up rickety stairs and down several narrow corridors. Along with the typing and shorthand lessons I was expected to take, the time spent on the stone was geared to teaching me the nuts and bolts of the newspaper trade. The paper was in its last days under the regime of hot metal. Stories and headlines were still made up in lead, then hammered into place on the page before being placed on the ancient printing machines.

The stone was the preserve of the printers. They were tough, suspicious Limerick men who would have regarded the arrival of a Corkman in their midst with moderate alarm, fearing perhaps that I was the advance guard of an invasion from the south. But when it was mentioned that I was John B. Keane's nephew they softened. Through Ireland his name acted as a passport to welcome.

The age of lead was noisy, dirty, time-consuming and glorious. But it would be gone in a few years. I had entered newspapers at a time of rapid change. In Britain the great printing unions would soon by humbled by Murdoch; the cold wind blew across the Irish Sea and their Irish counterparts were forced to accept radically altered working conditions and redundancies. Computers would simplify printing and accelerate the process of newsgathering and production. I didn't know it then, but I was witnessing the end of the industrial age in newspapers.

Mr first writings were modest. They were little stories based on press conferences: a junior minister's pronouncements on road safety; a row over licensing hours; a new route from Shannon airport to New York. When my first by-line appeared I proudly sent a copy to my mother and grandmother. John B called me from Listowel with congratulations. I loved turning up at press conferences and announcing myself as the *Leader* man: the paper was well respected and influential. Frequently, if you were late for an event it would be delayed until your arrival.

Some time in my first year I went to Halligan with a bright idea for boosting the circulation of our Tuesday evening tabloid edition.

'Why not have a Bonny Baby competition?' I asked.

'As long as you run it and make sure none of the pictures get lost. Baby pictures are important to the women of Limerick,' the editor replied.

The competition was a success. Circulation rose moderately and there were slaps on the back for me, even from the normally acerbic Liddy. I cannot remember which ham-fed cherub from the city of Limerick won the prize, but I do know that misfortune soon followed. I had placed the pictures of the finalists in a shoe box and given them to the photographer working with me on the competition. He later claimed that he had given the box back to me, which may well have been true. But somewhere between us both the box was lost. Soon the switchboard screamed with aural assaults of furious mothers. The girls in the font office were tormented. Worse still, one of the mothers was a paper seller with a stall directly in front of the *Leader* office. For several months I slunk in and out of the office by the back door, a skulking figure hurrying along the Limerick backstreets.

In the editorial office I was frequently reminded of my place. Wind-ups were part of my initiation, I was sent to find a rubber mallet, a glass hammer, the 'eye-kit' for photographs in which people squinted at the camera flash. 'That allows the boys back on the stone to open the eyes,' was the helpful explanation. I asked for this device at one of Limerick's leading photographic agencies, only to be laughed onto the street. 'Was it Liddy sent you,' the proprietor asked. In this case Liddy was innocent.

Another reporter was rumoured to have been sent to a City Council meeting with an important letter for the city manager. It was the week before St Patrick's Day, an important fact in the entertainment that followed. My colleague raced breathlessly into the chamber and approached the Manager's secretary. The manager was a powerful figure. He allowed the politicians to think they ran the city but he drew up the plans and signed the cheques.

The secretary passed the letter to the Manager who paused in the outrolling of some councillor's speech to read the contents. He began to heave with laughter then passed the letter back to his secretary who gave it back to the reporter. I will spare him the embarrassment and substitute a different name. The message read as follows:

'My name is John Breen and I want my arse painted green for St. Patrick's Day.'
The reporter quickly made his excuse and left.

From *All of These People: A Memoir*, Harper-Collins, 2005.

Does anyone give a Curse?
Rev. Frank Moriarty, C.C.

JIMMY Walsh hefted the twin burdens of his shoulders and munched his knuckles. The nails on his fingers had been chewed deep below the quick. He screwed his eyes and shook his head as if 'twas full of chickens coming home to roost. 'I don't smoke,' he said, "tisn't good for you.' He wanted his fare to Dublin. Wiping perspiration from his forehead, he laid his palm on the table between us and outlines of moisture collected into his finger prints. Jimmy Walsh, 28 years old, single, has no fixed abode. He talks:

'I don't recall much of when I was young. My sisters' names: Eileen, Margaret and Bridget. I'm the only one that was ever in trouble. Mitching from school started it. My father used flake me when he found out. But he couldn't make me cry; only once when I was drunk. I was never any good at the books. Then I was caught – stealing a bicycle.

'The Court said my father couldn't look after me and I was sent away to the Reformatory. My mother was crying. That's the hardest thing I ever saw in my life, her crying, and I wanted just to run away forever. I was about ten or eleven and they gave me two years. You had lessons all day and I remember you got a number and 'twas on everything you had so's you'd know it belonged to you. When I went home things were hard, all the other kids jeering and saying you were put away.

'I was sent to the Industrial School then for robbing gas meters and stealing a case of lemonade from a van. We had to get up for Mass every morning. You couldn't pretend even you were sick and you'd wash in freezing cold water. Some of the lads ran away and we cheered. They were brought back always, even the two who stole a car and drove to Sligo in it. They crashed into a bus. We had to wash the floors and polish everyplace and that was alright I suppose for them that were orphans.

'I got one holiday but my father wouldn't let me home. So I ran away. I was caught after a few hours, and I was taken to the hall where the whole school was gathered and I got thirty strokes of the cane. Then all my head was shaved badly. Some of the other boys said I was right tough because I talked while I was working and gave the Brother guff. I never got any letters from home or a parcel. I don't think that was fair – me having nothing to share with the others. When my time was up, my father said I was man enough to go fend for myself and that I wasn't to go near them at home. 'Tis a hard thing to have your own people say that. It makes you afraid that you haven't any place to call your own, no place to creep into and hide and to be alone and safe.

'There was a priest said to me the other day, 'You should be shamed of yourself, a fine, sturdy-looking young fella like you, begging like this. Go and get a steady job for yourself.' Ashamed he said I should be. But he gave me five bob and told me not to come back. Why didn't he want me back and still give me the five bob? I took it.

'I could get no job that suited me, what with my record and all. So one day I met a man who was looking for workers to go picking spuds in Scotland. He paid our fare over. They gave us plenty of grub, cuts of bread, and big cans of as much as you could drink. We'd have to be in the potato fields before you could see a stem in the morning's dark. The tractors had their headlights on. 'Twas rough labour when your hands got cut-sore and red raw with the cold, that you could hardly wash the wet clay off them. The bending was cruel on the back and at night you'd be so bone weary that you'd want to sleep with all your clothes on. I stuck it only two months. All the few pounds I got went on coming home.

'I heard my mother had died but I couldn't face the funeral. When I remember her 'tis to see her darning socks for me. I find that sad – just all her love woven in thread for me to have. I prayed for her though – the Rosary, I think it made some difference to her, don't you?

'I got a job with a circus. You'd be on the road at all hours after striking the tent. I must have seen every town worth talking about in Ireland. Hard work 'twas surely, but a great and cheap way to see the countryside. That was only for the four summer months, and one day in Galway they told me to go. I stayed around the West for a while working odd days for farmers. They didn't pay much but with a fair bed secure in the barn and a few bob in the pocket. But with harvesting and turf-saving time over, I had to wandering again. The West is a hungry place and wet with it. When the hunger hits you and you drenched and drowneded, you think you'll faint and, maybe, die in a ditch.

'I hitched a lift to Dublin. I got a lift from a bishop once, went right out of his way, and then gave me a pound. I was in mortal dread all the time I'd slip a curse of something, and that he'd make a reddening. Thinking back he was a kind man and I don't think he'd have minded a bit.

'I was sleeping rough in the hedges and the fields, anyplace I could bed down for a warm. Then one day I was so famished I tried to steal a box of tomatoes from a shop. The Guards caught me breaking in and I was sent to Mountjoy for a month. The grub wasn't any good and 'twas fierce to be in the dark at night thinking about too many things. They gave me sixpence a day for working at sweeping up the yard.

'When I came out I stayed in a hostel. They don't charge only a shilling and in the morning you can get lashings of bread and margarine and big mugs of tea. In the winter the chapels are the warmest places and no one bothers you drying up at one of the radiators. I had a lot of jobs, sweeping up in a cattle mart, and digging in a gravel pit, and road work with the Council, but I couldn't stick it. Then I came to Shannon. They said there is plenty of work there, but I couldn't find it.

'People tell you, 'why can't you work for your living?' I stayed a few nights in the Home. They are full up so I had to sleep on the floor with two blankets the nightman gave me. Another man, casual like me there, was drunk and he kept wanting to fight me. I don't think they'll let me back. I saw one of my sisters in the street, but I didn't know where to go with my face. She's married. He's in the bank or insurance or something. I couldn't be a bother to them, they have their own troubles I suppose. Sometimes because people are your own family is the reason to have nothing to do with them. But it's sad not to have a place of you own, even a bed. 'Tis hard to beg for it too.'

His lips quivered and I could see his jaw muscles twitch and knot under the seams of skin. His fingers curled as though to receive a gift. Tears leaked into his voice. But he needed more than a handkerchief or a shoulder to cry on. And there are so many like him. You step out of their way on a city street; you see them slouched in the mouth of a laneway, looking with continental distance in their eyes and balanced on the fine life-line between destitution and crime and the madness of their terrible loneliness.

And nobody gives a damn.

From *Catholic Life*, Summer, 1968.

Words spoken at the graveside of Jim Kemmy
Mount Saint Lawrence Cemetery, Limerick, 29 September, 1997.
Gearóid O Tuathaigh

WE have come here today to take our leave of a man whose life, though sadly cut short too soon, was lived to the full. A man of many talents and varied accomplishments, Jim Kemmy's life was yet all of a piece. Stonemason and socialist, trade unionist and political activist, writer and historian, parliamentarian and humanist, Jim Kemmy was, by any standards, a big man. Big in heart and big in frame, he was a towering presence in the life of Limerick for more than three decades, and, to many others elsewhere in Ireland and beyond, he was very often the voice of Limerick; in the sense that not only the cadences of accent and idiom but the very recounting of the city's proud history and the right of its people to fair play – in the Dáil and in the media – assumed a compelling force and authenticity when spoken by Jim. In this context, it is only right to remark on the widespread feelings of pride that attached to his election – after a long wait – as Mayor of Limerick.

In the days that have passed since Jim's death many attributes have been paid to his significant contributions to Irish political life, and in particular to the warm and humane dimension he gave to the cause he championed. These tributes have been genuine and just. Others, more qualified than I, have spoken of his political 'witness', as it were, in Ireland, for almost three decades of unprecedented change in Irish society.

Many indeed were the causes championed and battles fought in those decades, as those whose views he challenged and those whose views he changed can well testify. Frequently engaged in bruising controversy, his steady commitment to a socialist and libertarian view of human fulfilment and dignity never slackened or wavered throughout a political career that was never routine, never complacent, never opportunist. I feel very honoured that Jim should have indicated a wish before he died that I should add a few words at his graveside to the many tributes that have already been paid to his memory by political and other friends and colleagues.

I think he would have expected me to speak of him as an historian and as a very remarkable Limerick man, and it is in these terms that I will speak of him for a few moments before we depart from this grave. Jim Kemmy had an insatiable interest in the history of this city, and an inexhaustible energy for researching, reclaiming and sharing with his own, and with the wider public, his knowledge of and his enthusiasm for local history. And, of course, his interest and knowledge and enthusiasm was rooted in a boundless affection for his native place. He knew every path and pavement, every lane and court, every row, bow and alleyway of this city (and he knew well also 'Limerick in exile' – in Kilkee).

The time and dedication he gave to researching, understanding, preserving and publishing the history of his native city and its people constitutes a truly heroic service. The work which he performed on the many committees and societies on which he served (or the cultural initiatives which he frequently launched) – relating to labour, history, literary and artistic events, the preservation of historic monuments and buildings, the theatre, and many other examples – this work has undoubtedly left its mark on the life of the city.

It was the Welsh scholar, E. Estyn Evans, who first suggested that the 'personality' of any place was principally constituted by three main elements: habitat, heritage and history. So far as this city is concerned, it is hard for me to think of another in this, or indeed in any earlier generation, who gave such devotion to researching and understanding these elements of the personality of Limerick, or who scrutinised that personality with such unsparing candour and celebrated it with such unashamed pride as did Jim Kemmy. In short, he was steeped in the habitat, heritage and history of Limerick.

Jim Kemmy was an historian engagé. He held his own views firmly and he expressed them clearly, not to say trenchantly. But it was neither necessary, nor was it always the case, that one had to agree with his views in order to recognise in him (as other historians did) that stubborn refusal to defer to received wisdom, to the official rhetoric of 'authority', or to any dogma (whatever its ideological origins) which failed to take account of the frailty, the longings, the complexities and the contradictions of ordinary human beings, buffeted by history and circumstances, by their own hopes, fears and desires. He showed an uncompromising scruple for evidence in support of any and all historical claims.

It is his publications on history that we come closest, I believe, to the core of that passion, idealism and energy that kept the mighty engines of enquiry pumping away over the decades. *The Old Limerick Journal*, which he edited, the many individual contributions that were his own (including the study of the Limerick Soviet and numerous essays in the Journal), and the wonderful *Limerick Anthology* published at Christmas 1996 – these will surely be an enduring monument to Jim Kemmy, the historian and writer.

May I, very briefly, illustrate his characteristic style, by referring to one or two exemplary excerpts from his writings. Here is his editorial in the summer 1982 edition of the Old Limerick Journal; it is entitled, In Praise of Local History:

"For most people, once they leave school, local history is the most common and popular form of history they come into contact with. The reason is easily explainable. Local history can often be more interesting and more personal than other varieties. And readers will be immediately familiar with the names of people, places and buildings in their own locality.

Local history can serve other important functions. The broad canvas of man's historical development could well be described as a gigantic jigsaw. The documentation of history can be likened to the piecing together of a series of the small parts that go to make up the whole seamless picture. So the efforts of local historians can be a reliable source of materials for the general historian.

A relatively small number of dedicated enthusiasts throughout the country have given generously of their time and energies in the cause of local history. Their work of documenting and interpreting the story of their own people and places has added much to our understanding of history. Their quiet labours among forgotten records have brought clarity and light to hitherto dark and obscure corners of the past . . . .

Recent years have brought increased awareness and appreciation of what local history should be all about. While it must take into account of the passing parade of prelates, merchant princes and landlords across the centuries, the world of the common man – the story of the countless hundreds of thousands of ordinary people who struggled for survival and left little wealth or glory behind them."

This is a good example of what I've referred to: firm views plainly stated, the enthusiasm for knowledge, and the commitment to investigating and presenting the evidence, and letting readers reach their own conclusions. A further example of this characteristic style can be found in Jim's Preface to the Limerick Anthology:

"In his preface to his History, John Ferrar gives this attractive description of the vocation of the historian:

"To the love of literary pursuits the world is indebted for the preservation of its antiquities, so leading to an enlightened mind. The honest desire of rescuing our History from oblivion, of transmitting remarkable events to posterity, supports the historian in his undertaking, renders him superior to every difficulty, and repays the toll of reading and collating a number of manuscripts and old books."

This summarises succinctly the essence of the commitment that inspired not only the Anthology but the entire life's work in history and writing. But it seems to me that it does even more. The tone and vocabulary – 'the common bond of enthusiasm and tolerance' that he recognised in John Ferrar and Kate O'Brien; the sense of moral purpose conveyed by the word 'toil', in this context of historical research: these seem to me to be especially revealing. They place Jim Kemmy within a particular radical, dissenting tradition of the broad labour movement of the 19th century, especially but not exclusively to Britain. It is the tradition of Kier Hardie and Durham miners, of working men's reading societies and mechanics' institutes, of William Thompson and the early leaders of the Irish trade union and labour movement. Among contemporary historians, it is the company of E.P. Thompson and of Ralph Samuel, and others, determined to rescue the story and struggles of the common people from the terrible condescension of posterity.

In a certain sense, though utterly unsympathetic to cant or slack sentimentality, Jim Kemmy was a labour 'romantic'; he felt part of the romance of the historic project of working-class emancipation, with its strong 19th century idealistic strain. He spoke and wrote often (as in his moving 'The Death of a Cabin Boy' in the Anthology) of the need to record and respect 'the short and simple annals of the poor.' But it wasn't only the still, sad music of humanity that moved him, but also its more joyous, celebratory note. Indeed, when I spoke in my opening remarks of his full and fulfilling life being all of a piece, what I had in mind was the sense that that in all the political ups and downs, the battles lost and battles won, what sustained Jim Kemmy throughout was probably a profound conviction that, whatever the immediate clamour, he could hear and was in step with the deep, insistent rhythm of the march of the common man towards liberty, dignity and a place in the sun.

May the memory of his towering and combative presence remain with those who knew him; and when they too have passed on, may the record of his achievements continue to excite admiration and respect, and to offer inspiration to others. Or, as Jim himself might have put it, let the record stand.

And, for Jim, I am sure that I am not alone in thinking that for many a year to come I will see him in O'Mahony's on a Saturday afternoon, browsing through books, the bundle of proofs of his latest project tucked under his arm, his head slightly thrown back, ready for a chat or challenge with whoever came the way. Indeed, his presence will be felt for a very long time in many different parts of this city. As John Francis O'Donnell once wrote in his poem evoking memories of historic Limerick (which Jim published in the Journal):

> *And, as I pace each still and storied street,*
> *The pageants of forgotten days arise;*
> *I feel the tumult and the gathering heat,*
> *I hear the measured fall of warrior feet,*
> *I see the banners in the narrow skies.*
> *Cries and rejoicings burthen the warm air –*
> *Some foe has perished, some good deed been done,*
> *Some toil has borrowed comfort of the sun,*
> *And poured a moment's light upon despair.*

Jim Kemmy's toil has richly earned the comfort of the sun.
Atque in perpetuum, frater, ave atque vale.
And, let us go in peace from this place.

From the *Old Limerick Journal*, No. 34, Summer 1998.

Acknowledgments to Publishers

Every effort has been made by the publishers to trace all copyright holders. Those who have inadvertently been overlooked, and who wish to contact the publishers, will be made the usual and appropriate arrangements.

The O'Brien Press for extracts from *I Will In Me Politics*, by Pat Shortt.

Merlin Publishing for an extract (pp 126-5) from *Rucks, Mauls and Gaelic Football,* by Moss Keane with Billy Keane.

Michael McCarthy for extracts (pp 127-8, 148-5) from *High Tension, Life on the Shannon Scheme*.

Criostoir O'Flynn for extracts (pp 109-5, 290-8) from *There is an Isle, A Limerick Boyhood*.

Valerie Sweeney, for an extract (pp41-5) from *Shannon Airport: A Unique Story of Survival*.

Roisin Meaney for an extract (pp 176-11) from *The Daisy Picker*.

The Collins Press, for an extract (pp 65-6) from *A Spring in my Step*, by Joan McDonnell.

Poolbeg Press for an extract (pp 26-6) from *The People who Drank Water from the River* by James Kennedy.

Blackstaff Press for an extract (pp185-7) from *Pinhead Duffy* by Helena Close.

Micheal Curtin for *Defining A Limerickman* and extracts from chapter *After Fr. Cletus*, from *Sing*!

P. J. Browne for extracts (pp90-3, 30-5) from *Unfulfilled Promises, Memories of Donogh O'Malley*.

Des Fogerty for an extract (pp123-5) from *Sean South of Garryowen*.

Fr. Frank Moriarty for an extract from *Catholic Life*.

Alan English for an extract (pp 104-5) from *Stand Up and Fight*.

Pat Doran for extracts from *A Clune's Lane Fisherman*.

Vincent Carroll for extracts from *No Lock on the Door* by Joe Carroll.

Eoin Devereux for extracts (pp69-2, 78-30) from *Last Word by the Listener* (Séamus Ó'Cinnéide).

Four Courts Press for extract (pp 24-3) from *Bishop Edward Thomas O'Dwyer of Limerick, 1842-1917* by Thomas J. Morrissey.

Michael Quinlan for extracts from *Mickey Slabdabber*.

Revival Press for poems from *Revival Poetry Journal*.

Denis Leonard, Limerick Civic Trust.

Larry Walsh, Editor *Old Limerick Journal*, for extracts.

Helena Close for extracts, *Pinhead Duffy*.

Hannan family for extracts, *Historical Reflections*.

www.ingramcontent.com/pod-product-compliance
Ingram Content Group UK Ltd.
Pitfield, Milton Keynes, MK11 3LW, UK
UKHW022230230426
12048UKWH00016BA/1162